15.00
75K
2 vols

THE INTERNATIONAL MONETARY FUND

1966–1971

Volume I: Narrative

THE INTERNATIONAL MONETARY FUND 1966-1971

The System Under Stress

VOLUME I: Narrative

By
Margaret Garritsen de Vries

INTERNATIONAL MONETARY FUND
WASHINGTON, D.C.
1976

© 1986 International Monetary Fund

ISBN 0-939934-09-4 (v.I)
ISBN 0-939934-11-6 (set)

De Vries, Margaret Garritsen, 1922–
    The International Monetary Fund, 1966–1971: the system under stress. Washington, D.C., International Monetary Fund, 1976.
    2 v.
    Sequel to The International Monetary Fund, 1945–1965: twenty years of international monetary cooperation, by J. K. Horsefield and others, published by the Fund in 1969.

    CONTENTS: v.1, Narrative, by Margaret Garritsen de Vries.—v.2, Documents, edited by Margaret Garritsen de Vries.

    1. International Monetary Fund. 2. International finance. 3. International liquidity. 4. Special drawing rights. 5. Foreign exchange. I. Title.

Foreword

This history of the International Monetary Fund for the years 1966 through 1971 in two volumes is a sequel to three earlier volumes, which recounted the origins of the Fund and covered the first twenty years of its existence, from 1945 to 1965.

The six years now reviewed were momentous ones in international monetary relationships, and therefore for the Fund. In this period, the first amendment of the Articles of Agreement took place when the Fund was entrusted with authority for creation of a new reserve asset, the special drawing right. There was also a substantially increased use of the Fund's resources, accompanied by a sizable increase in members' quotas and by important changes in the Fund's policies governing the use of its financial resources. In addition, the Fund endeavored to serve an enlarged membership better by undertaking a number of new responsibilities and activities, primarily in the fields of technical assistance and training.

Outstanding as were the foregoing developments, however, it was the emergence of severe crises concerning gold and exchange rates from 1967/68 onward that catapulted international monetary events to the forefront of world attention and presented problems and challenges to the world's economic and financial authorities that were the most difficult since the inception of the Fund.

The Fund's role in all these events is described in Volume I, *Narrative*. Volume II reproduces the most important documents published by the Fund from 1966 until the end of 1971 and makes available for the first time seven draft outlines for reserve-creating schemes that were prepared in the Fund as part of the process by which special drawing rights were established.

With the advent of the SDR, the period reviewed may in some respects be seen as a special high point in the Fund's history. The period was, however, also marked by a series of monetary crises that culminated in the collapse of the Bretton Woods system, as described in the closing chapters of Volume I. Subsequently, there were discussions and actions pertinent to reforming the monetary system which are, indeed, still going on. Many of the problems for which solutions have been sought in the years after 1971 thus originated in the period described here. Hence, in publishing these volumes, the Fund hopes to promote understanding of its present, as well as of its past, work.

This history has been written by Margaret Garritsen de Vries, an economist and the Fund's Historian, a staff member who has been associated with the Fund since 1946. She has had full access to the Fund's records and has benefited from comments on the manuscript from her staff colleagues and members of the

FOREWORD

Executive Board, in both their personal and their official capacities. In these respects, these volumes are, as Pierre-Paul Schweitzer stated in his Foreword to the earlier volumes, "history written from the inside." At the same time, they are the personal responsibility of the author, and no statement or opinion expressed should be understood as committing the Fund in any way.

December 1976

H. Johannes Witteveen
Managing Director
International Monetary Fund

Contents

                                                                    Page

Foreword   v

Preface to Volume 1   xv

Chronology of Principal Events, 1966–71   xviii

Introduction   3

PART ONE   *The Birth of SDRs*

CHAPTER 1: EARLY DISCUSSIONS OF LIQUIDITY (Before 1963) . . .   11

Studies Before Convertibility, 11; Aftermath of Convertibility, 13; The Fund
Adapts Its Policies, 15; Proposals for Expanding World Liquidity, 17; The
Fund's Reactions to Proposals, 21

CHAPTER 2: DEBATE ON LIQUIDITY INTENSIFIED (1963–64)   25

Official Positions Develop, 26; Framework for the Fund's Study of Liquidity,
31; The Fund Adjusts Policies on Its Resources, 32; General Subject of
Liquidity Examined, 34; Group of Ten Reports, 35; Positions at Tokyo, 38

CHAPTER 3: EXPLORING TECHNIQUES FOR RESERVE
             CREATION (1964–65)   43

Deliberate Reserve Creation Studied, 43; Two Possible Techniques for
Creating Reserves, 46; Studies Accelerated, 51; Proposals for CRUs, 53;
Reactions of Management and Staff to CRU Proposals, 57; Ossola Group
Report, 58; France and United States Take Opposing Positions, 61;
Managing Director's Assessment and Action, 64; Agreement by Group of
Ten on Contingency Planning, 69

CHAPTER 4: SEARCH FOR A CONTINGENCY PLAN
             FOR RESERVE CREATION (1965–66)   74

Economic Circumstances Facilitate Agreement, 74; Intensified Discussions
by Group of Ten, 76; Emphasis on a Limited Group Continues, 78; Response
of Developing Countries, 82; Background to Managing Director's Proposals,

Page

86; Managing Director's Proposals, 91; Universality Accepted by Group of Ten, 95; Reasons for Acceptance of Universal Scheme, 99; Widening the Discussions, 100

CHAPTER 5: PROGRESS TOWARD A PLAN FOR RESERVE CREATION (October 1, 1966–April 15, 1967) 104

Arrangements for Joint Meetings, 105; Purpose of Reserve Creation Discussed, 108; Form of Deliberately Created Reserves Considered, 111; Question of Compulsory Reconstitution, 113; Question of Use and Transfer of a New Reserve, 114; Financing of Reserve Creation, 117; First Joint Meeting, 119; Question of Decision Making, 121; Second Joint Meeting, 126; Aftermath of First and Second Joint Meetings, 127; Plans Redrafted, 127; Attempts to Gain Momentum, 130

CHAPTER 6: SDRs TAKE SHAPE (April 16–September 30, 1967) 138

Developments in World Reserves, 139; Third Joint Meeting, 141; Decision to Draft a Tentative Outline, 143; Rules for Use and Transfer, 147; Fourth Joint Meeting, 150; Drafting a Final Outline, 153; Outline Agreed by Group of Ten, 155; Approval of Outline by Board of Governors, 158; Only an Outline, 160

CHAPTER 7: AMENDING THE ARTICLES (1967–68) 166

The Fund's Task, 166; Defining Currency Convertible in Fact, 168; Stockholm Meeting of the Group of Ten, 170; Decision Taken and Resolution Adopted, 175

CHAPTER 8: SDRs ENTER INTO FORCE (1968–69) 176

Amendment of By-Laws and Rules and Regulations, 177; Two Separate Accounts, 178; Allocations and Cancellations of SDRs, 180; Operations and Transactions in SDRs, 182; Designation, 184; Reconstitution, 186; Gold-Value Guarantee, 186; Significance of the New Asset, 187

CHAPTER 9: HOW SDRs EVOLVED: A SYNOPSIS 190

PART TWO *Allocation and First Use of SDRs*

CHAPTER 10: DECISION TO ALLOCATE SDRs (1969) 209

Circumstances Leading to Activation, 209; Staff Preparation, 212; Consultations Process Begins, 214; Proposal Formulated, 217; Approval by Board of Governors, 219; A Word in Retrospect, 220

Page

CHAPTER 11: PREPARING FOR SDR ALLOCATION (1969) 222

Specifying Currencies Convertible in Fact, 223; First Designation Plan, 226; Acceptance of SDRs for Charges and Repurchases, 229; Exclusion from Monetary Reserve Calculations, 230

CHAPTER 12: TWO YEARS OF EXPERIENCE WITH SDRs (1970–71) 232

Allocations Made, 232; Disclosing Transactions, 233; Transactions Through the General Account, 234; Experience with Designation Plans, 237; Requirement of Need, 242; Total Use of SDRs, 243; An Accepted Reserve, 244

PART THREE
General Resources: New Challenges and Responses

CHAPTER 13: CHANGES IN RULES AND PRACTICES 253

An 85 Per Cent Majority for Several Decisions, 254; Amendments Governing Use of Resources, 255; Amendments Governing Repurchases, 258; Interpretation of the Articles, 259

CHAPTER 14: COMPENSATORY FINANCING EXTENDED AND
LIBERALIZED 261

The Changes of 1966, 261; Usage Increases, 263; Compensatory Financing Becomes Important, 266

CHAPTER 15: FINANCING BUFFER STOCKS 269

Prelude, 269; African Members Press for Special Study, 270; Report by Staff, 272; Views of Executive Directors and Governors, 276; Intensified Study, 278; A Decision Reached, 279; The Decision Implemented, 282; Consultations to Include Commodities, 284

CHAPTER 16: QUOTAS ENLARGED 287

Growth from 1966 to 1969, 288; Fifth General Review Begins, 289; Agreement Reached on Fifth General Review, 295; New Quotas Become Effective, 300; Other Increases in Quotas During 1969–71, 301; Policy on Small Quotas, 302; Quota Formula to Be Reviewed, 303

CHAPTER 17: INCREASES IN DRAWINGS 309

Total Drawings, 310; Gold Tranche Drawings, 312; Direct Purchases in Credit Tranches, 316; Drawings Under Stand-By Arrangements, 320; Waivers, 322; Currencies Selected: Use of Past Principles, 322; Currencies Selected: Additional Developments, 324; Special Problems After August 15, 1971, 326

Page

CHAPTER 18: CONTINUED EVOLUTION OF STAND-BY
ARRANGEMENTS 338

Stand-By Arrangement for United Kingdom, 1967, 338; Terms of Stand-By
Arrangements Reviewed, 343; Stand-By Arrangement for United Kingdom,
1969, 348; Dramatic Improvement in U.K. Economic Situation, 349; United
Kingdom Repays the Fund, 351; Stand-By Arrangement for France, 352;
Rapid Recovery of French Economy, 354; Stand-By Arrangements for Devel-
oping Members, 358; Financial Programming—A Major Activity, 363;
Programming Methodology Under Study, 366; Expediting Purchases Under
Stand-By Arrangements, 368

CHAPTER 19: OTHER DEVELOPMENTS IN THE FUND'S
FINANCES 370

General Arrangements to Borrow Renewed, 370; Activation of General
Arrangements to Borrow, 374; Bilateral Borrowing, 376; Review of Charges,
378; Repurchases, 381; Investment of the Fund's Assets, 383; The Fund's
Budget, 385; Net Income Is Distributed, 388; Turnabout in Financial Operations, 392

PART FOUR *Gold*

CHAPTER 20: GOLD: NEW PROBLEMS, NEW POLICIES 401

Calm Before the Storm: 1965, 401; Gold Pool Abolished, 403; Two-Tier
Gold Market, 405; South African Gold: The Problem, 409; Fund Gold
Purchases Begin, 415; Fund Sells Gold, 416; General Deposits of Gold, 420;
Gold Subsidies and Transactions Service, 423; Basic Questions About Gold
Develop, 425

PART FIVE *Exchange Rates in Crisis*

CHAPTER 21: DEVALUATION OF STERLING (1967) 431

Prelude to Devaluation, 431; Notification to Fund, 433; The Fund's Delibera-
tions, 434; Limited Devaluations of Other Currencies, 437; U.K. Economy
Fails to Respond, 440; Evaluation of Improvement in U.K. Economy, 443;
Sterling Devaluation as Seen at the Time, 446

CHAPTER 22: ADJUSTMENTS IN RATES FOR FRENCH FRANC
AND DEUTSCHE MARK (1969) 449

Prelude to Devaluation of Franc, 449; Meeting at Bonn, 450; Decision to
Devalue the Franc, 453; The Fund's Deliberations on Franc Devaluation,

455; French Franc Area Alters Its Rates, 457; Sequel to Devaluation of Franc, 458; Deutsche Mark Is Revalued, 458; Difficulties After Revaluation of Deutsche Mark, 462

CHAPTER 23: OTHER ADJUSTMENTS IN EXCHANGE RATES
(1966–70)   465

Initial Par Values, 465; Changes in Monetary Units, 466; Devaluation of Indian Rupee, 468; Devaluation by Ghana, 471; Devaluation by Finland, 472; Devaluation by Iceland, 473; Devaluation by Turkey, 474; Devaluation by Ecuador, 475; Canada Returns to a Floating Rate, 476; Canada Continues to Have a Floating Rate, 480

CHAPTER 24: EXAMINING THE EXCHANGE RATE MECHANISM
(1969–70)   483

U.S. Deficit, 485; Tighter U.S. Measures in 1968, 487; Discussions of U.S. Deficit, 488; Countries in Surplus, 493; The Problem of Adjustment, 495; Increasingly Disruptive Capital Flows, 496; Initial Review of Exchange Rate Mechanism, 500; Governors' Positions, 503; Continued Review by Executive Directors, 504; Agreement by Executive Directors, 512; Reactions of Governors, 514; After Copenhagen, 515

CHAPTER 25: COLLAPSE OF THE PAR VALUE SYSTEM
(January 1–August 15, 1971)   517

Par Value and Other Adjustments, 517; Fresh Disturbances in European Markets, 519; New Measures by European Countries, 522; Difficult Issues Arise, 524; United States Suspends Convertibility, 527; Implications for the Fund, 530

CHAPTER 26: ROAD TO THE SMITHSONIAN AGREEMENT
(August 16–December 18, 1971)   531

Fund's Immediate Response to U.S. Announcement, 531; Exchange Rate Realignment—A Sensitive Issue, 534; Mr. Schweitzer's Concerns and Responses, 538; Variety of Exchange Rates Introduced, 541; Group of Ten Meetings, 543; 1971 Annual Meeting, 545; After the 1971 Annual Meeting, 548; Group of Ten Meets Again, 551; Developing Countries Present Their Views, 552; Smithsonian Agreement, 553

CHAPTER 27: A TEMPORARY REGIME ESTABLISHED
(December 18–31, 1971)   557

Consideration of Central Rates, 557; Decision Adopted, 559; Rates Communicated, 559; The Fund's Operations Restored, 563; World Payments Situation at the End of 1971, 564; International Monetary Reform—the Next Step, 564; A Backward Glance, 565

PART SIX *The Fund as an Institution*

Page

CHAPTER 28: GROWTH OF RESPONSIBILITIES 569

Increases in Membership, 569; Continued Importance of Annual Consultations, 570; Trends in Exchange Restrictions, 573; Developments in Annual Consultations, 575; Technical Assistance Evolves into a Large Program, 578; Technical Assistance in Central Banking, 579; Technical Assistance in Fiscal Affairs, 582; Technical Assistance in Statistics, 584; General Technical Assistance, 587; Special Program for Zaïre Ended, 588; Growth of IMF Institute, 588

CHAPTER 29: FURTHER EXPANSION OF ACTIVITIES 591

Payments Arrears Defined as Restrictions, 591; Greater Concern with External Debt Service, 593; External Debt of Ghana, 597; External Debt: A Long-Term Problem, 600; The Fund as a Center for Information, 601; Relations with UN, GATT, and OECD, 604; Relations with Other Organizations, 608; Cooperation with the World Bank, 610

CHAPTER 30: COMPLEXITIES IN THE PROCESS OF
            POLICYMAKING 616

Membership: Formation of Groups, 616; Board of Governors: Growth in Size and Powers, 620; Executive Board: Increasing Functions, 622; Executive Board: Changes in Composition, 625; Executive Board: Composition at End of 1971, 627; Executive Board: Size and Structure, 630; Managing Director, 632; Deputy Managing Director, 635; Staff: Organization and Expansion, 636; Staff: Teamwork, Anonymity, and Long Service, 640; New Headquarters Building, 649; The Fund as 1971 Ended, 650

APPENDICES

APPENDIX A–1: Appointed Executive Directors and Their Alternates, Article XII, Section 3(*b*)(i) 655

APPENDIX A–2: Elected Executive Directors and Their Alternates, Article XII, Section 3(*b*)(iii) 657

APPENDIX A–3: Elected Executive Directors and Their Alternates, Article XII, Section 3(*b*)(iv) 662

APPENDIX B: Management and Senior Staff 663

APPENDIX C: Organizational Chart 667

TABLES

Page

1. Participants and Observers at First and Second Joint Meetings of Executive Directors of Fund and Deputies of Group of Ten, 1966–67   134

2. Participants and Observers at Third and Fourth Joint Meetings of Executive Directors of Fund and Deputies of Group of Ten, 1967..   162

3. Allocations of Special Drawing Rights, 1970–72   248

4. Purchases and Repurchases Under Decision on Compensatory Financing of Export Fluctuations, February 27, 1963–April 30, 1972   268

5. Quotas of Members on Selected Dates   306

6. Drawings from the Fund, 1966–71   330

7. Stand-By Arrangements Approved, January 1, 1966–December 31, 1971   333

8. Drawings and Repurchases by Currency, Calendar Years, 1966–71..   337

9. Borrowing by Fund Under General Arrangements to Borrow, 1966–71   374

10. Financing of Drawings by France and United Kingdom Involving Activation of General Arrangements to Borrow, 1966–71   375

11. Charges on Fund's Holdings of Member's Currency in Excess of Member's Quota Resulting from Transactions Effected from May 1, 1963 to December 31, 1971   380

12. Total Purchases and Repurchases by Members, Fiscal Years Ended April 30, 1966–71   383

13. Repurchases of Currencies, Fiscal Years Ended April 30, 1966–71 ...   395

14. Income and Expenditure of Fund, Fiscal Years Ended April 30, 1966–71   397

15. Changes in Par Values, November 18–27, 1967   438

16. Initial Par Values Established, 1966–70   466

17. Exchange Rate Relationships Resulting from Smithsonian Agreement, December 18, 1971   555

18. Par Values Maintained Unchanged as of December 31, 1971   560

19. Par Values Changed, December 18–31, 1971   561

20. Central Rates Established, December 18–31, 1971   562

□   □   □   □   □   □

Index   669

Publications Cited   695

Illustrations

Facing page

Pierre-Paul Schweitzer, Chairman of Executive Board and Managing
Director 90

Meeting of 1966–68 Executive Board 118

Museum of Modern Art, Rio de Janeiro, Site of 1967 Annual Meeting ... 158

President Lyndon B. Johnson, Pierre-Paul Schweitzer, Managing Director,
and Henry H. Fowler, Governor for United States 176

Meeting of 1968–70 Executive Board 222

Meeting of 1970–72 Executive Board 298

Joint Session of Boards of Governors of Fund and World Bank at an
Annual Meeting 620

Frank A. Southard, Jr., Deputy Managing Director 636

Headquarters, Washington, 1973 650

Preface to Volume I

The history of the Fund for the six years 1966 through 1971 differs in many ways from that of the Fund's first twenty years. Innovative changes were introduced into the original design of the Bretton Woods system. Yet, notwithstanding these changes, such severe stress developed in that system as to cause its eventual collapse. Several of the monetary and financial questions discussed in the Fund in the period reviewed here were new to the international scene and involved highly technical matters with widespread implications for the monetary system. These questions engaged the interest of economists and monetary specialists to an extent that had not occurred since the discussions attending the birth of the Fund in 1944.

Moreover, in the second half of the 1960s, the Fund's activities and decisions became increasingly interwoven with discussions in and decisions by other forums, most notably the Group of Ten but also the European Economic Community and groups formed by developing countries. Also, to an extent greater than in the preceding twenty years, in the six years reviewed here events taking place in the Fund were directly and quickly influenced by economic and monetary developments taking place in the world as a whole and in individual member countries, especially as one monetary crisis after another erupted. Literally, the events of yesterday bore heavily on today's discussions and decisions. This situation was quite unlike that of the Bretton Woods discussions, in which the circumstances of war were, in a sense, ignored while the participants planned for a world yet to come into being after World War II. Furthermore, the questions involved in 1966–71 were of such consequence as to concern officials at the very highest political levels; and the circumstances were conducive to the public expression of views on these questions while negotiations had not yet been completed.

These factors have necessarily influenced my writing. I have organized this history around what I see as the four main areas in which the Fund's further evolution as an international monetary organization took place: the establishment of special drawing rights (SDRs); the unprecedented recourse by members to the financial resources of the Fund and important changes in policies affecting the use of those resources; the emergence of severe disturbances in gold and exchange markets that brought to an end the international monetary system created at Bretton Woods; and, with the growth of membership, the gradual assumption by the Fund of new responsibilities and activities. In my descriptions, I have tried especially to bring out the major issues that were involved insofar as the Fund was concerned and the reasoning that underlay the Fund's actions and decisions. As in the volumes relating the Fund's history for earlier years, the primary focus is on the Executive Board and the principal source of information has been the minutes of the Executive Board's meetings and informal sessions. However, to a considerably greater extent than was done in the earlier volumes, I have included material describing the staff's analyses, the considerations behind several of the decisions of the Managing Director, the nature of economic and monetary developments influencing negotiations, and related discussions and decisions taking place outside the Fund. This material has all been based on the Fund's documents and records.

My aim has been to describe the Fund's actions objectively. Since this is a history of events that are relatively near in time, there are instances, particularly in the final chapters, where I have regarded my task as mainly reportorial, and where I have refrained from analysis or interpretation.

Finally, some material has been included so that this history of the Fund for the years 1966–71 may be fairly self-contained, that is, so that readers do not necessarily have to have read the history of the Fund for earlier years.

A few techniques for identifying officials in a relatively simple way have been adopted. Those appointed by member countries as Governors of the Fund and of the World Bank have been referred to in these capacities, especially when they attended Annual Meetings, rather than in their capacities as officials of their home countries, usually Ministers of Finance or Governors of central banks. The Managing Director, who is also the Chairman of the Executive Board, is referred to as the Managing Director, thus avoiding the need to distinguish in which capacity he may have been acting at the time. The full name of an Executive Director and, as an approximation to the identification of his constituency, his country of nationality are given the first time he is mentioned; his country of nationality is repeated the first time he is mentioned in each of the subsequent parts into which the volume is divided. A similar course has been followed for Alternate Executive Directors, each of whom is also linked, on the first occasion he is mentioned, to the Executive Director who appointed him. Thereafter surnames only are used. The first mention of an Executive Director or of an Alternate Executive Director may come in a series of names and, consequently, there is at times a mixture of given names and surnames, especially in the later parts of the volume. The procedure may, therefore, be confusing for those reading only certain parts, but any alternative seemed to be even more complicated and repetitive of given names.

There is another point concerning the members of the Executive Board to which the reader should be alerted. During the period reviewed here, changes were made in appointed Executive Directors and, following the customary biennial elections of Executive Directors, newly elected Directors took office on November 1 of 1966, 1968, and 1970. For ease of exposition, changes in Executive Directors have not been spelled out in Parts One through Five. A brief description of the changes in the composition of the Executive Board from 1966 through 1971 is given in Part Six (Chapter 30). A complete listing of the

Executive Directors and their Alternates and of the countries appointing or electing them and the years in which they served is given in Appendix A–1, Appendix A–2, and Appendix A–3.

The names of some member countries were changed in the period reviewed here. However, the names in effect on December 31, 1971 have been used throughout the volume.

I am very much indebted to numerous colleagues both on the staff and on the Executive Board for their many comments. Unfortunately, I cannot mention all of their names here. I have especially warm feelings for several who have been exceptionally close to this history of the Fund. Frank A. Southard, Jr., Deputy Managing Director from November 1, 1962 until March 1, 1974, made several suggestions and read most of the manuscript; his extensive personal files and notes of meetings at which he presided or in which he took part provided me with much essential information and with background for understanding the formal documents. Joseph Gold, the General Counsel, and J. J. Polak, the Economic Counsellor, have answered queries, provided explanations and interpretations, and read and commented on draft copy, thereby enabling me to make more accurate and more complete than would otherwise have been possible descriptions of many events in which they participated. Fred Hirsch's comments on an early draft of the chapters on SDRs prompted me to make extensive revisions. J. Keith Horsefield, responsible for the history of the Fund for 1945 to 1965, read this sequel and made many suggestions. Philine Lachman read the manuscript with a lawyer's eye.

Marie C. Stark, Archivist, and her assistant, Milton K. Chamberlain, sorted out the materials that I needed from among the Fund's voluminous records and documents; their intimate familiarity with these records and documents made my hours of research most fruitful. Martin L. Loftus and Charles O. Olsen, then Librarian and Assistant Librarian, respectively, of the Joint Bank-Fund Library, and their staff helped me to keep abreast of related current literature.

Helen G. (Becky) Burrows was my assistant throughout most of the project, typing drafts, preparing statistical tables and Appendices, and making editorial suggestions; in all these capacities she was invaluable. Faye L. Olin performed secretarial and editorial duties in the later stages of the project.

Jane B. Evensen, Editor, assisted by Jennie Lee Carter, painstakingly edited the final manuscript and saw the volumes through to publication. Surinder Nath worked on the index. The Graphics Section helped in several ways with the production process; Joseph J. Diana assisted with photographs, and Toshiko Habir designed the dust jacket.

Needless to say, any shortcomings, errors, or blemishes that remain are my responsibility.

December 1976   M. G. de V.

Chronology of Principal Events, 1966–71[1]

1966

February 23   A general increase in Fund quotas of 25 per cent, together with special increases for 16 countries, became effective, which would, when all members had consented to their increases, expand the Fund's resources from $16 billion to $21 billion.

June 3   The Executive Board concurred in a proposal by India to change the par value of the rupee from 21 U.S. cents per rupee to 13.3333 U.S. cents per rupee, to be effective on June 5 (Washington time).

September 20   The Executive Board took a decision extending and liberalizing the compensatory financing facility.

1967

July 7   The Executive Board concurred in a proposal by Ghana to change the par value of the new cedi from 140 U.S. cents per new cedi to 98 U.S. cents per new cedi, to be effective on July 8.

September 29   The Board of Governors approved the "Outline of a Facility Based on Special Drawing Rights in the Fund," and asked that the Executive Directors proceed with work on drafting amendments to the Articles of Agreement.

September 29   The Board of Governors adopted a resolution asking for a study by the Fund and the World Bank of the problem of stabilization of the prices of primary products.

October 11   The Executive Board concurred in a proposal by Finland to change the par value of the markka from 31.25 U.S. cents per markka to 23.8097 U.S. cents per markka, to be effective on October 12.

November 18   The Executive Board concurred in a proposal by the United Kingdom to change the par value of the pound sterling from $2.80 to $2.40 per pound sterling, effective that same date.

November 18–27   The Executive Board concurred in proposals by Ireland, Israel, Cyprus, Guyana, Malawi, New Zealand, Spain,

---

[1] Includes all changes in par values before August 15, 1971.

Ceylon, Denmark, Jamaica, Sierra Leone, Trinidad and Tobago, and Iceland to change their par values, and in a proposal by The Gambia to change its exchange rate.

November 29   The Executive Board approved a stand-by arrangement for the United Kingdom for $1.4 billion.

1968

March 16–17   The central banks of seven countries agreed to buy and sell gold at the official price of $35 an ounce only in transactions with monetary authorities, and a two-tier market for gold emerged.

April 16   The Executive Board completed its work on the proposed amendments to the Articles of Agreement establishing an SDR facility in the Fund and making certain changes in the Fund's rules and practices; the amendments were to be transmitted to the Board of Governors for consideration and approval.

May 31   The Board of Governors approved the proposed amendments to the Articles of Agreement, which were then submitted to members for acceptance.

June 4   The French franc had come under pressure and France made a gold tranche purchase of $745 million from the Fund.

June 19   The United Kingdom drew the $1.4 billion authorized under its stand-by arrangement.

September 20   The Executive Board, having reviewed the Fund's policy on the use of its resources under stand-by arrangements, adopted guidelines to ensure uniform and equitable treatment for all members.

November 11   The Executive Board concurred in a proposal by Iceland to change the par value of the króna from 1.75439 U.S. cents per króna to 1.13636 U.S. cents per króna, to be effective on November 12.

November 20–22 After a new exchange crisis had forced the closing of markets in France, the Federal Republic of Germany, the United Kingdom, and other countries, the Group of Ten met at the ministerial level in Bonn to discuss the measures to be taken, including, inter alia, possible adjustments in the exchange rates of the deutsche mark and the French franc. (No exchange rate action was agreed upon.)

| December 31 | Drawings from the Fund for the year totaled $3.5 billion, the largest annual amount since the Fund commenced operations in 1947. |

1969

June 20	The Executive Board approved another stand-by arrangement for the United Kingdom, for $1.0 billion.
June 25	The Executive Board approved a facility to finance international buffer stocks of primary products.
July 28	The amendments to the Articles of Agreement entered into force.
August 6	The Special Drawing Account came into existence.
August 10	The Executive Board concurred in a proposal by France to change the par value of the franc from 0.180 gram of gold per franc to 0.160 gram of gold per franc, effective the same day.
September 19	The Executive Board approved a stand-by arrangement for France for $985 million, and shortly thereafter France purchased $500 million under the arrangement.
September 29	The Federal Republic of Germany informed the Fund that it could not maintain rates for the deutsche mark within prescribed limits around the par value, and thus the rate for the deutsche mark was allowed to float.
October 3	The Board of Governors approved the Managing Director's proposal to allocate SDRs over a first basic period of three years beginning January 1, 1970.
October 17	The Executive Board agreed to a second renewal of the General Arrangements to Borrow for five years beginning October 24, 1970.
October 24	The Executive Board concurred in a proposal by the Federal Republic of Germany to change the par value of the deutsche mark from 25 U.S. cents per deutsche mark to 27.3224 U.S. cents per deutsche mark, to be effective on October 26. This revaluation ended the floating rate for the deutsche mark.
November 7	The Executive Directors continued with the review of the role of exchange rates in the adjustment of international payments that they had begun somewhat earlier in connection with their Annual Report for 1969.
December 1–30	The Executive Board took a series of decisions preparatory to putting the Special Drawing Account into operation.

December 30	The Executive Board took a decision whereby as a matter of policy the Fund would buy gold from South Africa.
December 31	Drawings from the Fund for the year totaled $2.5 billion, the largest so far for any year except 1968.

1970

January 1	The first allocation of SDRs was made.
February 2	France drew the remaining $485 million authorized under its stand-by arrangement.
February 9	The Board of Governors approved increases in quotas under the fifth general review. Fund quotas would be increased from $21.3 billion to $28.9 billion if all members increased their quotas to the maximum proposed.
May 31	Canada informed the Fund that it would not maintain the exchange rate of the Canadian dollar within its present margins, and the rate for the Canadian dollar once again was allowed to float.
August 9	The Executive Board concurred in a proposal by Turkey to change the par value of the lira from 11.1111 U.S. cents per lira to 6.66667 U.S. cents per lira.
August 14	The Executive Board concurred in a proposal by Ecuador to change the par value of the sucre from 5.55556 U.S. cents per sucre to 4.00000 U.S. cents per sucre, to be effective on August 17.
September 13	The Executive Board reported to the Board of Governors on the role of exchange rates in the adjustment of international payments.
September 25	Closing the Twenty-Fifth Annual Meeting of the Board of Governors, Mr. Hédi Nouira, Chairman, observed that, on the subject of exchange rate flexibility, "there seems to be a consensus in favor of further study by the Fund but against any radical or major changes."
October 26	The Executive Board decided that restrictions resulting in payments arrears were exchange restrictions subject to the Fund's approval.
November 25	The Executive Board took a decision that enabled members to use the buffer stock financing facility in connection with their contributions under the Fourth International Tin Agreement.

1971

January 1	The second allocation of SDRs was made.
January 23	The Executive Board concurred in a proposal by Yugoslavia to change the par value of the dinar from 8.0000 U.S. cents per dinar to 6.66667 U.S. cents per dinar.
May 9–11	To stem capital inflows, the Federal Republic of Germany and the Netherlands allowed the rates for their currencies to float, the Belgo-Luxembourg Exchange Institute enlarged its free market for capital transactions, and Austria revalued its currency.
July 16	The first purchases under the buffer stock financing facility were made, by Bolivia and Indonesia. (Malaysia purchased under the facility on August 10.)
August 15	The United States informed the Fund that it would no longer freely buy and sell gold for the settlement of international transactions, thus suspending the convertibility of officially held dollars.
August 16–28	Members introduced a variety of exchange rate arrangements, with rates for several major currencies allowed to float.
October 1	The Board of Governors adopted a resolution calling for study of measures to improve or reform the international monetary system.
December 17–18	The Group of Ten decided, as part of the Smithsonian agreement, on a realignment of the currencies of the major industrial countries.
December 18	The Executive Board took a decision establishing a temporary regime of central rates and wider margins.

THE INTERNATIONAL MONETARY FUND

1966–1971

Volume I: Narrative

"If we consider the international monetary system not only as a structure, but also, as I believe we must, as the way in which that structure is used, it is quite evident that we do not have the same system now as we had five, let alone ten, years ago."

—Pierre-Paul Schweitzer, Managing Director, addressing the International Financial Conference in Geneva on May 19, 1970.

Introduction

*T*HE SIX YEARS from January 1, 1966 to December 31, 1971 were extremely important ones in the history of the International Monetary Fund. They were filled with turbulence and fundamental change in the international monetary system, all of which directly affected the functions and activities of the Fund. At the beginning of this period—in January 1966—it was already apparent that the world economic environment was changing radically. Among other things, short-term flows of capital were becoming larger and more difficult to manage by the methods that had been devised in the early 1960s. Moreover, concern that the supply of liquidity in the monetary system might prove insufficient had intensified, and monetary officials were in the midst of a debate on the need to introduce some innovative mechanism for deliberately creating reserves to augment that liquidity. Eventually, in 1969, special drawing rights (SDRs) were established in the Fund. The advent of SDRs was certainly the zenith of the Fund's first twenty-five years. And later, when full-scale reform of the international monetary system was being negotiated, many monetary experts were to look upon their establishment as the first part of a general monetary reform.

The years 1966 through 1971 featured, however, not only the creation of SDRs but also the onset of the disturbances that caused the breakdown of the Bretton Woods system and the need for discussions on monetary reform.

Even before the first SDRs could be allocated, the international monetary system was being subjected to stresses and strains more severe than any experienced since World War II. The imbalance in international payments and the flows of short-term capital from one money center to another that had emerged in the late 1950s and the early 1960s became steadily greater, and the resulting problems became increasingly harder to solve, or even to alleviate. Consequently, exchange crises became a regular feature of the international scene, especially after November 1967. News that traditionally had been relegated to the financial pages made front-page headlines when, in the next three and a half years, sterling was devalued, a single official price for gold was abandoned and a two-tier gold market set up, the French franc was devalued, the deutsche mark was revalued, and floating exchange rates for the Canadian dollar, the deutsche mark, and the Netherlands guilder were introduced. Then, on August 15, 1971, came the suspension by the United States of convertibility into gold of officially held dollars. As a result, two basic tenets of the Fund's Articles of Agreement—the system of agreed par values and the convertibility of dollars into gold—were no longer operative. The system designed at Bretton

3

Woods a quarter of a century before had collapsed. The Ministers and Central Bank Governors of the Group of Ten, meeting at the Smithsonian Institution in Washington in December 1971, reached agreement on the realignment of the currencies of their countries, and subsequently the Fund's Executive Board adopted a decision on a temporary regime of central rates and wider exchange rate margins. The crisis was so profound, however, that virtually everyone recognized the urgent need for a thoroughgoing reform of the international monetary system.

Thus this period in the Fund's history, one of trying to hold together the Bretton Woods system through severe stresses and strains, was distinctly different from either the preceding twenty years or the years following 1971. In the two decades 1945–65 there had been tremendous progress toward the attainment of the goals for which the Fund had been established. Reconstruction of the economies devastated by World War II had been accomplished, and the world had benefited from a signal expansion of international trade and investment. Most members of the Fund had achieved agreed par values or, at least, fixed exchange rates. Currency convertibility had been restored. Restrictions on current international payments were far fewer than they had been for decades, and even controls on capital, permitted by the Fund's Articles of Agreement, had been reduced much more than had been thought likely. The International Monetary Fund had become a successful instrument for international cooperation and consultation in the monetary and financial fields.[1] The years immediately after 1971 formed another epoch, one characterized primarily by a very ambitious attempt to achieve a multifaceted reconstruction of the international monetary system.

SCOPE AND COVERAGE OF THIS NARRATIVE

At the outset of the period 1966–71 the world's monetary officials were deliberating the problem of international liquidity. They had been discussing this problem for several years, but they were by no means agreed that the supply of liquidity in the international monetary system was actually inadequate or that unusual new arrangements for creating liquidity were necessary. Consensus on any particular mechanism for deliberate creation of reserves was even more remote. It was agreed only that it was important to formulate a plan for

---

[1] The story of the Fund's genesis and of its activities to the end of 1965 has been related at length in *The International Monetary Fund, 1945–1965; Twenty Years of International Monetary Cooperation*: Vol. I, *Chronicle*, by J. Keith Horsefield; Vol. II, *Analysis*, by Margaret G. de Vries and J. Keith Horsefield with the collaboration of Joseph Gold, Mary H. Gumbart, Gertrud Lovasy, and Emil G. Spitzer and edited by J. Keith Horsefield; Vol. III, *Documents*, edited by J. Keith Horsefield (Washington, 1969). Hereinafter cited as *History, 1945–65*.

creating reserves should the need arise in the future. In the next few years continuous discussion took place, inside and outside the Fund, both about issues and about particular proposals, until August 1969 when the facility for special drawing rights (SDRs) became a part of the structure of the Fund.

The establishment of SDRs was, without doubt, the most striking achievement of the Fund in the years 1966–71. Hence, after a description (in Chapters 1, 2, and 3 and a part of Chapter 4) of what transpired with regard to international liquidity before 1966, the rest of Part One and all of Part Two of this volume are devoted to tracing the evolution of SDRs and the first two years of experience with them.

The earlier history of the Fund discussed at some length the subject of the adequacy of the world's reserves and the two relevant Fund reports issued during the 1950s, but described only briefly the stirring of concern about international liquidity and the Fund's attention to it, through 1965, as reflected in the Annual Reports of the Executive Directors and the Annual Meetings of the Board of Governors. In this volume, therefore, only a few paragraphs are devoted to the events of the 1950s, but developments from 1960 through 1965 are treated more fully. Chapter 1 describes what happened in the field of international liquidity before 1963. Following the pattern of Volume I, *Chronicle*, of the earlier history, Chapters 2–8 of the present volume, which deal with the birth of SDRs, trace the events in 12-month intervals from one Annual Meeting to the next; the Annual Meetings usually brought to a head the debates and negotiations of the preceding year, and in nearly every year the Board of Governors took actions that helped to resolve the impasses that had been blocking further progress. The chapters on other topics are not so arranged, but cover time periods suitable to the topic.

Part Three examines the developments in 1966–71 that pertain to the use of the Fund's regular resources, which were placed in a General Account after the introduction of SDRs. The economic and financial circumstances of the late 1960s and early 1970s presented several challenges to the Fund with respect to the use of its general resources, and the Fund responded in a number of ways. Changes were made in the original provisions of the Articles of Agreement governing use of resources and repurchases (Chapter 13). The compensatory financing facility, set up in February 1963 to give assistance to primary producing members experiencing temporary shortfalls in their export earnings, was extended and liberalized, and for the first time many countries began to make drawings for this purpose (Chapter 14). Developing countries also sought assistance from the Fund and the World Bank on the problem of stabilizing primary product prices, and after considerable study the Fund introduced a facility for financing buffer stocks (Chapter 15). To meet the unprecedented recourse to the Fund's resources by both industrial and developing countries, members' quotas in the Fund were enlarged, particularly by a third round of general quota increases (Chapter 16). Drawings from the Fund were significantly higher than in any other period since the Fund commenced operations in 1947 (Chapter 17).

Most drawings took place under stand-by arrangements. Because of the expanded use of this instrument, the Executive Board reviewed the Fund's policy on the use of its resources under stand-by arrangements and adopted guidelines to ensure uniform and equitable treatment for all members. Financial programming associated with stand-by arrangements became one of the Fund's major activities. These developments, together with some description of the stand-by arrangements agreed with two industrial and three developing members and the related economic circumstances, form the subject of Chapter 18. Augmented drawings, as well as other factors, had important ramifications for the Fund's other financial operations and transactions, such as the charges on drawings, the policies on repurchases, its own budget, the size of its net income, the distribution of some of that income, and the investment of its assets. These developments in the Fund's other finances are taken up in Chapter 19.

In a period filled with dramatic events, some of the most interesting pertained to gold: there was the breakup of the single market for gold transactions, the introduction of a two-tier market for gold, and new developments in the Fund's policies toward purchases and sales of gold, including gold from South Africa. These events are discussed in Part Four (Chapter 20).

Consequential as were the foregoing developments, it was the disturbances in exchange markets that presented the most difficulty for the world's financial authorities. Hence, another major portion of the volume, Part Five, deals with exchange rates. During the years covered here there were a number of important changes in exchange rates. Among the major currencies, there were, first, the devaluation of sterling in November 1967 (described in Chapter 21), and then the devaluation of the French franc in August 1969 and the revaluation of the deutsche mark in October 1969 (described in Chapter 22). There were also devaluations of the Indian rupee (1966), the Ghanaian cedi and the Finnish markka (1967), the Icelandic króna (1968), and the Turkish lira and the Ecuadoran sucre (1970). Also in 1970 Canada reintroduced a fluctuating rate. These developments, together with a description of the initial par values established and the new monetary units introduced from 1966 to 1970, are covered in Chapter 23.

Recurrent crises in exchange markets led to calls for reform of the international monetary system, particularly to proposals for changing the par value system. Hence, international monetary officials had to direct their attention to the broad question: should the mechanism by which exchange rates were adjusted be altered, and if so, how? Chapter 24 describes the review of the mechanism of exchange rate adjustment that the Executive Directors undertook in 1969 and 1970. In 1971 there occurred events in the field of exchange rates that were even more reverberating than those that had taken place earlier, and the system of par values was suspended for what was considered to be a temporary period.

These events are set forth in Chapters 25, 26, and 27. Chapter 25 deals with the events from January 1 through August 15, 1971 that culminated in the suspension by the United States of the convertibility of officially held dollars into gold. Chapter 26 describes at some length the difficult negotiations preceding the Smithsonian agreement of December 1971, and Chapter 27 explains the temporary regime of central rates and wider margins that the Fund thereupon established.

Finally, Part Six (Chapters 28–30) presents an overview of how the Fund grew and changed as an institution during the six years ended with 1971. The Fund had to assume new responsibilities and functions as the world of international monetary and financial affairs expanded and became more complex. Consultations with members were expanded, technical assistance to members became much more extensive, new responsibilities were assumed with regard to external debt negotiations of members, and the Fund became a center for the collection and dissemination of information on economic and financial problems.

PART ONE

The Birth of SDRs

CHAPTER

1

Early Discussions of Liquidity

(Before 1963)

Q*UESTIONS ABOUT THE ADEQUACY* of the world's supply of reserves had arisen as early as 1953. It was not until after external convertibility of the Western European currencies had been restored toward the end of 1958, however, that international liquidity emerged as an issue in international financial discussions, and monetary experts and officials began to advance proposals for expanding or improving international liquidity.

STUDIES BEFORE CONVERTIBILITY

Reserve Adequacy—1953

The Economic and Social Council of the United Nations (Ecosoc) passed a resolution on July 10, 1952 which, inter alia, asked the Fund to keep under continuous review the adequacy of monetary reserves and to furnish an analysis on the subject for the meeting of the Ecosoc in 1953. As a result, the Fund staff prepared a draft report on "The Adequacy of Monetary Reserves" in April 1953. This report was discussed in the Executive Board in May and after revision was sent to the Ecosoc in June, being described as a technical analysis and not a statement of the Fund's policy.

The report, which was later published, explained that the adequacy of reserves depended on the prospective problems that confronted a country and, therefore, would differ from country to country and from problem to problem.[1] From there the report surveyed in detail the complexity of the concept of reserves and the varied factors entering into the determination of their adequacy. It also provided comparisons between the principal monetary reserves data for 1928, 1938, and 1951, and discussed the influences which, in these years, had made a given amount of reserves more (or less) adequate than previously.

---

[1] See *History, 1945–65*, Vol. I, pp. 334–35. The report was published in *Staff Papers*, Vol. III (1953–54), pp. 181–227, and in *History, 1945–65*, Vol. III, pp. 311–48.

Its conclusions consisted of four alternative definitions of adequacy. At the one end, (i), reserves might be considered adequate if they enabled a country in bad years, by recourse to intensified restrictions, to maintain its external debt payments and to purchase the goods and services necessary to avoid hardships to the population or dislocation of its economy. At the other extreme, (iv), reserves might be considered adequate if they permitted a country to maintain currency convertibility even through severe depressions (though not through prolonged periods of international deflation such as occurred in the 1930s) without the need to resort either to restrictions or to domestic deflation. Two intermediate definitions would have linked adequacy to the maintenance of currency convertibility, except in a severe depression, with (ii) and without (iii) the use of restrictions. The report suggested that almost all countries, assuming the adoption of appropriate policies, would have reserves that were adequate under definition (i), many would qualify under definition (ii), some under definition (iii), and a few under definition (iv).

A Second Report on Reserve Adequacy—1958

Following the report made in 1953, the Fund kept in view the possibility that it might have to expand its resources. In 1956 the staff made a fresh study of international liquidity, and reference to a possible need for increases in members' reserves other than in gold was made in a memorandum sent to the Executive Board in May 1956. In May 1957 South Africa, especially concerned about the position and price of monetary gold, asked that the staff undertake a study of the factors affecting the present state of international liquidity, and during the Annual Meeting in September 1957 several Governors made reference to a possible inadequacy of monetary reserves.

In April 1958 a staff working party, following up on these remarks, pointed out that the Fund might expect to be faced with requests for drawings which might be quite considerable in relation to the Fund's available resources. The working party saw no reason to anticipate that the Fund would exhaust its liquid resources by the end of 1958, but regarded it as desirable that the adequacy of the Fund's resources to meet prospective requirements be kept under review.

The outcome of this review was a report entitled *International Reserves and Liquidity*, published later in 1958.[2] This report reflected primarily the views of the Managing Director, Mr. Per Jacobsson, who expressly stated in the foreword that it did not necessarily represent the views of the Executive Directors. The report argued that the adequacy of international liquidity did not depend solely, or even mainly, on the volume of reserves in relation to the volume of world trade. Rather, reserve adequacy depended on a combination of factors: the level and distribution of country reserves, the existence of suffi-

---

[2] See *History, 1945–65*, Vol. I, pp. 447–48, and Vol. III, pp. 349–420.

cient facilities for international credit and borrowing, and the soundness of the international financial structure, including the appropriateness of prevailing exchange rates.

The report concluded that, although under certain fairly specific and broad conditions the existing gold and foreign exchange reserves, estimated at $52.9 billion, should not be considered inadequate, circumstances in which greater reserves would be needed could easily be envisaged. The stability of balances of payments was very uncertain, the Fund's aid had been sought in the sterling crisis of 1956, in the boom of 1957, and in the recession of 1958, and the Fund was likely to be called upon in currency crises in the future. In the light of these circumstances, it was doubtful that the Fund's resources were sufficient for future action.

This report was instrumental in bringing about, in 1959, the first enlargement of Fund quotas, and a sizable one at that. A general increase in quotas of 50 per cent, together with special increases in the quotas of Canada, the Federal Republic of Germany, Japan, and several other countries, resulted in an expansion of the resources of the Fund by about $6 billion, to more than $14 billion.

AFTERMATH OF CONVERTIBILITY

The establishment of external convertibility for 14 European currencies at the end of 1958, the subsequent virtual elimination of exchange restrictions, including the gradual relaxation of controls on capital transfers, and the eventual spread of external convertibility to other currencies, including the Japanese yen, added a new dimension to the question of the adequacy of world reserves. A liberal trade and exchange regime and unprecedented levels of world output and prosperity had expanded international trade in goods and services and the flow of investment capital across national boundaries to magnitudes far beyond what anyone had imagined possible a decade before. But it was not only long-term capital investment that rose rapidly. Transfers of short-term capital—previously curtailed by restrictions or by special exchange rates—also began to take place on an increasingly large scale. As exchange restrictions were lifted, greater freedom was given to banks and to private individuals in European countries to hold liquid assets in other countries. Moreover, once the European countries had accepted the obligations of Article VIII of the Fund's Articles of Agreement in February 1961, governments were seen as being formally committed to complete and lasting convertibility for their currencies. The lifting of restrictions that had taken place did not have to be regarded as temporary. Within a few years' time short-term capital was being transferred with relative frequency and in massive amounts. Initially, such transfers were made in response to

13

differences in interest rates between various countries. But after the revaluation of the deutsche mark and the Netherlands guilder in March 1961, anticipations of possible changes in par values—and even of changes in political leadership— began to touch off flows of funds of a speculative nature as well.

Short-term capital movements began seriously to disrupt the balance of payments positions of the major industrial nations. Sterling, for example, beginning in the 1960s was subjected from time to time to severe strains in the world's exchange markets, at least partly because of rather sharp movements of short-term capital, and capital flows in unexpectedly large magnitudes and flights from dollars into gold started to aggravate the balance of payments deficits of the United States also. Short-term capital movements became greater as vast holdings—in the billions—of dollars and of liquid assets denominated in dollars were accumulated by European central banks and by private commercial banks, traders, investors, and other international financiers—the building up of such dollar balances being the way, along with the use of gold reserves, in which the U.S. payments deficits were financed.

At first, in order to finance short-term capital movements, substantial amounts of reserves were utilized and there was extensive recourse to the Fund.[3] Financial officials realized, however, that further steps would have to be taken.

At their monthly meeting in March 1961 at the Bank for International Settlements (BIS) in Basle, the Governors of the central banks of Belgium, France, the Federal Republic of Germany, Italy, the Netherlands, Sweden, and the United Kingdom agreed to cooperate closely in foreign exchange markets to assist any currency that was in difficulty because of speculation. They would hold each other's currencies to a greater extent than before, instead of converting them immediately into gold or dollars, and they would provide each other with short-term loans of needed currencies to help finance sudden flights of capital.

After the inauguration of this Basle Agreement, a series of national and international arrangements was gradually worked out in the next several years by which central banks agreed to cooperate with each other. Defenses against speculative runs were strengthened in 1962 with the introduction of "swap" facilities by the United States. These arrangements provided for reciprocal lines of credit, that is, for the exchange of a specified amount of dollars against an equivalent amount of the currency of the other participant, which might be called upon by either party when considered necessary; the swaps were subject to reversal at a future date.

Like the Basle facilities, the swap arrangements were used extensively as soon as they were set up, and within a short time a network of swap arrangements and credit lines was developed. The leading proponent of this form of bilateral cooperation was Mr. Robert V. Roosa, then Under Secretary

---

[3] See *History, 1945–65*, Vol. I, pp. 486–87.

for Monetary Affairs in the U.S. Treasury, who worked out many of the arrangements. These and similar arrangements were heavily used in the next several years.

Central banks also began to work more closely together to reduce the likelihood that speculative capital movements would take place. For instance, they attempted to coordinate their monetary policies, deliberately influencing their short-term interest rates so as not to induce disturbing capital movements. In order to affect the cost of the forward exchange cover necessary for speculative operations, central banks of industrial countries began to intervene on a large scale in forward exchange markets and to try to coordinate their intervention. For the first time since before World War II the United States, in 1961, entered into exchange transactions for monetary purposes, selling exchange in the forward markets of Europe. Gradually arrangements were made between the European countries and the United States permitting the latter, in cooperation with the European central banks, to operate in spot and forward exchange markets in Europe.

Another evidence of the collaborative efforts of financial authorities to defend the international monetary system was the institution in 1961 of the so-called Gold Pool. As the gold reserves of the United States began to decline, enhancing speculation that the official price of gold, $35 an ounce, would be raised, and as pressure on the Bank of England to intervene in the London gold market to keep the price from rising became intense, an informal arrangement was formed: the central banks of Belgium, France, the Federal Republic of Germany, Italy, the Netherlands, Switzerland, and the United States would share with the Bank of England the burden of intervention in the London gold market to hold the market price of gold at, or close to, the official price.[4]

THE FUND ADAPTS ITS POLICIES

Two facets of the Fund's response to the evolving world monetary situation have already been mentioned: a large increase in quotas approved in 1959 and the provision of access to its resources on a scale greater than before. For the time being this was thought to be enough. Nevertheless, international liquidity began to claim an increasing share of the Fund's attention.

The Fund's first official pronouncements on the subject came in the Annual Reports for 1960 and 1961 and in the speeches of Governors at the Annual Meetings in those years. The Annual Report for 1960 took an optimistic view of the world liquidity problem. Stressing that international liquidity included not only gold and foreign exchange directly owned by members but also

---

[4] For further details on inter-central-bank cooperation and on the institution of the Gold Pool, see *History, 1945–65*, Vol. I, pp. 482–85.

members' positions in the Fund, the Report noted that the supply of world liquidity had actually expanded. Following the 1959 enlargement of quotas there had been an increase of about $1 billion in the gold holdings of the Fund, and if account was taken of the increase in the Fund's holdings not only of gold but also of currencies suitable for international settlements, the growth of resources available through the Fund was several times that of the decrease in reserves directly owned by members.

At the 1960 Annual Meeting those Governors who referred to the matter expressed agreement with this view, and in his closing speech Mr. Jacobsson cited a consensus that there was "no lack of international liquidity." [5] This remained the official view of the Fund for some time to come, but it was coupled with an apprehension that the situation might not remain favorable and with emphasis on the important role in world reserves to be played by the resources which the Fund controlled.

The Annual Report for 1961 stressed again the part played in members' reserves by their drawing rights in the Fund.[6] On the assumption that all members were eligible to purchase foreign exchange equivalent to their gold subscriptions plus 100 per cent of their quotas in the Fund, drawing rights in the Fund amounted to $18.1 billion at the end of 1960. Drawing rights calculated in this way were thus almost as large at the end of 1960 as the total of all exchange reserves held by national monetary authorities.

Considerably more attention was paid to the liquidity problem during the 1961 Annual Meeting. Two or three Governors believed that, reinforced by the availability of the Fund's resources, international liquidity was adequate to meet the world's needs. Mr. M. W. Holtrop (Netherlands) even concluded that of late, because of balance of payments deficits of the key-currency countries, there had been an oversupply of liquidity that exceeded the desired increment of reserves by the main reserve-holding countries.[7] But the more general view was that care would be needed to ensure that no lack of reserves developed.

In 1961 the Executive Directors began an examination of the ways in which access to the Fund's resources might be increased. Between July 1961 and July 1962 they took three landmark decisions that substantially improved the Fund's ability to give financial assistance to its members.

(1) A decision taken in July 1961 made clear that members could, in certain circumstances, use the Fund's resources to meet balance of payments deficits that

---

[5] Concluding Remarks by the Managing Director, *Summary Proceedings of the Fifteenth Annual Meeting of the Board of Governors, 1960* (Washington, 1960). (Hereinafter cited as *Summary Proceedings, 19—.*)

[6] *Annual Report of the Executive Directors for the Fiscal Year Ended April 30, 1961* (Washington, 1961), p. 114. (Hereinafter cited as *Annual Report, 19—.*)

[7] Statement by the Governor of the Fund for the Netherlands, *Summary Proceedings, 1961,* pp. 113–14.

went beyond the current account and were attributable, in whole or in part, to capital transfers which were not large or sustained. Thus any doubt that the Fund's resources could, in given circumstances, be used for that purpose was removed.

(2) A decision taken in July 1962 established principles for the selection of currencies to be used in members' transactions with the Fund, both drawings and repurchases. The decision gave assurance that transactions would take place in a broad range of currencies, and no longer primarily in dollars. It put into application the consequences for the Fund's transactions of the acceptance of Article VIII obligations by most European countries in February 1961.

(3) On January 5, 1962 a decision was taken by the Executive Directors approving the General Arrangements to Borrow, and by October 24, 1962 enough participants had acceded to the Arrangements to bring them into operation. By these Arrangements, the Fund enlarged by $6 billion the resources to which it had access.[8]

PROPOSALS FOR EXPANDING WORLD LIQUIDITY

Meanwhile a few economists, looking upon the network of swaps and similar arrangements as ad hoc financing of crises, began to advocate what they considered to be more permanent solutions to the increasingly apparent defects of the international monetary system. Most of the proposals involved, in one way or another, new functions for the Fund.

Triffin Plan

Professor Robert Triffin, of Yale University, was undoubtedly the front-runner in advocating broad reforms of the international monetary system. As early as 1959 he proposed that an enlarged and modified International Monetary Fund be assigned the job of providing a new kind of reserve in the required amounts.[9]

---

[8] More information on these decisions, and the circumstances leading up to them, can be found in *History, 1945–65*, Vol. I, pp. 502–20.

[9] Mr. Triffin's views were put forward initially in 1959 in two articles, "The Return to Convertibility: 1926–1931 and 1958— ? or, Convertibility and the Morning After," Banca Nazionale del Lavoro, *Quarterly Review*, March 1959, pp. 3–57, and "Tomorrow's Convertibility: Aims and Means of International Monetary Policy," Banca Nazionale del Lavoro, *Quarterly Review*, June 1959, pp. 131–200. Further development of his views can be found in "Statement," in *Employment, Growth and Price Levels*, U.S. Congress, Joint Economic Committee (Hearings), 86th Cong., 1st sess., October 26–30, 1959 (Washington, 1959), Part 9A, pp. 2905–54. A detailed exposition of his proposals was set forth in his *Gold and the Dollar Crisis: The Future of Convertibility* (New Haven, 1960).

His reasoning was based on the belief that the gold exchange standard as it had developed was basically unsatisfactory. Under that standard, countries held their reserves in the form of gold and a few national currencies, especially dollars and, to some extent, sterling. The production of new gold was insufficient to meet the growing needs for reserves as trade and other international transactions expanded. Reliance on national currencies as supplementary reserves was haphazard and dangerous. It was haphazard because the growth of reserves was tied to the existence of balance of payments deficits in the United States and the United Kingdom and, in effect, to the domestic policies pursued by these two countries. It was dangerous because foreign-held dollar and sterling balances represented short-term indebtedness of the countries whose currencies were being used as reserves, an indebtedness that weakened the net reserve positions of these countries. Even without any further growth of dollar and sterling balances, the stability of the international monetary system was already jeopardized by the risk of runs on currencies and of flights into gold.

What the world needed, Mr. Triffin argued, was a kind of international reserve which could be augmented appropriately in accordance with international liquidity requirements. The Triffin Plan was in effect two-pronged: it provided not only for an expansion of international reserves but also for a stable structure of reserves. Fund members should agree not to keep any of their official reserves in the national currencies of other countries but to keep all of their reserves in the form of deposits in an extended version of the Fund. Members would thus hold reserves in only two forms, gold and deposits in the Fund. The latter would be used along with gold in international settlements. They might be considered as good as gold, or even better, since they would not only carry a guarantee against exchange rate depreciation but would also earn interest.

In order that the total amount of international liquidity should grow, Mr. Triffin further proposed that the Fund be empowered to create new deposits. Such deposits would arise when the Fund, as appropriately altered, made loans to its members that were analogous to drawings from the Fund but were divorced from Fund quotas, and when the Fund made investments in short-term or long-term government securities of its members. To keep liquidity from becoming excessive, the lending capacity of the Fund would be limited.

In effect, Mr. Triffin proposed to give the Fund the power to create a new kind of money—an international money—and to add to the quantity of this money in accordance with international liquidity requirements as determined by its members. The Fund would be an international central bank for central banks, with the responsibility and the authority to do for central banks internationally what central banks already did for commercial banks nationally. Thus a system would be created that could be rationally managed to stabilize the structure of international reserves and to expand reserves in accordance with need.

In many respects, Mr. Triffin's proposal was similar to the Keynes Plan of 1942–43.[10] That Plan had provided that the monetary reserves of central banks consist of only gold and bancor, an international currency unit made up of deposits with the Clearing Union, and had provided for the creation of new bancor credit deposits. Under the Keynes Plan, central banks were to be allowed, when necessary, to overdraw their accounts with the Clearing Union.

Stamp Plan

The Honorable Arthur Maxwell Stamp, of the United Kingdom, also came up with ideas in 1960 which he modified in 1962 and which ultimately became known as the Stamp Plan.[11] His plan provided a mechanism whereby the needs of the industrial countries for additional liquidity, together with the needs of the developing countries for additional foreign capital, could be met simultaneously. According to the 1962 version of his plan, the Fund would create a new form of credit by issuing certificates, denominated in U.S. dollars at a par value based on gold at $35 an ounce, which would be convertible into currencies held by the Fund. Member countries would agree to receive these certificates from central banks or from monetary authorities in settlement of international obligations, up to a total amount equal to their quotas in the Fund. They would hold these certificates as reserves and would undertake to use them in payment only if they were under balance of payments pressure and not for the purpose of adding to their gold or dollar reserves.

The Fund would lend the certificates to the International Development Association (IDA), an affiliate of the World Bank, for 50 years. The IDA, in turn, would allocate them to the developing countries under an agreed program. The country receiving the certificates would use them to buy capital goods in the industrial countries by tendering them to the central bank of the industrial country concerned and acquiring the necessary national currency. The returns which the IDA received on its investments would be paid to the Fund as interest on the certificates. This interest would be credited, as far as practicable, to the members of the Fund that held certificates, in proportion to their holdings.

Other Proposals

In the early 1960s several economists made a number of other suggestions as to how the supply of international liquidity might be enlarged. Most of

---

[10] *Proposals for an International Currency (or Clearing) Union;* see *History, 1945–65,* Vol. III, pp. 3–36.

[11] Maxwell Stamp, "The Fund and the Future," *Lloyds Bank Review,* October 1958, pp. 1–20, "Changes in the World's Payments System," *Moorgate and Wall Street,* Spring 1961, pp. 3–22, and "The Stamp Plan—1962 Version," *Moorgate and Wall Street,* Autumn 1962, pp. 5–17.

these proposals were not as far-reaching as the Triffin and Stamp Plans: point-edly, they did not call for the centralization of reserves in the Fund or for the expansion of reserves through the Fund.

Professor A. C. L. Day, of the London School of Economics, proposed that the Fund be transformed into an international central bank, with its own unit of account, free to accept deposit liabilities or extend overdraft facilities to the central banks of member countries.[12] Unlike Mr. Triffin, Mr. Day would not have required central banks to hold stated proportions of their reserves in the form of deposits with the Fund. The Day Plan was submitted to, and endorsed by, the Radcliffe Committee.[13]

Other plans, such as those of Mr. Edward M. Bernstein, of the United States, formerly Director of the Fund's Research and Statistics Department, did not involve such drastic changes in the functions of the Fund or in the nature of the official reserves that countries held.[14] Some of these plans would simply have enlarged the number of currencies used as reserve currencies. Central banks would hold various European currencies, such as deutsche mark, French francs, or Swiss francs, in their reserves in addition to dollars and sterling. The gold exchange standard would thus be given a broader base through a system of "multiple reserve currencies." Some suggestions for such a multiple-currency approach included the idea that some major industrial countries would coordinate their monetary policies so as to reduce capital movements.

Additional suggestions involved the extension of mutual assistance among central banks. Many ideas were forthcoming as to how central banks could extend short-term credit to one another, by ad hoc agreements or stand-by

---

[12] A. C. L. Day, "Memorandum of Evidence," in *Principal Memoranda of Evidence*, [Radcliffe] Committee on the Working of the Monetary System, Vol. 3 (London, 1960), p. 75. See also his "The World's Payments System," in *International Payments Imbalances and Need for Strengthening International Financial Arrangements*, U.S. Congress, Joint Economic Committee (Hearings Before the Subcommittee on International Exchange and Payments), 87th Cong., 1st sess., May 16–June 21, 1961 (Washington, 1961), pp. 325–30.

[13] [Radcliffe] Committee on the Working of the Monetary System, *Report* (London, Cmnd. 827, 1959), pp. 241 and 247–48.

[14] See, for example, "International Effects of U.S. Economic Policy," in *Employment, Growth and Price Levels*, U.S. Congress, Joint Economic Committee (Study Paper No. 16), 86th Cong., 2nd sess. (Washington, 1960), pp. 85–86, "The Adequacy of United States Gold Reserves," *American Economic Review* (Papers and Proceedings of the Seventy-Third Annual Meeting of the American Economic Association), Vol. 51 (1961), pp. 439–46, and "Statement: The Problem of International Monetary Reserves," in *International Payments Imbalances and Need for Strengthening International Financial Arrangements*, U.S. Congress, Joint Economic Committee (Hearings Before the Subcommittee on International Exchange and Payments), 87th Cong., 1st sess., May 16–June 21, 1961 (Washington, 1961), pp. 107–37. Mr. Bernstein had advanced these ideas as early as October 1958 at a seminar in international economics at Harvard University.

arrangements. Some proposals involved the Fund's acting as intermediary between the lending and the borrowing central bank.[15]

While these proposals for ways to enhance world liquidity were being made, some economists had begun to advocate radically different methods for dealing with the problem of possible deficiencies of liquidity in the monetary system. Several, such as Sir Roy Harrod, of Oxford University, Jacques Rueff, of France, and Michael Heilperin, Professor, Graduate Institute of International Studies, Geneva, urged that the price of gold be sharply increased—possibly doubled (from $35 an ounce to $70 an ounce) or even tripled. Such a change in the price of gold would swell the supply of liquidity by upvaluing both the existing gold stocks held as monetary reserves and the annual additions to these stocks. Hence, they argued, there would be no need to do anything further. Others, most notably Professor Milton Friedman, of the University of Chicago, proposed the introduction of freely flexible exchange rates. Rates which equated demand and supply for exchange, they contended, would do away with any need to expand world liquidity. Central banks would be relieved of any function in the international payments system and would not need to hold reserves for the purpose of making foreign payments.

THE FUND'S REACTIONS TO PROPOSALS

We have already noted that the Fund's primary preoccupation in respect of international liquidity at the beginning of the 1960s was with devising new techniques and policies so that the resources under its control could be used more effectively and enlarged. It was at this time—from February 1961 to January 1962—that the General Arrangements to Borrow were worked out. These Arrangements came about as a result of proposals, initiated by Mr. Jacobsson and some Governors, for the Fund to borrow from the central banks in the countries receiving capital inflows and to make the borrowed funds available to the central banks suffering from capital outflows.[16]

Suggestions for raising the price of gold or for abandoning the par value system were not taken seriously by the authorities responsible for making

---

[15] Many of these proposals have been brought together in one volume in *World Monetary Reform: Plans and Issues*, Herbert G. Grubel, ed. (Stanford, 1963). Also, a comparison of the various proposals coming forward at this time can be found in Fritz Machlup, *Plans for Reform of the International Monetary System*, Special Papers in International Economics, No. 3, Princeton University (Princeton, 1962).

[16] Mr. Jacobsson first made public his proposals in April 1961; see "Fund Report at Ecosoc," *International Financial News Survey*, Vol. 13 (1961), pp. 121–27. He also publicized them at the 1961 Annual Meeting; see both Opening Address and Concluding Remarks by the Managing Director, *Summary Proceedings, 1961*, pp. 28–29 and 157–58. For a detailed description of how the General Arrangements to Borrow came into being, see *History, 1945–65*, Vol. I, pp. 507–16.

monetary decisions, including those in the Fund. The proposals for enlarging the supply of world liquidity, especially the more radical Triffin and Stamp Plans, were also received with coolness. Mr. Jacobsson clearly did not share the fears of those who foresaw a scramble for international reserves, nor did he concur with the predictions made by Mr. Triffin that the catastrophic collapse of the international monetary system of the 1930s was bound to be repeated.

Mr. Jacobsson's view, as expressed in his speeches and articles, was that the gold exchange standard had performed well the two functions required of an international monetary system: it had kept exchange rates stable and it had provided sufficient liquidity.[17] He believed that the problem of a shortage of international liquidity was not yet so acute as to require concerted action by monetary authorities. If the problem arose, monetary authorities could agree on solutions. His beliefs along these lines were reinforced by the 1959 increase in Fund quotas and the completion of the General Arrangements to Borrow in 1961–62.

Mr. Oscar L. Altman, then Advisor in the Research and Statistics Department, also set forth his personal views to the effect that Mr. Triffin had overstated the risks of instability in the structure of international reserves and had understated the ability of the key-currency countries to meet the risks to which they were exposed.[18] Mr. Altman, too, pointed to the much larger resources of the Fund following the 1959 increase in quotas and to the wider assortment of convertible currencies that had become available, and thought that the Fund was quite able to help countries in deficit.

Moreover, Mr. Altman argued, the volume of reserves and the volume of trade were not mechanically related. The demand for reserves was rather the result of the policy decisions of a relatively small number of countries. Furthermore, the adequacy of the reserve position of any country was influenced not only by its gross reserves but also by its debtor or creditor position in the Fund, the size of its unused drawing rights in the Fund, the amount of its outstanding and overdue short-term commercial debt, official short-term borrowings, gold pledges, banks' holdings and other private holdings of exchange, and the like. Accordingly, should the need to expand liquidity arise, the existing international financial machinery was the best means for doing so. Nothing so drastic as the Triffin Plan was necessary. Indeed, an expanded Fund as envisaged in Mr. Triffin's proposals would be faced with a host of new problems, unduly complicating its actions and policies.

---

[17] See, for example, his Opening Address to the 1962 Annual Meeting, *Summary Proceedings, 1962*, pp. 26ff, and his "The Two Functions of an International Monetary Standard: Stability and Liquidity," in *World Monetary Reform: Plans and Issues*, Herbert G. Grubel, ed. (Stanford, 1963), pp. 227–37.

[18] Oscar L. Altman, "Professor Triffin on International Liquidity and the Role of the Fund," and Robert Triffin, "A Brief for the Defense," *Staff Papers*, Vol. 8 (1960–61), pp. 151–91 and 192–94. Also, Robert Triffin, "Altman on Triffin: A Rebuttal," Banca Nazionale del Lavoro, *Quarterly Review*, March 1961, pp. 31–50.

New Studies of Liquidity

Nonetheless, the questions raised were very important and the staff of the Fund began to explore in greater depth than previously how a scarcity of liquidity might manifest itself and what methods were available for influencing and controlling the amount and the distribution of liquidity.[19] By what criteria could one judge the need for liquidity in the international monetary system? If the value of world trade was a relevant but not a sufficient consideration, what other factors had to be taken into account? Once it had been determined what the optimal level of liquidity was, what kind of international arrangements could best supply additional liquidity?

At this time the concepts of conditional and unconditional liquidity were refined and the distinction between them made clear. Conditional liquidity was defined as potential access to reserves, such as the resources of the Fund, subject to the observance of certain conditions as to the use to be made of them or as to the general economic policies to be pursued by the recipient. Unconditional liquidity, as the term implies, was defined as access to resources without any conditions being attached. These terms were later to be used with increasing frequency.

Zolotas and Maudling Plans

That the problem of liquidity was beginning to attract greater official attention was evidenced by new proposals made by Governors during the 1962 Annual Meeting. In general, the Governors who spoke about liquidity commended the various measures taken by central banks and by the Fund to deal with the problems created by capital movements; with these measures, they believed that the level of world liquidity was adequate. Nonetheless, two Governors advanced proposals to ensure that, in the future, as world trade continued to expand, the volume of liquidity could be appropriately enlarged.

Mr. Xenophon Zolotas (Greece) proposed a multiple-currency gold exchange standard, the main features of which would be (1) the reciprocal accumulation by major trading countries of reserve balances in each other's currencies, (2) a gold guarantee by the major countries on foreign official reserve deposits, and (3) preferential interest rate and tax treatment for foreign official depositors of reserve balances, which could possibly be extended to foreign private holders of short-term assets.[20]

---

[19] See, for example, J. Marcus Fleming, "International Liquidity: Ends and Means," *Staff Papers*, Vol. 8 (1960–61), pp. 439–63. Mr. Fleming's article appeared in the same volume of *Staff Papers* as Mr. Altman's article cited in the preceding footnote. Monetary experts could thus see that different approaches to the problem of liquidity were being studied by the Fund staff.

[20] Statement by the Governor of the Fund for Greece, *Summary Proceedings, 1962*, pp. 111–12.

Reflecting the importance attached in the United Kingdom to some new arrangement for providing liquidity, Mr. Reginald Maudling (United Kingdom) proposed a scheme that had been worked out in the Bank of England, labeled the "mutual currency account." Building on the cooperation that central banks had already initiated by holding each other's currencies, Mr. Maudling's plan was to widen the system still further. He described his plan as follows: "By this I have in mind an arrangement of a multilateral character under which countries could continue to acquire the currency of another country which was temporarily surplus in the markets and use it to establish claims on a mutual currency account which they could themselves use when their situations were reversed. Such claims on the account would attract the guarantee that attaches to holdings in the Fund." [21]

In his concluding remarks at the 1962 Annual Meeting Mr. Jacobsson took note of these suggestions, promising that they would be studied carefully.

---

[21] Statement by the Governor of the Fund and the World Bank for the United Kingdom, *Summary Proceedings, 1962*, pp. 67–68.

CHAPTER

2

Debate on Liquidity Intensified

(1963–64)

BY APRIL 1963 THE SITUATION HAD CHANGED considerably. Most central bankers and monetary officials had begun seriously to question whether the world's supply of liquidity would continue to be sufficient, especially as the world economy in general, and international trade in particular, expanded further.

Two developments brought about this heightened interest in the liquidity problem. *First*, in 1962 members' official reserves (including their gold tranche positions in the Fund)[1] did not grow, whereas in the previous three years they had risen from some $60 billion to about $65 billion.[2] There had been, in particular, a notable change in gold reserves: in most postwar years some $500–700 million of gold had been added to the official holdings of countries and international agencies, but the figure was much smaller in 1960 and again in 1962. Political and economic uncertainties had led to abnormally large private hoarding of gold. Meanwhile, world trade had been continuing to rise by an average of 8 per cent per annum.

Second, central bankers and other financial officials were coming to the realization that, as the United States succeeded in its efforts to reduce its payments deficit, there would be a slowdown in the growth of the exchange holdings of other countries and thereby in the growth of world reserves. Insofar as U.S. deficits had been financed by other countries accumulating

---

[1] Gold tranche position: the amount a member could draw without increasing the Fund's holdings of its currency beyond 100 per cent of its quota, excluding certain holdings arising from compensatory financing operations. For each member, that amount began by being equivalent to the member's gold subscription to the Fund, and it was for this reason that the tranche was called the gold tranche. Further information on the nature of the gold tranche can be found in Joseph Gold, *The Stand-By Arrangements of the International Monetary Fund: A Commentary on Their Formal, Legal, and Financial Aspects* (Washington, 1970), pp. 13–14 (hereinafter cited as Gold, *Stand-By Arrangements*), and in Chap. 13 below, pp. 255–56.

[2] Because of the absence of data for other countries, the Fund's statistics for the total official reserves of the world during the years covered in this volume were those for the members of the Fund plus Switzerland.

liquid claims on the United States, these deficits had led to increases in the world totals for international reserves. Since increases in liquid claims on the United States had, since 1958, been enlarging world reserves by nearly $1 billion a year, the elimination of the U.S. balance of payments deficit would dry up the largest source of additions to reserves.

On July 18, 1963, President John F. Kennedy called attention to the latter problem in a special message to the Congress on the U.S. balance of payments: "One of the reasons that new sources of liquidity may well be needed is that, as we close our payments gap, we will cut down our provision of dollars to the rest of the world." [3] At the opening session of the 1963 Annual Meeting of the Board of Governors in Washington, on September 30, 1963, President Kennedy again referred to the problem of world reserves posed by the elimination of the U.S. payments deficit, and announced that "the United States, therefore, stands ready to support such measures as may be necessary to increase international liquidity." [4]

OFFICIAL POSITIONS DEVELOP

Accelerated interest within the Fund in the subject of liquidity was reflected in the Annual Report for 1963.[5] As the Report was drafted, the line of thought of the two previous years, that the Fund was already a principal supplier of international liquidity, was developed further. It was to influence the liquidity debate for years to come. The figures for reserves published in the Report included members' gold tranche positions in the Fund along with their holdings of gold and foreign exchange. The inclusion was explained in the following way: since February 1952 members had been able to count on receiving the overwhelming benefit of any doubt for drawings in the gold tranche, and the clarification of July 1961 that the Fund's resources could in certain circumstances be used to meet deficits arising from capital transfers had made these gold tranche positions virtually freely usable.

Furthermore, the Report noted, international liquidity, a broader concept than that of reserves, included credit tranche positions in the Fund, defining credit tranche position as the amount a member could draw beyond the gold tranche before the Fund's holdings of that member's currency reached 200 per cent of its quota.[6]

At this time, too, the conviction began to develop that additions to conditional liquidity, such as those created by the Fund, were more to be desired

---

[3] *Department of State Bulletin*, Vol. 49 (1963), p. 259.

[4] Address by the President of the United States, *Summary Proceedings, 1963*, p. 5.

[5] *Annual Report, 1963*, Chap. 3.

[6] Drawings beyond this point could be permitted by waiver.

than expansion of unconditional liquidity. This view, which was held by several Executive Directors but was expressed most strongly by Mr. Pieter Lieftinck (Netherlands), stemmed from an apprehension that too easy access to reserves would encourage inflationary policies.[7] Hence, the Executive Directors strengthened a passage drafted by the staff for the 1963 Annual Report to read as follows:

> If improvement or enlargement of the credit facilities is needed, it may be more important and feasible to concentrate on the adaptation or enlargement of the existing multilateral arrangements through the Fund than to seek to establish supplementary or alternative arrangements outside. In this connection, it should be evident that the Fund, in its further evolution, would be capable of accommodating itself to the emerging needs for such enlarged facilities.[8]

Regarding the adequacy of such international liquidity as already existed, including positions in the Fund, the Executive Directors concluded that the supply available in 1963 was large, stating that "most countries already have sufficient reserves or access to credit arrangements, particularly in the Fund, to finance the kind of disequilibria that might occur." [9] It was a guarded conclusion, however, and concern was expressed for the adequacy of liquidity in the future:

> . . . if a substantial proportion of [liquidity] is, for one reason or another, considered to be available "for emergency use only," then the risk is correspondingly increased, not only of slowing down the world economy but also of being unable smoothly to deal with emergencies. . . .
>
> The quantitative and qualitative adequacy of the international liquidity structure requires continued close attention. The Fund must keep developments in this field under constant review in order to anticipate the problems that might arise. In this way, the Fund will be in a position in good time to take, or to propose to its members, any requisite action.[10]

Active Role for the Fund

Mr. Pierre-Paul Schweitzer became Managing Director on September 1, 1963, succeeding Mr. Jacobsson, who died suddenly in May. After being Managing Director for one month, Mr. Schweitzer, in his first opening address to the Board of Governors, set out an active role for the Fund in any delibera-

---

[7] In the text of this history, Executive Directors are identified by the country of their nationality. For the Directors that are elected, however, this is only an indication of their constituencies. A complete listing of the Executive Directors, their Alternates, and the countries that appointed or elected them (as well as the country of nationality of both the Directors and their Alternates) for the period 1966–71 is given in Appendices A–1, A–2, and A–3, to this volume. Management and senior staff as of the end of 1971 are listed in Appendix B. The same kind of information for the period 1946–68 is given in Appendices A and B to Vol. I of *History, 1945–65*.

[8] *Annual Report, 1963*, p. 51.

[9] *Annual Report, 1963*, p. 51.

[10] *Annual Report, 1963*, pp. 51–52.

tions concerning liquidity that might ensue. He was, of course, aware that the Finance Ministers and Central Bank Governors of the ten countries participating in the General Arrangements to Borrow—Belgium, Canada, France, the Federal Republic of Germany, Italy, Japan, the Netherlands, Sweden, the United Kingdom, and the United States—now meeting together from time to time as the Group of Ten, had decided in the summer of 1963 to consult among themselves during the next 12 months on problems of international liquidity and the international monetary system and were planning to issue a press release on this subject during the Annual Meeting. Mr. Schweitzer expressed his belief that "insofar as it is found necessary from time to time to expand the level of world liquidity by international action, the Fund will be found to be the instrument through which the bulk of the required expansion can most suitably be carried out," and explained that "the provision of supplementary international liquidity is, after all, one of the principal reasons for which the Fund was set up and is a matter with which it is concerned from day to day." [11]

He went on to say that the Fund's policies and practices could be modified, and if need be the Articles of Agreement could be amended, to enable the Fund to continue to play an effective role in the provision of international liquidity. And he announced that in the coming year the Fund would develop and intensify its study of international liquidity.

Most Governors, especially those representing countries outside the Group of Ten, welcomed the proposed inquiries by the Fund. This position was exemplified by the words of Mr. Harold Holt (Australia), who commended the Fund for its decision to develop and intensify its study of international liquidity, stressing that all countries had a direct and vital interest in the matter: "That is why so many of us believe that the Fund should continue to exercise a leadership in this field and why, in our judgment, decisions finally adopted should be decisions taken by the Fund after due process." [12]

Group of Ten Studies

The Finance Ministers and Central Bank Governors of the Group of Ten held a special meeting during the course of the 1963 Annual Meeting, after which they announced their intended studies. In their communiqué they "noted that the present national reserves of member countries, supplemented as they are by the resources of the IMF, as well as by a network of bilateral facilities, seemed fully adequate in present circumstances to cope with possible threats to the stability of the international payments system." But it appeared to them "to be useful to undertake a thorough examination of the outlook for the

---

[11] Opening Address by the Managing Director, *Summary Proceedings, 1963*, p. 29.

[12] Statement by the Governor of the Fund and the World Bank for Australia, *Summary Proceedings, 1963*, p. 71.

functioning of the international monetary system and of its probable future needs for liquidity."[13] The communiqué also specified two premises for their studies: fixed exchange rates would continue to be the basis of the international monetary system, and the price of gold would remain unchanged.

The Group of Ten noted with approval Mr. Schweitzer's statement that the Fund would "develop and intensify its studies of these long-run questions" and instructed their Deputies, in carrying out their studies, to maintain close working relations with the Fund and with other international bodies concerned with monetary matters. As for the Fund, Mr. Schweitzer, discussing the outcome of the Annual Meeting with the Executive Directors on October 16, 1963, said that he visualized a very close working relationship between the Fund and the Group of Ten in their parallel examinations. There would be a full interchange of ideas. He himself would participate in the meetings of the Group of Ten at the ministerial level, and he would send representatives to the meetings of the Deputies. The staff would produce memoranda for the Executive Board as its studies progressed, and copies of these would be available, through the Executive Directors, to the monetary authorities of the members of the Group of Ten.

Thus, following the 1963 Annual Meeting, intensive studies concerning liquidity and the broader topic of the international monetary system began both in the Fund and in the Group of Ten. These important issues also attracted considerable attention among economists outside official circles. Not since the Fund had been created had international monetary subjects so engaged the interest of specialists everywhere.[14]

Expansion of Liquidity versus Balance of Payments Adjustment

The speeches of the Governors at the 1963 Annual Meeting revealed a divergence of view between those who favored expansion of the world's supply of liquidity and those who emphasized elimination of balance of payments disequilibria. This controversy was to surface many times in the coming years. The fear expressed by those who urged elimination of balance of payments deficits before world liquidity was expanded was this: Would not too much liquidity tempt the large industrial countries that had been running persistent deficits, especially the United Kingdom and the United States, to pay too little heed to their deficits and to engage in overexpansive financial policies?

Mr. Valéry Giscard d'Estaing (France), in particular, voiced his fears of this risk, a position he was to repeat for the next several years. At the 1963

---

[13] Statement Issued on October 2, 1963 by the Secretary of the Treasury of the United States on Behalf of the "Group of 10" Members of the Fund, *Summary Proceedings, 1963*, pp. 285–86.

[14] For example, Fritz Machlup and Burton G. Malkiel, eds., *International Monetary Arrangements—The Problem of Choice: Report on the Deliberations of an International Study Group of 32 Economists* (Princeton, 1964).

Annual Meeting he contended that the fundamental difficulties confronting the international monetary system were not due to any shortage of international liquidity but to three structural weaknesses in the system: (a) the lack of mechanisms to correct balance of payments deficits; (b) the asymmetry between countries whose currencies were held as reserves by other countries, and which thereby had an easy means of financing deficits, and the rest of the world, which had no such means; and (c) the unevenness between countries of the risks of holding reserves, depending upon the type of reserve—those countries that held gold running the least risk that their holdings would be subjected to devaluation.[15]

The U.S. authorities, however, considered the conflict between the need to expand liquidity and the need to restore balance of payments equilibrium more apparent than real. Mr. C. Douglas Dillon (United States) wanted to make it "crystal clear: the United States does not view possible improvements in the methods of supplying international liquidity as relieving it of the compelling and immediate task of reducing its own payments deficit." Adjustments in balance of payments situations that were in chronic deficit or surplus had to take place. The critical question was how the adjustments were to be made. Balance could be—and too often in the past had been—forced by measures that endangered domestic stability or the prospects for growing international trade.[16]

Others, including Mr. Schweitzer, took the position that whether what was needed was more liquidity or better equilibrium depended on the time span one had in mind:

> International liquidity . . . consists of international reserves and other resources which are at the disposal of monetary authorities and which serve to finance balance of payments deficits, and thus provide time to make any adjustments that may be required to eliminate those deficits without resort to measures that would be damaging to the prosperity of the countries concerned or to the rest of the world.[17]

Mr. Maudling (United Kingdom) took a similar line:

> The primary purpose of international liquidity is to give time for individual countries to make adjustments in their balance of payments without sharp changes in the volume of imports or in the growth of domestic demand. But at the same time the availability of liquid resources should not be such as to promote, or encourage countries to tolerate, the continuance of basically unsound domestic or international positions in the guise of temporary fluctuations. The basic dilemma is clear. If adequate resources are not available automatically or nearly automatically, their usefulness in times of trouble may be problematic;

---

[15] Statement by the Governor of the World Bank for France, *Summary Proceedings, 1963*, pp. 60–61.

[16] Statement by the Governor of the Fund and the World Bank for the United States, *Summary Proceedings, 1963*, pp. 44 and 52.

[17] Opening Address by the Managing Director, *Summary Proceedings, 1963*, p. 27.

but to the extent to which they are automatically available, they may present a temptation to refrain from the necessary corrections of policy.[18]

FRAMEWORK FOR THE FUND'S STUDY OF LIQUIDITY

In undertaking its examination of international liquidity, a first task of the Fund staff was to identify the areas of research in which work would be needed. On October 31, 1963, the Managing Director sent to the Executive Board a memorandum proposing that studies be made of four main subjects: the need for international liquidity; the supply and management of international liquidity; the liquidity of the Fund itself; and the operational and policy issues arising with regard to the size of the Fund's resources and their use.

On January 10, 1964, he elaborated. Liquidity was not an end in itself, it was merely a means to the attainment of the common objectives of the Fund's members: high levels of employment and growth, the absence of restrictions on trade and payments, and stability of prices and exchange rates. The need for liquidity was not a simple numerical concept; its composition— as between gold, foreign exchange, and credit facilities—the way in which it was distributed among countries, and the manner in which it was created were all relevant to assessing its adequacy. Any appraisal of the need for liquidity would also have to make assumptions regarding the way in which countries were likely to respond to changes in the amount of liquidity available; this in turn depended on their balance of payments policies in general. The Fund's studies, like those of the Group of Ten, would also be based on the assumptions that fixed par values and freedom from restrictions on payments would be continued. There was no official support for fluctuating exchange rates or a return to restrictions as a means of easing pressures on available liquidity.

The dilemma of choosing between expanded liquidity and balance of payments adjustment was posed mainly by the deficit in the U.S. balance of payments. Here Mr. Schweitzer believed that there was general agreement among the U.S. authorities that the balance of payments must be brought into equilibrium as quickly as possible "without resorting to measures destructive of national or international prosperity," the words of Article I of the Fund Agreement. As the United States had substantial means with which to finance its deficit while it was achieving a reasonable equilibrium in its payments position, the international monetary system still had much strength.

The present adequacy of international liquidity was not a matter for concern. The problem, if there was a problem, was for the longer run. Accordingly, the Fund's work should not be done in haste. On the contrary, an undue

---

[18] Statement by the Governor of the Fund for the United Kingdom, *Summary Proceedings, 1963*, p. 65.

display of urgency might easily create expectations of specific proposals by certain dates and give the impression that the Fund itself lacked confidence in the present monetary system. Care was necessary that confidence in reserve currencies not be undermined as revolutionary proposals were discussed. It was, moreover, essential that new grafts to the international monetary system not damage the plant they were intended to improve.

Mr. Schweitzer further suggested that, as part of the Fund's study of liquidity, the general adequacy of quotas and the Fund's policies on gold tranche drawings also be examined. But in addition he thought that, if it should be found necessary to create more international liquidity of the unconditional variety, the Fund could be adapted to enable it to provide such liquidity. Therefore, he asked the staff to explore possible techniques.

The Executive Directors, sensitive to the attention being given to the subject by the Group of Ten, on the whole reacted very favorably to the Managing Director's suggestions. Mr. William B. Dale (United States) thought that history might well record that the initiative from the Fund in the field of international liquidity began with this statement. Mr. A. F. W. Plumptre (Canada) noted that a general view seemed to be forming that some sort of alterations to the international monetary system would, after study, prove to be desirable. The problem for the Fund was that future changes or adaptations or improvements could come within the structure of the Fund or from outside. The Fund could acquire increasing functions and responsibilities or it could sit passively and watch its influence and authority drift away.

When the Executive Directors continued their discussion of the Managing Director's statement in informal session on January 17 and 20, 1964, most of the Directors for countries not in the Group of Ten commended the broad range of the Managing Director's speech. Mr. J. M. Garland (Australia), for example, noted that the statement did not ignore the groups who were watching these discussions rather anxiously over the shoulders, as it were, of the main participants. The Managing Director had outlined a positive role for the Fund and had given the Fund a strong and stimulating lead.

THE FUND ADJUSTS POLICIES ON ITS RESOURCES

The question of how the Fund's policies regarding its resources might be adapted to provide additional liquidity to its members was tackled first. In the next several months, the Executive Board took decisions further liberalizing gold tranche drawings and recommending a second round of increases in quotas.

Although the Annual Report for 1963 had included gold tranche positions in the Fund as part of members' official reserves, a few limitations on members' access to these positions still remained, and these might inhibit some members from including them in their reserve figures. One such limitation was time: the procedure for handling requests for drawings, including the preparation of a staff memorandum, its consideration by the Executive Board, the dispatch of instructions to the Fund's depository to transfer the appropriate currency, and the actual transfer, took a full week. Therefore, in December 1963 the staff suggested some modifications in procedure that would permit gold tranche drawings to take place more quickly and more nearly automatically. After several discussions, the Executive Board took a decision on August 3, 1964 putting these modifications into effect.[19] Later, when the Articles were amended, gold tranche drawings became legally automatic.

The other drawing facilities of the Fund, in the credit tranches, were much larger, totaling about $13.4 billion at the end of 1962. But even these were below what they had been two years before, in spite of an expanded membership and some adjustments of quotas. Hence, it was to this important segment of liquidity that the Fund began to direct its attention late in 1963. The emphasis on credit tranches was in line with two Fund views—that the Fund was an important source of international liquidity, and that the conditional liquidity which it provided had advantages over unconditional liquidity.

After considerable discussion, the Executive Board concluded in mid-1964 that there was a case for a second round of increases in quotas. The normal practice would have been to begin a quinquennial review of quotas at the end of 1964 with a view to reaching a decision by the end of 1965, but there seemed to be merit in considering quotas as promptly as possible after the Annual Meeting, which was to be held in Tokyo in September.[20]

At the 1964 Annual Meeting the Governors resolved unanimously that the Executive Directors should proceed to consider the question of adjusting the quotas of members of the Fund and at an early date submit an appropriate proposal to the Board of Governors. The Governors' speeches made it clear, however, that there were differences of view with respect to the size and urgency of a general increase in quotas and with respect to the amount and number of special adjustments of quotas.

Action on this second round of quota increases was actually not completed until early in 1966, the process proving to be longer than that of the third quinquennial review of 1959. On February 24, 1965, the Executive Board adopted a report, *Increases in Quotas of Members—Fourth Quinquennial Review*, that included two resolutions: one proposed a general increase of 25 per cent in all quotas, the second proposed special increases for 16 members.[21] By March 31, 1965, both resolutions had been adopted by the Governors. By February 23, 1966, members representing the required two thirds of the total of

---

[19] For a fuller discussion, see *History, 1945–65,* Vol. I, pp. 564–67.

[20] This fourth quinquennial review of quotas was covered in *History, 1945–65,* Vol. I, pp. 574–85, and Vol. III, pp. 458–65.

[21] The report was published in *History, 1945–65,* Vol. III, pp. 458–65.

quotas had consented to increases in their quotas. On March 9, 1966, the Executive Board decided that the fourth quinquennial review of quotas had been completed. As a result of that review the Fund's assets were, in the course of the next two years, expanded from $16 billion to close to $21 billion.

GENERAL SUBJECT OF LIQUIDITY EXAMINED

In addition to these actions by the Fund affecting conditional liquidity, in 1963–64 the staff began intensive studies of a number of basic questions concerning liquidity in general: How could the world's requirements for liquidity be judged? Was the present total satisfactory? What were the relative functions of conditional and unconditional liquidity? How might the Fund expand unconditional liquidity? [22] What were the issues involved in managing international liquidity? [23]

These studies were exploratory. Among other things, they revealed that it was going to be difficult not only to judge the need for international liquidity but also to obtain a consensus among countries that any given expansion or contraction of liquidity was desirable. A further tentative conclusion was that the advantages of conditional liquidity from an international standpoint were such that the need for conditional liquidity should be fully met before any scheme for unconditional liquidity was established. Nonetheless, it was possible that the long-term upward trend in liquid reserves would be inadequate and would need to be supplemented by some form of unconditional or nearly unconditional liquidity. This type of liquidity, too, could be provided through the Fund.

The staff studies also noted that much of the discussion about the inadequacy of international liquidity, or projections of its future inadequacy, disguised in technical dress problems that were really political. Issues that greatly affected countries' interests were at stake: How much discipline would countries have to impose on their balance of payments? Who would own the bulk of the world's reserves?

Although the topic of liquidity was not discussed at length in the Executive Board for several months following the Annual Meeting, the Directors were kept abreast of developments by papers prepared by the staff, by oral reports from the staff and from the Managing Director, and through informal seminars of staff and Executive Directors. Consideration of the drafts of Chapters 3 and 4 of the Annual Report for 1964, entitled "International Liquidity: The Issues" and "The Fund and International Liquidity," provided an opportunity

---

[22] J. Marcus Fleming, "The Fund and International Liquidity," *Staff Papers*, Vol. 11 (1964), pp. 177–215.

[23] Oscar L. Altman, "The Management of International Liquidity," *Staff Papers*, Vol. 11 (1964), pp. 216–47.

to review the topic. Although some Directors were reluctant to have much detail in the Annual Report, it was the consensus that the Fund's Report had to go into matters in as much depth as would the forthcoming report of the Deputies of the Group of Ten. These chapters became the vehicle by which the Fund's views on liquidity in mid-1964 were made public. The Executive Directors stated their view that

> the determination as to whether the available supply of liquidity is adequate or inadequate must always be a matter of judgment, and a collective judgment is particularly difficult to arrive at because the balance of advantage, at any rate in the short run, may be different with respect to, and in the opinion of, different countries. Action in the liquidity field which absorbs unemployment in one country may promote excessive demand in another, and any change in the supply of international liquidity is likely to involve some transfer of resources, at least temporarily, between countries.[24]

Following this carefully qualified position, the Executive Directors concluded that the general level of international liquidity was broadly satisfactory, but that this did not mean that its distribution among countries or the supply of each type of liquidity was equally satisfactory. Emphasis was placed on the fact that, as the United States reduced its payments deficit, the expansion of holdings of dollars as reserves would not continue at the same rapid rate. Therefore, it was desirable and timely to explore possible ways to meet any inadequacies in the supply of international liquidity. However, any new arrangements for creating liquidity should be based on a multilateral institutional approach, which would be open to a worldwide membership and which would ensure that liquidity was made available on appropriate terms and conditions.

The Report also made clear that the Fund might enhance the supply of unconditional liquidity in a number of ways. One way was to give members firmer assurance of access to the credit tranches. Another was to allow members, on the occasion of quota increases, to pay their gold subscriptions to the Fund in some other form so that they could retain their gold. A third possibility was investment by the Fund: the Fund might purchase assets, other than the currencies which it acquired in connection with drawings, for the purpose of enhancing members' international liquidity. The Executive Directors intended to give these matters further study in the year ahead.

GROUP OF TEN REPORTS

Deputies' Emphasis on Multilateral Surveillance

Paralleling the Fund's studies were those of the Group of Ten. During the period spanning late 1963 and early 1964 the Deputies of the Group of Ten

---

[24] *Annual Report, 1964*, pp. 28–29.

held several informal meetings, where they spoke in their personal capacities. In April 1964 they began to take committed positions, as representatives of their countries, and thereafter held frequent formal meetings. Mr. Robert V. Roosa (United States) was chairman until October 1964, when Mr. Otmar Emminger (Federal Republic of Germany) became chairman.

On June 15 and 16, 1964, the Deputies presented to their Ministers and Governors the report which they had prepared in response to the request of the previous September.[25] This report, largely the work of Mr. Emminger, Mr. André de Lattre (France), Mr. Roosa, and Mr. Emile van Lennep (Netherlands), was published two months later as an Annex to the Group of Ten's Ministerial Statement.[26] By design, it was released to the public on the same day, August 10, 1964, as the Fund's 1964 Annual Report. The reports were closely linked. The Managing Director had participated in the meetings of the Ministers and Governors in Paris in December 1963 and June 1964; Mr. J. J. Polak, Director of the Research and Statistics Department, had participated in the Deputies' meetings; and the technical papers prepared by the Fund staff had been made available to the Deputies.

The Deputies' report stressed the relationship between the process of adjustment and the need for international liquidity. Therefore, before examining the liquidity problem it was necessary to look into the procedures for maintaining balance of payments equilibrium and for correcting imbalances when they occurred. The Deputies suggested that Working Party 3 of the Economic Policy Committee of the OECD should study how the members of the OECD, both individually and collectively, and compatibly with the pursuit of essential domestic objectives, could in the future preserve better balance of payments equilibrium and achieve faster and more effective adjustment of imbalances.

The Deputies further proposed that the processes of multilateral surveillance be continued and intensified. These were techniques, including the Fund's consultations, whereby officials from participating countries could review from time to time the balance of payments positions of other participants, the measures taken to adjust balances, and the means of financing them. All countries of the Group of Ten should provide the BIS with statistical data bearing on the means used to finance surpluses or deficits in their external accounts, and these data would be combined by the BIS and supplied in confidence to all participants and to Working Party 3 of the OECD.

Ossola Group Established

The Deputies' report also reviewed briefly various methods of meeting possible future needs to expand reserve assets, apart from the two methods

---

[25] See pp. 28–29 above.

[26] Group of Ten, *Ministerial Statement of the Group of Ten and Annex Prepared by Deputies* ([Washington], 1964).

already existing under the gold exchange standard—the flow into monetary reserves of new gold and of additional currency balances. Two proposals were considered—one for the introduction, through an agreement among the countries in the Group of Ten, of a new reserve asset, which would be created according to appraisals of an overall need for reserves; the other for a form of international asset similar to the gold tranche or similar claims on the Fund, the volume of which could, if necessary, be enlarged to meet an agreed need.

But proposals of this kind raised complex questions. How would any new reserve asset be made compatible with the existing international monetary system? How could liquidity be directed to the point of greatest legitimate need at any given time? How could the volume of reserves be adapted to global needs rather than to the shortages of reserves of individual countries? What effects would a new reserve asset have on the relations of the Group of Ten with the rest of the world? What machinery would be required for controlling the volume and distribution of the reserves that were created? What would be the desirability of creating a reserve asset for a limited group as opposed to an asset available on a worldwide basis?

To examine these and other similar questions, the Deputies established a group to study "owned" reserves—a term used to describe reserves that countries had at their own disposal, as distinct from "borrowed" reserves, which more closely resembled credit. This Study Group on the Creation of Reserve Assets became more widely known as the Ossola Group, after its chairman, Mr. Rinaldo Ossola, of the Bank of Italy.

Ministerial Statement

The Ministerial Statement issued by the Group of Ten on August 10, 1964 reflected the relatively small area of agreement among these countries. The Finance Ministers and Central Bank Governors of the Group, under the chairmanship of Mr. Giscard d'Estaing, agreed that supplies of gold and reserve currencies were fully adequate for the present and possibly for the immediate future. They were willing also to state that the continuing growth in the volume of world trade and payments was likely to entail a need for more international liquidity. But they were much less definite about how this need might be met: it might possibly be met by an expansion of credit facilities and, in the longer run, perhaps by some new form of reserve asset. Meanwhile, they agreed to support a moderate general increase in Fund quotas during 1965 and to re-examine the question of renewing the General Arrangements to Borrow.

The Ministers and Governors elaborated their position. The smooth functioning of the international monetary system depended on the avoidance of major and persistent payments imbalances and on the effective use of appropriate policies by national governments to correct imbalances when they occurred. Therefore, as a sequel to the study of liquidity by the Group of Ten, they agreed to the suggestion made by their Deputies and invited Working Party 3 of the OECD to embark on a study of the balance of payments adjustment process.

That the area of disagreement among the Group of Ten was still wide was more evident in the reactions to the Ministerial Statement than in the statement itself. One particularly strong reaction, for instance, was that of the Subcommittee on International Finance of the U.S. House of Representatives' Committee on Banking and Currency (under the chairmanship of Mr. Henry S. Reuss). That subcommittee issued a press release expressing its disappointment that these recommendations went only a little way toward providing necessary improvements in the international monetary system. The subcommittee urged that the U.S. monetary authorities give full support to the suggestion of the Fund's Managing Director for creating liquidity in some way through the Fund.

POSITIONS AT TOKYO

As a result of these discussions and reports, the points at issue in the debate on international liquidity had become a great deal clearer by the time of the Nineteenth Annual Meeting, in Tokyo in September 1964. A more sophisticated terminology had emerged: terms like conditional and unconditional liquidity, owned as against borrowed reserves, and multilateral surveillance were now used frequently. But even more important, the speeches of the Governors gave, for the first time, some indication to the world at large of the positions of the major countries. As these positions became known, it became more possible than before for informed public opinion—as expressed, for example, by members of the U.S. Congress and the British Parliament and by private bankers and monetary specialists—to participate in the shaping of governmental attitudes.

Areas of Agreement

Mr. Holtrop (Netherlands) found in the three reports—the Fund's Annual Report, the Ministerial Statement of the Group of Ten, and the report of the academic economists [27]—evidence that general agreement seemed to have been reached on at least four important propositions.[28] *One*, there was agreement that the proper functioning of the international payments system depended on

---

[27] See footnote 14 above.

[28] Statement by the Governor of the Fund for the Netherlands, *Summary Proceedings, 1964*, pp. 63–64.

the pursuit of national policies aimed at the avoidance or early correction of major and persistent imbalances. From this it followed that the proper function of reserves, and of international liquidity generally, was not the provision of real resources, but only the cushioning of such reversible imbalances as were unconnected with the movement of real resources and the temporary financing of more fundamental imbalances during the period necessary for corrective measures to become effective.

Two, there was agreement that the supply of international liquidity should be neither too abundant nor insufficient. At the one extreme, corrective internal policies might be delayed too long and inflationary tendencies would prevail; at the other extreme, the system would be threatened by deflationary bias and by the pursuit of policies, such as restrictions and protectionism, inimical to international cooperation. The present supply of liquidity seemed ample, if not overabundant; at any rate, there was no immediate shortage.

Three, there was agreement that it was both unlikely and undesirable that in the future the supply of international liquidity, originating from the balance of payments deficit of the United States, should continue to flow at the same rate as in the past. On the other hand, if and when this supply came to a stop, the problem of a deficiency of international liquidity might become a reality.

Four, there seemed to be rather general agreement that it would not be prudent to allow the provision of an appropriate supply of reserves, or of liquidity, to continue in the future to depend solely on the vagaries of the supply of gold for monetary purposes, supplemented by the accidental deficits of reserve currency countries and the credit facilities of the Fund in their present form. Instead, other techniques for creating reserves would have to be seriously considered.

Divergence of Views

Despite these areas of agreement, there were even more areas of disagreement, and the Managing Director, in his remarks at the closing session of the Tokyo meeting, referred to a "stimulating divergence of views." [29] Strong differences of opinion still attended the question of how urgently something needed to be done about expanding the supply of liquidity. Several of the Governors for the countries of the Group of Ten insisted that the emphasis should be placed on members' policies in respect of balance of payments adjustment rather than on ways to increase total liquidity. Mr. Karl Blessing (Federal Republic of Germany) and Mr. Emilio Colombo (Italy) took this line. [30] Mr. Giscard d'Estaing again stressed the risk of inflation if liquidity became excessive, and

---

[29] Concluding Remarks by the Managing Director, *Summary Proceedings, 1964*, p. 198.

[30] Statements by the Governors of the Fund for the Federal Republic of Germany and Italy, *Summary Proceedings, 1964*, pp. 53 and 108.

this time he also emphasized the role of gold in the international monetary system:

> The world monetary system must be set in concentric circles: the first one being gold, and then, the second, if necessary, recourse to deliberate and concerted creation of either reserve assets or credit facilities.
>
> The inner circle is gold.
>
> Experience in recent years has shown us that, aside from any theoretical preference, gold remains the essential basis of the world payments system.[31]

At the same time, he did not believe that the rate at which gold was mined would spontaneously adjust its volume to world needs. Thus, it might be necessary to seek out supplementary sources for supplying owned reserves, but the creation and volume of any new reserve asset would have to be governed by strict rules.[32]

Mr. Holtrop and others welcomed the agreement of the countries of the Group of Ten on multilateral surveillance as a means of adapting credit facilities to the particular type of imbalance that might have to be financed.[33] In fact, a great deal was heard about multilateral surveillance during the Tokyo meeting. It was defined by Mr. Maudling as follows:

> This phrase was very carefully chosen because the possible alternative of "discipline" has a different significance in different languages. It is intended to represent a step forward along the road of increasing consultation and cooperation in monetary and economic affairs which we have been following ever since the end of the war. Our agreement does not give any member of the Group of Ten, or indeed the Group as such, a veto on the setting-up of new facilities within the Group or between members of it, or on the use of existing facilities. It does, however, recognize very clearly that agreements made between individual countries may well be of close interest to other members of the Group, and that the interest of these other members should be taken fully into account when new arrangements are made.[34]

A second big area in which agreement was still far from being achieved was whether new liquidity should be channeled through the Fund or should be provided by some other agency. This question turned on the parallel question whether any innovative forms of liquidity should be available universally—that is, to all countries—or to a limited group of countries.

The view that the Fund was the appropriate agency for administering international liquidity because of its worldwide membership was voiced by many Governors for developing countries. The remarks of the Chairman of

---

[31] Statement by the Governor of the World Bank for France, *Summary Proceedings, 1964*, p. 205.

[32] *Ibid.*, pp. 206–207.

[33] Statement by the Governor of the Fund for the Netherlands, *Summary Proceedings, 1964*, pp. 67–68.

[34] Statement by the Governor of the Fund for the United Kingdom, *Summary Proceedings, 1964*, pp. 166–67.

the 1964 Annual Meeting, Mr. Francisco Aquino h., the Governor for El Salvador, are an example:

> The problem of international liquidity is one which rightly concerns all members of the Fund. It is true, perhaps, that the efficiency of the international monetary system is largely dependent on the effective cooperation of a relatively small number of countries; but it serves the interests of all. . . .
>
> I should like, therefore, to urge that whatever action may be the outcome of the present deliberations in the Fund and elsewhere will be taken within a truly multilateral framework such as that provided by our meeting.[35]

Some of the Governors for the countries of the Group of Ten cited the advantages of international credit arrangements. Mr. Dillon thought that it was "highly significant" that the studies both by the Group of Ten and by the Fund had concluded that the present system was functioning well and that any changes should be designed, in the words of the Fund's Annual Report, to "supplement and improve the system where changes are indicated, rather than to look for a replacement of the system by a totally different one.[36] Mr. Maudling likewise believed that the best course was to build on the Fund:

> I think, indeed, there is danger in too much emphasis on owned reserves as opposed to credit facilities. In the Fund, we have a system which operates by making available to deficit countries on a temporary basis the currencies of surplus countries. I believe that, for many purposes, such a system may be the most suitable and flexible instrument.[37]

Nevertheless, voices were heard against this view. Mr. Colombo suggested that the need for developing countries to participate in the distribution of additional international liquidity should be satisfied by the general increase in quotas that was being recommended, and Mr. Holtrop explained his Government's position favoring a limited participation.[38]

Managing Director's Position

Mr. Schweitzer made it abundantly evident, both in his opening address and in his concluding remarks, that he was in favor of a universal approach through the Fund. In his opening address he said that

> where decisions are taken to create and administer liquidity by deliberate international action, it is particularly important that the advantages of the multilateral institutional approach be kept in mind. An international organization provides the forum for a balanced consideration, and hence the best reconciliation,

---

[35] Opening Address by the Chairman, *Summary Proceedings, 1964*, pp. 10–11.

[36] Statement by the Governor of the Fund and the World Bank for the United States, *Summary Proceedings, 1964*, p. 42, and *Annual Report, 1964*, p. 32.

[37] Statement by the Governor of the Fund for the United Kingdom, *Summary Proceedings, 1964*, p. 168.

[38] Statements by the Governors of the Fund for Italy and the Netherlands, *Summary Proceedings, 1964*, pp. 106 and 68–69.

of the various objectives in the international financial field as they affect all countries.[39]

And in his concluding remarks he said:

A large number of members have emphasized in varying degrees the need to take such further steps as may be desirable to strengthen international liquidity within the framework of the Fund rather than on a more restricted basis. I would here again stress what I said in my opening remarks to this meeting. The world cannot be clearly divided into two groups, the developing and the industrial countries.[40]

In summing up the 1964 Annual Meeting, Mr. Schweitzer was particularly heartened that the multilateral institutional approach to the liquidity question had been given such widespread support. He called attention to the fact that multilateral surveillance, and even discipline, on a truly multilateral basis had long been part and parcel of the Fund's operations. And he noted a consensus among the Governors that another increase in Fund quotas was not a solution to the liquidity problems that might arise in the future; therefore, the Fund would continue to study the problems involved in the creation of liquidity.

---

[39] Opening Address by the Managing Director, *Summary Proceedings, 1964,* p. 28.

[40] Concluding Remarks by the Managing Director, *Summary Proceedings, 1964,* p. 200.

CHAPTER

3

Exploring Techniques for Reserve Creation

(1964–65)

$\mathcal{F}$OLLOWING THE ANNUAL MEETING IN TOKYO in September 1964, the Fund accelerated its search for answers to the perplexing questions related to international liquidity and for ways to augment the volume of liquidity that the Fund was providing through existing methods. Primary attention was devoted to the latter. In line with the resolution adopted by the Governors at Tokyo to the effect that the Executive Directors should consider the question of a general adjustment of quotas, the second round of general increases became the main focus of the Fund's work on liquidity in 1964–65. By February 1965, the report requested by the Governors had been prepared by the staff and adopted by the Executive Board.[1]

DELIBERATE RESERVE CREATION STUDIED

Attention to the enlargement of quotas reflected the Fund's emphasis at the time on the expansion of conditional liquidity. The 1965 Annual Report stated that "ideally, countries' needs for additional liquidity could be met by adequate increases in conditional liquidity."[2] But the Fund was also aware, and this too was spelled out in the 1965 Annual Report, that in practice most countries did not regard conditional and unconditional liquidity as equivalent. For various reasons, countries liked to have the major proportion of their liquidity freely available, that is, without conditions. Consequently, even if conditional liquidity were to be expanded, some countries might still attempt to increase their owned reserves by adopting balance of payments policies which, from an international point of view, might be regarded as undesirable.

---

[1] See Chap. 2, pp. 33–34, above.

[2] *Annual Report, 1965*, p. 15.

Therefore, as a second important part of their work on liquidity during 1964–65, the Executive Directors and the staff intensified their examination, begun the previous year, of the ways in which the Fund might bring more unconditional liquidity into existence.

This examination was concerned principally with the problems and techniques involved in "deliberate reserve creation," the term now used to distinguish the creation of reserves through some collective or international action from additions to reserves stemming from the traditional sources of gold production and the building up of balances in the currencies of particular countries.

In addition, the Executive Directors and the staff, mindful that the discussions concerning liquidity had led to suggestions that the operation of the whole international monetary system be reviewed, undertook to appraise how well the existing system had been functioning.

Building on Existing System

The Fund approached its examination of the techniques for increasing liquidity with caution. Compared with the existing mechanisms, any method for deliberate creation of reserves was unprecedented. Several important and entirely new issues had to be thought through, and answers had to be found to a number of questions that monetary officials had not covered in past discussions: How should the world's need for reserves be measured? In what form should any new reserves be made available? Who would create such reserves, and how? What would be the position in the international payments system of the novel reserve units compared with gold and foreign exchange reserves? How should these units be distributed initially—that is, how broad should be the group of countries that would first receive the newly created liquidity, either to spend or to add to reserves? What institutional provisions should be made to ensure proper management of the volume and functioning of the new reserves?

Both the Managing Director, Mr. Schweitzer, and the Deputy Managing Director, Mr. Frank A. Southard, Jr., made it clear that they were looking for solutions based on the existing international monetary system. Earlier, in a speech in March 1964, for example, Mr. Southard had pointed out that the studies in process looked to arrangements which, with emphasis primarily on gradual evolution rather than on the adoption of spectacular remedies, would provide for an adequate growth of liquidity and continuing improvement in international financial cooperation.[3]

---

[3] Speech by Frank A. Southard, Jr., to the Jno. E. Owens Memorial Foundation in Dallas, Texas, March 27, 1964, reproduced in Supplement to *International Financial News Survey*, Vol. 16 (1964), pp. 113–16. Reference is to p. 115.

On his way back to Washington from the Tokyo meeting, Mr. Schweitzer, in a speech at Bombay University, repeated this theme, saying, "it seems to us that the task of ensuring an adequate supply of liquidity does not require any drastic overhaul of the present arrangements." [4]

Wanted: A Universal Scheme

The management of the Fund was also looking for techniques that would, or could eventually, encompass all countries—not only all the industrial countries, which still held differing views, but also the developing countries. The Managing Director stressed repeatedly that he favored a mechanism for creating liquidity that was all-embracing. Addressing the National Foreign Trade Convention in New York on November 16, 1964, for example, Mr. Schweitzer dealt with the then controversial question of the size of the group of countries which should participate in any new arrangements for the creation of international liquidity, and spelled out why he believed all countries ought to be included:

> First, decisions determining the creation of new international liquidity directly affect all the world. Too little liquidity could permit a crisis to develop in which most of the world would tend toward economic stagnation and would suffer from declining trade. Excessive creation of liquidity would lead to inflation with its attendant instability and a tendency for excessive fluctuations in the terms of trade. The fact that all countries are vitally affected by whatever action may be taken would suggest that all should have some voice in the decision.
>
> Second, the benefits of participating in the creation of reserves are substantial. Those countries included in the arrangements have at their disposal liquidity created through cooperative action, liquidity which those outside any such arrangement have to earn with balance of payments surpluses. It would seem equitable that all countries should have an opportunity to participate in the benefits, and it would seem particularly regrettable if the poorer countries were those excluded.
>
> Finally, any division of the 102 countries which are Fund members raises problems of defining the groups and drawing a line between them. An examination of various criteria for such a division will, I believe, show that there is no basis for a sharp line of demarcation. In particular, the criterion which is often regarded as the most relevant in making such a division—that is, the level of a country's reserves—does not correspond to the grouping usually suggested. There are among countries outside the major industrial group a number that hold relatively high reserves. Furthermore, as there is a continuous gradation of industrialization in the countries of the world, it is impossible to draw the line clearly between industrial and nonindustrial countries. [5]

---

[4] Speech by the Managing Director before the University School of Economics, Bombay University, September 29, 1964, reproduced in Supplement to *International Financial News Survey*, Vol. 16 (1964), pp. 361–64. Reference is to p. 362.

[5] Speech by the Managing Director to the National Foreign Trade Convention, New York, November 16, 1964, reproduced in *International Financial News Survey*, Vol. 16 (1964), pp. 441–45. Quotation is from pp. 444–45.

In Mr. Schweitzer's view these considerations, among others, weighed heavily in favor of using the Fund for any liquidity-creating arrangements. The Fund was the truly worldwide organization already operating in this field. In this area, as in others, he believed that the Fund could, "through responsible leadership, provide the unifying force among all countries, industrialized and agricultural, developed and developing, creditor and debtor, rich and poor." Futhermore, he was optimistic that an appropriate solution would be found: "I feel confident that, in spite of different attitudes and opinions among countries on particular questions, this [international] cooperation will continue to strengthen and will provide conditions which will further enhance the growth of the world economy and the expansion of international trade." [6]

TWO POSSIBLE TECHNIQUES FOR CREATING RESERVES

With these terms of reference—a scheme that was universal and that worked within the principles of the existing international monetary system—the staff, in the latter part of 1964 and the first nine months of 1965, began to explore in more detail the ways in which the Fund might create additional reserves. Two main possible methods were devised. One, the drawing facilities made available by the Fund on a virtually automatic basis could be extended. Two, as an alternative, arrangements could be set up that would be similar to open market operations in domestic monetary creation: the Fund could, for instance, purchase assets from the national monetary authorities of participants in a liquidity scheme. This second method was called Fund "investment," the Fund's purchasing of assets being considered equivalent to the Fund's investing in participating countries. The investment involved might be in currency or in gold.[7] Under the first method, countries' reserves would increase in the form of liquid claims on the Fund; under the second, by additions to their gold or foreign exchange holdings. In the 1965 Annual Report the term "investment" was replaced by the phrase "the acquisition by the Fund of 'special assets'," a phrase which, although less brief, conveyed a clearer picture of the nature of the operation.[8]

As consideration of these two techniques within the Fund proceeded during the next several months, they came to be referred to, in a kind of shorthand, as (1) the extension of automatism and (2) the exchange of assets (more fully, the acquisition of assets and claims).

Consideration of a third technique was more or less dropped. This technique involved the transfer of gold stocks, by some means not yet specified,

---

[6] *Ibid.* Quotation is from p. 445.

[7] *Annual Report, 1964*, pp. 38–39.

[8] *Annual Report, 1965*, p. 19.

from the Fund's ownership to that of its members, thereby enhancing members' gold reserves, or, alternatively, the acceptance by the Fund of gold certificates in lieu of gold subscriptions in connection with quota increases; the latter would *pro tanto* have the effect of providing members with gold tranche positions without corresponding reductions in their gold reserves. The aim of this technique, however implemented, was to limit the increase in the Fund's stock of physical gold resulting from gold subscription payments. In this way the amount of gold held by members would not be reduced when their drawing positions in the Fund were enlarged. Given the relatively small size of the Fund's gold holdings, the staff thought that it was unlikely that changes in these holdings would contribute much toward enlarging countries' reserves.

The studies prepared by the staff on these reserve-creating techniques were intended primarily as a way to examine the possible methods by which the Fund could expand liquidity. No official position—preferring either technique—was taken by the Executive Board. The two techniques—the extension of automatism and the acquisition of assets—contained several features that were later incorporated into subsequent proposals and some that eventually became features of SDRs. A description of the two techniques and of their relative merits, as seen at the time, follows.

Extension of Automatism

The simplest way for the Fund to increase unconditional liquidity was to extend to its members, through its drawing facilities, a greater amount of what the Fund called quasi-automatic liquidity. The discussions on international liquidity that had gone on thus far had made it clear that total international liquidity consisted of a broad range of types of liquidity, running from reserves in the form of gold and foreign exchange to credit facilities. The Fund already provided liquidity over this whole range. At one end, gold tranche and super gold tranche positions and claims under the General Arrangements to Borrow fell within the concept of reserves and constituted unconditional, or quasi-automatic, liquidity.[9] In the middle, drawing facilities in the first credit tranche represented liquidity of the conditional type, although the conditionality was relatively slight. Then, as a member moved into the higher credit tranches or on to the upper end of the liquidity scale, requests for drawings were subject to more stringent conditions.

Quasi-automatic drawing facilities could be extended beyond the gold tranche into some part of the credit tranches. The Executive Board could, for example, take a decision under which the ratio of the Fund's holdings of a

---

[9] Super gold tranche position: the difference between the Fund's holdings of a member's currency and 75 per cent of the member's quota when those holdings were less than 75 per cent. (For the definition of gold tranche position, see Chap. 2, footnote 1, above.)

member's currency to the level of quota up to which members could draw on a virtually automatic basis could be raised from the 100 per cent already in operation to some higher percentage of quota, e.g., 105 per cent after one year, 110 per cent after two years, and so on. Such a decision could apply either to all members or only to such members as satisfied certain criteria. The extension of automaticity into the Fund's credit tranches would be tantamount to the creation of unconditional liquidity.

Because less systematic thought had been given to the possibilities involved in creating reserves through the extension of automatic drawing rights in the Fund than to the more unusual and spectacular methods suggested for reserve creation, the staff examined at some length the details and implications of this means of creating liquidity. If this method was to be used, a number of questions had to be answered. One of these was the question whether an extension of quasi-automatic drawing facilities should be accompanied by a corresponding extension of the Fund's total drawing facilities. If it was not, there would be some contraction in the amount of conditional drawing facilities available to members, unconditional liquidity having merely been substituted for conditional liquidity.

In particular, countries following conservative financial policies would ordinarily have unused drawing facilities in the gold tranche, and, should their payments positions require them to request drawings in the first credit tranche, they would have no difficulty in obtaining the requested drawings. For these countries, liquidity would not be greatly enhanced by any decision that was limited to giving gold tranche treatment to facilities previously available under the rules governing the first credit tranche. To make extended automatism a more effective way of increasing reserves, it would be necessary to raise correspondingly the maximum level of holdings (presently 125 per cent of quota) that applied to the first credit tranche facilities. Even then, a country would sacrifice an equivalent amount of conditional liquidity for the added unconditional liquidity it acquired, but the amount forgone would lie in the higher credit tranches.

Still other questions attended the expansion of liquidity via extended automatism: Should extended automaticity of drawings be applied to all members, possibly in proportion to quotas, or should it be circumscribed in some way? Even if greater automaticity of drawings was applied to all members, it would enlarge access to the Fund on gold tranche terms only for members that were not, at the time, using the Fund's resources beyond the new point to which quasi-automatic (or unconditional) drawing rights were extended; countries that had already used their resources in the Fund beyond this point would not acquire the new additions to their reserve positions in the Fund until they had brought down the Fund's holdings of their currencies into the area of automatism. In other words, what had become known as the "self-qualifying principle" might be used: while access to more unconditional liquidity was, in theory, available to all countries, only those in or close to the gold tranche would actually acquire reserves.

Alternatively, the extension of automatic drawing rights could be confined to some selected category of countries. The ease of drawing could be related, for example, to a country's record of performance in the Fund. A condition might be that the country had accepted the obligations of Article VIII. Or a condition for a country's receiving greater quasi-automatic drawing facilities might be that the country stood ready to lend to the Fund additional amounts of its currency. If the latter criterion was used, the Fund's liquidity would be simultaneously strengthened.

The staff noted that members' credit positions in the Fund in mid-1965 were such that the amounts of new liquidity created would be substantially greater if automatism was extended to all members rather than confined to some narrower group. The staff noted further that, if reserve creation through extended automaticity of drawings on the Fund was actually to enlarge liquid reserves, countries would have to consider as part of their reserves the full amount of their access to the Fund on gold tranche terms. In other words, countries would have to include in their reserves the amount of drawing facilities available in the gold tranche as defined at that time, the amount in the first credit tranche that would become available on the same terms, claims on the Fund that some countries may have accumulated under the General Arrangements to Borrow, and any claims on the Fund that would arise under new arrangements.

Another question was whether any extension of automatic drawing facilities should be carried out in units as large as a complete credit tranche or in smaller units. Minimum additions to reserves through an increase in quasi-automatic drawing rights need not be as sizable as 25 per cent of quota, the percentage by which gold and credit tranches were presently divided. The magnitude of reserve creation required at annual intervals would probably be smaller—perhaps 5 per cent, rather than 25 per cent, of quota.

A more fundamental problem was how the Fund was to be provided with any supplementary resources that might be necessary for the extension of quasi-automatic drawing rights. These resources could, in theory, be provided by a more rapid growth in quotas than normally took place; however, because such increases in quotas would cause a corresponding growth not only in quasi-automatic drawing facilities but also in conditional drawing facilities, complicated adjustments would have to be made in all of the Fund's policies on drawings.

Finally, there was the question whether quasi-automatic drawing facilities should occasionally be contracted as well as expanded. The contraction of drawing rights might be especially difficult.

49

Acquisition of Assets and Claims

A second major way in which the Fund could create reserves was through an operation whereby the Fund simultaneously obtained special assets and assumed additional liabilities. The Fund could purchase securities from participants and create for these participants some liquid loan claims on the Fund that these participants would treat as reserves. From the asset side, this form of reserve creation was described as the acquisition by the Fund of "special assets." From the liability side, which indicated more clearly that new reserves would thus be created, this technique was called the creation of loan claims, or "special claims," on the Fund.

The staff explored a number of technical questions presented by this type of reserve creation: What kind of special assets should the Fund purchase? What principles would govern the distribution of purchases among countries? What institutional machinery could be established to enable the Fund and the countries concerned to agree on the amount, the country distribution, and the nature of the assets to be acquired (or, reciprocally, the liquid claims to be created)?

It was necessary that the country distribution of these claims not be based on the balance of payments needs of individual countries. Otherwise, were the Fund to distribute loan claims under some new facility for the same purpose as its usual drawings, the Fund's regular drawing policies would become confused and undermined. The total amount of the loan claims to be distributed by the Fund should rather be decided on the basis of general liquidity considerations.

Study of this technique of reserve creation also involved thinking through the characteristics that the liquid claims to be created should have so as to be acceptable to countries as reserves. As a starting point, the staff thought that the liabilities would have to have at least the same three characteristics as claims under the General Arrangements to Borrow: (1) they would have to be encashable for useful currency at least as freely as gold tranche positions or be transferable directly to other members; (2) they should have a gold-value guarantee; and (3) they ought to receive a modest rate of interest reflecting the gold value of the claim.

There was also the further question of how the Fund would finance these additional claims. The strain on the Fund's own resources was likely to require an extension of them either by larger subscriptions or by greater borrowing by the Fund.

The staff, at this juncture, worked out schemes to illustrate to the Executive Directors and to the Group of Ten precisely how the Fund might go about acquiring assets out of borrowed resources and then creating reserves in the form of claims on itself. One such scheme entailed a free acceptance, at least within quantitative limits, of loan claims by other participants. Under another scheme, both the use and the acceptance of loan claims on the Fund would be governed by the principle that such claims would be held by participants in a proportion corresponding to their reserve holdings in other forms. Either scheme involved prior agreement on the types of assets to be purchased that gave rise to liquid claims, and possibly on the principles governing the distribution among participants of these purchases. Under either scheme, appropriate machinery would be established, presumably including the Fund and those countries that had undertaken to lend to the Fund, so that periodic decisions could be made, perhaps at six-month intervals and on the basis of a proposal by the Managing Director of the Fund, concerning the amount, the country distribution, the maturity, and any other features of the assets to be acquired or liquidated over the ensuing six months.

Relative Merits of the Two Techniques

Discussion at an informal seminar of Executive Directors and staff in June 1965 revealed no strong preference for either of the two methods. The staff thought that they ought to be judged mainly on the basis of technical considerations; political considerations were secondary. An important consideration of a technical nature was that the extension of automatism would not require amendment of the Articles but the acquisition of special assets would, and at this time the staff was not at all certain that members would look favorably on amending the Articles. In addition, the amount and distribution of reserve creation through extended automatism would probably be linked to the Fund's quotas, whereas new reserves could conceivably be allocated on some different principle under the special assets technique. Furthermore, extended automatism would, at least for some countries, involve merely a substitution of unconditional for conditional liquidity. The effects on the Fund's own liquidity of various techniques of reserve creation through the Fund also had to be taken into account.[10]

After this examination of the ways in which the Fund might create reserves, it was concluded that further exploration was necessary to judge which basic method would prove the more satisfactory. It was also recognized that some combination of methods might produce the most acceptable results.

STUDIES ACCELERATED

After mid-1965, the Fund accelerated its studies of reserve-creating mechanisms. Several reasons prompted this acceleration. For one, now that it had become widely accepted that the traditional sources of reserve growth would be

---

[10] These effects were discussed by J. Marcus Fleming in his "Effects of Various Types of Fund Reserve Creation on Fund Liquidity," *Staff Papers*, Vol. 12 (1965), pp. 163–88.

insufficient for any supplementary liquidity that might, in the future, have to be injected into the international monetary system, there was a proliferation of suggested liquidity arrangements. Schemes that had been advocated in the past were refined and additional ones were recommended.

Another reason for the Fund's intensification of its study of reserve creation was that the countries of the Group of Ten, through the Ossola Group, were exploring methods by which new reserves might be created, and Mr. Ossola had suggested that high priority be given to a comparative assessment of the proposals for collective reserve units (CRUs) that were then being advanced and of the possible techniques for creating reserves through the Fund. As early as during the second meeting of the Ossola Group, in June 1964, Mr. Ossola and delegates from practically all of its members, notably the United States and the United Kingdom, had strongly urged Mr. J. Marcus Fleming, Deputy Director of the Research and Statistics Department, who was the representative of the Managing Director to the Ossola Group, to request the Fund to produce for the third meeting, to be held in July 1964, a paper, however rough and informal, which would set out the possibilities of creating reserve assets through the Fund. Such a preliminary staff paper was prepared and transmitted. When the Ossola Group started to hold frequent meetings after October 1964, requests were often made for the Fund to present additional papers clarifying various schemes. In response, the staff studies discussed in the preceding section were made available to this Study Group.[11]

A further sense of urgency was imparted to the endeavors both of the Fund and of the Deputies of the Group of Ten as the U.S. Government took measures, early in 1965, to cope with the substantial balance of payments deficit that had re-emerged after the first quarter of 1964. After six years of deficits, the U.S. balance of payments had, at the beginning of 1964, come close to equilibrium for the first time since the trough of the 1961 recession. Moreover, the combined balance of payments of the six member countries of the EEC, which had been in surplus for many years, had also been brought to near equilibrium early in 1964. This pattern of relative stability was not maintained, however. Later in 1964 there was not only a major deterioration in the balance of payments of the United Kingdom but, more significantly, the reappearance of a sizable deficit in the balance of payments of the United States and of a large overall surplus in the combined balance of payments of the EEC countries.

In February 1965, the U.S. Government announced a comprehensive program to reduce its payments deficit.[12] It was accordingly expected that, should that deficit be eliminated, the situation regarding world liquidity could change fundamentally. The rest of the world, which had run a large aggregate

---

[11] The deliberations of the Ossola Group and its report are discussed at greater length later in this chapter; see pp. 58–61 below.

[12] This program is discussed in more detail later in this chapter (pp. 63–64), as well as in Chaps. 24, 25, and 26.

balance of payments surplus for many years, would cease to do so. Further increases in international reserves would be limited largely to the amount added to world monetary gold holdings. Already in the first quarter of 1965 international reserves had fallen by about $800 million, a drop that was in contrast to the situation in 1963 and 1964. In 1963 the increase in world reserves, $3.4 billion, had been higher than in any year since World War II, and in 1964 the increase had been $2.5 billion.

In these circumstances it was generally recognized—and the Fund's Annual Report for 1965 expressed that recognition—that consideration should continue to be given to the twin problems of international liquidity and the workings of the international monetary system.[13]

PROPOSALS FOR CRUs

Among the proposals for reserve creation were three or four involving a collective or composite reserve unit (CRU).

The first such proposal was made late in 1963 by Mr. Bernstein.[14] He was building on an idea of Professor S. Posthuma, of the Netherlands, who earlier in 1963 had suggested that the burden of maintaining the gold exchange standard could be shared more equitably and the system greatly strengthened if all the big industrial countries would hold an agreed proportion of their reserves in foreign exchange rather than in gold.[15] Mr. Bernstein thought that some agreement among the countries of the Group of Ten, plus Switzerland, to standardize the composition of their holdings of gold and foreign exchange and the use of these holdings in international settlements could help to alleviate any possible shortage of world liquidity. Accordingly, he recommended that the large industrial countries establish a new international reserve unit, equivalent to gold, consisting of a stated proportion of each of the 11 currencies concerned. A reserve unit might consist, for example, of about 50 cents in U.S. currency and lesser amounts of pounds sterling, French francs, deutsche mark, guilders, lire, Canadian dollars, yen, etc. The participating countries would be free to hold their reserves in any form, but holdings of gold would have to be matched by a minimum amount of holdings in reserve units. The ultimate objective would be for each country to hold reserve units totaling at least one half of its gold reserves.

---

[13] *Annual Report, 1965*, Chap. 2.

[14] Edward M. Bernstein, "A Practical Program for International Monetary Reserves," Model, Roland & Co., *Quarterly Review and Investment Survey*, Fourth Quarter, 1963, pp. 1–8.

[15] S. Posthuma, "The International Monetary System," Banca Nazionale del Lavoro, *Quarterly Review*, September 1963, pp. 239–61.

To create the reserve units, each participating country would deposit its own currency with the International Monetary Fund, acting as trustee, in an amount equal to its pro rata share of the reserve units to be created. In return, each country would be given a credit on the books of the trustee, denominated in reserve units. The currencies held by the Fund would be guaranteed against loss from exchange depreciation. The participating countries would be obliged, when requested by the monetary authorities of other countries, to convert balances of their currencies into gold and reserve units.

Mr. Bernstein saw as the advantage of his proposal that it would involve little change in the international monetary system. Gold would remain the basis for the value of currencies, the new reserve unit would have a fixed gold value, and official holdings of the currencies of the participating countries would be convertible into gold, although only in combination with reserve units. With such a system, the monetary reserves of the 11 countries could continue to grow without being hampered by a potential inadequacy of monetary gold. The system would also help to equalize, for all participating countries, the ratio of gold to foreign exchange in their reserves. Finally, all 11 currencies would be used as foreign exchange reserves, thus eliminating any inequities that might occur from the use of only a few reserve currencies. Later, Mr. Bernstein refined and elaborated his ideas.[16]

Mr. Robert V. Roosa, Under Secretary of the U.S. Treasury, in The Elihu Root Lectures for 1964–65, proposed another type of CRU.[17] A third scheme for a CRU was prepared by French experts and outlined in a speech by Mr. Giscard d'Estaing, Minister of Economy and Finance, at the Institut d'Etudes Bancaires et Financières, in Paris, on June 15, 1965.[18]

Features in Common

These proposals for a collective or composite reserve unit were carefully examined by the Fund staff. The several schemes were seen to be similar in their basic characteristics. *First*, a reserve unit, or CRU, was to come into being. It was to be a unit for transfer from one monetary authority to another, and was not to be used by monetary authorities for direct intervention in exchange markets. The unit would be created by an exchange of liabilities or

---

[16] See "Further Evolution of the International Monetary System," *Moorgate and Wall Street*, Summer 1965, pp. 51–70; also four papers in *Guidelines for International Monetary Reform*, U.S. Congress, Joint Economic Committee (Hearings Before the Subcommittee on International Exchange and Payments), 89th Cong., 1st sess. (Washington, 1965), Part 2, Supplement, pp. 230–81.

[17] The lectures were sponsored by the Council on Foreign Relations, New York, and were subsequently published as a book entitled *Monetary Reform for the World Economy* (New York, 1965).

[18] "La politique monétaire internationale de la France," in *Exposés de M. Valéry Giscard d'Estaing, Ministre des Finances et des Affaires Economiques, sur les problèmes monétaires internationaux* (Paris, 1965) and in *Les problèmes monétaires internationaux* (Paris, 1965), pp. 39–55; reprinted in *Problèmes Economiques*, August 1965, pp. 1–7.

claims between a trustee and each participating country. The units issued as liabilities of the trustee would be secured by counterpart assets, such as deposits by participants of gold or of promissory notes equivalent in amount to the value of the units distributed to them. Participants would accept the liabilities of the trustee as reserves but need not deduct from their reserves their liabilities to the trustee, since the latter would remain dormant until such time as the scheme was liquidated or any participant withdrew. In other words, the contributions of the participants were to be in the nature of IOUs acquired by the trustee and normally retained unused.

What was essential to the process of creating reserves was not so much the acquisition of assets that might remain unusable as the willingness of the participants, within certain limits or through certain procedures, to accept them in settlement of international transactions. The contributions under the CRU schemes thus differed from the quota subscriptions to the Fund, which resulted in a pool of currencies for use in the Fund's operations.

A *second* feature common to CRU schemes was that agreed amounts of CRUs would be created by a relatively small group of countries. Some schemes limited participation to the countries of the Group of Ten; some also included Switzerland. A few suggested that the countries of the Group of Ten be augmented by a small number of other countries. However, no proposal included anything like all members of the Fund.

Third, the amount of CRUs to be created was to depend upon the group's collective appraisal of the world's need for reserves. *Finally*, the initial distribution of CRUs was to be made to each participant according to some agreed formula without reference to its balance of payments position. Points three and four meant that both the creation and the distribution of CRUs were to take place without regard to the balance of payments situation of individual countries, that is, the creation and distribution of CRUs were not to be linked to the actual financing of external payments deficits.

The Issue of Decision Making

In the view of the Fund staff, one of the principal decisions that had to be made in respect of any scheme of reserve creation, whether a CRU or some other arrangement, concerned the amount of reserve units that would be periodically created or canceled. How would the amounts of reserves to be created be determined? More specifically, who would make such decisions? This issue of decision making was crucial, and one that was still unresolved. Each devotee of CRUs had a different suggestion. The French authorities believed that such decision making was basic; hence, their proposal called for "the rule of unanimity"—all participants in any scheme would have to consent to any creation of reserves. Mr. Bernstein's original proposal had not dealt with this subject, but he later suggested that the participating countries might enter into an agreement to create a stated amount of reserve units each year for five years. As an illustration, he mentioned annual amounts of $1–1.5 billion. Any change from the level agreed to in the initial agreement would be subject to unanimous consent.

Mr. Roosa had come up with fairly elaborate rules for the decision-making process. The decisions on the amounts of reserves to be created would be ratified by the same majority as that required to amend the Articles of Agreement of the Fund, i.e., three fifths of the members having four fifths of the total voting power. He further suggested that proposals for changing the amounts should be handled analogously to proposals for activating the General Arrangements to Borrow, in that initiation and approval would be distinguished from each other. A proposal could only be initiated by a "Governors' Committee on Fund Units," a committee to be formed in which each participant would be represented and would have voting rights based on the accumulated amount of its contribution. Nonparticipants would also be represented, but with a minority vote.

Given the condition that any participant would be free to take up all, or part, or none, of its potential share in each new increment of reserve units, Mr. Roosa thought that it should be possible to reach decisions in the Governors' Committee without insisting on unanimity. A proposal initiated in this fashion would then be presented for approval to all the Fund Governors and decided on the basis of, perhaps, a two-thirds vote weighted by existing quotas. The Roosa formula, while providing for a multilateral process of decision making, preserved for each country the right not to accept its share in a given distribution of new reserve units.

Many elements of this formula were later to find their way into the decision-making process agreed for the creation of SDRs.

Size of the Group

The question of the size of the group to be included in any CRU scheme, although essentially political, had, by the middle of 1965, taken on economic overtones. The advocates of CRUs thought that participation had to be limited because the international economic behavior of the industrial countries differed from that of the developing ones. In their view, the industrial countries needed substantial reserves, not because they wanted to acquire real resources from other countries but because they needed adequate reserves to help to finance, temporarily, the large and growing amounts of world trade and financial transactions. They wished to have the freedom of action that would come with having sufficient liquidity but did not intend that this should have a permanent effect on their demand for real resources. It was, therefore, possible for them to think about creating liquidity in advance of need and distributing it unconditionally to a small number of countries.

The number of countries was small because most other countries were chronically short of reserves and, if given more, would consider them as capital and proceed to spend them. Industrial countries would find themselves buying back with larger exports of goods and services the newly created reserves that had been given to the developing countries. Furthermore, if the developing countries were made participants in a CRU scheme, they might find the CRU route a most attractive way to obtain funds for economic development, and vote for annual increments of CRUs in excess of the global needs for liquidity. Hence, proponents of CRU schemes thought that not all countries could be made participants.

When the Executive Board was considering the draft Annual Report for 1965, the question of the size of the group turned very much around this economic issue. There was considerable discussion about the transfer of real resources involved in any new reserve asset. Executive Directors for the continental European members of the Group of Ten urged that increases in international liquidity should not be effected in such a way as to result in the transfer of real resources. Their wish was that increased liquidity should be provided only to countries that, in general, would hold it in the form of additions to their reserves; they therefore considered that the machinery which evolved should exclude the developing countries from participating in any distribution of international liquidity.

Executive Directors for the developing countries were strongly opposed to this view. They suggested that the objective of increasing international liquidity, that is, to ensure the smooth functioning of international trade, could best be achieved if the additional liquidity was moved into the hands of those who were prepared to spend it, rather than confining it to those who would merely hold it.

REACTIONS OF MANAGEMENT AND STAFF TO CRU PROPOSALS

It was in this atmosphere that the management and staff, in mid-1965, began to explore how the Fund should react to the various proposals for CRUs. They strongly preferred the reserve-creating techniques which they themselves were working out. While the CRU proposals limited the distribution of new reserves to a few countries, the techniques being studied in the Fund would be applied to all Fund members. Indeed, there was concern that the establishment of a CRU on a narrow basis in the Group of Ten could have disastrous effects on the international monetary system. CRUs could not take the place of dollars and sterling in world reserves, least of all in the reserves of the countries outside the Group of Ten. Financial authorities of nonindustrial countries were already asking the Fund's officers how they should operate if CRUs came into being.

There might be an even greater stimulus than there had been in the past for the developing countries to establish their own regional payments arrangements.

On the other hand, some of the staff advocated that the Fund at least keep the door open for a Fund-managed CRU scheme. They thought that, given the divergent views prevailing among the Group of Ten in the spring of 1965, the only scheme on which it might be possible to achieve a consensus would be some kind of CRU arrangement. In fact, the staff noted a convergence of thinking among the monetary authorities of the United States, just before the 1965 Annual Meeting, toward a CRU arrangement operated through the Fund, and thought that at least eight of the other nine countries of the Group of Ten might be in favor of some sort of "CRU in the Fund."

The staff therefore considered whether it was possible that a CRU scheme might be so framed that the criteria by which countries were initially admitted to the scheme would be defensible by the Fund's standards—such as that all Article VIII countries would be eligible to participate, and that the scheme would be open ended, that is, other countries could join later. If the CRU had a broad base and was not rigidly tied to gold, the Fund might be able to examine such an arrangement with an open mind.

After consideration, however, the Managing Director decided not to support any of the CRU schemes in his public statements and not to use any of them as a basis for the Fund's techniques. He preferred the stand that he had been taking over the past year, namely, that all Fund members must be included in any new reserve arrangements.

The management and staff had several reservations about CRUs. They doubted that the criteria that the Fund would want to apply for participation in a CRU scheme could be negotiated with the countries in the Group of Ten. Furthermore, even if some open-ended scheme were to be negotiated right away, it would not begin to operate until the countries of the Group of Ten had resolved their much more fundamental differences on whether there was any need at all to create additional liquidity. They also believed that in circumstances where agreement among the Group of Ten to create liquidity could be obtained—for example, if the world economic situation looked very unsatisfactory—any CRU scheme, with its emphasis on distributing reserves to a limited group, might be quite ineffective in stimulating world recovery. Yet staving off recession was one of the principal objectives of greater world liquidity.

OSSOLA GROUP REPORT

From May 1964 to July 1965, concurrently with the developments just described, the Ossola Group had also been examining the possibilities of deliberate reserve creation. Fund staff had regularly attended the meetings of this group.

Following preliminary meetings in May, June, and July 1964, the group met in Rome for five days, October 26–30, 1964, to scrutinize alternative approaches to the creation of reserves: the various CRU proposals, the techniques of creating reserves through the Fund, a suggestion from the Canadian representatives for a Reserve Depository, and the Maudling plan, also referred to as the mutual currency account, in which the representatives of the United Kingdom still had an interest.[19]

As these meetings progressed, it quickly became evident that the CRU schemes, especially in their original forms, did not have wide support. The features of CRU proposals that particularly gave rise to questions were the relationship between any CRU and gold and the possible adverse repercussions that a CRU scheme would have on reserve currencies. Some participants in the Ossola Group were definitely opposed to CRU schemes, preferring the Fund's techniques as being more flexible, as being more acceptable politically, and as not requiring new institutional arrangements. Hence, when the Ossola Group met the next time, in Paris, December 14–16, 1964, little attention was paid to the CRU schemes; they were referred to only occasionally by way of comparison with the possibilities of creating reserves through the Fund.

The Ossola Group responded somewhat more favorably to the techniques possible through the Fund. The extension of automatism to the credit tranches gained some adherents, since it had the advantage of keeping intact the liquidity of the Fund. There was a willingness in the Ossola Group also to consider the technique of Fund investment (acquisition of special assets), but there was a desire to narrow the number of possible variants of such a scheme and to clarify the means by which such investment would be financed.

By April 1965 it was evident that the countries of the Group of Ten, through the Ossola Group, were searching for more common ground among themselves but had not yet reached it. The report of the Ossola Group was sent to the Deputies of the Group of Ten on May 31, 1965, and on July 5, 1965 the Deputies decided that the report should be published, subject to agreement of the Ministers. Publication was set for August 10, 1965, again, as in the previous year, to coincide with publication of the Fund's Annual Report.[20]

Mr. Emminger, chairman of the Deputies, in a foreword addressed to the Ministers, made it clear that the members of the Ossola Group had been acting as individual experts rather than as representatives of their respective governments, that the findings did not commit any participating country, and that the

---

[19] See Chap. 1 above, p. 24.

[20] Group of Ten, *Report of the Study Group on the Creation of Reserve Assets* (Washington, 1965). For a brief summary of the report, see *International Financial News Survey*, Vol. 17 (1965), p. 297.

Study Group had not attempted to pass final judgments on or express prefer-ences for individual proposals. Its mandate had been "to assemble the elements necessary for an evaluation by the Deputies of the various proposals." It had not, for example, undertaken to expand the area of common ground, to suggest compromises between opposing views, or to reduce the range of choice among alternative proposals. The report classified the different types of proposals as follows:

1. Creation of reserve assets by a group of countries
   a. Collective Reserve Unit scheme
   b. Group schemes associated with the Fund
2. Creation of reserve assets through the Fund
   a. Normal drawings in credit tranches
   b. Enlargement of automatic drawing rights in the Fund
   c. Extension of the gold tranche without gold payment on the occasion of quota increases
   d. Special operation by the Fund
3. Schemes to provide holders of currency with an alternative asset
   a. Conversion of currency balances into reserve positions in the Fund
   b. Mutual Currency Account

Detailed comparisons were made of the proposals. Further, the report cautiously noted that, while reserve assets might continue to be created by the Fund in the course of assisting individual countries with balance of payments deficits, a situation might arise in which the total stock of reserve assets was inadequate. Attention was called to the general agreement which had been reached that, in these circumstances, deliberate across-the-board creation of more reserve assets would be desirable. The report also went on to recognize that, whatever the form of reserve creation, countries had to be prepared to accept the reserve assets in question in sufficient quantity to ensure that the possessors of these assets could use them in settlements between monetary authorities.

That differences of view on several questions persisted was also pointed out. These questions were (1) the nature of a link between gold and the new reserve asset, the closeness of that link, and its consequences for the existing international monetary system; (2) the number of countries that would par-ticipate in the management and distribution of new reserve assets; (3) the role of the Fund in any scheme for deliberate reserve creation; and (4) the rules for making decisions on liquidity creation.

With regard to the Fund, the report of the Ossola Group revealed that the general view of the Deputies was that the Fund had important advantages as a center for any new functions that might be needed for the deliberate creation of reserve assets. Various means were considered for dealing with the problem of the Fund's own liquidity should new reserve assets be both created by, and transferred through, the Fund. The group also stated the majority view that the provision of capital to developing countries was a problem distinct from the creation of reserves, and that there were disadvantages in any attempt to combine the objective of long-term development finance with the objective of greater liquidity, that is, to provide flexibility in the use of domestic monetary policy. But on these issues, as on many other questions, there had been little agreement within the Ossola Group, and the report spelled out the nature of the disagreements.

FRANCE AND UNITED STATES TAKE OPPOSING POSITIONS

As the several ways suggested for creating liquidity were extensively examined and discussed, not only within the Fund and within the Group of Ten but also within the national governments of the major industrial countries, the positions and attitudes toward the various techniques began to crystallize. There were many statements of national objectives and vigorous exchanges of views; opposing opinions were voiced, not only within the Ossola Group but also publicly. Some of the ideas being formulated by the Fund staff were disclosed to economists outside the Fund to help advance technical discussions.[21]

France Advocates Return to Gold Standard

The position of the French Government, that gold was the crux of the international monetary system, had been repeated time and again, in both private and public meetings. During 1964–65 that view became more deeply entrenched in the minds of the French officials. President Charles de Gaulle and Mr. Giscard d'Estaing both called for a more pronounced role for gold in the international monetary system.[22] In a press conference on February 4, 1965, President de Gaulle asked for the total abolition of the gold exchange standard and an immediate return to the gold standard, that is, that balance of payments deficits be settled only in gold. The Fund, the Group of Ten, and the EEC should, he stated, start negotiations to this end.

The French press suggested that what particularly troubled President de Gaulle and French monetary leaders about the continued U.S. balance of payments deficit was the extremely large outflows of long-term capital from the United States. These capital outflows reflected substantial investments by U.S. companies in European firms.

---

[21] See J. J. Polak, "The Report of the International Monetary Fund," *American Economic Review* (Papers and Proceedings of the Seventy-Seventh Annual Meeting of the American Economic Association), Vol. 55 (1965), pp. 158–65.

[22] *Le Monde*, Paris, February 6 and 13, 1965.

In a speech at the University of Paris on February 11, 1965, Mr. Giscard d'Estaing elaborated the French objections to the existing international monetary system. *First*, the gold exchange standard of the existing system lacked what he called reciprocity. The reserve currency countries—such as the United States and the United Kingdom—could incur payments deficits indefinitely because trading partners would accumulate the currencies of reserve centers, that is, dollars or sterling. Countries whose currencies were not held by other countries as reserves had to settle their deficits in gold or through international credit facilities. The need to correct payments deficits quickly was, therefore, not the same for all countries.

Second, the gold exchange standard lacked strength. While the U.S. dollar remained a strong currency from a national point of view, the assumption that dollars held by foreigners could be converted into gold had become increasingly questionable.

Third, a better mechanism for balance of payments adjustment than was assured under the gold exchange standard was essential. Otherwise, the payments deficits of reserve center countries would continue to persist.

Finally, the gold exchange standard did not provide international liquidity sufficient to permit the growth of the world economy without inflationary pressures. (In other words, the gold exchange standard required payments deficits by reserve centers and the building up of large balances by other countries of the currencies of the reserve centers. Both the deficits and the accumulation of balances were inflationary.)

Mr. Giscard d'Estaing also made more specific the proposal of President de Gaulle for an immediate return to the gold standard by suggesting that (1) the big countries publicly declare that they would henceforth settle their payments deficits only in gold and not through the creation of additional reserve monies; (2) additional liquidity should be provided only through the use of the Fund's resources, so as to avoid the financing of payments deficits that were of a fundamental character; and (3) the creation of additional international liquidity should be made dependent on a reform of the present system. Central bank reserves should ultimately consist only of gold and of owned reserves based on gold, with foreign currencies being held only as working balances. The process of eliminating the existing international holdings of reserve currencies could be achieved by the repayment of foreign debt. In the meantime, these holdings—most of which were invested in U.S. Treasury securities—should not receive interest. In the event that an international shortage of the means of payment were to develop, additional reserves based on gold could be created by a joint decision of the countries whose currencies were convertible into gold.

Consistent with these views, Mr. Giscard d'Estaing stated that hereafter France would use only gold to settle any deficits it might incur. On June 15, 1965, he reiterated the French position that gold should be the center of the international monetary system and put forward his own proposal for collective reserve units.[23]

United States Calls for Special Conference

On July 10, 1965, a sharp impetus was given to the debate by the United States. In a bold speech to the Virginia State Bar Association, Mr. Henry H. Fowler, who had been appointed by President Lyndon B. Johnson to be Secretary of the Treasury in his new administration, announced that the United States

> stands prepared to attend and participate in an international monetary conference that would consider what steps we might jointly take to secure substantial improvements in international monetary arrangements. . . .
>
> Our suggestion is that the work of preparation be undertaken by a Preparatory Committee which could be given its terms of reference at the time of the annual meeting of the International Monetary Fund this September.[24]

Also in mid-1965, as preparation for a possible international monetary conference, the U.S. Congress—through the Subcommittee on International Exchange and Payments of the Joint Economic Committee—held hearings at which a number of experts presented their views.

This stronger push by the United States came in the wake of the measures for dealing with the U.S. balance of payments problem (mentioned earlier in this chapter) which President Johnson announced in a special message to the U.S. Congress on February 10, 1965, less than a week after President de Gaulle had asked for a return to the gold standard.

Among the U.S. measures announced at that time were several aimed at stemming the outflow of private U.S. capital, especially of transfers for direct investment in Europe. President Johnson invoked his statutory authority to apply the interest equalization tax, which the United States had introduced in 1963, to bank loans with maturities of one year or more and asked Congress to extend this tax beyond its expiry date of December 31, 1965 and to broaden it to cover nonbank credits of one to three years' maturity; previously the tax had not been applicable to nonbank credits of less than three years nor to any bank loans. (Subsequently, on October 9, 1965, a new Act extended the interest equalization tax through July 31, 1967 and broadened its coverage to include nonbank debt obligations of one year or more to maturity.)

In addition, on February 10, 1965 there was instituted a new voluntary foreign credit restraint program. Sets of guidelines were subsequently arranged by which banks, nonbank financial institutions, and nonfinancial businesses were asked to limit their foreign undertakings. Financial institutions were

---

[23] Referred to in the section on Proposals for CRUs, p. 54 above.

[24] U.S. Treasury Department, Press Release, July 11, 1965, and reported briefly in *International Financial News Survey*, Vol. 17 (1965), p. 251.

requested to limit the increase in their foreign credits so that by March 1966, at the latest, they would not be more than 5 per cent in excess of their December 1964 levels. The ceiling of 5 per cent for expansion of lendings by financial institutions other than banks was to apply only to loans and investments with maturities of up to ten years. Within these overall limits, priority was to be given to export financing, special care was to be exercised to avoid possible adverse effects on Canada, Japan, and the United Kingdom, and credits to the developing countries were to be given preference. Industrial enterprises were asked to take steps to improve their individual payments balances—by expanding export and other receipts from abroad and by transferring income receipts from, and limiting outflows of capital to, developed countries other than Canada; they were to report on the results to the Secretary of Commerce.

Meanwhile, the other countries in the Group of Ten were continuing to formulate their positions and were considering, within their own governments and with each other, the merits of the various liquidity schemes being proposed, including those put forward by the staff of the Fund.

MANAGING DIRECTOR'S ASSESSMENT AND ACTION

These circumstances were conducive to further action by the Fund. In a speech on June 2, 1965 at the Institut d'Etudes Bancaires et Financières, in Paris, the Managing Director deliberately expressed his views publicly on the dilemma of whether liquidity ought to be increased or the international monetary system altered.[25] He took a broad position, explaining that any plans for the future must grow out of answers to three basic questions: What is the nature of the international monetary system and what do we want it to accomplish? To what extent has the present system succeeded or failed? How can the international monetary system be improved?

Defends Existing System

Mr. Schweitzer described the existing international monetary system as a complex of international rules and understandings, which included the par value system, convertibility, and the absence of exchange restrictions, as well as the arrangements under which countries held their external reserves in the form partly of gold, partly of convertible currencies, and partly of claims on the Fund. The system combined two complementary features, the financing of imbalances and the elimination of imbalances; and the task of managing the system was, in large measure, to strike a balance between the two. The Fund,

---

[25] Speech by the Managing Director at the Institut d'Etudes Bancaires et Financières, Paris, June 2, 1965, reproduced in Supplement to *International Financial News Survey*, Vol. 17 (1965), pp. 209–16.

as the international organization at the center of the system, had had this primary and crucial task.

But he also stressed that it was not enough that international payments should balance. The aim had to be the achievement of equilibrium with the least possible sacrifice of the generally accepted objectives of economic policy: full employment, an adequate rate of growth, reasonable price stability, and freedom from restrictions on current international transactions.

Noting that a return to the gold standard was being advocated in some quarters, Mr. Schweitzer said that he preferred the existing system. He asked monetary authorities to recall that, when the gold standard was in operation, its successes in terms of external balance were attained at the expense of internal objectives, and he underscored his rejection of a return to the gold standard by observing that, in the current world, national authorities placed a high priority on the management of their domestic economies.

Presenting the conclusions of the appraisal of the international monetary system that the Fund staff had undertaken during 1964 and the early part of 1965, Mr. Schweitzer observed that that system had operated fairly well, although a distinction had to be made between the developing countries and the industrial ones. By and large, the developing countries, hampered by structural problems, especially the unsatisfactory development of their export earnings, had found it difficult to achieve simultaneously the goals of rapid growth and internal and external stability. Restrictions on imports and on payments for invisibles had often been resorted to, exchange rates had been depreciated, and internal imbalances had interfered with growth.

On the other hand, for the industrial countries the system had, until the mid-1960s, worked with a very high degree of success. Between 1950 and 1964, production in the industrial countries had expanded at a rate of more than 5 per cent per annum, while the labor force had grown only by 1.3 per cent per annum; the large pockets of structural unemployment, which had at one time existed in most European countries and which had seemed likely to persist, had been largely absorbed. Great progress had also been made in removing barriers to trade and shifting from bilateral to multilateral payments. All the major industrial countries had accepted the obligations of Article VIII of the Fund Agreement.

In defending the present international monetary system, Mr. Schweitzer made it clear that he regarded some of the arguments criticizing the gold exchange standard as being of doubtful relevance. He thought that the argument that the system provided an unfair advantage to one or two reserve currency countries, in that it permitted them to finance their balance of payments deficits painlessly and automatically, was overstated. The real point was that, so long as a reserve center was strong and enjoyed unquestioned confidence, it could finance a proportion of its deficit through an accumulation of liabilities to foreign monetary holders; but as soon as that confidence was weakened, the pressures on the reserve center became at least as strong as, if not stronger than, those on other countries. What he thought was a valid point of objection to the gold exchange standard was that the supply of reserves created depended on the somewhat accidental circumstance of whether the reserve currency countries happened to be running deficits or surpluses, and also on whether there did or did not happen to be confidence in the future value of their currencies.

Notes New Problems

Despite the success of the existing system, the Managing Director recognized that, in the last few years, the unexpected magnitude of short-term capital movements between the main industrial countries had brought new problems. Capital movements were the more difficult to deal with since there were no agreed answers as yet as to the best method of handling them. Should they be considered temporary and financed by the use of reserves? Should current account balances be radically altered to accommodate them? Or, should capital flows be restrained by the use of controls?

A second element which made managing the international monetary system more difficult than it had been was that changes in general price levels between deficit and surplus countries could not be counted on to correct deficit and surplus positions. Modern conditions made economies more rigid and deficit countries could not force down their price levels without provoking substantial unemployment. At best they might be able to stabilize prices. On the other hand, countries in surplus resisted any addition, through increases in their monetary reserves, to the inflationary pressures already prevalent in their economies.

Suggests Elements of a Solution

From the above analysis Mr. Schweitzer deduced that the aim should be to supplement and not to supplant the present system. This process, he stressed, would be greatly facilitated if the payments deficits of the United States and the United Kingdom were corrected. Then, aggregate official holdings of dollars and sterling would become a relatively stable part of world reserves and it would not be necessary to transfer these holdings to the Fund in exchange for gold-guaranteed claims on the Fund, as some had been suggesting. He also concluded that a change in the price of gold would not improve the system of reserve creation; such a change would serve mainly to augment initially the value of gold holdings and would not add much to subsequent accruals to reserves.

The Managing Director once again outlined some of the reasons why he preferred the schemes for creating liquidity through the Fund. In the first place, the Fund was already equipped to finance the temporary balance of payments deficits of its members, including those of the industrial countries, by a mixture of conditional and unconditional liquidity. A second advantage lay in the variety and flexibility of the methods of creating reserve assets that were available through the Fund.

But, more importantly, it seemed to him to be highly desirable for the maintenance of good relations among countries in all stages of development that the richer nations of the world should not appear to be clubbing together to create reserves—out of nothing as it were—for themselves alone. By entrusting this function to the Fund, all countries, in proportion to their role in the world economy, could be given their due share both in the control over the creation of reserves and in the benefits of that creation. It need not be feared that countries urgently needing resources for development, or for other purposes, would run away with the process of reserve creation or that creditor countries would be faced with burdens which they were not willing to assume. The Fund had amply demonstrated that it could administer a worldwide pool of resources guided by policies to assure the proper use of those resources.

Attempts a Governors' Resolution

When several monetary officials of the EEC countries protested this speech by the Managing Director on the ground that it was premature for the Fund to say anything about the possibilities of creating liquidity through the Fund, Mr. Schweitzer took the view that the Fund could not remain silent while the Group of Ten spoke freely. It also appeared that the countries of the Group of Ten, urged on by those in the EEC, might decide to study international monetary questions on their own without putting their decision up for discussion or approval by the Fund's Board of Governors.

In these circumstances, Mr. Schweitzer favored what appeared to be the onset of a more activist and broader approach by U.S. officials. Recognizing that a committee of Governors of the Fund could be a useful addition to the Fund's machinery, even if a world monetary conference was never convened, and whatever the outcome with respect to international liquidity, the view developed within the Fund management that the preparatory committee for an international conference suggested in Mr. Fowler's speech could be a committee composed of Fund Governors. Such a committee, with the Managing Director as chairman, should have a balanced composition of about 15 Governors— probably the Governors for the countries in the Group of Ten but also 5 other Governors (such as those for Australia, India, a Middle Eastern member, an African member, and a Latin American member). Appropriate relations between the committee and the Executive Directors would be specified.

Accordingly, while the U.S. authorities considered the terms of reference for a preparatory committee, and while U.S. technical staff evaluated the various proposals for reserve creation, the Managing Director attempted to obtain support for a resolution of the Board of Governors at the Twentieth Annual Meeting, which would take place in a few weeks. The resolution would be directed to answering such questions as by what mechanism the liquidity discussions could be brought into the Fund, how the Executive Directors and the Group of Ten could collaborate, and what the composition of a preparatory committee would be.

It began to appear, however, that such a resolution would cause undue controversy. The U.S. authorities were willing to bring the discussions on liquidity into the Fund, but several European countries wished to keep them within the Group of Ten. Mr. Schweitzer dropped his efforts to obtain a resolution. But this attempt in 1965 to get a committee of the Board of Governors as part of the Fund's machinery was in a sense a forerunner of proposals that the Managing Director made on several subsequent occasions and was thus a lineal ancestor of the Committee on Reform of the International Monetary System and Related Issues (Committee of Twenty) that was established in 1972.

States Again: "Liquidity Is the Business of the Fund"

In his opening address at the Twentieth Annual Meeting, on September 27, 1965 in Washington, the Managing Director repeated his conviction that the Fund was "ideally and flexibly constructed to perform the new tasks and to provide the new facilities that may be found to be needed in the course of the continuing evolution of the international monetary system," and he repeated what he had said to the Governors two years before, that "international liquidity is the business of the Fund." [26] The staff would, he said, intensify its studies and would present the results to the Executive Directors for their consideration. Further, he believed that it would be very useful to seek ways by which the efforts of the Executive Directors and those of the Deputies of the Group of Ten could be directed toward a consensus on desirable lines of action. He suggested that the Board of Governors would serve ideally as the appropriate forum should an international monetary conference be considered necessary.[27]

Mr. Schweitzer was also more specific concerning the criteria that should be kept in the forefront as this work proceeded. *First*, the functioning of the international monetary system and the adequacy of the sources of international liquidity were matters of concern to all members. *Second*, new or improved facilities should be designed with the requirements of all members in mind. *Third*, this comprehensive approach, while it did not preclude the possibility

---

[26] Opening Address by the Managing Director, *Summary Proceedings, 1965*, pp. 31 and 30.

[27] *Ibid.*, p. 30.

that new facilities would be available to countries meeting reasonable and agreed tests, meant that any new facility should be available to all countries which could meet those tests. *Fourth*, the new facility should be so constructed as to ensure that additional liquidity was not created in a measure that would have an inflationary impact on the world economy, and there must be adequate safeguards to protect the quality of members' reserves.[28]

The Managing Director's remarks were endorsed by several Governors, especially by Governors for countries not in the Group of Ten.[29]

AGREEMENT BY GROUP OF TEN ON CONTINGENCY PLANNING

At the 1965 Annual Meeting, the differences that had existed in earlier years among the Governors for the countries in the Group of Ten continued. Messrs. Colombo (Italy), Blessing (Federal Republic of Germany), and Giscard d'Estaing (France) reiterated the warnings that they had given in 1964: excessive liquidity would result in persistent inflation; countries in deficit should give priority to attaining balance of payments equilibrium.

Mr. Colombo, taking the line of the report of the Deputies of the Group of Ten of May 1964 and the 1964 Annual Report of the Fund, thought that gold and reserve currency assets, together with a wide range of credit facilities, were fully adequate for present needs and most probably for some years to come. There was, therefore, no case at present for any further increase in the volume of liquidity, and, in fact, the problem really came down to avoiding any decrease in unconditional liquidity.[30]

Mr. Blessing stated similarly that he could see no urgent need for additional liquidity, especially in view of the considerable increase in Fund quotas that was now taking place. Multilateral surveillance within the Group of Ten had represented a useful step in the direction of stricter balance of payments discipline, but he believed that still more should be done to lay down specific rules of conduct for adjusting external disequilibria.[31]

Mr. Giscard d'Estaing took the same tack. He believed that the problem to be dealt with in the immediate future was one of too much liquidity rather than too little. He advocated "a discipline equally urging all countries to adjust their domestic economies to external financial balance requirements,

---

[28] *Ibid.*, pp. 30–31.

[29] For example, Statements by the Governor of the World Bank for Iran, the Governor of the Fund for Iraq, the Governor of the Fund and the World Bank for Australia, and the Governor of the Fund for New Zealand, *Summary Proceedings, 1965*, pp. 65, 74, 78–79, and 156.

[30] Statement by the Governor of the Fund for Italy, *Summary Proceedings, 1965*, pp. 41–42.

[31] Statement by the Governor of the Fund for the Federal Republic of Germany, *Summary Proceedings, 1965*, p. 117.

without excessive delay, although naturally without undue rigor." His conclusion was that "the main contribution by reserve currency countries to an international monetary reform is the restoration of a durable balance in their external accounts. This preconditions the study of any other device." [32]

Other Governors for the countries in the Group of Ten agreed. Indeed, the idea that there was nothing urgent about supplementing the volume of world reserves had been almost universally accepted for about a year by the officials of the Group of Ten.

Along with this emphasis by the countries of the EEC on attaining payments equilibrium and on discipline, there were reassurances at the 1965 Annual Meeting from the United Kingdom and the United States that measures were being taken to rectify their balance of payments deficits. Mr. James Callaghan (United Kingdom) reported that the United Kingdom was "firmly set on the course of recovery from the serious balance of payments deficit we suffered in 1964 and from the consequential period of uncertainty for sterling that followed. As a result of the drastic measures we have taken, our overseas deficit is being steadily reduced and this, together with the assistance we have received, has made it clear to all that the present parity of the pound sterling is not in question." [33] He proceeded to outline the measures being taken by his Government for the betterment of the U.K. balance of payments.[34]

Mr. Fowler, at the first of four Annual Meetings he was to attend, cited various facts and figures showing a significant improvement in the U.S. balance of payments. He further stated that the programs would be "vigorously pursued until we are certain that the conditions have been created in which equilibrium in our international accounts can be sustained." [35]

First Phase of Contingency Planning

In this environment it was possible for the Ministers and Central Bank Governors of the Group of Ten to agree only to draw up a plan for reserve creation that could be put into effect should the need arise. The wording of a communiqué that they issued on the second day of the 1965 Annual Meeting revealed the complex process by which even this degree of agreement had been attained.[36] They noted with approval that the program of multilateral surveillance that they had recommended in August 1964 had been put into effect,

---

[32] Statement by the Governor of the World Bank for France, *Summary Proceedings, 1965*, pp. 123–26. Quotations are from pp. 123 and 124.

[33] Statement by the Governor of the Fund for the United Kingdom, *Summary Proceedings, 1965*, pp. 85–86.

[34] *Ibid.*, pp. 86–87.

[35] Statement by the Governor of the Fund and the World Bank for the United States, *Summary Proceedings, 1965*, p. 103.

[36] Communiqué of the Ministers and Governors of the "Group of Ten" Issued on September 28, 1965, *Summary Proceedings, 1965*, pp. 279–81.

that the deficit in the U.S. balance of payments was being corrected, and that the United States had expressed its determination to maintain equilibrium in its balance of payments. Only after making these points did the Ministers and Governors conclude that it was important to undertake, as soon as possible, "contingency planning" so as to ensure that the future needs of the world for reserves would be adequately met.

Paragraph 7 of the communiqué stated that, as the first phase of contingency planning, the Ministers and Governors had given instructions to their Deputies to resume on an intensified basis their previous discussions and to report to the Ministers, in the spring of 1966, on the scope and basis of agreement that could be reached on improvements needed in the international monetary system, including arrangements for the future creation of reserve assets, as and when needed. It was also specified that during these discussions it would be desirable for the Deputies to continue to have the active participation of representatives of the Managing Director of the Fund, the OECD, and the BIS.

The remarks made by the Governors for the countries of the Group of Ten in the days that followed their communiqué indicated that there were differences in the sense of urgency with which they viewed the need for any liquidity plan. Mr. Callaghan, welcoming the initiative that Mr. Fowler had taken in July, was eager to proceed: "The time has come for negotiation leading to the preparation of a plan that can be put into effect as soon as agreement exists on the need to do so." Agreeing with the Governor for Italy that the problem of any new arrangements for reserve creation was essentially political, Mr. Callaghan argued that now was the time for governments to see how far they were prepared to forgo their own particular preferences in the interests of securing agreement. He suggested, too, that a careful reading of the report by the Ossola Group "leads to the conclusion that positions which may seem very far apart are in fact preferences about different ways of achieving the same end." He thought that any differences were not irreconcilable.[37]

Mr. Walter L. Gordon (Canada) stated the situation as follows:

> Discussions concerning the international monetary system have continued in the Fund, in OECD, and among the Deputies of the Group of Ten. But we have not reached firm conclusions as to what needs to be done to improve the international system, and the time has come to increase the tempo of our work. We cannot wait until the need for action is upon us before reaching agreement upon the most appropriate solution.[38]

But even among those who attached the least urgency to the need for reform, there was at least a willingness to engage in formulating a contingency

---

[37] Statement by the Governor of the Fund for the United Kingdom, *Summary Proceedings, 1965*, pp. 88 and 89. Mr. Fowler's speech was discussed above, p. 63.

[38] Statement by the Governor of the Fund and the World Bank for Canada, *Summary Proceedings, 1965*, p. 55.

plan. Mr. Blessing indicated that, while he did not share the view that the disappearance of the U.S. payments deficit must necessarily lead to an immediate shortage of liquidity, his Government agreed to "contingency planning with a view to providing suitable machinery for increasing liquidity if the need for it were really to arise." [39] Mr. Colombo similarly did not disagree that preparations ought to be made in good time.[40]

Thus the road had been paved for the countries of the Group of Ten to come to the same conclusion as had the Executive Directors of the Fund—that it was important to consider well in advance the principles and techniques by which liquidity would be expanded should the need for such expansion arise.[41]

Second Phase of Contingency Planning

The communiqué issued by the Group of Ten on September 28, 1965 also explicitly recognized that, once the countries of the Group of Ten had reached "a basis for agreement on essential points," discussions would have to include the countries outside the Group. Thus, the last paragraph of the communiqué read:

> 9. The Ministers and Governors recognize that, as soon as a basis for agreement on essential points has been reached, it will be necessary to proceed from this first phase to a broader consideration of the questions that affect the world economy as a whole. They have agreed that it would be very useful to seek ways by which the efforts of the Executive Board of the Fund and those of the Deputies of the Group of Ten can be directed toward a consensus as to desirable lines of action, and they have instructed their Deputies to work out during the coming year, in close consultation with the Managing Director of the Fund, procedures to achieve this aim, with a view to preparing for the final enactment of any new arrangements at an appropriate forum for international discussions.[42]

Here again, the speeches made during the Annual Meeting revealed considerable differences of approach. Some European Governors still held the view that reserve assets were not to be created for purposes of economic development. Mr. Colombo, for instance, was emphatic in his view that "the decision to create new reserve assets should not be made to depend upon the needs to finance external deficits or the economic development of the less developed countries; these requirements should continue to be financed by traditional means." [43]

---

[39] Statement by the Governor of the Fund for the Federal Republic of Germany, *Summary Proceedings, 1965*, p. 118.

[40] Statement by the Governor of the Fund for Italy, *Summary Proceedings, 1965*, p. 42.

[41] *Annual Report, 1965*, p. 19.

[42] Communiqué of the Ministers and Governors of the "Group of Ten" Issued on September 28, 1965, *Summary Proceedings, 1965*, p. 281.

[43] Statement by the Governor of the Fund for Italy, *Summary Proceedings, 1965*, p. 43.

Mr. Blessing repeated the view that the responsibility lay with a limited group:

> It seems to me that the responsibility connected with any creation of additional liquidity should be borne by a limited group of industrial countries, as only those industrial countries are in a position to back such a scheme by their own resources. This does not mean that other countries are excluded later on from such deliberations nor does it necessarily mean that newly created liquidity would be distributed only to assist this limited group.[44]

On the other hand, the Governors for the United Kingdom and the United States were much more eager to extend the discussions beyond the Group of Ten. Mr. Callaghan looked forward to the time when the results of the efforts of the Fund and the Group of Ten could be brought together. He explicitly interpreted paragraph 9 of the communiqué in these words:

> I take this to mean that, at the next stage, countries which are not included in the earlier discussions will be brought fully into the picture before there is any final enactment of such new arrangements as may be agreed. This stage is necessary in order to ensure that the basic interests of all members of the Fund are adequately represented and appropriately considered, for all countries have a vital interest in such arrangements. Only after this has been completed should we be able to proceed to the final stage of enacting the new arrangements at an international conference.[45]

Mr. Fowler explained at length the importance to the United States of the "second phase" of preparation. This phase should, he stressed, be designed primarily to assure that the basic interests of all members of the Fund in new arrangements for the future of the world monetary system would be adequately and appropriately considered and represented before significant intergovernmental agreements for formal structural improvements of the monetary system were concluded. Insisting that "all the countries of the free world have a fair and reasonable claim that their views must be heard and considered at an appropriate stage in the process of international monetary improvement," he welcomed paragraph 9.[46]

■ ■ ■ ■ ■ ■

As suggested by his brief remarks at the closing session of the 1965 Annual Meeting, Mr. Schweitzer was encouraged by what he saw as overwhelming agreement on three points—that liquidity was a matter that concerned all countries; that the interests of all members were best reconciled by international discussion in the Fund; and that general action to deal with the problem of liquidity should be taken within the framework of the Fund.[47]

[44] Statement by the Governor of the Fund for the Federal Republic of Germany, *Summary Proceedings, 1965*, p. 119.

[45] Statement by the Governor of the Fund for the United Kingdom, *Summary Proceedings, 1965*, p. 89.

[46] Statement by the Governor of the Fund and the World Bank for the United States, *Summary Proceedings, 1965*, pp. 106–107.

[47] Concluding Remarks by the Managing Director, *Summary Proceedings, 1965*, p. 226.

CHAPTER
4

Search for a Contingency Plan
for Reserve Creation
(1965–66)

*I*N CONTRAST TO THE EXPLORATORY NATURE of the discussions that
had taken place in 1964–65, the discussions in 1965–66 were intentionally
directed toward laying a basis for further action. Both the Group of Ten, in its
communiqué of September 28, 1965, and the Fund had expressed a desire to
reach a consensus about reserve creation. For much of the year, however, there
was little momentum in the discussions. It was only after the Fund took an
important initiative in March 1966 that a consensus on which further action
could be based began to appear possible.

ECONOMIC CIRCUMSTANCES FACILITATE AGREEMENT

In the meantime, evolving economic circumstances also were conducive
to a reconciliation of the strong differences of view about the need for reserve
creation that had persisted. One such circumstance was that the deficits of the
two reserve currency countries, the United Kingdom and the United States, and
the surpluses of continental European countries were declining. The U.K.
authorities had instituted several measures to restore domestic and external
equilibrium, and the U.K. deficit on current and long-term capital account,
which had been $2.2 billion in 1964, was reduced to less than half that amount
in 1965. Similarly, the balance of payments deficit of the United States turned
out to be lower in 1965 than in any year since the late 1950s, when it first
became a problem. The net outflow of private capital from the United States
had been curtailed by official programs for limiting capital outflow and by a
progressive tightening of monetary and credit policies. Interest rates in the
United States moved upward quite markedly: after January 1966 the yield
on Treasury bills was at a height that had been touched only briefly after the

stock market crash late in 1929, and the yield on medium-term government bonds was higher than at any time since shortly after World War I.

Reduction of the U.S. and U.K. deficits helped the discussions to progress. Since the French in particular had been insistent that the deficits of reserve currency countries be eliminated prior to agreement on any plan to create liquidity, the remarks of Mr. Giscard d'Estaing before the National Assembly on October 13, 1965 are noteworthy. Calling attention to the change of tone and attitude which had characterized the Annual Meeting just concluded, he said that he was impressed that the reserve currency countries had specifically confirmed that they now realized the necessity of restoring equilibrium in their balances of payments prior to any new action.

The second economic circumstance conducive to progress in the discussions about the need for reserve creation was that, as some officials had expected and feared, world reserves did not increase as much as they had in the past. Some new form of international reserve asset or mechanism for enlarging liquidity was, therefore, considered to be much more essential than it had been earlier. For the first time in the postwar period all the industrial countries either were enjoying virtually full employment or, as was the case for France, Italy, and Japan, were again entering an expansionary phase of the business cycle following a period of recession. As a consequence, many authorities believed that reserves in the traditional form of gold and dollars were not increasing sufficiently to finance the volume of world trade and other international transactions associated with such worldwide prosperity. The concern about the rate of growth of reserves was the greater because private gold hoarding in 1965 reached another high. The official dollar holdings of a number of European countries declined, partly because they became reluctant to hold continuously larger amounts of dollars, and in contrast to their earlier practice they requested the U.S. Treasury to convert dollars into gold. Inasmuch as the official dollar holdings of non-industrial countries rose substantially, there was little change in the aggregate official dollar holdings of all countries. But even then, the increase in world reserves for 1965 turned out to be only $1.7 billion, much smaller than that for 1964 and only about half the annual average for the preceding decade. Moreover, much of the increase in total world reserves that did take place in 1965 was attributable to transactions by the Fund.

Thus, the experience of 1965 suggested that the continuance of balance of payments deficits in the countries that were reserve centers was no longer necessarily bringing about a growth in world reserves. Indeed, sterling balances had not shown an upward trend during the entire postwar period; consequently, it could not be said that the U.K. payments deficit had been adding to international reserves. And in 1965 it became apparent that deficits in the U.S. balance of payments did not inevitably contribute to an increase in world reserves either: the U.S. deficit in 1965 was not financed by an increase in foreign dollar holdings.

INTENSIFIED DISCUSSIONS BY GROUP OF TEN

Against this background, the Deputies of the Finance Ministers and Central Bank Governors of the Group of Ten began to meet regularly. In the year ended September 1966, they met as frequently as every five or six weeks, usually in Paris but also in Washington, April 19–22, in Rome, May 17–19, and in Frankfurt, June 22–24. Mr. Emminger (Federal Republic of Germany) continued to serve as chairman until after the "Outline of a Facility Based on Special Drawing Rights in the Fund" was agreed to in September 1967. Technical monetary specialists usually accompanied the Deputies to the meetings. Many of the Deputies also continued to meet as members of Working Party 3 of the Economic Policy Committee of the OECD, which was under the chairmanship of Mr. Emile van Lennep, of the Netherlands.

Even some of the procedural arrangements suggested a more determined effort on the part of the Deputies to try to achieve a consensus among themselves. Instead of the arrangement under which the functions of a secretariat had been performed by staff members from national delegations, a three-man secretariat, consisting of one person each from the Fund, the OECD, and the BIS, was formed to keep records of the discussions. Papers indicating positions or outlining proposals were prepared by the staffs of the national delegations. Studies by the Fund staff on relevant topics were made available to the authorities of the countries in the Group of Ten as well as to observers from Switzerland, the OECD, and the BIS.

Closer Liaison with Executive Directors

At the outset of the year starting in September 1965, a somewhat closer official liaison between the Deputies and the Executive Directors of the Fund was established. During an informal session of the Fund's Executive Board on November 3, 1965, several Directors, finding their position vis-à-vis the Deputies increasingly awkward, argued that a fuller exchange of information between themselves and the Deputies was desirable if a contingency plan for reserve creation acceptable both to the Group of Ten and to the Fund was to be found. Otherwise, the two bodies might come up with divergent plans.

At the next meeting of the Deputies, two days after the Executive Board's informal session, it was agreed that the representatives of the Managing Director, following consultation with the chairman of the Deputies, might report back to the Executive Directors on the trend of the proceedings without disclosing positions of individual Deputies. Conversely, the Managing Director's representatives would interpret to the Deputies the current thinking of the Executive Directors without identifying the views of individual Directors.

The representatives of the Managing Director to the meetings of the Deputies of the Group of Ten throughout the years covered in this volume were Mr. J. J. Polak, appointed to be The Economic Counsellor in May 1966, who attended the meetings regularly, and Mr. Joseph Gold, appointed to be The General Counsel in May 1966, who attended whenever legal questions were being discussed.[1] These two senior staff officials participated actively in the discussions of the Deputies—advancing and defending many of the basic principles that were ultimately adopted—and reported to the Executive Directors within a few days after attending each meeting. Mr. J. Marcus Fleming, Deputy Director of the Research and Statistics Department, and Mr. George Nicoletopoulos, Deputy General Counsel, represented the Managing Director at these meetings when Mr. Polak and/or Mr. Gold could not attend. In addition, the Director of the Office in Europe, Mr. Jean-Paul Sallé, attended some of the meetings.

Provisional Positions

When the Deputies met on November 5 and 6, 1965 to begin consideration of a contingency plan, it was in an atmosphere more of prenegotiation than of negotiation. Most governments, still with an open mind on the major issues, sought clarification of technical points and expressed only provisional positions. The basic question of whether any new reserves were needed at all was still of intense interest. Most of the Deputies had come to believe that reserve creation would probably have very little immediate influence on world economic conditions—in alleviating cyclical swings, for example, and particularly in cushioning recessions. Creation of reserves would therefore have to be guided by longer-run or secular trends, with adjustments of requirements for reserves in the short term being handled by credit facilities.

The majority of Deputies remained convinced that responsibility for creation of reserves should rest with a limited group of countries, although that limited group need not necessarily be the Group of Ten. A variety of views prevailed, however, as to the size of the group that should participate in the distribution of the reserves that were created. Whether distribution should be in proportion to Fund quotas or in proportion to Fund quotas plus commitments under the General Arrangements to Borrow was also far from settled. Most Deputies appeared to favor some kind of relation between reserve creation and the Fund, but most had no strong preference between the two methods being developed by the staff for creating reserves through the Fund—automatic drawing rights or acquisition of special assets.

When the Deputies next met, on December 14 and 15, 1965, the discussions, as in the past, were exploratory and still were not yet aimed at coming

---

[1] Mr. Gold was also the Director of the Legal Department and Mr. Polak the Director of the Research and Statistics Department. The latter department, when the Bureau of Statistics was formed on May 1, 1968, was renamed the Research Department, which had been its name before May 1, 1955.

to any conclusions. Three questions were discussed. The first concerned the relation that any new reserve asset would have to already existing reserves. A minority of the Deputies believed that, before any reserves were created, agreement should be reached on limiting the amount of dollars that would be held in official reserves, particularly in the official reserves of the countries in the Group of Ten.

The second question concerned the process of decision making. One suggestion that found considerable support was that decisions for creating new reserves should be taken in two steps: there would first be a proposal by an international authority, which might be the Managing Director of the Fund, and then a vote would be taken on the proposal, which would be approved only if a specified number of countries voted for it.

The third question concerned the possibility of some parallel reserve creation for other countries if the reserve creation plan then being debated was limited to a small group. There was a growing realization in the Group of Ten that something substantial would have to be done for the countries outside the Group. A few Deputies had begun to think that there might be two parallel schemes—a worldwide scheme for all Fund members and another scheme for countries subject to large-scale capital movements, such as the countries of the Group of Ten. There was also increasing receptivity to the idea that some portion of the reserves created for a small group might be set aside for the countries outside the group and that this "set-aside" might be on the order of 25 per cent of the total reserves to be created.

EMPHASIS ON A LIMITED GROUP CONTINUES

The Group of Ten used several arguments to explain why they continued to insist on a basic scheme that limited the number of participants rather than to accept a scheme that included all countries. One argument was that some countries needed reserves to hold while others needed reserves to spend; therefore, two different types of reserves seemed to have logic in an economic sense. Second, the monetary authorities of the countries in the Group of Ten argued that they consulted closely with each other on their balance of payments policies and might eventually adopt a set of rules for balance of payments adjustment or a special regime for working out multilateral surveillance which could be implemented, for example, through Working Party 3 of the OECD. Third, there was a preoccupation in the Group of Ten with what was called the backing for any international asset that might be created and a desire that only countries with the financial resources to do so should undertake such backing. A fourth argument, closely related to the third, was the belief that participants in the inner group should have sufficient financial resources so that, if a created reserve unit was presented to them for conversion, they would be able to provide convertible currencies.

Still a fifth argument advanced for limiting participation in any scheme for reserve creation stemmed from the need to provide for the liquidation of any scheme and for the possible withdrawal of a participant. The monetary authorities of the countries in the Group of Ten thought that participants in a reserve plan would wish to be able to calculate, at any time, what their financial obligations would be should the scheme be ended. Furthermore, a country had to be able to withdraw, or to be expelled if it misbehaved. They believed that, if new reserve assets were distributed to all Fund members, some of the developing countries would not, in the event of liquidity or withdrawal, be able to repay their shares in convertible currencies or gold. Hence, a loss would have to be distributed among the remaining participants; and rules covering the distribution of that loss would have to be prearranged.

Nevertheless, while emphasizing schemes with limited participation, the Group of Ten began to devise ways in which some other reserve asset, in addition, might be provided for countries excluded from the limited schemes.

Four Plans Suggested

The emerging views of the Group of Ten began to take more specific shape early in 1966. Four plans for deliberate reserve creation were presented by national delegations when the Deputies met in Paris from January 31 to February 2, 1966. Mr. Emminger presented a "Draft Outline of a Scheme for Reserve Creation," which was a compromise between the ideas of Belgium, the Federal Republic of Germany, Italy, and the Netherlands, with the views of France taken into account. The Deputies from the United States submitted an "Outline of a Possible Dual Approach to the Creation of Reserve Assets." The Deputies from the United Kingdom presented a paper, "International Monetary Reform—Summary of United Kingdom Views," and the Deputies from Canada a paper, "Future Creation of Reserve Assets—Some Views of the Canadian Delegation."

These four schemes had several features in common. All provided for the creation of a reserve asset by, and under the responsibility of, a limited group of countries. The group would not be a closed one; new participants would be accepted if they met a certain number of qualitative tests and, at the same time, had sufficient importance in world financial transactions. A figure of 15 countries in total was often mentioned. The distribution of the new reserve asset was to be based in some way on Fund quotas. The amount of reserve assets to be created was to be determined on the basis of trends in world reserves, not on short-term considerations. Periodic decisions—say, every three to five years—were to be taken on the amount to be created during each interval.

More specifically, all four schemes provided for new reserve units, the term used to characterize a new reserve asset that was not in the form of drawing rights in the Fund. The terms used in the discussions were now becoming refined, and the term reserve asset was considered the broader term used to denote a new asset that might be in the form either of drawing rights or of reserve units. The reserve units in the schemes submitted by national delegations to the Deputies of the Group of Ten in January 1966 could be transferred directly between participants and would be backed by a pool of national currencies contributed by participants. The gold value of these currency contributions was to be guaranteed, but the currency balances themselves were to remain blocked or dormant and were to be used only in connection with either the liquidation of the scheme or the withdrawal from the scheme by individual members.

Three of the papers submitted by national delegations to the Deputies also contained proposals for another type of new reserve that would go to countries excluded from the limited scheme, or for a second new reserve that would go to all countries. The U.S. plan suggested unconditional liquidity in the form of "special reserve drawing rights" (SRDR)—the first time that term was used—for all Fund members. These were to be distinct and separate from other drawing rights in the Fund and might be used without regard to a member's ordinary position in the Fund. They were to be available on terms similar to those applying to drawings in the gold tranche. The plan submitted by the United Kingdom provided for creation of unconditional liquidity for members left out of the reserve unit scheme by extending gold tranche facilities in the Fund across the board, without payment of gold subscriptions.

The plans put forward by the United States and the United Kingdom, and Mr. Emminger's plan as well, also made suggestions for added liquidity, possibly conditional, that would apply only to countries excluded from the limited scheme. The United States suggested that participants of the limited group allocate to the Fund an appropriate portion of the reserve units received, which would administer them for the benefit of those members excluded from receiving reserve units direct. Alternatively, instead of allocating reserve units to the Fund, participants might allocate to the Fund an equivalent amount in their own currencies. The U.K. scheme called for expanding the compensatory financing facility of the Fund (as had been suggested by the Fund staff) [2] and for making a proportion (25 per cent) of the new reserve units available to an international institution, such as the Fund, for provision of added conditional liquidity.

The Emminger scheme noted that countries outside the Group of Ten might also have increasing needs for international liquidity and that these would have to be covered through the Fund, either in the course of its customary

[2] See Chap. 14 below.

activities or by way of special and enlarged facilities, such as more compensatory financing. To meet the Fund's need for more resources in this connection, it was suggested that the participants in the group receiving reserve units should extend credit lines to the Fund, possibly amounting to 25 per cent of each participant's quota in the scheme. The Fund would utilize these credit lines to permit additional drawings to be made by countries outside the limited group. The Canadian scheme made no special provisions for countries outside the limited reserve unit arrangement.

Criticism and Defense of Limited Group

The idea that there might be parallel types of reserve creation—a reserve unit for a limited or inner group and conditional drawing rights for all countries, plus, for countries not receiving the reserve unit, possible conditional credit facilities financed by the inner group—was labeled "the dual approach." It was an approach which the Managing Director consistently rejected, as described later in this chapter. Moreover, the decision of the Group of Ten to take upon themselves the task of trying to achieve a consensus on the principles of a plan to create liquidity began to be rather widely criticized, and even greater objections were being voiced about the possibility that a mechanism would be introduced to distribute new reserves only to a small group of industrial nations. During the 1965 Annual Meeting, Mr. Holt (Australia) had, for example, stated forcefully that "it would not be acceptable to the great majority of members [of the Fund] to have decisions on matters so vitally affecting every one of us determined in substance, if not also in form, by a small and strictly limited group. . . . The Group of Ten, whatever its voting strength, can in no sense claim to be fully representative of this world institution [that is, the Fund] nor, I imagine, would it claim to be so." Moreover, Mr. Holt took a stand in advance against any proposals by the Group of Ten that would limit the creation and distribution of new reserves to a small and exclusive group: "Some of those outside the Group are ready and able to assume the obligations involved. They would feel discriminated against if they were denied the opportunity to join in the arrangements made and share in the mutual extension of credits. . . ." [3]

In January 1966, Mr. Emminger, referring to the remarks of the Governor for Australia, as well as to those of other Governors at the Annual Meeting, publicly defended both the procedures being followed by the Group of Ten and the limited scheme approach.[4] He stressed the difficulties that even a limited group of countries had in formulating rules for balance of payments policy, but he emphasized even more the argument that only a limited number of industrial countries with strong currencies could bear the responsibilities involved. A new

[3] Statement by the Governor of the Fund and the World Bank for Australia, *Summary Proceedings*, 1965, pp. 79 and 80.

[4] "Zehner-Gruppe und Reform des Weltwährungssystems," Deutsche Bundesbank, *Auszüge aus Presseartikeln*, January 26, 1966, pp. 1–6.

type of reserve unit, which would complement gold and the dollar, needed the backing of strong currencies if it was to be a universally acceptable, fully valid means of payment for international obligations. Phrasing his statement so that he spoke for the other countries of the EEC as well as for the Federal Republic of Germany, Mr. Emminger explained that the development of the world's reserve system which the EEC countries had in mind simply meant the taking over, by a group of countries qualified to do so, of a responsibility that had been borne thus far in the postwar period by the United States alone.

RESPONSE OF DEVELOPING COUNTRIES

While the above discussions and studies were going on within the Group of Ten, the developing countries were becoming disturbed by the prospect that new reserve assets might be created by and for the industrial nations alone. Their interest in the monetary arrangements that were being considered was accelerated by the fact that some of them were having their own financial problems. The balance of payments position of the primary producing countries as a group did not prove to be especially unfavorable in 1965; in fact, they had an aggregate surplus. Also, commodity markets had strengthened, and with high and rising demand in the industrial countries, the export earnings of the primary producing countries increased rapidly. But there were wide differences among countries. The surplus of the primary producing countries as a whole reflected a very large surplus ($1.4 billion) for the least developed of these countries and a substantial deficit ($0.7 billion) for the more developed.[5]

Of greater concern to the developing countries than their current payments and reserve positions, however, was that the flow of long-term financial resources to them in the last few years had, in the aggregate, been stagnating.[6] This leveling off of long-term capital inflow was the more disturbing because the amount of incoming capital already was low. It had failed to grow in a period in which the industrial countries had achieved a continued and substantial rise in their gross national products. The proportion of the aggregate gross national product of the industrial countries devoted to the net flow of aid and long-term capital to the developing countries had fallen to less than 2/3 of 1 per cent. Progress toward easing the terms on which these resources were provided had also been limited.

[5] With the exception of the classification used in *International Financial Statistics*, which was somewhat different, the Fund used the following classification of members plus Switzerland in its statistics during the period covered by this history:

Industrial countries: Austria, Belgium, Canada, Denmark, France, the Federal Republic of Germany, Italy, Japan, Luxembourg, the Netherlands, Norway, Sweden, Switzerland, the United Kingdom, and the United States.

Primary producing countries in more developed areas: Australia, Finland, Greece, Iceland, Ireland, Malta, New Zealand, Portugal, South Africa, Spain, Turkey, and Yugoslavia.

Primary producing countries in less developed areas: all other members.

[6] *Annual Report, 1966,* pp. 83–88 and 105–11.

Action Through the United Nations

By the latter part of 1965 the developing countries had begun to undertake work of their own on the subject of world liquidity. In September the United Nations Conference on Trade and Development (UNCTAD) sent to the Fund a working paper prepared in the UNCTAD secretariat, which described developments in the international monetary system for the period 1958–65 and emphasized the interest of the developing countries in the world liquidity problems being discussed and in the prospect for an international monetary conference such as had been suggested by the United States. This paper had been prepared to assist the Expert Group on International Monetary Issues that had been appointed by the UNCTAD in August.

The Expert Group held meetings in New York from October 11 to 29, 1965, which Fund staff attended as observers. The subsequent report of the group was strongly in favor of a reform of the international monetary system that would make that system more responsive to the needs for economic growth of both developed and developing countries. Noting that, as a result of a growing fear of a shortage of liquidity, the developed countries had tended recently to adopt less expansionary policies, to limit the scale and liberal character of their assistance to developing countries, and to continue their restrictive trade policies, the report concluded that the general level of the world's reserves was inadequate and should be expanded.[7]

After examining the needs of the developing countries, the Expert Group rejected the view that the essential need of developing countries was for additional long-term aid rather than for liquidity. The liquidity needs of developing countries were, in fact, considered to be greater relative to their imports than those of the developed countries, and it was believed that those needs would increase with the growth of their economies. Furthermore, most developing countries were conscious of the advantages of having adequate reserves and would hold such reserves if the pressure of competing demands on convertible

---

[7] The report, entitled *International Monetary Issues and the Developing Countries*, was published by the United Nations as UN document TD/B/32 and TD/B/C.3/6, New York, 1965. The members of the group originally appointed were V. S. Alkhimov, Head, Foreign Currency Department, Ministry of Foreign Trade of the U.S.S.R.; Gamani Corea, Permanent Secretary, Ministry of National Planning and Economic Affairs, Ceylon; Octavio A. Dias Carneiro, formerly Chief of Economic Department of the Foreign Ministry, Brazil; Jorge González del Valle, Alternate Executive Director, International Monetary Fund; Julius Hájek, Director of the Foreign Exchange Department of the Ministry of Finance, Czechoslovakia, and Associate Member of the Prague Research Institute of Finance; Lord Kahn, Fellow of King's College and Professor of Economics in the University of Cambridge, England; Amon Nikoi, Executive Director, International Monetary Fund; I. G. Patel, Chief Economic Adviser, Ministry of Finance, India; Pierre Sanner, Director of Studies, Banque Centrale des Etats de l'Afrique de l'Ouest; Tibor Scitovsky, Professor of Economics, University of California; and T. W. Swan, Professor of Economics, Research School of Social Sciences, Australian National University. Owing to the inability of I. G. Patel to be present throughout the group's meetings, K. N. Raj, Professor of Monetary Economics, Delhi School of Economics, University of Delhi, was appointed as an additional member.

funds was lessened. In this connection, reform of the international monetary system should be accompanied by the adoption of trade and aid policies that would contribute to the solution of the problem of structural disequilibrium in developing countries.

The report asserted that the pressing needs of the developing countries for additional liquidity should be provided in part by expanding reserves and in part by increasing the amount of credit available from the Fund and other sources, recommending, inter alia, enlargement and liberalization of the Fund's compensatory financing facility. The conclusions were that (1) the establishment of a link between the creation of international liquidity and the provision of development finance was both feasible and desirable and would be detrimental to neither; (2) the reform of the international monetary system should be truly international; and (3) developing countries should be represented in the discussions leading to monetary reform, and in the operation of the new arrangements, in accordance with the degree of their interests and concern.

The UNCTAD report was discussed by the UNCTAD Committee on Invisibles and Financing Related to Trade, in Geneva in December 1965 and again in New York from January 27 to February 4, 1966, after which the committee endorsed the main conclusions of the Expert Group's report. The committee placed particular emphasis on the idea that all countries that were prepared to take part in the new monetary arrangements and to acquire the rights and accept the obligations inherent in such arrangements should be eligible to participate in the creation of reserve assets.

The follow-up to these studies and discussions by developing countries was to come later, in December 1966, when the General Assembly of the United Nations, at its twenty-first session, adopted a resolution on international monetary reform. The resolution had been proposed by the delegation from Ceylon and had been supported by the delegations of several other developing countries. The resolution requested "the Secretary-General of the United Nations Conference on Trade and Development to consult with the Managing Director of the International Monetary Fund on the progress of activity relating to international monetary reform and to report to the Trade and Development Board at its fifth session through the Committee on Invisibles and Financing Related to Trade." [8]

Further Action

In addition to action through the United Nations, the developing countries, during the year 1965–66, found still other forums through which to make their views known. In March 1966 four monetary officials, requested to do so by the Inter-American Committee on the Alliance for Progress (CIAP), issued a

---

[8] UN General Assembly Resolution (International Monetary Reform) 2208 (XXI), December 17, 1966.

report entitled *International Monetary Reform and Latin America*.[9] Endorsing
the report of the UNCTAD experts, they stressed the need of the developing
countries in general, and of the Latin American countries in particular, for
increased liquidity and suggested that the Latin American countries pool the
increase in their directly owned reserves that would accrue under any new
arrangements. They also urged that serious consideration be given to the idea
of linking the creation of reserve units with the provision of more financial
assistance to the developing countries. This report was presented to the seventh
meeting of the CIAP, which was held in Buenos Aires on March 12–15, 1966,
and was circulated to the fourth annual meeting of the Inter-American Economic
and Social Council, which was held at both the expert and the ministerial level.

The views of Latin American monetary officials on international monetary
reform were put forward again, on April 22, 1966, when the Governors of the
central banks of Latin America, meeting in Runaway Bay, Jamaica, issued what
was referred to as the Declaration of Jamaica. In a significant shift of attitude
toward the Fund from that prevalent in the 1950s, these Latin American
monetary officials endorsed the Fund, stating that the present mechanisms of the
international monetary system should be preserved to the greatest extent
possible and that the Fund, with any needed modifications, should continue to
be the center of that system. Access to new liquidity was no substitute for an
improvement of the Latin American countries' relative position within the Fund.
Such improvement, the Governors explained, could be brought about by increasing members' quotas and, in particular, by increasing the ratio of unconditional
drawing rights to quotas, expanding the compensatory financing facility, and
linking repurchase obligations under that facility to the recovery of export
earnings.

In May 1966, the developing countries took still other action concerning
the prospect of a new mechanism for enlarging world liquidity. A "Group of
Thirty-One" developing countries, noting that the Group of Ten was then
meeting in Rome and might agree on a scheme for reserve creation in which
only a few leading countries would be able to participate, reiterated a principle
which had been enunciated in the earlier meetings of the Committee on Invisibles
and Financing Related to Trade:

> Monetary management and co-operation should be truly international and
> . . . all countries, which are prepared to share in both the benefits and obligations
> of such new monetary arrangements as may be devised, should be eligible to
> participate in the creation of new reserve assets. The adoption of any scheme
> which is limited to a small group of countries will be a serious violation of this
> principle and will endanger the development of international monetary
> co-operation.[10]

---

[9] The four officials were Alexandre Kafka (Brazil), Javier Márquez (Mexico), Geoffrey
Maynard (United Kingdom), and Victor L. Urquidi (Mexico).

[10] UN document TD/B/75, par. 3, May 31, 1966.

BACKGROUND TO MANAGING DIRECTOR'S PROPOSALS

It was against this background of continued emphasis by the Group of Ten on limited schemes and increasing concern by the developing countries that they would be excluded from new forms of reserves that the Fund took an important initiative. In March 1966 the Managing Director circulated to the Executive Board and to the Group of Ten two proposals for creating liquidity through the Fund. These proposals very much helped to advance the discussions in the Group of Ten; and later their presentation was considered a significant turning point on the road to SDRs. A series of events within the Fund immediately preceded these proposals.

Initiative Suggested by Staff

For some months, at least since December 1965, the Managing Director's representatives to the meetings of the Deputies of the Group of Ten—the General Counsel and the Economic Counsellor—had been suggesting that it was opportune for the Fund to put forward its own proposals. Most of the country delegations to the meetings of the Deputies of the Group of Ten recognized that the Fund had spent more time exploring the subject of international liquidity than had the national governments of the Group of Ten. Moreover, the effect of the 1965 Annual Meeting had been to make it necessary for the Group of Ten to come up with a proposal that was, in a real sense, acceptable to the other members of the Fund. For these reasons, a concrete proposal by the Managing Director might serve as a fulcrum for the discussions of the Deputies.

The Research and Statistics Department had, in fact, started to sketch the outlines of a Fund scheme, and the Legal Department had begun to investigate whether a reserve-creating scheme could be established within the Fund and what amendments of the Articles would be required.

Further, in an attempt to provide answers to the difficult questions that were still outstanding, the staff had undertaken two comprehensive studies. The first, completed in December 1965, was directed to the question of the number of countries that should participate in the creation and distribution of any new reserve asset, and to the related issue of the criteria on which such creation and distribution should be based. To ascertain the implications of distributing new reserves to all Fund members, rather than to a limited few, this study quantified the effects, country by country, of distributing new reserves to all members on the basis of the various criteria—each participant's holdings of gold, holdings of total reserves, and Fund quota—that had been talked about in Deputies' meetings and in informal sessions of the Executive Directors. This examination showed that the distribution of $1 billion of new reserve assets, using any of the alternative bases, would not result in a large amount of new reserve assets for developing countries, nor, indeed, for all countries outside the Group of Ten, taken as a whole. In other words, should new reserve assets be distributed on the basis of any of the criteria that were being considered, the bulk would go to the countries in the Group of Ten. The staff believed that this finding might help to demonstrate to the monetary authorities of the Group of Ten—especially to those in the United States and the United Kingdom who were beginning to feel that restricting the scheme to the large industrial nations might be politically embarrassing—that participation by all Fund members might not be much more costly financially than a scheme with limited participation.

The second study by the Fund staff, completed in January 1966, attempted to answer the questions on the adequacy of world reserves that were constantly recurring in the discussions and were hampering consideration of what mechanisms could be used for reserve creation.[11] Was the existing level of reserves sufficient? Was the rate of growth of world reserves satisfactory? When would the need for supplementing existing reserves arise? How large a supplement would be required? How might the need for such a supplement be determined? The staff paper concentrated on how to measure the need for reserves and, in particular, how to distill quantitative estimates of reserve needs from the general criteria for reserve adequacy that had been discussed in the preceding two years. The trends of reserve movements since World War II—actually based on the period from 1951 or 1952 to 1964, inclusive—for several groups of countries were charted and examined. Statistical relations between the levels of reserves and the value of international trade over time, and between the rates of growth of reserves and the growth in the value of international trade, were investigated.

The conclusion of this examination was that quantitative assessment of the need for international reserves was very difficult. It involved, for instance, a number of judgments on which reasonable people might disagree—such as, whether aggregate demand was insufficient or excessive; whether too much or too little time was available for balance of payments adjustment; and what distribution of the burden of adjustment between countries in deficit and countries in surplus was appropriate.

Hence, hard decisions lay ahead as to the amount of world liquidity to be created that would be most conducive to high employment and growth in all countries, internal and external stability throughout the world, and freedom from restrictions on international transactions, the basic objectives of reserve creation. The criteria for the appropriate regulation of the supply of international reserves were much more complicated and their application much more uncertain than for the regulation of domestic monetary policy. The

---

11 The study was later published in the Appendix to *International Reserves: Needs and Availability*, papers and proceedings of a seminar at the Fund (Washington, 1970), pp. 369–422.

type of information needed for easy determination of how the supply of reserves should be adjusted from month to month in accordance with changing international economic conditions was not available; in fact, there was no agreement on precisely what information was required or on how to evaluate such information. Therefore, if the international community was to undertake the task of adjusting this supply by deliberate international action, it would have to proceed by agreeing on an estimate of the probable need for increases in reserves for a considerable period ahead, and the estimate would need to be revised at not too frequent intervals, perhaps on the basis of rules set down in advance.

Another part of the staff's examination of the world's stock of reserves was directed to ascertaining the differences between the amounts of reserves held by developing countries and the amounts held by developed countries. One of the conclusions was that developing countries had the same ratio of reserves to imports as did developed countries.[12]

Dual Approach Rejected

Meanwhile, the Managing Director continued to look upon the dual approach advocated in the Group of Ten as undesirable. Interpreting it as meaning that the two groups into which the Fund's membership would be divided would probably receive proportionately equal amounts of new liquidity, but the reserves of the inner group would be of one kind and those of the nonparticipating group of another kind, Mr. Schweitzer put a "separate but equal" stigma on the dual approach. Although Mr. Dale explained that the intention of the United States in the Group of Ten discussions was that there should be two kinds of assets, drawing rights and reserve units, and that at least the drawing rights should be shared universally and fully among the two groups, several Executive Directors for the developing members continued in the informal sessions of the Executive Board to consider a dual approach as discriminatory. Nevertheless, the idea persisted, and as late as May 1966 the Managing Director reported to the Executive Directors that there was still wide support for a dual approach among the Deputies of the Group of Ten.

Action Urged by Executive Directors

In these circumstances, the Executive Directors also urged that the Fund take action. In November 1965 they had begun a series of informal sessions on the subject of reserve creation that continued throughout the following year, concurrently with the discussions going on in the Group of Ten. The Directors were especially interested in what they referred to as the path-breaking staff paper—described above—which tried to quantify the global need for reserves. On this topic, the Directors for several developing countries, particularly Messrs. J. J. Anjaria (India), Luis Escobar (Chile), and Paul L. Faber (Guinea),

---

[12] *Annual Report, 1966*, pp. 12–14.

took the occasion to point out that the staff's findings demonstrated that the need for reserves was not confined to any particular group of countries.

In February 1966, at a regular session of the Executive Board, after the Directors had heard a staff report on the latest meeting of the Deputies of the Group of Ten, Mr. Ahmed Zaki Saad (Egypt) made a very strong plea for the Fund to advance its own proposals. He had difficulty not with the details but with the circumstances in which the current proposals for reserve creation were being made. The four plans put forward in the Group of Ten, described earlier in this chapter, purported to raise various questions affecting the Fund and its operations—possible increases in automatic drawing rights in the Fund, the creation and distribution of some sort of new unit from which most of the Fund's members might be excluded, and the making available of new resources in some form for use by the Fund. If these plans were worth considering, why not submit them to the Fund through the Executive Directors concerned? The Fund could not delegate its functions and its duties to the Group of Ten or to any other group. Recalling that great efforts had been made to make the Fund a worldwide institution, Mr. Saad thought that the leading members of the Fund should ask themselves whether they were not, perhaps quite inadvertently, undermining the authority and role of the Fund by imposing subtle barriers to the effective consideration by the Executive Board of matters of great importance to the whole of the Fund's membership.

Mr. Saad's remarks were endorsed by most of the Executive Directors for the countries other than those in the Group of Ten, especially by Messrs. Anjaria and Faber and by Messrs. Antonio de Abreu Coutinho (Brazil, Alternate to Mr. Mauricio Chagas Bicalho, Brazil), Amon Nikoi (Ghana), and Enrique Tejera-París (Venezuela). Mr. M. W. O'Donnell (Australia), although recognizing a distinction of interest between countries of the Group of Ten and other countries, also supported Mr. Saad's views by explicitly agreeing that the Fund should be more positive and active in this matter. If there was to be a solution acceptable to all Fund members, there must be more rapid progress toward finding a consensus within the Fund, and the Fund must urgently attempt to disentangle the main threads of the whole liquidity fabric and to reach broad conclusions to which all could subscribe.

Managing Director Again Speaks Out for Universal Plan

Meanwhile, the Managing Director persisted in his view that all Fund members ought to be included in any scheme of reserve creation and that the Fund ought to be the instrument for any new facility. He referred to the dual approach as a retrogressive development in international monetary relations. When the Executive Directors, in January 1966 in informal session, discussed the staff paper on distribution of reserves, Mr. Schweitzer argued that it would be difficult to find generally acceptable criteria to distinguish between participants and nonparticipants in any arrangement for reserve creation. Moreover, he did not agree that there was a difference in the behavior of countries concerning their reserves. The Fund had often urged its developing members to increase their reserves, pointing out to them, both in general and in individual cases, the severe problems that arose when members tried to conduct their external transactions with inadequate reserves. In a number of its stand-by arrangements, the Fund had even asked for a kind of reserve commitment. Hence, it was almost impossible, he thought, to make a clear-cut distinction between members that needed an increase in reserves to keep and hold and those that did not. As a matter of fact, the aggregate amount of reserves held by developing countries was substantial.

Regarding the global need for reserves, Mr. Schweitzer said at an informal session in February 1966 that, in his view, the significance of the staff paper on that subject lay not so much in its conclusions as in its demonstration that the Fund was the only institution able to take the first step, that is, to try to quantify the need for reserves.

Mr. Schweitzer stressed that any scheme for reserve creation must "start out from the recognition of the legitimate reserve needs of developed and developing countries alike."[13] He voiced these views not only to the Executive Directors and to other monetary authorities whenever the occasion arose but also to the public several times during the latter part of 1965 and the first few months of 1966. In an address before the Federation of German Industries, at Kronberg im Taunus, on April 25, 1966, for example, he explained in detail how a reserve unit scheme could cover all Fund members and emphasized the compelling reasons for avoiding any division of countries into two groups.[14] He had grave misgivings about the dual approach. In the first place, he could not accept the view that all but a few members of the Fund had little or no need of reserves and were not capable of keeping any that they might receive. Secondly, he could see no way to divide the member countries of the Fund in an objective and nondiscriminatory manner "into the reliable few and the less responsible many."[15] The process of balance of payments adjustment by any group of countries could not be governed by pre-set rules. Moreover, even if the second part of a dual package, namely, what was termed the set-aside for countries excluded from the reserve creation itself, seemed to be generous, any attempt to divide the countries of the world into separate groups would be bitterly resented and could bring grave damage to the cause of international cooperation in monetary and economic matters: "One of the outstanding achievements of the past twenty years has been the common commitment of all countries to avoid the destructive beggar-my-neighbor policies prevalent in the

---

[13] Address at Ecosoc, February 24, 1966. Published in Supplement to *International Financial News Survey*, Vol. 18 (1966), pp. 65–68. Reference is to p. 68.

[14] Speech published in Supplement to *International Financial News Survey*, Vol. 18 (1966), pp. 141–44.

[15] *Ibid.*, p. 143.

Pierre-Paul Schweitzer, Chairman of Executive Board and Managing Director,
September 1, 1963–August 31, 1973

1930s. It would not be wise for the main industrial countries to put in danger the continued observance of international economic regulation." [16]

He was, nonetheless, optimistic that new monetary arrangements could be agreed that would satisfy the concerns of those who feared an uncontrolled transfer of resources. But he saw control over the transfer of resources being exercised not by limiting participation in a reserve scheme to an exclusive group of a few industrial countries, but through rules governing the use of the new assets. He noted further that, on the assumption that distribution of new liquidity was in proportion to the size of a country's quota in the Fund, a universally applied scheme would mean that just over one quarter of the new liquidity would go to the developing countries. The possibility of a long-term transfer of resources was, therefore, small, perhaps no greater than what would be involved in a dual scheme with a set-aside for nonparticipants. Such a set-aside, it had been widely suggested, would also be in the region of one quarter of the total. Accordingly, the Managing Director stated his preference among schemes in these words: "If the choice of a universal rather than dual scheme did increase slightly the risk of a long-term transfer, it would in my opinion be a small price to pay to avoid the political and economic dangers of dividing the free world into two or more groups of countries." [17]

MANAGING DIRECTOR'S PROPOSALS

This was the background when, in March 1966, the Managing Director sent a note to the Executive Board with a staff paper outlining two plans for reserve creation through the Fund.[18] In this note he stated that his proposals had been guided by the general considerations which had governed his approach to the subject of international liquidity. The first was the connection between conditional and unconditional liquidity. There could be no question about the value of conditional liquidity which made reserves available to members on the basis of the steps they took to achieve needed adjustment in their external payments position. At the same time, members wished to have growing amounts of reserves at their disposal in the form of unconditional liquidity. The needs of an expanding world economy would thus require increases in both of these types of liquidity in an appropriate mixture. The Fund already had the task of providing the bulk of conditional liquidity, the amount of which could be adapted periodically through the quinquennial reviews of quotas. The second general consideration was that reserve creation had to be seen as a

---

[16] *Ibid.*, p. 144.

[17] *Ibid.*

[18] The two plans, and some supplementary notes that were circulated later in the month, are published below, Vol. II, pp. 3–7 and 8–14. The plans, presented as Part I and Part II of the staff paper, are referred to in the discussion here as Plan I and Plan II.

means to the attainment of objectives to which the Fund's members attached importance: high employment, economic growth, freedom of international transactions from restrictions, and international payments equilibrium.

The Managing Director outlined two schemes because there was still a considerable divergence of views among the monetary officials of the large industrial countries on the most desirable form for reserve creation. Both schemes built on the techniques explored by the staff the year before, and both were based on the principle that reserve creation was the concern of all Fund members and that all members should participate, with due safeguards, in decisions for reserve creation and in the distribution of the created reserves, with such participation being based on members' quotas.

Plan I provided for an extension in the Fund of quasi-automatic drawing rights of the gold tranche type. The Fund was to be prepared to waive the limits on its holdings of a member's currency by the amount of the special reserve facility. Members would be free to decide whether to use the special reserve facility before or after using any part of their regular drawing rights in the Fund. Members would become entitled to participate in any increase in the special reserve facility allocated to them if they granted to the Fund a line of credit equal to the increase.

Plan II was to involve the issuance of reserve units by a new organization, the International Reserve Fund (IRF), which would be an affiliate of the Fund in the same sense as the International Finance Corporation (IFC) was an affiliate of the World Bank and membership in which would be open to all Fund members. On the adoption of a decision by the IRF to increase reserves, all members of the IRF wishing to do so would exchange claims with the IRF in accordance with the rules of that institution. Members participating in this exchange would acquire claims on the IRF expressed in IRF units of a certain weight of gold, and the IRF would acquire corresponding claims on its members. The exchange of claims between the IRF and participants in the increases in question would be in amounts broadly in proportion to the participants' quotas in the Fund. On the occasion of any creation of reserve units, participants that had made a net use of the conditional drawing facilities of the Fund would be required to reconstitute those facilities through repurchase up to an amount equal to the new reserve units they received. There could be provisions according to which, by agreement between the Fund and the IRF, the allocation of reserve units to a member on the occasion of a reserve increase could be deferred or withheld.

Differences Between the Two Plans

Plan I could be implemented without amendment of the Articles and was based on techniques that the Fund had long used. Plan II, on the other hand, was not designed to fit into the framework of the existing Articles. If established within the Fund without a separation of accounts between regular drawing facilities and the new reserve units, Plan II would involve extensive amendment of the Articles. If established within the Fund with a separation of accounts, Plan II would not involve elaborate amendment, but some amendment would nevertheless be necessary. Plan II would also involve most members in new domestic legislation related to their belonging to the Fund.

A technical difference between drawing rights (Plan I) and reserve units (Plan II) arose from the manner in which reserves were to be transferred. Under Plan I, participants would use reserves in the form of automatic drawing rights in the same way as they already used existing drawing facilities in the Fund, that is, by purchasing foreign currency from the Fund in exchange for their own. By so doing, they would use up an equivalent amount of their automatic drawing rights and create an equivalent addition to the drawing rights of the participants whose currencies were purchased. Drawing rights would thus be effectively transferred from the drawer to the drawee, and the currencies purchased would be used directly, or after conversion, for the settlement of international transactions. Under Plan II, reserves created in the form of reserve units would be utilized by a direct transfer of units from one participant to another. The participant receiving the reserve unit was to provide in exchange its own or some other currency, which, in turn, could then be used for the settlement of international transactions. In brief, under Plan II the transfer of reserves created would take place directly between participants, while under Plan I transfer would be effected indirectly through the Fund.

Similarities in the Two Plans

Under both plans, all participants benefiting from the distribution of additional reserves were to have corresponding obligations to accept transfers of such reserves, whether directly or through the Fund. These obligations were, however, to be limited. In the reserve unit scheme (Plan II), the limits were to be set at, say, three times the cumulative amount of reserves issued to each country, or lower in certain circumstances. In the drawing rights scheme (Plan I), the limits were to be set by the lines of credit which each participant would have to extend to the Fund; these lines of credit were to be provided in the participant's own currency. Insofar as a participant's line of credit was drawn upon by the Fund, the participant was to acquire a liquid claim against the Fund which was to be a reserve asset of the same general type as a gold tranche position.

The amount of the line of credit to be given by each participant could be set equal to the cumulative amount of the special reserve facility allocated to it. In that event, the maximum reserve position in the Fund that any participant might be obliged to hold as a consequence of this scheme was to be equal to twice the amounts allocated to it. The obligation to provide financing, that is, to receive transfers, in connection with this scheme could in practice be kept somewhat lower than twice the allocations to a participant because it was envisaged that the resources to meet the Fund's traditional drawings and drawings on the new facility would be pooled.

In both plans, transfers were to be subject to an element of guidance—in Plan I through the policy of the Fund on the selection of currencies to be drawn, and in Plan II either through general rules to be agreed or through guidance to be applied in particular cases by the Fund. Both plans aimed at avoiding the necessity for participants in balance of payments difficulties to accept transfers from other participants and at bringing about a general proportionality between holdings of the new reserves and other forms of reserves. In the drawing rights scheme (Plan I), the Fund's repurchase provisions were to apply, but the participant was not to be expected to represent to the Fund that it intended to repurchase within a period of three to five years; this feature of Plan I was similar to the Fund policy then applicable to gold tranche drawings. In the reserve unit scheme (Plan II), the reconstitution of holdings of the new reserve units after use was to be left to the functioning of the transfer mechanism. Under both plans, the reserves created were to be used in the first instance to cancel out any outstanding net indebtedness of the participants concerned resulting from their previous use of the traditional facilities in the Fund.

In both schemes the creation of additional reserves was to be the subject of international decision at intervals of, say, five years, with certain limited possibilities of variation from year to year. It was suggested that decisions would be taken by the Executive Board of the Fund or by the appropriate organ of the affiliate, and that reserves would be created under these decisions when a sufficient proportion of participants able to provide resources to support the reserve creation had agreed to do so.

Meanwhile, as these proposals were being advanced, the staff was making a further study of the characteristics that any reserve assets must possess to assure their acceptability.[19]

Executive Directors' Positions

In informal sessions in March and April 1966, the Executive Directors held preliminary discussions on the two plans proposed by the Managing Director. They welcomed the imaginative techniques, noted that it was obviously possible to reproduce within the Fund any scheme that could be decided upon outside the Fund, and found this to be a factor in favor of finding a solution within the Fund.

At one session, Mr. O'Donnell urged that the Fund push on with its studies of the problem of international liquidity and that the Executive Directors continue their discussions with the aim of trying to reach generally acceptable

---

[19] J. Marcus Fleming, "Use and Acceptance of Reserve Claims," *Staff Papers*, Vol. 13 (1966), pp. 443–52.

conclusions. He attacked the notion, apparently held by most of the Deputies of the Group of Ten, that participation in any arrangements to create reserves had to be limited to a small group of countries. He objected to the establishment of "a group of 'second-class' participants."

The Directors' discussions were aimed at clarifying the implications of the two types of reserve creation; therefore, they did not attempt to reach any conclusions as to the desirability of these plans. But many favored Plan I, at least initially, as being easier to institute than Plan II; Plan II, possibly more flexible, might be put into effect later or introduced over time.

In the Annual Report for 1966, some of the details of these proposals were made public.[20] Since they had not been acted upon by the Executive Board, they were referred to as proposals of the Managing Director. In the Annual Report it was also noted that alternative provisions could be formulated for a number of features in these proposals and that such alternatives would be considered in further discussions.

UNIVERSALITY ACCEPTED BY GROUP OF TEN

Deputies Agree on Some Principles

During the month of May 1966, some of the Deputies of the Group of Ten became less inclined to the dual approach and more receptive to a universal approach. On May 27, 1966 the Economic Counsellor, reporting to the Executive Board on the meeting of the Deputies in Rome on May 17–19, 1966, observed that this meeting was the first at which the suggestion of a universal distribution of reserve units had been favorably commented upon by a number of Deputies. In the Deputies' report that was being prepared, the need for any reserves that would be created to be distributed to all countries was likely to be a central theme, and the problem of the form of reserve creation, previously paramount, would be presented as a subsidiary question.

Several Executive Directors queried the nature of the change in the Deputies' thinking. Had not the Group of Ten in effect recognized the universality of reserve needs earlier, even with the dual approach? Mr. Southard, Acting Chairman of the Board, explained that it now seemed likely that the Deputies' report would contain a well-balanced presentation of various possible schemes of reserve creation, including the two Fund plans. This careful balance had not been so certain a few weeks earlier.

When the Deputies' report was released on August 25, 1966—timed as in previous years to coincide with the release to the public of the Fund's Annual Report—the point was made in Chapter 3 (paragraph 42) that any plans for reserve creation should be either in the Fund or closely associated with it.

---

[20] *Annual Report, 1966,* pp. 18–20.

The report contained an extensive discussion of the various plans for reserve creation and (in the annex) a description of the individual plans.[21]

Although the Deputies did not have a fully developed contingency plan, they had achieved a consensus on certain basic principles for the creation of reserves. *First*, deliberate reserve creation should be neither geared nor directed to financing the payments deficits of individual countries. Rather, it should take place on the basis of a collective judgment of the reserve needs of the world as a whole, for a certain period ahead, without any attempt to counteract the world cyclical conditions by the adjustment of reserve creation. *Second*, deliberate reserve creation should consist of unconditional liquidity to be made available to all members of the Fund. *Third*, although all countries had a legitimate interest in the adequacy of international reserves, a group of major countries with a key role in the functioning of the international monetary system had a particular responsibility for the financial backing for any reserve assets that were created. Consequently, whatever process of decision making was established should reflect, on the one hand, the interest of all countries in the smooth working of the monetary system and, on the other, the special responsibility of the major industrial countries.

No Consensus by Deputies on Other Questions

The Deputies had still not resolved other issues, however. One unsettled question was the long-standing one of the need to meet any deficiency in the world's supply of liquidity versus the need to improve the process of balance of payments adjustment. This question had been debated since 1963, but as yet there was no real meeting of minds. Multilateral surveillance for the European countries had come to mean, essentially, first the provision through the BIS to Working Party 3 of the OECD of detailed information on how balance of payments deficits were financed and then discussions in that Working Party of particular cases of disequilibrium. Such discussions, however, had not so far culminated in the adoption of specific recommendations either for deficit or for surplus countries.

Nor had the special study of balance of payments adjustment by Working Party 3 produced the results hoped for. The advocates of that study had thought that Working Party 3 might adopt rules for some automatic link between movements in reserves and financial policies, similar to that which had prevailed under the classic gold standard. For example, the supply of money in any country, after allowance for the expansion required for the normal increase in real national income, would spontaneously rise or fall with external surpluses

---

[21] Group of Ten, *Communiqué of Ministers and Governors and Report of Deputies* ([Frankfurt], 1966). The report was transmitted to the Ministers and Governors on July 8, 1966 and released on August 25, 1966. The communiqué was issued at the conclusion of the Ministers' and Governors' meeting on July 25–26, 1966 in The Hague. See also *International Financial News Survey*, Vol. 18 (1966), pp. 245–46 and 285–86.

or deficits, and then monetary authorities would have to offset the inflationary consequences of what were regarded as "excess changes in the money supply" by the use of nonmonetary policies, particularly of fiscal policies.

Most members of Working Party 3, however, had been unable to adopt this type of multilateral surveillance because they regarded it as too mechanical and as an impairment of central bank autonomy. They preferred a system in which situations of imbalance would be considered on their merits and remedies applied that followed certain guidelines. In the report of Working Party 3 of August 1966, therefore, three typical situations were distinguished and appropriate action was recommended for each situation. But even these conclusions did not meet with enthusiastic response.

When the Deputies dealt with the question of balance of payments adjustment in their report of August 1966, they put forward various possible ways to link reserve creation to measures to correct balance of payments disequilibria. Most of these ways involved placing conditions on the use of new reserve units. Some Deputies went so far as to suggest that reserve units could be transferable only if accompanied by transfers of gold, so that countries in deficit would have an incentive to correct their disequilibria. Another suggestion was that countries in the Group of Ten agree on some kind of "harmonization" in the composition of their reserves, that is, that they reach some understanding on the proportions of their total reserves to be held in gold and in dollars. This suggestion had also been made by a number of Governors at the 1965 Annual Meeting. A third suggestion was that countries with drawings outstanding in the Fund's credit tranches immediately use their allocation of new reserve units to repurchase their currencies from the Fund. Yet another idea was that there should be rules limiting the "average net use" of new reserves.

Distinction Between Contingency Planning and Activation

The closest link between reserve creation and improvement of the adjustment process lay in still another principle expressed in the Deputies' report of August 1966. This was that activation of any plan—that is, the first actual creation of reserves, as distinguished from contingency planning—should not be undertaken until a separate and new decision had been taken that there was a clear need for reserves and that certain additional conditions had been fulfilled.

The possible activation of any reserve plan had emerged as an important issue. It was clearer now than it had been a year earlier that any plan for reserve creation was likely to be put into operation very soon after it was worked out. In short, the planning was for a contingency that was almost certain to arise, and in the words of Mr. Frederick L. Deming, Under Secretary of the U.S. Treasury for Monetary Affairs, the pertinent question was not if the plan would be activated but when.[22]

---

[22] Remarks at the Third International Investment Symposium, Boston, Massachusetts; see U.S. Treasury Department, Press Release, July 14, 1966, p. 13.

Expectation that any reserve plan would have to be activated reflected the slower rate of increase in world reserves in 1966 and the fact that the increase that was taking place was itself drawn from special and reversible sources—for example, from the transfer into reserves early in 1966 of the proceeds of what had been a second line of reserves held in U.S. securities by the British Government.

At the same time, those who were concerned about inflationary pressures, and who therefore wanted to delay actual creation of reserves, had much to support their concern. For many industrial countries, the expansionary forces of 1965 became inflationary pressures in 1966. While both private investment and public sector expenditure were advancing sharply in almost all the industrial countries, only France, Italy, and Japan had had a significant margin of unutilized economic capacity at the beginning of 1966. This conjuncture of demand forces exerted growing pressure, in the industrial countries other than France, Italy, and Japan, on financial markets, on interest rates, and on prices.

Moreover, in dealing with these inflationary pressures, most industrial countries either delayed fiscal action or employed it only moderately, placing emphasis on monetary policy. The heavy use of monetary policy instruments was not very successful in reducing payments disequilibrium or in inducing equilibrating capital flows. As a result, those who were most disturbed by the continuing imbalances in international payments began to stress the need for a clear distinction between contingency planning and activation of any new plan.

Meeting at Ministerial Level

At their meeting in The Hague on July 25 and 26, 1966, in which Mr. Schweitzer took part, the Ministers and Governors of the Group of Ten did not seem to feel that it was urgent to formulate a specific contingency plan. They expressed the hope that Working Party 3 of the OECD would continue its work and repeated their earlier agreement that, while there was currently no general reserve shortage, existing reserves might have to be supplemented in the future.[23]

Nonetheless, some progress had been made. At the ministerial level, as at the deputy level, the Group of Ten achieved a consensus on several of the basic principles of a liquidity plan. With the exception of one delegation, the Ministers and Governors agreed with their Deputies on the need to distinguish between the establishment of a contingency plan and its activation. They further agreed that the prerequisites for activation should include the attainment of better balance of payments equilibrium by all participants in the scheme and the likelihood of a better working of the adjustment process in the future. They agreed that decisions on the activation of any contingency plan and decisions

---

[23] Communiqué of the ministerial meeting of the Group of Ten; cited above in footnote 21 of this chapter.

to be taken later regarding reserve creation would recognize that, while all countries had an interest in the smooth working of the international monetary system, the responsibility for providing a substantial part of the financial strength behind any new asset would fall on a limited group. In effect, they had come around to accepting a universal scheme. To reconcile the interests of all with the special responsibility of a limited group, the Ministers and Governors further concluded that proposals for reserve creation should be considered both by the limited group and by the Fund.

Thus, while a few officials continued to reiterate, during the next several months, their partiality for a limited approach to reserve creation, the issue of universality was no longer a matter of major disagreement, and other issues, such as the characteristics that any new reserve asset should have, became primary.

REASONS FOR ACCEPTANCE OF UNIVERSAL SCHEME

A number of reasons for the Group of Ten's change in attitude from favoring a limited approach to acceptance of the idea of a universal scheme can be identified. The critical remarks of the Governors for countries outside the Group of Ten during the 1965 Annual Meeting, the adverse reactions to the dual approach expressed in early 1966 by the Executive Directors for the countries outside the Group of Ten and by the Managing Director, and the formal endorsement of a universal scheme by developing countries as a group—as, for example, in the UNCTAD report—all had an impact. Undoubtedly, too, some of the countries in the Group of Ten wanted to avoid the political awkwardness of supporting schemes to create money for the large industrial nations only.

There were, as well, difficulties in finding a suitable definition of the countries to be included in a limited scheme. Would countries that were neither industrial nor developing—Australia, for example—be included? Would countries that had particularly close trading and financial affiliations with countries that were part of the limited scheme also be admitted? The latter question concerned especially the members of the overseas sterling area, which were linked to the United Kingdom.

Nor should the Fund's efforts on behalf of a plan that would include all Fund members be underestimated. Probably most significant in this regard were the several public pronouncements of the Managing Director, who expressed over and over again his firm rejection of anything but a truly universal and international approach.

Possibly the Managing Director's recitals of the Fund's experiences persuaded the European countries in the Group of Ten to give up, at least for the time being, the hope for uniform rules for balance of payments adjustment.

The possibility that some type of multilateral surveillance could be applied in conjunction with a scheme to create liquidity had been an important motivation for the officials of France and the Federal Republic of Germany, for example, to limit the scheme to the major countries because they were thought to be more likely to adhere to special balance of payments rules. However, Mr. Schweitzer had stressed that the whole experience of the Fund for twenty years bore witness to the dangers of supposing that predetermined rules of balance of payments adjustment could apply to different country circumstances. No two situations were ever identical. But the most important factor facilitating the relinquishment by European authorities of the concepts of multilateral surveillance or close supervision was undoubtedly the safeguard that they suggested for any reserve creation scheme: once the scheme was agreed, it would not be activated until a further mutual decision was taken. In effect, the controversy shifted from the rules to be applied to balance of payments adjustment to the rules to be applied to the use of reserve units and how decisions for reserve creation and activation would be arrived at.

Especially persuasive were the specific proposals made by the Managing Director in March 1966. They provided the Group of Ten with concrete illustrations of how universal liquidity could be created through the Fund. The work of the Fund staff also helped to lay to rest many concerns about the economic and financial consequences of a universal scheme. That the Managing Director's proposals had been subject to a full exchange of views in the Executive Board was also significant: they could rightfully be regarded as reflecting an international position, as against the position of the few countries composing the Group of Ten.

WIDENING THE DISCUSSIONS

A Committee of Governors?

The important question of how the actions and discussions of the Group of Ten and of the Fund might be coordinated—that is, how the "second phase" of contingency planning might be implemented—was to occupy the attention of the Executive Board during the next few months before the 1966 Annual Meeting. Although the participation of the representatives of the Managing Director in meetings of the Deputies of the Group of Ten had produced a kind of coordination, there was an emerging view that more formal machinery was required. At a meeting of the Executive Board on May 27, 1966, the Economic Counsellor had reported that the Deputies of the Group of Ten, at their Rome meeting on May 17–19, had begun to give attention to the "second phase" of the deliberations on liquidity, that is, the matter of drawing into the discussions countries other than those of the Group of Ten. The Deputies had given some consideration to the possibility that the Governors of the Fund, at the Annual Meeting in September, might appoint a special advisory committee. This committee could be asked to work out a specific plan for deliberate reserve creation for subsequent decision by the Board of Governors.

Executive Directors' Reactions

Many Executive Directors expressed concern about the implications of a special advisory committee of Governors. Accordingly, the Executive Board held three informal sessions in June and July 1966 to discuss how the second phase of the deliberations on liquidity might be implemented. At the first of these sessions the Chairman outlined three possible alternatives: (1) the whole matter of liquidity could be referred to the Fund's Executive Board for consideration and report to the Board of Governors; (2) parallel consideration in the Executive Board and in the Deputies of the Group of Ten could continue; and (3) the Board of Governors could refer the matter to a special committee.

Although he considered the first alternative as the most satisfactory, Mr. Schweitzer did not himself think that it was likely to come about. The second alternative did not represent much of a forward step. Therefore, he saw some merit in the third alternative. As one possible variant of this third alternative, the U.S. authorities had come up with a specific proposal for a committee of 20 Governors. Another possibility, which he tended to favor, was a committee to advise the Board of Governors that would consist of all of the individual Executive Directors of the Fund plus the Deputies of the Group of Ten—in effect a merger into a single committee of the Executive Directors and the Deputies.

Several Executive Directors for countries not in the Group of Ten—e.g., Messrs. Escobar, Nikoi, and Tejera-París—had strong reservations about adding to the discussions another limited group of countries. Many countries would still be excluded. The subject matter being considered was clearly the province of the Executive Board of the Fund. On the other hand, Mr. O'Donnell welcomed the proposals for a second phase, which would broaden the base of the discussions before the countries of the Group of Ten had reached a firm position.

The Executive Directors for the countries in the Group of Ten spoke only in their personal, not in their official, capacities. They argued that any solution had to be practicable and feasible. Mr. Sergio Siglienti (Italy) noted the progress that had been made toward bringing the Fund and the Group of Ten closer together and commended the efforts made by the Managing Director and by the staff. Since these efforts had been inspired by the ideas being expressed by the Executive Directors, the Board had played a more important part in what had been achieved than some Executive Directors took credit for. The problem now was to find a way to recognize formally the role that the Board should continue to play. Mr. René Larre (France) did not favor the U.S. proposal for a committee of Governors. While the Managing Director's proposal for a joint committee of the Executive Directors and the Deputies of the Group of Ten required more reflection, he was concerned that the countries of the Group of Ten would have double representation. Mr. Horst Ungerer (Federal Republic of Germany, Alternate to Mr. Ernst vom Hofe, Federal Republic of Germany) had other problems with the U.S. proposal: How would the limited number of countries not in the Group of Ten be chosen? What would be the link between the committee of Governors and the Executive Board?

Joint Meetings Suggested

Mr. Emminger, as chairman of the Deputies of the Group of Ten, after sounding out the views of the other Deputies, proposed in July 1966 in a letter to the Managing Director that joint meetings of the Deputies and the Executive Directors be held, with the aim of reaching a consensus on arrangements for creating liquidity. Shortly thereafter, the Executive Directors considered a reply to this letter in two informal sessions. On the understanding that Executive Directors would participate fully and that there would be a free exchange of documents, most Directors were in favor of the joint meetings and asked Mr. Schweitzer to talk informally with Mr. Emminger about how they might be conducted. This he did when he attended the meeting of the Ministers and Central Bank Governors of the Group of Ten in The Hague on July 25–26.

In September 1966, the Managing Director again endeavored to obtain the support of the Executive Board for a draft resolution to be presented to the Board of Governors at the Annual Meeting. Such a resolution would, in effect, ask the Executive Directors to proceed with their work on liquidity and indicate that such work would include joint meetings with the Deputies. Although such a resolution was not legally necessary, Mr. Schweitzer believed that its passage by the Governors would focus attention on the role that the Fund had been playing, and would continue to play, in the field of international liquidity. Envisaging the possibility that the Ministers and Governors of the Group of Ten might take the occasion of the Annual Meeting to reiterate their views and recommendations on this subject, the Managing Director did not think it would be advisable for the Board of Governors to remain silent. It proved difficult, however, to obtain a text that commanded the general support of the Executive Board, and Mr. Schweitzer once more decided not to press for a resolution.

At the Twenty-First Annual Meeting, which was held in Washington from September 26 to 30, 1966, the Managing Director expressed the view that there were no technical reasons why concentrated work could not provide the Governors with fully developed suggestions for arrangements for reserve creation in time for the next Annual Meeting, and that informal meetings between the Executive Directors of the Fund and the Deputies would help the work along.[24]

---

[24] Opening Address by the Managing Director, *Summary Proceedings, 1966*, pp. 19 and 20.

Several Governors, especially those for Canada, the United Kingdom, and the United States, urged that specific proposals be ready for the next Annual Meeting and welcomed the idea of joint informal meetings.[25] Mr. Schweitzer replied that he was confident that the Executive Directors stood ready to consult with other groups where this promised to be productive and said that arrangements for informal meetings with the Deputies of the Group of Ten were being discussed.[26]

---

[25] Statements by the Governor of the Fund and the World Bank for Canada, the Governor of the Fund for the United Kingdom, and the Governor of the Fund and the World Bank for the United States, *Summary Proceedings, 1966,* pp. 33–34, 61, and 113.

[26] Concluding Remarks by the Managing Director, *Summary Proceedings, 1966,* p. 209.

CHAPTER 5

Progress Toward a Plan for Reserve Creation

(October 1, 1966–April 15, 1967)

*D*ISCUSSIONS ON RESERVE CREATION entered their fourth year. This year proved to be one of tremendous, and eventually fruitful, activity. The most appropriate way for the Group of Ten to confer with representatives of other countries—often referred to as the second phase of the deliberations—was found to be joint meetings of Executive Directors of the Fund and Deputies of the Group of Ten. Four such meetings were held between November 1966 and June 1967. The Managing Director also had consultations with the Secretary-General of the UNCTAD, Mr. Raul Prebisch, and in March 1967 an Executive Board seminar was held with members of the secretariat of that organization in order to give the developing countries an opportunity to express their special concerns about reserve creation.

In addition to their joint meetings, the Executive Directors and the Deputies met separately to consider questions coming up in the joint meetings. From November 1966 to the middle of August 1967 the Executive Directors held more than three dozen informal sessions on liquidity. Also, early in 1967 officials of the six member countries of the EEC—Belgium, France, the Federal Republic of Germany, Italy, Luxembourg, and the Netherlands—met at both the technical and the ministerial level to try to reach a unified position on a plan.

For most of the year, prospects for agreement on a specific plan seemed as dim as ever. As late as April 1967 the officials of the Group of Ten still held widely differing views on most of the key issues. From May to the end of August, however, efforts were enhanced to reach agreement on some plan and events moved swiftly. The principal points of a plan were thus worked out so that at the Twenty-Second Annual Meeting, in Rio de Janeiro late in September 1967, the Board of Governors had before it for approval an "Outline of a Facility Based on Special Drawing Rights in the Fund." On September 29, 1967, the significant step was taken: the Board of Governors adopted a resolution instructing the Executive Directors to convert the Outline into a legal instrument in the form of amendments to the Fund's Articles of Agreement.

These developments are described in detail in this and the following chapter. The present chapter recounts what happened until the middle of April 1967, when the members of the EEC came to an understanding among themselves, an achievement which gave impetus to agreement among the Group of Ten. Chapter 6 explains how the features of the Outline emerged during the following five and a half months, culminating in adoption of the resolution at the Annual Meeting in Rio de Janeiro in September.

ARRANGEMENTS FOR JOINT MEETINGS

Joint meetings between the Executive Directors and the Deputies of the Group of Ten were without precedent. Before the meetings were agreed, several questions had to be resolved to allay the fears of those Directors who were especially exercised lest the Fund's role in any such discussions be underplayed.

At the meeting of the Finance Ministers and Central Bank Governors of the Group of Ten on September 25, 1966, the Managing Director had explained the views and attitudes of Executive Directors for several countries that were not in the Group of Ten. He drew the attention of the Ministers and Governors to the fact that the Executive Board had been able to produce a unanimous section on international liquidity in the Fund's Annual Report for 1966. In his opinion, this indicated that the views of the financial officials of the countries outside the Group of Ten were not radically different from the views of the officials of the countries in the Group. He stressed, however, that what did concern the members of the Fund that were not in the Group was their role in the process by which broad agreement was to be reached on any new measures for creating liquidity. The members of the Fund that were not part of the Group were unwilling to be assigned a secondary role in negotiations affecting the monetary system for the whole world. In the view of the Executive Directors for these countries, subordinate participation was not justified by the economic behavior of the countries concerned: a large percentage of the non-industrial countries had been striving continuously and successfully to maintain sound and convertible currencies and to build up their reserves to reasonable working levels.

Mr. Schweitzer explained that countries outside the Group of Ten accepted the Fund's system of weighted voting—which gave most of the votes to the countries in the Group of Ten—because all members had a fair and adequate opportunity for group discussion and decision. These members regarded with dismay anything that disturbed the unity of the Fund because they saw in such a development their relegation to a status in which they would not enjoy, as a right, a due voice in international debate. Their fears were intensified when language was used, procedures followed, and proposals made that appeared to pay less than adequate regard to their interests.

The concerns of the Executive Directors for countries that were not in the Group of Ten regarding their participation in the discussions going on were again made evident in October 1966 when, following his informal talks with Mr. Emminger, the Managing Director discussed with the Executive Directors the form of the forthcoming joint meetings. The meetings were to be informal and would not take on the character of a session of the Executive Board. The first meeting would be held in Washington on November 28 and 29, 1966, and subsequent meetings would be held alternately in Washington and outside the United States. All meetings would be under the joint chairmanship of the Managing Director and the chairman of the Deputies. The chairmen would confer throughout the meetings on the conduct of the meetings, but the Managing Director would preside at meetings in Washington and the chairman of the Deputies at meetings outside Washington. Executive Directors, Alternate Executive Directors, the Deputies of the Finance Ministers and Central Bank Governors of the Group of Ten (two Deputies for each country), and their alternates would attend the joint meetings, together with the Managing Director, the Deputy Managing Director, and some senior officials of the Fund staff. Observers from the Swiss Government, the BIS, and the OECD would also be invited. The Secretary of the Fund would prepare an informal record similar to the Secretary's journal of informal sessions of the Executive Board.

Many Executive Directors still questioned the proposed arrangements. Did not the procedures imply that the Group of Ten, a limited group, was placing itself on the same level as the Fund, an international body? Should not the Executive Directors maintain their position by insisting that the chair should be held by the Chairman of the Executive Board, and that all joint meetings should be held at the Fund's headquarters and conform to the normal procedures of the Fund? Should not the Executive Directors have similar discussions with other agencies, such as the UNCTAD and the Inter-American Committee on the Alliance for Progress (CIAP)?

The Managing Director replied that the purpose of the joint meetings was, essentially, to advance international agreement on ways to create liquidity. The only purpose of his proposals on procedures was to have some practical arrangements for moving the discussions forward. The arrangements should not be construed as being a meeting of the Executive Board, in its capacity as the legal organ of the Fund, with the Deputies of the Group of Ten, in the manner of a meeting of two international institutions, each having to safeguard its international status. What he was proposing was, in effect, that the Executive Directors should meet as individuals, informally, with other individuals who were Deputies of the Ministers and Governors of the Group of Ten, in order to exchange views.

As to the place of meeting, it was a matter of courtesy to the Deputies to alternate meetings between Washington and Europe since the Deputies were busy in their home countries at other jobs while the Executive Directors devoted full time to these matters. Regarding the question of chairmanship, joint chairmanship was preferable to alternating the chairmanship between the Managing Director of the Fund and the Chairman of the Deputies, which had initially been suggested by the Deputies.

After further talks with Mr. Emminger about the arrangements, Mr. Schweitzer returned to the Executive Board on October 19, 1966 and explained that it was not feasible to modify the arrangements outlined above. He ascertained that the Executive Board was willing to proceed on that basis. Messrs. Schweitzer and Emminger then worked out the physical arrangements—dates, hours, agenda, size of delegations, simultaneous interpretation from French to English and from English to French, record keeping, and seating arrangements. The Deputies approved the arrangements made by Mr. Emminger on November 16, 1966 (in Paris), and on November 23, 1966 the Executive Directors in informal session agreed to the arrangements made by the Managing Director.

Before the first joint meeting with the Deputies, the Executive Directors held several informal sessions to consider the broad questions on which the discussions at the joint meetings were to focus. Also, in order to be in a position to present the views of the developing members of the Fund more effectively at the prospective joint meetings, the nine Executive Directors elected by developing members began in the latter months of 1966 to meet informally among themselves as a "G-9 Caucus," or "Group of Nine."

The informal sessions held by the Executive Directors as a whole revealed both the nature of the questions concerning reserve creation that remained outstanding and the opinions of individual Executive Directors. Many of the attitudes expressed, especially by the Executive Directors for the countries in the Group of Ten, were similar to the positions that had been, and were being, taken by representatives of those countries in Group of Ten meetings. These questions were considered: (1) What should be the purpose of reserve creation? (2) What form—reserve units or drawing rights in the Fund—should deliberately created reserves take? (3) Should countries already indebted to the Fund be obliged to use their new reserves in the first instance to pay off their Fund obligations? (4) What conditions should govern the transfer of the new reserves? (5) How should reserve creation be financed?

At this juncture, a clarification is necessary about the terminology used in the discussions of reserve creation in this chapter and in Chapter 6. The EEC countries, especially France, preferring to regard any new mechanism for creating liquidity as a credit arrangement rather than a means of providing a new form of reserve, regarded the concept of a "reserve asset" as unacceptable. In formal negotiations, therefore, such as meetings at the ministerial level or even in some of the discussions at the joint meetings between Executive Directors and the Deputies, monetary officials, when seeking a term to designate a new reserve—which could be in the form either of a drawing right or of a reserve unit—or when describing the ways in which a possible new mechanism for reserve creation might work, rarely used the term *reserve asset*. They used instead the more general terms *reserve creation* and *deliberately created reserves*. Nevertheless, the term reserve asset was singularly useful in discussions among technicians and was commonly used not only by the Fund staff but also by the Executive Directors in their informal discussions. Hence, in reporting here the discussions that took place within the Fund, the term *reserve asset* is often used, while in reporting discussions within the Group of Ten, or in joint meetings between the Deputies and Executive Directors, the terms *reserve creation* and *deliberately created reserves* are used.

PURPOSE OF RESERVE CREATION DISCUSSED

Based on Global Need

Consensus seemed to have been reached by the latter part of 1966 regarding the purpose of reserve creation. The purpose was to supply additional liquidity to the world economy as and when needed: the global need for reserves was to be provided for. In view of all the discussions that had been going on thus far as to whether reserve creation was, or was not, necessary for the monetary system, most agreement about the purpose of reserve creation was really in negative terms—that is, what its purpose was *not* to be. It was agreed, in particular, that the purpose of reserve creation should not be to provide countries with a means of financing balance of payments deficits, nor with a means of financing economic development.

By this time, it was also the accepted view that the global need for reserves should be assessed for a period of some three to five years ahead. It had been realized gradually that it would not be possible to alter world liquidity in accordance with changes in the business cycle in the same way that central banks managed short-term changes in the supply of domestic liquidity. The idea, current a few years earlier, that world reserve policy might be used to iron out short-term fluctuations in the world business cycle had been abandoned. The greatest risk that an inadequate amount of world reserves might present to the international economy was no longer regarded as the risk of deflation and unemployment but rather the risk of widespread restrictions on international trade and capital movements and a decreased willingness on the part of creditor countries to give aid to developing countries.

The staff reported to the Executive Board that the Deputies of the Group of Ten saw as an additional purpose of reserve creation that a specific plan for enhancing world liquidity would help to establish confidence in the entire international monetary system. Once the major countries had agreed on a plan, the excessive disappearance of gold into private hoards might stop and it might be unnecessary actually to create as many reserves as the then existing rate of gold hoarding might suggest were needed.

Relation to Conditional Liquidity

Despite their general agreement on the purpose of reserve creation, the Executive Directors, in their informal discussions, brought up a number of questions relating to the need for reserves and how that need would be determined. Mr. Anjaria wished to know how global, or universal, needs for reserves would be defined. What exactly was meant by reserve creation being adapted to the world's need for liquidity? Mr. Alexandre Kafka (Brazil) stressed the insistence of Latin American officials that all countries, not only the economically big ones, could and should assume responsibility for the financial backing of any new reserve asset. Mr. Lieftinck raised a question that he was to bring up frequently in later discussions: What was the relationship between the need for new reserves and the amount of, or need for, conditional liquidity in the traditional form of larger quotas in the Fund? More specifically, how would one judge whether it was the creation of new reserves or an increase in members' quotas in the Fund that was necessary?

Mr. Lieftinck explained his position. He found the reasoning in the report of the Deputies of the Group of Ten not very convincing. They had been fearful that any creation of reserves would be dangerous: these reserves might be misused and have undesirable repercussions on the world economy. Consequently, suggestions for establishing safeguards had crept into their proposals. They had even gone so far as to distinguish between a limited group, which would set its own safeguards and standards, and countries not in the Group of Ten, for whom the Group of Ten would probably also set safeguards. Indeed, the Deputies had suggested some built-in safeguards against overuse of the new reserves in the form of minimum and maximum limits on the holdings of new reserves, a reference to the harmonizing of reserve ratios that had come up in the Group of Ten's discussions in 1965–66 when the prospect of agreeing on other methods of enforcing discipline seemed remote.

It was Mr. Lieftinck's view that the logical conclusion of this philosophy of subjecting the use of a new reserve asset to rules would come very close to what the Fund was already doing. The Fund did exercise discipline over the use of its resources. Was not the solution to the need for augmenting world liquidity, therefore, an increase in conditional liquidity, that is, increases in Fund quotas? In his opinion, the problem of the relationship between conditional and unconditional liquidity should be further explored.

Mr. Jorge González del Valle (Guatemala) supported Mr. Lieftinck's view that the advantages of any scheme for creating a special reserve over the simpler and better-known procedure of increases in Fund quotas should be studied closely. In this context, he referred to the Declaration of Jamaica, in which the Governors of the central banks of Latin America had urged that the role of the Fund be strengthened, among other ways, through a more dynamic procedure for revising and adjusting quotas and through more flexible access to the Fund's resources, including an increase in unconditional drawing rights.[1] He also emphasized that the Fund's policies for providing conditional liquidity could be improved so as to strengthen the process of balance of payments adjustment. Such an improvement could reduce the need for additional reserves or for reserve creation.

Mr. Adolfo C. Diz (Argentina) pointed to a number of important problems concerning the timing of reserve creation. There were likely to be substantial delays between the recognition of a need to create reserves and the time when reserves were created, and between the time when reserves were created and the time when the effects of the reserve creation were felt.

Relation to Development Finance

In the discussions concerning the purpose of creating a reserve asset, it was inevitable that the question of the link with development finance, which had come up frequently in past discussions of reserve creation, would be raised again.

Mr. Faber pointed out that, for developing countries, the main benefit of reserve creation was a speeding up of their rate of development, not the maintenance of external payments equilibrium. For developing countries, reserves not only served the long-term need of financing development but were essential in the short term to enable development programs to be continued during times of emergency. Mr. Larre agreed with Mr. Faber that the developing countries were not being offered much by the various schemes that were to be considered at the joint meetings, and suggested that the Executive Directors hold joint meetings with the UNCTAD also.

Mr. Dale gave two reasons why the U.S. authorities were inclined to think that there should not be a link between reserve creation and development finance. First, the questions concerning deliberate reserve creation were sufficiently complex without bringing in considerations of development aid. Second, were such a link to be effected, the U.S. Congress might well reduce the amounts of other foreign aid programs; hence, the developing countries might not achieve any net gain from linking development aid to reserve creation.

In Mr. Dale's view, the question of the relationship between development aid and reserve creation was in the process of being resolved satisfactorily. He recalled that initially some monetary authorities had held the view, first advanced by Mr. Stamp, that only the developing countries should receive new reserve assets, although these reserve assets would later be earned by industrial countries. An opposing group had taken the position that new reserve assets should go wholly to the industrial countries, and that there should be no permanent transfer of resources to the developing countries. At a second

---

[1] See Chap. 4 above, p. 85.

stage of the discussions, both of these positions had been softened. The group advocating reserve assets only for developing countries had moved to the position that all countries should participate in the initial distribution. The group advocating reserve assets only for industrial nations had proposed what had been called a dual approach: new reserves would be distributed to a limited number of countries but, in addition, a certain amount of resources would be set aside, possibly through the International Development Association or through the Fund, from which assistance or additional drawing rights might be made available to countries not participating in the scheme. The third stage of the discussions had now been reached. A universal approach, involving creation of an identical reserve asset for all countries, had been accepted, in effect overcoming the problem of linking reserve creation and development financing.

FORM OF DELIBERATELY CREATED RESERVES CONSIDERED

When the Executive Directors moved on to the matter of the form that the deliberately created reserves might take, the Economic Counsellor first reviewed for them the ways in which the views of the Deputies of the Group of Ten on the various proposals for reserve creation had evolved. Originally the Group of Ten had had before it the Bernstein plan and the French proposal, both of which were schemes to create reserve units (CRUs) and were entirely limited to the Group of Ten. During the next three years those delegations of the Group of Ten that favored any reserve creation at all had indicated a preference for some kind of reserve unit, such as the CRU. The Belgian delegation had consistently favored some method of reserve creation through the Fund.

As the Deputies had come to the realization that something would have to be done for the countries not in the Group of Ten, they had attempted to make certain that the new reserves that these countries would receive were as good as the units to be distributed to the Group of Ten. There had been a shift by several Deputies away from the idea of reserve units for some countries and a different sort of reserve for others, say, drawing rights in the Fund, toward the idea of reserve units for all. The latter had been, of course, the concept behind the Fund's Plan II.[2]

There were a number of differences between the schemes put forward by various delegations at the Deputies' meetings during 1966 and the Fund's Plan II; but these differences were in the area either of the process of decision making or of arrangements for making good any losses should the scheme be liquidated. More specifically, Canada, Japan, and the United Kingdom within the Group of Ten favored reserve units for all, but this view had not yet been accepted by most members of the EEC; Belgium, for example, had a preference

---

[2] See Chap. 4 above, p. 92.

for drawing rights, as in the Fund's Plan I. For a long time the U.S. position had been, in effect, to support both kinds of reserve asset, under a combined drawing rights–reserve unit scheme.

Mr. S. J. Handfield-Jones (Canada) and Mr. J. M. Stevens, later Sir John (United Kingdom), confirmed that their Governments were in favor of a scheme based on reserve units rather than one based on drawing rights. Reserve units seemed to be endowed with more of the qualities of money and to satisfy better the motives that induced countries to hold owned reserves. Thus, reserve units would be more effective than drawing rights in sustaining confidence in the new reserves. Moreover, reserve units were more clearly distinguishable from existing drawing rights in the Fund than some kind of unconditional drawing rights would be, and therefore ran less risk of impairing the Fund's normal standards of conditionality. In addition, while some countries were treating their traditional drawing rights in the Fund as part of their reserves, others were not; hence, there was still a need to get the world at large to regard drawing rights in the Fund as part of reserves.

As he had on other occasions, Mr. André van Campenhout (Belgium) remained in favor of drawing rights. His argument was based in part on the Fund's long experience with drawing rights and in part on the idea that a drawing rights scheme was better adapted for maintaining a proper balance between conditional and unconditional liquidity. He endorsed Mr. Lieftinck's comments in favor of doing as much as possible through conditional liquidity. Mr. vom Hofe saw merit in the idea that had been suggested by the Managing Director of starting with drawing rights and shifting to reserve units later on. Mr. Siglienti and Mr. Otto Schelin (Denmark, Alternate to Mr. Kurt Eklöf, Sweden) confirmed that the positions of their countries on the question of drawing rights or reserve units were flexible.

Taking the line again of doing more through conditional liquidity, Mr. Lieftinck contended that the choice between reserve units and drawing rights was too restricted. Although the Managing Director's proposals for creating reserves had contained suggestions for setting up an affiliate organization of the Fund, he preferred to see a solution that would incorporate reserve creation into the existing mechanism of the Fund. More attention ought to be paid, for example, to ways to augment reserves that involved increases in Fund quotas. It might be possible, for instance, to link the creation of reserve units to the gold payments due in connection with quota increases. Possibly there could be quota increases without members making gold payments. Or members might use reserve units to pay the required gold subscriptions.

Mr. Larre, stating that he understood from the staff that there was no substantial difference between the schemes for reserve units and those for drawing rights, questioned whether this was actually so. In line with the French view that what was being discussed was not a new reserve but a new form of credit, Mr. Larre referred to "creditor countries." He explained why he thought that, from the viewpoint of the creditor country, the schemes for drawing rights might be significantly different from those for reserve units. Under a drawing rights scheme, the creditor country would presumably be consulted when its currency was to be drawn; it could therefore object to the drawing on balance of payments grounds. Under a reserve unit scheme, the creditor would not normally have an option to object.

The Economic Counsellor replied that it was possible to make the two types of scheme identical. One of the reasons why reserve unit schemes were preferred by some officials was that they were envisaged as being devoid of "guidance," that is, suggestions (presumably from the Fund) as to which currencies should be made available when a participant presented reserve units for conversion. He himself, however, could not imagine a scheme that would not involve at least some guidance; a member needing to encash reserve units would have to be able to turn to some organization to nominate a recipient that would exchange convertible currency for reserve units. Schemes involving drawing rights were based on arrangements already in operation that provided such guidance. Hence, differences in regard to guidance were not inherent in the two kinds of scheme.

QUESTION OF COMPULSORY RECONSTITUTION

Another difficult question that was still unresolved late in 1966 concerned the compulsory reconstitution of credit tranche positions in the Fund. Should countries that were indebted to the Fund—that is, members whose currencies were held by the Fund in amounts equivalent to more than 100 per cent of their quotas—be obliged to use newly distributed reserves to repurchase from the Fund before they could make any other use of them? When the Executive Directors discussed this question in informal session prior to their first joint meeting with the Deputies, the staff presented two arguments for compulsory reconstitution of Fund positions. First, countries that were indebted to the Fund could be considered the least entitled to obtain new freely available drawing rights or reserve units. Second, a provision requiring reconstitution of Fund positions was a more effective and permanent way of achieving one of the conditions sought by the Deputies of the Group of Ten for activation of any plan. One of the main reasons for delaying activation until certain conditions were fulfilled was a desire not to make new reserve units available to countries whose currencies were held as reserves so long as they were still running balance of payments deficits. Making activation of a contingency plan dependent on the absence of balance of payments deficits in a few key countries, however, was not, in the staff's opinion, a good solution. Presumably, even after activation, most countries, including reserve currency countries, would from time to time incur balance of payments deficits. Compulsory reconstitution would solve the problem of relating reserve creation to the elimination of balance of payments deficits by use of a general provision which was not directed in particular toward countries that were reserve centers but which would apply to any country that had already drawn on the Fund.

The positions expressed by the Executive Directors on the question of compulsory reconstitution suggested that this issue was going to be a bristly one, and so it did later prove to be. Mr. Dale said that the U.S. authorities had recently come to believe that the notion of compulsory reconstitution of credit tranche positions in the Fund required further thought. Initially the U.S. authorities had favored a version of this provision because there had been concern over the extent to which a distribution of new reserve assets beyond a limited group might give rise to transfers of real resources. For several reasons, however, the U.S. attitude on this question was changing. *One*, the focus of the discussions had shifted from international liquidity toward reserves; the mechanism now being discussed was for the purpose of creating reserves, that is, unconditional liquidity rather than conditional liquidity. The effect of requiring reconstitution of members' positions in the Fund was to make the new liquidity conditional rather than unconditional. *Two*, the U.S. view was that reserve creation should not be related to a country's balance of payments position; but requiring reconstitution of a credit tranche position involved relating the type of liquidity a country would gain from the new mechanism to its past balance of payments position. *Three*, many countries that were indebted to the Fund might be indebted also to other creditors. Why should the debts to the Fund be singled out for reconstitution or repayment?

In contrast to Mr. Dale's position questioning the concept of compulsory reconstitution was the position of some of the European Executive Directors. Messrs. vom Hofe, van Campenhout, and Lieftinck all definitely preferred the idea of compulsory reconstitution of Fund credit tranche positions with the new reserves. Hence, the staff was asked to study carefully the relationship between the provision for compulsory reconstitution in a reserve creation plan and the automatic repurchase obligations of Article V, Section 7, of the Fund Agreement.

QUESTION OF USE AND TRANSFER OF A NEW RESERVE

Another question still to be answered concerned the conditions that would govern the use and transfer of a new reserve. The Deputies of the Group of Ten, especially in the Ossola Group, had already devoted much attention to the rules of transfer for any reserve asset. Nonetheless, by November 1966 the characteristics to be given to a new reserve asset regarding its usability and transferability remained one of the most controversial of the unsettled issues. Determining these characteristics had been difficult, partly because very technical subjects were involved and many alternative suggestions had been advanced, but also because the characteristics attached to any new reserve asset involved the relation of the reserve asset to gold. Some officials emphatically did not want the new reserve asset to supplant gold or even to resemble gold. At the same time, the issue was an important one because the characteristics attached to a new reserve asset greatly affected its acceptability as a reserve.

At an informal session of the Executive Directors early in November 1966, Mr. Fleming, who had attended meetings of the Ossola Group, summarized the thinking thus far. Two points concerning the transferability and usability of a reserve asset had already been established. First, the freedom to transfer and to use reserve assets was dependent on the existence of firm obligations by participants in the reserve-creating scheme to accept them in exchange for convertible currency. Second, participants' willingness to accept and hold reserve assets must substantially exceed the amount in existence.

The issue that had been prominent earlier, in 1964–65 when the Ossola Group was meeting—whether transfers of reserve units would take place directly between participants or indirectly through some intermediary—was no longer vital. The crucial question now was the degree of freedom that should govern transfers. Should use of a reserve unit be determined only at the discretion of the participant holding the unit, or should the participant have to present a case that it had a need to use it? Would a participant making a transfer of units be free to decide to which other participant it would pass the units? How could the desire of the transferor for maximum freedom of use be reconciled with the desire of the transferee for protection from an undue accumulation of reserve units?

Mr. Fleming explained that in the early stages of the discussions on liquidity it had been suggested, as in the CRU proposals, that both the occasion for use of reserve units and the direction of transfer would be predetermined by fixing uniform ratios between a participant's holdings of reserve units and its total reserves. Participants would be able to transfer reserve units only in accordance with pre-set ratios between their holdings of the new units and their holdings of reserves in other forms, such as gold and foreign exchange. Later on, the inclination of the officials of the Group of Ten had been to favor giving maximum freedom to the transferor, both as to the occasion of use and as to the direction of transfer. Now, the Group was leaning toward limitations on both use and transfer so as to provide safeguards for the transferees.

At the end of November 1966, the Deputies of the Group of Ten set up a Working Party on Provisions to Ensure Acceptability of a New Reserve Asset, also under the chairmanship of Mr. Ossola, to study further the conditions governing use and transfer of a new reserve.[3] Mr. Fleming, who attended

---

[3] Because many of the Deputies were very concerned about the effect on gold of a new reserve asset and the relationships between the two, they also set up another working party, under the chairmanship of Mr. G. A. Kessler, of the Netherlands, to study the role of gold in the monetary system.

meetings of this Working Party, again reported to the Executive Directors in January 1967. The views of the Deputies were still not sufficiently definitive. While some attention was being given to the characteristics that would make the new reserve asset "like gold," this approach had not provided much guidance on what characteristics were actually to be given to a new reserve asset, especially as no one was in favor of making the asset convertible into gold. Three main viewpoints were being expressed, with many subvariants, combinations, and refinements.

One view still favored a gold-transfer ratio approach: transfers of reserve units would be made in some proportion to the gold holdings of the transferring country. A second favored fairly free transferability, but with certain provisos: the transfer should not be intended to change the composition of total reserves, and limits should be established on the obligations of countries to hold reserve units that were transferred to them, limits that might be two or three times the amounts of reserve units originally distributed to them. A third view favored provisions essentially similar to those which governed the Fund's transactions and which had been suggested by the Managing Director in the proposals he had put forward in March 1966. Transfer would be free, subject to balance of payments need. The direction of transfer would be guided by an agent, although possibly in a rather loose way—for example, by setting up a list of participants to which transfers should not be made and other lists of participants to which they would be permitted or encouraged. There would be holding limits and possibly reconstitution obligations. There was also a view held by some that the transferee would best be safeguarded by making the reserve unit so attractive that participants would not worry about how many they received.

The view of the staff was that at least a moral check on the use of new reserves ought to be set up by confining their use to situations of clear-cut balance of payments need. Also, the staff preferred a form of transferability that would be subject to some degree of guidance: there would be an attempt to steer the transfer of reserve units away from countries that were in payments difficulties and toward countries that had payments surpluses, or that had a smaller ratio of the reserve units to total reserves than the general average of other countries.

Messrs. Stevens, vom Hofe, and Lieftinck all stated that the new reserve unit must be "as good as gold." Therefore, its use ought to be made as free as possible. But it might not be feasible to make it fully usable until it had become accepted in international financial transactions. Hence, more guidance and control might be needed at the outset than would be necessary later. Mr. Lieftinck stressed the need for the new unit to have a gold-value guarantee, to bear interest, and to be usable in reconstituting credit tranche positions in the Fund. He also favored transfers through the Fund, at least in the initial phases, as this would help to establish an orderly and controlled market for the new reserves.

Also in January 1967, the Executive Directors considered a staff paper on how participants might use new reserve units in their transactions with the Fund. It was apparent that much more thought would have to be given to the nature of reserve units and how they would be used and transferred. Nearly all of the Executive Directors voiced concern that the Fund might become loaded down with new units and become illiquid.

FINANCING OF RESERVE CREATION

When informal discussions by the Executive Directors on how reserve creation should be financed got under way in November 1966, the Economic Counsellor reported that the term *financing of reserve creation* was a relatively new one. There was not likely to be any problem of financing when the new reserves were initially distributed. Reserves would be distributed to all participants, presumably all Fund members, and, although some consideration had been given to the possibility that a participant would "opt out" of the scheme, it might be assumed that normally all participants would accept the new reserves allocated to them rather than forgo them. Moreover, the total amount of reserves to be created would also have been determined before distribution.

The problem of financing would arise after the initial distribution, when some participants would want to reduce their holdings of the new reserves in order to finance a balance of payments deficit. The new reserves would then move to other participants according to the rules that would have been established for accepting and holding them. The basic question, therefore, concerned which participants were likely to be on the receiving end and in what amounts.

Staff studies had revealed that, contrary to initial impressions, the desire of the Fund's members to increase their reserves in the long run included not only the industrial countries but the developing countries as well. There was consequently no reason to presume that, over a sufficiently long period, any particular group of countries was likely to absorb most of the new reserves. Accordingly, the rules for accepting the new reserves could, from the beginning of the scheme, be based on the principle of universality, that is, that additional reserves would be absorbed by all participants that had reasonably strong balance of payments and reserve positions.

Mr. Kafka thought that the question of financing reserve creation centered on the nature of the economic burden involved. There were, he noted, three ways in which reserve creation might become a burden to the countries that found themselves accepting created reserves in payment of goods and services. The first was that they might be called upon to deliver so-called vehicle currencies, or other reserves (such as gold) that could be transformed into usable currencies. The second was that countries might be called upon to make permanent transfers of real resources. The third way in which reserve creation might become a burden was that, even if there were no permanent transfers of resources, it was conceivable that a rapid expenditure of the new reserves might lead to worldwide inflation. As a result, after several years the new reserves would have lost purchasing power. The countries that had received them initially would, after a time, be transferring them in exchange for goods and services at much higher prices; in turn, countries earning reserves later on through surpluses would be achieving such surpluses at relatively inflated prices. Thus, because of the gradual loss of value of the new reserves via the inflation process, there would be a real burden involved for those countries that had earned and held reserves at an earlier time.

Mr. Larre thought of the financing problem in terms of the balance and liquidity of a scheme, that is, in terms of the arrangements needed to ensure that the scheme would not break down. How was any scheme to be made financially sound? If countries were willing to make open-ended commitments as to what they would accept as a line of credit or as reserve units, then there could be a scheme with foolproof stability and liquidity. If there were limitations on the commitments of participants, then there was a risk of illiquidity. Since countries did want some limits on their commitments to accept deliberately created reserves, clearly there was a problem as to how to make the scheme work.

Mr. Siglienti would avoid using the term burden. It was difficult not only to identify the burden of any liquidity scheme, but even to define what was meant by that term. The discussions in the Group of Ten and in the Fund had shown that the deficit countries were somewhat more eager than the surplus countries to find a solution to the liquidity problem; this had led to the notion that the debtors would find a solution for their deficits through the creation of liquidity and the creditors would bear the burden. One had to assume that there would be no excess creation of any new liquidity instrument. Otherwise, the surplus countries would have to engage, unwillingly, in a transfer of real resources. Surplus countries wanted to protect themselves. Because no acceptable objective criteria were available as to what amount of reserves to create, these countries wished to have a major influence in any decisions relating to the creation of new reserves.

Mr. O'Donnell emphasized that the pattern of surpluses and deficits was continuously changing; hence, the so-called burden was likely to be a shifting one. He also believed that, if one really wanted to tie the new reserve unit closely to gold, the straightforward way to do it would be to increase the price of gold. Indeed, raising the price of gold would obviate the need for any new reserve asset. In the absence of this simple solution, much time and attention had to be devoted to discussing ways to introduce a new reserve asset, and how to give it features that made it "as good as gold" or "like gold."

The informal discussions of the Executive Directors on the question of financing reserve creation clarified the point that the question of backing for any new reserve instrument, another question frequently coming up, basically

Meeting of 1966–68 Executive Board

involved the provisions required to liquidate any reserve-creating scheme. At the time any scheme might be ended, the new units would have to be turned in for something, that is, for whatever backing these new units had. Presumably, the countries with the strongest currencies would have to provide such backing, which was another reason why the major industrial countries believed that they needed a major voice in any decisions concerning the amount of new reserves to be created.

FIRST JOINT MEETING

The first of the four joint meetings on reserve creation between Executive Directors and the Deputies of the Group of Ten was held in Washington on November 28, 29, and 30, 1966, immediately following the informal discussions of the Executive Directors described above. In addition to the participants and observers (see Table 1, pages 134–37 below), there was a secretariat made up of two members of the Fund staff and three persons from the Group of Ten, one of the latter being a member of the Fund's Office in Europe who had been temporarily assigned to assist the Deputies.[4]

At the first joint meeting, the ground covered was much the same as that covered by the Executive Directors in their informal sessions: (1) the aims of reserve creation, especially the need for reserves and its relationship to policies for balance of payments adjustment and to the supply of conditional liquidity; (2) the nature and form of deliberately created reserves, especially the choice among (a) reserve units for all, (b) Fund drawing rights for all, and (c) reserve units for a limited group and Fund drawing rights for others; (3) the distribution of deliberately created reserves, with emphasis on the criterion to be used for distribution and the question of requiring participants to reconstitute their use of conditional drawing rights in the Fund with newly distributed reserves; (4) the utilization of new reserve assets, including conditions for the transfer of and for assuring the acceptance of these assets; and (5) the conditions and circumstances for the activation of a contingency plan.

The meeting revealed that important differences of opinion on most of these issues persisted. There was much more discussion than had been anticipated by the Executive Directors on the question of the need for reserves. At the outset of the meeting, Mr. Maurice Pérouse (France) reiterated the position that the French authorities had been taking right along. The most important requirement of the international monetary system was restoring equilibrium to the balance of payments of the reserve currency countries. Creating reserves

---

[4] The secretariats for the other three meetings were similar to that for the first meeting. Tables 1 and 2 give the names of the participants and observers at the four joint meetings, along with their titles or positions, and thus identify these persons more fully than has been done in the text. Table 1 is on pp. 134–37 below; Table 2 is at the end of Chap. 6, on pp. 162–65 below.

would not solve any basic problem because there was no immediate unsatisfied need for reserves. He referred to the view held by some that there was currently an excess supply of world reserves and that it was doubtful that a shortage would arise in the foreseeable future. Mr. Pérouse stressed that the French authorities would, accordingly, give greatest attention to what measures were being proposed to improve the machinery for balance of payments adjustment. Plans for creation of liquidity were secondary.

Mr. Cecil de Strycker (Belgium), Mr. van Lennep (Netherlands), and Mr. Ossola (Italy) took moderate positions on this point but nonetheless made it clear that the creation of an unconditional reserve asset must not undermine international monetary stability. There had to be assurance that countries would observe the rules of monetary discipline and that if they had external deficits they would adopt the necessary adjustment processes. In effect, what was under consideration was how to determine in quantitative and qualitative terms when, and in what amounts, new reserves would be created and how to define with precision the conditions that would apply to the use of new reserves.

Addressing himself to the point that Mr. Lieftinck had so often raised, that the Deputies' report had laid stress on unconditional rather than on conditional liquidity, Mr. Emminger explained that, following the increase in Fund quotas in 1965, the Deputies had considered the supply of conditional liquidity sufficient. He also pointed out many of the difficulties that would be involved in recognizing the existence of a world shortage of reserves and, therefore, the precise time when activation of a contingency plan would be needed.

Little agreement existed on the type of new reserves to be created. Significantly, Mr. Deming and Mr. J. Dewey Daane (both of the United States) and Mr. van Lennep and Mr. Kessler (both of the Netherlands) took a position that they had not taken before—in favor of reserve units for all countries. This position had been expressed previously by the Japanese, the Canadian, and the British participants in Group of Ten meetings, and they restated it in the first joint meeting. Nonetheless, many Deputies continued to think that the rules for use of any reserve unit might be differentiated between groups of countries: industrial countries might be subject to different rules than developing countries. Moreover, only what might be considered as negative progress was made concerning the criterion by which a new reserve might be distributed: that is, any alternative to the use of quotas in the Fund as a criterion did not gain much support.

There was considerable discussion about the character of any new reserve asset, that is, about how it might be made "like gold." Several suggestions were put forward to link the new unit closely with gold and traditional reserves, such as through the "harmonization of reserve ratios." This concept involved instituting procedures whereby new reserve assets would be used and held in a ratio to total reserve holdings similar for all participants. Another principle being evolved was that participants would not use their new reserves to alter the composition of their total reserve holdings. Both of these ideas were aimed at avoiding the possibility that some participants would unload their new reserves in order to switch into traditional reserve forms at the expense of other participants who would then be obliged to hold excessive amounts of the new form of reserve.

Because of these areas of difference, the first joint meeting ended with most of the basic questions still unanswered.

From the outset, however, the joint meetings were considered useful. Immediately after the first one, Mr. Handfield-Jones, for instance, noted that the participants had buried the suspicions and mistrusts which had previously existed between the Deputies of the Group of Ten and the Executive Directors and that this type of unity made negotiations possible. Mr. Anjaria commented that one of the discoveries, at least for those countries not in the Group of Ten, had been that the countries of the Group of Ten were not, by any means, a solid phalanx. Like the Executive Directors, the Deputies were struggling to find a solution that would command maximum acceptance.

Making some observations to the Executive Directors about the first joint meeting, the Economic Counsellor said that contrary to what many had antici-pated, the physical size of the meeting had not proved to be a handicap—or at least not more so than the usual separate meetings of the Executive Board or of the Deputies—and that the meeting had disproved the proposition, often expressed, that no progress could be made in the larger group so long as no agreement had been reached in a smaller one. Mr. Emminger similarly expressed his satisfaction with the meeting.

This atmosphere of friendly, informal interchange continued through the other three joint meetings.

QUESTION OF DECISION MAKING

The most difficult and sensitive question in the entire debate had not yet been discussed: How should decisions be made for the entry into force of any liquidity scheme and for the creation and recall of new reserve assets?

Fund Staff Suggests Some Voting Arrangements

By late in 1966 it had become apparent that the EEC countries were concerned that they would not have a great enough influence in the decisions that would have to be taken in the Fund affecting the supply of world liquidity. In particular, they believed that they required special voting arrangements to protect them from the possibility that participants with large payments deficits, such as the United Kingdom and the United States, might outvote them in a new reserve arrangement. At the same time, the authorities of the United Kingdom and the United States had come to a recognition of what was being referred to as a fact of life—that the Six had become economically very powerful.

These considerations lay behind a statement by the staff to the Executive Directors regarding illustrative voting provisions when the Directors explored the voting question in informal sessions in January 1967, before the second joint meeting. Each participant in an affiliate agency of the Fund would have a quota proportional to, or equal to, its quota in the Fund. That quota could serve as the basis for distributing the new reserves, for specifying the limits, if any, on the obligations to accept a transfer of new reserves from other members, and for voting.

The staff went on to suggest that a majority of 85 per cent of the voting power represented by these total quotas could reasonably be required for the entry into force of any reserve creation scheme that was decided on and a majority of 80 per cent for the actual periodic creation of reserves that would subsequently take place. The rationale of these percentages was as follows. For a liquidity plan to enter into force, significant action had to be taken, such as amending the Fund's Articles of Agreement. Hence it appeared advisable to make certain that entry into force was accepted by virtually all members. It was also desirable to ensure that most of the large countries potentially in surplus as well as a high proportion of all members of the Fund would participate in the new scheme. Therefore, for the new scheme to take effect it did not seem unreasonable to require a participation representing as much as 85 per cent of total quotas.

The figure of 80 per cent for actual reserve creation, once the scheme had entered into force, corresponded to the majority applicable to decisions to change Fund quotas that was provided in Article III, Section 2, of the existing Articles. A second factor in favor of the 80 per cent figure was that this majority would make it likely that reserve creation would have the support not only of the total number of participants but also of the majority of the large participants that had balance of payments surpluses, and that any decision to recall or cancel reserves that had previously been created would have the support not only of participants in general but also of the majority of participants in balance of payments deficit.

The staff described two techniques whereby the influence of the participants that were, at any time, creditors under the scheme could be enhanced. There could be adjusted weighted voting, similar to that in Article XII, Section 5 (b), of the existing Articles. Voting in the affiliate could be adjusted, for example, on the basis of the difference between participants' actual holdings of new reserve assets and the total they had received in distributions. Participants that had accumulated reserve assets would thus have more voice than other participants in the decision-making process. Account could be taken not only of creditor, but also of debtor, positions. The second technique by which creditors could be protected was by a provision for "opting out" from a specified distribution under the scheme. Such a right could be given to a participant which dissented from any particular decision to create reserves.

In the belief that the need for reserve creation should be reviewed at regular intervals, the staff suggested an interval of every five years. In this way, the need for reserve creation would be reviewed at the same time as the need for a general increase in Fund quotas was being reviewed.

The significance of the percentages suggested by the staff was underscored in a statement by Mr. Handfield-Jones showing how he had calculated possible alternative distributions of votes. The figures suggested by the staff meant that, under the then existing division of voting power in the Fund, the EEC, when voting as a group, would have a veto over the entry into force of a new liquidity mechanism but not over subsequent reserve creation. The voting power in the Board of Governors of the EEC countries, taken together, made up 16.8 per cent of the total on November 30, 1966. Mr. Handfield-Jones called attention to the two opposing principles that were involved in deciding what majority should be required for the approval of a proposal to create reserves. On the one hand, deliberate creation of reserves was a sufficiently serious matter to require a large measure of international agreement; unpalatable decisions should not be imposed on important groups of countries. On the other hand, one would not wish to paralyze the ability of the international community to act by giving a veto to every individual member or to an unduly small aggregate of the votes. These opposing principles left only a limited range of compromise. Mr. Handfield-Jones suspected that 80 per cent would be regarded as the minimum, and he doubted whether any figure above 85 per cent would be widely accepted, even if agreement could be reached that the 80 per cent currently required by the Fund's Articles for quota increases could be higher.

Ancillary Questions

As the Executive Directors considered the process of decision making, it was evident that, in addition to the questions concerning the size of the majorities required for the acceptance of any liquidity scheme and for subsequent reserve creation, and whether and how weighted voting should be adjusted for creditor-debtor positions, a number of other questions concerning voting techniques would have to be answered. Should there be basic votes, equivalent to the existing basic votes in the Fund of 250 votes per country? Should the distribution of votes be based on Fund quotas alone, or should commitments under the General Arrangements to Borrow also be included, as was recommended by some Executive Directors? Should there be split voting, with votes cast on a country-by-country basis, as was done when the Governors voted on quotas, or should there be bloc voting, as was done when the Executive Directors voted, casting the total votes of all the countries that elected them? Split voting would present problems for the Executive Directors who were elected by several countries. It would also give each country a possible veto over activation of the plan or over subsequent reserve creation, and it was contrary to the customary weighted voting used in the Fund's normal operations. A further question was whether, if an opting out technique was introduced, a country should lose some votes, that is, those pertaining to a particular distribution of reserve units, when it did opt out.

Arguments in Favor of High Majorities

The Executive Directors appointed or elected by the countries in the EEC argued strongly in favor of the 85 per cent majority for all decisions relating to the new reserve mechanism. Messrs. van Campenhout and Lieftinck saw no logic in requiring one majority for the acceptance of a contingency plan and another for the activation of that plan. The 85 per cent majority should apply to both. Mr. Siglienti also considered that, as the creation of a reserve asset was different from anything the Fund had previously done, a decision-making procedure closely related to the economic power of the different countries was necessary. For example, more account would have to be taken of the levels of trade and reserves and less of national income than presumably was done in calculating Fund quotas. Furthermore, he thought that a high majority for activation was preferable to at least some of the preconditions for activation that had been suggested in various discussions of that topic, and that, in general, the countries that had accumulated the new reserves should have more voice than others in the decision-making process.

Mr. Larre, again expressing France's concerns about the inflationary impact of deliberate reserve creation, explained at length why the French authorities favored a procedure for decision making that called for the unanimous agreement of all participants before reserves could be created. They believed that any authority which had the power to create money would be under tremendous pressure to do so, and to do so on an extensive scale. Specifically, once the contingency plan had been agreed, there would be great pressure to activate it—pressure from debtor countries and from developing countries. Pressure might even come from the Fund, which would then have this new means of avoiding having to seek increases in more traditional resources from possibly reluctant members. Moreover, there might be pressure from some creditor countries which feared that they might become debtors or which, taking a long view of the international situation, thought that the main threat in the world was not inflation but recession and therefore considered it better to err on the side of excessive, rather than inadequate, money creation.

Further, the French authorities believed that reserve creation in the international sphere would not be controlled by the one limit that sooner or later worked on monetary policy in the domestic sphere, namely, the balance of payments position. Consequently, there was a genuine danger of excessive reserve creation, which would have serious inflationary consequences both for the international economy and for the economies of those countries which were more susceptible to inflationary pressures.

Mr. Larre thought that the way to get around these fears and dangers was to have checks and balances in the decision-making process. Provisions for opting out could not alone give a participant sufficient assurance that the scheme would not damage its national interests because pressure to create new units which would affect that participant could clearly be generated by other participants. The only real safeguard would be to require unanimity in the decision-making process. Unanimity could be a permanent rule under the scheme or it could apply for an initial period until experience with the scheme had been gained. But there might be other ways around these difficulties. For example, because creditors were likely to feel more pressure on their economies from a liquidity scheme than from their quotas in the Fund, more weight in voting under the scheme might be given to creditor positions.

Mr. Larre's statements also reflected a French view that was beginning to evolve in favor of a scheme based on drawing rights. He said that, although any scheme for creating reserves would tend to be inflationary, a drawing rights scheme was less prone to be inflationary than a reserve unit scheme. Moreover, a scheme that included a gold-transfer ratio, that is, a scheme under which new reserves would be transferred among participants only in some ratio to the participants' holdings of gold, would not be as inflationary initially as one which did not contain this kind of limitation. Therefore, before the issue of the decision-making process could be decided, agreement had to be reached on what sort of scheme it would apply to.

Mr. O'Donnell thought that there was a case for having an 85 per cent majority for both entry into force of a contingency plan and activation of that plan, and agreed with Mr. Siglienti that a high majority for activation was preferable to at least some of the preconditions that had been suggested.

It was evident that obtaining a meeting of the minds on this issue of voting was going to be unusually difficult. Mr. Saad said several times that he would reject any voting provisions for a new Fund affiliate, or in the Fund itself, that would have the effect of endowing any group of countries with the right to veto any decision. To think in terms of an affiliate of the Fund with special provisions for voting could mean the Fund's losing its standing in the world. Furthermore, the Fund and any affiliate should not have different provisions for voting. The Fund already provided adequate safeguards for surplus countries.

Several Executive Directors, especially Messrs. Stevens, Kafka, and Nikoi, argued that the crucial element in the decision-making process was the procedure by which proposals to create reserves were to be made. The procedure suggested by the staff was that proposals to create reserves would, after appropriate consultation with participating governments, be made by the Managing Director. These three Directors hoped that consultation procedures could be worked out which would ensure that the Executive Board would have a full opportunity to concur in any proposals that might be made. Mr. O'Donnell made the point that the Managing Director ought to be careful to consult the participants that were likely to have to provide resources in the event of an increase in created reserves, although it was hard to be sure in advance which participants these would be.

SECOND JOINT MEETING

The second joint meeting of Executive Directors and the Deputies of the Group of Ten took place on January 25 and 26, 1967 in London.[5] In line with the practice of the Ministers and Governors of the Group of Ten of electing one of their number to serve as chairman, and of rotating that chairmanship, Mr. Callaghan, U.K. Chancellor of the Exchequer, was then chairman of the Group at the ministerial level. At this meeting, some of the same ground that had been covered at the first joint meeting had to be gone over again. Mr. Pérouse emphasized that, in addition to examining plans for reserve creation, the position of gold in the international monetary system and the improvement of international credit facilities ought also to be studied. Nonetheless, in order not to divert attention from developing a reserve plan, the other Deputies and the Executive Directors agreed that the agenda for the meeting should be planned so that there would first be an exchange of views on (1) the conditions and circumstances for activating a contingency plan, (2) the process of decision making, and (3) the possibility of setting up reserve units in the Fund for all countries.

The meeting showed that, although there were still marked differences on certain topics, there appeared to be a growing convergence of opinion on some features of a plan for reserve creation. There was now no dissent from the concept that, if reserve creation took the form of a reserve unit scheme, it would be operated through the Fund, possibly through an affiliate, with the Managing Director of the Fund acting as managing director of the affiliate as well. There was also general recognition that the conditions for activation of a contingency plan could not be defined exactly, either quantitatively or qualitatively. Some discussants thought that an adequate voting requirement for activation would be a sufficient safeguard against premature activation. There was also some support for the idea that the same voting majorities should be used both for activation of the scheme and for subsequent creations of reserves. General agreement appeared to exist as well on the proposition that satisfactory consultation by the Managing Director prior to making proposals for reserve creation would go far to resolve the difficulties involved in decision making.

On the other hand, there was no broad support for any particular contingency plan or for any specific decision-making process. A scheme consisting

---

[5] See Table 1 for a list of the participants (pp. 134–37 below).

of reserve units in the Fund was still considered illustrative: it was a technical topic worthy of further exploration. With regard to the decision-making process, positions were preliminary. While the idea of weighted voting, based, for example, on quotas in the Fund, met with general approval, positions differed on a suggestion by Mr. Pérouse that votes be adjusted so as to give more votes to creditors and reduce the votes of debtors. In addition, some of the Deputies from EEC countries favored the idea that a participant could choose not to receive an allocation of new units, that is, that it would be possible for a participant to opt out of any distribution decided upon.

AFTERMATH OF FIRST AND SECOND JOINT MEETINGS

The differences of opinion prevailing after these two joint meetings seemed, to the Executive Directors, to revolve mainly around the question whether a plan to create liquidity should be based on reserve units or on drawing rights. Some of the European Directors, especially Mr. Larre, began to express the view that reserve units were, in effect, more like new money or reserves, whereas drawing rights were more analogous to credit, and they tended to favor the latter. Mr. Larre's position was in line with the resolution that had been adopted by the Finance Ministers of the EEC, meeting in The Hague in January 1967. In a development which Mr. Larre called the most important of the early weeks of 1967, the Ministers had agreed among themselves that the Monetary Committee of the EEC should, immediately, undertake a thorough exploration of the "credit facilities" that could be obtained within the framework of the Fund.

Hence, Mr. Larre requested that the staff consider more carefully the possibilities of schemes based on the Fund's traditional methods. Noting that Messrs. Lieftinck and van Campenhout had some time earlier suggested that liquidity creation might be tied to increases in Fund quotas or to a broadening of the automaticity of gold tranche drawings, Mr. Larre asked why the staff had not considered techniques of this type. Had not the Fund, fearful of being overtaken by the Group of Ten, rushed into the study of a new reserve unit without giving equal consideration to the facilities that could be provided within the framework of its own organization? Mr. Lieftinck, discerning what he believed was an increasingly favorable disposition among the countries of the Group of Ten to a drawing rights scheme, likewise requested that the staff examine not only how a reserve unit scheme based in the Fund might work but also how a drawing rights scheme could be devised.

PLANS REDRAFTED

Two detailed plans for creation of liquidity, "Outline of an Illustrative Reserve Unit Scheme" and "Outline of an Illustrative Scheme for a Special

Reserve Facility Based on Drawing Rights in the Fund," were prepared by the staff and circulated to the Executive Directors in February 1967.[6] A further paper compared the corresponding provisions of the two illustrative schemes. Both schemes were built on the Managing Director's proposals of March 1966, which in turn had been based on schemes drafted earlier. Several elaborations had been worked out in order to show how a fully developed scheme would look. The reserve unit scheme, which involved an International Reserve Organization as an affiliate of the Fund, contained illustrative details as to how decisions on the amount and timing of reserve units to be created and distributed would be taken. A mechanism for transferring reserve units among the members of the organization was suggested.

The illustrative drawing rights scheme, as now drafted, represented an attempt to have a scheme comparable in most respects to the illustrative reserve unit scheme. It differed significantly from the Managing Director's Plan I of March 1966. Plan I had involved an extension into the credit tranches of the quasi-automatic drawing rights that members already enjoyed in the gold tranche. A member would have been able to exercise those rights after it had used its gold tranche and at whatever point it chose until it had exhausted its rights in the credit tranches. No amendment of the Articles of Agreement was involved. In the illustrative drawing rights scheme of February 1967, however, "special drawing rights," a term now being used in the plans being drafted in the Fund, were to be established, which a member could use at any time regardless of that member's gold and credit tranche positions. These special drawing rights could be thought of as having a completely floating character, that is, they could be used quite independently of the Fund's usual drawing rights. They could constitute a separate account within the Fund. Like the reserve unit scheme, the drawing rights scheme now entailed amendment of the Articles.

Executive Directors' Consideration of Illustrative Schemes

In the next few weeks, the Executive Directors held numerous informal sessions to consider these illustrative schemes. Mr. Larre wanted to discuss only the drawing rights scheme. But many Directors preferred the reserve unit scheme; these included Mr. Dale, Mr. Handfield-Jones, Mr. B. K. Madan (India), Mr. Hideo Suzuki (Japan), and Mr. Douglas W. G. Wass (United Kingdom, Alternate to Mr. Stevens). Some of their reasons were new, others had been mentioned before. Reserve units seemed to have more the quality of international legal tender; they looked more credible as a supplement to, or substitute for, gold. Drawing rights might be construed as a right to borrow or as a simple extension of the existing Fund credit facilities and therefore could not compete with reserve units in being accepted as a new asset. Reserve units could be used

---

[6] Published below in Vol. II, pp. 15–23 and 24–29.

directly in transactions between monetary authorities, their transfer not being dependent upon an intermediary agent or upon some method for guiding the transfer. A system of reserve units for unconditional liquidity would be separate from the operation of the Fund system for conditional liquidity, thus providing a clear-cut distinction between conditional and unconditional liquidity.

Because he wanted the reserve units to be as much as possible like legal tender, Mr. Handfield-Jones had difficulties with the transfer arrangements which the staff had proposed for the reserve unit scheme. As he understood it, there was envisaged a system of guided transfers in which one country would transfer units to another country on the advice of the Fund affiliate. Presumably, in giving its advice, this affiliate would draw on the long experience that the Fund had had with the operation of the policy on selection of currencies already governing the Fund's ordinary drawings. One could not know how such a system would work in practice, however, or whether the Fund's existing policy on selection of currencies was strong enough to bear the heavy additional burden of serving as a guide to the transfer of a deliberately created international reserve unit. More importantly, by recourse to the principle of guided transfer the opportunity would be missed of endowing the reserve unit with a truly monetary quality. In a drawing rights scheme there must inevitably be guidance, but in a unit scheme there could be something much closer to free transfer and to the quality of legal tender.

Mr. Handfield-Jones therefore circulated his own memorandum suggesting alternative transfer arrangements for a reserve unit scheme. He proposed in effect a flexible version of the concept of linking holdings of the new units to holdings of gold. In the absence of a voluntary transfer arrangement between participants, transfers would be made in such a way that the ratios between the gold holdings and the reserve unit holdings of two participants would tend to be equalized. But, normally, reserve units and gold would be transferred voluntarily.

Other Executive Directors did not favor this proposed link. Mr. van Campenhout repeated his preference for a drawing rights scheme. Several Executive Directors expressed no strong preference for either scheme; these included Mr. Torben Friis (Denmark), Mr. Kafka, Mr. Saad, and Mr. Siglienti.

A number of technical points were discussed during the Executive Directors' informal sessions. The extent to which the Fund as agent would direct transfers between participants, that is, "guide" transfers, was a point on which there were differences of opinion. On the one hand, the Executive Directors for the United Kingdom, Italy, and the Nordic countries wanted a minimum of guidance and of rules of transfer so as to improve the reserve nature of the new asset. On the other hand, the staff argued that guidance and transfer rules of some kind were necessary in practice to ensure the workability of the new asset. A number of criteria were suggested for transfers, but the staff argued that it was simplest to decide upon transfer practices that were similar to those which the Fund had built up over the years for its policies on regular drawings.

Deputies Discuss Illustrative Schemes

From March 30 to April 1, 1967, a few weeks before the third joint meeting with Executive Directors was scheduled to take place, the Deputies of the Group of Ten met in The Hague, also to discuss these two illustrative schemes. A number of Deputies from EEC countries that had previously indicated a preference for reserve units put forward suggestions for drawing rights of a type that closely resembled reserve units in many of their formal characteristics—a similarity already found in the Fund's illustrative scheme for drawing rights. For example, the new drawing rights would be operated through a special account in the Fund, that is, they would be financed by techniques that separated them from the general resources of the Fund. They would be directly transferable between participants according to rules of use and transfer rather than being transferable via an exchange of currencies through the Fund.. These suggestions were received with interest, but without immediate acceptance, both by other Deputies of the Group of Ten who still preferred reserve units and by Deputies from those EEC countries that continued to favor drawing rights.

ATTEMPTS TO GAIN MOMENTUM

In March and April 1967, a strong push was made within the Fund and by the United States finally to get agreement on a contingency plan for reserve creation. Moreover, the EEC countries seemed to be coming around to agreement on a plan.

In the Fund

As the Deputies of the Group of Ten and the Executive Directors determined their positions on these questions and schemes in the early months of 1967, the Managing Director and Mr. Emminger consulted frequently on the agenda of the forthcoming joint meetings and exchanged information about the thinking of their groups. Meanwhile, as both groups discussed extensively the two illustrative schemes that had been prepared by the Fund staff, the records of several of the informal sessions of the Executive Directors were made available to the Deputies of the Group of Ten and the minutes of some of the meetings of the Deputies were made available to the Executive Directors. The evolution of the thinking of each group was thus familiar to the other.

In order to facilitate agreement on a plan, the General Counsel and the Economic Counsellor in March 1967 suggested to the Managing Director a procedure aimed at a resolution for adoption by the Board of Governors, which was to meet in Rio de Janeiro in September. Such a resolution would instruct the Executive Directors to prepare, in a reasonably short time, a concrete proposal in legal form for member governments to adopt. To get such a resolution ready in time, negotiations on a text would have to be started as soon as possible after the fourth joint meeting of Executive Directors and Deputies, scheduled for Paris in June 1967.

The staff thought that the greatest step forward in this process would be to have a choice made between the two illustrative schemes. It appeared that the scheme for drawing rights had a better chance than that for reserve units of being accepted by the EEC, and hence by the other countries in the Group of Ten. If agreement could be reached on an outline for one particular plan before the third joint meeting, to be held in Washington at the end of April 1967, attention could then be devoted to specific features of that plan. Further changes could be made at the fourth joint meeting. The revised plan could then be submitted to the Governors; precise drafting would be reserved until after the Annual Meeting.

Strong U.S. Statement

Addressing the American Bankers Association at Pebble Beach, California, on March 17, 1967, nearly two years after he had suggested an international monetary conference,[7] the Secretary of the U.S. Treasury, Mr. Fowler, gave what was regarded by many monetary officials as a tough speech. He was worried about the recession in the world economy and about the slowing down in the growth of world reserves, and he urged immediate agreement on a meaningful liquidity plan so that it could be presented to the Board of Governors in September. The speech was considered tough because, to many, it implied that, in the absence of agreement, the U.S. authorities might take unilateral action, possibly suspending conversion into gold of official dollar balances held abroad. At the time some officials were also concerned that the United States might arrange some kind of "dollar bloc," that is, enter into bilateral agreements with countries holding large amounts of dollar balances that had not been converting their dollars into gold.

EEC Works Toward a Common Position

The third significant event of March–April 1967 was that the EEC countries also seemed to be arriving at a common position. It has already been noted that in January 1967 the Monetary Committee of the EEC was assigned the task of studying the possibility of expanding liquidity through the credit facilities of the Fund. In February the French authorities formed a position that combined a possible unified EEC position on such credit facilities with a number of suggestions for changes in the existing practices of the Fund. These suggestions involved an increase in the voting power of the EEC countries in the Fund through selective increases in the quotas assigned to them and a suggestion that the rules governing voting power in the Fund be changed so as to give more

---

[7] See Chap. 3, p. 63 above.

votes to members with creditor positions in the Fund and fewer votes to members with debtor positions.

The French suggestions involved, as well, some changes for the role of gold in the Fund. The dollar, defined in the Articles in terms of the weight of fine gold as of a certain date, would no longer be used to express par values or used as the Fund's unit of account; instead, some unit defined in terms of a given weight of fine gold would be used. Gold tranche drawings would be made a matter of legal right under the Articles, rather than by Executive Board decision, a suggestion that had already been made several times by the Belgian authorities. The power of the Fund to waive the gold-value guarantee of its assets in case of a uniform proportionate devaluation of member currencies should be abolished. Further suggestions were made so as to strengthen the discipline the Fund applied to countries in deficit. The Fund should emphasize the conditional and temporary character of its financial assistance.

Most of these suggestions for changes in the Fund's practices involved amending the Articles.

By early in April 1967, the six countries of the EEC had not reached agreement either on the plan they would accept or on the conditions they would attach to their willingness to move on any plan. But it was thought that the French authorities might finally agree at the ministerial level to a plan to create unconditional liquidity. They might agree because it appeared that the French authorities were aware that their position—against any reserve plan—ran the risk that other countries would agree on a plan even if France abstained. The alternative suggestions made by France had not found support. The U.S. authorities had not accepted the ideas that the French authorities had proposed for changing the General Arrangements to Borrow as a way to expand international liquidity, and most of the European countries were also against increasing quotas in the Fund until the next quinquennial review.

Meeting in Munich on April 17, 1967, the Finance Ministers of the six countries of the EEC approved the recommendations that had been made by the Monetary Committee of the EEC.[8] That committee had proposed that there be opened in the Fund new automatic drawing rights, with both accounting and financing separated from other drawing rights in the Fund, which would be usable in accordance with well-defined rules drawn up in advance and directly transferable between the monetary authorities of the member countries. Furthermore, when the Fund's Articles of Agreement were amended to include such new drawing rights, other amendments should be made. Many of these amendments were along the lines of the earlier French suggestions. Conditions

---

[8] Robert Henrion, Minister of Finance, Belgium; Michel Debré, Minister of Economy and Finance, France; J. Schoellhorn, Secretary of State, and Franz Josef Strauss, Minister of Finance, Federal Republic of Germany; Emilio Colombo, Minister of the Treasury, and Athos Valeschi, Secretary of State, Italy; Pierre Werner, President of the Government and Minister of Finance, Luxembourg; and H. Johannes Witteveen, Deputy Prime Minister and Minister of Finance, Netherlands.

attached to drawing rights in the credit tranches should be tightened. The definition of par values and of the Fund's unit of account should be simplified by retaining only the reference to a weight of fine gold. An 85 per cent voting majority should be required for various decisions in the Fund, particularly those for general changes in quotas and for the creation of additional reserves, and this majority ought to include at least half the major creditor countries.

In their communiqué, the Finance Ministers indicated that, because of the economic strength of their six countries and their union in the EEC, they must, in any event, be assured of a proper influence in the Fund, particularly in respect of voting. Accordingly, they supported the idea that new automatic drawing rights, separate from the Fund's traditional operations, could be established.

■　■　■　■　■　■

The kernel of a contingency plan for reserve creation was at last forming. Nonetheless, it was apparent that negotiation of the precise features of such a plan was not going to be easy.

Table 1. Participants and Observers at First and Second
Joint Meetings of Executive Directors of Fund
and Deputies of Group of Ten, 1966–67 [1]

INTERNATIONAL MONETARY FUND

Management
Pierre-Paul Schweitzer, Managing Director (1,2)
Frank A. Southard, Jr., Deputy Managing Director (1)

Executive Directors and Alternates [2]	**Constituency** [3]
J.J. Anjaria (1,2) *Arun K. Banerji (1,2)*	India
William B. Dale (1,2) *John S. Hooker (1,2)*	United States
Adolfo C. Diz (1) *Yamandú S. Patrón (2)*	Argentina, Bolivia, Chile, Ecuador, Paraguay, Uruguay
Paul L. Faber (1,2)	Burundi, Guinea, Kenya, Liberia, Malawi, Mali, Nigeria, Sierra Leone, Sudan, Tanzania, Trinidad and Tobago, Uganda, Zambia
Torben Friis (1,2) *Jorma Aranko (1,2)*	Denmark, Finland, Iceland, Norway, Sweden
Jorge González del Valle (1,2) *Alfredo Phillips O. (1,2)*	Costa Rica, El Salvador, Guatemala, Honduras, Mexico, Nicaragua, Venezuela
S.J. Handfield-Jones (1,2) *Patrick M. Reid (1,2)*	Canada, Guyana, Ireland, Jamaica
Alexandre Kafka (1) *Paulo H. Pereira Lira (1,2)*	Brazil, Colombia, Dominican Republic, Haiti, Panama, Peru
René Larre (1,2) *Gérard M. Teyssier (1,2)*	France
Pieter Lieftinck (1,2) *H.M.H.A. van der Valk (1,2)*	Cyprus, Israel, Netherlands, Yugoslavia
Amon Nikoi (1,2)	Algeria, Ghana, Laos, Libyan Arab Republic, Malaysia, Morocco, Singapore, Tunisia
M.W. O'Donnell (1,2) *A.M. de Villiers (1,2)* *J.O. Stone (2)* [4]	Australia, New Zealand, South Africa
Sergio Siglienti (1,2) *Costa P. Caranicas (1,2)*	Greece, Italy, Portugal, Spain
J.M. Stevens (1,2) *Douglas W. G. Wass (1,2)*	United Kingdom
Hideo Suzuki (1,2) *Eiji Ozaki (1,2)*	Burma, Ceylon, Japan, Nepal, Thailand
Beue Tann (1) *Chi-Ling Chow (1,2)*	Republic of China, Korea, Viet-Nam
André van Campenhout (1,2) *Herman Biron (1,2)*	Austria, Belgium, Luxembourg, Turkey

Table 1 (*continued*). Participants and Observers at First and
Second Joint Meetings of Executive Directors of Fund
and Deputies of Group of Ten, 1966–67 [1]

Executive Directors and Alternates [2]

Ernst vom Hofe (1,2)
Horst Ungerer (1,2)

Antoine W. Yaméogo (1,2)
Léon M. Rajaobelina (1,2)

Constituency [3]

Federal Republic of Germany

Cameroon, Central African
Republic, Chad, Dahomey,
Gabon, Ivory Coast, Malagasy
Republic, Mauritania, Niger,
People's Republic of the Congo,
Rwanda, Senegal, Togo, Upper
Volta, Zaïre

Staff [5]

Joseph Gold, The General Counsel (1,2)
J.J. Polak, The Economic Counsellor (1,2)
Roman L. Horne, Secretary of the Fund (1)
W. Lawrence Hebbard, Secretary of the Fund (2)
Jean-Paul Sallé, Director, Office in Europe (1,2)
J. Marcus Fleming, Deputy Director, Research
   and Statistics Department (1,2)
George Nicoletopoulos, Deputy General Counsel (1,2)

GROUP OF TEN

Deputies

Alternates

BELGIUM

Cecil de Strycker, Director,
National Bank of Belgium (1,2)

Marcel D'Haeze, Director of the
Treasury and Public Debt, Ministry
of Finance (1,2)

*Jacques Mertens de Wilmars, Adviser
to the Board, National Bank of
Belgium (1,2)*

*R. van der Branden, Belgian
Financial Adviser to Organization for
Economic Cooperation and
Development (2)*

CANADA

A.B. Hockin, Assistant Deputy
Minister of Finance, Department
of Finance (1,2)

R.W. Lawson, Deputy Governor,
Bank of Canada (1,2)

*W.A. Kennett, Adviser, Department
of Finance (1,2)*

*W.C. Hood, Adviser, Bank of Canada
(1,2)*

FRANCE

Maurice Pérouse, Director of
Treasury, Ministry of Economy
and Finance (1,2)

Pierre Esteva, Secretary General,
National Council of Credit (1)

B. Clappier, Deputy Governor,
Bank of France (2)

*Pierre Esteva, Secretary General,
National Council of Credit (2)*

*Daniel Deguen, Assistant Director
of Treasury, Ministry of Economy
and Finance (1,2)*

135

Table 1 (*continued*). Participants and Observers at First and
Second Joint Meetings of Executive Directors of Fund
and Deputies of Group of Ten, 1966–67 [1]

Deputies   *Alternates*

FEDERAL REPUBLIC OF GERMANY

Otmar Emminger, Member, Board of   *Wolfgang Rieke, Division Chief,*
Directors, Deutsche Bundesbank (1,2)   *Deutsche Bundesbank (1,2)*
Rolf Gocht, Assistant Secretary,   *Lore Fuenfgelt, Division Chief,*
Ministry of Economic Affairs (1,2)   *Ministry of Economic Affairs (1,2)*

ITALY

                                               Silvano Montanaro, International
Rinaldo Ossola, Director of the   *Economics Research Department,*
International Economics Research   *Bank of Italy (1)*
Department, Bank of Italy (1,2)   *L. Fronzoni, Representative in*
                                               Brussels, Bank of Italy (2)
                                               Florio Gradi, Representative in
Giorgio Rota, Chief Inspector,   *United States, Italian Exchange Office (1)*
Ministry of the Treasury (1,2)   *E. Valle, Representative in Paris,*
                                               Bank of Italy (2)

JAPAN

Yusuke Kashiwagi, Director,   *Keijiro Tanaka, Chief, International*
International Finance Bureau,   *Organizations Section, International*
Ministry of Finance (1,2)   *Finance Bureau, Ministry of Finance*
                                               (1,2)
Haruo Mayekawa, Executive   *Daizo Hoshino, Adviser, Bank of Japan*
Director, Bank of Japan (1,2)   *(1,2)*

NETHERLANDS

E. van Lennep, Treasurer General,   *D.M.N. van Wensveen, Head, Inter-*
Ministry of Finance (1,2)   *national Monetary Affairs Department,*
                                               Ministry of Finance (1,2)
G.A. Kessler, Managing Director,   *Baron A.W.R. MacKay, Deputy Director,*
Netherlands Bank (1,2)   *Netherlands Bank (1,2)*

SWEDEN

Sven F. Joge, Deputy Governor,   *A. Lindå, Head of Division,*
Sveriges Riksbank (1,2)   *Sveriges Riksbank (1,2)*
                                               L. Klackenberg, Counsellor,
                                               Ministry of Finance (2)

UNITED KINGDOM

Sir Denis Rickett,   *D.F. Hubback, H.M. Treasury (1)*
Second Secretary of the Treasury   *L.P. Thompson-McCausland,*
(1,2)   *H.M. Treasury (2)*
C.J. Morse, Executive Director,   *C.W. McMahon, Adviser to the*
Bank of England (1,2)   *Governors, Bank of England (1,2)*

Table 1 *(concluded)*. Participants and Observers at First and Second Joint Meetings of Executive Directors of Fund and Deputies of Group of Ten, 1966–67 [1]

Deputies	***Alternates***
	UNITED STATES
Frederick L. Deming, Under Secretary of the Treasury for Monetary Affairs (1,2)	*George H. Willis, Deputy to the Assistant Secretary for International Monetary Affairs (1,2)*
J. Dewey Daane, Member, Board of Governors of the Federal Reserve System (1,2)	*Robert Solomon, Adviser to Board of Governors of the Federal Reserve System (1,2)*

Observers	***Alternates***
M. Iklé, Managing Director, Swiss National Bank (1,2)	*J. Lademann, Director, Swiss National Bank (1,2)*
Jean Cottier, Deputy Secretary General, Organization for Economic Cooperation and Development (1,2)	*S. Marris, Organization for Economic Cooperation and Development (1,2)*
Milton Gilbert, Economic Adviser, Bank for International Settlements (1,2)	

[1] First meeting, November 28–30, 1966, Washington; second meeting, January 25–26, 1967, London. The numbers in parentheses indicate which of the two meetings the individual attended.

[2] Alternate Executive Directors, always appointed by the Executive Director, are indicated by italic type.

[3] Only 19 of the 20 constituencies that appointed or elected Executive Directors were represented at the joint meetings because neither Mr. Ahmed Zaki Saad (Egypt) nor his Alternate, Mr. Albert Mansour (Egypt), attended. See also Chap. 30, p. 626.

[4] Mr. Stone was Executive Director elect when he attended the second meeting.

[5] Not including two persons who served as members of the secretariat.

CHAPTER
6

SDRs Take Shape
(April 16–September 30, 1967)

*O*NCE THE EEC COUNTRIES HAD DECIDED that new arrangements
for the creation of liquidity in the Fund might be established if a number
of changes were made in the Fund's policies governing its regular resources and
if a sufficiently large majority of the voting power in the Board of Governors
was required for actual reserve creation, a compromise began to emerge. Many
more meetings were held and tentative outlines drafted, however, before the
precise characteristics of the new arrangements were determined. Preferences
for certain features of these arrangements gradually became clear; the arrangements should be based on new automatic drawing rights rather than on reserve
units; a facility should be set up with resources separate from the Fund's
traditional drawing rights; and no backing in the sense of a pool of currencies
would be needed if the obligations of participants in the facility to accept the
new drawing rights were specified. New tentative outlines were drafted in the
Fund. Yet many questions remained unanswered, in particular the question of
the size of the voting majority to be required for approval of the actual creation
of new drawing rights and the question of the rules that would apply to
reconstitution of the drawing rights after participants had received and used
them. At one meeting in July and another in August of 1967, the Finance
Ministers and Central Bank Governors of the countries of the Group of Ten
provided the answers. The Executive Directors then worked out and approved
for submission to the Board of Governors a final Outline, and this was adopted
by the Board of Governors at their Annual Meeting in Rio de Janeiro in
September.

Among the factors that helped to foster agreement on a final Outline was
the growing concern about developments in world reserves.[1] These developments were, at least in part, responsible for the heightened eagerness of the
U.S. authorities for a liquidity plan. The Fund, too, regarded the changes taking
place in the level and composition of world reserves as indicative both of the

---

[1] The reader is reminded that the term world reserves as used by the Fund meant
the reserves of its members plus Switzerland.

need for a plan to supplement world reserves and of the form that a new reserve might take. The Fund, therefore, devoted an entire chapter to the subject of reserves in the Annual Report for 1967.[2] A brief recounting of what was occurring with respect to reserves is thus important background to the discussions described later in this chapter.

DEVELOPMENTS IN WORLD RESERVES

We have already noted in Chapter 4 that the rate of growth of world reserves slowed down in both 1965 and 1966. In the 12 months to the end of March 1967 the reserves of the industrial countries, taken as a group, actually declined. During the next 12 months, ended March 1968, this decline was to extend to the total of world reserves. Moreover, not only were there actual declines in world reserves, but there were also significant changes in their composition. Gold continued to be the largest component, constituting $40.9 billion, or about 57 per cent of the total of $71.5 billion at the end of 1966. But for many years this percentage had been falling, mainly because of the reduced weight in total world reserves of the United States, which held a particularly high proportion of its reserves in gold. Furthermore, additions to the supply of gold held by national monetary authorities were becoming smaller. Between 1948 and 1964 the gold added to official monetary reserves had averaged annually about 1.4 per cent of existing gold reserves. After 1964 these additions ceased, and by December 1966 the gold holdings of national monetary authorities were no higher than they had been two years before.

In 1966, for the first time since just after World War I, gold actually started to flow out of some official stocks. Private demand for gold for hoarding, manufacture of jewelry, and industrial use was very much on the increase and, indeed, in anticipation of a price rise, hoarding of gold was to become intense late in 1967 and early in 1968.[3] By the end of March 1968 the gold holdings of national monetary authorities, at $37.8 billion, were lower than at any time in more than a decade.

Foreign exchange holdings at the end of 1966, at $24.3 billion, made up 34 per cent of world reserves. But in the three years 1964–66, allowing for the effect of special financing transactions, growth in this component of reserves had also shown signs of coming to a halt. From the late 1930s until about the end of 1964, foreign exchange had constituted the most rapidly growing form of world reserves in absolute amounts, and usually in percentage terms as well. After the end of World War II virtually the whole increase had been in the form of liquid claims on the United States. In 1951 holdings of dollars in official reserves, at $4.2 billion, had still been only about half the size of official holdings of sterling. Throughout the postwar period, sterling holdings had

---

[2] *Annual Report, 1967*, Chap. 2 (pp. 11–25).

[3] Chap. 20 below recounts developments in gold markets.

remained roughly stable, while official dollar holdings had increased steadily. By 1962, therefore, official dollar holdings were about twice as large as official sterling holdings. Official reserves held in other currencies, mostly French francs, were much smaller.

After 1964 official holdings of foreign exchange had been dominated by special influences and had moved rather erratically, partly in connection with drawings on credits from central banks; these transactions had somewhat blurred the distinction between the different currency components of foreign exchange reserves and involved large shifts in foreign exchange holdings between countries. On balance, in 1965 and 1966 there had been a substantially slower accumulation of foreign exchange reserves than in prior periods.

In contrast to the declines in reserves held in the traditional forms of gold and foreign exchange, reserve positions in the Fund had risen by exceptional amounts. Following the quota increases agreed in 1965, some 70 per cent of the growth in total world reserves in the two years 1965–66 had been accounted for by positions in the Fund; reserves in this form had risen by $2.2 billion, to $6.3 billion.

To the Fund, these developments suggested that members were making important changes in their reserve policies. Countries that were reserve centers had become eager to avoid weakening their liquidity positions. Faced with payments deficits, the United Kingdom and the United States preferred to obtain credit, either through swap facilities or from the Fund, and to incur repayment obligations, rather than to draw down their gold and exchange reserves or further enlarge their liquid liabilities.

A noteworthy decrease in official gold movements was also evidence that the role of gold in the international monetary system was changing. Reserve centers needing to finance reserve losses and payments deficits were making settlements insofar as possible in forms other than gold. A number of large countries with payments surpluses had received gold for only a very small part of their monetary surpluses and for a still smaller part of their basic payments surpluses. The degree to which members financed deficits and surpluses in forms other than gold bore little relation to the average ratios of gold in their reserves. This suggested some lessening of the influence of traditional reserve policies on the composition of members' reserves. In effect, in the interest of joint responsibility for the working of the international monetary system, countries seemed to have imposed upon themselves some restraint in the accumulation of gold reserves.

These movements in reserves and shifts in policies influenced the thinking of monetary officials in 1967 both about the need for new reserves and about the type of new reserve that would be acceptable. It seemed probable that, in the absence of international action, not much further increase in the stock of world reserves could be expected. Although there might be some disagreement among officials as to the seriousness of such a situation in the short run, it was hard to conceive that, in the long run, a constant reserve supply could meet the needs of a rapidly expanding world economy. Moreover, data showing that reserves in the form of positions in the Fund were growing very fast helped to demonstrate the point, made repeatedly in the Annual Reports, in the speeches of the Managing Director, and by his representatives at international discussions, that reserve positions in the Fund were genuine reserves.

THIRD JOINT MEETING

The Need for Reserves

These developments, however, did not by any means produce ready agreement that a reserve plan was urgent. French monetary officials continued to be concerned lest any contingency plan agreed upon should be activated forthwith. The external position of the United Kingdom had deteriorated in 1966, amid circumstances that worsened in 1967 and were to culminate in a devaluation of the pound by the end of the year.[4] Similarly, by the end of 1966 the U.S. balance of payments had again deteriorated and was in a precarious position. Although the capital balance had improved, military expenditures associated with the hostilities in Viet-Nam had accelerated and imports were increasing rapidly. The current account surplus had thus fallen to its lowest level since 1960.

Consequently, while the main focus of the third joint meeting of Executive Directors and Deputies of the Group of Ten, which was held in Washington on April 24–26, 1967, was to be the two illustrative schemes for reserve creation that had been prepared in the Fund, the French Deputies wanted to discuss again how the actual need for reserve creation was to be determined.[5] The U.S. Deputies had circulated a paper (dated April 13, 1967 and entitled "The Need for Reserves") that contained a number of suggestions for measuring the global need for reserves. But Mr. Pérouse did not regard any quantification as appropriate, and doubted the validity even of qualitative criteria. Instead, he reiterated, it was essential for countries that had been in chronic deficit to restore equilibrium to their balances of payments. Several Executive Directors—Mr. González del Valle, Mr. Diz, Mr. Handfield-Jones, and Mr. J. O. Stone (Australia)— found the U.S. techniques helpful, explaining that some quantitative determination of the need for reserves was going to be necessary to supplement qualitative criteria. Mr. Madan stated that he deduced from their previous reports that both the Deputies and the Executive Directors could recognize the symptoms of economic disorder that would be the prelude to decisions to create reserves: trends toward restrictions on international trade and payments; recourse to domestic policies that were inimical to growth and employment; excessive

---

[4] The 1967 devaluation of sterling is the subject of Chap. 21 below.

[5] Table 2 lists the names and positions of the participants in the third joint meeting; see pp. 162–65 below.

141

amounts of speculative capital movements. The difficulties of assessing these symptoms should not be exaggerated. As for the improvement of the adjustment process, in Mr. Madan's view, this was a long-term structural matter that encompassed more than the management of its balance of payments by a single country. National economic policies might have to be coordinated, and countries with payments surpluses, as well as those with deficits, might have to take measures to smooth the necessary readjustments.

The Managing Director recommended that not too much time be devoted to considering the precise urgency of the need for reserves; it was better, he said, to determine the general criteria for reserve creation that were to be written into the contingency plan. Following Mr. Schweitzer's intervention, the two illustrative schemes that had been prepared in the Fund were taken up.[6]

Features of a Plan

Instead of considering one illustrative scheme at a time, the Executive Directors and the Deputies discussed the elements common to both schemes:

(1) the rules that would apply to the creation and distribution of any new reserve, whether a drawing right or a reserve unit;

(2) the provisions that would govern the use and transfer of either drawing rights or reserve units;

(3) the financial resources that would "back" either scheme including, in the case of the drawing rights scheme, the question whether the resources would be merged with other resources of the Fund or would be separate;

(4) what kind of reconstitution or repayment process, if any, ought to be instituted; and

(5) what decision-making process ought to be written into the plan.

No consensus was reached on any of these points. Although some progress was made regarding the transfer and use of any new reserve, differences persisted on many of the most important elements of any scheme, including the form of any new reserve. Some Deputies and Executive Directors, those, for example, from Canada, the United Kingdom, and the United States, remained very much in favor of reserve units; others, mainly from the EEC countries, would agree only to drawing rights.

In all the main areas, agreement remained elusive. Specifically the issues that were still undecided were (1) the entry into force of any scheme and the way decisions would be taken, especially decisions to activate the scheme, that is, actually to create new reserves; (2) the use, transfer, and acceptability of the new reserves, including how they could be used, how they could be trans-

---

[6] "Outline of an Illustrative Reserve Unit Scheme" (February 23, 1967), and "Outline of an Illustrative Scheme for a Special Reserve Facility Based on Drawing Rights in the Fund" (February 28, 1967); Vol. II below, pp. 15–23 and 24–29.

ferred—either directly or indirectly—and with what obligations to accept and to hold them; (3) the nature of the resources backing these schemes and, in the case of the drawing rights scheme, whether the resources would be merged with other resources of the Fund or whether they would be segregated; and (4) whether there would be any reconstitution or repurchase provisions linked with the prolonged or extensive use of these assets.

All of these areas involved the basic characteristics of any new drawing rights or reserve units. Among the Deputies, Mr. Deming and Mr. Sven F. Joge (Sweden) went so far during the meeting as to wonder whether efforts to design a truly evolutionary contingency plan should be temporarily abandoned.

On the other hand, as the Executive Directors observed in an informal session two weeks later, there had been some worthwhile achievements at the meeting. The role of the Fund in whatever arrangement was agreed was no longer in doubt. The need for some supplement to reserves of an unconditional type in the international monetary system was generally acknowledged—the term *reserve asset* now being used fairly generally in the discussions to refer either to reserve units or to drawing rights. And the principle of universality— that all members of the Fund would participate in whatever distribution of reserve assets was made—had been accepted.

DECISION TO DRAFT A TENTATIVE OUTLINE

To facilitate agreement on the issues still outstanding after the third joint meeting, the Fund staff prepared technical papers on particular topics: the use and transfer of reserve assets, the choice between merged and separate resources in the Fund for a new reserve facility, and illustrative examples of voting provisions in reserve asset schemes.

Simultaneously, the U.S. authorities, in an effort to pull together the results agreed upon so far, submitted two papers to the Group of Ten: "Outline of a Drawing Unit Reserve Asset (Dura) Plan" and "Revision of the Fund Illustrative Reserve Unit Scheme." The first of these papers advocated that there be established a new instrument, called a "drawing unit reserve asset." This term yielded the acronym *dura*, something like the bancor and unitas that had been advocated more than twenty years before by the Fund's founders.[7] As an offset to the EEC proposal that an 85 per cent voting majority plus the agreement of most creditor countries be required to activate any plan or subsequently to create reserves under that plan, the United States put forward what was called the "band" proposal, that is, a voting majority of between 75 per cent and 90 per cent would be required, the lower percentage applying to the smallest amounts of reserve creation and the higher percentage to the largest amounts.

---

[7] See *History, 1945–65*, Vol. I, pp. 18 and 36.

Late in May 1967, several Executive Directors, fearing that the Group of Ten might go on indefinitely considering and reconsidering alternative features of a plan and aware that the Deputies were not resolving their differences very quickly, suggested that the staff draft an outline of a scheme for the fourth joint meeting. Such an outline would not be rigid on any matters on which the discussions of the Deputies of the Group of Ten revealed that country delegations continued to hold contrasting positions. Alternative formulations of certain provisions would be necessary, and some blanks would be left to be filled in later. An outline of this type, although incomplete, would nonetheless give the officials concerned a document that would highlight the points on which they could agree and those on which they differed. Delegations to the fourth joint meeting could indicate what changes they wanted and an amended version could then be presented to the Board of Governors at the Annual Meeting in Rio de Janeiro in September.

Although a few Executive Directors, notably Mr. Larre, preferred that an exhaustive and substantive discussion of the vital questions still to be resolved precede attempts by the staff to draft such an outline, it was agreed that the staff should go ahead.

Convergence of Drawing Rights and Reserve Units

At the end of May 1967, Mr. Schweitzer wrote to Mr. Emminger informing him of the decision to draft an outline and enclosed a copy of the outline that was then being circulated to the Executive Board: "An Outline of a Reserve Facility Based on Drawing Rights in the Fund," dated May 29, 1967. Since this outline described only a facility based on drawing rights, a companion paper describing a facility based on reserve units was circulated about a week later: "An Outline of a Reserve Facility Based on Reserve Units and Administered by a Fund Affiliate," dated June 8, 1967. After the tentative outline on drawing rights was discussed in informal session by the Executive Directors, a revised version was issued, also dated June 8.[8] The two schemes outlined were simpler than the illustrative schemes drawn up in February 1967 in that they contained only brief references to subjects not yet fully discussed and left blanks for the figures for the voting majority needed for the decision-making process.

The tentative outlines of June 8, 1967 were very like each other, in contrast to the two plans that had been drawn up in February 1967. These had had features in common but had still attempted to present the Deputies with two distinct alternatives.

One of the reasons why the outlines of June 1967 were virtually identical was that when discussion began to center on the characteristics of the schemes rather than on one scheme versus another, many officials realized that the crux of any scheme was the characteristics attached to the reserve asset rather than

[8] All three tentative outlines are published below, Vol. II, pp. 30–34, 35–39, and 40–44.

the name given to it. Once these characteristics were determined, it would be immaterial whether the resulting bundle was called a drawing right or a reserve unit. This realization—that either drawing rights or reserve units could serve equally well—meant that reconciliation among the disagreeing parties might be made possible by compromise on what the asset was called. The staff, in preparing the tentative outline on drawing rights and in revising it, in effect transferred to the drawing rights plan many of the features that had been formerly associated only with reserve unit plans.

No Backing Needed

Another idea that was gradually receding was that backing was necessary for any reserve that was created, except in the event of withdrawal of a participant or liquidation of the scheme. It had become evident that the essential value of the new reserve asset derived from the obligation of participants to accept it, in much the same way as the value of domestic fiduciary money derives its value from its status as legal tender. The resources of the new scheme, therefore, did not have to consist either of a pool of currencies or of lines of credit. They could consist of the obligation on the part of the participants in the scheme to accept drawing rights, or reserve units, from other participants in exchange for an equal amount of convertible currency. The drawing country would thus acquire currencies not out of resources held by the Fund but in the form of convertible currency to be delivered by the participants drawn upon, either directly or indirectly through the intermediacy of the Fund.

This development in thinking is reflected in the plans that the Fund evolved over time. In February 1967, in drafting the "Outline of an Illustrative Reserve Unit Scheme," the staff had questioned the earlier supposition of Plan I of the Managing Director's proposals of March 1966 that a member would deposit with the supervising agency currency equivalent to the new units, and had pointed out that this deposit would serve no purpose except when a participant withdrew from the plan or it was liquidated. Therefore, if the plan made appropriate provision for these events, it could dispense with the deposit of currency. It had been further realized that, on these occasions, the reserve asset represented obligations of the issuer of the asset and these obligations could be fulfilled in ways other than the deposit of currencies by participants with the issuer.

The reserve unit scheme of February 1967 had contained details on how to settle accounts with a participant who withdrew from the scheme, as well as for liquidation of the scheme. The tentative outlines of June 1967 likewise did not provide for backing for the new reserve asset in the sense of a pool of currencies. Emphasis shifted to making precise the obligation of participants to accept the new assets. Some illustrative obligations were written into both the February 1967 schemes and the tentative outlines of June 1967.

Separate Resources in Any Event

Both of the tentative outlines of June 1967 provided for a separation of the new reserve assets from the Fund's traditional operations. The reserve drawing rights plan would have established a separate Reserve Drawing Account in the Fund, and the regular resources of the Fund were referred to as the General Account; any member of the Fund could become a "participant" in the Reserve Drawing Account. The reserve unit plan provided for an International Reserve Organization, this time referred to as an International Reserve Union (IRU), as an affiliate of the Fund in which membership would be open to all of the Fund's members.

In the paper on the choice between merged and separate resources, the staff concluded that merging the new facilities with the regular facilities of the Fund would not necessarily achieve much economy in the resources required. Furthermore, pooling the resources for the two facilities would deprive members of their right to decide the extent to which they would actually commit themselves to finance either of the two kinds of Fund facility, particularly if they intended to participate in only one of them.

The Executive Directors had additional reasons for wanting the two facilities separated. As Mr. vom Hofe observed, if the resources of the two facilities were merged, the Fund's policies on drawings and repurchases would inevitably influence the provisions attached to the new scheme. It might, for example, be impossible to apply liberal transfer rules to the new facility. Mr. Faber stressed that separation of the two facilities would make it clear that the new scheme was self-supporting. The Executive Directors emphasized that, when a new facility distinct from the Fund's normal operations was set up, two separate sets of accounts would be required. Separate accounts were essential because the new facility would have a completely different financial structure from that of the rest of the Fund. Countries' drawings under the new facility would have to be distinguished from their usual drawings. It was also vital that the new facility not be subsidized by the Fund, nor be used to finance the Fund. In addition, because there would be limits to participants' obligations to accept the new asset, it would not be a complete substitute for gold; the extent to which the Fund's resources in the two kinds of facility could be substituted for each other or combined should therefore also be restricted.

Executive Directors' Reactions

In sum, both tentative outlines of June 1967 provided that the new facility, whatever its name, would be separate from the rest of the Fund's operations and that no backing would be needed in any case. They were also very much alike in their provisions for the distribution (or issuance) of reserve drawing rights (or units), for the voting procedure necessary to make decisions on creation, for a participant (or member) being able to opt out of a given distribution of drawing rights (or units), for the cancellation of drawing rights (or units), and for their use and transfer.

When the tentative outlines were considered by the Executive Directors in informal session in June 1967, Mr. vom Hofe and Mr. Larre, noting the similarities, characterized them, somewhat unfavorably, as "identical twins." Mr. vom Hofe wondered whether those who had favored reserve units would find the outline on units to their liking. Mr. Larre thought that what the staff had drawn up under the title of a drawing rights scheme was in fact a reserve unit scheme, and he hoped that the discussions would "progress back" to the "genuine" drawing rights scheme of March 1966.

Mr. Handfield-Jones and Mr. Dale, both of whom had favored reserve units, agreed that the two outlines were very similar in substance. In reply to Mr. Larre, Mr. Handfield-Jones stated that, conversely, one could conclude that the reserve unit scheme was really a drawing rights scheme. Mr. Handfield-Jones and Mr. Dale stressed an important difference between the two outlines so far as their appearance was concerned: a reserve unit was preferable to a drawing right in that world public opinion would find a reserve unit a more convincing new asset than a drawing right. But they welcomed the convergence of views on so many points of a reserve plan.

Not only was the form of reserve creation still undecided, but other issues were also still unresolved: the rules for use and transfer; the conditions under which a participant could choose not to receive a given distribution, that is, to opt out; and the much argued subjects of reconstitution and voting majorities.

RULES FOR USE AND TRANSFER

The issue whether the transfer of drawing rights should be "direct," from one participant to another, or "indirect," through some intermediary such as the Fund, had been resolved by June 1967. All transferability was considered to be, in effect, indirect: The bookkeeping was to be done by the Fund, and there could be no transfer of the new asset without a change in ownership being recorded on the books of the Fund. But much had to be made more precise here, too, especially as it became apparent that the new facility would have resources and accounts separate from the Fund's regular resources and accounts. Mr. Suzuki, for instance, was anxious for a clarification of how the recording and accounting system for the new facility would work: What kind of a balance sheet would the reserve drawing account have, since it could not be a conventional one? Would the recording differ for direct and indirect transfers? Would the Fund have to hold currencies or counterpart deposits as transfers were made that would have to show on the Fund's books?

Guided Transfer?

There were other unanswered questions regarding transfers of the new reserve asset: Should transferability be voluntary, or guided by the Fund in the sense that the Fund would designate which participants should encash the new reserve unit? If transfers were to be guided, what rules would govern such guidance? Should transfers be subject to some test that the transferring country had a suitable defined need?

The EEC countries had been advocating different transfer rules for creditors than for debtors. If a country was in a net creditor position in the system and found a country in a net debtor position that was willing to accept its drawing rights, the creditor country should be free to effect a direct transfer. But a country that was in a debtor position should, when utilizing its drawing rights, be subject to guidance, to a test of balance of payments need, and to rules for reconstitution. Mr. Larre expressed this thought in the Executive Board and believed that most, if not all, transfers would have to be guided. This was not to say that he liked guidance, but if the scheme was to work one had to accept it. Moreover, in his view it would be very difficult to mix guided transfers with voluntary transfers. If guided transfers were to be the rule, voluntary transfers should be the exception, perhaps limited to transfers from a creditor to a debtor.

A related issue was precisely how the Fund would guide transfers. The positions of the Executive Directors for the EEC countries were similar to those being expressed by their representatives at Group of Ten meetings. Mr. Larre was in favor of letting the Fund choose the currencies to be provided, but according to given rules. Mr. Herman Biron (Belgium, Alternate to Mr. van Campenhout) suggested that it would be preferable to specify in detail the rules for transfers in the amended Articles. Mr. Siglienti and Mr. Larre both believed that the provisions for converting drawing rights into currency should be closely related to those for normal drawings on the Fund.

The complications of working out rules for the use and transfer of a reserve asset were suggested by a number of questions that Mr. Diz raised. Might not the size of a particular transaction have a bearing on how transfer was to be made? Could the Fund direct transfers to a member that was ready, even when it had reached the limit of its holdings, to accept more units; or would the member have to rely on voluntary transfers if it wanted its holdings to go beyond the limits established? Would any acceptance limits established apply only to guided transfers, so that voluntary transfers could be accepted over and above those limits? Would voluntary transfers that had already been accepted be taken into account when the Fund considered the direction in which to guide additional transfers? And what would the transferor receive in exchange for the reserve units or drawing rights that it was transferring? Mr. Faber and Mr. Madan, too, raised questions about how "large" or "excessive" or "sustained" use of the new units would be defined.

Balance of Payments Test?

While the staff had been working on the tentative outlines, they had sought the views of the Executive Directors also about whether participants would be able to exchange the new assets for convertible currency for any reason at all or whether they would be unable to transfer the new assets unless they had some need to do so. The staff believed that it would be safer if the plan was based on the principle that transfer of the new assets was subject to a test of need. The logic of reconstitution was that some kind of test of need was required. If countries were expected to reconstitute their positions when they could or when such reconstitution was necessary, it was implied that they would not transfer the assets in the first place unless they had some kind of need to do so. Furthermore, complete freedom of transfer would have adverse implications for the liquidity of the scheme, although the effects might not be very important statistically. If many small countries decided to transfer most of their new assets to the reserve centers, the acceptance limits of the reserve centers would, to that extent, be filled up.

The position of Mr. Larre was that a test of balance of payments need was very important. He reasoned that a new reserve could only be used in one of two ways, either to meet a balance of payments need or to change the composition of one's reserves. He believed that virtually everyone was on record as not wanting the new reserve to be used to change the composition of reserves and was surprised that some were reluctant to accept a test of need. But other Executive Directors favored freedom of use of the new asset, in that transfer, possibly direct, would be permitted even where a balance of payments need was not proved. In their view, the safeguard that there must be a willing transferee was sufficient. Where the transferor sought guidance as to when and to whom to transfer the asset, however, it would be appropriate to have a test of need.

Freely Usable or Not?

The issue underlying the rules for the use of the new reserve asset really revolved around the question of how freely usable the new asset would be. Positions differed between those, such as in the United States, the United Kingdom, and the Fund, who wanted the asset to be free of restrictions so that it would quickly become acceptable as a substitute for traditional reserves, and those, like the French, who wanted to retain a unique role for gold and to place limitations on the use of the new asset.

Messrs. Dale, González del Valle, Handfield-Jones, Kafka, Lieftinck, and Alfredo Phillips O. (Mexico) stressed that they wanted the new asset to be founded on the concept of a reserve asset and not on a credit concept; the new reserves to be created were supposed to be unconditional assets, not conditional ones. They exhibited the same fear of overrestricting the new asset that was even more evident later when the rules for reconstitution were discussed. They

149

worried that the new reserve asset would be encumbered with features that made it little different from the Fund's usual drawing facilities. If use of the new asset was to be subject to a balance of payments test, if there was to be guided transferability with the Fund directing the transfer of the new asset in much the same way that the Fund already provided guidance for the selection of currencies for its normal transactions, and if rigid rules for reconstituting members' positions in the new assets were drawn up, what was the difference between the new asset and the Fund's usual facilities? Mr. Lieftinck said pointedly that a drawing rights scheme with separate resources and hemmed in by restraints was very similar to the Fund's gold tranche and super gold tranche arrangements. Yet the new reserve was to be sufficiently novel and distinctive so as to justify changes in the Fund's voting structure and decision-making process.

This issue as to how much the new reserve would be subject to constraints was to be basic to the discussions of the next two or three months.

FOURTH JOINT MEETING

When the Executive Directors and the Deputies of the Group of Ten, meeting independently in late May and early June, considered the tentative outlines and the provisions that might go into a revised outline, it became clear that some of the EEC countries had a strong preference for drawing rights rather than reserve units.[9] To these countries, drawing rights seemed more in the nature of a familiar form of credit than of "new money" which might compete with, or supplant, gold. Nevertheless, both of the June outlines were presented for consideration at the fourth joint meeting of Executive Directors and Deputies of the Group of Ten (held in Paris on June 19–21, 1967), and at that meeting no firm decision was taken on whether the new reserve facility would be based on drawing rights or on reserve units. In the discussions, however, more attention was given to the drawing rights scheme and the term drawing rights was used fairly freely to characterize the new reserve that was likely to be created.[10]

Some Issues Resolved

Broad agreement was reached on many points. Any new reserve would have a gold-value guarantee and would earn interest. The new reserve facility would be administered by the Fund, either in the Fund itself or through an

---

[9] In May 1967 Mr. Emminger also circulated a paper for consideration by the Deputies— "Outline of a Reserve Drawing Rights (RDR) Scheme."

[10] The names and positions of the participants in the fourth joint meeting are given in Table 2; see below, pp. 162–65.

affiliate, but in any event would be kept separate, both in accounting and use, from the Fund's regular resources. All members of the Fund would be entitled to participate. Specified prerequisites for the initial creation of new reserves would have to be met. Distributions, now called *allocations*, would be made on the basis of the world's long-term need for reserves, normally for periods of five years, and would be distributed to participants in proportion to their Fund quotas. The Managing Director would make proposals for allocations (previously called creation) after consulting members to make sure that any proposal would be supported by a large majority.

As the drawing rights scheme was being discussed, some principles concerning the use and acceptance of the new drawing rights were also agreed. A participant would normally use its drawing rights only for balance of payments needs and not solely for changing the composition of its reserves. The Fund should see to it that currencies were requested from participants that had strong balance of payments and reserve positions, but it should aim at asking for currencies from these participants in such a way that their holdings of the new drawing rights in relation to their total reserves would approach more or less equal ratios. Participants should be obliged to provide their currency for use by other members up to a certain multiple of the drawing rights allocated to them. Drawing rights under the new facility, after they had been used in a large measure and over an extended period, should be subject to reconstitution.

Issues Not Yet Resolved

Nevertheless, because there were still strong differences of opinion on several matters, a number of questions remained open. A choice among three possibilities for the voting majority necessary before reserves could be created was left in the outline: One possibility was the proposal of the EEC countries that called for a majority of 85 per cent of the total voting power of the participants plus one half of the major creditor countries. The second was the U.S. "band" proposal, which called for a range of from 75 per cent to 90 per cent of the total voting power of the participants. A third possibility, suggested by the Fund staff, left open the required percentage but proposed that the voting power be adjusted according to the individual creditor positions of countries participating in the scheme. Some of the Executive Directors for developing countries, Mr. Kafka, for instance, argued against larger votes being given to countries that were creditors in the scheme.

One suggestion concerning voting, which was made by Mr. Joge during the fourth joint meeting, considerably disturbed most of the Executive Directors—that the Executive Directors cast their votes on reserve proposals according to the instructions given them by the individual countries that had appointed or elected them to the Board instead of on a bloc basis as they usually did. Most Directors were strongly opposed to such "separate" or "split" voting. Mr. vom Hofe, for example, considered that such a procedure would destroy the meaning and importance of the Executive Board. It would not be possible to confine this procedure to voting on reserve questions. Countries that were unable to nominate an Executive Director of their own would soon insist that this kind of voting procedure apply to other matters. The result would be that Executive Directors would not be able to change their minds on major problems or explain their motives to one another or negotiate compromises acceptable to all the participants for whom they spoke, because every Executive Director would have binding instructions. Similarly, Mr. Siglienti thought that split voting would open a Pandora's box, with more disadvantages than advantages. Messrs. Biron, Handfield-Jones, Kafka, Lieftinck, Madan, Stone, Wass, and Antoine W. Yaméogo (Upper Volta) also expressed vigorous opposition to split voting.

Also left open were the provisions concerning reconstitution of participants' positions in the new drawing rights. Five alternative formulations regarding reconstitution remained in the outline after the fourth joint meeting. The basic questions still unanswered were the following: Should the reconstitution obligations arise only in cases where a large and persistent use of the new drawing rights affected adversely the liquidity of the whole scheme, or should reconstitution be the more general rule? Should it be left to the Fund to determine in each case what constituted a large and sustained use of the new drawing rights, or should there be precise rules, and if so, what rules? Should a participant's full initial position be reconstituted, or rather the use of the new drawing rights in proportion to the participant's use of its total reserves? Should the precise rules and definition of the reconstitution obligation be laid down now or later, and should they be revised in the light of subsequent experience?

Another unresolved question was whether the new facility should be run by an affiliate organization of the Fund or by the Fund itself. It had become evident that an affiliate of the Fund, requiring a new organization and another set of voting procedures, need not be established at all. As the General Counsel reported to the Executive Directors in June 1967, the simplest way to put a plan into legal effect was to attach another Article (or Articles) to the existing Articles of Agreement. With the additional Articles, there could be, under the aegis of the Fund, two separate accounts—one for the Fund's general facilities and another for the proposed facility. In order to have a legal bridge between these two accounts, some amendments to individual Articles might also have to be made, but no new distinct structure such as the IRF, or the IRU, or some other organization, need be set up.[11]

Also unsettled was whether a participant would be able to opt out from the beginning of the scheme or only after a certain minimum distribution of new drawing rights had been made. The staff had proposed that opting out

---

[11] For a detailed discussion of the choices and the reasons for the final technique chosen, see Joseph Gold, "Legal Technique in the Creation of a New International Reserve Asset: Special Drawing Rights and the Amendment of the Articles of Agreement of the International Monetary Fund," *Case Western Reserve Journal of International Law*, Vol. 1 (1969), pp. 105–23.

should occur only after an amount of new drawing rights equal to 50 per cent of Fund quotas had been distributed; this amount would help the scheme to get going before participants began to opt out. And it was not yet clear whether, in the event that it was a drawing rights scheme that emerged, the name of the new assets should be simply "special drawing rights," or whether it should be "special reserve drawing rights" in order to emphasize the reserve character of the assets.

Results Uncertain

Because these crucial points of difference had not been reconciled, many Executive Directors, for instance, Mr. González del Valle, Mr. Kafka, and Mr. Stone, regarded the fourth joint meeting as anticlimactic. In their view, the future course of action was uncertain. Should more joint meetings with the Deputies be held before the Annual Meeting? Could an outline be ready for the Annual Meeting, or might negotiations have to continue after the Annual Meeting?

At a press conference after the fourth joint meeting, Mr. Emminger and Mr. Schweitzer made public their uncertainty about what had been achieved.[12] While important progress toward agreement on a plan had been made with the acceptance by all countries of the principle of reconstitution or reimbursement in case of "excessive use," the precise form of reconstitution and, in particular, the definition of excessive use would have to be considered at a ministerial meeting of the Group of Ten. When Mr. Emminger was asked what he thought were the prospects for the achievement of concrete results at the ministerial level, he replied that, in his opinion, the chances for a positive outcome "were somewhat more than 50 per cent."

DRAFTING A FINAL OUTLINE

Following the fourth joint meeting, the staff prepared a draft of a final outline as a working document to set out the major unsettled issues as fully and as clearly as possible. The topics on which views differed were put between brackets, and alternative proposals on a number of subjects were included. The facility described was to be based on drawing rights.

In drafting this working document, and later the amendments to the Articles, great care was taken to find a terminology that would not jeopardize the compromise that seemed to be emerging.[13] Since the concept of a reserve

---

[12] *International Financial News Survey*, Vol. 19 (1967), pp. 205–206.

[13] How the choice of language influenced the drafting of the final Outline and later on also the amendments to the Articles has been described by Joseph Gold in his *Special Drawing Rights: The Role of Language*, IMF Pamphlet Series, No. 15 (Washington, 1971). (Hereinafter cited as Gold, *Special Drawing Rights: Role of Language*.)

asset was still unacceptable to some of the negotiating countries, terms like assets, reserves, and even reserve drawing rights and special reserve drawing rights—terms that had been used in the past—were shunned. The final outline spoke throughout of *special drawing rights.* An initial sentence was introduced to indicate the purpose of the new facility: "The facility described in this Outline is intended to meet the need, as and when it arises, for a supplement to existing reserve assets." [14] The words *a supplement to existing reserve assets* had been substituted for the language of previous documents, which had referred to supplementing existing forms of reserves with additional reserve assets.

Avoidance of a vocabulary that suggested the bringing into existence of new reserve assets or the transmission of reserve assets among participants in operations and transactions was the reason for what the General Counsel has characterized as "a less energetic terminology" that had been used in earlier discussions. Words like creation, distribution, issuance, and transfer disappeared. *Allocation* was substituted for distribution and issuance, and *cancellation* was preferred to recall. Transfer, transferor, and transferee were avoided in favor of formulations involving the word *use.* Even the title of the outline referred to a facility *based* on special drawing rights. Some words, like *reconstitution,* were entirely novel, not having been applied before to a medium of exchange.

The choice of this terminology was quite deliberate. Its use was instrumental in reconciling opposing positions. Words were selected that were not only innocuous but in some ways ambiguous, so as to make agreement possible. In the words of the General Counsel, it "enabled the proponents of divergent views to insist that their opinions had prevailed." [15] Each participant in the Special Drawing Account could decide for itself, for example, whether special drawing rights were or were not reserve assets.

The effort expended in the search for a suitable terminology was only part of the much larger effort required to reach final agreement, but it was considerable. The merit of this careful terminology has been recognized even by those not directly involved in its selection. Professor Fritz Machlup, for example, has praised the negotiators for finding a solution to their difficulties by avoiding all terms that had established connotations in economics:

> This conflict was resolved, almost miraculously, by extraordinarily efficient mediators applying the recipe of avoiding all the words which the nations had written on their banners and for which they were valiantly battling. The words "credit," "credit facility," "reserve asset," "reserve units," "borrowed reserves," "owned reserves," "loans," "repayments"—all of them were, with great circumspection, avoided in the Outline drafted. Words not burdened with a history of controversy, not associated with recognizable ideologies, and not widely used in monetary theories, words, therefore, with still neutral and not always fixed

---

[14] Gold, *Special Drawing Rights: Role of Language,* p. 18.
[15] Gold, *Special Drawing Rights: Role of Language,* p. 2.

connotations were put in place of the old, battle-scarred and now banished words.[16]

OUTLINE AGREED BY GROUP OF TEN

The continuing differences of view on a number of key points among the countries of the Group of Ten had to be settled at the highest level. Early in June 1967 the Finance Ministers of the EEC countries had reached agreement on several points. They favored a new facility in the framework of the Fund, with separate accounting but no affiliate organization. Transferability was a technical rather than a political question. An 85 per cent voting majority should be required for allocation of any new reserve. Any new reserve should be subject to reconstitution. And the establishment of a new reserve should be paralleled by "improvements in the practices of the Fund."

Changes in Fund's Rules and Practices

The last point had reference to changes in the Fund's rules and practices that the French authorities had suggested some months before.[17] Subsequently, on June 26, 1967, a memorandum was addressed to the Managing Director by the five Executive Directors for the six countries of the EEC—Messrs. van Campenhout, Lieftinck, Larre, Siglienti, and vom Hofe. This memorandum proposed that the Fund staff undertake a study of certain subjects corresponding to those that had been included in a report of the Monetary Committee of the EEC (dated April 11, 1967) which, because of their operational character, raised technical questions. The subjects included making drawings in the gold tranche legally automatic, tightening conditions on drawings in the credit tranches, and redefining par values only in terms of gold rather than in terms of U.S. dollars or gold. By August 1967 the staff had prepared a paper dealing with the legal points taken up in the memorandum, and the Executive Board agreed that, along with the outline for a reserve facility, it would review these practices of the Fund.[18]

Voting Issue Decided

After the EEC ministerial agreement in June, the Finance Ministers and Central Bank Governors of the Group of Ten met twice, in London in July and August, under the chairmanship of Mr. Callaghan, U.K. Chancellor of the Exchequer.

---

[16] Fritz Machlup, *Remaking the International Monetary System: The Rio Agreement and Beyond*, Committee for Economic Development, Supplementary Paper No. 24 (Baltimore, 1968), p. 9.

[17] See Chap. 5 above, pp. 131–32.

[18] These changes in the Fund's rules and practices are described in detail in Chap. 13 below.

At their meeting on July 17 and 18, 1967, the question of the voting majority came close to resolution. A majority of 85 per cent of the total voting power of the Board of Governors would be required for decisions involving the basic periods for allocation and cancellation of the new special drawing rights, for the amounts to be allocated, and for the rate of allocation. The Managing Director told the Ministers that several of the Executive Directors, especially those appointed or elected by developing countries, objected to voting arrangements that gave effective veto power to an individual country and felt strongly that the rest of the EEC proposal—that at least half the major creditor countries ought to concur in any decision about special drawing rights—should not be a part of the voting arrangement. Hence, this feature was not included in the final Outline.

Reconstitution Unresolved

Opposing views on reconstitution persisted, however. Mr. Debré, Minister of Economy and Finance, France, continued to believe that strict rules on reconstitution were essential and should be spelled out. The new unit was a credit and not a reserve. It had to be repaid. But he would limit the precise rules for reconstitution to the first five-year period, after which the rules could be reassessed. The opposing view, presented mainly by Mr. Fowler, Secretary of the Treasury, United States, was that if the new asset was surrounded by rules it might never become accepted as a reserve.

Mr. Colombo, Minister of the Treasury, Italy, supporting an idea offered at the fourth joint meeting of Executive Directors and Deputies by Mr. Ossola, introduced the principle of harmonization, according to which participants would from time to time be asked to reconstitute their outstanding special drawing rights to the extent necessary to restore the reserve position that would have obtained if they had used their special drawing rights in the same proportion as their total reserves. This arrangement would, he argued, both ensure the liquidity of the new scheme and facilitate a better working of the adjustment process, the two aims of reconstitution, without detracting from the credibility of the asset, since the new asset would be closely tied to traditional reserve assets. The alternative principle for reconstitution that had been suggested by the French authorities at previous discussions, a formula based on the average net use by a participant of its special drawing rights, had the disadvantage, Mr. Colombo thought, of freezing debtor positions below a certain ceiling. The principle of harmonization could best be implemented, he believed, in a system of guided transferability.

Renewed Efforts to Reach Agreement

If an outline was to be ready for the Annual Meeting in September, time was running out. The Deputies of the Group of Ten hoped to work intensively during the latter part of July and in August to resolve the areas of difference among their countries without another meeting of the Finance Ministers and Central Bank Governors. But, as the Managing Director had made clear at the ministerial meeting in July, the document that was to go to the Fund's Governors must be in the form of a resolution proposed by the Executive Board, to which would be attached an outline that the Executive Directors had approved. The outline as agreed by the Group of Ten would, therefore, have to come back to the Executive Directors, and they in turn would have to have enough time to examine it, to agree on a draft resolution, and to confer with their authorities. That was the only way in which to get "proposals acceptable to all," the phrase of the communiqué of the Group of Ten itself.[19]

In the next weeks there were to be extremely intensive negotiations by the Executive Directors and by the Deputies of the Group of Ten. As background to these negotiations, the Fund staff had prepared papers explaining some suggested provisions: why the obligation of each participant to accept the new drawing rights should equal twice the amount distributed, so that each participant would be obliged to hold the new drawing rights in amounts up to three times its net cumulative allocation; what opting out arrangements should apply; and what provisions should govern reconstitution.

Several Executive Directors objected to mechanical formulas and rigid requirements for reconstitution. Mr. Madan noted that the Ossola concept of harmonization was based on the proportionality of use of new assets in relation to other reserves by transferor countries as against proportionality of the holdings of new assets, both of which were possible ways of harmonizing reserves. Because the use of traditional reserves was sometimes subject to statutory requirements, there was an important difference between these two techniques of harmonization. Mr. Dale agreed that it was difficult to know exactly what different formulas would mean. Both Mr. Madan and Mr. Stone emphasized that any provisions for reconstitution should take into account the diversity of balance of payments situations that member countries would encounter over the years ahead.

By the end of July 1967, following a meeting in Paris on July 27 and 28, the Deputies of the Group of Ten had agreed on a version of the outline to put before their Ministers and Governors at a second meeting set for late in August in London. The word reserve had been dropped from the name of the facility, leaving the term *special drawing rights*. There was to be a separate account in the Fund rather than an affiliate. The section on opting out was put in general language, to be settled after the Annual Meeting in Rio de Janeiro. There were still two proposals on voting. The distinction between the concept of direct and indirect transfers and the concept of guided and unguided transfers

---

[19] Communiqué of the Ministers and Central Bank Governors of the Group of Ten, July 18, 1967, *International Financial News Survey*, Vol. 19 (1967), p. 229.

was not maintained. The Fund would make the rules governing the extent to which all transactions should be guided.

The five alternative formulations for reconstitution were reduced to two. The first was based essentially on a net average use, a French proposal explained by Mr. Paul Mentré (France, Alternate to Mr. Larre). Reconstitution would be based on the average debit position of a drawing participant calculated on the basis of the last four years; it would never exceed 50 per cent of a participant's average allocations of drawing rights over this reference period. The second alternative for reconstitution was based on the principle of the proportionality of use along the lines of the ideas for harmonization.

Rules for Reconstitution Agreed

At their meeting in London on August 26, the Ministers and Governors of the Group of Ten agreed finally on the general principles for reconstitution and on the rules for reconstitution to be applied during the first basic period. These were ideas that had been suggested by the Fund's General Counsel at a meeting of the Deputies. The proposal that finally broke the deadlock over the reconstitution provisions was that they could be changed later without the need to amend the Articles. Participants that used their special drawing rights would incur an obligation to reconstitute their positions in accordance with principles which would take account of the amount and duration of the use. The reconstitution principles would be laid down in the Rules and Regulations of the Fund rather than in the Articles of Agreement. For drawings made in the first basic period of five years, the principal rule of reconstitution should be that over any period of five years a member's net average use of the new facility should not exceed 70 per cent of its net cumulative allocation. Participants should also pay due regard to the desirability of pursuing over time a balanced relationship between their holdings of special drawing rights and other reserves. These reconstitution provisions were to be reviewed before the end of the first period.

APPROVAL OF OUTLINE BY BOARD OF GOVERNORS

The Executive Board approved the draft Outline on September 6, 1967, and two days later approved the text of a draft resolution for transmission to the Governors. Mr. Saad had proposed that the voting majority required for decisions on the basic period for, timing of, and rate of allocation of, special drawing rights should be 80 per cent of the total voting power of the participants, and not 85 per cent, and wanted his opposition to the proposed 85 per cent majority to be recorded at a formal Executive Board meeting and also at the meeting of the Board of Governors. He abstained from approving the draft Outline.

Museum of Modern Art, Rio de Janeiro, site of 1967 Annual Meeting of Board of Governors, at which Outline of SDR facility was approved

On September 11 the Fund released the text of an "Outline of a Facility Based on Special Drawing Rights in the Fund."

At the closing session of the Annual Meeting in Rio de Janeiro (September 29, 1967), the Board of Governors adopted the resolution, to which was attached the Outline.[20] It requested the Executive Directors to proceed with work relating both to the establishment in the Fund of a new facility based on the Outline and to improvements in the rules and practices of the Fund, and to propose amendments to the Articles on these matters. There had been some feeling, especially by the U.S. authorities, that the new facility and the so-called reform of the Fund should not be linked in the same resolution because, inter alia, the reform had not had adequate consideration and it might take longer to get approval in the U.S. Congress for it than for the special drawing rights facility. It was not even certain that the staff could prepare in time all the needed amendments for both the new facility and the changes in rules and practices. It was nevertheless agreed that both topics should be combined in a single resolution.

The Managing Director described the proposed new arrangements for international liquidity as the most significant development in international financial cooperation since Bretton Woods.[21] Most of the Governors shared his view. Mr. Karl Schiller (Federal Republic of Germany) commented on the importance of tying the reform of the Fund to the establishment of the new drawing rights.[22] Mr. Callaghan (United Kingdom) called attention to the importance of the universality of the scheme.[23] Governors for the developing countries also supported the scheme, both because it was universally applied and because it operated through the Fund.

Mr. Callaghan and Mr. Fowler expressed their intention of treating the new drawing rights as "front-line" or "first-line" reserves.[24] Mr. Debré (France), in contrast, took the position that the introduction of special drawing rights in no way constituted "a revolutionary step." They did not and could not "establish a new currency designed to replace gold." The plan provided for "the possible extending of credit facilities." The nature of the proposed new facility was "a limited but important one."[25]

---

[20] The "Outline of a Facility Based on Special Drawing Rights in the Fund" is reproduced below, Vol. II, pp. 47–51. Resolution No. 22-8 is also reproduced below, Vol. II, pp. 54–55.

[21] Opening Address by the Managing Director, *Summary Proceedings, 1967*, p. 21.

[22] Statement by the Governor of the World Bank for the Federal Republic of Germany, *Summary Proceedings, 1967*, p. 46.

[23] Statement by the Governor of the Fund for the United Kingdom, *Summary Proceedings, 1967*, p. 58.

[24] Statements by the Governor of the Fund for the United Kingdom and the Governor of the Fund and the World Bank for the United States, *Summary Proceedings, 1967*, pp. 58 and 82.

[25] Statement by the Governor of the World Bank for France, *Summary Proceedings, 1967*, p. 67.

ONLY AN OUTLINE

Thus, finally, after years of negotiation, a contingency plan for reserve creation was agreed, with the cumbersome name, "Outline of a Facility Based on Special Drawing Rights in the Fund." The plan was still an outline: the precise drafting of an amendment to the Articles of Agreement was yet to come. The particular considerations that would govern the activation of the plan, as well as the principles on which all decisions to allocate the new asset were to be based, would be described in an introductory section of the amendment and, to the extent necessary, in a report explaining the amendment.

Nonetheless, the basic ingredients of a contingency plan had been decided. Deliberate creation of liquidity, when it was considered necessary, was to be accomplished through the International Monetary Fund, not through any of the other arrangements that had been proposed. The new facility was to be set up through amendment of the Articles. Thus the existing organizational structure of the Fund would be used and there would be no need for a separate affiliate. New reserves would take the form of so-called drawing rights, not reserve units, and the drawing rights would be special ones, entirely separate from existing drawing rights in the Fund. Participation in the new arrangements would be open to all Fund members; distribution of the new asset would not be restricted to a limited group. There would be no currency contribution or financial backing required of the participants; the character of the special drawing right as an asset would depend entirely on the obligation of participants to exchange it for convertible currency. Limits to this obligation were spelled out in the Outline as were the general principles that the Fund would use to guide the transfer of the special drawing rights. Procedures for deciding how often, exactly when, and in what amounts the special drawing rights were to be allocated were also set out; an 85 per cent majority of the total voting power of the participants for these decisions to become effective was also to be required.

For use of the new drawing rights there would be a balance of payments test. The Outline provided for guided as well as for some voluntary transfers. Guidance by the Fund would be basically similar to the practices already followed in the Fund for selecting the currencies to be used when a member drew from the Fund; that is, participants with strong balance of payments and healthy reserve positions would encash the special drawing rights and in such amounts that participants would hold over time equal ratios of them to their total reserves. This rule of equalizing the ratios of special drawing rights to participants' total reserves would be supplemented by a special provision permitting a reserve center that wanted to buy balances of its currency held by another country to direct its drawing specifically to that country, provided that the latter agreed.

There would also be an obligation by participants to reconstitute their positions, and the Outline specified the principles on which the rules and regulations governing reconstitution would be based. For those participants that were unhappy with the detailed rules for reconstitution, the Outline provided that the rules would be reviewed before the end of the first, and of each subsequent, period in which special drawing rights were allocated and that new rules could be adopted if necessary. For those participants that continued firm in their conviction that strict rules for reconstitution were essential, the Outline specifically noted that the same 85 per cent majority of voting power that was required for decisions to allocate special drawing rights would also be required for decisions to adopt, amend, or abrogate rules for reconstitution.[26]

The Fund now turned to the major task of incorporating the new facility into its Articles.

---

[26] The Outline has been discussed in detail by Joseph Gold, "The Next Stage in the Development of International Monetary Law: The Deliberate Control of Liquidity," *American Journal of International Law*, Vol. 62 (1968), pp. 365–402.

Table 2. Participants and Observers at Third and Fourth Joint Meetings of Executive Directors of Fund and Deputies of Group of Ten, 1967 [1]

INTERNATIONAL MONETARY FUND

Management

Pierre-Paul Schweitzer, Managing Director (3,4)
Frank A. Southard, Jr., Deputy Managing Director (3)

Executive Directors and Alternates [2]	Constituency [3]
William B. Dale (3,4) *John S. Hooker (3,4)*	United States
Adolfo C. Diz (3,4) *Yamandú S. Patrón (3,4)*	Argentina, Bolivia, Chile, Ecuador, Paraguay, Uruguay
Paul L. Faber (3,4) *Leonard A. Williams (3,4)*	Burundi, Guinea, Kenya, Liberia, Malawi, Mali, Nigeria, Sierra Leone, Sudan, Tanzania, Trinidad and Tobago, Uganda, Zambia
Torben Friis (3,4) *Jorma Aranko (3,4)*	Denmark, Finland, Iceland, Norway, Sweden
Jorge González del Valle (3,4) *Alfredo Phillips O. (3,4)*	Costa Rica, El Salvador, Guatemala, Honduras, Mexico, Nicaragua, Venezuela
S.J. Handfield-Jones (3,4) *Patrick M. Reid (3,4)*	Canada, Guyana, Ireland, Jamaica
Alexandre Kafka (3,4) *Paulo H. Pereira Lira (3,4)*	Brazil, Colombia, Dominican Republic, Haiti, Panama, Peru
René Larre (3,4) *Gérard M. Teyssier (3,4)*	France
Pieter Lieftinck (3,4) *H.M.H.A. van der Valk (3,4)*	Cyprus, Israel, Netherlands, Yugoslavia
B.K. Madan (3,4) *Arun K. Banerji (3,4)*	India
Amon Nikoi (3,4) *Muhamad Barmawie Alwie (3)*	Algeria, Ghana, Laos, Libyan Arab Republic, Malaysia, Morocco, Singapore, Tunisia
Sergio Siglienti (3,4) *Costa P. Caranicas (3,4)*	Greece, Italy, Portugal, Spain
J.M. Stevens (3,4) *Douglas W.G. Wass (3,4)*	United Kingdom
J.O. Stone (3,4) *A.M. de Villiers (3,4)*	Australia, New Zealand, South Africa
Hideo Suzuki (3,4) *Eiji Ozaki (3,4)*	Burma, Ceylon, Japan, Nepal, Thailand
Beue Tann (3) *Chi-Ling Chow (3,4)*	Republic of China, Korea, Viet-Nam
André van Campenhout (3,4) *Herman Biron (3,4)*	Austria, Belgium, Luxembourg, Turkey

Table 2 (*continued*). Participants and Observers at Third and Fourth Joint Meetings of Executive Directors of Fund and Deputies of Group of Ten, 1967 [1]

Executive Directors and Alternates [2]

Ernst vom Hofe (3,4)
Horst Ungerer (3,4)

Antoine W. Yaméogo (3,4)
Léon M. Rajaobelina (3,4)

Constituency [3]

Federal Republic of Germany

Cameroon, Central African Republic, Chad, Dahomey, Gabon, Ivory Coast, Malagasy Republic, Mauritania, Niger, People's Republic of the Congo, Rwanda, Senegal, Togo, Upper Volta, Zaïre

Staff [4]

Joseph Gold, The General Counsel (3,4)
J.J. Polak, The Economic Counsellor (3,4)
W. Lawrence Hebbard, Secretary of the Fund (3,4)
Jean-Paul Sallé, Director, Office in Europe (3,4)
J. Marcus Fleming, Deputy Director,
    Research and Statistics Department (3,4)
George Nicoletopoulos, Deputy General Counsel (3,4)
F.L. Hall, Personal Assistant to the
    Managing Director (3,4)

GROUP OF TEN

Deputies

Alternates

BELGIUM

Cecil de Strycker, Director, National Bank of Belgium (3,4)

Jacques Mertens de Wilmars, Adviser to the Board, National Bank of Belgium (3,4)

Marcel D'Haeze, Director of the Treasury and Public Debt, Ministry of Finance (3,4)

CANADA

A.B. Hockin, Assistant Deputy Minister of Finance, Department of Finance (3,4)

W.A. Kennett, Adviser, Department of Finance (3,4)

R.W. Lawson, Deputy Governor, Bank of Canada (3,4)

W.C. Hood, Adviser, Bank of Canada (3,4)

FRANCE

Maurice Pérouse, Director of Treasury, Ministry of Economy and Finance (3,4)

Jean-Yves Haberer, Technical Counsellor to the Minister of Finance (3,4)

Bernard Clappier, Deputy Governor, Bank of France (3,4)

Daniel Deguen, Assistant Director of Treasury, Ministry of Economy and Finance (3,4)

Table 2 (*continued*). Participants and Observers at Third and
Fourth Joint Meetings of Executive Directors of Fund
and Deputies of Group of Ten, 1967 [1]

Deputies	**Alternates**
	FEDERAL REPUBLIC OF GERMANY
Otmar Emminger, Member, Board of Directors, Deutsche Bundesbank (3,4)	*Wolfgang Rieke, Division Chief, Deutsche Bundesbank (3,4)*
	Erich Stoffers, Office of Executive Director for Federal Republic of Germany, International Monetary Fund (3)
Lore Fuenfgelt, Division Chief, Ministry of Economic Affairs (3,4)	*W. Flandorffer, German Delegation to Organization for Economic Cooperation and Development (4)*
	ITALY
Rinaldo Ossola, Director of the International Economics Research Department, Bank of Italy (3,4)	*L. Fronzoni, Representative in Brussels, Bank of Italy (3)*
	E. Valle, Representative in Paris, Bank of Italy (4)
	L. Fronzoni, Representative in Brussels, Bank of Italy (4)
Giorgio Rota, Chief Inspector, Ministry of the Treasury (3,4)	*or*
	S. Montanaro, International Economics Research Department, Bank of Italy (4)
	JAPAN
Yusuke Kashiwagi, Director, International Finance Bureau, Ministry of Finance (3,4)	*Keijiro Tanaka, Chief, International Organizations Section, International Finance Bureau, Ministry of Finance (3,4)*
Haruo Mayekawa, Executive Director, Bank of Japan (3,4)	*Daizo Hoshino, Adviser, Bank of Japan (3,4)*
	NETHERLANDS
E. van Lennep, Treasurer General, Ministry of Finance (3,4)	*D.M.N. van Wensveen, Head, International Monetary Affairs Department, Ministry of Finance (3,4)*
G.A. Kessler, Managing Director, Netherlands Bank (3,4)	*Baron A.W.R. MacKay, Deputy Director, Netherlands Bank (3,4)*
	SWEDEN
Sven F. Joge, Deputy Governor, Sveriges Riksbank (3,4)	*A. Lindå, Head of Division, Sveriges Riksbank (3,4)*
L. Klackenberg, Counsellor, Ministry of Finance (3,4)	*J. Nipstad, Ministry of Finance (3,4)*
	UNITED KINGDOM
	D.F. Hubback, H.M. Treasury (3)
Sir Denis Rickett, Second Secretary of the Treasury (3,4)	*or*
	L.P. Thompson-McCausland, H.M. Treasury (3,4)
C.J. Morse, Executive Director, Bank of England (3,4)	*C.W. McMahon, Adviser to the Governors, Bank of England (3,4)*

Table 2 (*concluded*). Participants and Observers at Third and
Fourth Joint Meetings of Executive Directors of Fund
and Deputies of Group of Ten, 1967 [1]

Deputies	Alternates
UNITED STATES	
Frederick L. Deming, Under Secretary of the Treasury for Monetary Affairs (3,4)	*George H. Willis, Deputy to the Assistant Secretary for International Monetary Affairs (3,4)*
J. Dewey Daane, Member, Board of Governors of the Federal Reserve System (3,4)	*Robert Solomon, Adviser to Board of Governors of the Federal Reserve System (3,4)*

Observers	Alternates
M. Iklé, Managing Director, Swiss National Bank (3,4)	*J. Lademann, Director, Swiss National Bank (3,4)*
Jean Cottier, Deputy Secretary General, Organization for Economic Cooperation and Development (3,4)	*J.C.R. Dow, Assistant Secretary General for Economics and Statistics, Organization for Economic Cooperation and Development (3)*
Milton Gilbert, Economic Adviser, Bank for International Settlements (3,4)	

[1] Third meeting, April 24–26, 1967, Washington; fourth meeting, June 19–21, 1967, Paris. The numbers in parentheses indicate which of the two meetings the individual attended.

[2] Alternate Executive Directors, always appointed by the Executive Director, are indicated by italic type.

[3] Only 19 of the 20 constituencies that appointed or elected Executive Directors were represented at the joint meetings because neither Mr. Ahmed Zaki Saad (Egypt) nor his Alternate, Mr. Albert Mansour (Egypt), attended. See also Chap. 30, p. 626.

[4] Not including two persons who served as members of the secretariat.

CHAPTER
7

Amending the Articles
(1967–68)

THE MOST DIFFICULT DISCUSSIONS and negotiations still lay ahead. The Outline had intentionally been couched in general terms. Now agreement was needed on the precise language that would be needed in the amendments to the Articles of Agreement and to the By-Laws and the Rules and Regulations as well, to make the new facility part of the machinery of the Fund and to put into effect the various modifications in the rules and practices of the Fund. Many of the issues involved were in the province of international law. The General Counsel has described elsewhere some of the legal problems presented.[1]

The Deputies of the Group of Ten (under the chairmanship of Mr. Ossola, whom they had elected in September 1967 to succeed Mr. Emminger) continued to meet during the winter of 1967 and the spring of 1968. But they acknowledged that the Board of Governors had entrusted the Executive Directors with the task of drafting amendments on the basis of the Outline, and that their role was to help the Executive Directors to reach agreement in the event of conflicting opinions. At the request of the EEC countries, the Finance Ministers and Central Bank Governors of the Group of Ten met in Stockholm at the end of March 1968 to discuss a number of continuing differences. These differences were resolved at that meeting. The Executive Directors then combined the various draft amendments into a final draft, called the "proposed amendment," for submission to the Board of Governors.

THE FUND'S TASK

A comparative glance at the Outline and at the Articles as they were amended suggests what was involved.[2] The relatively short Outline was

---

[1] In addition to the articles by Joseph Gold referred to in the preceding chapter, see also the following by him: *History, 1945–65*, Vol. II, pp. 595–99; *The Reform of the Fund*, IMF Pamphlet Series, No. 12 (Washington, 1969); and *Special Drawing Rights: Character and Use*, IMF Pamphlet Series, No. 13, 2nd ed. (Washington, 1970).

[2] Both the Outline and the amended Articles of Agreement are reproduced in Vol. II below, pp.47–51 and 97–157.

translated into 13 new Articles (Articles XXI through XXXII to follow the original Articles I to XX and an Introductory Article to precede Article I); Schedules F through I were added to the original Schedules A through E; and substantial changes were made in several of the original Articles. In order to make the new facility for special drawing rights [3] operative, provisions had to be drafted for many topics that had not been specified in the Outline. Provision had to be made, among other things, for a Special Drawing Account separate from the Fund's traditional mechanism, now to be called the General Account; for specifying the technique by which members could become participants in the Special Drawing Account; and for administering the two Accounts and indicating the connection between them. Details also had to be supplied specifying how the Fund would apply the suggested criteria of balance of payments positions and reserve holdings when it designated participants to encash SDRs, and how reconstitution of SDRs would be achieved. Terms like *currency convertible in fact*, which had been used in the Outline to refer to what a participant would receive for its SDRs, had to be defined. The exchange rates that would apply to transactions involving SDRs had to be determined.

All these provisions were meticulously drafted in four to five months, beginning late in 1967. The staff prepared a number of drafts of a proposed amendment, as well as many papers on individual topics to explain how the suggested provisions would operate, and worked very closely with the Executive Directors in their ensuing consideration of the draft amendments. The General Counsel and the Economic Counsellor and other staff of the Legal and Research Departments carried out these staff functions, assisted by members of the staff of other departments.

The Executive Directors began to consider the text of a proposed amendment on December 1, 1967. Before the discussions were finished, on April 16, 1968, they had devoted 74 sessions and nearly 170 hours to a section-by-section, even word-by-word, deliberation of each provision. As in the drafting of the Outline, the Executive Directors and Alternate Executive Directors, individually and collectively, played an extremely active role. They devoted themselves to clarifying the implications of possible alternative features, to examining the nuances of different terms and expressions, to agreeing on compromise provisions, and to suggesting specific language. Mr. Saad continued to express his disapproval of an 85 per cent voting majority, and he reserved his position on the role of the Executive Directors and the Managing Director in the decision-making process to be set up for the new facility. Some of the provisions proposed as amendments to the Articles were based on practices and policies that had evolved in the Fund's regular transactions. Others were based on the original Articles. Still other provisions deliberately departed from the original Articles.[4] An even finer net than had been used in drafting the Outline was

---

[3] Hereinafter referred to, for the most part, as SDRs.

[4] For a discussion of which of the provisions dealing with the SDR facility were in each of these categories, see *History, 1945–65*, Vol. II, pp. 597–99.

used to filter out language that could prejudice the compromise reached among the disagreeing parties. For instance, where the Outline had referred to "special drawing rights and other reserves," such expressions as "gross reserves" or "reserves" were, for the most part, avoided in the Articles when those concepts included special drawing rights.

DEFINING CURRENCY CONVERTIBLE IN FACT

Illustrative of the care taken in drafting the amendments is the attention given to the term *currency convertible in fact*. When the Outline was drafted, this term was taken from the provisions in the General Arrangements to Borrow. There it had been used in the provisions governing repayment by the Fund of any loans made to it by participants in the Arrangements. The aim had been to set standards of convertibility for the currencies used by the Fund in repayments under the Arrangements that were stricter than those for the currencies of members that had assumed the obligations of Article VIII. In the late 1950s and early 1960s the Fund had formulated standards for determining which exchange restrictions it would approve when a member wished to assume the obligations of Article VIII.[5] Once a member had met these standards, its currency was considered "convertible." However, even a currency that was convertible in the sense that the member was fulfilling the obligations of Article VIII might be subject to certain restrictions, for instance, restrictions on current transactions that had been approved by the Fund or restrictions on capital transfers that did not require the Fund's approval.

Under the General Arrangements to Borrow, it was intended that the Fund should not be able to repay loans in a currency so restricted. Hence, the term *currency convertible in fact* was coined as the Fund was, in effect, gradually evolving different concepts of currency convertibility.[6] The term had not been defined in the decision setting forth the General Arrangements in the belief that it would be easy to recognize such a currency without a definition.

Sharpening the Definition

The phrase *currency convertible in fact* was adopted for the Outline and for the amendments for the same reason that it was used in the General Arrangements—because of the conviction that a transferor of SDRs should receive a currency that met certain standards of convertibility not necessarily attained by a currency that was convertible under Article VIII. As the drafting of the amendments progressed, it became obvious that the concept would have to be sharply defined. A transferor of SDRs had to be assured that it could obtain,

---

[5] See *History, 1945–65*, Vol. I, pp. 477–81, and Vol. II, pp. 283–88.

[6] These concepts have been described in Joseph Gold, *The Fund's Concepts of Convertibility*, IMF Pamphlet Series, No. 14 (Washington, 1971); the concept of currency convertible in fact is discussed on pp. 30–33 and 37–53.

directly or indirectly, the currency it needed; therefore, some procedure had to exist for converting promptly, and with a minimum of inconvenience, the currency received into the currency wanted. At the same time, the transferee had to have some option as to which currency it would provide to the transferor. Thus it was important to make sure that the transferor would receive "equal value" for the SDRs it surrendered regardless of which currency was provided to it. This "principle of equal value" required that, in the determination of the quantity of convertible currency to be provided against SDRs, account had to be taken of the exchange rate at which this quantity of currency could be sold. This is why the concept of currency convertible in fact as eventually defined in Article XXXII (*b*) was intertwined with the provisions for determining appropriate exchange rates as eventually specified in Article XXV, Section 8.

Interconvertibility

Initially, the staff had in mind that there would normally be only one central currency (under Article XXXII (*b*) (1)), probably the U.S. dollar, and a number of currencies (under Article XXXII (*b*) (2)) that would be convertible into that currency. But after several days of discussion and the preparation of separate technical papers on possible procedures for obtaining specific currencies against SDRs and on exchange rates for transactions in SDRs, it was decided to widen the definition of currency convertible in fact so as to include more than one central currency. Some members of the Executive Board, especially Mr. Mentré, were eager to allow for the possibility that at least a few currencies—those that were readily obtainable and usable in international financial transactions—would serve as basic reference currencies. In the view of the French authorities there was what they termed an "asymmetry" in the present international monetary system, where the dollar was the "fixed star," an asymmetry that they believed should not be cemented into the SDR scheme.

A system of *interconvertible currencies*, later currencies identified in Article XXXII (*b*) (1), was eventually agreed. In the amended Articles, Article XXXII (*b*) thus defined currency convertible in fact as follows:

(1) a participant's currency for which a procedure exists for the conversion of balances of the currency obtained in transactions involving special drawing rights into each other currency for which such procedure exists, at rates of exchange prescribed under Article XXV, Section 8, and which is the currency of a participant that

    (i) has accepted the obligations of Article VIII, Sections 2, 3, and 4, or

    (ii) for the settlement of international transactions in fact freely buys and sells gold within the limits prescribed by the Fund under Section 2 of Article IV; or

(2) currency convertible into a currency described in paragraph (1) above at rates of exchange prescribed under Article XXV, Section 8.

A transferee of SDRs might determine which currency within this definition it would provide to the transferor. But the amended Articles stated the principle that the transferor must receive the same value whatever currency was provided and whichever participant provided it. Thus, Article XXV, Section 8, on exchange rates read:

> (*a*) The exchange rates for operations or transactions between participants shall be such that a participant using special drawing rights shall receive the same value whatever currencies might be provided and whichever participants provide those currencies, and the Fund shall adopt regulations to give effect to this principle.

> (*b*) The Fund shall consult a participant on the procedure for determining rates of exchange for its currency.

> (*c*) For the purpose of this provision the term participant includes a terminating participant.

Accordingly, if two currencies had the same par value but one was at a discount and the other at a premium in the market, the transferee of SDRs would have to provide more units of the former currency and fewer of the latter than it would have to provide on the basis of par values.

The word *interconvertible* was used in the Executive Directors' report to the Board of Governors on the proposed amendment but was not incorporated into the Articles. The word meant that balances in a currency of the first category (Article XXXII (*b*) (1)) obtained in a transaction involving SDRs had to be convertible, at rates of exchange prescribed under Article XXV, Section 8, into any other currency of the first category that the transferor of SDRs wanted. The obligation to ensure conversion fell on the participant that issued the currency concerned; it was not satisfied by directing the transferor to the exchange market. In other words, if country A wanted to transfer SDRs for U.S. dollars and country B, the transferee, provided sterling, the United Kingdom would have to convert the sterling into U.S. dollars; or if country B provided French francs, France would have to convert them into U.S. dollars.

Other currencies could qualify as convertible in fact of the second category, under Article XXXII (*b*) (2). These currencies had to be convertible by the issuer into at least one currency of the first category at rates of exchange prescribed under Article XXV, Section 8. The difference between currencies of the two categories was that every currency of the first category had to be interconvertible with all other currencies of the first category. Currencies of the second category might be convertible into various currencies of the first category, but convertibility into a single currency of the first category sufficed. Interconvertibility was not necessary.

STOCKHOLM MEETING OF THE GROUP OF TEN

Early in March 1968 the monetary officials of the countries of the EEC requested that the Finance Ministers and Central Bank Governors of the Group of Ten meet again. The French authorities, in particular, were distressed because the draft amendments seemed to be going beyond the dictates of the Outline. Special drawing rights, in the opinion of Mr. Debré (France), were not being made the supplementary credit that the French had thought would be useful but were being made into a "money."

What especially alarmed the French authorities, however, was the sharp deterioration that had occurred in the international monetary situation. The external payments deficits of the United Kingdom and the United States had grown larger than ever in 1967, and the payments surplus of continental Europe had remained sizable. Not only had the U.K. current account position worsened in 1967, but short-term capital had moved out of sterling in mammoth amounts, and sterling had had to be devalued in November 1967. Even after devaluation, the U.K. balance of payments had not begun to show much, if any, improvement, and sterling was still in trouble.

It was the serious worsening in the U.S. position, however, that was most worrisome. With an upsurge of imports into the United States late in 1967 and early in 1968, the U.S. payments deficit had become unusually large, and in the aftermath of the devaluation of sterling, speculative pressures had shifted to the dollar. On January 1, 1968, the U.S. authorities had announced stricter and broader measures of financial restraint, but, although these measures had had some effect, the deficit in the first quarter of 1968, at an annual rate of about $2 billion, remained unsatisfactory in light of the requirements of the international monetary situation and of the U.S. goal to bring the balance of payments to equilibrium, or close to equilibrium, in 1968.[7] Less than two weeks before the ministerial meeting of the Group of Ten was to take place, the situation became acute. Renewed movements of funds out of dollars and into continental currencies and gold brought about the end of the Gold Pool on March 18, 1968—thereby cutting off the official supply of gold to private buyers—and the establishment of a two-price system for gold.[8]

The heavy strains to which the international monetary system was subjected during these months had put international monetary cooperation to its severest test in a long time.

Such were the circumstances in which the Finance Ministers and Central Bank Governors of the Group of Ten met in Stockholm on March 29 and 30, 1968, under the chairmanship of Mr. Krister Wickman, Minister of Economic Affairs of Sweden. The Managing Director took part in the meeting, and most of the Executive Directors for the countries of the Group of Ten were present.

Mr. Debré pointed out that the strains in the international monetary system, especially pressures on the two reserve currencies, which the French authorities had been fearing for some time were now materializing. He urged

---

[7] Developments in the U.S. balance of payments position are taken up in Chaps. 24, 25, and 26 below.

[8] See Chap. 20 below.

once more that gold, rather than national currencies, be the basis of the monetary system and that gold be immediately revalued.

Mr. Debré also protested several features of the SDRs as they were developing in the discussions of the draft amendments, features which, he said, contradicted the understandings reached by the Group of Ten in London in July and August 1967 and which had been written into the Outline. The SDRs were becoming more of a replacement for gold and less of a supplementary credit. Being considered, for instance, were suggestions that holders other than participants might deal in SDRs; that participants that had voted against or opted out of an allocation might still be obliged to take a minimum amount of SDRs; and, most troublesome of all, that the Fund would be empowered to accept SDRs in its General Account in payment of gold subscriptions and in repurchases, which, Mr. Debré thought, was directly contrary to what had been agreed at Bretton Woods. SDRs should be held in the General Account only to defray the costs of operating the new facility.

Most of the other Ministers, while sympathetic with Mr. Debré's concerns about the seriousness of the international monetary situation, were not responsive to his suggestion to raise the price of gold. Several Ministers were willing to accept features for SDRs that would make them readily acceptable in international financial transactions even though these features might be a little beyond the prescription of the Outline. However, they were even more anxious that the SDR facility, so close to fruition, should not be jeopardized at this point. They insisted that the Stockholm meeting produce clear-cut and workable decisions. This attitude, plus reassurance by Mr. Fowler (United States) that his authorities were giving the U.S. balance of payments deficit top priority and his noting that the United States would receive only one fourth of SDR allocations, helped to get agreement on a compromise. In these negotiations, the EEC countries other than France labored to win acceptance of features for the SDR facility that might enable France to agree to the facility later.

Compromises

The situation that would have to exist before the SDR facility was activated was made very specific. It was decided to add as the first special consideration a requirement that a collective judgment must be obtained that there was a global need to supplement reserves. The other two special considerations, which had already been agreed, were the attainment of a better balance of payments equilibrium and the likelihood of a better working of the adjustment process in the future.[9]

A clear agreement was also reached, as proposed by the French authorities, that provision be made for a participant to opt out of any proposed allocation,

---

[9] The second and third special considerations were agreed by the Ministers and Governors of the Group of Ten at their meeting in The Hague in July 1966; see Chap. 4 above, p. 98.

in which event a participant so electing would not be obliged to receive any part of that allocation of SDRs. Opting back in, however, would be at the discretion of the Fund and not a right of a participant. It was further agreed that SDRs would not be used to pay gold subscriptions to the Fund, but, as a concession on the other side, it was agreed that the Fund could accept SDRs in repurchases and in payment of charges.

There were still other compromises. Provision would be made for the possibility of holders of SDRs other than participants in the Special Drawing Account; but the categories of possible other holders would be limited to nonmembers of the Fund, members that had chosen not to become participants, and institutions that performed central banking functions for more than one member. The last category could include the BIS and regional organizations in which members or their central banks pooled some of their reserves; other international organizations and private parties were not to be among the possible other holders. The Board of Governors would determine the terms and conditions on which any of the prescribed other holders might use SDRs in operations and transactions with participants. Decisions prescribing other holders and establishing these terms and conditions were to be taken by a majority of 85 per cent of the total voting power.

It was also accepted that, when the Executive Board voted on issues concerning SDRs, Directors would cast the votes they held as a bloc, rather than split their votes according to the wishes of the individual members that had elected them. The Managing Director made a strong case at the Stockholm meeting for bloc voting by the Executive Directors, as any other technique would be difficult for Directors who were elected by a number of members.

Even with these compromises, Mr. Debré reserved the position of the French authorities on the proposed amendment, pending a final text.

Connection Between SDR Facility and Changes in Rules and Practices of Fund

A matter of particular interest at Stockholm was whether changes in certain of the existing rules and practices of the Fund should go into effect at the same time as the SDR facility. The resolution adopted by the Board of Governors at the Annual Meeting in Rio de Janeiro several months earlier specified that the Executive Board should study and report on both subjects at the same time. The Governors for the EEC countries had insisted that the establishment of the SDR facility and the changes in rules and practices of the Fund must be regarded as contemporaneous projects. At the Annual Meeting, however, the Governors for the United Kingdom and the United States took the position that the changes in rules and practices ought not to be regarded as a precondition to taking action on the SDR facility, especially if they turned out to be complicated or controversial.[10]

---

[10] Statements by the Governor of the Fund for the United Kingdom and the Governor of the Fund and the World Bank for the United States, *Summary Proceedings, 1967*, pp. 59 and 84–85.

Some Executive Directors, especially those for developing members, were also disturbed about the interconnection between the introduction of the SDR facility and the other amendments. On March 26, 1968, at a meeting of the Executive Board on the eve of the Stockholm meeting, Mr. Madan made an impassioned plea on behalf of Messrs. Kafka, Yaméogo, Diz, González del Valle, Leonard A. Williams (Trinidad and Tobago, Alternate to Mr. Faber), and Nikoi. Recognizing that the Stockholm meeting would be a meeting of the Group of Ten, they nonetheless asked the Managing Director to bring their views to the attention of the participants of that meeting. Mr. Madan stressed that, while the question of a mechanism for creating new reserves had been under consideration for a long time, the question of the proposed alterations in the rules and practices of the Fund had come on the scene only recently. Nevertheless, it had been considered logical and desirable to proceed with both at the same time. Now there was much discussion of activating the SDR facility—as distinct from the creation or institution of a facility. These Executive Directors did not want the changes in rules and practices being suggested to cause an undue delay in this possible activation. Mr. Madan stated that he was not sure that the developing members, as they undertook to pass enabling legislation to accept the amendments, would understand why there had to be changes that seemed to make it more difficult for members to draw on the Fund's regular resources, in exchange for some "nonactivated or unactivated" scheme. Changes in the Fund's rules and practices were bound to be interpreted as tightening the previous policies of the Fund regarding its resources. Consequently, these changes should be made simultaneously with activation of the new facility, not just with its incorporation into the Articles. Mr. Madan emphasized that, if some authorities believed that at least some of the changes in the rules and practices of the Fund should be put into force immediately, even in advance of activation of the SDR facility, some other of the provisions—such as those that barred further quasi-automaticity in the credit tranches, the new repurchase provisions, and the 85 per cent voting majority for general quota increases—should not be brought into effect before the first allocation of SDRs.

It was agreed at the Stockholm meeting that the proposed amendments would be presented in a single document. Thus, the changes in the Fund's rules and practices would become effective when the amendments relating to the new reserve facility took effect, whatever might be the lapse of time before activation of the facility. Nevertheless, Mr. Madan's statement on behalf of the developing members was favorably received at the Stockholm meeting by some Ministers and Governors. Mr. Dale, in assuring Mr. Madan of this at a meeting of the Executive Board shortly after the Stockholm meeting, said he believed that the somewhat obscure sentence about the interconnection in the ministerial communiqué should be read in terms more of its spirit than of its precise legal meaning. It had been included as an attempt to assure those who were concerned about the appearance of greater restriction following the changes that at least some Ministers and Governors in the Group of Ten had tried, and would continue to try, to ensure that any such changes would be applied in a spirit that was in accordance with that expressed in Mr. Madan's statement.

Since the Executive Directors had devoted many sessions to considering changes in the Fund's rules and practices, these draft amendments were ready for submission to the Board of Governors along with the draft amendments to establish special drawing rights.

DECISION TAKEN AND RESOLUTION ADOPTED

A draft, and a redraft, of the report of the Executive Directors to the Board of Governors covering the new facility and the changes in the Fund's rules and practices were considered at several sessions of the Executive Board.[11] The deadline of March 31, 1968 specified in the Board of Governors' resolution was not quite met. But on April 16, 1968 the Executive Board took a decision to adopt the report and to recommend the adoption by the Board of Governors of a resolution approving the proposed amendment.[12] The report, to which was annexed the recommendations of the Executive Board as well as the Outline on which the proposed amendment was based, was submitted to the Governors on the following day and was made public on April 22, 1968.[13]

The Governors approved the proposed amendment, without meeting, effective May 31, 1968.[14] France was the only large member of the Fund that did not vote in favor of it. The proposed amendment was then submitted to all members for their acceptance. Before the proposed amendment could enter into force, it had to be accepted by three fifths of the members having four fifths of the total voting power. For most members this acceptance involved legislative action. In addition, members having 75 per cent of the total of quotas had to deposit instruments of participation in the Special Drawing Account before the Account could become operational. At the Twenty-Third Annual Meeting, held in Washington from September 30 to October 4, 1968, Mr. Schweitzer urged all members, small and large, to take the necessary steps as soon as possible. Agreement on the SDR facility had shaped the course for a rational response in the event of a future need to supplement reserves, but such a response required that the facility be established with minimum delay.[15]

---

[11] The changes in the rules and practices of the Fund are dealt with in Chap. 13 below.

[12] E.B. Decision No. 2493-(68/74), April 16, 1968; Vol. II below, p. 216.

[13] *Establishment of a Facility Based on Special Drawing Rights in the International Monetary Fund and Modifications in the Rules and Practices of the Fund: A Report by the Executive Directors to the Board of Governors Proposing Amendment of the Articles of Agreement* (Washington, April 1968), 80 pp. Also published in Vol. II below, pp. 52–94.

[14] Resolution No. 23-5, *Summary Proceedings, 1968*, pp. 293–94.

[15] Opening Address by the Managing Director, *Summary Proceedings, 1968*, pp. 24–25.

CHAPTER

8

SDRs Enter into Force
(1968–69)

O N JULY 28, 1969 THE AMENDMENT to the Articles of Agreement establishing SDRs and amending the original Articles to change certain of the Fund's rules and practices became effective for all members of the Fund. This was a little more than a year after the proposed amendment was approved by the Board of Governors (May 31, 1968). An interval was necessary because many of the members of the Fund had to pass enabling legislation in order to accept the proposed amendment. By July 28, 1969, acceptances had been received by 69 of the then 111 Fund members—that is, by three fifths of the members having four fifths of the total voting power, as provided in Article XVII (*a*).

The United States had been among the first to accept the amendment. President Lyndon B. Johnson had proudly announced the U.S. acceptance to the Governors on September 30, 1968, as he addressed them at the Annual Meeting.[1] The U.S. acceptance thus had come exactly five years after President Kennedy had suggested the need for action with regard to international liquidity. Only eight of the countries in the Group of Ten, however, were in the initial group accepting the new facility by July 1969; Italy and France accepted later, Italy on October 2, 1969 and France on December 30, 1969.

Once the proposed amendment had been accepted, the Special Drawing Account was to come into existence when Fund members having 75 per cent of the total quotas had deposited instruments of participation. That condition was satisfied on August 6, 1969, a little more than a week after the amendment became effective. The participants in the Special Drawing Account—numbering 50 on that date—were thereby enabled to take decisions with respect to the management of the Account, including any allocation of SDRs.

In his concluding remarks to the Board of Governors at the 1969 Annual Meeting, the Managing Director characterized the establishment and activation of the SDR facility as "a momentous innovation in the international monetary

---

[1] Address by the President of the United States, *Summary Proceedings, 1968*, p. 2.

President Lyndon B. Johnson, *left*, with Managing Director, *center*, and Henry H. Fowler, Governor for United States, at 1968 Annual Meeting

system—a landmark in the process of international monetary cooperation." [2] What was significant about the advent of SDRs was that there was instituted a unique type of reserve, one that had never before existed, issued by an international agency rather than by any national government, and used by governments, along with gold and foreign exchange, to settle international accounts. A mechanism had been agreed for the deliberate creation of reserves to inject liquidity into the international monetary system, should the need arise.

Because of their novelty, and because they resembled gold more than they did anything else, SDRs were initially referred to by financial journalists and laymen as "paper gold." But within a very short time the term by which the Fund and technicians called them, SDRs, had gained wide acceptance. Most significant of all was that the Fund had been given the kind of reserve-creating powers that had been denied it at its inception.

AMENDMENT OF BY-LAWS AND RULES AND REGULATIONS

After the amendment to the Articles became effective, it was possible to adopt the amendments to the By-Laws and to the Rules and Regulations of the Fund that were necessary both because of the Special Drawing Account and because of the changes in the rules and practices of the Fund.

The amended By-Laws spelled out, for example, that in matters pertaining exclusively to the Special Drawing Account, only those Governors and Executive Directors could vote who had been appointed or elected by Fund members that had become participants in the Special Drawing Account. Other amendments to the By-Laws related to the Executive Directors' Annual Report to the Board of Governors: that Report was hereafter to include a review of the operation of the Special Drawing Account and of the adequacy of global reserves and to extend to the Special Drawing Account the annual external audit of the financial records and the operations and transactions of the Fund. More far-reaching additions were needed in the Rules and Regulations. For one thing, the Rules and Regulations had to include a description of the various operational steps that would apply to the use of SDRs.

The Executive Directors had considered a first draft of the amendments to the By-Laws and the Rules and Regulations during the course of their discussions of the proposed amendment to the Articles. They considered a redraft more carefully over the three months from mid-June to mid-September 1969. On September 18, 1969 the Executive Board approved the texts of these amendments, and on October 2, 1969 the Board of Governors adopted Resolutions Nos. 24-9 and 24-10 stating that the amendments of the By-Laws should take effect and that the Governors had reviewed the amendments to the Rules

---

[2] Concluding Remarks by the Managing Director, *Summary Proceedings, 1969*, p. 250.

and Regulations recommended by the Executive Board and had no changes to suggest.[3] One By-Law, Section 23, pertaining to the establishment of a Committee on Interpretation of the Board of Governors, had not, however, been adopted by the end of 1971.

The amended Rules and Regulations helped to give operational substance to the new facility.[4] They specified, for example, the methods for deciding which currencies were convertible in fact and how exchange rates would be determined in connection with transfers of SDRs. They detailed the procedures for the provision and conversion of currency in exchange for SDRs and for designating participants to provide currency. They directed the Fund to make calculations for each participant at the end of given calendar intervals so as to determine whether, and to what extent, a participant would need to acquire and hold SDRs between the date of the calculation and the end of any five-year period in order to enable the participant to observe its reconstitution obligation. They provided for the procedures to deal with a participant's failure to fulfill its obligations that involved or could lead to the suspension of the participant's right to use SDRs.

■ ■ ■ ■ ■ ■

A summary description of the SDR facility as it finally emerged follows.[5] This description lays the framework for the discussion, in Chapters 10, 11, and 12, of the activation of the facility in January 1970 and operations and transactions in SDRs in 1970 and 1971.

TWO SEPARATE ACCOUNTS

After the establishment of the SDR facility, the Fund set up two separate accounts, a General Account and a Special Drawing Account. The Fund's operations and transactions involving SDRs were conducted through the Special Drawing Account. All other operations and transactions of the Fund, including transactions of an administrative character, were conducted through the General Account. Operations and transactions involving the acceptance or holding of SDRs in the General Account or the use of SDRs so held were carried out through, and recorded in, both Accounts.

The Board of Governors and the Executive Board functioned for the Special Drawing Account as well as for the General Account. But when deci-

---

[3] *Summary Proceedings, 1969*, pp. 260-75 and 320-25.

[4] The By-Laws and the Rules and Regulations, as amended to March 20, 1972, are reproduced in Vol. II below, pp. 158-91.

[5] See also Joseph Gold, *Special Drawing Rights: Character and Use*, IMF Pamphlet Series, No. 13, 2nd ed. (Washington, 1970); and J. J. Polak, *Some Reflections on the Nature of Special Drawing Rights*, IMF Pamphlet Series, No. 16 (Washington, 1971).

sions were taken on matters pertaining exclusively to SDRs, those entitled to vote could cast only the votes of the participants in the Special Drawing Account, and the special majorities that were specified for certain decisions were based on the total voting power of those participants only. No special provision was introduced with respect to the voting strength of a participant on matters pertaining to the Special Drawing Account: a member that was a participant thus had the same voting strength (250 basic votes plus 1 additional vote for each part of its quota equivalent to US$100,000) whether an issue related to the General Account or to the Special Drawing Account.

Each member of the Fund was entitled to become a participant in the Special Drawing Account, but was not required to participate. Participation involved the assumption of both financial and nonfinancial obligations, and in order to become a participant a member had to deposit with the Fund an instrument setting forth that it undertook all these obligations and that it had taken all the steps necessary in accordance with its own domestic law to enable it to carry them out.

The basic financial obligation each participant assumed was the obligation to provide currency convertible in fact to another participant that was using its SDRs in a transaction subject to designation. The participant providing convertible currency received an equivalent amount of SDRs. In other words, a participant designated by the Fund to do so was obliged to provide convertible currency in return for SDRs. This obligation to accept SDRs was not unlimited, however; it ceased at the point at which a participant's holdings of SDRs were three times its net cumulative allocation, that is, its obligation could extend up to a total amount equivalent to twice the net amount of SDRs allocated to the participant. The obligation could be extended beyond this limit to a higher limit agreed between a participant and the Fund.

The currency obtained by a participant in return for its SDRs was thus not drawn from any pool of resources of gold or currency held by the Fund in the Special Drawing Account. Participants that received allocations of SDRs were not required to deposit an equivalent amount in gold or currencies for the purpose of subsequent operations or transactions in SDRs or for any other purpose. Only in the abnormal circumstances of the withdrawal of a participant from the Special Drawing Account or the liquidation of the Account would the Fund hold any gold or currency in that Account, and then only temporarily and in order to facilitate the settlements that were involved in these phenomena. This was one of the most fundamental differences between the two Accounts. In the General Account the Fund held large resources of gold and currencies. The Special Drawing Account did not contain even the resources with which to cover the administrative expenses of running the Account. These expenses were paid out of the General Account, subject to reimbursement by assessments levied in SDRs on all participants.

ALLOCATIONS AND CANCELLATIONS OF SDRs

Basic Principles and Techniques

Article XXIV, Section 1, stated the basic principles and considerations governing allocation and cancellation of SDRs:

> (a) In all its decisions with respect to the allocation and cancellation of special drawing rights the Fund shall seek to meet the long-term global need, as and when it arises, to supplement existing reserve assets in such manner as will promote the attainment of its purposes and will avoid economic stagnation and deflation as well as excess demand and inflation in the world.

> (b) The first decision to allocate special drawing rights shall take into account, as special considerations, a collective judgment that there is a global need to supplement reserves, and the attainment of a better balance of payments equilibrium, as well as the likelihood of a better working of the adjustment process in the future.

It was thus a global shortage of unconditional liquidity that had to guide the Fund in reaching a decision on whether to generate SDRs. Decisions were not to be determined by the desire of one or more participants for additional reserves in order to enable them to defer the measures necessary to correct balance of payments disequilibrium. The need that SDRs was intended to satisfy had to be not only *global* but also *long-term*. In taking its decisions, the Fund was to deal with long-term trends in the needs of the community of its members. It was not intended, therefore, that the Fund should attempt the short-run management of the volume of international liquidity in the way that national monetary authorities regulate domestic liquidity.

The general formulation in the amendments, which related decisions to allocate or to cancel SDRs to the attainment of the Fund's purposes and to worldwide inflation and deflation, recognized that there were no agreed mathematical or mechanical tests by which to determine whether there was too little, enough, or too much liquidity in the international monetary system. In effect, a qualitative judgment had to be made. The first decision to allocate SDRs had to take into account three "special considerations": (1) a collective judgment that there was a global need to supplement reserves; (2) the attainment of a better balance of payments equilibrium; and (3) the likelihood of a better working of the adjustment process in the future.

Decisions to allocate SDRs were made for basic periods, which normally were to be five years in duration and which were to run consecutively. A basic period could be an empty period, in which there was neither allocation nor cancellation. The length of the normal basic period was an expression of the principle that the Fund was to be dealing with long-term trends in reserves. The choice of five years had also been intended to make it possible to deal simultaneously with the levels of both conditional and unconditional liquidity, since under the then existing Articles the Fund had to review the adequacy of quotas at intervals not exceeding five years.

Allocations that were decided upon were normally to be made annually so as to provide for a steady expansion or contraction in the volume of SDRs outstanding. Allocations were made on the basis of participants' quotas in the Fund on the date of the relevant decision to allocate, unless the Fund decided that allocations were to be made at different intervals or were to be based on quotas at different dates. A decision to allocate expressed the amount to be allocated as a uniform percentage of quota for all participants rather than as an absolute amount. Provision was also made for determining the amounts of SDRs to be canceled in the event of decisions to cancel.

A participant whose Governor did not vote in favor of a decision under which allocations for a basic period were being made did not have to receive allocations under that decision if it did not wish to do so. In other words, a participant might "opt out" of a decision to allocate SDRs over a basic period by not voting for the related decision and by informing the Fund that it wanted no allocation under the decision. Subsequently it might, if the Fund permitted, "opt back in" and receive later allocations made during the remainder of the basic period. A participant was required to receive SDRs allocated to it if its Governor voted in favor of the decision under which the allocations were made. A member that became a participant after a basic period had started did not receive allocations during that basic period, unless the Fund decided that the member would start to receive allocations beginning with the next allocation after it became a participant. It was expected that normally the Fund would so decide.

Allocations of SDRs might be made only to participants, but the holding of SDRs was not restricted to participants. The Fund itself was authorized to accept and hold SDRs in, and use them through, the General Account; and by an 85 per cent majority of the total voting power, the Fund might permit nonmembers, members that were not participants, and institutions that performed the functions of a central bank for more than one member, to engage in operations and transactions involving SDRs.

Procedure for Making Decisions

The procedure for arriving at decisions on allocations and cancellations of SDRs defined precisely the roles of the Managing Director, the Executive Board, and the Board of Governors. The Managing Director must make a proposal. But he must first satisfy himself that the proposal would be consistent with the principles and special considerations governing allocations and cancellations, and he must then conduct such consultations as would enable him to determine that there was broad support among participants for the proposal. The Managing Director also had some guidance for determining when to consider the possibility of making proposals. In accordance with the concept of consecutive basic periods, he was directed to make a proposal not later than six months before the end of each basic period or within six months of any request for a proposal by the Board of Governors or the Executive Board. He might, however, make a report instead of a proposal if he concluded that there was no proposal that commanded broad support among participants.

The Executive Board then had to concur in the Managing Director's proposal before it could be presented to the Board of Governors. A decision to concur required a majority of the votes cast. The Executive Board might refuse to concur but it had no authority to change a proposal. If it concurred, the proposal still went forward as the proposal of the Managing Director, for which he continued to have responsibility. It was, of course, unlikely that the Executive Board would withhold its concurrence, since the Managing Director would have determined beforehand whether there was the broad support necessary for a proposal.

The last step in the procedure was the decision by the Board of Governors; the Board of Governors could not delegate to the Executive Board the authority to take decisions on allocations or cancellations of SDRs. A decision approving the Managing Director's proposal as transmitted to the Board of Governors, or with modifications determined by the Board of Governors, could be adopted only if the very high majority of 85 per cent of the total voting power of participants was in favor of the decision. With such a majority, a decision to make allocations of SDRs had to win the support of almost the whole community of participants, including many, and perhaps most, of those in balance of payments surplus. These participants were likely to be the most vigilant in ensuring that allocations did not outstrip the global need for reserves.

Once allocations of SDRs were made, each holder received interest on the amount of its holdings and each participant paid charges on its net cumulative allocation. The rates of interest and charges were the same, so that a participant holding more SDRs than its net cumulative allocation received a net payment, and one holding less made a net payment. Charges and interest were payable in SDRs. The initial rate was set at 1½ per cent per annum, but the Fund might change this rate. The payment of interest, which did not exist for gold reserves, was intended to be an inducement to hold SDRs.

OPERATIONS AND TRANSACTIONS IN SDRs

There was, in effect, a requirement of need before a participant used SDRs: A participant was expected to transfer its SDRs to another participant only to meet balance of payments needs or because of adverse developments in its official reserves. The provision regarding developments in reserves had been intended to indicate that the participant might have a need to use SDRs even if developments in its reserves were attributable to conversions of balances in its currency rather than to a balance of payments deficit. But, in particular, a participant was not expected to use its SDRs for the sole purpose of changing the composition of its reserves as between SDRs and holdings of gold, foreign exchange, and its reserve position in the Fund. This basic principle of need protected other participants from the risk that a participant that had no economic justification for the use of SDRs might be tempted to use them solely in order to get rid of them and to obtain reserve assets that it preferred.

Despite the foregoing, a participant's use of SDRs was unconditional, clearly not to be challenged in any circumstances. The use of SDRs was not dependent, for instance, in any way on a participant's use of the Fund's regular resources, nor could a participant's use of SDRs be questioned on the basis of the economic and financial policies that it was pursuing. If a participant could be prevented from using its SDRs because its policies were regarded, for example, as inadequate to correct its external payments difficulties, SDRs would be subject to the conditionality associated with drawing rights in the Fund's General Account. SDRs, in contrast to regular drawings from the Fund beyond the gold tranche, represented unconditional liquidity. Hence, in effect a participant was entitled to transfer its SDRs but was not expected to do this unless it had a need to do so because of its balance of payments or because of developments in its reserves.

By the same reasoning, there was no provision in the Articles which declared that a participant could use no more than a proportion of its net cumulative allocation of SDRs: a participant was able to use its SDRs until none remained. Use beyond a certain average proportion over time, however, might require the participant to restore its holdings to a certain extent (described below in the section on Reconstitution).

The principle that a participant was expected to use its SDRs only when in need protected transferees. On the other hand, the fact that the use of SDRs was immune from challenge protected transferors. The tests for ascertaining whether a transfer of SDRs was proper were not applied by the Fund before a transfer was made, and the Fund could not obstruct a transfer even if it could be demonstrated that there was no balance of payments or reserve need. All of these provisions emphasized the asset-like character of SDRs.

To balance the interests of participants, however, the Fund might make representations to a participant that had not fulfilled the expectation. The Executive Board could decide *ex post* that a participant had failed to meet the test of need when it used its SDRs. That participant was then subject to designation by the Fund as a transferee of SDRs even though it would not otherwise have been subject to designation. Designation for that purpose was limited to the amount of SDRs that the participant had used in nonconformity with the expectation as to need.

A participant transferred its SDRs to another participant designated by the Fund and obtained currency convertible in fact. (SDRs could not be used in transactions with private parties in the market.) The term currency convertible in fact was defined in the Articles, and the Rules and Regulations set up procedures by which the Fund might determine which currencies qualified to be termed convertible in fact.

When a participant wished to use its SDRs, it informed the Fund so that the Fund could give instructions to the participant or participants that it designated to provide currency convertible in fact. If the transferor of SDRs wished to receive a particular currency convertible in fact, it must request that in the notice sent to the Fund, but the transferor was not required to express a preference for a currency if it was content to receive any currency convertible in fact. The designated participant might provide any currency convertible in fact. If the currency provided was not the currency convertible in fact requested by the transferor, then the country that had issued the currency provided must convert it into the currency requested.

Instructions for conversion when a participant transferred SDRs to a designated participant were given by the Fund so as to avoid procedures that might be inadequate or unfamiliar if conversions had to be arranged between participants. The Fund encouraged participants to inform it of the currency convertible in fact that they were likely to provide when designated and of the currency convertible in fact that they were likely to request when transferring SDRs. The rules stated that instructions for the provision or conversion of currency were to be carried out promptly, and the objective was to see that the transferor received the currency it had requested two business days after the Fund received the communication requesting the currency or as soon as possible thereafter.

The preceding chapter pointed to the close relation between the definitions of currency convertible in fact and the exchange rates applicable to various currencies. The purpose of the provisions of the amended Articles regarding exchange rates was to specify that in operations or transactions between participants in the Special Drawing Account the transferor must receive the same value, whatever currency was provided and whichever participant provided it.

DESIGNATION

It will be recalled that one of the most important issues that had to be resolved in determining the qualities of a reserve asset was whether a participant wishing to use the asset should be able to decide for itself on the identity of the transferee or whether there should be a system of guidance. The solution finally agreed upon was a system of guidance by the Fund.

Under the system of guidance, the Fund was to channel the flow of SDRs toward appropriate transferees. The general principles to be used for designation and the rules for the first basic period were specified in the Articles. Briefly, a participant was to be subject to designation if its balance of payments and gross reserve positions were sufficiently strong, or possibly if it had a strong reserve position even though it had a moderate balance of payments deficit. Designations of participants were also to aim over time at a balanced or equitable distribution of SDRs among participants.

Much discussion had attended the concept of a balanced or equitable distribution of SDRs among participants and how to achieve it. There had been great concern that some participants would make excessive use of their SDRs compared with other components of their reserves; by the same token, other participants would have to hold excessive amounts of the new assets. Finally, it was agreed that the criterion would be an approach to equality in the ratios of participants' holdings of SDRs in excess of their net cumulative allocations to their official holdings of gold and foreign exchange. These ratios were to be "harmonized" over time. Notwithstanding the importance for designation of the principles of a strong balance of payments and reserve position and of harmonization of the ratios of holdings of SDRs of participants, priority was normally to be given to designations to ensure certain operational objectives of the Special Drawing Account: to help participants observe their obligations to reconstitute, to correct any failure by participants to observe the expectation as to need when using SDRs, or to provide participants with the SDRs that they owed the Fund because they did not hold enough to meet their shares of a cancellation.

In accordance with the Rules and Regulations, the Executive Board was to adopt a designation plan at quarterly intervals. This plan would list the participants subject to designation during that quarter and the amounts for which they would be designated. All participants subject to designation in the forthcoming quarter had to be included in the plan. The total amount of all designations equaled the amount considered appropriate. If this forecast turned out to be wrong, a supplementary plan was to be adopted by the Executive Board. In addition, should any participant, an Executive Director, or the Managing Director so request, the Executive Board might review a plan and amend it if considered necessary. This amendment might be desirable, for example, if an unexpected and serious change occurred in the balance of payments and reserve position of a participant. The extent to which participants were actually designated depended on the volume of transactions involving designation that occurred.

The acceptance of SDRs by designated participants was, of course, the rock on which the use of SDRs rested. But participants were not obligated to accept SDRs without limit. A participant's obligation to accept further SDRs ceased at the point at which its holdings in excess of its net cumulative allocation reached twice that amount. That is to say, a participant could not be required to hold more SDRs than three times its net cumulative allocation.

RECONSTITUTION

One of the most controversial of all the questions debated in the course of setting up the new reserve facility, and the last to be resolved, was whether a participant that used its SDRs should be bound to restore its holdings of them. The solution was a pragmatic compromise. A participant would be entitled to use all of its SDRs and would not be required to retain a permanent minimum balance. But it would be required to maintain a certain average balance in its holdings over time, and the maintenance of this average balance might require a participant to reconstitute its holdings of SDRs. A participant's net use of SDRs had to be such that the average of its daily holdings of SDRs over any five-year period would be not less than 30 per cent of the average of its daily net cumulative allocation over the same period. If a participant used no more than 70 per cent of its average net cumulative allocation at all times, it would have automatically fulfilled this obligation. If it used more than 70 per cent for some part of a five-year period, it would have to increase its holdings above 30 per cent for a period long enough to bring its use for the whole five-year period to no more than 70 per cent on the average.

The main mechanism for the reconstitution of SDRs was the designation of participants to accept transfers of SDRs from other participants. The Fund would make calculations for each participant to determine whether and to what extent a participant would need to acquire and hold SDRs between the date of the calculation and the end of any five-year period in order to enable the participant to observe its obligation to reconstitute. Under the Rules and Regulations, when these calculations showed that a participant needed to obtain SDRs for any reconstitution period in an amount per quarter that equaled or exceeded 10 per cent of the participant's net cumulative allocation at the end of the period, the participant was subject to designation "as of the beginning of the calendar quarter following the calculation, for an amount of special drawing rights equal to the largest amount per quarter calculated for any reconstitution period." [6]

GOLD-VALUE GUARANTEE

The value of SDRs was stated in terms of gold and not in terms of any national currency, with the unit of value equivalent to 0.888671 gram of fine gold. (This was the gold content of the U.S. dollar of the weight and fineness in effect on July 1, 1944 and also the value of the dollar when the SDR facility came into being in August 1969.) Participants that received SDRs, whether by allocation or by subsequent transfer, could be certain that there would never

---

[6] Rule P-4. Reproduced in Vol. II below, p. 189.

be a reduction in the gold value of their SDRs, and, therefore, they could accept them without fear of loss. In effect, SDRs enjoyed an absolute guarantee of the maintenance of their gold value. Changes in the par values of currencies in terms of gold did not affect the gold value of SDRs. If a currency was devalued in terms of gold, an SDR commanded more units of that currency on a transfer of SDRs than it did before the devaluation. Moreover, even a uniform proportionate change of par values in terms of gold—equivalent to a change in the price of gold in terms of currencies—could not affect the gold value of the SDR.

This feature of SDRs—the fixed gold value—became of even greater importance after August 15, 1971, when the exchange rate for the U.S. dollar in terms of other currencies was no longer fixed but an SDR retained its specified value.

SIGNIFICANCE OF THE NEW ASSET

The significance of an arrangement whereby the Fund could create reserves was commented upon by President Johnson in mid-1968 when he signed into law the U.S. Special Drawing Rights Act:

> For the first time in the world's financial history, nations will be able to create international reserves by deliberate and joint decision—and in amounts needed to support sound growth in world trade and payments.[7]

To bring the idea into reality had required an intensive period of study, negotiation, and, finally, legislation. The process had seemed long and drawn out to the watching public and to the financial markets, as well as to those intimately involved. That the negotiations were so prolonged—they had taken longer than those that had preceded the birth of the Fund itself in 1944—and that substantial compromise was required of all parties reflected the nearly equal financial strength of the major industrial countries. Unlike the situation toward the close of World War II, one or two economically dominant countries could not, in the second half of the 1960 decade, draw up an international monetary arrangement to which other countries could be expected to adhere.

To most the effort seemed worthwhile. The Managing Director, for example, said that "given the novelty, the complexity, and the responsibility of the task, I am convinced that the time invested in building a sound structure, and in developing the understanding necessary for the proper use of that structure, has been well justified."[8]

The new drawing rights were certainly novel, and were unlike any other reserve asset or money. Their uniqueness has been described by the General Counsel of the Fund in these words:

---

[7] *Department of State Bulletin*, Vol. 59 (1968), p. 49.

[8] Opening Address by the Managing Director, *Summary Proceedings, 1969*, p. 11.

The characteristics of special drawing rights are not the result of any single approach. They are the distillation of a chemistry—some might say an alchemy—in which many theories and many compromises, economic, legal, and political, went into the alembic. The product cannot be classified according to such familiar categories as "legal tender," "money," or "credit." Special drawing rights are *sui generis*.[9]

It seemed that the Fund could create reserves, as it were, out of nothing; it did not need to hold a corresponding amount of financial resources. Just how revolutionary the introduction of SDRs was may be noted by recalling some of the views prevalent at the time of the Bretton Woods Conference. A document issued by the U.S. Treasury in June 1944, for example, explained that the International Monetary Fund then being proposed would not have any means of creating, holding, or transferring currencies or deposits that did not originate with the member countries themselves. It was explicitly noted that the creation of credit was to remain exclusively a function of the monetary authorities of member countries. Among the reasons cited for preferring this arrangement to one permitting the Fund to create some new or special monetary unit was the following:

> . . . The financial strength and stability will be greater in the case of a Fund which possesses a substantial amount of tangible resources for carrying on its operations than in the case of an international institution which has no resources other than an agreement on the part of member countries to accept the credits created by that institution in exchange for real goods and services.[10]

By coincidence, the date on which the amendment to the Articles became effective, July 28, 1969, was 25 years almost to the week after the date, July 22, 1944, on which the original Articles were adopted at the Bretton Woods Conference. The advance made in that interval was that the Fund was at last to be given the power to create reserves that it had not received at Bretton Woods.

Many of the disputes that had attended the formation of SDRs subsided rather quickly. Whether they were or were not to be called reserve assets, for instance, soon was no longer a question that provoked ardent dispute. By the time of the 1969 Annual Meeting, where a decision was taken to activate the new facility, Mr. Giscard d'Estaing was calling the SDR a reserve asset, and no longer was insisting on the term "credit":

> . . . I wish to inform you of the reasons for which France has taken the decision to participate in the activation of the SDR system. First, as the Managing Director of the Fund has so aptly reminded us, the system is now in existence: we have ourselves always considered that alongside conditional liquidities there was room in the modern world for a new reserve asset of an unconditional type, designed to supplement gold and foreign exchange in the

---

[9] Gold, *Special Drawing Rights: Character and Use*, p. 28; cited above in footnote 5 of this chapter.

[10] *Questions and Answers on the International Monetary Fund* (June 10, 1944), reply to Question 15. Reproduced in *History 1945–65*, Vol. III, pp. 136–82; reference is to p. 154.

holdings of the central banks. This was the purport of the proposal that we made for the creation of a collective reserve unit, or CRU.[11]

A complex of reasons explains why the dream of many monetary theorists— a mechanism for deliberate creation of international reserves—finally became a reality. Foremost was the persistence of the officials involved. Time and again the monetary authorities of the ten largest industrial countries came together at the highest level to try to resolve their differences. What prompted their frequent meetings was not their fears that the supplies of gold or other reserves in the world were declining or that a shortage of reserves was imminent. Indeed, after the SDR facility was activated in 1970 some observers still did not see much evidence of the need for more reserves in the monetary system. The reason for trying to reach agreement on SDRs was rather that, after 1964–65, the monetary officials of the countries in the Group of Ten were forced to deal more and more often with monetary crises. These officials hoped that somehow, in ways that were not yet clear, the new supplement to the gold exchange standard would alleviate monetary crises and ease their problems.

Another reason why agreement finally came about in spite of differing opinions was that the new facility was initially looked upon as an experiment: participants took a wait-and-see attitude. Some of the rules, for example, were specified for the first basic period only and were to be reviewed later; and some were to be determined only after the facility had been in use for a period of time.

That the final scheme was an international one—open to all Fund members—rather than the limited arrangement initially envisaged was, of course, politically expedient to the countries in the Group of Ten. Many of them had a strong desire not to offend countries outside the Group. For political as well as other reasons, the United States, for instance, was especially eager to please Australia and was very sensitive to the views that had been expressed by Mr. Holt when he was the Treasurer of that country.[12] Moreover, since the countries in the Group of Ten had become nearly equal in economic strength, and no one country or countries in the Group could insist on its own ideas, it was all the more likely that, once they had reached accord among themselves on the features of any arrangement, the final arrangement would have to become operable through some neutral agency, such as an international organization.

That deliberate reserve creation took the form of special drawing rights in the Fund was, in no small part, a tribute to the intensive efforts of the Executive Directors, the Managing Director, and the staff. Their expertise and experience had enabled them to bring forth a host of studies, plans, and suggestions, and to convince the officials of the countries in the Group of Ten that the Fund was the appropriate agency to operate any new reserve facility.

---

[11] Statement by the Governor of the World Bank for France, *Summary Proceedings, 1969*, p. 58.

[12] See, for example, Chap. 4, p. 81.

CHAPTER
9

How SDRs Evolved:
A Synopsis

*T*HE PRINCIPAL EVENTS bearing on the creation of SDRs are listed here in brief form and chronological order. This synopsis has three objectives: (1) to juxtapose the developments in different forums (such as in the Fund, in the Group of Ten, and among technical experts) that were taking place concurrently; (2) to highlight the dates and decisions of the most fruitful of the numerous meetings that took place; and (3) to bring to the forefront the nature of the Fund's part in the formation of SDRs.

As a corollary, this synopsis brings out the modifications in several of the Fund's policies on the use of its resources and in its financial structure that took place partly in response to, or at least in the course of, the prolonged deliberations on international liquidity, especially in the early 1960s. Among the by-products of the discussions of liquidity were increases in Fund quotas, the establishment of the General Arrangements to Borrow, changes in the policies on purchases in the gold tranche, and the extension and liberalization of the compensatory financing facility. These by-products are described in separate chapters below or in the earlier history. It is worthwhile, however, to note here their geneses in the discussions that eventually led to SDRs.

1950s

April–October 1953	At the request of Ecosoc, the Fund studied world reserve adequacy and in a report, "The Adequacy of Monetary Reserves," defined adequacy.
August–September 1958	A study by the Fund staff on international liquidity, presented to the Annual Meeting (New Delhi), examined the subject of reserves afresh and questioned the adequacy of the Fund's resources, then about $9 billion.
December 1958	External convertibility was established for the currencies of 14 European countries. Thus, a majority of the Fund's members

now permitted nonresidents to transfer current earnings of their currencies to any other country.

March 1959 — Robert Triffin, Yale University, proposed that an enlarged and amended Fund should provide a new kind of international reserve and that all reserves except gold should be centralized in the Fund.

September 1959 — A 50 per cent general increase in quotas and special increases in the quotas of certain countries became effective, expanding the Fund's resources by about $6 billion, to more than $14 billion.

1960

January–December — As world trade increased rapidly, as movements of short-term capital began to take place relatively freely, and as pressures on gold reserves emerged, several monetary experts made proposals for expanding world liquidity:

Maxwell Stamp, United Kingdom, proposed the Stamp Plan. The Plan combined the needs of the industrial countries for additional liquidity with the needs of the developing countries for more capital.

Edward M. Bernstein, United States, and Robert V. Roosa, U.S. Treasury, suggested that the gold exchange standard be broadened by a system of "multiple reserve currencies." On the other hand, Jacques Rueff, France, advocated increasing the price of gold, and Milton Friedman, University of Chicago, advocated introducing freely flexible exchange rates as an alternative to expanding reserves.

September — The Fund's Annual Report stressed that the concept of international liquidity was broader than that of international reserves and should include the gold and foreign exchange held by the Fund.

September — The Managing Director, Per Jacobsson, at the Annual Meeting (Washington), observed that most Governors believed that the emerging problem of international movements of funds could be met within the existing international financial system and that there was no lack of international liquidity.

1961

February — Nine European countries accepted the obligations of Article VIII of the Fund Agreement; hence, they were committed to convertibility of their currencies, and liquid funds began to flow more freely than ever across national boundaries and into a greater number of convertible currencies.

March
To cope with increased short-term capital flows, which were aggravating payments imbalances in several industrial countries, inter-central-bank cooperation was strengthened. Under the Basle Agreement, the Governors of the central banks of Belgium, France, the Federal Republic of Germany, Italy, the Netherlands, Sweden, and the United Kingdom agreed to hold each other's currencies to a greater extent than before and to lend needed currencies to each other.

July
The Executive Board took a decision to permit members to use the Fund's resources to meet balance of payments deficits that were attributable to capital transfers.

September
The Fund's Annual Report observed that members were increasingly regarding their drawing rights in the Fund as part of their reserves.

September
The Managing Director, Per Jacobsson, at the Annual Meeting (Vienna), emphasized the steps that the Fund was taking to help meet the impact of international movements of private funds and stressed the need to enlarge the Fund's resources for emergencies, such as arrangements for the Fund to borrow from its principal members.

October
The London Gold Pool was formed, an arrangement whereby a number of countries agreed to share the burden of intervention in the London gold market to keep fluctuations in the price of gold within a reasonable range.

1962

February
The United States, through the Federal Reserve System, introduced "swap" facilities, i.e., the central banks of the main industrial countries would provide each other with reciprocal lines of credit.

July
The Executive Board took a decision which widened the selection of currencies that could be used in members' transactions with the Fund, thus augmenting considerably the Fund's supply of usable resources.

September
The Fund's Annual Report described the problems created by the growing volatility of short-term capital and how these problems were being handled by the strengthening of inter-central-bank cooperation and by new measures being taken by the Fund.

September	The Managing Director, Per Jacobsson, at the Annual Meeting (Washington), spelled out the reasons for his confidence in the existing international monetary system and reiterated his view that there was, as yet, no liquidity crisis.
September	Xenophon Zolotas, Greece, at the Annual Meeting (Washington), proposed a multiple-currency gold exchange standard.
September	Reginald Maudling, United Kingdom, at the Annual Meeting (Washington), proposed a mutual currency account.
October	The General Arrangements to Borrow entered into force, enlarging by $6 billion the resources to which the Fund had access.

1963

April–July	Many central bankers, while recognizing that the existing volume of world liquidity might be adequate, began to question whether it would continue to be so in the future. The world's holdings of official reserves had ceased to grow and there was a widening realization that, as the United States closed its balance of payments gap, the supply of dollar reserves for other countries would be reduced. On the other hand, some monetary officials in Europe contended that the major problem was not the supply of liquidity but rather how to improve the process of balance of payments adjustment.
July	The countries in the Group of Ten prepared to discuss the question of liquidity among themselves during the forthcoming Annual Meeting of the Fund.
September	The Fund's Annual Report stressed the central role of the Fund in matters concerning international liquidity.
October	The Managing Director, Pierre-Paul Schweitzer, announced at the Annual Meeting (Washington), that the Fund would intensify its study of international liquidity, the functioning of the international monetary system, and the role of the Fund in that field.
October	Valéry Giscard d'Estaing, France, at the Annual Meeting (Washington), repeated his view that the fundamental difficulty with the international monetary system was not a shortage of liquidity but a lack of mechanisms for correcting balance of payments disequilibria.

October — The Finance Ministers and Central Bank Governors of the Group of Ten, after a special meeting during the Fund's Annual Meeting, instructed their Deputies to undertake a thorough examination of the international monetary system and of the probable future need for liquidity. The terms of reference for these studies specified that a system of fixed exchange rates would continue to prevail and that the price of gold would remain unchanged. They also urged the reserve currency countries to eliminate their payments deficits. The Deputies were instructed to maintain close working relations with the Fund.

October — The Managing Director, Pierre-Paul Schweitzer, outlined for the Executive Board a program of studies on liquidity on which the Fund would begin.

October — Edward M. Bernstein, United States, proposed that the countries of the Group of Ten, plus Switzerland, should establish a composite reserve unit (CRU) equivalent to gold, consisting of a stated proportion of each of their currencies.

1964

January — The Executive Directors held informal sessions to discuss the studies on liquidity that the Fund would undertake. The Managing Director, Pierre-Paul Schweitzer, suggested that, as part of these studies, the general adequacy of Fund quotas and the Fund's policies on gold tranche drawings should be examined.

August — The Executive Board took a decision which modified the Fund's procedures so that gold tranche drawings could take place more quickly and more nearly automatically.

August — The Fund's Annual Report (Chapters 3 and 4) dealt at length with the subject of liquidity. A distinction was made between conditional and unconditional liquidity, and it was noted that the Fund had been much the largest creator of conditional liquidity, in the form of drawing rights financed under the Fund's system of quotas. The Report concluded (1) that there was a case for a second round of increases in Fund quotas, (2) that the general level of liquidity then existing was broadly satisfactory but that some inadequacies might arise in the future, and (3) that any new liquidity arrangements or mechanism should be based on a multilateral institutional approach.

August — A report by the Deputies of the Group of Ten (1) suggested that Working Party 3 of the OECD should study how members of the OECD could achieve faster and more effective adjustment of their payments imbalances, (2) proposed that multilateral surveillance be continued and intensified, and (3) established a Study Group on the Creation of Reserve Assets, under the chairmanship of Rinaldo Ossola, Italy, to consider the need for a new reserve asset.

August   The Finance Ministers and Central Bank Governors of the Group of Ten agreed that supplies of gold and reserve currencies were fully adequate for the present, but approved the formation of the Ossola Group to study future needs. They agreed also to support a moderate increase in Fund quotas during 1965 and to re-examine the question of renewing the General Arrangements to Borrow.

August   The report on a series of informal conferences held in Bellagio by an unofficial group of academic and government economists was published. In general, these economists concluded that various alternative solutions to the existing international monetary problems—such as a multiple reserve currency system, flexible exchange rates, a semiautomatic gold standard, or the centralization of all reserves—were not so diametrically opposed as they once had thought.

September   At the Annual Meeting (Tokyo), Governors still expressed divergent views on how urgently something needed to be done about expanding the supply of liquidity. The Managing Director, Pierre-Paul Schweitzer, was strongly in favor of having any new arrangements undertaken in the Fund and of including all members in any such arrangements.

September   The Board of Governors, at the Annual Meeting (Tokyo), resolved that the Executive Directors should consider an increase in Fund quotas and submit an appropriate proposal at an early date.

October   The Fund staff, partly in response to requests from the Deputies of the Group of Ten, began to explore ways by which the Fund might engage in deliberate reserve creation. Two techniques were examined: (1) extension of quasi-automatic drawing facilities and (2) acquisition of special assets and assumption of additional liabilities.

1965

February   President Charles de Gaulle, France, and his Minister of Economy and Finance, Valéry Giscard d'Estaing, called for a return to the gold standard.

March	The Board of Governors adopted resolutions proposing an increase of 25 per cent in the quotas of all Fund members and special increases for 16 members.
March	Robert V. Roosa, U.S. Treasury, proposed that a type of CRU be established by the main industrial countries.
March	Valéry Giscard d'Estaing, Minister of Economy and Finance, France, put forward a French version of a CRU plan.
June	The Managing Director, Pierre-Paul Schweitzer, speaking in Paris, (1) observed that the present international monetary system had worked well, but that large short-term capital movements had caused difficulties, (2) rejected the need for a change in the price of gold, (3) advocated correction of balance of payments deficits by the United Kingdom and the United States, and (4) expressed a preference for liquidity schemes which operated through the Fund with participation by all members.
July	Henry H. Fowler, Secretary of the U.S. Treasury, considered early action on liquidity essential and urged establishment of a preparatory committee to arrange for an international monetary conference.
August	The report of the Ossola Group was published. Various techniques for deliberate reserve creation were examined, but no preference was expressed. Differences of view still persisted on such questions as the nature of a link between any new reserve asset and gold, the number of participating countries, the role of the Fund in any scheme, and the rules by which decisions to create liquidity would be made.
August	The Fund's Annual Report described several problems of principle and technique that were involved in any scheme for reserve creation and concluded that, even if there was no need for immediate creation of additional reserves, it was important to consider well in advance the many questions involved. The Report also suggested ways in which reserves could be created through the Fund.
September	During the Annual Meeting (Washington), the Finance Ministers and Central Bank Governors of the Group of Ten issued a communiqué reporting their agreement to draw up a plan for reserve creation that could be put into effect should the need arise, i.e., a contingency plan. They also recognized that, once the countries of the Group of Ten had agreed on essential points, a second phase of the discussions should include coun-

tries outside the Group of Ten. They instructed their Deputies to work out with the Managing Director of the Fund procedures by which the efforts of the Executive Directors of the Fund and of the Deputies of the Group of Ten could be directed toward a consensus.

September   The Managing Director, Pierre-Paul Schweitzer, at the Annual Meeting (Washington), (1) reiterated his belief that international liquidity was the business of the Fund, (2) suggested that, rather than a special international monetary conference, the Board of Governors of the Fund would serve ideally as a way to bring together high-level financial and monetary authorities, and (3) again advocated that any new liquidity facilities should be available to all Fund members.

November   The Expert Group on International Monetary Issues set up by the UNCTAD in September, after holding meetings in New York in October, issued a report, *International Monetary Issues and the Developing Countries.* The report recommended, inter alia, enlarging and liberalizing the Fund's compensatory financing facility and concluded that (1) the establishment of a link between the creation of international liquidity and the provision of development finance was both feasible and desirable, (2) the reform of the international monetary system should be truly international, and (3) developing countries should be represented in the discussions leading to monetary reform and in the operation of any new arrangements.

November   It was agreed that the Managing Director's representatives at the meetings of the Deputies of the Group of Ten could report on the proceedings, in general terms, to the Executive Directors.

November   The staff and the Executive Board began to consider extending the Fund's compensatory financing facility.

1966

January   Four plans for deliberate reserve creation were submitted to the Deputies of the Group of Ten—by the United States, by Otmar Emminger, by the United Kingdom, and by Canada. All four provided for creation of a reserve asset by a limited group of countries. Three of the plans provided for a "dual approach," i.e., for two kinds of co-existing arrangements, a new reserve asset for a limited group of countries and some kind of additional drawing rights in the Fund—the U.S. plan called them "special reserve drawing rights"—either for all countries or for those not included in the reserve asset scheme.

February	A special session of the UNCTAD Committee on Invisibles and Financing Related to Trade, meeting in New York, endorsed the report of the UNCTAD group of experts that had been issued in November 1965.
February	Several Executive Directors elected by countries not in the Group of Ten, uneasy about the discussions going on in the Deputies of that Group, as well as about a possible "dual approach," made a plea for the Fund to submit its own proposals for deliberate reserve creation.
February	The second general increase in Fund quotas, along with special increases for some countries, became effective for those members that had consented to increases in their quotas. With the consent of all members to the increases, the Fund's resources would be expanded from $16 billion to $21 billion.
March	At the request of the Inter-American Committee on the Alliance for Progress (CIAP), four monetary officials issued a report, *International Monetary Reform and Latin America*, which endorsed the report of the UNCTAD group of experts (issued in November 1965) and stressed Latin America's need for increased liquidity.
March	The Managing Director, Pierre-Paul Schweitzer, sent to the Executive Board two alternative plans for reserve creation. Plan I would use the Fund's existing machinery to extend quasi-automatic drawing rights of the gold tranche type. Plan II would involve the issuance of reserve units by a newly organized Fund affiliate (the International Reserve Fund, or IRF), membership in which would be open to all Fund members.
March–April	The Executive Directors in informal session held preliminary discussions of the two plans for reserve creation proposed by the Managing Director. Since these proposals had not been acted upon by the Executive Board, they were referred to as those of the Managing Director and were sent as such to the Deputies of the Group of Ten.
April	The Governors of the central banks of Latin America, meeting in Runaway Bay, Jamaica, expressed their views on international monetary reform in the Declaration of Jamaica. They advocated the preservation to the greatest extent possible of the existing mechanisms of the international monetary system, including the Fund as the center, and suggested further improvements within the Fund that would enlarge and facilitate the access of Latin American countries to the Fund's resources.

April	A number of academic economists and some of the officials of Working Party 3 of the OECD met in Princeton, New Jersey, for the second of two series of discussions on adjustment of international payments imbalances. (The first series had been held in Zürich, Switzerland, in January.)
April	The Managing Director, Pierre-Paul Schweitzer, addressing the Federation of German Industries at Kronberg im Taunus, Germany, emphasized the importance of avoiding any division of countries into two groups, as through a dual approach, and explained how a reserve unit scheme could cover all Fund members.
May	Among the countries of the Group of Ten, support for a universal approach to deliberate reserve creation, as against a dual approach, began to increase.
May	A "Group of Thirty-One" developing countries reiterated a principle enunciated earlier by the UNCTAD Committee on Invisibles and Financing Related to Trade—that all countries should be eligible to participate in any deliberate creation of reserve assets.
July	The Deputies of the Group of Ten sent their report on a contingency plan for reserve creation to the Ministers and Governors. While no specific plan was presented, certain principles were enunciated: (1) deliberate reserve creation should take place on the basis of a collective judgment of the world's reserve needs and not be directed to financing the payments deficits of individual countries; (2) deliberate reserve creation should consist of unconditional liquidity to be made available to all members of the Fund; (3) the process of decision making for reserve creation should reflect the special responsibility of the major industrial countries for the international monetary system; and (4) activation of any plan, that is, the actual creation of reserves as distinguished from contingency planning, would not take place until a separate and new decision had been taken that there was a clear need for supplementary reserves and that certain additional conditions had been fulfilled. (The Deputies' Report was released to the public in August.)
July	The Finance Ministers and Central Bank Governors of the Group of Ten, after meeting in The Hague, issued a communiqué agreeing with the principles set forth in the report of the Deputies. They also reviewed the report of Working Party 3 of the OECD and expressed their hope that the Working Party would continue its work.

August	Some of the details of the Managing Director's proposals for reserve creation were made public in the Fund's Annual Report (Chapter 2).
September	The Executive Board took a decision liberalizing and extending the Fund's compensatory financing facility.
September	The Managing Director, Pierre-Paul Schweitzer, at the Annual Meeting (Washington), indicated that he knew of no technical reasons why concentrated work could not provide the Governors with fully developed suggestions for reserve creation in time for the next Annual Meeting. He announced that arrangements for informal meetings between Executive Directors and the Deputies of the Group of Ten were being discussed. At the ministerial meeting of the Group of Ten, he explained why the Executive Directors for the countries not in the Group of Ten did not want subordinate participation.
October–November	The Executive Directors agreed to meet with the Deputies of the Group of Ten.
October–November	The Executive Directors considered in informal sessions the procedures to be followed in their joint meetings with the Deputies of the Group of Ten and the questions to be discussed.
November	The first joint meeting of Executive Directors and the Deputies of the Group of Ten was held in Washington to discuss, inter alia, the aims and form of reserve creation, the criteria for distributing new reserves, how new reserves would be transferred and their acceptance assured, and the conditions necessary for actually creating reserves under a contingency plan.

1967

January	The second joint meeting of Executive Directors and the Deputies of the Group of Ten was held in London. The nature and form of deliberately created reserves and the utilization, transfer, and acceptance of new reserve assets were still being debated, but emphasis was on the process to be used for making decisions concerning reserve creation and on the possibility of setting up reserve units in the Fund. There was still no broad support for any one decision-making process or for any particular reserve unit plan.
January	The Finance Ministers of the six countries of the EEC, meeting in The Hague, requested their experts, through the Monetary Committee of the EEC, to study "almost immediately" ways of improving international credit facilities within the Fund. It

began to appear that the EEC countries might combine their agreement on a plan for deliberate reserve creation with suggested changes in the Fund's voting structure and in the Fund's policies on the use of its resources.

February   Some Executive Directors, believing that an important part of the continuing differences of view revolved around the question whether a plan to create liquidity should be based on reserve units or on drawing rights, and influenced by the decision of the EEC in January, urged the staff to focus on how a liquidity scheme based on the familiar mechanisms of the Fund could be set up.

February   Two detailed plans for creation of liquidity, prepared by the staff, were circulated to the Executive Directors: "Outline of an Illustrative Reserve Unit Scheme," requiring a Fund affiliate organization, and "Outline of an Illustrative Scheme for a Special Reserve Facility Based on Drawing Rights in the Fund."

March   Henry H. Fowler, Secretary of the U.S. Treasury, addressing the American Bankers' Association at Pebble Beach, California, gave added impetus to a move toward a specific contingency plan for reserve creation by urging immediate agreement on such a plan.

March   The Managing Director and the staff suggested a procedure aimed at a resolution for adoption by the Board of Governors at their Annual Meeting in September. The resolution would instruct the Executive Directors, presumably working jointly with the Deputies of the Group of Ten, to prepare, in a reasonably short time, a concrete proposal in legal form for governments to adopt. First, a choice would have to be made between the two basic types of reserve plan. The features of the chosen plan could then be discussed at the third joint meeting of Executive Directors and the Deputies of the Group of Ten, and a final draft agreed at the fourth joint meeting.

March–
April   The Executive Directors considered the two illustrative schemes that had been circulated to them in February. What the merits of reserve units as against drawing rights were, how strict the rules attending the transfer of units from one participant to another should be, and how the Fund would "guide" such transfers were among the principal points debated. The records of the sessions of the Executive Directors were made available to the Deputies of the Group of Ten and the minutes of some of the meetings of the Deputies, being held concurrently, were made available to the Executive Directors.

April	The Finance Ministers of the EEC countries, after meeting in Munich, issued a communiqué stating their approval of the recommendations of the Monetary Committee of the EEC. That committee had proposed (1) that any increase in international liquidity be based on an extension of the credit facilities of the Fund, (2) that new automatic drawing rights, entirely separate from other drawing rights, could be established in the Fund, and (3) that, when the Fund's Articles were amended to include these new drawing rights, other amendments should be made, including a provision that an 85 per cent voting majority be required for various decisions in the Fund, particularly those for general changes in quotas and for the actual creation of additional reserves under a new facility.
April	The third joint meeting of Executive Directors and the Deputies of the Group of Ten was held in Washington. The two illustrative schemes for reserve creation were considered. Following the meeting, agreed answers still had to be found for (1) the decision-making process, (2) the rules for the use, transfer, and acceptability of the new reserve, (3) the nature of the resources backing the new reserves and whether such resources would be merged with or separated from other resources of the Fund, and (4) whether there would be any reconstitution or repurchase provisions linked with the prolonged or extensive use of the new reserve assets.
May	Otmar Emminger, Federal Republic of Germany, chairman of the Deputies, prepared an "Outline of a Reserve Drawing Rights Scheme," for consideration by the Deputies.
May–June	The Fund staff issued separate papers on the four main issues on which agreement had still to be reached: the decision-making process, the rules for use of the new reserve, its financing, and reconstitution.
May–June	During a meeting of the Deputies, the U.S. delegation, in an effort to pull together the results agreed on so far, submitted two papers on reserve creation.
May–June	Several Executive Directors advocated that, instead of revising the illustrative schemes to meet comments made at the third joint meeting, the staff should draft an outline to be considered at the fourth joint meeting.
May–June	The staff prepared two outlines: "An Outline of a Reserve Facility Based on Drawing Rights in the Fund" was circulated to the Executive Board and sent by Mr. Schweitzer to Mr. Emminger, chairman of the Deputies of the Group of Ten;

"An Outline of a Reserve Facility Based on Reserve Units and Administered by a Fund Affiliate" was circulated to the Executive Board about a week later, as was a revision of the first outline.

May–
June

The above papers were considered separately both by the Executive Directors and by the Deputies. Consensus was developing on some of the features that the final outline should have, but still being hotly debated were the rules for use and transfer of the new drawing rights, the provisions that should govern the reconstitution of those rights, and the procedures for making decisions to create such drawing rights.

June

The fourth joint meeting of Executive Directors and the Deputies of the Group of Ten was held in Paris. Most of the points to be included in a final outline were agreed. It began to be clearer that there need not be a Fund affiliate and that the resources of the new scheme did not have to consist of a pool of currencies or of lines of credit; they could consist of the obligation on the part of participants to accept drawing rights from other participants in exchange for an equal amount of convertible currency. However, two subjects were to be referred to the Ministers and Governors of the Group of Ten: the provisions for reconstitution and for the voting majorities that would be necessary to create liquidity.

June

The five Executive Directors appointed or elected by the six countries of the EEC sent a memorandum to the Managing Director suggesting certain changes in the Fund's rules and practices.

July–
August

The Ministers and Governors of the Group of Ten met in London twice and the Deputies met several times. As background for these meetings, the Fund staff, as requested by the Deputies, had prepared papers on the two aspects of special drawing rights on which agreement had not yet been reached, namely, voting procedures and reconstitution obligations. After considerable discussion, the Ministers and Governors agreed that decisions on the basic period for, timing of, and amount and rate of allocation of, what were now being called *special drawing rights* should be taken by the Board of Governors of the Fund by a majority of 85 per cent of the total voting power, that the process by which proposals for allocating special drawing rights would come about would be a complicated one involving the Managing Director, the Executive Board, consultations with countries, and the Board of Governors, and that participants would incur reconstitution obligations according to rules that would be specified in the Rules and Regulations of the Fund rather than put into the amended Articles.

September | The Fund's Annual Report for 1967 devoted an entire chapter to developments in world reserves. It called attention to (1) the continued slowing down in the rate of growth of world reserves, (2) the declining proportion of gold and currencies in total reserves and the increasing proportion of reserve positions in the Fund, and (3) the enhanced financing of payments deficits by reserve currency countries through credit facilities, as against drawing down gold reserves or enlarging liquid liabilities.

September | The Executive Board approved the "Outline of a Facility Based on Special Drawing Rights in the Fund" and the text of a draft resolution for transmission to the Board of Governors.

September | The Board of Governors, at the Annual Meeting (Rio de Janeiro), adopted a resolution, to which was attached the Outline, requesting the Executive Directors to submit to them not later than March 31, 1968 a report proposing amendments to the Articles of Agreement and to the By-Laws.

December | The Executive Board began consideration of a draft of a proposed amendment of the Articles of Agreement.

1968

January–
March | The Executive Board continued its intensive deliberations on a number of drafts of a proposed amendment of the Articles of Agreement and a related report to the Board of Governors.

March | The Ministers and Governors of the Group of Ten met in Stockholm to resolve their differences on ten points still at issue. They approved a draft of the proposed amendment to the Articles of Agreement. The Executive Directors would iron out further details and prepare the final draft. The French delegation reserved its position on the proposed amendment, pending a final text.

April | The Executive Board took a decision to adopt the report, *Establishment of a Facility Based on Special Drawing Rights in the International Monetary Fund and Modifications in the Rules and Practices of the Fund,* and recommended that the Board of Governors adopt a resolution approving the proposed amendment to the Articles of Agreement.

May — The Board of Governors, without meeting, approved the proposed amendment and directed the Secretary of the Fund to ask all members whether they would accept it.

1969

July — Following acceptance by three fifths of the Fund's members having four fifths of the total voting power, as required by the Articles of Agreement, the amendment to the Articles became effective for all members.

August — Members having 75 per cent of the total of quotas in the Fund had deposited instruments of participation, and the Special Drawing Account was established.

September — The draft amendments to the Rules and Regulations relating to the amended Articles were adopted by the Executive Board.

October — The Board of Governors, at the Annual Meeting (Washington), resolved that it had reviewed the amendments to the Rules and Regulations adopted by the Executive Board and had no changes to suggest.

October — The Board of Governors, at the Annual Meeting (Washington), adopted the amendments to the By-Laws relating to the amended Articles.

PART TWO

Allocation and First Use of SDRs

"In my judgment, the experience up to now with the operation of the special drawing rights facility has been highly successful, and it can be stated that the SDR has become established as a reserve asset."

—PIERRE-PAUL SCHWEITZER, Managing Director, addressing the Twenty-Fifth Annual Meeting of the Board of Governors on September 21, 1970.

10

Decision to Allocate SDRs
(1969)

$\mathcal{E}$CONOMIC CIRCUMSTANCES IN 1969 were conducive to an early activation of the SDR facility. Official holdings of gold and foreign exchange had been declining for several years, and at the end of 1968 the world reserve situation was considered tight. The balance of payments of the United Kingdom and the United States—countries that were reserve centers—had begun to improve in 1969, and, consequently, reserves in the form of sterling and dollars were expected to decline further in the near future. Moreover, in contrast to its previous balance of payments surpluses, France had begun to encounter deficits and to experience substantial losses of reserves during the second half of 1968 and the first half of 1969. These developments were sufficiently indicative of potential shortages in the world supply of liquidity that officials of European countries—including the French authorities—who for some years had been voicing strong opposition to activation of the new facility were now more inclined to proceed. Thus, by the time the Special Drawing Account was established in August 1969, the process of deciding to allocate SDRs was well under way.

CIRCUMSTANCES LEADING TO ACTIVATION

The world reserves situation at the end of 1968 was considered tight mainly because there had been a marked decline in traditional reserves and because further declines were expected. By the end of 1968 the decline in world reserves in the form of gold had become substantial. In the four years 1965–68, official holdings of gold had fallen by almost $2 billion. The outflow of gold from official holdings had been $1.7 billion in the first quarter of 1968 alone, when speculative demand for gold had soared preceding the suspension of Gold Pool operations in March 1968.

Equally noteworthy was that countries' reserves in the form of dollars were no longer being augmented as a consequence of the U.S. payments deficit.

Only a relatively small proportion of the U.S. deficits in 1965–68 had been financed by the accumulation of official claims on the United States; instead they had been financed primarily by a drop of over $4.6 billion in U.S. monetary gold. Official claims on the United States payable in dollars had actually declined. In addition, official holdings of sterling, other than holdings that arose mainly out of special arrangements to assist the United Kingdom in its external crises, had shown a net decline of $1.7 billion over the four years 1965–68.

As a result of these influences, world reserves held in traditional forms— gold, claims on the United States payable in dollars, and what might be termed normal sterling—had declined by $4.4 billion in the four years ended 1968. There had been a $2.8 billion increase in total foreign exchange holdings, but this increase was attributable mainly to larger reserve positions in the Fund. The potential shortage of world reserves was revealed also by the fact that world reserves had been declining in relation to the value of world trade. Calculations made by the Fund staff showed that for a group of 60 countries there had been a steep and fairly regular decline in the ratio of reserves to imports for the period 1952–68, broken only in 1952–53 and 1957–58, when temporary setbacks in trade had occurred.

Further Declines in Reserves Expected

An even greater shortage of world reserves appeared to be in the offing. By the first quarter of 1969 the United Kingdom's large current account deficits of 1967 and 1968 had been sharply reduced, and refluxes of short-term capital were enabling the U.K. authorities to repay some of the substantial official debt which they had incurred in the previous two years. Liabilities in sterling were thus declining.

An even more significant factor signaling prospective decreases in world reserves was the turnabout in 1968 and the first half of 1969 in the capital accounts of the United States. On January 1, 1968, President Johnson had announced a series of measures aimed at reducing the U.S. overall balance of payments deficit for the coming year. The previously voluntary controls on capital exports had been made mandatory in order to reduce outflows to the developed countries. In particular, curbs had been placed on direct investments in developed countries financed out of funds obtained in the United States, or out of funds borrowed at short term abroad, or out of profits earned abroad. The voluntary program for banks and other financial institutions that had been in effect for the previous few years had also been made more restrictive, to induce a net repatriation of funds from continental Western Europe. These measures were expected to improve the U.S. balance of payments by $1.5 billion. Additionally, in August 1968 a 25 per cent increase in the rates of the U.S. interest equalization tax on new foreign portfolio investments by U.S. residents had been introduced.

Another factor that had operated to improve the external capital accounts of the United States in 1968 and the first half of 1969 was the progressive tightening of general financial conditions in the United States from the latter part of 1968 onward. U.S. banks had sought to mitigate the impact of stringent monetary policy by borrowing from their foreign branches, and U.S. corporations had borrowed abroad to meet part of their financial requirements. The U.S. payments position had benefited still further from sizable purchases of existing corporate securities on the U.S. stock market. That market was booming during this period, and capital inflow from this source alone had totaled $2.1 billion in 1968, more than double the inflow in 1967. Also, Europeans were more willing to acquire new securities issued by U.S. corporations to finance their foreign direct investment.

All of these circumstances had made for an exceedingly large favorable shift in the capital accounts of the United States. From 1967 to 1968 there had been, for example, a turnaround of $7.5 billion in the U.S. capital accounts. As a result, notwithstanding a worsening of the current account by some $2.6 billion, the overall balance of payments of the United States on the official settlements basis had shifted from a deficit of $3.4 billion in 1967 to a surplus of $1.6 billion in 1968.[1]

In the first quarter of 1969 the United States again had had a large surplus on the official settlements basis. It came to $1.7 billion, greater than for the whole year 1968. As a consequence, there had been a decline of $2.1 billion in other countries' official reserves, including a decline of $1.8 billion in their foreign exchange holdings.

Changes in EEC Positions

Juxtaposed against the improved balance of payments positions of the United Kingdom and the United States was the situation of France, which had radically worsened. Economic difficulties in France had caused extreme pressures on the franc in May and June 1968 and again in August and November, and French gold reserves had declined by $1.7 billion in 1968, the largest loss by a single country in a year in which several countries had lost reserves. The inverse of outward flows of capital from France had been massive inflows into the Federal Republic of Germany, with consequent heavy upward pressures on the deutsche mark.[2]

After the many exchange crises of 1968 and the first part of 1969, yet

---

[1] The balance as measured by the changes in U.S. official holdings of gold and convertible currencies, in liquid and certain nonliquid liabilities to foreign central banks and governments, and in the U.S. accounts with the International Monetary Fund. During the years covered in this history, the official settlements basis as a measure of the U.S. balance of payments position was distinguished from the liquidity basis, which took into account changes in liquid liabilities to all foreign entities, including private commercial banks.

[2] These developments in France and the Federal Republic of Germany are discussed below in Chaps. 18 (p. 352) and 22 (pp. 449–50 and 458–60).

another atmosphere of crisis greeted the opening of the Twenty-Fourth Annual Meeting, at which the Board of Governors was to decide on the Managing Director's proposal for the activation of the SDR facility. Just ten days before, on September 19, 1969, the Executive Board had approved a large stand-by arrangement for France, and on September 26, the Friday before the Annual Meeting opened, France had drawn about half of the amount of this stand-by arrangement. Furthermore, on Thursday and Friday before the Annual Meeting, another heavy flow of funds into the Federal Republic of Germany had forced that Government to take the emergency step of closing the foreign exchange markets. On Monday morning, September 29, it was announced that the authorities would reopen the exchange markets on the following day without a fixed rate for the deutsche mark. Many of the Governors learned for the first time about the decision to let the deutsche mark float as they listened to the Managing Director's opening address.[3]

Declines in world reserves and the prospect of further declines, together with the lessened deficits of the United Kingdom and the United States and heavy declines in France's reserves, had brought about a change in the attitude of the EEC countries toward an early activation of the SDR facility. This change in attitude had been evident on June 4 and 5 and on June 27, 1969, when many of the Deputies of the Group of Ten met as members of Working Party 3 of the Economic Policy Committee of the OECD, and also when they met as Deputies of the Group of Ten on June 6, 1969—their first meeting in over a year—and again at the end of the month. Several of them had stated that their countries could hardly accept any further losses in reserves without having to take corrective action. It was, they thought, more than likely that a global need for reserve creation was emerging—a need that would have to be met by the new method just agreed to in the amendment to the Fund's Articles.

There had been differences in emphasis—some countries putting greater stress on the risk that too long a delay in creating reserves would frustrate balance of payments adjustment, others worrying that too much reserve creation too early would interfere with countries' willingness to combat inflation. But in effect there had been a consensus among the Deputies that it would not be inappropriate to activate the SDR facility in the near future. Arrival at this consensus had been facilitated by assurances from the United States and the United Kingdom that the accruals to their reserves that would arise from the creation of SDRs would not interfere with their determination to proceed with the correction of their external payments imbalances.

STAFF PREPARATION

In March 1969, several months before the Special Drawing Account came into existence, the Managing Director had alerted the Executive Directors to the

---

[3] Opening Address by the Managing Director, *Summary Proceedings, 1969*, pp. 9–10.

need for the Fund to be ready for activation. The Directors had agreed that, while such preparation would not prejudge their positions on actual activation, it should nonetheless proceed.

As early as January 1969 the staff had begun to prepare papers relevant to activation—the issues that would have to be considered, the long-run trends in the rate of growth of world reserves, the interconnections between reserve availabilities and balance of payments adjustment, and various calculations projecting the need for increases in world reserves through 1973.

The staff regarded estimating the required amount of world reserve supplementation as one of the most difficult of the technical questions involved in the SDR exercise. It will be recalled that this had been one of the most persistent of the problems that plagued international monetary officials in their earlier negotiations. The discussions about international liquidity had, in fact, originated with a debate on whether additional reserves were or were not necessary for the smooth operation of the international monetary system. As the discussions had progressed, possible qualitative criteria and quantitative measures by which total reserve needs might be judged had been considered on several occasions.

The estimate that the staff arrived at for the required growth in world reserves was $4 billion to $5 billion a year. This represented an annual increase of 5–6 per cent, somewhat less than the trend in the rate of growth of world financial transactions. But the most uncertain element in the calculation for reserve supplementation, in the staff's opinion, was the extent to which gold and foreign exchange reserves might increase in the foreseeable future, especially over the next five years. The rather cautious estimate was that reserves other than SDRs might account for an increase in total world reserves of $1 billion to $1.5 billion a year. Hence, the staff had come to think in terms of allocations of SDRs of about $2.5 billion to $4 billion a year, starting in 1970, and a first basic period of five years, the normal period specified in the amended Articles.

Part of the staff's preparation for the activation of the SDR facility involved a special seminar on reserves. Because of the importance of the matter, and because so many experts had been suggesting a variety of views and techniques, the staff had proposed in 1968 that a round table or seminar on the subject of appraising world reserve requirements be held between the staff and academic specialists. The Executive Board had approved this proposal, and when the sessions were later held many Directors attended. In the course of 1968, however, the onrush of events accelerating activation of the SDR facility overtook the timing of the seminar, and it was not held until June 1–3, 1970, some eight months after the size of the allocations of SDRs had been agreed and five months after the first allocation had actually been made.

A brief digression to describe the seminar is, nonetheless, apropos. Twenty-two academic scholars from various parts of the world participated; economists from governmental institutions and commercial banks were not asked to attend on the ground that their positions would be taken to reflect the official views of their organizations. The seminar dealt with a wide variety of topics: the key issues in estimating the need for general reserve supplementation; the need for reserves by a single country; the practical techniques for assessing the need for world reserves; the relationship between international liquidity and balance of payments adjustment; and the bearing of the supply of other reserves on the need for SDRs.

For the staff it was particularly noteworthy that the academic specialists either broadly agreed with, or did not contest, the basis that the Fund had used for estimating reserve needs as a prerequisite to activating the new facility. The papers and proceedings of the seminar, together with several papers that the staff had prepared earlier in connection with activation, were published by the Fund.[4]

CONSULTATIONS PROCESS BEGINS

When the Executive Directors began in June 1969 in informal session to consider the possibility of activating the SDR facility, they were generally agreed that it was necessary to move rapidly if they did not want to be presented with a decision already taken by the Group of Ten. The Managing Director therefore put before them a statement for discussion at an informal session in July in which he indicated that the Fund was approaching attainment of the provision that members having 75 per cent of total quotas must deposit instruments of participation in the Special Drawing Account, and in which he stressed that, in his view, it would be unwise to delay any longer consideration of activation of this facility. Believing that considerable progress had been made toward a consensus that SDR allocations should begin and on the general magnitude of such allocations, and believing that in due course he would find the broad support on which to base a proposal for allocation, he suggested the ingredients of a proposal.

The first decision to allocate SDRs should be taken by the Board of Governors at the forthcoming Annual Meeting. Because this first decision would be one of the most momentous so far taken by the Board of Governors, it was proper that it be done in the course of the Annual Meeting, when Governors would have an opportunity to discuss the proposal. Mr. Schweitzer believed further that the decision by the Governors should not be merely a decision in principle to activate the facility but one that contained all the elements necessary to bring about allocations of SDRs during the first basic period. Thus, the decision would specify the start and the duration of the first basic period, the

---

[4] *International Reserves: Needs and Availability*, papers and proceedings of a seminar at the Fund (Washington, 1970).

rates of allocation in terms of percentages of quota, the dates as of which quotas would be used as the basis for these percentages, the dates when allocations would be made, and any other aspects of the allocation plan for the first basic period. He suggested a basic period of five years, with allocations to begin late in 1969 or at the beginning of January 1970 and, on the basis of the staff's calculations, proposed allocations in the middle of a range of $2.5 billion to $4 billion a year. He also thought that there would be a good case for some addition to these amounts at the beginning of the period to compensate for the slow growth of global reserves and the decline in official gold holdings in the last few years, an idea referred to initially by the staff and, as the discussions progressed, also by the Executive Directors, as "front-loading." In effect, the Managing Director was beginning the process of consultation that must precede his making a proposal to allocate SDRs.

Most Executive Directors agreed with the general tenor of the Managing Director's suggestion. However, Mr. Dale (United States) argued for larger annual allocations. Although he started from the same point of departure as the staff—that is, a future need for world reserves in the range of $4 billion to $5 billion a year—he did not wish to make the same downward adjustments as the staff had made for increases in reserves in the form of foreign holdings of U.S. dollar balances. The U.S. authorities did not want to assume that their dollar liabilities would increase in this way and in these amounts. Hence, Mr. Dale arrived at a minimum of $4.5 billion a year, a figure that was regarded by the U.S. authorities as the minimum appropriate one.

Mr. Plescoff (France) considered the timetable suggested by the Managing Director unrealistic. He noted that France had not yet become a participant in the Special Drawing Account, although it would be discussing such action in ten days' time at the next meeting of the Finance Ministers of the EEC countries, nor had it yet ratified the amendments to the Articles.

Tie-In with Quota Review

The fifth general review of quotas was also beginning to get under way.[5] Several Executive Directors urged that the magnitudes of the amounts involved in the two exercises—allocation of SDRs and increases in quotas—be considered more or less in concert. As the discussions continued, it became clear that the Executive Directors for some industrial countries, while willing to see the SDR facility activated, might then be inclined to cut back on quota increases. Mr. Madan (India), speaking at some length, presented the contrasting view of the developing members. Like the industrial countries, they, too, had been adversely affected by the steady erosion over the years in the supply of world liquidity, as evidenced in the shrinking proportion of reserves to imports or to

---

[5] Chap. 16 deals with this review of quotas.

international payments and the consequent retreat from freedom and multilateralism of international trade and capital movements. The developing members were definitely interested in the activation of the new facility. Nonetheless, they also wanted adequate provision to be made for an increase in conditional liquidity through a sizable expansion of Fund quotas. Furthermore, having in mind the strong hints from the members of the EEC that their quotas in the Fund ought to be greatly enlarged so as to reflect their enhanced economic position in the world, Mr. Madan said that the developing members would be opposed to appreciably large special readjustments in the structure of Fund quotas if these were detrimental to the developing members as a whole. Messrs. Phillips O. (Mexico), Kafka (Brazil), Escobar (Chile), Byanti Kharmawan (Indonesia), Léon M. Rajaobelina (Malagasy Republic, Alternate to Mr. Yaméogo, Upper Volta), and other Executive Directors for developing members agreed with Mr. Madan, wanting assurance that, when the decision was taken to activate the SDR facility, there would still be a satisfactory outcome of the quota review.

A way out of the dilemma was found mainly by shortening the first basic period for allocation of SDRs. The idea that the first basic period need not run for the full five years envisaged as normal had been expressed by the Deputies of the Group of Ten at their meetings in June, and the same idea was voiced in the Executive Board by Messrs. Guenther Schleiminger (Federal Republic of Germany), Stone (Australia), and Suzuki (Japan). But the dilemma was also resolved by lowering the magnitudes of both SDR allocations and quota increases.

Consensus on Amounts and Period

When attention turned to the amounts of SDR allocations and the length of the basic period that could be agreed upon, it was evident that some of the EEC countries considered excessive the Fund staff's estimates of global reserve needs. At the end of July the Managing Director informed the Executive Board that the Deputies of the Group of Ten had, subject to the approval of their Ministers, reached a consensus that they would support an eventual proposal for the activation of the SDR facility for an amount equivalent to $9.5 billion over a period of three years, on the basis of $3.5 billion for the first year and $3 billion for each of the two subsequent years. The Managing Director's representatives at the relevant meetings of the Deputies explained the circumstances to the Executive Board. At a morning meeting of the Deputies on July 24, the countries not in the EEC had continued to favor five years for the first basic period of allocation. The amounts these Deputies had preferred covered a wide range, some favoring $2.5–3 billion a year, others preferring $4–4.5 billion a year. The EEC countries, however, had wanted only $2.5 billion a year for three years. By the time the Deputies assembled for the afternoon meeting, a consensus had been reached.

The Managing Director was thus assured that he had the support required to go ahead with a proposal to allocate.

PROPOSAL FORMULATED

In August 1969, after the staff had had a chance to put together the main operative provisions of a first decision to allocate SDRs, the Executive Directors resumed their consideration of activation, again in informal session. Much of their discussion centered on how to translate the absolute amounts to be allocated into percentages of quota as required by the Articles. The three yearly allocations that had been agreed upon by monetary authorities—SDR 3.5 billion, SDR 3.0 billion, and SDR 3.0 billion—were more difficult to convert into percentages of quota for each participant than they would otherwise have been because the aggregate of participants' quotas was expected to be enlarged during the first basic period as a result of the general review of quotas then under way. Another complication was that, once the percentages of quota had been determined on the basis of total participation by all participants, the opting out by one or more participants would reduce the absolute amount of the total allocation concerned. In addition, provision had to be made for the receipt of SDRs by new participants joining the scheme, either between the time of the decision to allocate and the time of the first allocation, or later during the first basic period.

Part of the solution was for the Fund to use the authority it had under the amended Articles to let allocations and percentages be as of dates other than the date of the decision to allocate. It was proposed that the allocations to be made on January 1 of 1970, 1971, and 1972 should be based on the quotas of participants on the day before those dates, that is, December 31, 1969, December 31, 1970, and December 31, 1971, rather than on the quotas existing on the date of the decision to allocate, that is, October 3, 1969. The rest of the solution was to specify that the percentages worked out originally (17.5 per cent for the first allocation and 15 per cent for the second and third allocations) would be adjusted later so as to result in allocation of the agreed absolute amounts to participants that were members of the Fund on December 31, 1969. If new members joined the Fund and became participants in the Special Drawing Account, total allocations might increase beyond these amounts.

The Executive Directors took up a draft of a specific proposal by the Managing Director to allocate SDRs in the first basic period along these lines early in September 1969. Generally they favored it. They considered three years for the first basic period instead of five years to be justified, although they recognized, and some regretted, that the Managing Director had so restricted his proposal because of the preference of certain members. On September 12, the Executive Board formally concurred in the Managing Director's proposal for a first basic period of three years beginning January 1, 1970, with allocations to be made on January 1 of 1970, 1971, and 1972.

Some Serious Reservations

Despite the ready concurrence of the Executive Board and, later, of the Board of Governors in the Managing Director's proposal to activate the SDR facility, there had been some drama. Mr. Plescoff did not concur in the proposal: France, he stressed, had not yet taken a position on activation and was not yet a participant in the Special Drawing Account. By the time of the Annual Meeting, however, France had concurred in the proposal, and it became a participant at the end of 1969.

Mr. Stone abstained. In his personal view, and he stressed the point that this view was not shared by his Australian or New Zealand authorities, the provisions of the Articles requiring that before activation there should be attainment of a better balance of payments equilibrium and there should be the likelihood of a better working of the adjustment process in the future had not yet been met. He referred to reports on the Article VIII consultations with the United Kingdom and the United States that had been discussed in the Executive Board only a few months before.

In June, when the Executive Board had considered the request of the United Kingdom for a stand-by arrangement and had simultaneously taken up the 1969 consultation under Article VIII, Mr. Stone had voiced his uncertainty about the U.K. economy. Although the staff paper and most of the Executive Directors' views pointed to a boom in the United Kingdom, Mr. Stone suspected that certain recessive tendencies were developing. If so, the United Kingdom would be in the economically anomalous position of having a continuing external deficit together with an underemployment of domestic resources.

But it was in regard to the economy of the United States that Mr. Stone had had the most serious misgivings. In July, when the Article VIII consultation with the United States had come before the Executive Board, Mr. Stone had underscored the staff view that control of inflation in the United States was vital to checking the inflationary bias of the world economy, and that a strengthening of the U.S. balance of payments was a basic prerequisite for improving the international adjustment process and for restoring widespread confidence in the soundness and effectiveness of the international monetary system. Therefore, he had addressed himself to two questions which he regarded as pertinent to activation of the SDR facility: To what extent, as far as the U.S. economy was concerned, had a better balance of payments equilibrium been attained? To what extent was it reasonable to make the judgment, with regard to the U.S. economy, that there was a likelihood of a better working of the adjustment process in the future?

Mr. Stone analyzed at some length not only the separate elements of the U.S. balance of payments—the projected trade surplus for 1969, the relation between imports and estimated gross national product, the travel account and investment income flows, and the movements of capital—but also details of the U.S. domestic economy, and he concluded that the U.S. payments position was more unfavorable than it had been and that there had not been any improvement in the domestic sector of the economy. Furthermore, he found no convincing evidence that there was likely to be a better adjustment of the external position in the future.

APPROVAL BY BOARD OF GOVERNORS

On October 3, 1969, at the Twenty-Fourth Annual Meeting, in Washington, the Board of Governors adopted a resolution approving the Managing Director's proposal to allocate SDRs.[6] While the Governors for the United Kingdom and the United States expressed "wholehearted" and "full" support, respectively, for the activation of the SDR facility, the Governor for France was much less enthusiastic: France, he said, had gone along because the facility was in effect anyway and because France wanted to help to make certain that the new experiment was "managed in a rational fashion."[7]

The fact that the UNCTAD's Expert Group on International Monetary Issues had just met again in New York and had recommended the establishment of a link between SDRs and additional development assistance undoubtedly influenced the tenor of the remarks made at the Annual Meeting by the Governors for the developing members. Among the Expert Group had been, for example, Mr. Carlos Massad A., Governor for Chile, and Mr. Yaméogo, an Executive Director elected by several African members. While the Governors for the developing members expressed general satisfaction with the basis for the allocation of SDRs as proposed by the Managing Director, several of them urged that the opportunity be taken to do more to augment the financial aid available for development. For instance, Mr. L. K. Jha (India) urged that the whole question of a formal link between the creation of international liquidity and development finance, which had been shelved, be considered afresh.[8]

Mr. Colombo (Italy) reminded his colleagues that a year earlier he had suggested that, "following each allocation of SDRs, the major industrial countries should agree to make, in a manner to be agreed upon, a contribution to the IBRD or IDA equivalent to a portion of each country's SDR allocation."[9] He continued to believe that it was worthwhile to examine the possibility of

---

[6] Resolution No. 24-12; Vol. II below, pp. 262–63.

[7] Statements by the Governor of the Fund for the United Kingdom, the Governor of the Fund and the World Bank for the United States, and the Governor of the World Bank for France, *Summary Proceedings, 1969*, pp. 35, 52, and 58.

[8] Statement by the Governor of the Fund for India, *Summary Proceedings, 1969*, p. 73.

[9] Statement by the Governor of the Fund for Italy, *Summary Proceedings, 1969*, p. 71.

implementing this proposal. Several Governors for the developing members—among them Mr. Nawab Mozaffar Ali Khan Qizilbash (Pakistan), Mr. Ali bin Haji Ahmad (Malaysia), and Mr. Yadav Prasad Pant (Nepal)—seconded Mr. Colombo's suggestion.[10]

While some Governors for major industrial members continued to object to any specific link between reserve creation and development finance, others, such as Messrs. Roy Jenkins (United Kingdom) and Janko Smole (Yugoslavia), who were less concerned with a concrete link between SDRs and development aid, made it plain that they wished the more prosperous members to understand that the agreed allocation of SDRs would be expected to ease the transfer of resources from the richer to the poorer parts of the world.[11] Sharing this view, Mr. Schweitzer said that "conditions should now be favorable for a major improvement in the volume and quality of development aid and for a decisive check to regressive tendencies in trade and payments liberalization." [12]

■　■　■　■　■　■

The decision to activate the SDR facility greatly speeded up the rate at which Fund members became participants in the new arrangements. During the week of the 1969 Annual Meeting alone the number of participants grew from 68 to 74, and in the next three months 31 members deposited their instruments of participation, so that at midnight of December 31, 1969 there were 105 participants. Only 10 of the Fund's members—Ethiopia, Iraq, Kuwait, Lebanon, the Libyan Arab Republic, Nepal, Portugal, Saudi Arabia, Singapore, and Thailand—had not become participants by the end of 1969.

A WORD IN RETROSPECT

In view of the veritable explosion that took place in world reserves in 1970 and 1971, we may call attention here a little more fully to the reasons underlying the decision to activate the SDR facility. The official reasons were spelled out in the Annual Report for 1969 and in the Managing Director's report to the Board of Governors containing his proposal to allocate SDRs in the first basic period.[13] In addition, in an unusual instance of a full exposition of the background for a decision taken in the Fund, the staff's thinking that

---

[10] Statements by the Governors of the World Bank for Pakistan and Malaysia and the Governor of the Fund for Nepal, *Summary Proceedings, 1969*, pp. 22, 44–45, and 157–58.

[11] Statements by the Governor of the Fund for the United Kingdom and the Governor of the World Bank for Yugoslavia, *Summary Proceedings, 1969*, pp. 36 and 208.

[12] Concluding Remarks by the Managing Director, *Summary Proceedings, 1969*, p. 250.

[13] *Annual Report, 1969*, Chap. 2, and *A Report to the Board of Governors of the International Monetary Fund Containing the Managing Director's Proposal on the Allocation of Special Drawing Rights for the First Basic Period* (Washington, 1969); the latter is reproduced in Vol. II below, pp. 251–65.

underlay the SDR allocations was published as part of the papers and proceedings of the 1970 seminar on reserves.[14]

The report containing the Managing Director's proposal probably has the best explanation. In sum, that report reviewed the tight reserve situation then prevailing, noting that reserves had declined by over 50 per cent relative to world trade since the early 1950s. Admittedly it was difficult to judge the adequacy of the existing level of reserves, and the signals after about 1964 had been conflicting. Although world output and international trade had been expanding, despite declining reserves, there had, on the other hand, been increased reliance on restrictions and increased recourse to international financial assistance, including use of the Fund's resources, to meet payments deficits and to sustain reserves. The momentum of trade liberalization had also slackened. Above all, measures to restrict, attract, or, occasionally, repel capital flows had been applied or intensified for payments reasons in many countries, large and small.

Regarding the relationship between reserves and the adjustment process, the report stated that it appeared unlikely that reserve creation would significantly increase the imbalances of those countries which in the past had had the biggest deficits. The United States and the United Kingdom were under such strong pressure to correct their deficits that any relief afforded by a general expansion of reserves was likely to be negligible. The need to repay a large amount of indebtedness in a rather short period of time was likely to compel the United Kingdom to adopt policies that might even exceed the requirements of long-term adjustment. In the United States, the need to contain inflationary pressures would of itself be expected to induce the authorities to pursue demand management policies tending to strengthen the current account of the balance of payments. The measures being applied by the United States and the United Kingdom, as well as by France, then also in deficit, were specifically noted.

In these circumstances, the report went on, the supplementation of reserves would be most unlikely, on balance, to exercise any adverse effect on the adjustment process, and indeed if nothing were done to supplement reserves, the stabilization efforts that were being made by deficit countries might be frustrated by the defensive measures of others. In any event, a three-year interval, rather than a five-year one, had been used for the first basic period because estimation of reserve needs for five years ahead had been particularly difficult.

---

[14] *International Reserves;* cited above in footnote 4 of this chapter.

CHAPTER

11

Preparing for SDR Allocation
(1969)

$\mathcal{N}$UMEROUS DECISIONS of considerable importance had to be taken before SDRs could be allocated and put into use. Which currencies would be declared convertible in fact? How should the general principles governing designation of participants to receive transfers of SDRs be implemented? What particular plan for designating participants should be put into effect for the first quarter of 1970? How far should the Fund go in exercising its authority to accept SDRs in lieu of gold and members' currencies in its General Account?

As has been seen in the foregoing chapters, the step-by-step progress toward establishment and activation of the SDR facility involved numerous discussions and decisions by the Executive Board, the Group of Ten, and the Board of Governors. By contrast, the decisions that were necessary before the first allocations of SDRs could actually be made were taken, quite easily, by the Executive Board alone. Working in close cooperation, and with élan and an eagerness to make the SDR an effective instrument, the Executive Directors, including the Executive Director for France, took all the decisions necessary to give SDRs a fine start. In this the Executive Directors played a special and unique role in the establishment of the new facility.

Indeed, the last few months of 1969 were for the Executive Board more productive than any comparably short period in the six years reviewed in this history. While working intensively on the several new and difficult points that had to be settled before SDRs could be allocated, they were resolving other unusually troublesome issues as well—notably, the quota increase of 1970 and the South African gold problem.[1]

---

[1] Chap. 16 discusses the quota increase of 1970 and Chap. 20 the South African gold problem.

Meeting of 1968–70 Executive Board

SPECIFYING CURRENCIES CONVERTIBLE IN FACT

How Many Should There Be?

The question of which currencies should be declared convertible in fact, at least initially, had to be decided by the Executive Board before the date of the first allocation of SDRs, that is, before January 1, 1970. To make matters more complex, there were two categories of currencies convertible in fact. First, there were what were referred to as interconvertible currencies, those under Article XXXII (*b*) (1). These currencies were subject to the strictest test: in effect, issuers of currencies that were declared interconvertible guaranteed to convert their currencies at agreed rates of exchange into any other currencies declared interconvertible. Second, there were currencies that would not themselves be interconvertible but which would be convertible, under Article XXXII (*b*) (2), into at least one of the interconvertible currencies. The two types of currencies convertible in fact were referred to as Article XXXII (*b*) (1) and Article XXXII (*b*) (2) currencies.

It was with regard to the former—the interconvertible currencies—that the most difficulty existed. Here, two specific questions needed to be answered: what precise procedures would be required to ensure the interconvertibility of currencies declared to be convertible in fact under Article XXXII (*b*) (1), and how many currencies should be Article XXXII (*b*) (1) currencies, that is, should be interconvertible. Mr. Plescoff had already asked for a paper setting forth the staff's views on the criteria that the Fund should apply for satisfactory conversion procedures for an Article XXXII (*b*) (1) currency, and Mr. Dale had indicated reservations regarding such procedures.

In a memorandum sent to the Managing Director at the end of October 1969, the staff explained that the U.S. authorities, in the interests of keeping their own monetary arrangements simple, did not wish to have to introduce procedures for acquiring currencies that they might not otherwise hold in their reserves. Under the interconvertibility arrangements of the Articles, if a transferor of SDRs received U.S. dollars from a transferee, the United States would be obliged to convert those dollars into any other Article XXXII (*b*) (1) currency that the transferor might want. For ease of operation, the U.S. authorities preferred to keep the number of interconvertible currencies as small as possible.

On the other hand, the French and the Italian authorities had maintained during the negotiations leading to the SDR facility that some participants, countries in the French franc area, for instance, might want to exchange their SDRs for currencies other than the U.S. dollar. Therefore, a system of using only the U.S. dollar would not work smoothly because participants that did not hold or use dollars would have to make their own conversion arrangements.

The staff suggested a way out of this dilemma. In transactions subject to designation (the only type for which this problem of conversion existed), participants should be able to exchange SDRs, at appropriate rates of exchange, for their main reserve currency, which was normally also the currency they used in daily transactions. In turn, participants taking the SDRs should normally be able to satisfy their obligation to give currency by providing their principal reserve currency.

The staff further suggested that the participant's initiative to have its currency declared convertible in fact should take the form of a letter to the Fund describing the existing procedures for convertibility and containing a declaration of intent stating that all necessary conversions involving SDR transactions would be made in accordance with these procedures.

At first, only the United Kingdom and the United States proposed to make their currencies convertible in fact in the interconvertible sense of Article XXXII (b) (1). Mr. Seitaro Hattori (Japan, Alternate to Mr. Suzuki), Mr. Robert Johnstone (Canada), Mr. Lieftinck (Netherlands), Mr. Palamenghi-Crispi (Italy), and Mr. Schleiminger (Federal Republic of Germany), in fact, explicitly stated that their authorities were not intending to establish Article XXXII (b) (1) status for their currencies. They did not regard this kind of status for the currencies of their countries as a matter of prestige. On the contrary, there was a disadvantage, since the position of a currency convertible in fact was similar to a reserve currency. They believed, moreover, that the successful functioning of the SDR system would be very much aided if the number of interconvertible currencies was kept fairly small. Mr. Bruno de Maulde (France, Alternate to Mr. Plescoff) remarked that he had not been able to detect any keen interest among his authorities for making a declaration regarding the French franc.

While Mr. Schleiminger and some other Directors were willing to have a single Article XXXII (b) (1) currency, Mr. Lieftinck reported that the Netherlands authorities saw some merit in having more than one. It would be unwise to have many such currencies, as that would allow for more speculation than was desirable, but it would be advantageous to have one or two currencies additional to the U.S. dollar in a backup role. Otherwise, if something happened to a reserve currency, and it was the only one convertible in fact under Article XXXII (b) (1), it would be difficult for authorities in other countries to switch to a second reserve currency if that second country had not yet developed the practices and arrangements required for the easy functioning of the SDR system. Consequently, the Netherlands authorities favored having more than one currency convertible in fact from the outset.

The staff explained what it considered to be the advantages of a limited number of currencies or even of a single currency under Article XXXII (b) (1), from the point of view of the operation of the scheme. A single currency would simplify operations in SDRs. A designated participant would provide that currency and no other, and a user of SDRs would always know which currency it would receive from a designated participant. The user of SDRs would be able to make arrangements for conversion of the currency received into any other currency it might want to obtain. The disadvantage was that the user of SDRs would not enjoy an exchange rate prescribed by the Fund for that conversion.

At the end of the Executive Board's discussion, the Managing Director made a strong plea for participants wishing their currencies to be convertible in fact under Article XXXII (b) (1) to inform the Fund as soon as possible, in order to provide sufficient time for the arrangements to be submitted to the Executive Board and for members to know by January 1, 1970 which currencies would be available in return for SDRs.

Three Interconvertible Currencies and Five Additional Currencies Convertible in Fact

On December 31, 1969, the day before the first allocations of SDRs were to be made, the Executive Board considered a staff memorandum containing a letter from the Secretary of the U.S. Treasury advising the Fund of the intention of the U.S. authorities that the dollar should be a currency convertible in fact, and took a decision that the U.S. dollar was a currency convertible in fact in accordance with Article XXXII (b) (1), that is, that it was interconvertible.[2]

In February 1970 the Executive Board considered similar letters from the Governor of the Bank of England and the Director of Treasury of the French Ministry of Economy and Finance, as well as memoranda received by the Managing Director from the British and French authorities in January, advising of the intentions of these countries that the pound sterling and the French franc should be currencies convertible in fact in accordance with Article XXXII (b) (1). Contemporaneously, the Executive Board had before it letters to the Managing Director from the appropriate authorities and accompanying memoranda advising of the intention that the Belgian franc, the deutsche mark, the Italian lira, and the Mexican peso should be currencies convertible in fact in accordance with Article XXXII (b) (2), that is, that these currencies should not be interconvertible but should be convertible into at least one of the interconvertible currencies.

The staff explained what the Fund's concurrence in these intentions would mean for the conversion of SDRs. There would be three currencies convertible in fact under Article XXXII (b) (1), that is interconvertible: the U.S. dollar, the pound sterling, and the French franc. The U.S. authorities had entered into arrangements with the United Kingdom and France under which the United States could acquire at any time sterling or French francs in order to arrange for the conversion of U.S. dollars received by the transferor of SDRs into sterling or French francs, as the case might be. The United Kingdom and

---

[2] E.B. Decision No. 2918-(69/128) S, December 31, 1969; Vol. II below, p. 220.

France, for their part, would use procedures that already existed in their countries, that is, they would draw on their dollar balances, or sell gold and acquire dollars, should conversion of their currencies into U.S. dollars be needed. Arrangements had also been made between the United Kingdom and France so that each of those countries could arrange for conversion of their respective currencies whenever that should be necessary in connection with an SDR transaction.

The staff noted that if the Executive Board decided that the proposed currencies would be declared convertible in fact, there would be seven currencies in which the designated participants could fulfill their obligations to provide currency in return for SDRs. The Executive Board would also have to take decisions on the representative exchange rates at which conversions would take place. Those rates would serve as the exchange rates prescribed by the Fund in any transaction or operation connected with SDRs.

In February 1970 the Executive Board took a series of decisions regarding these currencies and the representative exchange rates.[3] The Netherlands Government subsequently requested the Fund to make similar arrangements for the guilder, and in March 1970 the Executive Board decided that the Netherlands guilder was a currency convertible in fact under Article XXXII (b) (2) and specified the method to be used to determine the necessary representative rate.[4] In August 1970 the Fund took note of a change in the procedure for the conversion of sterling, but sterling continued to be a currency convertible in fact in accordance with Article XXXII (b) (1). In May 1971, after a floating rate was introduced for the Netherlands guilder, the Fund took a second decision on the representative exchange rate for that currency.[5]

FIRST DESIGNATION PLAN

Under the new SDR facility the Fund was to ensure that a participant would be able to use its SDRs by designating participants to provide currency for specified amounts of SDRs. Rules for designation during the first basic period of allocation of SDRs were specified in the Articles, and the Rules and Regulations provided that at quarterly intervals the Executive Board should decide on a plan by which designations would be made.

---

[3] E.B. Decisions Nos. 2955-(70/8) S, 2956-(70/8) S, 2957-(70/8) S, 2958-(70/8) S, 2959-(70/8) S, 2960-(70/8) S, 2961-(70/8) S, 2962-(70/8) S, 2963-(70/8) S, 2964-(70/8) S, 2965-(70/8) S, and 2966-(70/8) S, all dated February 2, 1970 and reproduced in Vol. II below, pp. 220–22.

[4] E.B. Decisions Nos. 2988-(70/19) S and 2989-(70/19) S, March 5, 1970; Vol. II below, pp. 222–23.

[5] E.B. Decision No. 3338-(71/44) S, May 19, 1971; Vol. II below, p. 223.

General Techniques and Principles

Before the Board began its consideration of a first designation plan, the staff circulated a paper proposing a basis on which to establish quarterly designation plans. The speed with which transactions in SDRs were required to be carried out would make it difficult for the Executive Directors for participants subject to designation to be consulted at the time of a transaction, as was the procedure when a member's currency was drawn from the Fund's General Account.[6] The staff suggested, therefore, that some time before the end of each calendar quarter it would propose to the Executive Board a quarterly plan consisting of a list of participants to be designated and the maximum amounts for which each could be designated during the quarter without discussion or decision on individual transactions. After discussing the composition of the list and the amounts designated for each participant and after making any modifications it thought appropriate, the Executive Board would take a decision adopting the plan. This decision would govern designations until an amended plan, or the next quarterly plan, was adopted. Since unexpected changes in a participant's balance of payments and reserve position might warrant adjustment of the plan, the Board would have to review and, if necessary, amend the plan should the Managing Director, an Executive Director, or a participant so request. If at any time it appeared likely that the use of SDRs during a given calendar quarter might exceed the balance of the amount provided in an initial plan, the staff would propose a new plan for action by the Executive Board.

The following considerations guided the staff in proposing a designation plan for the first quarter, January 1–March 31, 1970.

First, the total amount provided should be large enough so that supplementary designation plans during the quarter would not ordinarily be necessary. Although the total amount for the first plan was largely a matter of conjecture, the staff proposed SDR 350 million, that is, 10 per cent of the first allocation.

Second, two groups of participants would be listed: (1) those considered to have a sufficiently strong balance of payments and reserve position, and (2) those that would receive SDRs to promote reconstitution or to reduce a negative balance of SDRs. The selection of a participant for the first group required a judgment as to its financial strength. The figures reported in the Fund's monthly statistical bulletin, *International Financial Statistics (IFS),* were taken as fulfilling the definition of "official holdings of gold and foreign exchange" for the first designation plan (Schedule F of the Articles), but the staff considered that this definition would have to be further explored. In like manner, as a preliminary measure of reserve strength, the staff used a participant's ratio of reserves to its Fund quota for the first plan, but realized the need to search for a better index.

---

[6] The procedures for selecting the currencies to be used in transactions and operations through the General Account are described in Chap. 17 below, pp. 322–26.

Third, in drawing up the first plan the staff was guided by the consideration that the number of designees should be large. A wide distribution of SDRs was in conformity with the concept of collective responsibility for the SDR scheme. Also, the greater the distribution of SDRs the more equally would any holdings of SDRs that were considered excessive be shared among participants.

Fourth, although all participants subject to designation were supposed to be included in the quarterly plan, the staff thought that, from an operational standpoint, the list of designees should, in practice, be confined to those that would be designated for at least SDR 1 million.

Fifth, the staff proposed that the amounts for designation in the first plan be, simply, a fixed percentage of official gold and foreign exchange holdings, the same percentage applying to each designated participant. While subsequent designation plans would have to be designed so as to promote a "balanced distribution" of SDRs, as provided in the Articles, the ratios of excess holdings of SDRs to official holdings of gold and foreign exchange at the onset of operations were equal (that is, zero) for all participants. Determination of the amounts for designation in later plans would be more complex as these ratios became unequal. Efforts toward harmonization of the composition of participants' reserves would then be necessary.

Sixth, the staff thought that it would be desirable for the Fund to have advance information from prospective users of SDRs so that it could, in turn, give some prior notice to the participants designated.

First Plan Approved

In December 1969, the Executive Board discussed the staff's proposals for a first quarterly designation plan. The Directors recognized the difficulties of determining the candidates for designation and of drawing up a specific plan. A balance had to be struck between the desire for automaticity in the working of a plan and the need for flexibility as the new mechanism was being tried. Gradually, as had happened with the currency budgets for the use of currencies in purchases and repurchases through the Fund's General Account, cumulative experience with SDRs would help with the compilation of designation plans and with actual designation within these plans. Meanwhile, most of the Executive Directors favored the staff's learn-as-you-go approach. Hence, the first designation plan, listing 23 participants, both industrial and developing countries, subject to designation for a maximum total of SDR 350 million, was agreed to with relative ease by most of the Executive Directors.

Messrs. Palamenghi-Crispi, de Maulde, and Lieftinck would have gone along with a figure somewhat higher than SDR 350 million, while Mr. Suzuki considered SDR 350 million too high. The Managing Director explained that the aggregate figure was the outcome of the judgment not of how many

SDRs should or could be used but of how many SDRs were likely to be used. It was in no way any kind of a limit. The staff observed that, if it were to propose an amount that overestimated the probable use of SDRs, members might be inconvenienced because they would have to rearrange their foreign exchange resources so as to take account of the higher amounts for which they might be liable.

Mr. Saad (Egypt) abstained from approving the plan. He explained that he had found it difficult to advise the members that elected him whether or not they should even become participants in the SDR scheme; four of the nonparticipants were among the countries that had elected him. He believed that there was no objective standard for designation, and most of his countries had large reserves. There was some question, he thought, as to what constituted a deficit in the balance of payments and what weight should be put on the reserves of a member, or on its levels of exports and imports. The criterion being used to judge strong reserves was a country's annual imports. Some small countries, however, might need to accumulate reserves, and their reserve strength was not necessarily related to the level of their annual imports.

ACCEPTANCE OF SDRs FOR CHARGES AND REPURCHASES

The Executive Board took yet another important decision with regard to the SDRs in December 1969. In a further effort to make SDRs an acceptable reserve, it authorized the Fund to go as far as it legally could to receive from participants their newly acquired SDRs without limitation for the payment of charges due to, and for voluntary repurchases from, the General Account.[7]

The Articles required the Fund to accept SDRs in compulsory repurchases and in reimbursement of the Fund by participants for the expenses of conducting the business of the Special Drawing Account, and authorized the Fund to accept SDRs in payment of any charges that arose from operations and transactions conducted through the General Account and in voluntary repurchases of participants' currencies held in the General Account. The question now was whether the Fund would use this authority.

The staff had hesitated to come forward with what might be considered to be a radical proposal, but finally decided to do so. The Fund's willingness to accept SDRs to the greatest extent possible, reasoned the staff, not only would help to establish the new unit but would be a convenience for both members and the Fund. Should SDRs not be acceptable to the Fund for voluntary repurchases, a member with a balance of payments need could use them nonetheless to obtain whatever currency was needed, as indicated in the Fund's currency budget, to repurchase from the General Account. Direct acceptance

---

[7] E.B. Decision No. 2901-(69/122) G/S, December 18, 1969, pars. 2 and 3; Vol. II below, p. 218.

by the Fund of SDRs would be less cumbersome. Moreover, the SDRs acquired by the Fund in this way would be useful since the Fund was permitted under the Articles to disburse SDRs in various ways. The Fund could also, if it found this to be necessary or desirable, use SDRs held in the General Account to replenish its holdings of the currency of any participant. In effect, the Fund would gain an asset that it could use in a manner similar to gold.

In considering the staff's proposal, some of the Executive Directors for European countries, although eager to build up the status of SDRs as being on an equal footing with other reserves, at first expressed concern about the future liquidity of the Fund. An excessive flow of SDRs from participants to the General Account might jeopardize, rather than help, the standing of the new asset. These Directors raised questions about the uses that could be made of SDRs that accumulated in the General Account. A few Directors suggested that participants might obtain guidance from the Fund on the amount of SDRs that could be used in voluntary repurchases, similar to the guidance given in the Fund's currency budgets on the currencies to be used in repurchases. The staff, however, underlined the similarity between SDRs and gold: members did not consult the Fund on the use of gold in repurchases. The Managing Director stated that he could not visualize an acceptable means of guidance for the use of SDRs in repurchases. What criterion, for instance, would govern the volume of SDRs that the Fund should accept in repurchases? If it was judged that too many SDRs had been received, would the Fund stop accepting them?

The Executive Directors went along with the staff's proposal with relatively little debate. Experience alone would indicate the amount of SDRs that would be desirable for the Fund to receive. Moreover, the decision was to be reviewed during the course of 1970, after the SDRs had been in use for a time. Meanwhile, it would do no harm for the Fund to accept some SDRs. Their decision was influenced in part by their realization, as they undertook the fifth general review of quotas, that the amount of gold the Fund would receive when quotas were increased might be limited.

Shortly thereafter the Board took a decision, without meeting, to reword the text of stand-by arrangements so as to note that repurchases could be made not only in gold or convertible currencies acceptable to the Fund, the way repurchases in stand-by arrangements had previously been stated, but also in SDRs in accordance with whatever Fund policies and practices were prevailing at the time of repurchase.[8]

EXCLUSION FROM MONETARY RESERVE CALCULATIONS

On December 18, 1969, the Executive Board decided also that, at least for the fiscal year ended April 30, 1970, calculations of members' monetary

---

[8] E.B. Decision No. 2944-(70/3) G/S, January 14, 1970; Vol. II below, p. 218.

reserves for the purpose of determining compulsory repurchase obligations should not include the increase in reserves resulting from the first allocation of SDRs.[9] The staff proposed this exclusion of SDRs from monetary reserve data on the grounds that members had received unexpected new reserves and had not yet had time to use them, or even to plan their use. Later on, a general decision might be taken on whether or not increases in monetary reserves resulting from SDR allocations should be taken into account in determining repurchase obligations.

As it happened, the Executive Board, in April 1970, decided that for the fiscal years ended April 30, 1971 and 1972 increases in monetary reserves resulting from allocations of SDRs again would not be taken into account in calculating monetary reserves and increases in them during those years.[10] While there were finely balanced arguments both in favor of and against such exclusion, the staff's proposal in favor of exclusion of SDRs from monetary reserves data was based largely on the argument that the Fund had a number of other ways to ensure that repurchases would take place; hence, it was unnecessary to use the newly allocated SDRs in a way to make members fulfill their repurchase obligations to the Fund. Messrs. C. P. C. de Kock (South Africa, Alternate to Mr. Stone), Lieftinck, and van Campenhout (Belgium) dissented from this second decision, contending that, for the purpose of calculating repurchase obligations, no distinction should be made between SDRs and other reserves: the Fund and its members considered SDRs part of reserves.

Because of the difference between the date of an SDR allocation, January 1, and the date of the end of the Fund's fiscal year, April 30, some related decisions were taken as well to clarify the precise amounts of SDRs that would be excluded.[11]

■   ■   ■   ■   ■   ■

After the various decisions described in this chapter had been taken, the staff prepared a Manual of Procedures to guide participants in the use of their newly acquired SDRs. The Manual was approved by the Executive Board and sent to the fiscal agencies and depositories of participants.[12]

---

[9] E.B. Decision No. 2901-(69/122) G/S, December 18, 1969, par. 1; Vol. II below, p. 217.

[10] E.B. Decision No. 3034-(70/38), April 29, 1970; Vol. II below, p. 217.

[11] E.B. Decisions Nos. 3032-(70/38) G/S, April 29, 1970, and 3320-(71/34) G/S, April 21, 1971; Vol. II below, pp. 217 and 218.

[12] *Special Drawing Account: Manual of Procedures [for] Operations and Transactions in Special Drawing Rights* (Washington, 1970); and Supplement No. 1, *Principles and Procedures for Reconstitution* (Washington, 1971); and Revised Supplement No. 1, *Principles and Procedures for Reconstitution* (Washington, 1973).

CHAPTER

12

Two Years of Experience with SDRs
(1970–71)

*W*HEN THE REQUISITE DECISIONS had been taken concerning the currencies that would be convertible in fact, the nature of the first designation plan, the manner of implementing the designation plans, and the acceptance by the Fund of SDRs in its General Account, the way had been cleared for the first allocation of SDRs. The first basic period was to run for the three years 1970–72, with allocations on January 1, 1970, 1971, and 1972.

ALLOCATIONS MADE

The amount of the first allocation, which had been planned at SDR 3,500 million, actually turned out to be SDR 3,414.1 million. The Republic of China exercised its option not to receive an allocation, which lowered the rate of allocation somewhat. The rate was equal to 16.8 per cent of participants' quotas, instead of 17.5 per cent as planned. The amounts of SDRs allocated to individual participants ranged from SDR 867,000,000 for the United States to SDR 504,000 for participants with the smallest quotas.

During 1970 membership in the Fund rose from 115 to 117 and participation in the Special Drawing Account from 105 to 110. The two new members—the Yemen Arab Republic and Barbados—became participants, and three other members—Iraq, Nepal, and Thailand—that had not previously been participants deposited their instruments of participation during the year. Having become participants after the start of the first basic period, these five countries requested that they be included in the next allocation, and the Fund decided that they would receive SDRs beginning with the allocation on January 1, 1971. The second allocation of SDRs was, therefore, to 109 participants, the Republic of China again opting not to receive its share of the allocation. This second allocation, SDR 2,949.3 million, was equal to 10.7 per cent of participants' quotas.

During 1971 Fiji, Oman, and Western Samoa joined the Fund and became participants in the Special Drawing Account. This raised the Fund's membership to 120 and participation in the Special Drawing Account to 113. On January 1, 1972 the Fund made a third allocation of SDRs in the amount of SDR 2,951.4 million to 112 participants—to all participants except the Republic of China. The rate of allocation for the third year was computed at 10.6 per cent of the quota as of December 31, 1971 of each participant receiving an allocation.

The amounts received by participants in each allocation are shown in Table 3 at the end of this chapter.

DISCLOSING TRANSACTIONS

Another matter that had to be decided—and that also proved easier than had been expected—was how much information concerning transactions in SDRs should be disclosed. The matter involved both information to be revealed within the Fund and information to be made public. As for internal information, each participant would receive confidential monthly reports listing the transactions in SDRs that had taken place plus a statement of its balances. The Executive Directors also wanted to have information on SDR transactions as currently as possible, but they recognized that transactions in reserves were often highly confidential. In particular, it was prudent not to reveal the identities of participants in designated transactions until the transaction had been completed. With regard to the information to be made public, the management and staff proposed that, unlike the situation with respect to use of the Fund's regular resources, press releases would not be issued on the occasion of transactions in SDRs. But there was a question of what should be published in *IFS*.

For the first few weeks after the first allocation, the Managing Director gave weekly oral reports to the Executive Board. Then, in February 1970, the staff began to supply confidential written reports, for use only within the Fund, containing data on the total of SDRs used in designated transactions, in repurchases from and payments of charges to the General Account, and in voluntary transactions. It was soon evident that the issue of making SDR transactions public was of no real concern. Many participants were themselves releasing data concerning such transactions.

Hence, the staff suggested that each issue of *IFS* should include information on SDRs through the end of the preceding month by (1) introducing a comprehensive table in the section on the Fund at the beginning of each issue to report SDR allocations, net use of SDRs, and SDR holdings; (2) adding a table to the international liquidity tables to report SDR holdings as a time series; and (3) adding a line in the country pages for holdings of SDRs. The Executive Directors agreed with these suggestions, and the March 1970 issue of *IFS* reported countries' holdings of SDRs for the first time.

TRANSACTIONS THROUGH THE GENERAL ACCOUNT

Repurchases and Payment of Charges

It became evident in the first few months of 1970 that the greatest use of SDRs by participants initially would be for repurchases from and charges payable to the Fund's General Account. Developing countries especially began to use their SDRs in this way. In the first six months of 1970, 46 participants used a total of SDR 549 million; of this amount, SDR 206 million was used by 22 participants to repurchase their currencies from the General Account, and SDR 56 million was used by 25 participants to pay charges due to the General Account. By April 30, 1971, when SDRs had been in use for 16 months, a total of SDR 1,450 million had been used, of which SDR 641 million had been transferred to the General Account, mainly in repurchases by the United Kingdom and India. From May 1, 1971 to April 30, 1972 (the Fund's 1971/72 fiscal year), participants transferred a total of SDR 540 million to the General Account, of which SDR 501 million was in repurchases, this figure again heavily influenced by the United Kingdom's use of its SDRs to repurchase sterling from the Fund.

Two factors contributed to this large transfer of SDRs to the General Account: transfers to the General Account were not subject to the requirement of need, and SDRs transferred to the Fund did not have to be converted into currency but served as a direct means of payment. The majority of participants engaging in these transactions had balance of payments problems, but the reserves of several were rising. Almost all participants holding SDRs at the time that a repurchase became due elected to make some use of them in this way, and many used their SDRs only for the purpose of repurchase from the Fund. For some, the use of SDRs reflected their generally low holdings of reserves: they might have used their SDRs to acquire currency if it had not been possible to use them in repurchases. For others, the relative interest yields on different reserve assets appeared to have influenced their decisions.

Decision Concerning General Account Is Reviewed

The staff's paper preparatory to the Executive Board's review of its decision of 1969 concerning the use of SDRs in repurchases and payment of charges was circulated in November 1970. The staff believed that the evidence available so far suggested that the Fund's decision permitting participants to transfer their SDRs to the General Account had operated in a generally satisfactory manner. That decision had underlined the usability of SDRs as a ready means for settling obligations to the General Account. The absence of limitations on the amount that could be used in this way had not so far had any harmful consequences, either for the SDR facility or for the General Account. The staff therefore recommended that the Fund continue to authorize the use of SDRs, without limitation and at the option of participants, to discharge repurchases outside Article V, Section 7 (*b*), and to settle all charges payable to the General Account, but also recommended that the decision be reviewed again before the end of 1971, should experience warrant, and in any event before the end of the first basic period, December 31, 1972.

In December 1970 the Executive Board undertook a review of the Fund's acceptance of SDRs simultaneously with a reconsideration of the principles and procedures of designation (described below). The two subjects were interrelated. Some Executive Directors or Alternates—Mr. Lieftinck and Mr. de Maulde, for example—believed that transactions in SDRs vis-à-vis the Fund's General Account had hampered the achievement of harmonization of the ratios of SDRs to total reserves held by participants. To achieve greater harmonization, there should be more transactions subject to designation and fewer vis-à-vis the General Account. But other Directors, such as Mr. Schleiminger, hoped that participants' freedom to engage in voluntary transactions and in transactions with the General Account—that is, in nondesignated transactions—would not be limited; such limitations would jeopardize the acceptability of SDRs as a reserve asset. The Executive Board agreed to continue the earlier decision regarding the receipt of SDRs in the General Account. It would review the decision again before December 31, 1971 or, in any event, before the end of the first basic period.[1] This review was delayed until after the end of 1971.

The Fund Uses Its SDR Holdings

The Articles also provided that, in agreement with a participant, the Fund could use the SDRs held in its General Account—that is, could use SDRs in lieu of gold or members' currencies. In addition, a participant that was obligated to acquire SDRs for certain purposes could obtain them from the General Account. In 1970 and 1971 the SDRs held by the Fund in its General Account were used in each of these ways.

In April 1970 the Executive Board agreed to a staff proposal that the Fund offer to pay participants, at their option, in SDRs the remuneration otherwise payable to members in gold or currency. In September 1970 the Board took a decision allowing the use of SDRs for payment of the net income that it proposed to distribute to members.[2] The staff's paper had shown that there were considerations both in favor of and against the use of the Fund's holdings of SDRs to pay distributions of net income and therefore recommended that the offer apply only to 1970. But in August 1971, the Executive Board took

---

[1] E.B. Decision No. 3188-(70/106) G/S, December 2, 1970; Vol. II below, p. 218.

[2] The payment of remuneration and the distribution of net income are covered in Chap. 19 (pp. 387–92). The decisions permitting the use of SDRs for these purposes, E.B. Decisions Nos. 3033-(70/38), April 29, 1970, and 3130-(70/87), September 11, 1970, are reproduced in Vol. II below, pp. 218–19.

a decision again permitting the use of SDRs in payment of the distribution of net income voted for the fiscal year ended April 30, 1971.[3]

At the time of the 1970 decisions, Mr. Stone and some other Executive Directors had expressed concern that, to the extent participants availed themselves of the option to receive SDRs in these transactions with the Fund, the ratios of their holdings of SDRs to their total reserves would be increased and the acceptance liability of those on the designation list would be commensurately reduced. However, for most Directors the persuasive argument in favor of using SDRs for remuneration and the distribution of net income was that further uses for SDRs would promote their acceptability as a reserve asset, especially in this formative period.

Several participants, including Canada, the Federal Republic of Germany, Italy, Japan, the Netherlands, and the United States, elected to receive SDRs in accordance with these two decisions. In 1970, the Fund transferred some SDR 18 million to 15 participants in payment of remuneration on net creditor positions and SDR 9 million to 14 participants in a distribution of net income. In 1971, 7 participants elected to receive a total of about SDR 15 million in payment of remuneration and some SDR 8 million in distribution of net income.

One of the most important uses that the Fund might make of its holdings of SDRs was for the replenishment of its holdings of any currency if it deemed this appropriate for the purpose of the operations and transactions that were conducted through the General Account.[4] This use of SDRs supplemented the sale of gold by the Fund and Fund borrowing from its members as a means of currency replenishment. In September 1970 the Fund proposed to replenish its holdings of members' currencies by sales of gold totaling the equivalent of $325 million. The members involved in these sales were given the option of receiving SDRs rather than gold; 3 of them elected to do so, receiving a total of SDR 68 million. Again, in April 1971, the Fund replenished its holdings of the currencies of 14 members for a total equivalent to $320 million, and 3 members elected to receive a total of SDR 56 million instead of gold.

Hence, during the period January 1, 1970 to April 30, 1971 the Fund transferred, in total, SDR 152 million from the General Account to participants. In the fiscal year 1971/72 the comparable figure was SDR 120 million.

An even more significant development concerning the use of the Fund's holdings of SDRs took place later in 1971. On August 4, the Executive Board considered a paper drafted by the staff in response to a suggestion by Mr. Palamenghi-Crispi that participants in the Special Drawing Account that were making purchases from the General Account should receive SDRs in lieu of currencies. The staff had not considered the case for using SDRs in drawings from the Fund a very strong one, but thought that it would be useful to

---

[3] E.B. Decision No. 3383-(71/81) G/S, August 2, 1971; Vol. II below, p. 219.

[4] Currency replenishment is discussed below in Chap. 19 (p. 375) and in Chap. 20 (pp. 417–20).

try such a use of SDRs in a modest way, so as to gain experience with additional types of SDR transactions. Some Directors favored the idea because this use of SDRs would increase transactions subject to designation and harmonization of participants' SDR holdings would thus be made easier. Others thought that SDRs would become more palatable politically through greater use. The relevant decision was taken in September.[5] However, by the end of 1971 no drawings using SDRs had taken place.

EXPERIENCE WITH DESIGNATION PLANS

Plans for Remainder of 1970

The first quarterly designation plan, as noted in the preceding chapter, had been for SDR 350 million. But the total use of SDRs in transactions subject to designation in the first quarter turned out to be only SDR 133 million, so that no participant was designated for more than 42 per cent of the maximum amount to which it was subject under the plan.

When the staff again proposed an amount of SDR 350 million for the second quarterly designation plan, April–June 1970, Mr. Stone queried the amount at some length. Too large a plan, he stressed, made it necessary for participants to keep their reserves in a more liquid form than might otherwise be required so that they could meet their designation obligations. But what was more important, in his view, was that the designation of amounts in excess of actual use made it difficult for the Fund to work toward equalizing for all participants the ratios of their holdings of SDRs to their aggregate reserve holdings.

The staff defended the amount proposed on the ground that the staff might have to return to the Executive Board for a decision on another plan should one large transaction take place. In the eyes of the users of SDRs the need for a new decision would limit the value of SDRs as a quickly available asset. The Executive Board approved the second designation plan for the larger amount.

As the actual use of SDRs with designation in the second quarter of 1970 was only SDR 114 million, the staff considered that a total of SDR 201 million would be appropriate for the third plan. By the time this plan was formulated, techniques had been worked out so that participants were sending to the Fund much more current data on their holdings of gold and foreign exchange; the third designation plan (for July–September 1970) was consequently based on reserve figures for dates no earlier than the end of April 1970.

---

[5] E.B. Decision No. 3414-(71/98) G/S, September 10, 1971; Vol. II below, p. 219.

Debate on Equalizing Ratios

When it came time to prepare the third quarterly designation plan, the staff, in response to requests from Executive Directors, explored a number of alternative technical formulas for selecting designees. Now that SDRs were in use, several Directors were extremely eager to make sure that designations took place in such a way as to fulfill the principle of equalizing the ratios between participants' holdings of SDRs and their other reserves, as expressed in the Articles.

Once again an important debate took place on the use and transfer of SDRs, this time with the focus on the procedures for designating participants to receive SDRs.[6] As in earlier discussions, the issue at stake was the relative ease or stringency with which the new reserve asset could be transferred between participants. Again, some Executive Directors were concerned that a few industrial countries might eventually have to hold the bulk of the SDRs while other Directors wanted to avoid making the use of SDRs so difficult that they would not become fully accepted as reserves.

The debate about equalizing the relative amounts of SDRs held by participants involved arguments and terminology that were more technical than any of the discussions concerning the establishment and initial use of SDRs. Some background may therefore be helpful.

When the amendments to the Articles were being drafted, there had been considerable debate in the Executive Board about the specific criteria on which to base the selection of designees. It was generally agreed that not only should the balance of payments and reserve position of a participant be taken into account, but so also should the amount of SDRs that a participant already held in its reserves. There had been disagreement, however, as to which ratio between SDRs and reserves should serve as the relevant measure of a participant's holdings of SDRs—the ratio of holdings of SDRs to official holdings of gold and foreign exchange or the ratio of holdings of SDRs in excess of a participant's net cumulative allocations to its official holdings of gold and foreign exchange. During the debate these two ratios came to be known as the "holdings ratio" and the "excess holdings ratio."

In the agreed amendment, the excess holdings ratio was the one accepted, at least for the first basic period, with provision for review of the rules for designation before the end of each basic period. Article XXV, Section 5, thus stated that participants were to be designated in such a way as to promote over time a balanced distribution of holdings of SDRs among them. Schedule F, specifying the rules for designation for the first basic period, stated that participants were to be designated for such amounts as would "promote over time equality in the ratios of the participants' holdings of special drawing

---

[6] The reader is reminded of the discussions described in Chaps. 5 and 6 above (pp. 114–17 and 147–50).

rights in excess of their net cumulative allocations to their official holdings of gold and foreign exchange."

Inasmuch as Schedule F referred to promoting equality in the ratios "over time," the issue that was raised early in 1970 when the Executive Board was considering actual designation plans concerned the speed with which that equality ought to be promoted. Since outright equality of the excess holdings ratios seemed to be difficult of attainment, certainly on a continuous basis, the objective of harmonization of the ratios came to be substituted—that is, the ratios of the participants should not diverge too much from each other. Attention centered on the following question: if the ratios of different participants did become diverse, how rapidly should they be brought closer together? This was referred to in the discussions as "catching up."

The Executive Directors devoted several sessions to the topic of methods of designating participants so as to facilitate harmonization of their holdings of SDRs. The method that harmonized ratios most quickly was referred to as the "filling-up" approach: participants with the lowest ratios would be designated before participants with higher ratios were designated. Variants of the filling-up approach would limit the amounts that participants with the lowest ratios would be designated for, permitting other participants to be designated for larger amounts. Under an alternative method—referred to as a "proportional" approach—the highest ratio existing for any participant would serve as a target in the designation of participants so as to attain harmonization of participants' ratios.

The staff, believing that whatever rules were agreed could not be uniformly applied and were likely to require modification from time to time, preferred flexible methods for achieving harmonization of participants' excess holdings ratios. But several Executive Directors wanted the catching-up process to occur as quickly as possible and were, therefore, not receptive to flexible methods. Other Directors considered catching up within a year's time to be adequate; they wanted the emphasis to be placed on participants' ability to absorb SDRs rather than on making sure that all participants held relatively the same amounts of SDRs in their reserves.

The solution lay in the use of a relatively large number of designees; this in effect spread out the flow of SDRs and minimized the catching-up problem. Hence, the designation plans for the first two quarters of 1970 included as many as 30 participants each.

By the inception of the designation plan for the fourth quarter of 1970, the catching-up issue was, at least temporarily, subordinate to the concern once again with the total size of the plan. The staff proposed an amount of SDR 200 million. Only SDR 20.7 million of the third plan had been used, however, and Mr. Stone again expressed concern about the consequences for the participants included in the designation list of plans that eventually proved to be excessive. The staff explained the difficulties involved in prognosticating the likely use of SDRs during any calendar quarter and again commented that it was preferable not to have to enlarge a designation plan later: the need for such action might cast some doubt on the immediate usability of the new reserve asset. Other Executive Directors favored a large safety margin in designation plans, believing that the irritation to participants of the drawing up of an additional plan outweighed that of having to make disposition for an amount of SDRs greater than had actually been needed. The Executive Board therefore approved the fourth designation plan for 1970 as drawn up by the staff, of which only SDR 23.3 million was actually used.

In December 1970 the Executive Directors again discussed a staff paper on the principles and procedures of designation for promoting over time equality among participants' excess holdings ratios. They observed that during the last few months of 1970 little progress had been made in raising excess holdings ratios that were low. They observed further that several problems were emerging that were jeopardizing harmonization of participants' excess holdings ratios. For example, none of the methods for designation seemed to ensure that participants would not be designated too frequently or for too large amounts in the light of the amount of SDRs that they already held. Therefore, whatever method for designation was used would have to be accompanied by some sort of protective device to ensure that participants' excess holdings ratios did not diverge too much, or that some participants were not designated excessively. The staff advised against the adoption of any procedure that was too fixed, since the SDR scheme was still in an experimental stage. In addition, once SDRs actually began to be used, it was apparent that the relatively low level of SDR transactions with designation and the marked variation from quarter to quarter in the volume of these transactions added to the difficulties of harmonizing or equalizing excess holdings ratios.

The Executive Directors still did not agree on a practicable formula to equalize or harmonize the relevant ratios. Some Directors pointed to the relatively large amounts of nondesignated transactions—voluntary transactions between participants and the use of SDRs in transactions through the Fund's General Account—as an important reason for the failure to achieve harmonization, and wondered whether it might not be advisable for the Fund to limit this use of SDRs. Other Directors, however—Mr. Dale, Mr. Palamenghi-Crispi, and Mr. Schleiminger, for example—did not support such limitations on the use of SDRs.

By the end of the fiscal year 1970/71, 28 participants had what were considered excess holdings of SDRs. Three had excess holdings ratios that were regarded as "high." Belgium and the Netherlands had high excess holdings ratios as a result of bilateral transactions with the United States. Canada's ratio had become high after it opted to receive SDRs instead of gold when the Fund replenished its holdings of Canadian dollars.

Plans for 1971

In the latter part of December 1970 the staff prepared the first quarterly designation plan for 1971, with special emphasis on the designation of participants with holdings considerably below their cumulative allocations. Designations were to be for a total amount of SDR 250 million. At the time, it appeared that there might be some seasonality in the use of SDRs: more than 45 per cent of the SDR 291 million of transactions with designation that had taken place in 1970 had been in the first quarter of the year. The staff considered it likely that SDR usage might be even higher in the first quarter of 1971 than it had been in the first quarter of 1970.

This designation plan was approved by the Executive Board in January 1971. Some six weeks later SDR transactions involving designation already totaled SDR 172 million and the staff proposed an amended plan for SDR 350 million, which was approved by the Executive Board in February. Transactions with designation for the first quarter of 1971 turned out to be SDR 207 million, much lower than the amount of the amended plan.

The second quarterly plan for 1971 was for SDR 250 million. The method used by the staff to arrive at the designations was the same as had been used since the middle of 1970. Basically, it was assumed that if the plan was fully used—that is, if the use of SDRs was such that the amounts of designation were realized in practice—participants would within a year reach a common excess holdings ratio. In other words, the staff was trying to determine a common ratio that all participants might attain by the end of the year if participants actually used SDRs in the amounts that the staff had estimated at the beginning of the year. The staff arrived at the common ratio by taking the ratio between the estimated annual use of SDRs and the total amount of SDRs that had been allocated. Actually, in the second quarter of 1971 SDR transactions subject to designation amounted to only SDR 10 million. The third and fourth quarterly plans for 1971 were each for SDR 200 million. In the third quarter there were five transactions with designations totaling SDR 69 million.

It was the small amount of SDR transactions requiring designation from March 1971 onward that had led Mr. Palamenghi-Crispi to suggest and the Executive Board to agree (as described above, page 236) that SDRs be used along with currencies when participants in the Special Drawing Account drew on the Fund's General Account. SDR transactions requiring designation would accordingly be larger since countries receiving SDRs from the Fund would have to acquire currencies through the designation process. Thus the Fund would be more able to influence the rate of harmonization of participants' excess holdings ratios.

By the time the fourth designation plan for 1971 was considered by the Executive Board, the international monetary situation had suddenly and completely changed. On August 15, 1971, the U.S. authorities had suspended the convertibility into gold of officially held dollars, thus removing what some considered to be the linchpin from the monetary system that had existed since World War II. Among other consequences, the Fund's General Account could not be operated in the normal way. Hence, the Executive Board was not certain how to proceed with the designation of SDRs for the rest of 1971 nor how participants might react to designation. Mr. Lieftinck thought that participants designated under the proposed plan would probably raise no objections because they would receive SDRs, which had a promising future, in exchange for dollars, which perhaps had a less certain future. But participants using their SDRs and receiving dollars might be reluctant to part with their SDRs. Therefore, it might be preferable to discontinue the use of SDRs for the time being, or at least not adopt a new designation plan. Mr. Kafka disagreed. An announcement by the Fund that the SDR scheme had been paralyzed by the U.S. action on August 15, 1971 would damage the prestige of the scheme. The Fund should go ahead with a designation plan for the fourth quarter of 1971. Other Executive Directors, including Mr. Lindsay B. Brand (Australia), agreed with Mr. Kafka, noting that countries that had elected them had been using SDRs after August 15, 1971. The plan for SDR 200 million was adopted, but only SDR 76 million was used.

REQUIREMENT OF NEED

Late in 1969 and early in 1970, as the Fund was making ready to begin transactions in SDRs, the staff had thought it would be useful to participants if they had some initial guidelines to enable them to decide whether they met the requirement of need expressed in the Articles. Many countries had been informally asking the staff of the various area departments about this point. The staff therefore suggested some general criteria, but when these were discussed by the Executive Board, the Directors expressed their preference for the time being for a pragmatic approach rather than for any rigid formula. Flexible rules regarding the requirement of need would, they believed, help establish the credibility of SDRs.

The staff thereafter formulated two principles to guide participants: (1) participants could use SDRs whenever they had a need to use reserves, and (2) participants could not use SDRs for the sole purpose of changing the amount of SDRs held in their total reserves. Participants were to be encouraged to make their own judgments.

During the first 16 months of operation of the new facility, as participants used their SDRs both through the process of designation and through voluntary bilateral arrangements, all of the transactions were subject to the requirement of balance of payments need. Later examination of these transactions showed that for the overwhelming majority, the use of SDRs had followed a period in which the users' gross reserves, excluding SDRs, had declined. In some instances, there had been no decline in reserves but the participant's reserves could be considered to be close to minimum working balances.

In April 1971 the staff reviewed this experience and devised a general statistical test that might provide the necessary information for *ex post* re-examination of the requirement of need for using SDRs. No Executive Board decision had been taken on such a test by the end of 1971. Meanwhile, the staff's procedures turned up two instances where the use of SDRs during 1971 appeared not to fulfill the requirement of need. The two participants concerned, Israel and Turkey, subsequently reversed this use of SDRs by acquiring SDRs from the Fund's General Account.

TOTAL USE OF SDRs

From January 1, 1970 to April 30, 1971, the first 16 months that SDRs were in existence, participants used SDRs in three ways: (1) to obtain currency convertible in fact from other participants designated by the Fund; (2) to obtain, in agreement with other participants, equivalent amounts of their own currencies held by those participants; and (3) to make repurchases from and pay charges and assessments to the General Account. The amounts involved were, respectively, SDR 503 million, SDR 306 million, and SDR 641 million, for a total of SDR 1,450 million. There was also a transfer of SDR 152 million from the General Account to participants, largely to replenish the Fund's holdings of those participants' currencies.

The second category of transactions involved only two participants, but the relative amounts were larger than those of transactions in the other two categories. The United States used SDR 286 million to obtain dollars, held mainly by Belgium and the Netherlands, and the United Kingdom transferred SDR 20 million to the Federal Republic of Germany. In May and July 1971 the United States used another SDR 305 million to reduce the dollar holdings of Belgium and the Netherlands.

The period after May 1, 1971 was one of considerable disturbance in the international monetary system, but the mechanism of the Special Drawing Account remained fully operative. Since a large number of countries experienced increases in gross reserves, fewer participants had a balance of payments need to use SDRs. Nevertheless, a small number of countries with balance of payments problems used substantial proportions of their SDR holdings to finance their deficits.

Under the Rules and Regulations of the Fund, the gold value of the SDR was translated into values in terms of currencies through the par value of the U.S. dollar and the market rates for other currencies against the U.S. dollar; as a

243

consequence, an expectation of an increase in the official price of gold, following the U.S. announcement of August 15, 1971, created a disincentive for participants to use their SDRs. In the absence of a change in the par value of the U.S. dollar, the amounts of currencies that could be obtained against SDRs continued to reflect the one-to-one relationship between the SDR and the dollar. Participants thus refrained from the use of SDRs.[7]

AN ACCEPTED RESERVE

Within less than two years—a remarkably short time—SDRs met and passed several important tests. All but seven of the Fund's members elected to become participants in the Special Drawing Account. Only one participant, the Republic of China, opted out from the allocations. Over half of the participants used at least some of their allocations, beyond the nominal amounts involved in paying their share of the annual assessments for the costs of operating the scheme. The conversion procedures agreed between the Fund and the issuers of the currencies functioned well. Some participants were both users and receivers of SDRs; a few voluntarily accepted SDRs from other participants in exchange for currency balances. When the Fund gave participants the option of receiving SDRs rather than gold in payment of remuneration on super gold tranche positions and for the replenishment of the Fund's currency holdings, and when the Fund gave participants the option of receiving SDRs rather than their own currency at the time it distributed net income, a number of participants took SDRs.

Indeed, after the middle of August 1971, when confidence in the U.S. dollar as a reserve currency was shaken, SDRs were thrust into the limelight. At the Twenty-Sixth Annual Meeting, held in Washington from September 27 to October 1, 1971, several Governors suggested that the par values of currencies might begin to be expressed in terms of SDRs. The SDR, rather than gold or the U.S. dollar, could accordingly become the numeraire of the world monetary system, that is, the unit in which international financial transactions were stated.[8] Some Governors went even further, suggesting that the SDR could become the main asset in which countries held their reserves or that countries' accumulated dollar reserves could be converted into a special issue of SDRs. Thus, by the end of 1971 it seemed clear that SDRs not only had been accepted

---

[7] For a review of the various transactions and operations in SDRs in the three years 1970–72, see Walter Habermeier, *Operations and Transactions in SDRs: The First Basic Period*, IMF Pamphlet Series, No. 17 (Washington, 1973).

[8] Statements by the Governors of the Fund for the United Kingdom and Italy and the Governor of the Fund and the World Bank for Japan, *Summary Proceedings, 1971*, pp. 32–33, 38, and 46.

as a new reserve asset but, in all probability, would have a wider role in the future.

The Link Issue Persists

A long-standing and still unanswered question concerned a possible link between the allocation of SDRs and the financing of the economic development of the developing nations. As part of their preparations for the Twenty-Fifth Annual Meeting, held in Copenhagen, September 21–25, 1970, the developing members, meeting as the Group of Seventy-Seven, had examined this issue afresh, and the topic had also been discussed at the Commonwealth Finance Ministers' meeting in Cyprus in September 1970. At the Annual Meeting in Copenhagen, many Governors for developing countries urged reconsideration of such a link.[9] Accordingly, in his concluding remarks Mr. Schweitzer indicated that the Executive Directors would want to give careful consideration to the Fund's program of work in this field.

The keen interest of developing members in establishing a link between SDR allocations and financing development was exemplified again in October 1970 when a document entitled *An International Development Strategy for the Second United Nations Development Decade* was adopted by the Second (Economic and Financial) Committee of the General Assembly.[10] In paragraph 52 of that document it was resolved that, as soon as adequate experience was available on the working of the SDR scheme, serious consideration should be given to the possibility of establishing a link between the allocation of new assets under that scheme and the provision of additional finance for economic development. But at that UN meeting reservations about such a link were expressed by several delegations, including those from Australia, Belgium, France, Japan, the Netherlands, Sweden, the United Kingdom, and the United States.

Early in 1971 the Fund staff submitted to the Executive Board a paper outlining the main issues that would have to be considered in any study of the desirability and feasibility of creating a link between SDR creation and development finance. And the Economic Counsellor explored informally the ideas of Mr. Manuel Pérez Guerrero, the successor to Mr. Prebisch as Secretary-General of the UNCTAD.

In April 1971 the Executive Board examined the merits of undertaking a study of a link between the SDR scheme and development finance, and the

---

[9] See, for example, Statements by Mr. Y. B. Chavan (Governor of the Fund and the World Bank for India), Mr. Francisco Morales Bermúdez (Governor of the World Bank for Peru), Mr. Mwai Kibaki (Governor of the Fund and the World Bank for Kenya), Mr. David Horowitz (Governor of the World Bank for Israel), Mr. Janko Smole (Governor of the World Bank for Yugoslavia), and Mr. N. M. Perera (Governor of the Fund and the World Bank for Ceylon), *Summary Proceedings, 1970*, pp. 43, 113, 141–42, 162–63, 164–65, and 177–80.

[10] UN document A/C.2/L.1104/Rev. 1.

scope of any such study. To assist the Executive Board in reaching a conclusion as to what might be studied first, the staff suggested two specific studies that might be given priority: (1) a comparison of the main types of link proposals and their implications for aid and for SDR allocations (to be done with the assistance of the World Bank staff), and (2) an analysis of the different link schemes from the point of view of the monetary character of SDRs and the longer-run developments envisaged for the SDR facility. These two proposed studies were approved by the Executive Board in May 1971.

At the 1971 Annual Meeting, although the Governors were very much occupied with the disruption in international finance that had existed since mid-August, several of those for developing members again referred to the link question. Mr. Horowitz, for example, again suggested that part of the SDRs be used to buy World Bank bonds.[11]

Concern about a link between SDR allocation and the provision of development finance was thus by no means ended as 1971 came to a close.

Other Issues

Additional questions were being considered and discussed within the Fund during 1971 with a view to improving and developing the operation of the SDR mechanism. What effects might the existence of SDRs have on the working of the gold exchange standard?[12] How should the yields on the various Fund-related reserve assets—the basic gold tranche, the super gold tranche, readily repayable claims arising out of borrowing by the Fund through the General Arrangements to Borrow, and SDRs—compare, and what considerations should govern the interest paid on these assets? Should they not receive equal interest? Could the Fund influence the asset preferences of countries by interest rate incentives? How should the reconstitution principles be applied? Outside experts as well as the Fund staff were beginning also to consider the new directions in respect of reserves that a reform of the international monetary system might take.[13]

As the first two years of experience with SDRs came to a close, the Executive Board, assuming that there would be no allocations of SDRs for a

---

[11] Statement by the Governor of the World Bank for Israel, *Summary Proceedings, 1971*, p. 77. See also Statements by the Governors of the Fund and the World Bank for Ceylon, India, and Korea, *ibid.*, pp. 114, 59, and 17.

[12] These effects were discussed by J. Marcus Fleming, "The SDR: Some Problems and Possibilities," *Staff Papers*, Vol. 18 (1971), pp. 25–47, and Fred Hirsch, "SDRs and the Working of the Gold Exchange Standard," *Staff Papers*, Vol. 18 (1971), pp. 221–53.

[13] Robert Triffin, "An Agreed International Monetary Standard," *Annals of International Studies*, Alumni Association of the Graduate Institute of International Studies (Geneva, 1970), pp. 214–23; and Edward M. Bernstein, "The Dollar is the Problem of the International Monetary System," *Quarterly Review and Investment Survey*, Model, Roland & Co., Second Quarter, 1971, pp. 1–12.

while after January 1, 1972, took a decision outlining how reconstitution of the existing amounts of SDRs might take place.[14]

■ ■ ■ ■ ■ ■

The SDR mechanism had been successfully launched. Its future was certainly not in question. The continuing deliberations about SDRs now involved ways of developing and expanding the role of the new asset in the international monetary system.

---

[14] E.B. Decision No. 3457-(71/121) G/S, December 3, 1971; Vol. II below, pp. 216–17.

Table 3. Allocations of Special Drawing Rights, 1970–72

(In millions of SDRs)

Participant [1]	January 1 1970	January 1 1971	January 1 1972
Afghanistan	4.9	4.0	3.9
Algeria	12.6	13.9	13.8
Argentina	58.8	47.1	46.6
Australia	84.0	71.2	70.5
Austria	29.4	18.7	28.6
Barbados	—	1.4	1.4
Belgium	70.9	69.6	68.9
Bolivia	4.9	4.0	3.9
Botswana	0.5	0.5	0.5
Brazil	58.8	47.1	46.6
Burma	8.1	6.4	6.4
Burundi	2.5	2.0	2.0
Cameroon	3.1	3.7	3.7
Canada	124.3	117.7	116.6
Central African Republic	1.6	1.4	1.4
Ceylon	13.1	10.5	10.4
Chad	1.7	1.4	1.4
Chile	21.0	16.9	16.7
Colombia	21.0	16.8	16.6
Congo, People's Republic of the	1.7	1.4	1.4
Costa Rica	4.2	3.4	3.4
Cyprus	3.4	2.8	2.8
Dahomey	1.7	1.4	1.4
Denmark	27.4	27.8	27.6
Dominican Republic	5.4	4.6	4.6
Ecuador	4.2	3.5	3.5
Egypt	25.2	20.1	19.9
El Salvador	4.2	3.7	3.7
Equatorial Guinea	1.0	0.9	0.8
Fiji	—	—	1.4
Finland	21.0	20.3	20.1
France	165.5	160.5	159.0
Gabon	1.6	1.6	1.6
Gambia, The	0.8	0.7	0.7
Germany, Federal Republic of	201.6	171.2	169.6
Ghana	11.6	9.3	9.2
Greece	16.8	14.8	14.6
Guatemala	4.2	3.9	3.8
Guinea	3.2	2.6	2.5
Guyana	2.5	2.1	2.1
Haiti	2.5	2.0	2.0
Honduras	3.2	2.7	2.6
Iceland	2.5	2.5	2.4
India	126.0	100.6	99.6
Indonesia	34.8	27.8	27.6

Table 3 (*continued*). Allocations of Special Drawing Rights, 1970–72

(In millions of SDRs)

| Participant [1] | January 1 | | |
	1970	1971	1972
Iran	21.0	20.5	20.4
Iraq	—	11.7	11.6
Ireland	13.4	12.9	12.8
Israel	15.1	13.9	13.8
Italy	105.0	107.0	106.0
Ivory Coast	3.2	5.6	5.5
Jamaica	6.4	5.7	5.6
Japan	121.8	128.4	127.2
Jordan	2.7	2.5	2.4
Kenya	5.4	5.1	5.1
Khmer Republic	3.2	2.7	2.6
Korea	8.4	5.4	8.5
Laos	1.7	1.4	1.4
Lesotho	0.5	0.5	0.5
Liberia	3.4	3.1	3.1
Luxembourg	3.2	2.0	2.1
Malagasy Republic	3.2	2.8	2.8
Malawi	1.9	1.6	1.6
Malaysia	21.0	19.9	19.7
Mali	2.9	2.4	2.3
Malta	1.7	1.7	1.7
Mauritania	1.7	1.4	1.4
Mauritius	2.7	2.4	2.3
Mexico	45.4	39.6	39.2
Morocco	15.1	12.1	12.0
Nepal	—	1.1	1.1
Netherlands	87.4	74.9	74.2
New Zealand	26.4	21.6	21.4
Nicaragua	3.2	2.9	2.9
Niger	1.7	1.4	1.4
Nigeria	16.8	14.4	14.3
Norway	25.2	25.7	25.4
Oman	—	—	0.7
Pakistan	31.6	25.1	24.9
Panama	4.7	3.9	3.8
Paraguay	2.5	2.0	2.0
Peru	14.3	13.2	13.0
Philippines	18.5	16.6	16.4
Rwanda	2.5	2.0	2.0
Senegal	4.2	3.6	3.6
Sierra Leone	2.5	2.7	2.6
Somalia	2.5	2.0	2.0
South Africa	33.6	21.4	33.9
Spain	42.0	42.3	41.9
Sudan	9.6	7.7	7.6

Table 3 (concluded). Allocations of Special Drawing Rights, 1970–72

(In millions of SDRs)

Participant [1]	January 1		
	1970	1971	1972
Swaziland	1.0	0.9	0.8
Sweden	37.8	34.8	34.4
Syrian Arab Republic	6.4	5.4	5.3
Tanzania	5.4	4.5	4.5
Thailand	—	14.3	14.2
Togo	1.9	1.6	1.6
Trinidad and Tobago	7.4	6.7	6.7
Tunisia	5.9	3.7	5.1
Turkey	18.1	16.2	16.0
Uganda	5.4	4.3	4.2
United Kingdom	409.9	299.6	296.8
United States	866.9	716.9	710.2
Upper Volta	1.7	1.4	1.4
Uruguay	9.2	7.4	7.3
Venezuela	42.0	35.3	35.0
Viet-Nam	6.6	6.6	6.6
Western Samoa	—	—	0.2
Yemen Arab Republic	—	1.1	1.1
Yemen, People's Democratic Republic of	3.7	3.1	3.1
Yugoslavia	25.2	22.1	21.9
Zaïre	15.1	12.1	12.0
Zambia	8.4	8.1	8.1
Totals [2]	3,414.1	2,949.3	2,951.4

[1] Names for participating countries are those in effect on December 31, 1971.

[2] Components may not add to totals because of rounding of figures for individual participants.

PART THREE

General Resources:
New Challenges and Responses

"The extension by the Fund of financial
assistance to members in support
of sound financial programs plays a
key role in the international adjustment
process."

—PIERRE-PAUL SCHWEITZER, Managing Director,
addressing the Twenty-Fourth Annual Meeting
of the Board of Governors on September 29, 1969.

CHAPTER

13

Changes in Rules and Practices

CHANGES IN THE FUND'S RULES AND PRACTICES that were made
when the Articles of Agreement were amended to incorporate the SDR
facility have been mentioned in earlier chapters. Since many of the changes
dealt with the resources held in the Fund's General Account, they are discussed
in more detail here in Part Three.

Most of the amendments involved were proposed by the six EEC countries,
although the amendments finally adopted were only a portion of what these
countries suggested initially.[1] As we have also seen, the EEC countries insisted
that these changes in the rules and practices be made effective simultaneously
with the establishment of the SDR facility.

Before the amendments relating to the General Account were approved
by the Board of Governors in May 1968, they had been the subject of intensive
deliberation, just as had the amendments dealing with the SDR facility. Successive drafts prepared by the staff had been considered at length by the
Executive Board, and before completion of the final draft the Finance Ministers
and Central Bank Governors of the Group of Ten, at their meeting in Stockholm
in March 1968, had agreed to the proposed changes.

This chapter summarizes the nature of these amendments. The General
Counsel discussed them in the earlier history and has elsewhere provided a
fuller description of them.[2] For a while they were referred to as "reform amendments." But, the word "reform," suggesting a radical overhaul of the Articles of
Agreement or sweeping modifications of them, was too strong. Certainly in
retrospect, and also in view of the deliberations after 1971 on reforming the
Fund, the changes made in 1969 were modest in number and effect.

---

[1] See above, Chap. 5, pp. 131–32.

[2] *History, 1945–65*, Vol. II, pp. 599–603; and Joseph Gold, *The Reform of the Fund*,
IMF Pamphlet Series, No. 12 (Washington, 1969).

AN 85 PER CENT MAJORITY FOR SEVERAL DECISIONS

One of the major developments in the world economy after the creation of the Fund in 1944 was the phenomenal increase in the economic and financial strength of the EEC countries. By the early 1960s this strength was reflected in the volume of the Fund's sales of their currencies. For many years after the Fund started transactions in 1947, most drawings from the Fund were in U.S. dollars. However, beginning with the 1960s Western European currencies had become convertible and the Fund's sales of Belgian francs, deutsche mark, French francs, Italian lire, and Netherlands guilders had become equally as great and, at times, even greater than sales of dollars. Nonetheless, the combined votes in the Fund of the six EEC countries represented only about 16.5 per cent of the total voting power, compared with 21–22 per cent for the United States.

Foremost among the amendments in their dramatic effect, therefore, were those that introduced the requirement of a special majority of 85 per cent of the total voting power of the Board of Governors for several decisions affecting the General Account. An 85 per cent majority was required for increases in quotas resulting from a general review; previously an 80 per cent majority had been required. A like majority was required for any decision dealing with the payments related to such increases. Two kinds of decision were affected by the latter provision: decisions dealing with payments of subscriptions due in connection with quota increases, such as a decision to reduce the proportion payable in gold, and decisions dealing with the mitigation of the effects of such payments. In 1964, for example, the Fund had decided to sell gold to reserve currency members in order to mitigate the effect on the gold holdings of these members when they sold gold to the Fund's other members to enable the latter to pay gold subscriptions due in connection with quota increases. These decisions had been taken by the Executive Board by a majority of the votes cast. The amendment to the Articles meant that decisions of this kind were to be reserved to the Board of Governors and would require a majority of 85 per cent of the total voting power. A majority of 85 per cent of the total voting power of the Board of Governors was also now required for uniform proportionate changes in par values; the original Articles had provided that the authority to take such a decision was reserved to the Board of Governors but could be taken by a majority of the votes cast.

The argument for an 85 per cent majority of the total voting power for these decisions related to the General Account was that there was a logical link between these decisions and decisions to allocate or cancel SDRs. The EEC countries argued that decisions to adjust all Fund quotas, to mitigate the secondary impact of the payment of subscriptions as a result of a general quota review, and to bring about a uniform proportionate change in the par values of all currencies, all affected the volume of world liquidity. Accordingly, they should command the same general support as decisions on allocations or cancellations of SDRs, which also required an 85 per cent majority of the total voting power of the Board of Governors.

The special majority required for adjustment of a member's quota not resulting from a general review, such as could be made in individual cases on the application of any member, was not changed, that is, a majority of 80 per cent of the total voting power of the Board of Governors continued to be required.

AMENDMENTS GOVERNING USE OF RESOURCES

Some of the amendments enacted into law features of the Fund's policies on the use of its resources that were already in practice. This was most notably the situation with respect to purchases in the gold tranche.

Very early in the discussions about world liquidity a number of suggestions had been made, especially by the Belgian authorities, for changes that would enhance the character of the Fund's gold tranche and persuade more members to regard it as a reserve asset. These suggestions had been considered informally by the Managing Director as early as 1964, and Messrs. Cecil de Strycker and Hubert Ansiaux (Belgium) had addressed remarks to this effect at the Annual Meetings in 1964 and 1965.[3] Thereafter, the Fund's management had discussed in some detail the views of the Belgian authorities on this matter and had ascertained the opinions of other members. Hence, there was considerable background to this amendment prior to the adoption by the Governors of the resolution at Rio de Janeiro in September 1967.[4]

The Articles as amended provided that a member was entitled, without challenge, to purchase from the Fund the currency of another member if the proposed purchase was a gold tranche purchase. Gold tranche purchases, which had been virtually automatic as a matter of policy, thus were made legally automatic under the Articles. This was the least controversial, although not the least complicated, of the amended rules and practices. Furthermore, the term *gold tranche purchase* was defined for the first time:

> Gold tranche purchase means a purchase by a member of the currency of another member in exchange for its own currency which does not cause the Fund's holdings of the member's currency to exceed one hundred per cent of its quota, provided that for the purposes of this definition the Fund may exclude purchases and holdings under policies on the use of its resources for compensatory financing of export fluctuations.[5]

---

[3] Statement by the Temporary Alternate Governor of the Fund for Belgium, *Summary Proceedings, 1964*, pp. 77–78, and Statement by the Governor of the Fund for Belgium, *Summary Proceedings, 1965*, pp. 131–32.

[4] Resolution No. 22-8, adopted September 29, 1967; Vol. II below, pp. 54–55.

[5] Article XIX (j).

There were also related amendments which could be described as improvements in the qualities of the gold tranche. For example, a member could make a request for a gold tranche purchase without challenge on the ground that the purchase was needed to meet a large or sustained flow of capital. Under the original Articles such drawings were permitted only in the super gold tranche and only in specific circumstances and in certain currencies.

Members were to be assured of remuneration on their super gold tranche positions, the term remuneration being used to indicate that it was not interest paid to a creditor and also to make the point that it was an expenditure which the Fund would have to make whatever its income position might be. The rate of remuneration was set at 1½ per cent per annum, but the Fund was authorized to make changes in this rate. Authority was conferred on the Fund to levy on members making gold tranche purchases a service charge lower than the former minimum (½ of 1 per cent) or to dispense with a service charge altogether.

In the light of the change in the status of the gold tranche, the Executive Board took a decision on September 15, 1969 making a number of changes in the Fund's operational practices with respect to gold tranche purchases. Gold tranche purchases should not await the Board's prior approval but should be effected automatically and as promptly as practicable, normally within two to three business days after the receipt of a valid request. The service charge on gold tranche purchases made after July 27, 1969 was abolished. The floating character of the compensatory financing facility was confirmed by deciding that the Fund's holdings of currency resulting from purchases under the compensatory financing decision would be excluded for the purposes of defining a gold tranche purchase. Stand-by arrangements would be worded so as to exclude purchases in the gold tranche.[6]

Shortly after the amendments had gone into effect, Rule I-9 of the Rules and Regulations was adopted, according to which remuneration was to be paid as of the end of the Fund's fiscal year in gold and the member's currency. In April 1970, as discussed in Chapter 12, the Fund decided to offer to pay remuneration in SDRs; as described in Chapter 19, remuneration was paid in May 1970 and May 1971.

The amendment making gold tranche purchases legally automatic was accompanied by others which made explicit what had been implicit before: that use of the Fund's resources must be temporary in character and that the Fund must adopt policies to this end. The fifth purpose of the Fund, stated in Article I, was amended by adding the word *temporarily*: "To give confidence to members by making the Fund's resources temporarily available to them under adequate safeguards, thus providing them with opportunity to correct maladjustments in their balance of payments without resorting to measures destructive of national or international prosperity." The last sentence of Article I was

---

[6] E.B. Decision No. 2836-(69/87), September 15, 1969; Vol. II below, pp. 202–203.

changed by adding the words *policies and:* "The Fund shall be guided in all its policies and decisions by the purposes set forth in this Article."

These amendments to Article I were given operational effect by two new subsections in Article V, Section 3, "Conditions governing use of the Fund's resources." Subsection (*c*) now stated that a member's use of the Fund's resources should be in accordance with the purposes of the Fund, and directed the Fund to adopt policies on use that would assist members to solve their balance of payments problems in a manner consistent with the purposes of the Fund and that would establish adequate safeguards for the temporary use of its resources. Subsection (*d*) now provided that the representation made by a member when it requested the use of the Fund's resources should be examined to determine whether the proposed purchase would be consistent with the provisions of the Articles and with the Fund's policies, subject to the exception for gold tranche purchases.

The foregoing amendments were not intended to introduce policies or practices different from those that the Fund had already developed, nor to make the rules with respect to the use of the Fund's general resources more restrictive than they had been. Nevertheless, these amendments did make an important change. The Fund no longer had the legal power to make the use of the Fund's resources, other than in the gold tranche, quasi-automatic or quasi-conditional. One of the consequences of this change, as will be seen in Chapter 16, was that in 1971 the Fund could not permit virtually unconditional drawings to help members to finance the quota increases authorized under the fifth general quota review of 1970, as had been done in connection with the previous general quota increase in 1965–66.

■ ■ ■ ■ ■ ■

Three factors were responsible for the amendments described thus far in this chapter.

One, there was a desire to crystallize a function of the Fund that had gradually evolved. The outside world tended to look upon a member's drawing from the Fund as a sign of the Fund's approbation of that member's economic and financial policies. A drawing from the Fund should, accordingly, mean that the Fund had put its stamp of approval on the member's policies.

Two, and more important, the SDR facility was to take care of any need for additions to liquidity of an unconditional nature. Unconditional liquidity should not be generated from the Fund's regular resources, except in the form of drawings in the gold tranche.

Three, the proponents of these amendments argued that it would not be logical to permit the creation of conditional liquidity through the General Account by a majority of votes cast while a higher majority for the same purpose was required for unconditional liquidity created through the Special Drawing Account.

AMENDMENTS GOVERNING REPURCHASES

Substantial changes were made in the original provisions of the Articles governing repurchase and the calculation of monetary reserves by which repurchase obligations were determined. These amendments formed the longest chain of all the amendments affecting the General Account.

The negotiation of these amendments stemmed from the thesis that two aspects of the original provisions were unsatisfactory insofar as they involved reserve currencies. One of these was that, when a member's monetary reserves were calculated for the purpose of determining the member's repurchase obligation, what were called its "currency liabilities" were deducted from its gross reserves (the currency liabilities of a member being the holdings of its currency by the monetary authorities, official institutions, and banks of other members). Some monetary officials contended that this calculation gave an undue advantage to the reserve currency countries. Because their currencies were held by other members, calculations for reserve currency countries included deductions to which the other members of the Fund were not entitled, and hence reserve currency countries were not subject to as stringent repurchase obligations as were other members.

A further objection to the original repurchase provisions related to what was known in the Fund as "abatement." Abatement was the principle by which a calculated repurchase obligation was canceled if it accrued in the currency of a member which the Fund could not accept because the Fund's holdings of that currency could not be increased above 75 per cent of the member's quota by repurchases. The member for which the obligation was calculated was not required to use another convertible currency or gold for the repurchase transaction.

Abatement was criticized because repurchase obligations resulted from an improvement in the member's monetary reserves and a member could be freed from discharging a repurchase obligation even if its monetary reserves had increased. The problem had become more acute since 1962 because the Fund had been unable to accept either U.S. dollars or pounds sterling in repurchase transactions. In order to enable members to carry out their repurchase commitments, and hence be able to continue to draw on the Fund's resources, the United States had arranged with the Fund in 1964 and 1965 to draw currencies that were acceptable to the Fund in repurchases and to make them available at par to countries that held U.S. dollars and needed to fulfill repurchase obligations or commitments. The arrangements between the United States and the Fund were technical rather than substantive. The currencies were drawn under a stand-by agreement (although they were in the gold tranche) and they were normally returned immediately to the Fund by the country making the repurchase. This procedure was, accordingly, sometimes called a turnstile operation.

Two basic amendments relating to repurchase were introduced. The first provided that currency liabilities would not be deductible in the calculation of monetary reserves. The second provided that repurchase obligations that had been abated because the Fund could not accept the currency in which they had accrued could be discharged in another convertible currency which the Fund could accept. In sum, these changes in the repurchase provisions involved the transition from a concept of monetary reserves net of currency liabilities to a gross concept and the effecting of repurchase transactions in a greater number of currencies. These changes affected both the amounts to be repurchased and the media in which repurchases were made.

These two amendments were accompanied by others, some of which were intended to soften the impact of the increase in repurchase obligations that might have followed from the two basic reforms just described. Allowance was to be made for any decreases during a year in the Fund's holdings of a member's currency; thus, the calculation of repurchase obligations at the end of the year could give credit to the member for any other repurchases made during the year. Also, repurchase obligations were to be limited to the equivalent of 25 per cent of quota for any financial year; any excess would be postponed. Furthermore, repurchase obligations that would reduce a member's monetary reserves below 150 per cent of its quota were to be abated; previously, the comparable figure had been 100 per cent of a member's quota.

INTERPRETATION OF THE ARTICLES

Article XVIII, the provision on interpretation of the Articles and a topic of fundamental importance in international law, was amended to change the procedure for dealing with questions of interpretation. The Executive Board would continue to take decisions on questions of interpretation as provided in the original Articles, and any member could appeal to the Board of Governors, whose decision was final. But questions of interpretation referred to the Board of Governors were now to be submitted within three months after the Executive Board's interpretation and would be considered by a Committee on Interpretation of the Board of Governors. The Board of Governors would establish the membership, procedures, and voting majorities of the committee, each member of which would have one vote. The decisions of this committee were now the only decisions within the structure of the Fund that were taken without weighted voting. This was particularly important because a decision of the committee would be deemed to be a decision of the Board of Governors unless the Board repudiated the decision by a majority of 85 per cent of the total voting power.

The possible size and composition of such a Committee on Interpretation of the Board of Governors were discussed by the Executive Board on several occasions, and the staff circulated a number of papers projecting alternative committee sizes and group formations and the corresponding percentages of quota and voting power that would be involved. But by the end of 1971 no consensus had been attained for a recommendation to the Board of Governors.

■　■　■　■　■　■

Part of the significance of the amendments to the Articles of Agreement that became effective in July 1969 was that they were the first modifications of the original Articles. However, as will be seen in Part Five, within a few months after these first amendments had gone into effect the possibility of additional and much more far-reaching amendments, especially concerning par values, was already under consideration. Moreover, the serious discussions about reforming the international monetary system that began at the end of 1971 were, in essence, deliberations concerning what basic alterations should be made in the Fund's Articles of Agreement.

Compensatory Financing
Extended and Liberalized

C OMPENSATORY FINANCING started on an upward course in the years
after 1965. The arrangements for compensatory financing of export
fluctuations that the Fund had introduced in February 1963, and which had
been little used, were extended and liberalized in 1966, and, when world prices
for primary products declined in 1966–68, developing countries began to turn
to these arrangements for financial assistance. Again, in the latter part of 1971,
despite an extraordinary boom in commodity markets, an upsurge in compensatory drawings began to take place. As 1971 came to an end, several
officials from developing countries were recommending further liberalizations
in the Fund's compensatory financing facility, recommendations which were
harbingers of more extensive changes in the facility in years to come.

THE CHANGES OF 1966

The changes in the Fund's compensatory financing arrangements that were
made in 1966 were an offshoot of the discussions on international liquidity.
When it appeared possible that any new scheme for deliberate creation of
reserves might be limited to the few big industrial countries, representatives
from some of these countries suggested that the Fund liberalize its policies on
the use of its resources by developing members. Attention focused particularly
on the compensatory financing facility. Reference has already been made in
Part One to proposals along these lines made by the United Kingdom in 1965.
These suggestions by the industrial countries paralleled similar calls for modi-
fying the Fund's compensatory financing facility by the UNCTAD in 1964 and
by a number of Governors for developing countries at the Fund's Annual Meeting in 1965.

As an aftermath of these recommendations, the Executive Board, in September 1966, after careful consideration, decided to extend and liberalize the com-

pensatory financing facility.[1] Since this action was reported in the earlier history, only the principal changes that were made in the facility will be noted here.[2]

First, the limit on outstanding drawings under the facility, which had been 25 per cent of a member's quota, was extended to 50 per cent. Except for export shortfalls resulting from disasters or major emergencies, however, outstanding compensatory drawings could not increase by more than 25 per cent of a member's quota in any 12-month period.

Second, when export shortfalls were calculated, greater weight than previously was to be given to qualitative estimates. Where countries had a rising trend of exports, explicit account was to be taken of this fact in calculating what were considered export shortfalls. In effect, if exports were not increasing at a sufficient rate, a shortfall in exports could be presumed to exist.

Third, compensatory drawings were separated from the other drawing facilities of the Fund in the sense that the amount of outstanding drawings that a member had under the compensatory financing facility was not to affect its ability to draw under the Fund's other policies. The compensatory financing facility was to float alongside the credit tranches. The importance of this change was that compensatory drawings were no longer to affect the policy criteria applied to a member's subsequent request for a regular drawing. Otherwise, later regular drawings would be subjected to the more severe criteria pertinent to drawings in the higher credit tranches.

Fourth, a member that made an ordinary drawing was permitted later to reclassify that drawing as one made under the compensatory financing facility. Such reclassification had to take place within six months of the initial drawing and the member had to meet the requirements for a compensatory drawing of the same amount at the time of the reclassification. In this way, the member's other drawing rights could be restored for use for regular drawings, or for a new stand-by arrangement upon the expiration of an existing stand-by arrangement.

Fifth, a change was made regarding repurchases. Members making drawings under the compensatory financing facility were expected to repurchase within three to five years, just as with regular drawings. But the 1966 decision included a provision (paragraph 7) linking repurchases of compensatory drawings more closely to the recovery of a member's exchange earnings, rather than making such repurchases subject to the usual three-to-five-year rule. It was provided that as soon as possible after the end of each of the four years following a compensatory drawing a member should, on the basis of a statistical determination that there existed what was called "excess exports" and on the basis of a

---

[1] E.B. Decision No. 1477-(63/8), February 27, 1963, as amended by E.B. Decision No. 2192-(66/81), September 20, 1966; Vol. II below, pp. 198–201.

[2] See *History, 1945–65*, Vol. II, pp. 424–27. The reader interested in the details is referred to the Fund's second report on compensatory financing, which was reproduced in Volume III of *History, 1945–65*, pp. 469–96.

recommendation by the Fund, repurchase an amount approximately equal to one half of the amount by which the member's exports in value terms exceeded, in the special language of the compensatory financing arrangements, the "medium-term (five-year) trend value" of its exports. However, the Fund's recommendation did not impose a legal obligation on the member to repurchase. The change regarding repurchases emphasized that use of the compensatory financing facility was geared to developments in a country's exports: through use of a statistical formula, not only were drawings associated with shortfalls in export earnings but repurchases were expected when export earnings exceeded a medium-term trend.

After the decision setting up the original compensatory financing facility was amended, members began to use the reclassification procedure. They also continued to use stand-by arrangements to alleviate general balance of payments deficits, deficits which were attributable in part to shortfalls in export earnings. Because a member could draw from the Fund for an export shortfall either under the policies governing regular drawings or under the compensatory financing facility, it was necessary to ensure that the sum of any drawings made with respect to a given shortfall did not exceed the amount of the shortfall. In other words, "double compensation" had to be avoided. In the first half of 1967 the staff suggested some techniques for preventing double compensation; these were agreed by the Executive Board in August 1967.[3]

Another decision relating to compensatory drawings was taken in June 1969, when the Fund approved an arrangement to assist members in financing contributions to international buffer stocks of primary products: it was decided to place a joint ceiling on drawings under the new buffer stock facility and those under the compensatory financing facility. Drawings under either facility could amount to the equivalent of 50 per cent of quota, but drawings under the two facilities taken together could not exceed 75 per cent of quota.[4]

USAGE INCREASES

After the compensatory financing facility was introduced in 1963, prices of many primary commodities turned sharply upward. Consequently, only three members made use of the facility during the first three years of its existence— Brazil and Egypt in 1963 and the Sudan in 1965, for a total of $87.25 million.[5]

In contrast, there was a notable acceleration of compensatory financing

---

[3] These techniques are described in Gold, *Stand-By Arrangements*, pp. 108–111.

[4] The buffer stock facility is described in Chap. 15.

[5] Strictly speaking this should be "the equivalent of $87.25 million," since drawings from the Fund were usually made in a parcel of currencies, not only in U.S. dollars. The constant repetition of the words "the equivalent of" in such instances would, however, be tedious, and they have been omitted here and in later chapters.

purchases almost immediately after the arrangements were extended and liberalized in September 1966. The Dominican Republic and Ghana drew amounts totaling $23.85 million in December 1966. Then, in the course of 1967 nine members—Burma, Ceylon, Colombia, Haiti, Iceland, India, Iraq, New Zealand, and the Syrian Arab Republic—all drew for a total of nearly $200 million. And in the first half of 1968 purchases under the facility were made by Afghanistan, Ceylon, Colombia, Egypt, Guatemala, and Uruguay for nearly $65 million; Colombia, Guatemala, and Iraq took advantage of the provision in the amended decision permitting part or all of other drawings to be reclassified as drawings under the compensatory financing arrangements. Table 4 at the end of this chapter gives the details of the transactions carried out under the compensatory financing decision from the time it was taken on February 27, 1963 until April 30, 1972, the end of the last fiscal year of the period covered by this history.

Factors on both the demand side and the supply side explain the step-up in the rate of drawings in the 18 months from December 1966 to June 1968. On the demand side, there was once again evidence of the well-known fact that fluctuations in the pace of economic activity in the industrial world have a direct and forceful impact on primary producing countries. Most primary producing countries were affected by the general slackening of economic growth in several industrial countries that occurred in 1966–67, and by the accompanying weakness of world market prices for many agricultural raw materials. In response to high interest rates, importers in industrial countries also drew down their inventories of many commodities, thereby preventing any significant increase in the volume of demand for these commodities. Hence, in 1966–68 primary producing countries suffered either much reduced rates of export growth or actual export declines. Only a few primary producing countries in special situations expanded their exports in these years.

Demand elements were not, however, the only cause of lower export earnings of primary producers in this 18-month span. The capacity to export of several countries was adversely affected by a number of factors—poor crops, dislocations in transport or other export servicing industries, and the closing of the Suez Canal and other repercussions of the six-day war in the Middle East in June 1967. Also contributing to export shortfalls in the first part of 1968 was the temporary lag in any expansion of the volume of exports following the currency devaluations of several developing countries in November 1967. In value terms, exports were down inasmuch as those devaluations and the devaluation of sterling had reduced export prices in terms of U.S. dollars. All in all, the value of exports of the primary producing countries was only 4 per cent higher in 1967 than in 1966, whereas it had been 8 per cent higher in 1966 than in 1965.

Conditions in commodity markets were reversed, however, in the latter part of 1968, and that year as a whole proved relatively favorable for exports of primary products. The rise in demand and in output in industrial countries in the second half of 1967 was the main factor underlying the return to more satisfactory growth for most primary product exports, but better conditions for producing crops in some exporting countries were also a factor.

The marked upturn in the export earnings of the primary producing countries was mirrored by diminished recourse to the compensatory financing facility in the second half of 1968. After the relatively extensive and frequent use of the facility in the preceding year and a half, in the remainder of 1968 only Iceland, whose exports were depressed by poor fish catches, made a compensatory financing purchase—for $3.75 million. This purchase was made possible by the provision in the amended decision for a limit of 50 per cent of quota on compensatory financing purchases, instead of 25 per cent.

Similarly, during 1969 and 1970 there was no widespread need for compensatory financing of export fluctuations. Exports of primary producing countries continued to expand: their value was 13 per cent higher in 1969 than in 1968 and 11 per cent higher in 1970 than in 1969. Only two countries, Ecuador and El Salvador, made use of the compensatory financing facility during 1969, each for $6.25 million, Ecuador using the reclassification procedure under the amended compensatory financing decision. In 1970 Burundi alone made a compensatory purchase, for $2.5 million.

The situation changed again in the last four months of 1971. Despite the generally favorable payments situations of most countries, once more there was recourse to the compensatory financing facility. In September Burma purchased $6.5 million to alleviate payments difficulties that had arisen from a temporary shortfall in its export earnings during the 12 months ended May 31, 1971. During the shortfall period, rice shipments had increased substantially but no gain in export earnings from rice had been achieved because world prices for rice had declined. In November the Executive Board approved a request by Jordan for a $4.5 million purchase. Jordan had experienced an export shortfall owing to incidents in the Jordan valley that had adversely affected horticultural production, an important source of its export earnings.

Another cause of the accelerated use of the compensatory financing facility in the latter part of 1971 was a sharp drop at that time in world market prices for copper. World market prices for virtually all primary metals were low late in 1971 partly as a result of depressed demand in industrial countries accompanying the reactions of buyers to the international financial disturbances that occurred after August 15, 1971. But lower prices for copper reflected as well the relatively ample supplies available.

The five major copper exporters among the developing countries—Chile, Peru, the Philippines, Zaïre, and Zambia—were all to resort to the compensatory financing facility in the next 17 months, going beyond the time frame of this history. Chile and Zambia drew first, in December 1971. Chile's copper earnings had dropped to 14 per cent below the pre-shortfall average, and to 19 per cent below the average for 1970, and it drew $39.5 million. Zambia's purchase of $19 million was to alleviate a shortfall for the 12 months ended June 30, 1971. Zambia's difficulties had been intensified by the flooding of a major mine, and its copper export earnings were down by 20 per cent compared with the pre-shortfall average.[6]

The first repurchases of drawings under the compensatory financing facility began in 1968. In January 1968 the staff had suggested a procedure to be followed in making recommendations to members for repurchases to take place out of their export excesses, as provided by paragraph (7) of the amended decision. Should calculations show that the member had an export excess, the Managing Director would notify the member by letter, recommend a repurchase of a specific amount, and inquire about the member's intention to repurchase. The Executive Board would be informed through semiannual reports on the situations in which such recommendations had become applicable and on the members' responses.

As time went on, such recommendations were sent to several members. Some members repurchased shortly after receiving the Fund's recommendation. Others represented that, despite the improvement in their exports, their balance of payments deficits, low reserves, or heavy external indebtedness made it difficult for them to repurchase at that time. (Amounts of repurchases, by member country, are given in Table 4.)

COMPENSATORY FINANCING BECOMES IMPORTANT

From September 20, 1966, when the facility was extended and liberalized, until December 31, 1971, total drawings under the compensatory financing facility came to $375 million, more than four times the amount used under the facility during the first three and a half years of its existence. Twenty-one members made compensatory drawings, five of them (Burma, Ceylon, Colombia, Haiti, and Iceland) twice, in contrast to the earlier use by only three members.

Thus a new upsurge in compensatory drawings was beginning as 1971 ended, despite the tremendous boom in commodity markets that was just getting under way. Strong demand in the industrial countries combined with supply shortages of several commodities was beginning to bring about unprecedented spurts in commodity prices. Commodity markets were soon to become so buoyant that, with the continuation and even intensification of inflation and the unsettling of exchange rates and the international monetary system after August 15, 1971, purchases of commodities and commodity stockpiling gradually became common hedges against inflation and against currency depreciation.

---

[6] Compensatory drawings were made by Peru in June 1972 and by Zaïre in July 1972 for $30.75 million and $28.25 million, respectively, and by the Philippines in May 1973 for $38.75 million.

Primary producing countries, as a group, accordingly began to experience unusually favorable balance of payments positions. Nevertheless, it was apparent that these developments did not obviate the need for compensatory drawings. The Fund's developing members had become so large in number and so diverse in circumstance that there were always exceptions to general trends. Thus, even amid prosperous world commodity markets, a number of members continued to suffer from the circumstances which the Fund's compensatory financing arrangements were intended to alleviate. Some members had adverse weather to contend with. Others exported commodities, such as rubber or copper, that did not share in the rise in commodity prices, at least not until much later. Still others were in the throes of special political difficulties that disrupted their production and export. In addition, the lag between commodity market developments and export returns necessitated calls on the compensatory financing facility despite the existence of a commodity boom.

At the close of 1971, the Fund's compensatory financing arrangements were thus at last coming into their own and it was evident that, in future, they would receive enhanced attention. Indeed, within three years after the facility was liberalized in September 1966, that is, by the time of the 1969 Annual Meeting, several Governors, including Mr. Ali Wardhana (Indonesia), Mr. Kuo-Hwa Yu (Republic of China), and Mr. Hassan Abbas Zaki (Egypt), were advocating further liberalization.[7] Suggestions for liberalization were made again at the Annual Meetings in 1970 and 1971 by a number of Governors, notably Mr. Diógenes H. Fernández (Dominican Republic), speaking on behalf of 19 Latin American members, and by Mr. Tan Siew Sin (Malaysia).[8] In 1971 Mr. Bernard Bidias à Ngon (Cameroon), speaking on behalf of 5 Central African nations, also criticized the facility as being "inadequate to resolve the problem of erratic movements in prices of raw materials."[9]

---

[7] Statements by the Governor of the World Bank for Indonesia, the Governor of the Fund for the Republic of China, and the Governor of the World Bank for Egypt, *Summary Proceedings, 1969*, pp. 84, 116, and 166.

[8] Statement by the Governor of the Fund and the World Bank for the Dominican Republic, *Summary Proceedings, 1970*, p. 105, and Statement by the Governor of the World Bank for Malaysia, *Summary Proceedings, 1971*, p. 50.

[9] Statement by the Governor of the Fund for Cameroon, *Summary Proceedings, 1971*, p. 137.

Table 4. Purchases and Repurchases Under Decision on
Compensatory Financing of Export Fluctuations,
February 27, 1963–April 30, 1972 [1]

(In millions of SDRs)

| Member | Purchases | | | Related Repurchases | | Outstanding Balance on April 30, 1972 |
	Date	Amount	Total	Under para. (7)	
Afghanistan	June 5, 1968	4.80	4.80	—	—
Argentina	Mar. 3, 1972	64.00	—	—	64.00
Brazil	June 7, 1963	60.00 [2]	60.00	—	—
Burma	Nov. 21, 1967	7.50	5.00	—	2.50
	Sept. 21, 1971	6.50	—	—	6.50
Burundi	June 9, 1970	2.50	0.50	0.50	2.00
Ceylon	Mar. 21, 1967	19.50	19.50	—	—
	Apr. 17, 1968	19.30	2.00	—	17.30
	Jan. 24, 1972 [3]	4.70 [3]	—	—	4.70
	Jan. 26, 1972	14.75	—	—	14.75
Chile	Dec. 14, 1971	39.50	—	—	39.50
Colombia	Mar. 22, 1967	18.90	18.90	7.70	—
	Apr. 19, 1968 [3]	0.95 [3]	0.95	0.95	—
	Apr. 19, 1968 [3]	0.95 [3]	0.95	0.95	—
Dominican Republic	Dec. 6, 1966	6.60	6.60	3.30	—
Ecuador	Oct. 15, 1969 [3]	3.50 [3]	3.50	—	—
	Oct. 15, 1969 [3]	2.75 [3]	2.75	—	—
Egypt	Oct. 15, 1963	16.00 [2]	16.00	—	—
	Mar. 18, 1968	23.00	—	—	23.00
El Salvador	Dec. 16, 1969	6.25	4.30	4.30	1.95
Ghana	Dec. 20, 1966	17.25	17.25	0.75	—
Guatemala	Feb. 5, 1968 [3]	3.00 [3]	3.00	1.60	—
	Feb. 5, 1968 [3]	3.25 [3]	3.25	—	—
Haiti	Aug. 11, 1967	1.30	1.30	0.12	—
	Dec. 6, 1967	1.00	0.63	0.20	0.37
Iceland	Nov. 10, 1967	3.75	3.75	3.75	—
	Nov. 26, 1968	3.75	3.75	3.75	—
India	Dec. 28, 1967	90.00	90.00	80.00	—
Iraq	Nov. 8, 1967 [3]	17.50 [3]	17.50	—	—
Jordan	Nov. 15, 1971	4.50	—	—	4.50
Khmer Republic	Mar. 14, 1972	6.25	—	—	6.25
New Zealand	May 10, 1967	29.20	29.20	—	—
Sudan	June 1, 1965	11.25 [2]	11.25	—	—
Syrian Arab Republic	Sept. 18, 1967	9.50	7.12	—	2.38
	Jan. 25, 1972	12.50	—	—	12.50
Uruguay	Feb. 7, 1968	9.50	7.20	5.00	2.30
Zambia	Dec. 14, 1971	19.00	—	—	19.00
		564.45	340.95	112.87	223.50

[1] Under E.B. Decision No. 1477-(63/8), February 27, 1963, as amended by E.B. Decision No. 2192-(66/81), September 20, 1966, except where noted. The decision as amended is reproduced below, Vol. II, pp. 198–201.

[2] Under E.B. Decision No. 1477-(63/8), February 27, 1963.

[3] Date and amount of reclassification of previous purchases.

CHAPTER 15

Financing Buffer Stocks

*B*UFFER STOCK FINANCING was the Fund's answer to the demands of
the developing countries in 1967 and 1968 that the Fund and the World
Bank pay greater heed to the problem of stabilization of prices of primary
products. For two decades developing countries had been calling attention to the
adverse consequences for their export earnings of the extreme fluctuations in
world commodity prices, although they had never specifically asked the two
Bretton Woods institutions to help find a solution. However, in the circumstances prevailing internationally in 1967—a renewed onset of falling commodity
prices in the midst of intensive consideration by the industrial countries of
how to change existing international monetary arrangements to aid their own
external payments problems—the developing countries considered the time ripe
to request, at a minimum, a special study of the problem of primary product
prices. After nearly two years of study and discussion, in June 1969 the Fund
introduced a facility for financing buffer stocks.

PRELUDE

The reversal in world prices of raw materials from the beginning of 1966
to the latter part of 1967 was swift and sharp. In the early months of 1966,
output in industrial countries had been rising more rapidly than at any time
since 1964 and raw material prices had risen steeply. But, in the second half
of 1966 and the first half of 1967, a slowing down of world industrial growth
precipitated very large declines in the prices of nearly all raw materials and
primary products. The prices of wool, rubber, tin, coffee, sisal, and lead dropped
markedly. For the first time since 1963 the maintenance of tin prices above
the floor established by the International Tin Agreement required intervention
through the international buffer stock. In contrast, when more normal growth
in the output of industrial countries had been maintained, as from mid-1964
through 1965, raw material prices had been more or less stable.

In 1967 most primary producing countries began to experience rather severe
balance of payments pressures. The most adversely affected were the African

countries. These countries were already suffering from a number of difficulties that reduced their exports in 1966–67: the outbreak of civil war in Nigeria, the closing of the Suez Canal because of hostilities in the Middle East, the unilateral declaration of independence by Rhodesia, and the poor agricultural harvests in several northern African countries. Moreover, the African countries exported mainly to Europe, and the slower growth of output in industrial Europe in 1966–67 compounded their export difficulties. Hence, the export earnings of Cameroon, Ethiopia, Kenya, Nigeria, Rhodesia, Senegal, Sierra Leone, Tanzania, Uganda, Zambia, and other African countries declined appreciably.

Because of the tremendous attention that had been given for some years, and was still being given, at the behest of the industrial countries, to the possibility of creating a new reserve asset to meet their possible needs for greater liquidity, it was to be expected that the Fund's developing members would take the occasion to request a review of their special needs. Not only had there been the deterioration in their foreign exchange earnings just described, but—what was more serious for most developing countries—the Decade of Development, as the United Nations had christened the 1960s, had not come close to being the era of economic advance originally hoped for.

The monetary and financial leaders of developing countries consequently intensified their efforts to bring attention to their common financial problems and to press their concerns in unison, not only in the Fund but in other forums. The UNCTAD, which had held a world conference in Geneva in 1964, was planning a second conference for February–March 1968 in New Delhi. Analogous to the Group of Ten of the industrial countries, the leaders of developing countries were beginning to assemble from time to time as the Group of Seventy-Seven.

These were among the facts to which Mr. Schweitzer directed the attention of the Governors at the Annual Meeting in Rio de Janeiro in September 1967.[1] Noting the severe impact that the deceleration of activity in the industrial world during 1966–67 had had on primary producing countries, he stressed the untimeliness of any setback for the less developed of these countries. The real gross national product of many less developed countries, he said, had grown more slowly from 1960 to 1965 than in the previous five years and, on a per capita basis, had risen only slightly or had even declined. Now, he feared, this situation had worsened.

AFRICAN MEMBERS PRESS FOR SPECIAL STUDY

These circumstances prompted the Governors for France and for 14 African members within the franc zone—Cameroon, the Central African Republic, the

---

[1] Opening Address by the Managing Director, *Summary Proceedings, 1967*, pp. 19–20.

People's Republic of the Congo, Ivory Coast, Dahomey, Gabon, Upper Volta, Madagascar, Mali, Mauritania, Niger, Senegal, Chad, and Togo [2]—to assemble in Dakar, Senegal, the week before the 1967 Annual Meeting and to agree to submit to the Governors of the Fund and the Bank a resolution concerning the stabilization of primary product prices. The interest shown in this subject by the Governors for these African members had been foreshadowed at the Annual Meeting the year before in the remarks of Mr. Mohamed Salem Ould M'Khaitirat (Mauritania). Speaking on behalf of the 7 countries of the West African Monetary Union (UMOA)—Dahomey, Ivory Coast, Upper Volta, Togo, Niger, Mauritania, and Senegal—he suggested that international aid take the form of stabilization of commodity prices.[3]

During the 1967 Annual Meeting, while for virtually all the Governors the most important topic was the proposed outline for establishment of the SDR facility, Mr. Debré (France) and the Governors of the Fund for several African members addressed themselves vigorously to the problem of prices of primary products. Mr. Debré wanted priority to be given "to an international organization of the market for certain raw materials and certain products, notably tropical products."[4]

Mr. Alexandre Banza (Central African Republic), giving the views of the five countries making up the Central African Customs and Economic Union (UDEAC)—Cameroon, the Central African Republic, the People's Republic of the Congo, Gabon, and Chad—talked about the particular plight of the producers of coffee, cocoa, cotton, bananas, and oilseeds.[5] Mr. Courmo Barcourgné (Niger), the Governor to speak this year for the 7 countries making up the West African Monetary Union, urged a study of the stabilization of commodity prices.[6]

Warmly seconding a resolution by the Board of Governors concerning prices of primary products was Mr. Tan (Malaysia). The commodity price problem became graphic as he cited price and quantity statistics for his country's main export, natural rubber. Between 1960 and 1966 the unit value of Malaysia's natural rubber exports had fallen from an average of 35 U.S. cents a pound to 21 U.S. cents a pound, and in 1967 the price fell further, to 15 U.S. cents a pound, the lowest in 18 years. As a result of falling commodity prices Malaysia had, since 1960, incurred a foreign exchange loss of the order of US$1,807 mil-

---

[2] These countries are listed in the same order in which they were listed in the Governors' resolution, that is, in the alphabetical order of their French names; see Vol. II below, p. 227.

[3] Statement by the Governor of the Fund for Mauritania, *Summary Proceedings, 1966*, p. 165.

[4] Statement by the Governor of the World Bank for France, *Summary Proceedings, 1967*, p. 72.

[5] Statement by the Governor of the Fund for the Central African Republic, *Summary Proceedings, 1967*, pp. 101–102.

[6] Statement by the Governor of the Fund for Niger, *Summary Proceedings, 1967*, p. 144.

lion, an amount equivalent to 6¾ times the total official net loans and grants that Malaysia had received during the six years 1961 through 1966.[7]

This much interest in some action on primary product prices was sufficient. On September 29, 1967, the same day on which they adopted the resolution approving the Outline for the SDR facility and calling for changes in the rules and practices of the Fund, the Board of Governors of the Fund adopted a resolution concerning primary product prices.[8] This resolution requested the staff of the Fund, together with the staff of the World Bank, to prepare a study of the problem of the stabilization of prices of primary products at remunerative levels and of possible solutions and their feasibility. The study was to be submitted to the Executive Directors, who were asked to transmit it to the Board of Governors with their comments, if possible by the time of the next Annual Meeting in 1968. A similar resolution was adopted by the Boards of Governors of the World Bank Group.

Many of the supporters of the resolution seemed to believe that, since the Fund and the World Bank had the financial wherewithal to support any plan that might be devised for the solution of the problem of primary product prices, there was a real distinction between a study of the problem by these Bretton Woods institutions and the studies by other groups.

Mr. Schweitzer welcomed the invitation to the Fund to study the stabilization of commodity prices. But he emphasized that a great deal of work in this area had been done and was currently being done in other international bodies, such as the UNCTAD and the Food and Agriculture Organization (FAO), and reminded the Governors that "there is no easy road toward fully satisfactory solutions of the problems related to the instability of commodity prices."[9]

REPORT BY STAFF

After the staffs of the Fund and the World Bank had exchanged views on the procedure to be followed in the preparation of this study, the Fund staff advised the Executive Directors that the study could best be divided into two parts. The first would cover the general commodity problem, including an evaluation of possible solutions to the instability of commodity prices, and would be worked on jointly by the staffs of both institutions. The second would discuss the role that the Fund or the World Bank might have in solving commodity problems, and would necessarily be prepared separately by each insti-

---

[7] Statement by the Governor of the Fund and the World Bank for Malaysia, *Summary Proceedings, 1967*, pp. 42–43.

[8] Resolution No. 22-9; Vol. II below, p. 227.

[9] Concluding Remarks by the Managing Director, *Summary Proceedings, 1967*, p. 242.

tution. In line with the desire of several of the Governors that the commodity study should involve a major effort—possibly comparable to that of the work on international liquidity—and in order to ease coordination with the World Bank, an interdepartmental staff group was designated to oversee the Fund's part of the study.

The Executive Directors, especially the Executive Directors elected by developing members, supported by the French Executive Director, expressed keen interest in the progress of the staff's work. For example, when the Directors gave their informal reactions to the 1967 Annual Meeting, shortly after they returned to Washington, Mr. Plescoff (France) underscored the necessity for a Fund-Bank study of commodity problems. The French authorities, he said, attached great importance to the resolution and believed that precise proposals should be presented to the Governors at the 1968 Annual Meeting. Early in 1968, when the UNCTAD adopted a resolution stressing the importance of the Fund-Bank study, Mr. Plescoff requested that the text of the UNCTAD resolution be distributed to the Executive Directors.[10] In July 1968 he was to tie together the commodity price question and the basic purposes of the Fund and of the World Bank, pointing out that the Brazilian delegation had circulated a proposal on the stabilization of prices of primary products at Bretton Woods at the time these organizations had been established.

Because of the intense interest of the Executive Directors, a provisional outline of Part I, prepared by a joint Fund-Bank working party, was sent to the Executive Board in April 1968 and discussed by the Board at two meetings on May 15, 1968. Mr. Yaméogo (Upper Volta), who had been elected by the African members that had initiated the Governors' resolution, commented favorably on the breadth and thoroughness of the study. He stressed that there were two major facets to the study of commodity prices. The first was the short-term instability of prices and earnings and how the consequences of such instability could be limited. The second was the long-term trend in the level of earnings of primary producing members. The first was in essence a problem of balance of payments adjustment while the second was basically a problem of economic development. He was pleased to note that the staff study recognized the distinction. Mr. Yaméogo, as well as Messrs. Diz (Argentina), Faber (Guinea), González del Valle (Guatemala), Kafka (Brazil), Madan (India), and Nikoi (Ghana), made a number of specific suggestions for the study. They urged especially that practical specific proposals be forthcoming, noting that the Fund had had some experience along these lines as a result of the compensatory financing facility.

In July 1968 preliminary texts of both Part I, the analytical part prepared jointly with the World Bank staff, and Part II, *Scope for Action by the Fund*, were sent to the Executive Board.

---

[10] UN document TD/11/RES/19, March 28, 1968.

Part I of the study, later published, took into account both the short-term and long-term situations in commodity markets.[11] It analyzed the trends in commodity trade, as well as the fluctuations of primary product prices, and it considered the measures that might be taken to reduce price fluctuations. In preparing the report, the staffs of the World Bank and the Fund drew widely on the work of the FAO, the CONTRACTING PARTIES to the GATT, and the UNCTAD, as well as of specialist commodity organizations, although the high priority given to completion of the study in time for presentation to the 1968 Annual Meeting necessarily limited consultation with these and other organizations.

This part of the report made several observations which formed the underpinnings for the policy action recommended in Part II. Among the observations were the following:

One, developing countries were still heavily dependent on a narrow range of primary products for most of their exports. Furthermore, the exports of most developing countries continued to be concentrated on a few commodities.

Two, world commodity markets had shown two major unfavorable characteristics. Their absorptive capacity had grown only slowly: technological developments, changes in consumer spending patterns, and protection given by industrial countries to their own primary products had all worked in the direction of slowing the growth of outlets for primary product exports. Commodity markets had also been subject to wide price fluctuations. The degree of price instability since the early 1950s appeared to be lower than in earlier decades, but it had remained substantial.

Three, a technique of price stabilization which was widely discussed but not much used was an international buffer stocking arrangement. This device was used in the International Tin Agreement, and was being envisaged in the cocoa agreement that had been under negotiation for several years. The objective of buffer stock operations was to keep the price of the commodity between certain agreed limits by a procedure in which the buffer stock agent bought the commodity when the price dropped below a floor and sold the commodity when the price rose above a pre-set ceiling. The staff's analysis showed that, when the objective of buffer stock operations was limited to smoothing fluctuations around a medium-term price trend, and when this trend was correctly identified, the quantities which the buffer stock agent had to buy or sell for stabilizing the price of the commodity canceled out within a reasonably short time. In other words, the quantities bought when prices were low equaled the quantities sold when prices were high.

Four, the international buffer stock device did not work equally well for all commodities. Much depended on the causes of the price instability of the given commodity. When the price instability resulted from shifts in demand as

---

[11] *The Problem of Stabilization of Prices of Primary Products: A Joint Staff Study (Part I),* International Bank for Reconstruction and Development and International Monetary Fund (Washington, 1969).

against shifts in supply, buffer stock operations tended to stabilize both product prices and export earnings. However, when price instability resulted from shifts in supply, buffer stock operations were not necessarily successful in stabilizing export earnings. These considerations, plus others, such as the perishability of some commodities, meant that the range of commodities for which buffer stock operations were appropriate might not be large. In determining the desirability of price stabilization through stocking operations, the benefits to producing and consuming countries had to be weighed against the costs of the stabilizing arrangement. These costs varied from commodity to commodity, depending on the size of the required stocks, the costs of storage, the rate of interest, and the duration of the stocking period.

Five, the level and trend of the export earnings of developing countries could be improved in a number of other ways, for instance, restrictions on primary products by importing countries could be removed and the output and exports of developing countries could be diversified over the long term.

The staff also examined, in Part II, the contribution that the Fund might make to the specific problems of countries producing primary products, over and above the functions the Fund performed in facilitating world trade generally. In two important fields of action for the Fund—consultations with members and the provision of financial resources—the staff offered recommendations.

Noting that the Fund's annual consultations under Articles VIII and XIV had broadened to include virtually all policies bearing on members' balance of payments positions, the staff suggested that consultations could include more intensive discussions of commodity problems. In consultations with developing members, the effects on production and export of primary commodities of such factors as exchange rate policies, taxation and subsidization, bilateral trading arrangements, and restrictions by other countries could all be more fully considered. In consultations with developed members, where less attention had been paid to commodity problems, the Fund could ask that officials direct their attention to the disadvantages to primary product producers, especially those with low incomes, of the policies being applied by developed countries to favor their own primary products.

Another part of the staff's suggestion was that the Fund periodically review with both producing and consuming members the outlook for particular commodities and their policies with respect to these commodities. These discussions, thought the staff, would encourage industrial members to remove government-sanctioned impediments to imports from primary producing members.

The staff believed further that the Fund's compensatory financing facility should be retained even if the Fund widened its policies, or introduced new ones, relating to primary products. The compensatory financing facility dealt with the problem of fluctuations in export earnings *after* the problem arose.

But there was another problem, namely, that of trying to prevent fluctuations in export earnings.

Therefore, in addition to the compensatory financing facility, there was merit in the Fund's providing buffer stock financing, especially as there had been a gap in this field. The two schemes would be complementary. Admittedly, problems of financing international buffer stocks had not necessarily been the main stumbling block in the formation of commodity agreements among countries. The costs and benefits of price stabilization were not easily ascertainable, and the interests of one country might conflict with those of another. Hence, agreement among countries was often difficult. Nonetheless, outside financing, as from the Fund, might help countries to work out and conclude appropriate agreements.

Such financing by the Fund should be on a modest scale, on a short-term repayment basis, in methods that were integrated with the Fund's existing policies on the use of its resources. The standard three-to-five-year rule on repurchase could apply to drawings for buffer stock financing, since stock transactions in any sound scheme could be expected roughly to balance out in the medium term. The close relationship between buffer stock financing for price stabilization and compensatory drawings for export shortfalls also made it reasonable that any assistance by the Fund to buffer stock financing should have a joint upper limit with compensatory financing drawings.

VIEWS OF EXECUTIVE DIRECTORS AND GOVERNORS

When the Executive Board began consideration of the staff's study on July 31, 1968, Mr. Southard, the Acting Chairman, noted that, as the Board had agreed, a representative of the staff of the World Bank was present and a representative of the Fund's staff had attended discussions of the Bank's Executive Board. Most members of the Executive Board commended the analysis, which contained new ideas on this often-studied topic. Mr. Rajaobelina (Malagasy Republic), however, expressed disappointment at the proposals for action. These consisted of (1) indirect assistance by the Fund to buffer stocks by allowing members to draw to finance contributions to stocks and (2) drawings to mitigate the effects of domestic stockbuilding. He hoped the Fund would be more liberal. Mr. Stone (Australia), reflecting the view of the Australian authorities that the crux of the commodity problem was that industrial countries protected their own agriculture, differed with the staff's reasoning. He contended that any solution to the problem of primary product prices should reduce, rather than increase, restraints on world trade. A vital criterion for any adequate solution, he suggested, was its effect on global real income. This criterion might require that any necessary restructuring of production or of demand occur in the economies of the industrialized countries rather than, as was usually assumed, in those of the developing countries. It was ironic, Mr. Stone continued, that restructuring of output should take place in the developing countries in order to correct supply gluts that had resulted largely from the failure of developed countries to undertake such restructuring themselves. The irony became more acute when one considered that the developed countries, compared with the developing ones, enjoyed considerably greater mobility of resources, much higher levels of technical skills, and a much greater availability of capital, all of which would make the task of restructuring easier for them.

Mr. Diz, in a detailed paper of his own, contended that the staff report had not provided a satisfactory empirical basis for action in the commodity field. The relationship between variations in the prices of different commodities and variations in the export earnings of developing countries was a complex, multifaceted one that needed further analysis if the Fund and the World Bank were to come up with useful recommendations.

Some Executive Directors favored the staff's idea that the Fund finance international buffer stocks. Mr. Lieftinck (Netherlands), for example, generally agreed with the staff's suggestions. Mr. Plescoff, on the other hand, like Mr. Rajaobelina, did not want the Fund restricted to the solutions available under its existing Articles. Similarly, Mr. Nikoi and Mr. Madan preferred broader solutions. Mr. Kafka, emphasizing that any proposals that might be devised only went a short way to solving the problems arising out of the instability of commodity prices, wanted to explore just how much might be done within the existing Articles before thought turned to possible amendments. For instance, might not rules on repurchase be altered? Might there not be a second compensatory tranche under the compensatory financing facility? Might not the formula for determining the extent of export shortfalls under that facility be re-examined? Mr. Dale (United States) raised a number of questions concerning the results of a buffer stock financing facility in the Fund and the ways in which the buffer stock arrangements that countries set up would be formulated and administered so that countries might qualify for assistance from the Fund. Several Executive Directors also noted the need for the Fund's action to be coordinated with the responsibilities and policies of the World Bank.

Because of the diversity of their views, and because the 1968 Annual Meeting was only weeks away, the Executive Directors, after considerable debate about procedures and after coordination with the Executive Directors of the World Bank, decided in September 1968 to transmit to the Board of Governors only Part I of the study and to inform the Governors that Part II had been begun and would be sent later. They attached a draft resolution for the Governors to consider to the effect that Part II should be completed not later than the 1969 Annual Meeting.

At the 1968 Annual Meeting, several Governors, including Mr. Ismail bin Mohamed Ali (Malaysia), Mr. François-Xavier Ortoli (France), and Mr. R. D.

Muldoon (New Zealand), indicated their disappointment at the results thus far achieved.[12] Then the Board of Governors considered and passed a second resolution on the stabilization of prices of primary products. This resolution urged that "specific financial measures" and other solutions to the commodity problem be considered, and that Part II of the study be completed not later than June 30, 1969.[13]

INTENSIFIED STUDY

Beginning in October 1968 and continuing for the next eight to nine months, the attention of the Executive Directors to the primary product price problem became a full-blown effort. The statistical material which had formed the empirical basis of Part I of the staff study was circulated to the Executive Board. A representative from the staff of the Fund regularly attended the meetings of an Executive Director–staff seminar on stabilization of prices of primary products that was inaugurated by the World Bank and was to go on for many months. In February and March 1969 the Fund staff prepared two further papers. The first spelled out criteria that the Fund could apply to international buffer stock proposals in order to determine whether or not they were worthy of Fund financial support. The second examined the possible effects of buffer stock financing on the liquidity of the Fund.

Developing countries continued to be very interested in the study. In January 1969 Mr. Prebisch, Secretary-General of the UNCTAD, wrote to Mr. Schweitzer drawing attention to the proposals concerning buffer stocks contained in the report of the UNCTAD Committee on Commodities, which had concluded its meetings in Geneva the previous November. Mr. Prebisch stressed that the proposals had been unanimously agreed by the members of the UNCTAD Committee, who attached great importance to the resources for financing buffer stocks that could be made available by international financial institutions.

At the Fourth Conference of Governors of the Central Banks in Southeast Asia, held in Bali, Indonesia, in February 1969, the Governors of the central banks of the Khmer Republic, Ceylon, Indonesia, Laos, Malaysia, Thailand, and South Viet-Nam, the Deputy Governor of the Central Bank of the Philippines, a representative of the Nepal Rastra Bank, and the Permanent Secretary of the Ministry of Finance, Singapore, adopted a joint position on the problems of stabilization of the prices of primary commodities. A report embodying this position was later transmitted to the Managing Director by Mr. Kharmawan (Indonesia). They advocated further liberalization of the Fund's compensatory

---

[12] Statements by the Alternate Governor of the Fund for Malaysia, the Governor of the World Bank for France, and the Governor of the Fund for New Zealand, *Summary Proceedings, 1968*, pp. 39–40, 75–77, and 148–49.

[13] Resolution No. 23-13; Vol. II below, p. 228.

financing facility and the introduction of a separate facility for financing buffer stocks. With regard to the latter, those Governors present at the Conference considered, inter alia, that the maximum period of three to five years for repayment of buffer stock assistance, as proposed by the staff, might not coincide with the price cycles of certain commodities. For such situations they thought it would be desirable to have available a refinancing facility, this refinancing to be done by both the Fund and the World Bank.

In mid-March 1969, the Executive Board began a paragraph-by-paragraph consideration of the staff's policy paper of the previous year in order to guide the staff in a redraft. In the midst of these discussions Mr. de Maulde (France) circulated a memorandum giving the views of the French authorities on the action the Fund and the World Bank could initiate in the field of stabilization of prices of primary products. These institutions could (1) help to solve the financing problems associated with the initial and operating stages of commodity agreements; (2) play a key role in the investment programs needed to diversify the output and exports of primary producing countries; and (3) adapt their traditional lending policies so that countries would have a strong incentive to reach and abide by international stabilization agreements.

The first form of assistance was the Fund's domain, while the second and third were matters for the World Bank Group. Any responsibilities that might devolve upon the Fund and the World Bank in connection with this minimum program would not require additional funding for these institutions nor more than a slight broadening of their existing activities.

The French authorities thus concluded that the Fund staff's proposals represented "a positive approach" to what the Fund could do. A consensus of the Executive Directors on a buffer stock financing arrangement seemed to be emerging.

A DECISION REACHED

The staff redraft of Part II of the study, *Scope for Action by the Fund*, completed in May 1969, reflected these views. Therefore, when this report came before the Board, most of the Executive Directors appointed or elected by industrial members—Messrs. Dale (United States), Johnstone (Canada), Lieftinck (Netherlands), Maude (United Kingdom), Palamenghi-Crispi (Italy), Plescoff (France), Schleiminger (Federal Republic of Germany), and van Campenhout (Belgium)—were in general accord with it. Several of the Executive Directors elected by developing members—Messrs. Kafka, Kharmawan, and Yaméogo in particular—regretted that the Board could not support more liberal action by the Fund in the commodity price field, but they went along with proposals that were acceptable to the other Executive Directors.

During the Executive Board's discussion much attention centered on the question of what limits should apply to drawings under the proposed buffer stock facility and on the question of how high should be the joint limits placed on buffer stock drawings and drawings under the existing compensatory financing facility. After consideration of a revised version of the staff report, the Executive Board, on June 25, 1969, adopted a decision to assist members in financing contributions to international buffer stocks, and on July 9 their report to the Board of Governors was made public.[14]

Elements of the Decision

The Executive Directors' report on buffer stock financing took the form first of having the Executive Directors state that they generally agreed with the suggestions for Fund policy that was set out in Part II of the staff's study. Then, there was a Board decision on buffer stock financing which contained a complex of features, fixing the terms and conditions of drawings. To help finance its contribution to an international buffer stock, a member might draw from the Fund amounts up to 50 per cent of its quota, without any limit—such as existed in the compensatory financing facility—on the amount that might be drawn in any 12-month period. However, drawings outstanding for the purpose of buffer stock financing and for compensatory financing of export fluctuations together might at no time exceed a common upper limit of 75 per cent of quota. To the extent that such drawings raised the Fund's holdings of a member's currency above 200 per cent of quota, the Fund was prepared to waive this limit on purchases. Buffer stock drawings were also conditional in the sense that a member drawing under the facility had to have a balance of payments need and had to agree to cooperate with the Fund to find solutions to its balance of payments difficulties.

Other features of the buffer stock financing facility were similar to, though not identical with, those of the compensatory financing facility. Drawings were to be additional to access to the Fund's regular resources: they were to be ignored in computing the amounts that members were normally able to draw under the Fund's usual tranche policies, and, more importantly, in determining the conditions to be applicable. An exception was that a member drawing under the buffer stock facility at a time when it still had gold tranche drawing rights at its disposal *pro tanto* lost such drawing rights, an exception that later was to require separate examination and decision of the legal question whether the Fund could challenge a member's representation of need when the purchase for buffer stock financing was also a gold tranche purchase. In August 1971 the Board decided that the Fund would not challenge a member's repre-

---

[14] E.B. Decision No. 2772-(69/47), June 25, 1969. The Executive Directors' report, their decision, and Part II of the staff's study are reproduced in Vol. II below, pp. 201 and 227–50.

sentation of need for a buffer stock drawing if the purchase was within the gold tranche.[15]

The standard three-to-five-year rule on repurchases applied to drawings for buffer stock financing. In addition, since drawings under this facility were in support of buffer stock operations of a revolving character, the decision established a rule requiring a member to repurchase from the Fund at an earlier date than the usual three to five years to the extent that the buffer stock agent distributed cash to its members.

Further criteria were set down to enable the Fund to judge the suitability of buffer stock arrangements for assistance. The Fund had to be satisfied that the arrangements were economically sound and that the transactions it was helping to finance were compatible with the Fund's purposes and with the requirement that the use of its resources be temporary. Certain general principles of intergovernmental relations laid down by the United Nations were, for example, expected to be observed in the conclusion and conduct of the international commodity agreements involving the buffer stock arrangements. The agreements had to take explicit account also of the effects of price stabilization objectives on the stabilization of export earnings: the Fund would have serious reservations about any scheme that appeared likely to destabilize export earnings for any number of members.

The nature of the price objectives of a stockholding scheme were also considered crucial. Schemes suitable for Fund financing were those aiming at the stabilization of prices around a medium-term trend, so that stock transactions could be expected roughly to balance out over a medium-term period. The Fund further regarded as an important test of any stabilization scheme the willingness of participating governments to commit some of their own resources to the scheme. Thus an appropriate part of the initial and operating costs of the buffer stock arrangement was to be met from resources other than those of the international financial institutions.

Paragraph 6 of the decision further stated that the Fund, in its consultations with members, would pay increased attention to their policies in the commodity field. The implementation of this paragraph is discussed in the last section of this chapter.

Some Disappointments

When the 1969 Annual Meeting took place the following September, several Governors from developing members—Mr. Qizilbash (Pakistan), Mr. Ahmad (Malaysia), and Mr. Wardhana (Indonesia)—expressed regrets that the outcome of the Fund-Bank exercise on the stabilization of primary product prices had been limited.[16] Other Governors, including Mr. Giscard d'Estaing

---

[15] E.B. Decision No. 3386-(71/83), August 6, 1971; Vol. II below, p. 203.

[16] Statements by the Governors of the World Bank for Pakistan, Malaysia, and Indonesia, *Summary Proceedings, 1969,* pp. 23, 46, and 84.

(France) and Mr. E. H. K. Mudenda (Zambia), had indicated satisfaction with the Fund's buffer stock financing decision.[17] Mr. Henri Konan Bédié (Ivory Coast), considering the solution temporary, made detailed suggestions for longer-run solutions.[18]

While the Fund's scheme was less criticized as time went on, the number of general comments on the need to stabilize commodity prices increased. At the 1970 Annual Meeting in Copenhagen, several Governors, especially for member countries in Africa, continued to voice concern that the problem of the stabilization of primary product prices had not been adequately dealt with. Mr. Hédi Nouira (Tunisia), who was Chairman of the 1970 meeting, so remarked in his opening address.[19] Similarly, Mr. Abdoulaye Lamana (Chad), speaking on behalf of Cameroon, the Central African Republic, the People's Republic of the Congo, and Gabon, said that the problem remained serious.[20] Mr. Muldoon (New Zealand) once again stressed that the primary product problem was a basic one.[21] And Mr. Tan was already suggesting a liberalization of the Fund's new facility.[22]

By the time of the 1971 Annual Meeting, however, the transformation of the international monetary scene brought about by the suspension of official dollar convertibility on August 15, 1971, and the crisis implications for both industrial and primary producing members, dominated the Governors' remarks, and for the time being the primary product problem was submerged.

THE DECISION IMPLEMENTED

In October and November 1970 the Fund examined the first use proposed for the new buffer stock financing facility.

The Fourth International Tin Agreement, negotiated in April–May 1970, was to enter into force on July 1, 1971, on expiry of the Third Agreement. Like the previous Agreements, the Fourth Agreement provided for the operation of an international buffer stock of tin to which participating countries were expected to make contributions.

---

[17] Statements by the Governor of the World Bank for France and the Governor of the Fund and the World Bank for Zambia, *Summary Proceedings, 1969,* pp. 61 and 151.

[18] Statement by the Governor of the Fund for Ivory Coast, *Summary Proceedings, 1969,* pp. 190–94.

[19] Opening Address by the Chairman of the Boards of Governors, *Summary Proceedings, 1970,* p. 12.

[20] Statement by the Governor of the Fund for Chad, *Summary Proceedings, 1970,* pp. 28–29.

[21] Statement by the Governor of the Fund for New Zealand, *Summary Proceedings, 1970,* p. 52.

[22] Statement by the Governor of the World Bank for Malaysia, *Summary Proceedings, 1970,* p. 62.

The staff prepared a report that examined (1) current conditions in the world tin market, (2) the operations of the first three International Tin Agreements, which had been in force since 1956, (3) the details of the Fourth Agreement, and (4) the suitability of the Tin Agreement for the Fund's assistance under its new buffer stock facility. On November 25, 1970, after several discussions of the question, the Executive Board took a decision to the effect that members could use the Fund's buffer stock financing facility in connection with the financing of the contributions that they were required to make to the international tin buffer stock to be established under the Fourth International Tin Agreement.[23] The Fund would expect that each participant in the Tin Agreement would meet from sources other than the Fund not less than one third of its share of the initial contribution of the cash equivalent of 7,500 tons of tin. This amount, that is, the amount to be furnished from sources other than the Fund, would correspond to one eighth of the total of compulsory producer contributions envisaged over the life of the scheme. The staff was to keep the Executive Board informed on the operation of the buffer stock and other developments in connection with the Fourth International Tin Agreement by reports to be made at least once a year, and the Fund might make such review of this decision as was appropriate in the light of these reports.

In June 1971, shortly before it was expected that requests for the use of the Fund's resources would be made under this decision, another problem arose. Some tin remained in the buffer stock at the conclusion of the old Agreement. Members wanted to receive credit for these past tin contributions as part of their new contributions and to draw equivalent amounts under the Fund's new buffer stock facility. The Executive Board decided in favor of this arrangement. Their decision was that any initial contribution that a member might make in kind (that is, in the form of tin metal) would be regarded as equivalent to contributions in cash and would be valued at the floor price ruling when the Agreement entered into force.[24] Messrs. Lieftinck, Schleiminger, and van Campenhout, believing that access to the buffer stock facility was being unduly widened, abstained from the decision. They were concerned that contributions in the form of tin metal, especially past contributions, did not directly affect a member's foreign exchange reserve position and hence did not meet the test of balance of payments need that was to govern drawings for buffer stock contributions.

The Fourth International Tin Agreement entered into force provisionally on July 1, 1971, and on July 1–5, at its first session under the Agreement, the International Tin Council determined the initial stock contributions to be made by the participating producing countries.

The new facility was used shortly thereafter by three members that were major tin exporters. On July 16, 1971, the Fund agreed to purchases by Bolivia

---

[23] E.B. Decision No. 3179-(70/102), November 25, 1970; Vol. II below, pp. 201–202.

[24] E.B. Decision No. 3351-(71/51), June 21, 1971; Vol. II below, p. 202.

and Indonesia of $2,974,000 and $1,887,000, respectively, under the terms of the buffer stock facility; and on August 6 the Fund agreed to a purchase of $7,293,240 by Malaysia under the facility.[25] Since Malaysia's request for a drawing under the buffer stock facility also involved a gold tranche purchase, the drawing had been held up pending the decision, referred to above, as to whether a member's claim that it had a balance of payments need could be challenged under these circumstances. At the end of October 1971 Bolivia and Indonesia again requested purchases under the facility of $1,545,000 and $980,000, respectively, and these requests were granted.

CONSULTATIONS TO INCLUDE COMMODITIES

In August 1970 the staff suggested a way to implement that part of the buffer stock decision relating to the taking up of commodity problems as part of the Fund's regular annual consultations. Here, the principal question for the Fund was the degree to which it should become involved in commodity problems that arose from restrictions or other trade practices by one member that adversely affected the commodity exports of another member.

The question was a thorny one. In the first place, as a general policy the Fund had not pursued questions relating to its members' trade practices and trade restrictions, as distinct from their restrictions on foreign exchange and payments. Matters pertaining to trade had been the prerogative of the GATT.[26] Yet the primary producing countries had become intensively concerned about the agricultural restrictions of the industrial countries and the resultant limitations on their access to the industrial countries' markets.

A number of developments in the late 1960s had brought about these concerns. Primary producing countries had been asked to limit their exports of meat and cotton textiles voluntarily. More stringent regulation of imports of meat had been introduced in European markets. Some primary producing countries had been having marketing difficulties as a consequence of preferences extended by the EEC countries to developing countries associated with the EEC. In addition, industrial countries were becoming increasingly self-sufficient in many materials, as a result both of the increasing importance of synthetic products and of the rapid growth of their own production of natural products, especially of agricultural goods sheltered by protective barriers and subsidies.

Questions concerning restrictions on commodity trade and of agricultural protection in industrial countries had come under active consideration by

---

[25] Amounts in respect of drawings are expressed here in dollars, although they may have been made in other currencies; see footnote 5 in Chap. 14 above.

[26] For a discussion of the distinction between the areas of jurisdiction of the GATT and the Fund, see *History, 1945–65*, Vol. II, Chap. 16, and also pp. 235–40.

various international organizations. The FAO and the UNCTAD, for instance, had been scrutinizing these questions. That the study of primary products by the Fund and the World Bank ought to be concerned with the agricultural protectionist policies of the industrial countries, even more than with buffer stock arrangements, had been the thrust of the remarks at the Annual Meetings by the Governors for Australia and New Zealand. Mr. Muldoon (New Zealand) had spoken on this point at some length at the Annual Meetings both in 1968 and in 1969. Similarly, Mr. Leslie H. E. Bury (Australia), at the 1969 Annual Meeting, stressed that the urgent need was for the industrial countries to reduce their protection and to adopt more liberal trading policies toward the importation of raw materials and foodstuffs.[27]

Against this background, the staff did not make specific suggestions, and awaited guidance from the Executive Directors as to how far they wished to extend their concern with commodity problems. It was the staff's view that the Fund's entrance into the field of restrictions on commodities should be a cautious and experimental one. Reasoning that the Fund had a special interest in those commodity trade practices that might cause use of the Fund's compensatory financing facility or that might affect the operations of buffer stock schemes where the Fund might be asked to commit resources, the staff suggested that the Fund's efforts, at least at the outset, be addressed to those commodity trade practices that were closely associated with balance of payments difficulties in primary producing members.

During consultation discussions the staff could encourage primary producing members to make known the specific situations that were aggravating their balance of payments difficulties. The issues selected for follow-up would be those that appeared to the Fund significantly to affect the payments situations or domestic equilibrium of members. The consultations with industrial members would not get into reviews of domestic agricultural policies but would, nonetheless, yield important information on commodity practices, including members' reasons for the specific policies criticized by primary producing members and the intent of the industrial members to ameliorate any adverse effects on other members. The effective contribution of the Fund would be to encourage members to give fuller consideration to the international implications of specific national actions and policies in the commodity field. Because of the newness of this consultation activity, the staff proposed to make progress reports to the Executive Directors from time to time.

In October 1970, after a very long session on this topic, the Executive Board endorsed the proposed procedure. Mr. de Maulde, Mr. Tom de Vries (Netherlands, Alternate to Mr. Lieftinck), Mr. Palamenghi-Crispi, and Mr. van Campenhout abstained.

---

[27] Statements by the Governor of the Fund for New Zealand and the Governor of the Fund and the World Bank for Australia, *Summary Proceedings, 1968*, pp. 147–49; *Summary Proceedings, 1969*, pp. 87–88 and 148.

■   ■   ■   ■   ■   ■

Thus, after 1965, the Fund's interest in the problems of primary commodities was stepped up appreciably. There was the enlarged access to its financial resources through the compensatory financing and buffer stock arrangements described in this chapter and the preceding one. In addition, as a further explicit recognition that what affects primary commodities impinges directly on members' balances of payments, the Fund greatly expanded its collaboration with specialized groups working on commodity problems.

To help to deal with the Fund's widening tasks in the commodity field, a Commodities Division in the Research Department was established in 1969.

As an illustration of the Fund's growing work in commodities, it may be noted that during the single fiscal year 1970/71 staff representatives attended the Seventeenth Session of the International Coffee Council in London, the Twenty-Ninth Plenary Meeting of the International Cotton Advisory Committee in Washington, and meetings of several bodies of the FAO—such as the Committee on Commodity Problems (CCP), the Consultative Committee on Tea, the Study Group on Rice, and the Consultative Committee of the CCP Study Group on Jute, Kenaf, and Allied Fibres. Staff representatives also went to the UN Wheat Conference, held to negotiate a new International Wheat Agreement to replace the International Grains Arrangement of 1967, which was due to expire on June 30, 1971; to the meetings of the UNCTAD Committee on Commodities, a permanent subcommittee of the UNCTAD set up a few years before; to the UNCTAD consultations on a draft International Cocoa Agreement; and to meetings of the International Tin Council's Interim Committee concerning the transition to the Fourth International Tin Agreement.

At the request of the International Coffee Organization, the Fund also entered into an informal arrangement to provide it with information on exchange rates in connection with payments by participants into the Organization's Diversification Fund.[28]

---

[28] That these trends would continue was evidenced by the fact that in 1972 and 1973, staff representatives were to participate in international discussions of still other commodities. But the most important event in the Fund's activities regarding commodities in these two years was the agreement by the Fund, on April 30, 1973, after the International Cocoa Agreement was signed, to permit the use of its buffer stock facility for cocoa.

CHAPTER
16

Quotas Enlarged

QUOTAS, A BASIC PART of the Fund's original financial structure, assumed increasing importance in the years 1966–71. As in the previous twenty years, so in the years 1966–71, each member, upon joining the Fund, was assigned a quota and was required to pay a subscription equal to that quota. All subscriptions were paid partly in gold and partly in the member's own currency, the gold portion normally amounting to 25 per cent of the member's quota. The aggregate of quotas was the principal determinant of the volume of currencies and of gold available to the Fund, although the Fund also had access to additional resources by borrowing. The quota determined the contribution of a member to the Fund's resources, the amount that the member might draw from the Fund, the member's basic voting rights, and—for a member that was a participant in the Special Drawing Account—its allocations of SDRs.

There were several reasons why quotas assumed a greater importance in the six years ended with 1971. Members were making heavy use of the Fund's resources. The discussions on international liquidity put considerable emphasis on the distinction between conditional and unconditional liquidity, and the volume of conditional liquidity was related to quotas. Members became more concerned about their relative voting positions in the Fund. And quotas were to be used to determine amounts of SDR allocations. Close attention to quotas meant that, when overall quotas were reviewed, the calculation of individual members' quotas and the relative share of different groups of countries in the total were carefully scrutinized. Moreover, because of emerging problems about gold, the payment of gold to the Fund in connection with increases in quota also received special study.

In the six years ended December 31, 1971, the aggregate of quotas in the Fund—often used as a measure of the size of the Fund—almost doubled, increasing from a little less than $16 billion to almost $29 billion. Important changes also took place in the relative position of members in the structure of quotas; accordingly, changes occurred both in the distribution of votes cast by the Executive Directors and in representation on the Executive Board.

GROWTH FROM 1966 TO 1969

The aggregate of quotas in the Fund on December 31, 1965 was $15,976 million. The first big jump thereafter came in the first few months of 1966 as a result of the fourth quinquennial review of quotas.[1] The general and selective increases in quotas that had been recommended by the Executive Board following that review, and which had been approved in two resolutions of the Board of Governors in March 1965, took effect in February 1966.[2] Within two months, that is, by April 30, 1966 (the end of the Fund's 1965/66 fiscal year), 78 members had consented to the authorized increases and 67 members had paid the required gold and currency subscriptions. Also by that date, Jamaica, Malaysia, Nicaragua, the Syrian Arab Republic, and Tunisia had taken up the increases in their quotas that had been approved under that part of the compensatory financing decision that provided for sympathetic consideration of requests for quota adjustments by certain primary producing countries, particularly those with relatively small quotas.[3] Quotas totaled $19,411 million on April 30, 1966. Table 5 (at the end of this chapter) gives the quotas for each member on that date and on April 30, 1968 and December 31, 1971.

During the next fiscal year, which ended on April 30, 1967, the total of quotas rose by $1.5 billion, to $20,921 million. Another 34 members had made effective the general and selective increases in their quotas that had been authorized in 1965; Malaysia had paid the last of three installments of a special increase in its quota that had been approved by the Board of Governors in September 1964; Singapore (on August 3, 1966) and Guyana (on September 26, 1966) had joined the Fund with quotas of $30 million and $15 million, respectively; and Indonesia, which had joined the Fund in April 1954 and withdrawn in August 1965, re-entered on February 21, 1967 with a quota of $207 million.

Late in 1967 the Executive Board extended to April 30, 1968 the period for consent under the first resolution of the Board of Governors, the 16 members that were entitled to special increases under the second resolution having already taken up their increases. Hence, quotas from this source rose again in the fiscal year 1967/68, by $65 million. Only 6 members (the Republic of China, Kuwait, Laos, Panama, Senegal, and Togo) had not consented to the changes in their quotas that had been authorized in 1965. The Republic of China had

---

[1] All figures in this chapter (as well as elsewhere in this history) pertaining to the Fund's accounts are given in U.S. dollars; the Fund's accounts were expressed in dollars until March 20, 1972. Moreover, for the most part, the figures in this chapter and in Chap. 19, both dealing with the Fund's accounts, are based on the fiscal year of the Fund (May 1–April 30). The Fund regularly publishes its financial data on a fiscal year basis in the Annual Reports. The figures given here thus can be compared with other readily available data.

[2] This quota exercise was summarized in Chap. 2, pp. 33–34.

[3] See par. 3 of E.B. Decision No. 1477-(63/8), February 27, 1963, as amended by E.B. Decision No. 2192-(66/81), September 20, 1966; Vol. II below, pp. 198–99.

not taken up any increase in its quota since joining the Fund in 1945. Senegal and Togo had declined increases.

A more important source of the rise in aggregate quotas in the year ended April 30, 1968 was the enlargement of the quotas of several members under the compensatory financing decision. The quotas of Korea, Nigeria, Peru, Uruguay, and Viet-Nam were increased by an aggregate of $128 million. In addition, The Gambia joined the Fund on September 21, 1967 with a quota of $5 million. On April 30, 1968 total quotas came to $21,119 million.

By April 30, 1969, quotas had risen by another $112 million, to $21,231 million. Only $32 million was accounted for by the admission of new members: Botswana (on July 24, 1968), Lesotho (on July 25, 1968), Malta (on September 11, 1968), and Mauritius (on September 23, 1968). The balance resulted from adjustments in quotas of existing members, mostly for members that had opted to pay in installments the additional subscriptions occasioned by the enlargements of their quotas authorized by the general increase of 1965. In addition, Burma, Cyprus, Panama, and Trinidad and Tobago increased their quotas under the compensatory financing decision, bringing the total number of quota adjustments effected under that provision to 30, for an aggregate increase of about $430 million. Panama's increase took into account the general increase authorized in 1965 that it had not taken up before the date of expiry.

FIFTH GENERAL REVIEW BEGINS

Under the Fund's procedures, the fifth general review of quotas was due to be completed not later than December 27, 1970, and the Executive Board was required to appoint a review committee one year in advance, that is, by no later than the end of December 1969.[4] The Executive Directors decided, however, to begin the quota review somewhat earlier with an informal exchange of views in mid-1969. The fourth quinquennial review of 1964–65 had taken the better part of two years, despite the discussions of quotas in connection with the 1963 decision on compensatory financing of export fluctuations and those that the Group of Ten had had in 1964. The fifth general review was likely to raise more intractable questions.

As has been seen in Chapter 10, one of the difficulties facing the fifth general review of quotas was that it began in 1969 when consideration was being given to the activation of the SDR facility. Some members had misgivings about agreeing to the allocation of SDRs, and some officials feared that if these members consented to a general enlargement of quotas it would

---

[4] One of the amendments to the Articles in 1969 altered the provision for reviews of quotas every five years (quinquennial reviews) to general reviews to be conducted at intervals of not more than five years.

be on the condition that there would be no early SDR allocations. At the very least, the magnitudes of the amounts involved in the two exercises would be interrelated.

Furthermore, because each participant's allocation of SDRs was to be based on its quota in the Fund, the Executive Directors, especially those elected by developing members, were eager that an understanding should be reached on what the quota increases were to be before any SDRs were allocated. In any event, some ingenious technique would have to be found to relate the SDR allocations, the first of which were expected to be made on January 1, 1970, to the quota changes resulting from the fifth general review of quotas, which was not expected to be completed until later in 1970.

Interest in the fifth general review of quotas was intense also because some of the largest members, including France, Italy, and Japan, had made it clear that, in addition to any general quota increase, they wanted substantial special increases in order to bring their quotas more into line with their stronger economic positions in the world. To arrive at these special increases on a consistent basis, there would have to be sizable special increases in the quotas of some other industrial members, including Belgium, Canada, the Federal Republic of Germany, and the Nordic countries. Thus, the upcoming quota review would affect not only the total size of the Fund but also the relative positions of members within the Fund, with resulting consequences for voting power and for representation on the Executive Board.

Another question was what part the Group of Ten would have in the quota review. Mr. Lieftinck told the Executive Directors, many of whom had not been on the Executive Board at the time of the fourth quinquennial review of quotas, that in his view the decision on the fourth quinquennial review had been taken outside the Fund and that the report of the Executive Board, which contained little economic rationale for the quota adjustment agreed upon, had reflected that situation. These were circumstances that he hoped would be avoided this time. Yet, in the meantime, the Group of Ten had become more active in international financial decisions.

Contrasting Views

The informal sessions of the Executive Directors in mid-1969 quickly brought out the major question on which debate was to center for the next several months: Should more emphasis be given to the general increase in quotas or to the selective increases? Because of the considerations mentioned in the preceding paragraphs, positions on this question differed substantially.

Data prepared by the staff showed that, given the rapid growth of world trade and payments during the mid-1960s, a general increase of reasonable size in Fund quotas was warranted. Calculations for members' quotas applying the Bretton Woods formula to national income, foreign exchange and gold reserves, average imports and exports, current services, and variations in trade and service accounts as of 1967 produced a total of quotas much higher than that based on data for 1962, the year used at the time of the previous review of quotas.[5] Even reducing the calculated quotas by one half, as had been done at the time of the fourth quinquennial review, yielded a total of $29.4 billion.

The Executive Directors elected by developing members were in favor of a large general increase. Messrs. Kafka and Madan contended that the world's need for much more conditional, as well as unconditional, liquidity was readily apparent. The shift in world finance to heavy reliance on bilateral swap transactions and temporary lines of credit had been unhealthy. The size of the Fund ought to keep pace with the rapidly expanding world economy. But the primary consideration influencing their position was that, with large selective quota increases in prospect for several industrial members, the relative position of developing members as a whole in the structure of Fund quotas was in danger of being reduced. Quotas calculated for individual members showed that the shares of the quotas of several Latin American members and of India in total Fund quotas were especially likely to become smaller. The shift in the structure of quotas toward industrial members would be diminished if the general increase in quotas was larger and the special increases not so large.

Messrs. Kafka and Madan favored a general increase of at least 25 per cent, and would have preferred an even larger increase. The total of quotas of the Fund, they thought, could easily be increased to $30 billion. Some other Executive Directors for developing members went even further. Mr. Phillips O. (Mexico) said that he had personally told the Governors for many Latin American members who would be attending the 1969 Annual Meeting that a general increase in quotas of less than 50 per cent would not meet their needs. Mr. Escobar (Chile) took issue with the staff's calculations. The use of official exchange rates to convert into dollars national income data initially expressed in local currency, he argued, yielded national income figures that were unduly low for members such as those in Latin America whose exchange rates had been substantially depreciated.

Mr. Stone was one of the few Executive Directors for the nonindustrial developed members who favored a general quota increase of considerable size. Inflation, he stated, had effectively reduced the real resources available to members from the existing level of quotas. Moreover, the quotas then being discussed were actually relevant to transactions some years hence, when world

---

[5] The so-called Bretton Woods formula was the one used at the Bretton Woods Conference to determine the quotas of the Fund's original members. The formula was: 2 per cent of national income for 1940; plus 5 per cent of holdings of gold and U.S. dollars as of July 1, 1943; plus 10 per cent of average annual imports, 1934–38; plus 10 per cent of the maximum variation of annual exports, 1934–38; the sum was then increased by the ratio of average annual exports, 1934–38, to national income.—Oscar L. Altman, "Quotas in the International Monetary Fund," *Staff Papers*, Vol. 5 (1956–57), pp. 129–50; reference is to pp. 138–39.

prices would be even higher and the volume of financial transactions much greater. Therefore, he believed that the quantity of the Fund's resources ought to be considerably enlarged. In addition, he wanted to strengthen the quality of the Fund's resources, stressing that a large increase in quotas would augment the Fund's holdings of gold.

The Executive Directors for the industrial countries were much less inclined to support a large general increase, although most of them favored some sort of balance between the general increase in quotas and the expected selective increases for individual members. Mr. Johnstone believed that the sum total of selective increases should be of roughly the same magnitude as that of the general increase. Mr. Lieftinck thought that it would be difficult, both psychologically and politically, to have a smaller increase in quotas overall than on the occasion of the fourth quinquennial review, so that a 25 per cent increase seemed logical. The question was whether that 25 per cent should be inclusive or exclusive of the selective increases. Mr. Suzuki (Japan) preferred a comparatively large SDR allocation rather than a substantial general increase in quotas and, regarding the quota review, thought that preference should go to the selective increases. Mr. Maude likewise considered that, because of the activation of the SDR facility, the case for a general quota increase was much less strong than otherwise. Indeed, he believed that any increase in quotas could be limited to the selective increases.

Limit Set by Group of Ten

The Executive Directors thus held contrasting views. Some Directors favored as a minimum a general increase of 25 per cent, which would amount to an expansion of the Fund's resources by $5.2 billion, plus whatever selective increases were agreed; other Directors wanted the emphasis placed on selective increases, which could themselves be as large as $5 billion. Reconciliation of these opposing views became quite complicated. The Group of Ten took the position that an upper limit should be placed on the amount of the increase in total Fund quotas. During the third week of July, Mr. Ossola, Chairman of the Deputies of the Group of Ten, informed Mr. Schweitzer that in the forthcoming general review the countries of the Group of Ten would support an overall increase in Fund quotas of 30 per cent, plus or minus 3 percentage points. The Deputies believed that, within this total increase of between $6 billion and $7 billion, it would be possible to combine a general increase of "reasonable" size with whatever selective adjustments were necessary. This consensus by the Deputies was accepted shortly afterwards at the ministerial level of the Group of Ten.

That the contrasting views expressed in July were deeply held was evident when the Executive Directors resumed their informal sessions in mid-August. Mr. Palamenghi-Crispi, Mr. Jacques Roelandts (Belgium, Alternate to Mr. van Campenhout), and Miss Lore Fuenfgelt (Federal Republic of Germany, Alternate to Mr. Schleiminger) emphasized that the figure of 30 per cent arrived at by the Group of Ten had been a compromise: it represented a one-third expansion of the Fund, which ought to be sufficient. The upper limit of 33 per cent consequently had to be regarded as nonnegotiable, that is, no figure higher than 33 per cent could be considered. On the other side, Mr. Kafka and Mr. Phillips O. objected that the Executive Board ought not to be faced with nonnegotiable limits.

Attempts at Reconciliation

In order to explore the implications of several possible combinations of general and selective quota increases, the staff calculated individual members' quotas on a number of different bases: a 25 per cent general increase and $2.8 billion in selective increases; a 25 per cent general increase and $3.5 billion in selective increases; and a 20 per cent general increase and $4.5 billion in selective increases. In line with expressions by the Executive Directors appointed or elected by the members concerned that their authorities would not take up their full potential quotas, considerable downward adjustments were then made in the calculated quotas for the United States and the Federal Republic of Germany, no selective quota increase was assigned to the United Kingdom, and no quota increase was calculated for the Republic of China. Still, the total increase exceeded the 33 per cent limit insisted upon by the Group of Ten.

The staff then made an informal suggestion that the size of the general quota increase might be differentiated by country groupings. For example, a general increase of 15 per cent might be applied to those members that belonged to the Group of Ten while a 25 per cent general increase would be applied to all other members. A general increase so differentiated would expand the Fund by $3.87 billion, and with selective quota increases of about $3.1 billion, a package could be reached just within the $7 billion upper limit set by the Group of Ten.

Some members of the Executive Board—Mr. de Maulde, Mr. Hattori (Japan), and Mr. Palamenghi-Crispi—favored such differentiation in the percentages used for a general quota increase. Mr. Palamenghi-Crispi suggested that the basis of the differentiation could be along lines other than membership in the Group of Ten. But most of the Executive Directors did not like differential percentages. Mr. Dale said that the U.S. authorities objected in principle to differentiation among the Fund's members. Mr. de Vries characterized differentiated rates for a general quota increase as the appearance of discrimination among the Fund's members and feared that such discrimination might then follow in other situations, such as in the allocation of SDRs or in the degree of conditionality applicable to drawings. Mr. Stone thought that, as a result of the differentiation suggested by the staff for the forthcoming quota increase, the Fund would be too small, and it would not acquire enough gold. Mr. Kafka reiterated his belief that the quotas of all members ought to be increased by at least 25 per cent if the general quota review was to be significant.

Hence, although many of the Executive Directors were anxious that their proposed resolution to the Board of Governors for the Twenty-Fourth Annual Meeting, to begin in Washington on September 29, 1969, should be as specific and quantitative as possible, it was clear that accord could be reached on a resolution couched in only the most general terms. The Board of Governors was invited to approve, in addition to the resolution on allocating SDRs, one asking the Executive Directors to proceed promptly with the consideration of the adjustment of the quotas of members and to submit an appropriate proposal not later than December 31, 1969. This resolution was adopted by the Board of Governors on October 3, 1969.[6]

A Solution Emerges

After the Annual Meeting the elements of a solution began to take shape. The Governors for a number of developing members had spoken both about the low share of the developing members in the existing structure of Fund quotas and the need for a large general increase. And the Governors for some of the industrial members, for example, Canada and Italy, had expressed their support for a general quota increase of meaningful size that would not reduce the relative position of the developing members as a whole.[7]

It appeared that most Executive Directors, including those for the industrial members, would accept a general increase of 25 per cent. However, a general increase of 25 per cent, plus $5 billion in selective increases, would lead to an overall increase in the size of the Fund of nearly 50 per cent and to a sharp reduction in the shares of members other than those belonging to the Group of Ten. In order to limit the total increase, it seemed likely that some of the countries in the Group of Ten would voluntarily agree not to take up the full quotas offered to them, provided a number of them agreed to do so. Belgium, the Federal Republic of Germany, the Netherlands, Sweden, the United Kingdom, and the United States would, it was believed, be willing to scale down considerably the quotas offered to them.

The problem that now emerged was, therefore, how to reconcile arithmetically a 25 per cent general increase and a number of sizable selective increases with the 33 per cent limit for the total increase. This problem was to be taken up by the Executive Board meeting as a Committee of the Whole on Review of Quotas. In accordance with the Fund's procedures, the Board appointed such a Committee of the Whole on November 5, 1969. The Committee consisted of all the Executive Directors, with the Managing Director as Chairman.

---

[6] Resolution No. 24-15; Vol. II below, p. 266.

[7] See references listed in *Summary Proceedings, 1969*, pp. 361–63.

The Economic Counsellor, reporting on the meeting of the Deputies of the Group of Ten that was held in Paris on October 31, 1969, said that he thought that the Deputies were prepared to go along with a somewhat higher upper limit—say 35 per cent—in order to accommodate their own requests for increases in their quotas that amounted to a 34.8 per cent increase. However, several Executive Directors, including Mr. Lieftinck and Mr. Schleiminger, favored the 33 per cent ceiling. Hence, another compromise was attempted. Among the members slated to get large selected increases in their quotas, in addition to countries in the Group of Ten, were 4 other industrial members (Austria, Denmark, Luxembourg, and Norway) and 11 nonindustrial developed members (Australia, Finland, Greece, Iceland, Ireland, New Zealand, Portugal, South Africa, Spain, Turkey, and Yugoslavia). Mr. Palamenghi-Crispi and Mr. Plescoff, therefore, urged these members to accept voluntarily quotas lower than those calculated, just as some of the countries in the Group of Ten were doing. And Mr. Lieftinck attempted to work out agreed reductions with Messrs. Eero Asp (Finland), Johnstone, Palamenghi-Crispi, Stone, and van Campenhout. But this attempt was unsuccessful. While the Nordic members were willing to scale down their increases, other members strongly resisted any reduction in their proposed quotas. Mr. Stone gave the Executive Directors a number of reasons why the industrial members other than those in the Group of Ten and the nonindustrial developed members should not necessarily volunteer to let their quotas be reduced below the calculated amounts. For several of these members the calculated increase from both the general quota increase and any special increase was less, or certainly not much more, than the 33 per cent average increase being considered for the Fund as a whole. Moreover, the proportion of Fund quotas represented by developing members could remain unchanged, a stated objective of the quota exercise, without reducing the quotas proposed for these middle countries, if sufficient adjustment was made in the quotas of the industrial countries.

AGREEMENT REACHED ON FIFTH GENERAL REVIEW

In accordance with the Executive Directors' request, the staff then compiled a list of potential quotas. Taking into account the smaller increases agreed by some of the countries in the Group of Ten and by the Nordic countries, and allowing for no increase in the quota of the Republic of China, in line with the report of Mr. Beue Tann (Republic of China) to the Committee of the Whole that that member did not intend to participate in the general increase in quotas, the total of quotas came to $28.9 billion, an increase of $7.6 billion, or 35.4 per cent, over the existing size of the Fund.

These potential quotas became the basis for the report of the Executive Directors to the Board of Governors. The United States, the member with the largest quota, accepted a quota of $6,700 million, which was just slightly above its previous quota enlarged by the 25 per cent general increase. The United Kingdom, which had the second largest quota, accepted a quota of $2,800 million, only 14.8 per cent above its previous quota. The United Kingdom thus did not receive even the full 25 per cent general increase. The Federal Republic of Germany, which had the third largest quota, agreed to $1,600 million, a 33 per cent enlargement. The largest quota increases in percentage terms were for Japan (65 per cent), Italy (60 per cent), Belgium (54 per cent), France (52 per cent), and Canada (49 per cent). France was to have a quota of $1,500 million, still the fourth largest in the Fund, followed by Japan ($1,200 million), Canada ($1,100 million), Italy ($1,000 million), and India ($940 million).

Many other members were offered quotas that were 40 per cent, or more, higher than their existing quotas. These members included not only Austria, Denmark, Finland, Iceland, Ireland, Norway, South Africa, and Spain among the industrial and the nonindustrial developed members mentioned earlier but also, among developing members, Algeria, Iran, Israel, Kenya, Korea, Malaysia, Peru, the Philippines, Saudi Arabia, Thailand, and Trinidad and Tobago. Several other members—including Australia, Greece, Iraq, Jamaica, Mexico, Nigeria, Tunisia, Turkey, and Yugoslavia—were offered quotas that were at least 30 per cent higher than their existing quotas.

Mr. Phillips O., supported by Mr. Kafka, suggested that the principles of rounding used in the staff's calculations should be changed somewhat. As in the fourth quinquennial review, quotas of less than $500 million had been rounded to the next higher $1 million and quotas of more than $500 million had been rounded to the next higher $5 million. The suggestion of Mr. Phillips O. was that quotas of up to $300 million be rounded to the next higher $1 million, that quotas between $300 million and $1,000 million be rounded to the next higher $5 million, and that quotas of more than $1,000 million be rounded to the next higher $10 million. These changes in rounding enlarged the potential quotas of Argentina, Brazil, Mexico, South Africa, and Venezuela. Very little was added to the sum total of quotas, and so alterations in quotas for these members were accepted.

The authorized quotas of six members (Cameroon, Ivory Coast, Kuwait, Lebanon, the Libyan Arab Republic, and Sierra Leone) also took account of the special increases to which they were entitled under the compensatory financing decision and which they had not yet taken up. Some members that had the right under the compensatory financing decision to claim increases in quota had not yet done so. The report of the Executive Directors recommended that where such a right had not yet been approved by the Board of Governors it would be superseded by the provisions of the resolution.

Because of these several adjustments in the quotas of individual members, the resolution proposed to the Governors did not describe the quota increase in general terms; instead, an annex attached to the resolution listed the maximum quota to which each member could consent.

Gold Payments and Alleviation of Impact

Before an increase in a member's quota could become effective, the member was required to pay a subscription equal to the increase in its quota, of which 25 per cent must be paid in gold and the remainder in its currency. In the past the Board of Governors had approved a number of different arrangements for mitigating the impact on members' reserves of gold payments to the Fund, necessitated by increases in quotas. To alleviate the direct, or primary, impact on their reserves, members had been permitted to increase their quotas by installments or to pay their subscription by means of special, unconditional drawings repayable in three years. In order to alleviate the indirect, or secondary, impact on the reserves of those members that had sold gold to other members so that the latter could pay their gold subscriptions, the Fund had sold gold to the former and had also made provision for gold from the Fund's resources to be placed on general deposit with the United States and the United Kingdom up to an amount not exceeding $350 million.

During the fifth general review the question again arose whether the burden of members' gold payments to the Fund should be alleviated and by what techniques. As the reader may recall, the possibility of using SDRs for gold in connection with quota increases had been explicitly rejected by the Finance Ministers and Central Bank Governors of the Group of Ten at Stockholm in March 1968.[8] The problem of mitigation of the impact of gold payments, therefore, continued to exist, although it seemed less severe than on previous occasions because members would simultaneously be receiving additional reserves in the form of SDRs.

Some new technique for mitigating the impact of gold payments was necessary, however, since two of the means used in connection with the fourth quinquennial review to mitigate the primary impact could not be used. Under the Articles, as amended, special drawings in the credit tranches could no longer be unconditional. Moreover, although it had been agreed that a member could take up only a part of its quota and then, so long as the period of consent remained in effect, could take up larger amounts at a later date, SDRs were to be allocated as a percentage of quota. Members' allocations of SDRs would thus be smaller if they took up their quota increases in installments.

This time the Executive Directors decided to exercise the discretion given to the Fund by Article III, Section 4 (*a*), to reduce the proportion of the increase in quota that had to be paid in gold. In accordance with that Article, a member was permitted to pay in gold only that proportion of 25 per cent of the increase in quota that the member's monetary reserves bear to the increased quota to

---

[8] See Chap. 7 above, p. 173.

which the member has consented, and to pay the balance of the increase in quota in the member's currency. The possibility of reducing the portion of quota increase payable in gold had been considered in connection with the third and fourth quinquennial reviews of quotas, but both times the Executive Directors had decided against it.

Despite these earlier rejections, the Executive Directors decided to consider such action in connection with the fifth general quota review. When the Committee of the Whole was considering mitigation of the impact of gold payments in November 1969, the Executive Directors favored the invocation of Article III, Section 4 (a), on a proportional basis, that is, reducing the gold payment required to the extent that a member's reserves fell below its new quota. Mr. Kharmawan and Mr. Rajaobelina preferred a total waiver of gold payments, but that would have meant much less gold being paid into the Fund. The Executive Directors decided further that any member paying less than 25 per cent of its quota increase in gold must undertake to repurchase the additional currency subscription beyond 75 per cent of the increase in quota, unless the Fund's holdings of that currency had otherwise been reduced, in five equal annual installments commencing one year after the date on which the quota increase became effective. As an additional technique for mitigation of the primary impact of gold payments, it was decided that members could consent to increases in quotas by installments.

Mitigation of the secondary impact of gold payments was also provided for. The Fund would sell gold up to a maximum amount of $700 million when it needed to replenish its holdings of the currencies of members from which gold had been purchased by other members. While the Executive Directors recognized that these triangular or turntable operations were somewhat artificial, adding nothing to total world liquidity, they thought that their objective justified these arrangements. Mr. Stone objected to this sale of gold by the Fund on the ground that the Fund thereby relinquished its right to a certain amount of gold emanating from the larger quotas. Several Executive Directors regretted that the new SDRs had not been given some kind of a role in the payment of quota increases. It was expected that most members wishing to buy gold for the purpose of paying their increased subscriptions to the Fund were likely to buy it from the United States, as they had done in the past, and that to a very large extent the sale of gold by the Fund would be to replenish its holdings of U.S. dollars. To the extent that the Fund did not have a need to replenish its holdings of U.S. dollars, it would be suggested to members that they purchase the gold from other members whose currencies the Fund did have a need to replenish.

Delaying the Consequences for Composition of the Executive Board

It was intended that the increases in quotas under the fifth general review should become effective sometime in 1970. This timing presented certain novel

Meeting of 1970–72 Executive Board

problems because it coincided with the regular election of Executive Directors, scheduled to take place during the 1970 Annual Meeting in Copenhagen. In the past, a regular election had never intervened between the time of the adoption by the Board of Governors of a resolution on quota increases and the effective date of most of the increases under it. In previous quota exercises, a minimum participation clause had been prescribed: quota increases became effective after members whose quotas represented a specified proportion of the total had consented to them.

However, it could not be known in advance when a minimum participation clause would be fulfilled, and on the occasion of the fifth general review this uncertainty could create difficulties in connection with the composition of the Executive Board. The increases in quotas might become effective too close to the time of the 1970 regular election to permit country groupings to be formed for electing Executive Directors. A similar difficulty attended a solution of letting the increase in any member's quota become effective when that member had consented to the increase and had paid the subscription. In the past, any change in the groupings of countries electing Executive Directors or in the number of votes that might be cast by members had been avoided during the period immediately preceding an election. Moreover, Japan, which would have the fifth largest quota, would have the right to appoint an Executive Director, while India would no longer have that right. It was desirable to give India time to become part of a country grouping that would elect an Executive Director.

The Executive Directors accordingly agreed that no quota increases under the fifth general review would become effective until after the 1970 regular election. They chose October 30, 1970 as the earliest date that quotas could become effective, a date after the regular election of Executive Directors but before December 31, 1970, which was the latest date on which increased quotas could serve as a basis for the allocation of SDRs on January 1, 1971.

Consequently, while members received their altered voting power on November 1, 1970, the full impact on the line-up of members appointing or electing Executive Directors did not occur until the 1972 regular election of Executive Directors. There was, however, an interim arrangement for part of the change that would eventually come about. On November 1, 1970 Japan appointed an Executive Director, but Burma, Ceylon, Laos, Malaysia, Nepal, Singapore, and Thailand did not cast votes for any of the Executive Directors elected in the 1970 regular election of Executive Directors and designated the Executive Director appointed by Japan to look after their interests in the Fund until the next regular election of Executive Directors. India continued to have an appointed Executive Director until the 1972 regular election of Executive Directors. (At that election, held in Washington in September 1972 during the Twenty-Seventh Annual Meeting, there were several shifts in the groupings of members electing Executive Directors. These shifts were especially marked for members in Asia. India, not having formerly been in a group electing an Executive Director, had to arrange such a group.)

Resolution Adopted

On December 24, 1969 the Executive Board considered a draft of the report it would make to the Board of Governors, to which was attached the proposed resolution, and adopted that report. The Board of Governors adopted the resolution (No. 25-3) effective February 9, 1970 by more than the newly required majority of 85 per cent of the total voting power. Members had until November 15, 1971 to consent to the increases in their quotas, unless the date was extended by the Executive Directors.[9]

NEW QUOTAS BECOME EFFECTIVE

Of the 116 members listed in the annex to the resolution, as amended to include the Khmer Republic (Cambodia) and the Yemen Arab Republic, 107 consented to increases in their quotas between October 30, 1970 and April 30, 1971. All of these had paid their increased subscriptions in full, and their new quotas had become effective. One member, Nepal, had paid one installment, thereby raising its quota only by one fifth of the increase to which it had consented. The total of Fund quotas on April 30, 1971 was $28,478 million.

By October 28, 1971, two weeks before the period of consent was due to elapse if it was not extended, Korea, Lebanon, and Tunisia had not yet notified their consents, and Kuwait, the Libyan Arab Republic, Luxembourg, and Singapore had consented to amounts less than those authorized. (The Executive Board extended the period, first to June 30, 1972 and then to December 31, 1972.) By the end of 1971 Korea and Tunisia had notified the Fund of their consents and only Lebanon had not consented to all or part of its increase.

Following these increases in quota under the fifth general review, there was a sharp rise in the Fund's holdings not only of members' currencies but also of gold. In the fiscal year 1970/71 members paid to the Fund $1,744 million in gold as a result of the payment of their increased subscriptions following the fifth general review. This was slightly less than 25 per cent of the aggregate increase in quotas. More than 20 members made reduced gold payments because their monetary reserves were less than their new quotas on the dates that they consented to their increased quotas. They paid $32 million, about half of what they would have paid had there been no reduction. These members undertook to repurchase in five equal annual installments, unless the Fund's holdings

---

[9] "Increases in Quotas of Members—Fifth General Review: Report of the Executive Directors to the Board of Governors, December 24, 1969," and Resolution No. 25-3; reproduced in Vol. II below, pp. 266–72.

of their currency were otherwise reduced, that portion of their local currency subscription which represented the difference between the actual amount of gold paid and 25 per cent of the increase in their quotas.

Seventy-five members bought gold from other members to pay all or part of their increased gold subscriptions to the Fund in 1970/71. Most purchases ($548 million) were from the United States; $16 million was from Austria. The Fund replenished its holdings of U.S. dollars and Austrian schillings by equivalent sales of gold to the United States and Austria. Very small amounts of gold were bought by Somalia from Italy and by Swaziland from South Africa, for which no mitigation was sought by Italy or South Africa.

In the eight months between the end of the fiscal year 1970/71 and the end of the calendar year 1971, seven members (Austria, Korea, Luxembourg, Portugal, Singapore, South Africa, and Tunisia) made their quotas effective. One member bought $7.5 million in gold from the Federal Republic of Germany to pay its subscription, and the Fund replenished its holdings of deutsche mark by an equivalent sale of gold to Germany.

OTHER INCREASES IN QUOTAS DURING 1969–71

From May 1, 1969 to the end of 1971, the total of Fund quotas also rose for reasons other than the fifth general review. In the fiscal year 1969/70 4 countries joined the Fund: Swaziland on September 22, 1969 with a quota of $6 million; the People's Democratic Republic of Yemen (Southern Yemen) on September 29, 1969 with a quota of $22 million; Equatorial Guinea on December 22, 1969 with a quota of $6 million; and the Khmer Republic (Cambodia) on December 31, 1969 with a quota of $19 million. In the same fiscal year, Zaïre and Jamaica increased their quotas under the compensatory financing decision, to $90 million and $38 million, respectively. These were the last quota increases under this decision because its provisions relating to quotas were superseded by the Board of Governors' resolution on the fifth general review of quotas.

In December 1969 the quota of Laos was increased from $7.5 million to $10 million, the amount that had previously been authorized in the course of the fourth quinquennial review, but that Laos had rejected. At the end of 1969, just before the first allocations of SDRs, Laos reversed itself for the second time and decided to take up the larger quota, and was permitted to do so. In addition, in fiscal 1969/70, quotas were increased for 14 other members that had elected to take up in five equal annual installments the quotas authorized for them under the fourth quinquennial review. In view of the forthcoming SDR allocations, 11 of these members (Algeria, Chad, the People's Republic of the Congo, Dahomey, Ivory Coast, Luxembourg, Malaysia, Mauritania, Morocco, Niger, and Upper Volta) accelerated payment of the fifth installment, thereby completing the total increases in their quotas under the fourth quinquennial review. The remaining 3—Cameroon, the Central African Republic, and Gabon—completed their installment payments in the fiscal year 1970/71.

All of the increases in quotas in the fiscal year 1969/70 were small. The aggregate of Fund quotas on April 30, 1970 was $21,349 million, only $118 million larger than the year before.

Aggregate quotas in the Fund on April 30, 1971, $28,478 million, were 33 per cent higher than they had been on April 30, 1970. Besides the quota increases under the fifth general review, this expansion reflected several small increases: three members paid their final installments under the fourth quinquennial review; on May 22, 1970 the Yemen Arab Republic joined the Fund with a quota of $8 million; and on December 29, 1970 Barbados became a member with a quota of $13 million.

In the last eight months of 1971, Fund quotas continued to grow as a result both of the fifth general review and of additions to membership. On May 28, 1971 Fiji became a member with a quota of $13 million; on December 23, 1971 Oman became a member with a quota of $7 million; and on December 28, 1971 Western Samoa became a member with a quota of $2 million.

The total of the Fund's quotas on December 31, 1971 stood at $28,808 million. (See Table 5 at the end of this chapter for the quota of each of the 120 members on that date.)

POLICY ON SMALL QUOTAS

The growth in membership after 1966 raised another question concerning quotas: Should the Fund's policy regarding small quotas be changed? After 1958 small countries seeking membership in the Fund had been offered minimum quotas in the range of $7.5 million to $11.25 million. Following the 25 per cent general increase in quotas effective under the fourth quinquennial review early in 1966, the applicable minimum would have been in the range of $10 million to $15 million. Several members did, in fact, ask for and receive increases in their quotas to $10 million. But when Zambia became a member in 1965 it was decided that quotas to be set for new members would not be adjusted to take account of the general increase under the fourth quinquennial review and that the applicable minimum would remain at $7.5 million.

Nonetheless, the staff believed that even this amount might be too large for some very small states that had become independent or were likely to become so in the future and that might apply for membership in the Fund. The economies of several countries, such as Botswana, The Gambia, Lesotho, and Western Samoa, that were then contemplating membership were extremely small when measured in terms of national income, imports and exports, foreign exchange reserves, and similar indicators of economic size. Calculations for quotas for these countries based on these indicators would yield quotas much below the minimum of $7.5 million. For some of these countries, quota calculations based on the relevant indicators would yield figures as low as $1 million to $2.5 million. Offering these prospective members unduly large quotas, even the applicable minimum of $7.5 million, could impose insuperable repurchase commitments on them when they became members and would also discriminate against other members.

The staff consequently recommended early in 1967 that the Fund should be prepared to consider offering small states a range of quotas below $7.5 million, with the understanding that this range should be appropriately related to the economic circumstances of each individual prospective member. For The Gambia, then an applicant for membership, the staff suggested a range of $4 million to $5 million. The lower figure, $4 million, resulted from a figure calculated in accordance with the Bretton Woods formula, which was then reduced in the same way as previous quota calculations for other members. The higher figure, $5 million, came from applying the ratio between quota and foreign trade that existed for several other small countries that were already members of the Fund.

The consensus of the Executive Board's committee on membership for The Gambia was to accept the staff's proposals. A quota of $5 million was accepted by the Executive Board and was approved by the Board of Governors in the membership resolution. Later in 1967 a quota for Botswana in the range of $2 million to $5 million was suggested, with the proviso that the quota chosen should be a multiple of $1 million. Botswana accepted a quota of $3 million.

In line with these precedents, in November 1967 the staff suggested a quota range of $3 million to $5 million for Lesotho. Lesotho accepted the lower figure. It was further agreed for both Botswana and Lesotho that they should pay not less than 3 per cent of their subscriptions in gold (compared with the usual 25 per cent) and the balance in their local currencies.

In 1969 the quotas for Swaziland and Equatorial Guinea were set at $6 million each, and in 1970, when the Yemen Arab Republic became a member, its quota was set at $8 million. As the year 1971 ended, Oman joined with a quota of $7 million and Western Samoa with a quota of $2 million, the smallest quota of all.

QUOTA FORMULA TO BE REVIEWED

During the 1969 Annual Meeting, some of the Governors for developing members had expressed dissatisfaction with the way in which quotas in the

Fund were determined. Mr. Jha (India) contended that the formulas used subjected developing members to a "double disability." When their gross national product and foreign trade figures declined, they received relatively smaller increases in quotas. Their access to the Fund's resources was accordingly increased to a much smaller extent than if they had not suffered such declines. Yet these were the very members that most needed to use the Fund's resources. In addition, poor members could not afford to lock up real resources for acquiring gold or foreign exchange. Mr. Jha further pointed to the large increase in the Fund's membership that had resulted from the accession of so many developing members during the twenty-five years since Bretton Woods. By 1969, developing members accounted for over four fifths of the total membership. It was important to ensure that the position in the Fund of these members, individually and collectively, improved substantially in consonance with their changed status and responsibilities.[10]

Mr. Massad (Chile) urged the Fund to institute an early study and review of the factors taken into account in the Bretton Woods formula for determining quotas. In part, he argued that developing members had more need than other countries for the Fund's resources. But he also appealed to the countries of the Group of Ten not to deprive the Fund as a multilateral organization of its full authority, and he urged that participation of all members be an actual fact.[11] Mr. Tiémoko Marc Garango (Upper Volta), on behalf of the West African Monetary Union (Ivory Coast, Dahomey, Upper Volta, Mauritania, Niger, Senegal, and Togo), suggested a review of voting power.[12]

When the Executive Directors resumed their deliberations on quotas after the 1969 Annual Meeting, Mr. Kafka underscored Mr. Massad's urgent request for a review of the quota formula. Mr. Escobar circulated a lengthy, technical paper prepared by his Alternate, Mr. Ricardo H. Arriazu (Argentina), containing calculations for the quotas of all members on the basis of a new formula. The formula stressed the increments in the variables of the Bretton Woods formula, that is, the increases in exports, imports, and national income taking place over a fairly long period of time, rather than the absolute values for these variables for a relatively short and outdated period of time, as in the Bretton Woods formula. Mr. Arriazu's formula, therefore, became known within the Fund as the "incremental approach" to quota calculations. In using that approach, Mr. Arriazu's rationale was that special weight ought to be given to the unusually rapid increases in trade and national income that many members had experienced in the years since the Bretton Woods formula was devised. In addition, his proposed formula used hypothetical exchange rates based on

---

[10] Statement by the Governor of the Fund for India, *Summary Proceedings, 1969*, pp. 74–75.

[11] Statement by the Governor of the Fund and the World Bank for Chile, *Summary Proceedings, 1969*, pp. 129–30.

[12] Statement by the Governor of the Fund for Upper Volta, *Summary Proceedings, 1969*, pp. 141–42.

purchasing power parity relationships (that is, relationships between exchange rates and prices) rather than actual exchange rates, to convert national income figures from local currencies into a common currency. Mr. Arriazu argued that the use of such hypothetical exchange rates would produce higher and more accurate figures for national income, especially for the developing countries, because these countries had depreciated their currencies relative to changes in their price levels to a far greater extent than had industrial countries.[13]

The case of Mexico was an example of the dissatisfaction of several developing members with the calculations produced by the Bretton Woods formula. Mr. Phillips O. had asked that Mexico's quota as calculated during the fifth general review be enlarged beyond the amount produced by the formula, basing his argument on the need to take into account items not included in the Bretton Woods formula. Mexico needed a larger quota, he said, because it was subject to large and volatile movements in capital owing to its substantial commercial and financial interchange with the United States and an open border that made enforcement of exchange controls impossible. Moreover, Mexico was an original Article VIII member and a net creditor to the Fund, factors also relevant to the quota of a member.

Because of these arguments, the Executive Directors, toward the end of 1970, agreed to a program of work that included a full review of the economic and statistical criteria used in determining quotas and a careful consideration of formulas that were alternative to the Bretton Woods formula, including the one proposed by Mr. Arriazu. Although this review did not take place in 1971, the staff was preparing a number of technical papers on the subject. As 1971 ended, it was clear that the whole problem of quotas in the Fund, including the methodology used in their calculation, and the payment of gold to the Fund as a result of increases in quotas, was going to be under extensive review in the foreseeable future.

---

[13] Estimates of the magnitudes of exchange rate changes in developing countries relative to those in other countries can be found in Margaret G. de Vries, "Exchange Depreciation in Developing Countries," *Staff Papers*, Vol. 15 (1968), pp. 560–78.

Table 5. Quotas of Members on Selected Dates [1]

(In millions of U.S. dollars)

Member	Apr. 30, 1966 [2]	Apr. 30, 1968 [3]	Dec. 31, 1971
Afghanistan	29.0	29.0	37.0
Algeria	63.0	69.0	130.0
Argentina	280.0	350.0	440.0
Australia	500.0	500.0	665.0
Austria	175.0	175.0	270.0
Barbados	•	•	13.0
Belgium	337.5	422.0	650.0
Bolivia	29.0	29.0	37.0
Botswana	•	•	5.0
Brazil	350.0	350.0	440.0
Burma	30.0	30.0	60.0
Burundi	15.0	15.0	19.0
Cameroon	15.0	16.6	35.0
Canada	550.0	740.0	1,100.0
Central African Republic	7.5	8.5	13.0
Ceylon	78.0	78.0	98.0
Chad	7.5	8.5	13.0
Chile	100.0	125.0	158.0
China, Republic of	550.0	550.0	550.0
Colombia	125.0	125.0	157.0
Congo, People's Republic of the	7.5	8.5	13.0
Costa Rica	20.0	25.0	32.0
Cyprus	15.0	15.0	26.0
Dahomey	7.5	8.5	13.0
Denmark	163.0	163.0	260.0
Dominican Republic	26.4	29.2	43.0
Ecuador	25.0	25.0	33.0
Egypt	150.0	150.0	188.0
El Salvador	25.0	25.0	35.0
Equatorial Guinea	•	•	8.0
Ethiopia	19.0	19.0	27.0
Fiji	•	•	13.0
Finland	125.0	125.0	190.0
France	787.5	985.0	1,500.0
Gabon	7.5	8.5	15.0
Gambia, The	•	5.0	7.0
Germany, Federal Republic of	787.5	1,200.0	1,600.0
Ghana	69.0	69.0	87.0
Greece	100.0	100.0	138.0
Guatemala	25.0	25.0	36.0
Guinea	15.0	19.0	24.0
Guyana	•	15.0	20.0
Haiti	15.0	15.0	19.0
Honduras	19.0	19.0	25.0
Iceland	15.0	15.0	23.0

Table 5 (*continued*). Quotas of Members on Selected Dates [1]

(In millions of U.S. dollars)

Member	Apr. 30, 1966 [2]	Apr. 30, 1968 [3]	Dec. 31, 1971
India	750.0	750.0	940.0
Indonesia	•	207.0	260.0
Iran	125.0	125.0	192.0
Iraq	80.0	80.0	109.0
Ireland	80.0	80.0	121.0
Israel	90.0	90.0	130.0
Italy	625.0	625.0	1,000.0
Ivory Coast	15.8	17.4	52.0
Jamaica	30.0	30.0	53.0
Japan	725.0	725.0	1,200.0
Jordan	13.0	16.0	23.0
Kenya	32.0	32.0	48.0
Khmer Republic	•	•	25.0
Korea	24.0	50.0	80.0
Kuwait	50.0	50.0	65.0
Laos	7.5	7.5	13.0
Lebanon	6.75	9.0	9.0
Lesotho	•	•	5.0
Liberia	20.0	20.0	29.0
Libyan Arab Republic	19.0	19.0	24.0
Luxembourg	15.0	16.6	20.0
Malagasy Republic	19.0	19.0	26.0
Malawi	11.25	11.25	15.0
Malaysia	84.17	115.0	186.0
Mali	17.0	17.0	22.0
Malta	•	•	16.0
Mauritania	8.0	9.0	13.0
Mauritius	•	•	22.0
Mexico	270.0	270.0	370.0
Morocco	75.6	82.8	113.0
Nepal	10.0	10.0	10.8
Netherlands	412.5	520.0	700.0
New Zealand	157.0	157.0	202.0
Nicaragua	19.0	19.0	27.0
Niger	7.5	8.5	13.0
Nigeria	50.0	100.0	135.0
Norway	100.0	150.0	240.0
Oman	•	•	7.0
Pakistan	188.0	188.0	235.0
Panama	11.25	11.25	36.0
Paraguay	15.0	15.0	19.0
Peru	47.0	85.0	123.0
Philippines	75.0	110.0	155.0
Portugal	75.0	75.0	117.0
Rwanda	12.0	15.0	19.0

Table 5 (concluded). Quotas of Members on Selected Dates [1]

(In millions of U.S. dollars)

Member	Apr. 30, 1966 [2]	Apr. 30, 1968 [3]	Dec. 31, 1971
Saudi Arabia	90.0	90.0	134.0
Senegal	25.0	25.0	34.0
Sierra Leone	15.0	15.0	25.0
Singapore	•	30.0	37.0
Somalia	15.0	15.0	19.0
South Africa	200.0	200.0	320.0
Spain	250.0	250.0	395.0
Sudan	57.0	57.0	72.0
Swaziland	•	•	8.0
Sweden	225.0	225.0	325.0
Syrian Arab Republic	38.0	38.0	50.0
Tanzania	25.0	32.0	42.0
Thailand	95.0	95.0	134.0
Togo	11.25	11.25	15.0
Trinidad and Tobago	25.0	25.0	63.0
Tunisia	28.0	35.0	48.0
Turkey	86.0	108.0	151.0
Uganda	32.0	32.0	40.0
United Kingdom	2,440.0	2,440.0	2,800.0
United States	5,160.0	5,160.0	6,700.0
Upper Volta	7.5	8.5	13.0
Uruguay	30.0	55.0	69.0
Venezuela	250.0	250.0	330.0
Viet-Nam	23.8	39.0	62.0
Western Samoa	•	•	2.0
Yemen Arab Republic	•	•	10.0
Yemen, People's Democratic Republic of	•	•	29.0
Yugoslavia	150.0	150.0	207.0
Zaïre	45.0	57.0	113.0
Zambia	50.0	50.0	76.0
Totals	19,411.27	21,119.35	28,807.8

[1] A dot (•) indicates that the country was not a member on the particular date or dates.

[2] By this date not all members had taken up the increases in quota authorized by the Board of Governors in March 1965.

[3] By this date all members had taken up the selective increases in quota authorized by the Board of Governors in March 1965; the period of consent for the general increase of 25 per cent that was authorized at the same time lapsed on April 30, 1968.

CHAPTER

17

Increases in Drawings

U*SE OF THE FUND'S RESOURCES* attained unexpectedly large magnitudes in the years 1966–71. An overview of the drawings that took place
is presented in this chapter: some statistics are given showing the amount and
nature of drawings made and the currencies in which they occurred, and the
modifications that were made in the Fund's policies on the selection of currencies
to be used in purchases and repurchases are described. In general, drawings
during 1966–71 were in accordance with policies that the Fund had formulated
during the previous twenty years.[1] However, many drawings resulted from
policies evolving during the years reviewed here, the policies already covered in
Chapters 13–15.

As the stand-by arrangement became the major vehicle by which the
Fund gave financial support to its members, an increasing proportion of drawings took place under such arrangements. The drawings described in this
chapter, therefore, include those made under stand-by arrangements. Discussion
of other aspects of stand-by arrangements relevant to the 1966–71 period is
deferred to Chapter 18. The reader should recall (as was noted in Chapter 13)
that, after September 15, 1969, amounts that might be drawn in the gold
tranche were excluded from stand-by arrangements. Because some stand-by
arrangements prior to September 1969 had been written to include gold tranche
drawings and because a few members did make such drawings, the change of
September 15, 1969 in the legal treatment of gold tranche drawings in stand-by
arrangements requires adaptation of the statistics for drawings under stand-by
arrangements to ensure comparability. Hence, all gold tranche drawings have
been excluded from drawings under stand-by arrangements.

---

[1] For a description of these policies, see *History, 1945–65*, Vol. II, Chaps. 18–21 and 23.

TOTAL DRAWINGS

During the six calendar years 1966–71 members purchased currencies from the Fund totaling $11.7 billion.[2] The significance of this amount can be better appreciated when it is realized that the amount exceeded the cumulative drawings made in the first two decades of the Fund's operations. Total drawings were rather small in 1966 and 1967, but in 1968 and 1969 they expanded to $3.5 billion and $2.5 billion, respectively—the largest amounts for any calendar year since the Fund commenced operations in 1947. It was in 1968 and 1969 that the payments imbalances of industrial members and the periodic crises in exchange markets impelled many industrial members (Belgium, Canada, France, the Federal Republic of Germany, the United Kingdom, and the United States) to have recourse to the Fund.

In 1970 and 1971 purchases dipped considerably because many countries had balance of payments surpluses as counterparts to the large deficits of the United States. In these two years purchases were $1.5 billion and $1.9 billion. In 1971 most members, experiencing unprecedented increases in their reserves, did not need to draw from the Fund. All but $500 million of the purchases in that year were by the United States. Nonetheless, even these lower levels of drawings in 1970 and 1971 were surpassed only in the peak years 1968 and 1969 and, earlier, in 1964 and 1965. Drawings under stand-by arrangements in 1971 (the U.S. drawings were gold tranche drawings and not under a stand-by arrangement) amounted to only $231 million, the smallest amount in 11 years, and were made by only 16 members (Burundi, Ceylon, Colombia, El Salvador, Guyana, Liberia, Mali, Morocco, Nicaragua, Peru, the Philippines, Tunisia, Turkey, Uganda, Uruguay, and Yugoslavia). In fact, the amount that the Fund approved in stand-by arrangements in total in 1971 came to only about $450 million, the lowest since the Fund's transactions took an upward surge in the mid-1950s, with the first large drawing by the United Kingdom.

By December 31, 1971 total purchases of currencies by members since the Fund began operations in 1947 amounted to over $23.2 billion. On that date outstanding drawings, that is, the total amount for which members still had undertakings and commitments to repurchase, were, of course, only a fraction of that figure. First, since 1947 repurchases had totaled over $15 billion. Second, the use in drawings and in repayment of borrowings by the Fund of currencies of which the Fund's holdings were in excess of 75 per cent of the members' quotas reduced the amount of outstanding drawings of the members whose currencies were thus used. Third, drawings in the super gold tranche, which were fairly large in 1966–71, were not subject to repurchase and hence did not add to outstanding drawings.

---

[2] Amounts of drawings have been expressed in dollars in this chapter, although many of them were made in other currencies; see footnote 5 in Chap. 14 above.

Outstanding drawings were at a record high figure of $5.7 billion in June 1968. However, a lower rate of purchases thereafter and very large repurchases reduced outstanding drawings at the end of 1971 to below $3 billion, the lowest since 1965.

Distribution Among Members

Of the total of $11.7 billion of drawings in 1966–71, nearly $8 billion was drawn by 8 industrial members.[3] The United Kingdom, the United States, and France each had more than one transaction with the Fund, making purchases for $2.5 billion, $2.4 billion, and $1.7 billion, respectively. The Federal Republic of Germany drew $540 million in November 1969, its first drawing since it had become a member in 1952. Canada drew $391 million in February 1968, Belgium drew $46.5 million in July 1969, and Italy drew $133 million in July 1970. Two transactions with Denmark—in May 1969 and July 1970—totaled $70 million. Consequently, of the 14 industrial countries that were members of the Fund, all but 6 (Austria, Japan, Luxembourg, the Netherlands, Norway, and Sweden) made drawings in 1966–71.

Sixty-nine nonindustrial members purchased currencies from the Fund in these years. Eight members among those classified as primary producing countries in more developed areas together drew over $1 billion: Iceland, Ireland, New Zealand, South Africa, Turkey, and Yugoslavia made more than one drawing; Finland and Spain drew once. Ireland's use of the Fund's resources was the first since it had become a member in 1957.

A total of $2.8 billion was drawn by primary producing countries in less developed areas in 1966–71. The geographic distribution of these drawings was as follows: [4]

(1) Drawings of about $1 billion were made by 19 members in *Latin America and the Caribbean:* Argentina, Bolivia, Brazil, Chile, Colombia, Costa Rica, the Dominican Republic, Ecuador, El Salvador, Guatemala, Guyana, Haiti, Honduras, Jamaica, Nicaragua, Panama, Peru, Trinidad and Tobago, and Uruguay. Among Latin American and Caribbean members, only Barbados, Mexico, Paraguay, and Venezuela did not draw during this period. (Barbados had become a member only in December 1970.) The drawings by Guyana, Jamaica, and Trinidad and Tobago were their first use of the Fund's resources. Chile, Colombia, and Peru were among those making the largest use in this region, and each made several drawings.

---

[3] For the Fund's classification of members as industrial or primary producing and further as primary producing in more developed areas and in less developed areas, see above, Chap. 4, footnote 5 (p. 82).

[4] The geographic groupings used here are those that were used in *International Financial Statistics* during 1966–71; they do not correspond to the groupings of members in the five area departments of the Fund.

(2) In *Asia*, drawings of another $1 billion were made by 12 members: Afghanistan, Burma, Ceylon, the Republic of China, India, Indonesia, the Khmer Republic, Korea, Laos, Malaysia, Pakistan, and the Philippines. Among these members, India drew sizable amounts twice, and Indonesia and the Philippines made frequent and relatively large use of the Fund's resources. Korea and Malaysia, which had joined the Fund in the 1950s, and Laos, which had joined in 1961, all used the Fund's resources for the first time, as did the Khmer Republic, a member only since the end of 1969. Likewise, the Republic of China made its first use of the Fund's resources. Among developing members in the region, Nepal, Singapore, Thailand, and Viet-Nam did not ask for the Fund's financial support, nor did Fiji and Western Samoa in the Western Pacific, countries that had become members only recently.

(3) In the *Middle East*, Cyprus, Egypt, Iran, Iraq, Israel, Jordan, the Syrian Arab Republic, and the Yemen Arab Republic made purchases totaling nearly $350 million. The purchases by Iraq, Jordan, and the Yemen Arab Republic were those members' first; Iraq was an original member, Jordan had joined the Fund in 1952, and the Yemen Arab Republic had joined in 1970. Kuwait, Lebanon, Saudi Arabia, and the People's Democratic Republic of Yemen did not draw in these years.

(4) Twenty-two *African* members drew a total of about $415 million. Among these were a number that were using the Fund's resources for the first time (the Central African Republic, Chad, Guinea, Lesotho, Malawi, Mauritania, Mauritius, Nigeria, Sierra Leone, Swaziland, Uganda, Upper Volta, and Zambia) as well as several that had drawn previously (Burundi, Ghana, Liberia, Mali, Morocco, Rwanda, Somalia, the Sudan, and Tunisia). The heaviest users were Ghana, Morocco, the Sudan, and Tunisia.

Table 6 at the end of the chapter lists the amounts drawn by each of the Fund's members in each of the six calendar years 1966–71.

GOLD TRANCHE DRAWINGS

Nearly half—about $5.3 billion—of the total drawings in 1966–71 represented drawings within the gold tranche or, in several instances, within the super gold tranche. Gold tranche and super gold tranche drawings accounted for all the purchases by industrial members except those that the United Kingdom and France made under stand-by arrangements.

By United States in 1966 and 1968

All of the drawings made by the United States were in the gold tranche. During 1966, U.S. purchases of currencies from the Fund amounted to $680 million. Of this total, $400 million in Canadian dollars and $30 million in deutsche mark represented the same kind of technical drawings that the United States had undertaken in 1964 and 1965: because the Fund already held dollars in an amount in excess of 75 per cent of the U.S. quota and could not accept dollars in repurchases, the United States made drawings in currencies that the Fund could accept and made these currencies available at par to countries that held U.S. dollars and wished to fulfill their repurchase obligations.[5] The remaining $250 million that the United States drew in 1966 was in Italian lire, drawn in August, to enable the United States to buy from Italy an equivalent amount of dollar holdings that had come about as a result of Italy's continuing balance of payments surplus.

The U.S. balance of payments deficit persisted after 1965 and showed signs of worsening. U.S. monetary officials, being under some pressure by their European counterparts to seek a large drawing from the Fund, explored informally with the Managing Director and the staff in 1966, and again in 1968, what might be involved in a drawing beyond the gold tranche. Such a drawing might extend partly into, or possibly would exhaust, the first credit tranche.

In the course of these talks the United States was informed that the Fund would prefer a stand-by arrangement rather than a large drawing that went beyond the gold tranche. In addition, any drawing extending into the first credit tranche would require an activation of the General Arrangements to Borrow. Third, the currencies that the United States would receive would be a package of currencies made up in accordance with the Fund's 1962 decision on currencies to be used in drawings and repurchases; a custom-made bundle of currencies was unlikely.[6] Finally, a stand-by arrangement would be easier to work out if domestic tax measures were enacted first.

These conditions posed some difficulties for the U.S. authorities. Arranging a stand-by agreement with the Fund might give the world the impression that the United States was anticipating an extremely large deficit and that it was ready to convert "excessive" amounts of dollars received by surplus countries into claims on the Fund. Moreover, the U.S. authorities might prefer being able to specify the currencies that they wished to draw from the Fund, and the amounts of these currencies, rather than receiving the currencies that would result from the Fund's usual policy on selection of currencies. The possibility of a stand-by arrangement was not pursued further by the U.S. authorities.

In March 1968 the U.S. Government submitted a request to the Fund for a purchase of $200 million made up of $15 million in Belgian francs, $35 million

---

[5] See *History, 1945–65*, Vol. I, pp. 530–31.

[6] Decision No. 1371-(62/36), July 20, 1962, and the accompanying statement set out criteria for currencies to be drawn that took into account the balance of payments and reserve positions of the members whose currencies were being considered as well as the Fund's holdings of these currencies. See section on Currencies Selected: Use of Past Principles, later in this chapter, and *History, 1945–65*, Vol. I, pp. 516–20, and Vol. II, pp. 448–59. For the text of the decision and the statement, see Vol. III of *History, 1945–65*, pp. 235–38.

in deutsche mark, $50 million in Italian lire, and $100 million in Netherlands guilders. The proposed drawing fell within the gold tranche, and little decision was involved for the Fund. The requested composition of currencies, however, was not in accord with the Fund's policy on selection of currencies.

The staff considered the U.S. request justified. The needs of the United States could not be met by drawing currencies other than those that the United States had asked for even if the alternative currencies could be converted. The Fund's policy on selection of currencies, so reasoned the staff, was predicated on the proposition that in a world where convertibility is assured by free exchange markets, members can use any convertible currency to defend their exchange rates and to protect their reserves. The same did not apply fully, especially in the short run, to a reserve center, such as was the United States. If a reserve center required a particular currency to meet its convertibility obligations, it could not in general obtain that currency by drawing some other currency from the Fund, unless the countries whose currencies were drawn would agree to convert them into gold. The reserve center would, therefore, normally be obliged to draw the specific currency necessary to fulfill its convertibility obligations.

Furthermore, because of the cumulative principle involved in the Fund's policy on selection of currencies, the staff believed that the drawing of an unusually large amount of certain currencies by the United States in a particular drawing would mean that rather less of these currencies would be drawn in the future. Hence, the underlying principle of a gradual approach toward equality for members in the ratios of their positions in the Fund to their total reserves would continue to be observed. Prior to placing the U.S. purchase transaction on the agenda of the Executive Board, the Managing Director consulted informally with the Executive Directors appointed or elected by members whose currencies would be drawn. Shortly thereafter, the Executive Board approved the purchase.

By United States in 1970 and 1971

The United States did not draw again for more than two years. Repurchases by the United States toward the end of 1968 had restored the U.S. gold tranche position by the end of that year, and on March 31, 1969 the Fund's holdings of U.S. dollars were below 75 per cent of the U.S. quota, that is, the United States had a super gold tranche position for the first time in five years.

In May 1970 the United States again came to the Fund, this time for a drawing of $150 million—$90 million in Belgian francs and $60 million in Netherlands guilders. The drawing was well within the super gold tranche, but once again the requested currency composition deviated from the Fund's usual policy on selection of currencies. After prior agreement by the Executive Directors concerned, the purchase was approved by the Executive Board. At the same time, the United States transferred SDR 10 million to Belgium and the same amount to the Netherlands, to complete repayment to these countries of short-term swap drawings that had been made from them by the Federal Reserve System in 1969 and early 1970.

It was during the first seven and a half months of 1971, before the U.S. monetary authorities decided to suspend convertibility of officially held dollars, that the United States made its largest drawings on the Fund. In these months the United States purchased $1,362 million. In January 1971 the United States purchased $125 million in Belgian francs and $125 million in Netherlands guilders. Again, in June, purchases were made for $150 million in Belgian francs and $100 million in Netherlands guilders. Then, on August 4, 1971, the Secretary of the U.S. Treasury, Mr. John B. Connally, requested the purchase of $862 million, of which $415 million was to be in Belgian francs and $447 million in Netherlands guilders. These purchases were to be used by the United States to meet demands by the authorities of Belgium and the Netherlands for conversions of their holdings of U.S. dollars. Again, the prospective U.S. purchase was within the gold tranche. However, the Managing Director consulted with the Executive Directors not only on the currencies to be used for the drawing but also on the need to revise, at least as far as repurchases were concerned, the Fund's currency budget for the third quarter of 1971 as a consequence of this drawing. The purchase was approved by the Executive Board on August 6, 1971.

By Other Members

Drawings by six of the seven other industrial members that made purchases in the six years 1966–71 (except those by France under a stand-by arrangement and all the drawings by the United Kingdom) were also in the gold tranche or the super gold tranche. Canada's drawing in February 1968 corresponded to the amount of its gold subscription to the Fund plus the amount of Canadian dollars purchased by other members from the Fund; about half of the drawing was in the super gold tranche. Similarly, France's drawing in June 1968 was partly in the super gold tranche; Denmark's drawing in May 1969 and that of Belgium in July 1969 made full use of those members' gold tranche positions; the Federal Republic of Germany's drawing in November 1969 was entirely in the super gold tranche; Denmark's drawing in July 1970 was within the gold tranche; and Italy's drawing in July 1970 represented a full use of its gold tranche position.

The drawing by Spain, the three by South Africa, and some of those by Finland, Ireland, and Yugoslavia, among the countries classified as primary producing countries in more developed areas, were also within the gold tranche or the super gold tranche.

In contrast to the large number and size of gold tranche drawings by industrial countries and primary producing countries in more developed areas, gold tranche drawings by primary producing countries in less developed areas in 1966–71 amounted to less than $350 million. Twenty-seven of these members made drawings within the gold tranche, particularly in 1970 and 1971: viz., in the Middle East (Iran, Iraq, Israel, the Syrian Arab Republic, and the Yemen Arab Republic), in Asia (the Republic of China, the Khmer Republic, Korea, Laos, Malaysia, and the Philippines), in Latin America and the Caribbean (Argentina, Chile, Costa Rica, Guyana, Honduras, Jamaica, Trinidad and Tobago, and Uruguay), and in Africa (the Central African Republic, Guinea, Lesotho, Mauritania, Nigeria, Swaziland, Uganda, and Upper Volta).

DIRECT PURCHASES IN CREDIT TRANCHES

Apart from gold tranche drawings, direct purchases (that is, drawings not under stand-by arrangements) were relatively rare in the years reviewed here. Only about $980 million was disbursed as a result of direct purchases in the credit tranches. This situation was a reversal from that of the past. From 1952 to the end of 1965, cumulative direct purchases had been much more common than drawings under stand-by arrangements.

A number of direct purchases were for the purpose of financing quota increases. During 1966 special purchases to help members finance quota increases following the fourth quinquennial review of quotas came to $240 million. Between March and August 1966, Argentina, Burundi, Ceylon, Colombia, Costa Rica, Cyprus, Ecuador, Egypt, Guinea, Haiti, India, Liberia, Mali, New Zealand, Pakistan, Somalia, the Sudan, the Syrian Arab Republic, Tunisia, the United Kingdom, and Yugoslavia made purchases for this purpose; the largest of these was one for $122.5 million made in March 1966 by the United Kingdom. In January 1968 Chile drew $6.25 million to help finance a belated increase in its quota, as authorized by the fourth quinquennial review.

In addition, during 1966, Liberia, the Syrian Arab Republic, and Tunisia drew a total of $3.2 million to finance increases in their quotas as permitted under the compensatory financing decision.

Many more direct purchases involved drawings in connection with the compensatory financing and buffer stock facilities. Of the drawings from the Fund from 1966 to 1971, $375 million represented the purchases by 22 members under the compensatory financing decision that have been described in Chapter 14. A further $14.8 million represented purchases by 3 members under the buffer stock facility that have been described in Chapter 15.

Beyond these drawings under special policies, the Executive Directors were inclined to regard as unusual any requests for direct purchases that went beyond the first credit tranche. Hence, of the direct purchases in the credit tranches that took place during 1966–71, all but two, by India and Egypt, were for amounts that did not exceed the first credit tranche (see below).

In First Credit Tranche

Each direct purchase in the first credit tranche had its own rationale and was nearly always accompanied by a letter of intent resembling the letters of intent accompanying stand-by arrangements.[7] These purchases are described below in chronological order, except that all purchases by a given member are treated together regardless of date.

In January 1966 the Executive Board agreed to a purchase by Argentina of $30 million. The Fund's analysis indicated that Argentina's economic situation and its position in the Fund were improving. After the proposed drawing and the repurchases that were expected during 1966, Argentina's position in the Fund would still be less than halfway through the first credit tranche, the lowest it had been for some years.

In the same month, Ireland made its first request to purchase; the amount, $22.5 million, was equal to half of its quota at that time. The Irish balance of payments had moved into deficit, and for the first time in many years there had been a loss of reserves. The request was accompanied by a letter from the Minister of Finance setting forth the Government's economic and financial policies and intentions. The Executive Board approved the purchase.

In May 1967 Iraq, an original member that had made its first drawing from the Fund only a few months before (a gold tranche drawing for $20 million in February), came to the Fund for a purchase of $20 million. Mr. Saad (Egypt) explained to the other Executive Directors that Iraq had suffered a serious decline in its foreign exchange earnings owing to the stoppage of oil flow through the pipelines during the first part of 1967. The Executive Board considered that Iraq's record in the Fund had been consistently good, that the drawing would be in the first credit tranche, and that Iraq was making reasonable efforts to meet its difficulties, and agreed to the drawing.

Two requests by the Dominican Republic, one in January 1969 for $6 million and a second in January 1971 for $7.5 million, came within the first credit tranche and were accompanied by letters stating the financial policy intentions of the member's authorities. The Executive Board approved both requests.

In August 1969 the Executive Board approved a request by Guinea to purchase $3.8 million. The member had purchased $1 million in July 1966, a gold tranche drawing. Some of the Executive Directors were concerned about Guinea's balance of payments, but they welcomed the member's request for a technical advisor and noted that the purchase would go only a small way into the first credit tranche. Consequently, in line with the Fund's tranche policies, the Fund needed only to be convinced that the member was making a reasonable effort toward improving its payments position, and did not need to require

---

[7] For an explanation of letters of intent accompanying stand-by arrangements and how they developed, see Gold, *Stand-By Arrangements*, especially pp. 57–64, and *History, 1945–65*, Vol. II, pp. 468–91.

that the member have a realistic exchange rate or a satisfactory program, as stipulated for drawings in the higher credit tranches. Guinea requested another purchase in May 1970, this time for $4.2 million in Japanese yen. Mr. Lieftinck pointed out the continuous difficulties that the country was facing, but joined the Executive Board in agreeing to the drawing since it was still within the first credit tranche.

In August 1969 the Executive Board approved a request from Haiti for a drawing of $1.5 million, an amount that covered the remainder of that member's first credit tranche position.

In September 1969, after some years of not having recourse to the Fund's resources, and following a gold tranche drawing for $22.5 million in May 1969, Israel asked the Fund for a further $22.5 million, an amount covered by the first credit tranche. The request was accompanied by a letter from the Minister of Finance to the Managing Director summarizing economic developments in Israel over the previous few years, the problems facing Israel's economy, and the essentials of their financial program. The staff, having recently completed a consultation mission and having revisited Israel to appraise this request for a drawing, concluded that the program represented a reasonable effort toward adjusting Israel's balance of payments. Mr. Lieftinck assured the Executive Board that the Government would take any additional measures that might become necessary for this purpose, and the Board agreed to the drawing.

In February 1971 Israel requested another drawing, this time for $20 million. Because of the increase in Israel's quota following the fifth general review of quotas, this drawing would bring the Fund's holdings of Israel pounds to 125 per cent of quota and hence within the first credit tranche. Since Israel, in 1969 and 1970, had taken many monetary and fiscal measures to reduce excessive demand and was expected to take additional measures to ease the situation further during 1971, the Executive Board approved the Israeli request.

The first action taken by the Fund in 1970 was to approve a request from Chad for a purchase of $3.8 million. Chad's quota had been increased, effective December 19, 1969, to $10 million, so that this purchase, Chad's first, involved the member's gold tranche position and about half of its first credit tranche.

There were also two purchases by Egypt, one in 1970 and one in 1971, that were in the first credit tranche; these are described below, following the description of Egypt's purchase in 1967, which went beyond the first credit tranche.

Beyond First Credit Tranche

Drawings for amounts that extended beyond the first credit tranche were subjected to much greater scrutiny.

In April 1966 India requested a purchase for $187.5 million, an amount equal to one tranche of India's quota, as recently increased by the fourth quinquennial review of quotas, and that would raise the Fund's holdings of Indian rupees to 153 per cent of quota. Despite the absence of the usual policy commitments for a drawing in the second credit tranche and beyond, the Executive Board agreed to the drawing. It did so on the grounds that India was confronted with a genuine emergency because of severe drought, that the purchase was for an unusually short term—the Indian authorities having agreed to repurchase by the end of 1967—and that a number of measures were being taken to strengthen the country's admittedly weak economy. Two months later, in June 1966, India devalued the rupee; this devaluation is described in Chapter 23.

In March 1968, simultaneously with a request for a drawing of $23 million under the compensatory financing facility, Egypt asked for a drawing of $40 million. While most of the Executive Directors had little difficulty with the compensatory financing drawing, some of them had doubts about the additional drawing. Mr. Lieftinck, for instance, recalled that the drawing by India early in 1966 had also not satisfied the Fund's conditions for drawings in the higher credit tranches, but that drawing had, at least, been for a more limited time than was usual. He was concerned about deviations from the two criteria customarily applied to a drawing in the higher credit tranches, namely, that it was in support of an exchange rate that was realistic and that the member would very soon be having its annual consultation with the Fund under Article XIV. He wanted assurance that the Egyptian purchase would be regarded as exceptional.

On the other hand, a majority of the Executive Directors welcomed the return to normal of Egypt's relations with the Fund, following the break that had occurred in the country's relations with the rest of the world in June 1967 after the six-day war in the Middle East, and they stressed the severity of Egypt's financial and economic difficulties. Not only had the Suez Canal been closed and this source of revenue lost to Egypt, but a heavy burden of foreign indebtedness had resulted in arrears of debt service. The Executive Board took explicit note of the letter of intent from the Minister of Economy setting forth the Government's economic and financial policies and intentions and declaring that Egypt would consult the Fund, and agreed to the purchase.

Egypt came to the Fund with requests to purchase twice more in the next few years—once in July 1970 for $17.5 million and again in September 1971 for $32 million. Because of intervening repurchases and because of the increase in Egypt's quota following the fifth general review, these purchases were both in the first credit tranche. Letters of policy intent accompanied the requests. The Executive Board approved both of these requests, noting the improvement in Egypt's general economic situation—owing especially to a record cotton crop and a buoyant demand for exports—and commending the introduction of a number of exchange measures in anticipation of a more comprehensive exchange reform.

DRAWINGS UNDER STAND-BY ARRANGEMENTS

The frequency with which the Fund approved stand-by arrangements and the volume of resources made available under these arrangements accelerated sharply in the latter part of the 1960s. As already noted, except for drawings within the gold tranche and drawings in accordance with special decisions (to finance quota increases or under the compensatory financing and buffer stock facilities), drawings by members without stand-by arrangements became more and more unusual.

During the six years 1966–71 the Fund approved stand-by arrangements for 42 members authorizing purchases totaling $6,834 million, an amount substantially larger than authorized under stand-by arrangements in the years from 1952, when they were inaugurated, until the end of 1965. Table 7 at the end of this chapter lists the members for which the Fund approved stand-by arrangements and the amounts authorized. Nine of these members—Burma, Ghana, Guyana, New Zealand, Rwanda, Sierra Leone, the Sudan, Uganda, and Zaïre—had not had stand-by arrangements before, and in February 1968 the first stand-by arrangement was approved for Indonesia since that member had rejoined the Fund.

There was a heavy concentration of stand-by arrangements in two annual periods—May 1, 1967 to April 30, 1968 and May 1, 1969 to April 30, 1970 (the Fund's fiscal years 1967/68 and 1969/70, respectively). In fact, in 1969/70 stand-by arrangements were approved for a total of $2,381 million, the largest amount that the Fund had yet approved in any one fiscal year. Thereafter, however, as the reserves of most members expanded, the number of stand-by arrangements and the amounts authorized dropped markedly.

Stand-by arrangements with two industrial members—the United Kingdom and France—accounted for $3,385 million of the $6,834 million total authorized under stand-by arrangements during the six years 1966–71. In November 1967 a stand-by arrangement for $1,400 million was approved for the United Kingdom and in June 1969 one was approved for $1,000 million. In June 1969 a stand-by arrangement for $985 million was approved for France. The circumstances of these stand-by arrangements are described in Chapter 18.

Four members for which stand-by arrangements were approved during 1966–71 were primary producing countries in more developed areas: Finland, New Zealand, Turkey, and Yugoslavia. There were five stand-by arrangements for Turkey, three for Yugoslavia, and one each for Finland and New Zealand.

Most of the arrangements approved during 1966–71, however, were for primary producing countries in less developed areas, and most represented a continuation or a renewal of the Fund's previous financial support, with the Fund approving stand-by arrangements year after year, or with only short intervals in between. Thus, during the six years reviewed here, six stand-by arrangements each were approved for Brazil, Colombia, and Korea, and five each for Burundi, Guatemala, Guyana, Liberia, Morocco, the Philippines, and Somalia: in other words, stand-by arrangements were approved for these members nearly every year. Other members, too, had rather regular support from the Fund in the form of stand-by arrangements. Four each were approved for Ceylon, Ghana, Honduras, Indonesia, Mali, Panama, Peru, Rwanda, and Tunisia. Those for Ghana and Rwanda were renewed each year from 1966 to 1969. Three each were approved for Afghanistan, Bolivia, Chile, Paraguay, Sierra Leone, and the Sudan between 1966 and 1969, so that these countries had almost continuous support in this four-year period. Three stand-by arrangements each were also approved for Ecuador, El Salvador, Haiti, Nicaragua, and Uruguay during the six-year period, but some of these were approved in 1970 and 1971, so that the authorizing of stand-by arrangements for these five members was not quite as regular as for the members mentioned earlier in this paragraph. Two stand-by arrangements were approved for Argentina and Costa Rica, and single stand-by arrangements were approved for Burma, Pakistan, Uganda, and Zaïre. (See Table 7.)

Nearly all of the amounts authorized by stand-by arrangements were actually drawn. In the six years 1966–71 a total of just under $5.4 billion was drawn under such arrangements.[8] Drawings under stand-by arrangements were small in 1966 and 1967—$261 million and $374 million, respectively— but swelled to $1.9 billion and $1.7 billion, respectively, in 1968 and 1969, when the United Kingdom and France drew the full amounts authorized by their stand-by arrangements. Drawings under stand-by arrangements totaled $919 million in 1970, but dropped to $231 million in 1971.

In June 1968 the United Kingdom drew in a single purchase the full amount ($1,400 million) of the stand-by arrangement approved in November 1967, and between June 1969 and March 1970 made four purchases for the full amount ($1,000 million) of the stand-by arrangement approved in June 1969. Under its stand-by arrangement of September 1969, France made a purchase shortly thereafter for $500 million and in February 1970 drew the remainder. How these drawings were financed is discussed in Chapter 19.

Other members also made a large number of purchases under their stand-by arrangements. A few (Ceylon, Colombia, Liberia, and Turkey) made purchases under their stand-by arrangements in each of the years 1966–71. Several others (Afghanistan, Burundi, Chile, El Salvador, Ghana, Guatemala, Mali, Nicaragua, Peru, the Philippines, and the Sudan) made purchases under their stand-by arrangements in at least four of the six years, and still others (Bolivia, Indonesia, Ecuador, Morocco, Panama, Rwanda, Uruguay, and Yugoslavia) drew at least twice. Burma, Finland, Iceland, and New Zealand used their stand-by arrangements in single drawings.

On the other hand, four members (Argentina, Korea, Paraguay, and

---

[8] The reader is reminded that this figure excludes gold tranche drawings made under stand-by arrangements prior to September 1969.

Zaïre) did not draw at all under their stand-by arrangements, and four (Brazil, Guyana, Sierra Leone, and Somalia) made use of only some of the several arrangements that were approved for them.

WAIVERS

Any drawing or stand-by arrangement that would increase the Fund's holdings of a member's currency by more than 25 per cent of its quota within any 12-month period (except to the extent that the Fund's holdings of the member's currency were less than 75 per cent of its quota) required a waiver under the Articles of Agreement.[9] After the mid-1950s, it became rather common practice for the Fund to grant such a waiver. During the fiscal year 1966/67, for example, waivers were granted for all the stand-by arrangements approved except those for Brazil and Turkey, and waivers were also granted for the direct purchases made by Ceylon, Costa Rica, Ghana, and Tunisia. During the fiscal year 1967/68, waivers were granted for all the stand-by arrangements approved except those for Brazil, Indonesia, Rwanda, and Turkey, and waivers were granted for direct purchases by Burma, Iraq, and Egypt. In the fiscal year 1969/70, waivers were granted for all the stand-by arrangements approved except those for Brazil, Liberia, Rwanda, Sierra Leone, the Sudan, and Tunisia, and waivers were granted for direct purchases by Burma and Iceland.

A waiver was also required for any drawing or stand-by arrangement the use of which would increase the Fund's holdings of a member's currency to more than 200 per cent of quota, and waivers had been granted for this purpose since 1963.[10] In the year 1967/68, for instance, such a waiver was granted to Ceylon, whose drawing brought the Fund's holdings of Ceylonese rupees to approximately 205 per cent of quota. In the next fiscal year such a waiver was granted to Ghana.

CURRENCIES SELECTED: USE OF PAST PRINCIPLES

Until August 15, 1971 the currencies in which purchases were made continued to be selected in accordance with the principles and procedures set forth in the statement approved by the Executive Board in July 1962 on the currencies to be drawn and to be used in repurchases (repurchases are discussed in Chapter 19).[11]

The guidelines for determining which currencies should be used in the Fund's transactions were to be the balance of payments and reserve positions

---

[9] See Article V, Sections 3 (*a*) (iii) and 4.

[10] *Ibid.*

[11] See footnote 6 in this chapter.

of members, the Fund's holdings of members' currencies, and the Fund's holdings of members' currencies compared to their quotas. Briefly, the economic concept involved was that reserves should, through the Fund, flow from countries with strong balances of payments to countries with weak ones. Ideally, therefore, each member's reserve position in the Fund should move in parallel with the movements in its gross reserves. The former quantity was defined as the gold tranche drawings that the member could make plus the amount of any indebtedness of the Fund that was readily repayable to the member under a loan agreement, including the General Arrangements to Borrow. Currencies used for drawings were to be those of members with strong balance of payments and reserve positions, while currencies used in repurchase were to be those of members whose balance of payments and reserve positions were relatively weak.

However, these economic considerations were overridden by legal constraints protecting the composition of the Fund's holdings of currencies and by attention to members' attitudes. On the repurchase side, the range of usable currencies was to be limited to those that were formally convertible under Article VIII and that the Fund did not hold in amounts above 75 per cent of quota. On the purchase side, as a matter of practice, the Fund traditionally did not allow a member's currency to be drawn without the agreement of that member.

The idea of the 1962 decision was that, subject to other constraints, the currencies to be used in purchases and repurchases would be selected in such a way that the ratio between a member's reserve position in the Fund and its gross holdings of gold and foreign exchange would be roughly equal for each member whose currency was used in the Fund's operations. In effect, the proportion of their reserves that members held in the form of positions in the Fund would be approximately the same for each member.

By 1966 the principles of the 1962 decision were well established and in operation. Gradually, it had become the responsibility of the staff to draw up for each quarter of the fiscal year what were called proposed target distributions of the currencies to be used in purchases and repurchases; that responsibility included deciding what specific methods or formulas to use for quantifying the guidelines of the 1962 decision. In July 1966 these staff functions were transferred from the Research and Statistics Department to the Treasurer's Department as part of a move to broaden the role in the Fund generally of the Treasurer's Department and to apply, to a greater extent than in the past, operational considerations to the formulation of the Fund's financial policies.

Part of the procedure was that, before the proposed target distributions were put into final form as currency budgets to be submitted to the Executive Board, the Executive Directors for the members whose currencies were involved were consulted by the management and the staff as to the acceptability of the proposed targets. These consultations brought occasional requests for changes in the targets for particular currencies and, in some instances, comments that approval of the target distributions did not necessarily imply approval of the rationale or methodology by which the staff had derived them.

The number of currencies in the currency budget was usually about 10 to 15, a small number compared with the number of participants, 25 to 30, that were usually included in the designation plans for the Special Drawing Account after that facility was activated.

In applying the guidelines for choosing amounts of particular currencies, the staff tried to equalize the ratios between members' reserve positions in the Fund and their gross holdings of gold and foreign exchange. In effect, purchases were distributed over the list of currencies in proportion to members' gross holdings of gold and foreign exchange, and repurchases were distributed in proportion to members' reserve positions in the Fund. The rationale of the procedure lay in the fact that when currencies were drawn the Fund's holdings of them tended to decline and when currencies were used to repurchase the Fund's holdings of them tended to be replenished; these movements were reflected in converse movements in the members' reserve positions in the Fund. A distribution of repurchases in proportion to members' reserve positions in the Fund thus tended to counterbalance the cumulative net use of currencies in purchases, leading to a gradual harmonization of the ratios between members' reserve positions in the Fund and their holdings of gold and foreign exchange.

Application of the guidelines for determining currency budgets did not take the form of a precise formula. Rather, the staff adapted the guidelines, fairly flexibly, to changing circumstances. The amounts derived from calculations were often modified by taking into account members' economic positions, members' attitudes toward having their currencies used in Fund transactions, and the composition of the Fund's currency holdings.

CURRENCIES SELECTED: ADDITIONAL DEVELOPMENTS

In the years 1966 through 1971, some modifications and adaptations were made in the drawing up of currency budgets. First, the number of currencies included was enlarged. As the aggregate amount of the Fund's transactions became much greater, especially in 1968 and 1969, the staff explored with the authorities of several members the possibility of expanding the list of currencies to be used in drawings. Many members accepted this use of their currencies, and the list gradually grew to 24 at the end of 1971. Brazilian cruzeiros, Finnish markkaa, Irish pounds, Kuwaiti dinars, Malaysian dollars, Norwegian kroner, South African rand, and Venezuelan bolívares were those added. Table 8 at the end of this chapter lists the currencies in which purchases, as well as repurchases, were made during the period 1966–71, and the related amounts.

The number of currencies used for repurchases remained considerably smaller than that for purchases (Table 8). Because Brazil, Finland, South Africa, Spain, and Venezuela had not yet accepted the obligations of Article VIII at the end of 1971, their currencies were not eligible to be used in repurchases. Although Ireland and Malaysia had accepted the obligations of Article VIII, no repurchases were made in their currencies. Moreover, between February and March 1967, as had happened between July and September 1965, repurchases were made almost exclusively in Japanese yen. The balance of payments position of Japan was weak at the time and the Fund especially chose that currency for use in repurchase.

The use of SDRs in repurchases was approved by the Executive Board in December 1969 (see Chapter 11). They were not included in the currency budgets because they were not currency, but members could opt to repurchase with SDRs instead of with the currencies listed in the budget. During 1970 and 1971 many members exercised this option. Moreover, on August 4, 1971, just before the suspension of official convertibility of the dollar on August 15, 1971, the Executive Board agreed that SDRs held in the General Account could be transferred to participants in the Special Drawing Account that were making purchases from the Fund. Because of the disruption in the Fund's normal operations after the middle of August, however, implementation of this decision was delayed until after the end of 1971.

The internal procedure used for agreeing on currency budgets was also modified. Beginning in 1969 all Executive Directors were invited to the consultations on these budgets. After gold tranche purchases were made automatic under the amended Articles, a simplified procedure for consulting with Executive Directors regarding the currencies to be drawn was introduced so that these purchases could be handled easily and speedily: consultations prior to a gold tranche drawing could take the form of a notification to the Executive Directors concerned that it was intended to use the currency or currencies of a member or members that had appointed or elected them.

With more currencies being used in repurchase, it was necessary to find some way to avoid large differences in the costs of various packages of currencies, especially after the exchange rates for some important currencies began to move more widely than before within the margins around par values. Accordingly, the staff began to make computations for the currency composition of each repurchase in such a way that its likely cost to the repurchasing member was as close as possible to the cost that would result from using the average exchange rate of all the currencies that could be used in repurchase.

Modification of Methodology

Toward the end of 1968 there was yet another modification in the Fund's policy on selection of currencies. The staff found it necessary to modify the method it had been using for determining the proposed target distributions of currencies that formed the basis for the quarterly currency budgets. The quarterly budget for November 1968–January 1969 was the first affected. The change was intended to hasten the catching up of the ratios between members' reserve positions in the Fund and their gross reserves. Rapid shifts in members' gold and foreign exchange reserves were taking place. As trade imbalances grew and as large capital movements began to occur, some members lost considerable amounts of reserves while others gained reserves. The ratios between members' reserve positions in the Fund and their holdings of gold and foreign exchange were becoming more unequal faster than could be offset by the operation of the Fund's currency budgets. The currency budget was not as effective as it might have been in this respect for several reasons. For one thing, many purchase transactions included in the currency budgets did not actually materialize. Some stand-by arrangements were not drawn upon. In addition, large drawings, those in excess of $100 million, did not take place within the framework of the regular currency budgets; they were the subject of separate arrangements and, in the instance of the U.S. drawings, involved specially requested currencies.

As a consequence, the staff began to reinforce the equalizing effects of transactions within the currency budget for members with ratios that were below average (that is, members with relatively low proportions of their reserves in the form of positions in the Fund) by using their currencies solely for drawings. The currencies of members with ratios that were above average (that is, members with relatively high proportions of their reserves in the form of positions in the Fund) were used only in repurchases.

This change in methodology was discussed by the Executive Board in October 1969, when Mr. Stone requested the Board's consideration of what was happening to reserve ratios and of the change in the techniques used by the staff to determine currency budgets. Having debated at great length harmonization of the ratios between participants' holdings of SDRs and their holdings of reserves in other forms in connection with the Special Drawing Account, the Executive Directors welcomed a discussion of the similar question raised by transactions through the General Account. How rapidly should the catching up of the relevant ratios proceed? The majority of the Executive Directors favored letting the staff have flexibility in applying the guidelines established by the decision of July 1962. They also agreed with the methodological change that accelerated the catching up of the ratios relevant to the General Account.

SPECIAL PROBLEMS AFTER AUGUST 15, 1971

Much more troublesome for the Fund's normal policy on selection of currencies to be used in purchases and repurchases—and, indeed, for the whole of the Fund's financial operations, both in the General Account and in the

Special Drawing Account—was the suspension by the U.S. authorities on August 15, 1971 of official convertibility of the dollar into gold and other reserve assets.[12] With rare exceptions, countries had been willing to retain, or even to augment, their holdings of U.S. dollars. After August 15, 1971 this willingness was substantially lessened. It became increasingly likely that the dollar price of gold would be raised, and members decidedly preferred to hold gold and SDRs rather than dollars. (The reader is reminded that the value of SDRs was constant in terms of grams of gold.)

These preferences affected members' attitudes regarding transactions with the Fund. On the one hand, members regarded purchases from the Fund as less attractive than before because the resulting liabilities were fixed in terms of gold. On the other hand, members considered it advantageous to repurchase outstanding drawings from the Fund with currencies, thereby reducing their liabilities expressed in terms of gold. However, the interest of members wanting to repurchase their currencies from the Fund conflicted with that of the members whose currencies would be used in repurchase. Members with super gold tranche positions in the Fund were reluctant to see these positions diminished by use of their currencies in repurchase. For one thing, such repurchases decreased their assets fixed in terms of gold. For another, the repurchasing member was likely to offer U.S. dollars, for which convertibility had been suspended, in exchange for the currencies needed to make the repurchase.

U.S. dollars could not be used directly in repurchase because the Fund's holdings of them were in excess of 75 per cent of the U.S. quota: following the purchases by the United States in June and on August 4, 1971, these holdings were 91.5 per cent of the U.S. quota.

By the same token, some participants in the Special Drawing Account that had been reluctant in 1970 and the first part of 1971 to be included in designation plans were now less reluctant. Because of the expectation of an early increase in the dollar price of gold, there was a desire to acquire SDRs, the value of which was expressed in terms of grams of gold.

The U.S. actions of August 15, 1971 presented a host of other problems, too, for the conduct of the Fund's operations, both in the General Account and in the Special Drawing Account. The Fund's financial operations were normally conducted on the basis of par values or, in the absence of agreed par values, on the basis of provisionally agreed exchange rates. For members with fluctuating exchange rates, certain rules had existed since June 1954 to allow transactions and computations in their currencies.[13] These rules had been used to cope with the situation arising from the introduction of fluctuating rates by Canada in 1970 and by the Federal Republic of Germany and the Netherlands in 1971. More explicitly, after the announcement by the Canadian authorities on May 31,

---

[12] The suspension of official dollar convertibility is discussed in Chap. 25.

[13] E.B. Decision No. 321-(54/32), June 15, 1954, as amended in 1961 and 1971; Vol. II below, pp. 193–94.

1970 that the exchange value of the Canadian dollar would not be maintained within the prescribed margins around the par value (see Chapter 23), the Executive Board decided on July 14, 1970 to apply these rules to the Canadian dollar. This decision had enabled the Fund in the second half of 1970 and the first half of 1971 to continue to use Canadian dollars in operations in the General Account and to adjust the valuation of its holdings of Canadian dollars. Similarly, on May 19, 1971, after the exchange rates for the deutsche mark and the Netherlands guilder were allowed to float (see Chapter 25), decisions were taken by the Executive Board to determine appropriate exchange rates for the Fund's transactions in deutsche mark and Netherlands guilders, so that these currencies could continue to be used in the Fund's financial operations.

After August 15, 1971 the exchange rates for almost all of the currencies that the Fund would use in drawings and repurchases and for other transactions and operations were not being effectively maintained within the margins around par values established under the Articles or by decisions of the Fund. Since the Fund had regularized operations only for three major currencies for which there were no par values—the Canadian dollar, the deutsche mark, and the Netherlands guilder—a widespread problem suddenly existed concerning the exchange rates at which the Fund's transactions in many other currencies would take place. Purchases and repurchases through the General Account could no longer be effected on the basis of agreed par values or of provisionally agreed exchange rates, and transactions in the Special Drawing Account could not be conducted on the basis of representative exchange rates.

Further, in the absence of agreed arrangements for convertibility, it might be difficult for members to use currencies which they held in their reserves but which could not be accepted by the Fund to acquire the currencies that were needed for their transactions with the Fund.

Finally, without agreement on the values to be used for currencies and gold, there was the problem of the valuation of the Fund's assets, which consisted of holdings of currencies and of gold.

In these circumstances, the staff worked out a series of ad hoc turnstile arrangements that would allow repurchases to be carried out. In October 1971 three members—Canada, France, and the Federal Republic of Germany—agreed to what amounted to a revolving fund in their currencies: Canadian dollars, French francs, and deutsche mark might be used for repurchases to the extent that drawings had been made since August 15, 1971 in these currencies, provided that consultation with the member preceded each transaction. By these arrangements, members avoided any enlargement of their U.S. dollar holdings as a result of transactions through the Fund. Nonetheless, the agreement permitted repurchases that might otherwise have had to be postponed.

During the latter part of 1971, the staff suggested some techniques that the Fund might use to facilitate orderly resumption of its financial operations, and these suggestions were considered by the Executive Directors. Any solution, however, had implications for the official dollar price of gold, and at the time the U.S. monetary authorities were insistent that that price should remain unchanged. Hence, it was only after the Smithsonian agreement in December 1971 had provided for an increase in the official dollar price of gold as part of a realignment of the exchange rates of the major industrial nations that the Executive Board was able to take a decision enabling the Fund's operations to be resumed in a more nearly normal way. The suggestions by the staff, the discussions of them by the Executive Board, and the Board's decision of January 4, 1972 are described in Chapters 26 and 27.

Factors other than the existence of special problems for the Fund's operations contributed to a diminution of the use made of the Fund's financial resources. This diminution, which had started early in 1971, became more pronounced after August and was to continue for many months to come. For one thing, an ample supply of international liquidity meant that many members' foreign exchange reserves were very high. For another, there was increasing reliance on exchange rate adjustments, rather than on the use of reserves, to meet pressures on the balance of payments.

Table 6. Drawings from the Fund, 1966–71 [1]

(In millions of U.S. dollars)

Member	1966	1967	1968	1969	1970	1971	Total
Afghanistan	9.1	4.0	4.8	13.0	4.0	—	34.9
Algeria	—	—	—	—	—	—	—
Argentina	47.5	—	—	—	—	5.2	52.7
Australia	—	—	—	—	—	—	—
Austria	—	—	—	—	—	—	—
Barbados	•	•	•	•	—	—	—
Belgium	—	—	—	46.5	—	—	46.5
Bolivia	—	—	12.0	11.0	—	4.5	27.5
Botswana	•	•	—	—	—	—	—
Brazil	—	—	75.0	—	—	—	75.0
Burma	—	15.0	4.5	—	12.0	6.5	38.0
Burundi	3.9	5.0	5.0	3.5	2.5	1.5	21.4
Cameroon	—	—	—	—	—	—	—
Canada	—	—	391.0	—	—	—	391.0
Central African Republic	—	—	—	—	—	1.3	1.3
Ceylon	30.2	25.8	35.8	13.0	9.5	14.0	128.3
Chad	—	—	—	—	3.8	—	3.8
Chile	30.0	10.0	43.2	29.0	—	77.5	189.7
China, Republic of	—	—	—	—	—	59.9	59.9
Colombia	37.8	71.4	34.8	33.2	29.2	30.0	236.4
Congo, People's Republic of the	—	—	—	—	—	—	—
Costa Rica	6.8	2.8	—	—	1.8	6.0	17.4
Cyprus	0.9	—	—	—	—	—	0.9
Dahomey	—	—	—	—	—	—	—
Denmark	—	—	—	45.0	25.0	—	70.0
Dominican Republic	6.6	—	—	14.0	—	7.5	28.1
Ecuador	6.2	—	—	18.0	10.0	—	34.2
Egypt	7.5	—	63.0	—	17.5	32.0	120.0
El Salvador	20.0	5.0	3.0	12.2	—	9.0	49.2
Equatorial Guinea	•	•	•	—	—	—	—
Ethiopia	—	—	—	—	—	—	—
Fiji	•	•	•	•	•	—	—
Finland	—	93.8	—	—	—	—	93.8
France	—	—	745.0	500.8	485.0	—	1,730.8
Gabon	—	—	—	—	—	—	—
Gambia, The	•	—	—	—	—	—	—
Germany, Federal Republic of	—	—	—	540.0	—	—	540.0
Ghana	52.2	25.0	10.0	5.0	2.0	—	94.2
Greece	—	—	—	—	—	—	—
Guatemala	7.0	10.0	3.0	6.0	—	—	26.0
Guinea	1.0	—	—	3.8	4.2	—	9.0
Guyana	—	—	—	—	—	4.0	4.0
Haiti	4.6	2.3	—	1.5	—	—	8.4
Honduras	2.5	—	—	—	6.3	—	8.8
Iceland	—	3.8	3.8	7.5	—	—	15.1

Table 6 (*continued*). Drawings from the Fund, 1966–71 [1]

(In millions of U.S. dollars)

Member	1966	1967	1968	1969	1970	1971	Total
India	225.0	90.0	—	—	—	—	315.0
Indonesia	•	—	45.0	65.8	38.0	2.9	151.7
Iran	—	—	46.5	—	16.8	—	63.3
Iraq	—	40.0	—	—	27.2	—	67.2
Ireland	22.5	—	—	—	40.0	—	62.5
Israel	—	—	—	45.0	—	20.0	65.0
Italy	—	—	—	—	133.0	—	133.0
Ivory Coast	—	—	—	—	—	—	—
Jamaica	—	—	—	—	3.8	—	3.8
Japan	—	—	—	—	—	—	—
Jordan	—	—	—	—	—	4.5	4.5
Kenya	—	—	—	—	—	—	—
Khmer Republic	•	•	•	—	—	6.3	6.3
Korea	—	—	12.5	—	—	7.5	20.0
Kuwait	—	—	—	—	—	—	—
Laos	—	—	—	—	0.5	—	0.5
Lebanon	—	—	—	—	—	—	—
Lesotho	•	•	—	—	0.6	—	0.6
Liberia	5.2	5.2	3.4	1.4	2.0	1.0	18.2
Libyan Arab Republic	—	—	—	—	—	—	—
Luxembourg	—	—	—	—	—	—	—
Malagasy Republic	—	—	—	—	—	—	—
Malawi	—	—	—	—	1.0	—	1.0
Malaysia	—	—	—	—	—	11.7	11.7
Mali	1.0	3.0	4.0	2.5	1.5	2.5	14.5
Malta	•	•	—	—	—	—	—
Mauritania	—	—	—	—	—	1.0	1.0
Mauritius	•	•	—	4.0	—	—	4.0
Mexico	—	—	—	—	—	—	—
Morocco	—	—	50.0	10.0	10.0	8.3	78.3
Nepal	—	—	—	—	—	—	—
Netherlands	—	—	—	—	—	—	—
New Zealand	8.0	89.2	—	—	—	—	97.2
Nicaragua	—	—	19.0	14.0	10.0	3.0	46.0
Niger	—	—	—	—	—	—	—
Nigeria	—	—	9.2	—	8.8	—	18.0
Norway	—	—	—	—	—	—	—
Oman	•	•	•	•	•	—	—
Pakistan	9.5	—	40.0	35.0	—	—	84.5
Panama	—	—	3.0	6.4	—	1.0	10.4
Paraguay	—	—	—	—	—	—	—
Peru	—	21.2	46.2	30.0	18.0	16.0	131.4
Philippines	—	27.5	55.0	—	27.5	35.0	145.0
Portugal	—	—	—	—	—	—	—
Rwanda	5.0	2.0	3.0	2.0	—	—	12.0

Table 6 (concluded). Drawings from the Fund, 1966–71 [1]

(In millions of U.S. dollars)

Member	1966	1967	1968	1969	1970	1971	Total
Saudi Arabia	—	—	—	—	—	—	—
Senegal	—	—	—	—	—	—	—
Sierra Leone	1.5	5.4	—	—	—	—	6.9
Singapore	—	—	—	—	—	—	—
Somalia	0.9	4.0	3.7	—	—	—	8.6
South Africa	—	—	62.0	66.2	125.0	—	253.2
Spain	—	166.0	—	—	—	—	166.0
Sudan	17.5	19.0	10.0	2.5	—	—	49.0
Swaziland	•	•	•	—	1.2	—	1.2
Sweden	—	—	—	—	—	—	—
Syrian Arab Republic	3.2	9.5	—	9.5	3.0	—	25.2
Tanzania	—	—	—	—	—	—	—
Thailand	—	—	—	—	—	—	—
Togo	—	—	—	—	—	—	—
Trinidad and Tobago	—	—	4.8	—	4.8	—	9.6
Tunisia	8.5	7.0	9.6	2.0	7.5	2.5	37.1
Turkey	21.5	27.0	27.0	10.0	75.0	15.0	175.5
Uganda	—	—	—	—	—	16.5	16.5
United Kingdom	122.5	—	1,400.0	850.0	150.0	—	2,522.5
United States	680.0	—	200.0	—	150.0	1,362.0	2,392.0
Upper Volta	—	—	—	—	0.8	—	0.8
Uruguay	5.0	—	29.5	1.8	40.3	9.5	86.1
Venezuela	—	—	—	—	—	—	—
Viet-Nam	—	—	—	—	—	—	—
Western Samoa	•	•	•	•	•	—	—
Yemen Arab Republic	•	•	•	•	0.5	—	0.5
Yemen, People's Democratic Republic of	•	•	•	—	—	—	—
Yugoslavia	37.5	45.0	—	—	—	96.3	178.8
Zaïre	—	—	—	—	—	—	—
Zambia	—	—	—	—	—	19.0	19.0
Total [2]	1,448.2	834.7	3,517.3	2,461.2	1,509.3	1,900.4	11,671.4

[1] A dot (•) indicates that the country was not a member at the time; a dash (—) indicates that no drawing was made.

[2] Components may not add to totals because of rounding of figures for individual members.

Table 7. Stand-By Arrangements Approved,
January 1, 1966–December 31, 1971

(In millions of U.S. dollars)

Member	Date of Inception	Amount of Arrangement
Afghanistan	August 1966	8.00
	July 1968	7.00
	October 1969	12.00
Argentina	May 1967	125.00
	April 1968	125.00
Bolivia	December 1966	18.00
	December 1967	20.00
	January 1969	20.00
Brazil	February 1966	125.00
	February 1967	30.00
	April 1968	87.50
	April 1969	50.00
	February 1970	50.00
	February 1971	50.00
Burma	November 1969	12.00
Burundi	March 1966	5.00
	March 1967	6.00
	March 1968	6.00
	April 1969	4.00
	June 1970	1.50
Ceylon	June 1966	25.00
	May 1968	19.50
	August 1969	19.50
	March 1971	24.50
Chile	March 1966	40.00
	March 1968	46.00
	April 1969	40.00
Colombia	January 1966	36.50
	April 1967	60.00
	April 1968	33.50
	April 1969	33.25
	April 1970	38.50
	April 1971	38.00
Costa Rica	March 1966	10.00
	August 1967	15.50
Ecuador	July 1966	13.00
	April 1969	18.00
	September 1970	22.00
El Salvador	December 1967	10.00
	July 1969	17.00
	December 1970	14.00
Finland	March 1967	93.75

333

Table 7 (*continued*). Stand-By Arrangements Approved,
January 1, 1966–December 31, 1971

(In millions of U.S. dollars)

Member	Date of Inception	Amount of Arrangement
France	September 1969	985.00
Ghana	May 1966	36.40
	May 1967	25.00
	May 1968	12.00
	May 1969	5.00
Guatemala	January 1966	15.00
	April 1967	13.40
	April 1968	10.00
	August 1969	12.00
	December 1970	14.00
Guyana	February 1967	7.50
	February 1968	4.00
	March 1969	4.00
	April 1970	3.00
	May 1971	4.00
Haiti	October 1966	4.00
	June 1970	2.20
	June 1971	3.00
Honduras	January 1966	10.00
	January 1968	11.00
	February 1969	11.00
	June 1971	15.00
Indonesia	February 1968	51.75
	April 1969	70.00
	April 1970	46.30
	April 1971	50.00
Korea	March 1966	12.00
	March 1967	18.00
	April 1968	25.00
	April 1969	25.00
	March 1970	25.00
	January 1971	25.00
Liberia	June 1966	6.00
	June 1967	4.40
	June 1968	3.20
	June 1969	2.00
	June 1970	2.00
Mali	August 1967	6.50
	August 1968	5.00
	October 1969	3.00
	July 1971	4.50

Table 7 (*continued*). Stand-By Arrangements Approved, January 1, 1966–December 31, 1971

(In millions of U.S. dollars)

Member	Date of Inception	Amount of Arrangement
Morocco	September 1966	50.00
	October 1967	50.00
	October 1968	27.00
	December 1969	25.00
	March 1971	30.00
New Zealand	October 1967	87.00
Nicaragua	March 1968	19.00
	May 1969	15.00
	August 1970	14.00
Pakistan	October 1968	75.00
Panama	May 1968	3.00
	January 1969	3.20
	February 1970	10.00
	March 1971	14.00
Paraguay	September 1966	7.50
	January 1968	8.00
	January 1969	7.50
Peru	March 1966	37.50
	August 1967	42.50
	November 1968	75.00
	April 1970	35.00
Philippines	April 1966	26.70
	January 1967	55.00
	March 1968	27.50
	February 1970	27.50
	March 1971	45.00
Rwanda	April 1966	5.00
	April 1967	2.00
	April 1968	3.00
	April 1969	2.00
Sierra Leone	November 1966	7.50
	January 1968	3.60
	March 1969	2.50
Somalia	January 1966	2.80
	January 1967	5.00
	January 1968	7.00
	January 1969	6.00
	January 1970	3.98
Sudan	September 1966	28.50
	September 1967	10.00
	December 1968	12.00

335

Table 7 (concluded). Stand-By Arrangements Approved, January 1, 1966–December 31, 1971

(In millions of U.S. dollars)

Member	Date of Inception	Amount of Arrangement
Tunisia	December 1966	9.60
	December 1967	9.61
	January 1969	6.00
	January 1970	7.50
Turkey	February 1966	21.50
	February 1967	27.00
	April 1968	27.00
	July 1969	27.00
	August 1970	90.00
Uganda	July 1971	10.00
United Kingdom	November 1967	1,400.00
	June 1969	1,000.00
Uruguay	June 1966	15.00
	March 1968	25.00
	May 1970	13.75[1]
Yugoslavia	January 1967	45.00
	February 1971[2]	51.75
	July 1971	83.50
Zaïre	July 1967	27.00

[1] After being fully utilized, the stand-by arrangement was augmented by $13.75 million because of repurchases in October and November 1970. The full amount of these augmentations was also utilized, and the stand-by arrangement was again augmented in May 1971 by $9.5 million because of repurchases.

[2] Canceled by Yugoslavia in July 1971, when the new stand-by arrangement for a larger amount was arranged.

Table 8. Drawings and Repurchases by Currency, Calendar Years, 1966–71

(In millions of U.S. dollars or equivalents)

Currency	Drawings	Repurchases
Argentine pesos	91.0	25.1
Australian dollars	265.3	238.4
Austrian schillings	142.0	70.1
Belgian francs	1,226.6	843.8
Brazilian cruzeiros	32.4	—
Canadian dollars	1,163.4	899.5
Danish kroner	36.0	52.1
Deutsche mark	2,103.9	1,050.2
Finnish markkaa	24.4	—
French francs	341.6	342.2
Irish pounds	64.2	—
Italian lire	1,164.0	763.5
Japanese yen	563.4	648.9
Kuwaiti dinars	5.0	5.0
Malaysian dollars	5.0	—
Mexican pesos	108.0	85.9
Netherlands guilders	1,252.9	899.3
Norwegian kroner	77.3	54.7
Pounds sterling	404.8	0.2
South African rand	204.0	—
Spanish pesetas	10.0	—
Swedish kronor	105.5	186.6
U.S. dollars	3,018.6	1,048.5
Venezuelan bolívares	37.3	—
Totals in currencies	12,446.6	7,214.1
Repurchases in gold		684.2
Repurchases in SDRs		593.8
Total repurchases		8,492.1

CHAPTER
18

Continued Evolution of
Stand-By Arrangements

STAND-BY ARRANGEMENTS became the crux of the Fund's policies on the use of its resources during the six years covered by this history. This was apparent in three ways. First, the authorities of member governments, the Executive Directors, the management, and the staff were all fairly much agreed that only in exceptional circumstances could a member draw in the credit tranches without the Fund's having authorized a detailed stand-by arrangement in advance. Second, requests for exceptional direct drawings were nearly always accompanied by letters of intent, which were not dissimilar to the letters of intent attached to stand-by arrangements. Third, after September 1968, any member making use of the Fund's resources beyond the first credit tranche was required to consult with the Fund from time to time, in addition to the regular Article VIII or Article XIV consultations, whether the member's use of the Fund's resources was under a stand-by arrangement or by direct purchase.

The previous chapter noted the expanded use of stand-by arrangements and described those approved from January 1966 through December 1971 and the amounts drawn. This chapter explains the circumstances attending the approval and use of some stand-by arrangements of particular interest and the continued evolution of the Fund's policies on stand-by arrangements.

STAND-BY ARRANGEMENT FOR UNITED KINGDOM, 1967

The Fund approved two stand-by arrangements for the United Kingdom during the years 1966–71, one in November 1967 and one in June 1969. The arrangement approved in November 1967 was in the main responsible for bringing about a general review in the middle of 1968 of the conditions that the Fund attached to stand-by arrangements. The review is discussed below in the section, Terms of Stand-By Arrangements Reviewed; a discussion of the 1969 arrangement follows that section.

Background and Request

The United Kingdom's recurrent balance of payments difficulties in the mid-1960s and the enlarged deficits in 1967 and 1968 had, as we have seen in Part Two, been part of the background to the discussions that led to the establishment of SDRs. While the discussions were still at a crucial stage, late in 1967, the external financial plight of the United Kingdom became acute, and in November 1967 there were both a devaluation of sterling and a request to the Fund for a stand-by arrangement. The devaluation is discussed in Chapter 21.

Sir Leslie O'Brien, Governor of the Bank of England, attending the Annual Meetings in Rio de Janeiro in September 1967 as Governor of the World Bank for the United Kingdom, alerted the Managing Director to the seriousness of the United Kingdom's financial troubles. The circumstances worsened in October and the first days of November, and U.K. officials called on the Fund's management in Washington early in November to discuss the possibility of financial assistance. Mr. Schweitzer told the U.K. authorities that there would be great interest in the corrective measures that would be pursued, and he explained the need for the full support of the other participants in the General Arrangements to Borrow, since those Arrangements would have to be activated to finance any U.K. drawing or stand-by arrangement.

Meanwhile, heavy pressure on sterling continued. Over the weekend of November 11–12, the U.K. authorities explored with the Fund's management, and also with the central bankers of the countries of the Group of Ten, meeting in Basle, how much financial assistance they might obtain to support sterling and stave off devaluation: as the United Kingdom wished to marshal a total of $3 billion, the amount obtained from other countries directly influenced the amount that the United Kingdom would wish to request from the Fund.

Devaluation was a step that the U.K. authorities were eager to avoid because, among other considerations, a devaluation of sterling, as had happened in 1949, might precipitate a series of devaluations of other currencies, including those of the EEC countries. Nevertheless, it was clear by Thursday, November 16, that a devaluation was imminent. Mr. Schweitzer told Mr. Maude that, in his view, a sterling devaluation, coupled with an adequate domestic program, would well support a request for a stand-by arrangement. An amount of $1.4 billion was agreed upon; that amount, if fully drawn, would bring the Fund's holdings of sterling to not quite 200 per cent of the U.K. quota.

At about midday on November 17, Mr. Maude handed to Mr. Schweitzer and Mr. Southard a memorandum addressed by Mr. Callaghan, the Chancellor of the Exchequer, to the Managing Director requesting the Fund's concurrence in a change in the par value of the pound sterling, giving the reasons for the proposed change, describing the related domestic measures that were being taken, and stating the United Kingdom's intention to request a stand-by arrangement in the amount of $1.4 billion.

The situation was of the utmost urgency. A staff mission left Washington that evening and arrived in London on Saturday, November 18, the day that the devaluation of sterling was announced, to discuss the terms of the stand-by arrangement. Meanwhile, some senior Fund staff were abroad, and the Managing Director asked them to explore informally both the moves that other countries might take in reaction to the devaluation of sterling and the willingness of the participants in the General Arrangements to Borrow to activate that facility. These advance preparations meant that at the same time that the United Kingdom was devaluing the pound the Managing Director was able to circulate to the Executive Directors preliminary figures on financing a stand-by arrangement, as well as to indicate the understanding of the management regarding the intentions of other members concerning their exchange rates (see Chapter 21). Meanwhile, the U.K. authorities had borrowed $1.6 billion from the central banks of the Group of Ten, so that the total of $3.0 billion that had been sought was in fact obtained.

The formal request to the Fund, along with the letter of intent, came from the Chancellor of the Exchequer on November 23. The requested stand-by arrangement was for 57.4 per cent of quota and, as noted above, could bring the Fund's holdings of sterling (taking into account a repurchase on November 20, 1967) to almost 200 per cent of the U.K. quota if fully drawn. In other words, the amount of the requested stand-by arrangement began in the upper reaches of the second credit tranche and ended in the uppermost reach of the fourth credit tranche.

The Fund's management supported the request for the stand-by arrangement. As described in Chapter 21, the staff's analysis was that the change in the parity for sterling, the supporting measures announced on November 18, and the policies to be introduced as outlined in the Government's letter of intent laid the basis for a substantial improvement in the balance of payments within the next 12 months and for further improvement thereafter. The measures already adopted included raising the bank rate from 6½ per cent to 8 per cent, the highest rate since 1914; reimposing severe but selective ceilings on bank credit to the private sector, except for exports; and tightening the terms of hire purchase (installment credit) on motorcars. A number of measures of fiscal restraint that were to become effective early in 1968 were also announced: the imposition of heavy taxes, mainly indirect ones, and an increase in the corporation tax, and reductions in public expenditures, both civil and defense, including investment by nationalized industries.

Executive Board's Discussion and Approval

The Executive Board considered the request on November 29, 1967, only 11 days after the devaluation and 12 days after the staff mission had left for London. (The Board had discussed devaluation of the pound sterling on November 18.) The U.K. stand-by arrangement of 1967 was thus the most quickly negotiated one in the history of the Fund to this time. It was also equal to the largest transaction in which the Fund had so far engaged—the U.K. drawing in May 1965. But most Executive Directors did not regard the amount as unduly large when considered as a percentage of the U.K. quota ($2,440 million).

The Managing Director was sensitive to the fact that the Executive Directors for developing countries, as well as monetary officials from those countries, would compare the terms of this stand-by arrangement with those of the stand-by arrangements that the Fund worked out with the members that elected them. The United Kingdom was the only large industrial member with which the Fund had so far negotiated a stand-by arrangement, whereas many stand-by arrangements had been approved for developing members. Hence, in an opening statement to the meeting of the Executive Board, Mr. Schweitzer took pains to explain the reasoning behind the proposed terms of the U.K. stand-by arrangement. Action was necessary to forestall or cope with an impairment of the international monetary system. There was a devaluation of a major currency, the need to support a return to confidence in that currency with maximum speed, and the need to maintain that confidence in the future. In these circumstances, it seemed to him that all of the financial support which the Fund could make available to the member ought to be forthcoming *en masse* whenever needed. This reasoning explained why no phasing of the amount available under the stand-by arrangement had been included.[1]

Nonetheless, the management and staff had made maximum and, Mr. Schweitzer thought, successful efforts to reach understandings on a program and had endeavored to find effective procedures other than phasing for following the progress of the United Kingdom while it was making a massive use of the Fund's resources. The Chancellor of the Exchequer had agreed to consult the Fund on a quarterly basis to review the U.K. economy and the balance of payments. If necessary, there would be more formal consultations, that is, at the Executive Board level, on any further action that might be required should the given policies not be producing the desired improvement in the balance of payments. In addition, the authorities stood ready to consult the Fund as long as the Fund's holdings of sterling were in excess of 125 per cent of quota.

Mr. Maude was able to announce at the Executive Board meeting that short-term funds had been flowing back to London from abroad and that the exchange rate for sterling being quoted in world markets was consistently above the new parity. He said that the U.K. authorities conceived of the future in two stages. In the first stage the aim was to increase employment at home while the external situation was being redressed; it would involve the measures already taken. The second stage was to come in a few months' time, when it

---

[1] I.e., no clauses providing for drawings by installments were included. In other words, the United Kingdom would be able to purchase the full amount in one transaction.

was expected that unemployment would be lower, the export drive would have become effective, and growth of the domestic economy would have picked up. Then tighter fiscal policies were to be considered.

All Executive Directors supported the request. Most of them commended the U.K. authorities for their courageous decision to change the par value of the pound and for their actions on the domestic front. They hoped that the devaluation and the associated domestic measures would lead to the decisive turning point that everyone desired. Some regretted the series of adverse external events that had frustrated the objectives of the policies of financial restraint that the authorities had followed in the last few years and that had affected not only the United Kingdom but the entire international financial community.

Several Directors, however, remained very much concerned about the U.K. economic situation and about the adequacy of the domestic measures being taken. Mr. Plescoff supported the stand-by arrangement because the United Kingdom needed urgently to repay its debts and confidence in sterling must be restored, but he believed that the supplementary policy measures announced were not adequate: for devaluation to be successful, it had to be accompanied by a comprehensive program of immediate restrictive measures designed to produce the necessary shift of real resources from domestic to external uses. Mr. Stone doubted that a substantial improvement in the United Kingdom's external position would come about in 1968. Mr. Diz commented on the difficulties of forecasting economic events, even for a member, like the United Kingdom, that had much economic data at its disposal and was rich in economic research.

Because of these uncertainties about the U.K. economy, the Executive Directors attached very great importance to the provisions, both in the letter of intent and in the stand-by arrangement, for frequent consultations between the U.K. authorities and the Fund.

There were, in addition, concerns of another type. Mr. Kafka, while supporting the proposed stand-by arrangement, drew particular attention to the fact that it contained no provisions for phasing, no performance clauses, and relatively few ceilings on variables, such as credit expansion, that were often subject to ceilings under the terms of stand-by arrangements (i.e., performance criteria). In other words, although this stand-by arrangement was in the highest credit tranches, it lacked both a quantitatively defined program and the usual clauses contained in stand-by arrangements. Instead, it included unusually far-reaching provisions for consultations.

Mr. Kafka thought that the U.K. stand-by arrangement would certainly be studied with great interest by members, and that many might wish the stand-by arrangements that were approved for them to be modeled on the same lines, unless it could be demonstrated that their situations differed substantially. Such demonstrations were difficult, or even impossible, however, unless there was a simple, readily understood criterion, such as the tranche position of a member.

Nearly all of the Executive Directors for the developing members supported Mr. Kafka's position. Mr. Phillips O. commented on the absence of quantitative targets in the U.K. stand-by arrangement and their replacement by a series of consultations and hoped that this type of stand-by arrangement would be more widely used in the Fund's operations, thus ensuring uniform standards for all members. Mr. Albert Mansour (Egypt, Alternate to Mr. Saad) and Mr. Williams (Trinidad and Tobago) hoped that the emphasis in the U.K. stand-by arrangement on general policy measures and consultations, rather than on quantitative targets and ceilings, signaled a departure from what they called the more rigid form of stand-by arrangement that had been customary.

Following these deliberations (on November 29, 1967), the Executive Board approved the United Kingdom's request for a stand-by arrangement for $1.4 billion.

TERMS OF STAND-BY ARRANGEMENTS REVIEWED

The discussion of the U.K. stand-by arrangement in November 1967 touched off a general review of the Fund's policy on the use of its resources under stand-by arrangements. In effect, the comments of several Executive Directors, especially those for the developing members, suggested that they had serious misgivings about the equality of treatment that members were receiving in respect of the terms of stand-by arrangements, particularly those applying to the higher credit tranches. Were industrial members subject to terms as severe as those being applied to developing members?

In the next seven or eight months, Mr. Diz, Mr. González del Valle, and Mr. Kafka, among other Executive Directors for the developing members, voiced their concern about the need for uniform treatment for all members in respect of the operative clauses in stand-by arrangements. They believed that the topic might be raised by some of the Governors at the forthcoming Annual Meeting. Therefore, it was agreed that the Executive Board would consider the provisions associated with stand-by arrangements and with use of the Fund's resources before then, and it did so in August and September 1968.

Deliberations

The terms of stand-by arrangements had developed gradually.[2] The overall examination in mid-1968 was thus, in a sense, the first of its kind, and was

---

[2] See *History, 1945–65*, Vol. I, pp. 321–32, 373–76, 429–33, and 488–91, and Vol. II, Chaps. 18, 20, 21, and 23.

to lead to another milestone decision on the use of the Fund's resources and stand-by arrangements.

When they began to consider this topic on August 14, 1968, the Executive Directors had before them a staff paper that evaluated existing policies on the use of the Fund's resources under stand-by arrangements and recommended the continuation of the same policies on stand-by arrangements that had been followed, including the recent arrangement with the United Kingdom. The staff suggested that appropriate clauses providing for consultation, phasing, and performance criteria should continue to be incorporated in all stand-by arrangements, with three exceptions: (1) performance clauses need not be put into stand-by arrangements that did not go beyond the first credit tranche; (2) phasing could be omitted from stand-by arrangements that did not go beyond the first credit tranche when the Fund did not advocate any major adjustments in the member's policies; and (3) phasing should not be stipulated when the stand-by arrangement had been requested to maintain confidence in the member's currency, ready availability of the full amount of the arrangement was considered essential as a deterrent to speculation, and maintenance of the value of the currency was important for the stability of several other currencies. In this third situation, the performance clauses would provide for consultation with the Fund even if the entire amount of the stand-by arrangement had already been purchased.

The staff gave two arguments in defense of the continuation of existing policy, that is, the use of stand-by arrangements more or less in their same form as the main vehicle for making the Fund's financial resources available to members. *One,* stand-by arrangements as they had evolved had successfully met the twin objectives of assuring members access to the Fund's resources on agreed terms and assuring the Fund that the use of its resources would be consistent with its Articles and with its tranche policies. *Two,* each stand-by arrangement had to be individually designed; no general rule for the number and content of performance criteria could be adopted. Because members had economies that operated in different ways, and because they had various types of institutional arrangements for implementing their monetary and financial policies, the economic effects of any ceilings and targets, such as limits on the expansion of money supply, credit ceilings, and the like, that might be included in performance clauses could not be the same for all members.

Inclusion of fiscal criteria, such as budgetary deficits, total budgetary expenditures, or particular categories thereof, had been relatively rare. If the Fund included fiscal criteria in performance clauses in stand-by arrangements, the impression might be created that the Fund was making a judgment on the priorities of the member: budgetary operations and the operations of public agencies reflected the social and economic priorities of the member, and usually came about after internal political compromises had been made. Moreover, fiscal criteria in performance clauses were normally not necessary because in most situations the substance of what they might achieve could be adequately handled by ceilings on aggregate credit expansion and credit expansion by the public sector. Furthermore, for many members fiscal data were both less reliable and less available than monetary data.

The Executive Board's discussion revealed the familiar dichotomy of view on a number of issues between Executive Directors for industrial members and Executive Directors for developing members. Messrs. Biron (Belgium), Dale, Hattori, Lieftinck, Mentré (France, now Alternate to Mr. Plescoff), Patrick M. Reid (Canada, Alternate to Mr. Handfield-Jones), and Schleiminger endorsed the continuation of the existing policies on the use of the Fund's resources and on stand-by arrangements. They recognized the importance of policies that gave equitable treatment to all members, but in their opinion the policies that the Fund had been following were in the right direction and were for the benefit of all members.

Several of them thought that performance clauses might be made even more specific. For instance, greater reliance on use of targets for fiscal policy was favored. Was it really true that monetary policy lent itself better to performance clauses than did fiscal policy? Mr. Schleiminger also wondered whether some "quantitative bench marks" might not be used to serve as "warning lights" when economic and monetary targets were not being observed. Such indicators of the country's economic situation had been used in the EEC and were being considered by Working Party 3 of the OECD. Mr. Lieftinck wanted more attention to be paid to the exchange rate policies of members that ran persistent balance of payments deficits and that were regularly drawing from the Fund in the higher credit tranches. It was essential that the Fund's resources not be used to support unrealistic rates of exchange.

Mr. Guy Huntrods (United Kingdom, Alternate to Mr. Maude) defended the absence of specific safeguards in the U.K. stand-by arrangement of November 1967. The U.K. economy was the subject of close examination by the Fund; therefore, the form of the stand-by arrangement did not mean that the United Kingdom could make use of the Fund's resources on terms that were any less stringent than those for other members. Performance criteria had been expressed largely in qualitative rather than in quantitative terms because the difficulties of accurate forecasting were particularly marked in the case of the United Kingdom. The letter of intent had included certain precise figures as goals, and the staff had frequently expressed their views in quantitative terms. But quantitative performance criteria would not have been effective and would have lessened the confidence-building effect of the stand-by arrangement, the key reason for having the arrangement.

Messrs. Diz, Faber, González del Valle, Kafka, Madan, Nikoi, Phillips O., Rajaobelina, and Yaméogo, in contrast, had much greater difficulty with the existing policies. Mr. Kafka wanted to know what specific criteria governed the number and content of performance clauses and the periodicity of drawings in stand-by arrangements that went above the first credit tranche. Was it not possible to spell out some minimum performance criteria which would ordinarily be both necessary and sufficient according to the tranche position? Messrs. González del Valle and Faber were also concerned that the differentiation in policy was between the first credit tranche and the other tranches. Mr. Diz questioned whether additional numbers of clauses and a complex system of safeguards had permitted larger amounts of funds to be authorized under stand-by arrangements: since 1959, when stand-by arrangements had become more complicated, the average amount of a stand-by arrangement had remained at about 50 per cent of quota. Mr. Madan argued that detailed conditions and clauses made for undesirable rigidities in a member's economic policies.

The Executive Directors for the developing members, pointing to the detailed figures in the staff paper which showed that the number of performance criteria in the stand-by arrangements for members in the Western Hemisphere and in Asia was on average much greater than for members in Europe, also raised other questions about the Fund's present policies on stand-by arrangements. Was there such a substantive difference between drawings in the first credit tranche and drawings in the upper credit tranches that no performance and phasing clauses were needed for the former while the latter required several specific ones? Since monetary ceilings and targets could not be forecast with certainty, how useful were such quantities at all in performance clauses? Did not the same reasons why fiscal criteria were not useful for performance clauses apply as well to monetary criteria?

Some Executive Directors, including Mr. Nikoi, urged that greater reliance be placed on regular consultations with the member rather than on quantitative safeguards written into performance clauses. Mr. Diz and Mr. Rajaobelina liked quantitative criteria because they were precise and objective, but they suggested that there might be some kind of consultation by geographic region so that members with similar economies could talk simultaneously to the Fund about their related economic problems and possible common solutions.

Decision on Stand-By Arrangements

The positions of Executive Directors were not as far apart, however, as this line of argument suggests. Those for industrial members agreed that equality of treatment for all members was essential and that such treatment should explicitly be seen as being equal. Those for developing members agreed that equality of treatment did not mean identity of treatment; in particular, it did not require identical performance clauses in stand-by arrangements. The issue of policy, therefore, came down to reconciling the need for flexibility with the requirement that all members be treated uniformly.

To this end, a comprehensive decision was taken on September 20, 1968, the basic elements of which were as follows: [3]

One, clauses requiring the member to remain in consultation with the Fund were to be included in all stand-by arrangements.

Two, provisions would be made for consultation with a member, from time to time, during the whole period in which the member was making use of the Fund's resources beyond the first credit tranche, whether or not that use resulted from a stand-by arrangement.

Three, clauses providing for phasing of the amounts that might be drawn, and clauses requiring the achievement of certain performance criteria if drawings were to continue, would be omitted in stand-by arrangements that did not go beyond the first credit tranche. (This provision brought the policy on the use of the Fund's resources in general and the policies on stand-by arrangements closer together.)

Four, in all other stand-by arrangements, phasing and performance clauses would normally be included, but they would be applicable only to purchases beyond the first credit tranche.

Five, in exceptional cases, phasing would not be stipulated if it was essential that the full amount of the stand-by arrangement be available promptly. In such a case, the performance clauses would require the member to consult the Fund about new or amended performance criteria even if there was nothing left to be drawn. This consultation was to include a discussion by the Executive Board that could culminate in a communication of their views to the member under Article XII, Section 8.

Six, performance clauses would be limited to stipulating criteria necessary to evaluate the implementation of the member's financial stabilization program, with a view to ensuring achievement of the objectives of that program.

Seven, language having a contractual flavor would be avoided in the documents relating to stand-by arrangements.

Shortly thereafter, standard texts were devised for the consultation and performance clauses in stand-by arrangements.[4] It was expected that the consultation clause would not have to be regularly "invoked." Rather, if the member's external situation caused concern, the staff would visit the country at least once a year, such visits to be arranged by mutual consent. Only where such visits could not be arranged would the "125 per cent" clause, as it was referred to within the Fund, be invoked (see the second basic element above).

---

[3] E.B. Decision No. 2603-(68/132), September 20, 1968. The full decision is reproduced in Vol. II below, p. 197.

[4] For an illustrative stand-by arrangement and a detailed commentary on each provision, see Gold, *Stand-By Arrangements*, Chaps. 2 and 3.

At the Twenty-Third Annual Meeting, Mr. Schweitzer, observing that the stand-by arrangement had become an increasingly effective tool of collaboration between the Fund and many members with widely differing situations, explained that the review that had just been completed had "sought primarily to preserve the uniform and equitable treatment of all members." He said that he was "confident that this basic principle will be upheld without impairment of necessary flexibility." [5]

STAND-BY ARRANGEMENT FOR UNITED KINGDOM, 1969

As is discussed in Chapter 21, the U.K. economy responded slowly to the 1967 devaluation of sterling. Early in 1969 the authorities indicated informally to the management and staff of the Fund that they would like to negotiate another one-year stand-by arrangement (the 1967 arrangement had expired in November 1968). The new arrangement would facilitate $1.3 billion of repurchases of sterling from the Fund regularly falling due between February 1969 and the end of May 1970; these were repurchases in connection with a drawing of $1,400 million in May 1965 and a drawing of $122.5 million in March 1966 in connection with payment of the gold portion of the increase in quota. Repurchases of the first two installments of part of the sterling held because of the 1965 drawing had already been made, in August and November 1968.

At the suggestion of the Managing Director, the U.K. authorities requested an amount of $1.0 billion, rather than an earlier-considered figure of $1.3 billion. They made repurchases totaling nearly $500 million in February, March, and May 1969, and the Fund's holdings of sterling at the end of May 1969 amounted to 173 per cent of quota, so that the stand-by arrangement would fall in the upper credit tranches.

The terms had been negotiated under the comprehensive decision of September 20, 1968. Although there were no performance criteria related to credit or fiscal policies, the Managing Director assured the Executive Board, when it considered the request on June 20, 1969, that he was satisfied that the stand-by arrangement was in accord with the Fund's current policy. The U.K. authorities had stated that, for the financial year ending in March 1970, their objective was to obtain a surplus of at least £300 million on the current and long-term capital accounts of the balance of payments, and they had specified how budgetary and monetary measures were working toward that end. They intended to limit domestic credit expansion to not more than £400 million, compared with some £1,225 million in the financial year 1968/69. Rather than performance criteria, the letter of intent and the stand-by arrangement provided for full-scale reviews of performance through consultations. Drawings under

---

[5] Opening Address by the Managing Director, *Summary Proceedings, 1968*, p. 27.

the stand-by arrangement, after the initial one, would be phased to follow such reviews. These terms were readily accepted by the Executive Board, especially because the Managing Director assured the Executive Directors that other members could, if they wished, also be considered eligible for this form of stand-by arrangement.

Reporting on developments in the U.K. economic situation, Mr. Maude said that the U.K. authorities agreed with the staff that the performance of the U.K. economy and the balance of payments position were beginning to look encouraging. The authorities were even more optimistic than the staff that the balance of payments surplus would be sizable in 1969/70. They believed that devaluation was having a powerful effect on exports, especially of manufactured goods, and that resources were being switched away from internal consumption and into exports on a significant scale. Mr. Maude also pointed out that U.K. monetary policy had now become extremely tight.

The 1969 Article VIII consultation was considered at the same time as the request for a stand-by arrangement. Most of the Executive Directors observed that pronounced improvements were beginning to take place in the United Kingdom's financial prospects. Mr. Dale said that he was able to welcome the proposed stand-by arrangement because of the comprehensiveness of the targets and programs of the U.K. authorities. Mr. Johnstone commented on the value to all members of the close working relationship that had been established between the Fund and the United Kingdom.

The discussion of the U.K. stand-by arrangement prompted other comments of a general nature. Mr. Schleiminger, as on other occasions, wondered how useful monetary policy was compared to fiscal policy. Mr. Lieftinck, Mr. Plescoff, and Mr. Stone pointed to the long time lag, more than a year, between the devaluation of the pound sterling and the implementation of firm budgetary and monetary restraints and suggested that the U.K. situation represented the failure generally of economic forecasting. Mr. Kafka and Mr. Williams were concerned about large outflows of private long-term capital to high-income countries in the sterling area. Mr. Madan was worried about the implications for developing members of the upward trend of interest rates in international money markets.

The stand-by arrangement was approved. One week later, on June 27, 1969, the United Kingdom purchased $500 million, one half of the amount authorized by the stand-by arrangement.

DRAMATIC IMPROVEMENT IN U.K. ECONOMIC SITUATION

By September 1969, when the first review of monetary and fiscal policies under the stand-by arrangement took place, the U.K. financial situation had clearly been reversed. Tight controls on public expenditures and heavy taxation had been continued, and the public debt had been managed in such a way as to yield substantial net sales of government securities to the nonbank public, rather than net purchases, as had been expected. Total bank credit had thus declined. Private consumption in real terms had fallen, largely reflecting the absorption of increasing money incomes through the massive increases in tax rates that had been put into effect in 1968. Pressure on foreign exchange reserves had moderated.

On September 17, 1969, the Executive Board adopted a decision to the effect that the United Kingdom had consulted on its monetary and fiscal programs in accordance with the stand-by arrangement and that no further understandings need be reached between the Fund and the United Kingdom to enable that member to make further purchases under the stand-by arrangement through September 30, 1969. On September 26, 1969 the United Kingdom purchased $175 million.

By December 1969, when the next quarterly review took place, a surplus in the foreign trade account, arising particularly from increases in exports, had emerged. The strengthening of the U.K. position was evident from what had been happening in the world's foreign exchange markets. During the first three quarters of 1969 there had been large-scale speculative international capital movements that had culminated in changes in the exchange rates for both the French franc and the deutsche mark in August and October 1969, respectively. Yet, for the first time in several years sterling had not come under pressure.

The Executive Board again agreed that the United Kingdom had consulted on its monetary and fiscal programs and could make further purchases under the stand-by arrangement through December 31, 1969. On December 29, 1969 the United Kingdom again purchased $175 million.

At the time of the third quarterly review in March 1970, a dramatic improvement in the balance of payments was clearly a reality. The surplus on current account in 1969, over £400 million, had been the largest ever recorded—in relation to the gross domestic product it was roughly equivalent to the large surplus of 1958—and a peak postdevaluation surplus of more than £800 million (annual rate, seasonally adjusted) had been achieved. This strengthening of the balance on current account had been accompanied by a pronounced shift in capital flows. With the continuation of stringent policies in the United Kingdom and a calmer climate in the exchange markets in late 1969 and the first part of 1970, short-term capital had flowed into London on a large scale. This inflow was supplemented by unusually large increases in official sterling holdings, reflecting exceptionally favorable developments in the balance of payments of the overseas sterling area as a whole.

It was in the light of these developments that the Executive Directors, many of whom congratulated the U.K. authorities on the success of their efforts, took a decision in March 1970 indicating that the United Kingdom had consulted the Fund under the stand-by arrangement concerning its monetary and fiscal programs and could draw the remainder of the amount authorized by the stand-by arrangement. On March 26, 1970 the United Kingdom did so, with a purchase for $150 million.

The model of the 1969 U.K. stand-by arrangement, in which the amounts that could be drawn were phased to come after consultations between the Fund and the member on the member's monetary and fiscal policies—in some respects a more stringent condition than the usual terms of stand-by arrangements—was not used again.

UNITED KINGDOM REPAYS THE FUND

Because of the vast improvement in the balance of payments that began in 1969 and continued through 1971, the U.K. authorities were able to repay external debts in very large amounts. In the 18 months to the end of June 1970, short-term and medium-term foreign obligations were reduced from over $8 billion to $3.5 billion. By the end of 1971 the United Kingdom had virtually eliminated its short-term and medium-term obligations. These repayments included repurchases of sterling held by the Fund. Consequently, also by the end of 1971 the Fund's holdings of sterling were below the level where further special consultations under stand-by arrangements were required.

The details of the repayments are as follows: Under the terms of the November 1967 stand-by arrangement, the $1.4 billion drawn in June 1968 was, to the extent that the outstanding amount had not otherwise been reduced (as through sales of sterling by the Fund to other members), to be repurchased beginning June 18, 1971. These obligations overlapped with repurchase obligations in respect of the $1.0 billion of drawings under the 1969 stand-by arrangement, which would begin to fall due in June 1972. Because of these overlapping repurchase obligations in respect of the drawings under these two stand-by arrangements, and in view of the U.K. balance of payments surplus, the U.K. authorities wanted to make some advance repurchases of the June 1968 drawing. Accordingly, on March 22, 1971 the Executive Board agreed to a U.K. proposal that the repurchase of the then outstanding amount ($1,324.75 million) be discharged in accordance with a schedule of eight quarterly installments that would start on or before March 31, 1971 and end on December 31, 1972. With Board approval, the United Kingdom repurchased, in advance, the first four installments, totaling $684.8 million, on March 31, 1971 and repurchased a further $614.1 million on August 9, 1971. These repurchases, together with the Fund's sales of sterling, completed the discharge of the outstanding balance of the $1.4 billion drawn in June 1968 and reduced the Fund's holdings of sterling from 139.8 per cent to 117.9 per cent of the U.K. quota of $2.8 billion.

STAND-BY ARRANGEMENT FOR FRANCE

During the years 1966–71 the Fund approved only one stand-by arrangement for an industrial member other than the two for the United Kingdom, the one with France of September 19, 1969. That stand-by arrangement followed strictly the form of the Fund's general decision on stand-by arrangements of September 1968.

Request Is Made

France's request to the Fund in September 1969 for a one-year stand-by arrangement followed a series of crises involving the French franc from the spring of 1968 onward, which culminated in a devaluation of the franc on August 10, 1969.[6] The use of its gold tranche in 1968 to make its first purchase from the Fund in more than a decade, described in Chapter 17, had been prompted by the first of these crises. Hence, in 1969 the Fund's holdings of French francs were equal to 100 per cent of quota.

Because of the frequency with which short-term capital funds had moved from French francs into deutsche mark in the previous 16 or 17 months, the French authorities feared that, even after devaluation of the franc, there would be more such movements. This fear was not unjustified. As we have seen in the discussion in Part Two, the 1969 Annual Meeting opened on September 29 in the midst of another crisis in European exchange markets. A renewed flow of funds into deutsche mark, including movements out of French francs, had forced the German exchange markets to close, and the German authorities had introduced a floating rate for the deutsche mark.

Because its reserves had already been seriously depleted by previous capital outflows, France wanted an arrangement with the Fund whereby during the next year it could, after making full use of any gold tranche position it might have, purchase from the Fund a sum equal to the whole French quota at the time ($985 million). The stand-by arrangement, if fully drawn, would thus bring the Fund's holdings of French francs to 200 per cent of quota.

Arriving in Paris on August 11, 1969, the day after the franc had been devalued, the staff team had to come quickly to an informal understanding with the French authorities, both on what might be the terms of such a stand-by arrangement and what stabilization plan would support it. In fact, negotiations were completed in ten days, when it became apparent that France would probably want to draw at least half of the amount of the stand-by arrangement in the next four weeks, that is, before the Annual Meeting, which was to be held in Washington at the end of September. That the package of currencies involved would necessitate activation of the General Arrangements to Borrow,

---

[6] The reader who wishes to look first at the events leading up to the devaluation is referred to Chap. 22.

that the amount of the stand-by arrangement would cover all four credit tranches, that negotiations were taking place under a relatively new general decision on stand-by arrangements, that any performance clauses would be closely examined to see if they were comparable to those that the Fund had included in the stand-by arrangements for other members, and that the various measures already taken by the French authorities to restore external equilibrium had by no means solved the crisis that was facing the French franc, all added to the complexities that attended the drafting of the stand-by arrangement.

As with the U.K. stand-by arrangement of the previous June, the working out by the staff and the French authorities of the proposed stand-by arrangement with France was done in a very short time.

Executive Board Approves

The official request for a stand-by arrangement was communicated to the Managing Director by Mr. Giscard d'Estaing, Minister of Economy and Finance, on August 27, 1969 and was considered by the Executive Board on September 19. As Mr. Plescoff indicated at the outset of the Board meeting, the Executive Directors were considering the French economy for the third time in 1969: they had discussed it in March in connection with the 1968 Article VIII consultation and in August when the par value of the franc had been changed.

In support of the request for a stand-by arrangement, the Executive Directors had before them details of a stabilization program, the main objective of which was equilibrium in the current account of the balance of payments by the end of June 1970. To this end the French Government had taken measures designed to eliminate excess demand in the domestic economy as rapidly as possible, to check the growth in imports, and to promote a shift in resources to the external sector. The deficit in the government budget was to be drastically reduced in 1969 and eliminated in 1970. Quantitative controls on bank credit were to be tightened and continued until mid-1970. Interest rates were to be raised. Extremely severe restrictions were to be imposed on consumer credit.

Mr. Plescoff said that the French authorities well understood that the goal of eliminating the current account deficit of the balance of payments by mid-1970 was a demanding one. But they considered it essential to establish confidence, both at home and abroad, in the new par value of the franc, and both the stand-by arrangement and the stabilization program were important in this regard. He went on to say that, if the Executive Board approved the request, the Bank of France would make an immediate drawing of $500 million under the stand-by arrangement and at the same time draw some $800,000 remaining in the gold tranche.

Before June 30, 1970 the French authorities were to review the country's economic and financial developments and prospects with the Fund; in addition, the Article VIII consultation would provide a further review of economic developments during the period of the stand-by arrangement.

The Executive Directors warmly supported the stand-by arrangement. Mr. Yaméogo, speaking after Mr. Plescoff, commended the courageous program of the Government and pointed out how much the stability of the franc meant to all members of the French franc area, which included the members that had elected him. The measures announced seemed fully adequate to re-establish equilibrium in France's balance of payments.

On the whole, the Executive Directors were satisfied with the stabilization policies proposed, although they recognized how difficult the achievement of budget equilibrium in 1970 and of current account equilibrium by the middle of that year would be. Mr. Johnstone suggested that perhaps these goals were more ambitious and precise than they need be. Mr. Palamenghi-Crispi, joined by Mr. Phillips O., was not at all certain that they could be achieved. Mr. Kafka noted that the stand-by arrangement was in full conformity with the Board's decision of September 20, 1968.

Several Executive Directors took the occasion to speculate generally as to what the deterioration in the French economic position and the proposed ways of dealing with it, taken in conjunction with the course of economic events in the United Kingdom and the United States, implied for the kinds of financial policies that would best be pursued by members. Mr. Schleiminger, for instance, observed that the experience of the United Kingdom and the United States had been that the fight against inflation could not be won without an aggressive monetary policy. Noting that the French Government's program put the burden of adjustment about evenly on monetary and fiscal policies, he stressed the need for France to keep the expansion of domestic credit well below the quantitative credit ceilings that had been agreed as part of the stand-by arrangement. Other Executive Directors, pointing out how much the rate of inflation and the balance of payments deficit in France, as in other countries, had departed from those forecast earlier, were concerned that economists had no very accurate guidelines for the economic consequences of monetary and fiscal policies. Mr. Lieftinck queried the relationship between monetary and fiscal policies and real economic phenomena: How sensitive to import competition would the French economy remain? What were the implications for agricultural production and imports? What rate of growth of the gross national product was envisaged? Mr. Suzuki noted the difficulty of holding wage increases to those that could be absorbed by rises in productivity.

Following this discussion, the stand-by arrangement was approved—on September 19, 1969.

RAPID RECOVERY OF FRENCH ECONOMY

The 1969 Article VIII consultation involved discussions between French officials and the staff in Paris in December 1969 and an Executive Board deliberation in March 1970. Meanwhile, France had drawn the entire amount of the stand-by arrangement ($985 million), raising the Fund's holdings of French francs to just under 200 per cent of quota.

A staff mission visited Paris from April 29 to May 12, 1970 so that the Executive Board could review the French economic position in full by June 30, as provided by the stand-by arrangement. It was found that the various commitments and undertakings included in the French program had all been carried out. The current account of the balance of payments had swung into surplus early in 1970. Thus, the objective of a current account surplus was achieved ahead of schedule.

When they met to conduct the review, on June 29, 1970, the Executive Directors congratulated the French authorities on the effectiveness of their stabilization efforts. Several of them, including Mr. Dale, nonetheless noted that, in addition to the tight reins on the domestic economy, there were external explanations for the sudden turnaround in the French current account. Coming as it did so rapidly after devaluation in August 1969, the improvement in the external account could not yet be attributable to the major effects of devaluation on the relative prices of French exports and imports. Because restrictive policies had been in force for a number of months prior to devaluation, the pressure of domestic demand had probably begun to subside by the time the franc was devalued. Hence, a change in the current account shortly after devaluation was facilitated. Another factor that had played a role in the quick recovery, and that had both enlarged the deficit before devaluation and reduced it afterward, was the prevalence of speculative imports in the earlier period. Large stocks of imported goods had been accumulated before August 1969 in anticipation of the change in par value, swelling the size of predevaluation imports; the subsequent depletion of these stocks helped to account for the sudden decline in imports after devaluation.

Another factor contributing to the improvement in the balance of payments was the continued buoyancy of demand for French exports. This had enabled exporters to keep the dollar prices of their goods relatively close to predevaluation levels. In addition, the outflow of speculative short-term funds had been sharply reversed when the deutsche mark was revalued in October 1969.

The next discussions with the French authorities were in connection with the 1970 Article VIII consultation. They took place at the staff level in December 1970 and in the Executive Board in March 1971. In December 1970 the economic situation in France was showing still further improvement. Helped by favorable external circumstances, the stabilization program had brought about a restoration of confidence in the franc and a shift of the necessary additional resources to the external sector without unduly restricting the growth of domestic demand, output, and employment. The overall balance of payments surplus for 1970 was sizable ($2.0 billion in contrast to a deficit of $1.1 billion for 1969), and net official reserves at the end of 1970 (nearly $5 billion) were about three times as large as they had been in August 1969.

There remained, however, a number of potential trouble spots in the domestic economy. The expansion of exports and of investment had put pressure on the capacity of a wide range of industries. To make up for commodity shortages, the volume of imports in 1970 was very much higher than had been foreseen. Consequently, while the authorities responded to the improvement in the balance of payments with a selective relaxation of fiscal policies, they resisted the temptation to pursue more expansive measures, even though unemployment was edging upward. In December 1970 a seminar similar to ones with U.K. officials was conducted in Paris between Fund staff and officials of the Bank of France and the Ministry of Economy and Finance.[7] The purpose was to consider on a technical basis the impact on aggregate economic activity of changes in the total supply of money and in its various components. Inasmuch as the emphasis was on the practical policies of France, the seminar turned out to be somewhat less general than those held with U.K. officials.

During 1971 the French economy continued to expand at a very satisfactory pace compared with the economies of its trading partners. Prices and wages rose fairly rapidly, but the increases were smaller than in most other industrial countries and France's competitive position remained strong. The progress made since 1969 by the French authorities in strengthening the overall balance of payments was further consolidated.

This success enabled France to repurchase from the Fund the extra francs held. Under the terms of the stand-by arrangement, special consultations were to be held in mid-1971, just a few months after the Article VIII consultation, if the Fund's holdings of French francs remained in excess of 125 per cent of quota. However, these consultations did not need to be held. On December 14, 1970 France paid in gold 25 per cent of the increase in quota authorized under the fifth general review of quotas. In addition, France discharged repurchase obligations in 1970 and early in 1971. By April 30, 1971 the Fund's holdings of francs were down to 75 per cent of quota. By August 1971, as a result of some sales of francs by the Fund, France had attained a small super gold tranche position.

Restrictions on Travel Allowances

In the course of their economic difficulties in 1968, the French authorities instituted exchange controls, in May and June and again in November. The controls comprised a comprehensive range of restraints on capital movements and certain restrictions on allowances for foreign travel by French residents.

---

[7] The seminars with U.K. officials are discussed in Chap. 21, pp. 443 and 445.

New restrictions by France were followed by comparable regulations on capital and travel by the African countries of the CFA franc area.

In memoranda to the Managing Director from Mr. Plescoff on November 25, 1968 and Mr. de Maulde on November 29, 1968, France provided details of these control measures and requested the approval of the Executive Board under Article VIII for such restrictions on payments and transfers for current international transactions as had been introduced. Capital controls not being subject to the Fund's jurisdiction, it was the restrictions relating to foreign travel that required the Fund's approval. The staff recommended approval of the restrictions on travel allowances on a temporary basis, that is, for a few months, and the Executive Board agreed. In March 1969 approval of these restrictions was extended through the end of 1969.

At the time the stand-by arrangement was approved in September 1969, the French authorities declared their intention to abolish the restrictions on allowances for travel as soon as the balance of payments position allowed. In view of the continuing payments difficulties, however, the Executive Board in December 1969 approved another extension of these exchange restrictions through December 31, 1970.

During 1970 the French authorities made substantial progress in easing both capital controls and restrictions on allowances for travel. With regard to the latter, they raised the limits within which the banks could make foreign exchange available for travel, and they usually authorized additional amounts for bona fide travel. The authorities defended the restrictions that remained as being necessary to prevent disguised capital flight: because they found it difficult to distinguish suspected capital transfers from legitimate tourist expenditures, the restrictions helped them to prevent illegal outflows of capital.

Mr. Marc Viénot (France) requested the Executive Board to approve the remaining restrictions for another year, and in December 1970 the Board approved their use until December 31, 1971. However, in view of France's strong balance of payments position, they, like the management and staff, had some reservations about the continuation of restrictions in France and so made their approval subject to review a few months later on the occasion of the 1970 Article VIII consultation.

In March 1971, just before that consultation in the Executive Board, the French authorities announced that the basic travel allowance was to be further increased. At the meeting of the Board, the Executive Directors commented favorably on France's general economic situation. They welcomed the relaxation of the restrictions on travel allowances, but urged that they be abolished as soon as possible. In the meantime, their extension was approved until the end of 1971.

In August 1971 there were further relaxations of these restrictions, and on December 27, 1971 the Fund was informed that the restrictions on allowances for travel had been abolished.

STAND-BY ARRANGEMENTS FOR DEVELOPING MEMBERS

Illustrative of the stand-by arrangements between developing members and the Fund are those for Colombia, Indonesia, and Brazil.

Colombia

Colombia had a stand-by arrangement with the Fund virtually continuously beginning in October 1959. The Colombian authorities undertook in September 1965 an exchange reform, most features of which were carried out during the course of 1966, supported by a stand-by arrangement approved in January 1966 for $36.5 million. However, a marked decline in world prices for coffee, which constituted about 65 per cent of Colombia's total export earnings, contributed to a serious deterioration in the country's payments position for 1966 as a whole. Extensive exchange controls and restrictions had to be reimposed in November 1966 and there was a renewed accumulation of payments arrears.

Consequently, in March 1967, with the help of the Fund staff, the Colombian authorities introduced another comprehensive financial program centering on a new exchange rate system. A dual market was introduced. A certificate rate primarily determined by market forces was to be applicable chiefly to trade transactions. Another rate applied to most capital movements and payments for invisibles. Most transactions remained subject to controls, but these controls were to be liberalized gradually. New tax measures were instituted to strengthen the fiscal situation, and current expenditures were to be limited. A cautious wage policy was to be continued and monetary controls improved. A one-year stand-by arrangement, this time for $60 million, nearly twice as large as Colombia's other stand-by arrangements, was approved in April to provide the Colombian authorities with a secondary line of reserves in the event of temporary balance of payments difficulties.

By the time this stand-by arrangement expired, in April 1968, the full amount had been drawn. Significant progress had been made, however, and the Fund authorized another stand-by arrangement, for $33.5 million, in that same month. The Colombian authorities were continuing the financial program and were now aiming at equilibrium in Colombia's external and budgetary finances and at still greater freedom in its international transactions. The balance of payments position was much stronger and controls were being relaxed.

Again, the amount of the stand-by arrangement was fully utilized and the financial program was remarkably successful. The flexible exchange rate was adjusted periodically and unification of the two exchange markets was achieved. Exports were somewhat diversified by the promotion of the so-called minor exports, that is, commodities other than coffee and petroleum.[8] Imports were gradually liberalized and exchange reserves increased. On the domestic front, the rate of increase of domestic prices had slowed, and in fact economic growth had accelerated since public investment had been able to expand.

In order to consolidate this progress, the Fund in April 1969 approved yet another stand-by arrangement for Colombia, the tenth for that member. The amount authorized was $33.25 million, and this was fully utilized by April 1970.

As Colombia continued to make progress, and wished to continue to keep its own rate of price increase low despite rising import prices associated with inflation in other parts of the world, and to continue to augment its exchange reserves, the Fund approved a stand-by arrangement for another year in April 1970, this time for $38.5 million. By April 1971 purchases under this arrangement totaled somewhat less than the full amount. Nonetheless, after the highest annual rate of growth since 1959, Colombia requested a stand-by arrangement for $38 million, which the Fund approved. At that time, Colombia asked also for technical assistance from the Fund to undertake a study of budgetary reform aimed at introducing effective procedures for controlling budgetary expenditures.

Indonesia

The new Indonesian Government that came into power in March 1966 adopted, in October 1966, a broadly based economic program aimed at slowing down the very high rate of inflation and at rehabilitating the national economy, which had deteriorated badly. The principal elements of this program were tightened credit policies and a balanced budget; the reduction of internal price distortions by increasing the prices of certain essential goods that had been subject to control and by raising the rates of tariff on public utilities charged by the Government; and the reactivation of market forces, especially in the foreign trade sector, by completely decontrolling imports and introducing a more realistic rate of exchange. With the agreement of creditor countries, repayments of external debt were also rescheduled.

Indonesia re-entered the Fund in February 1967 (having withdrawn from membership in August 1965) and in February 1968 asked for a stand-by arrangement for $51.75 million. Some success in reducing the rate of inflation was already being achieved, and a stronger anti-inflationary effort was being planned. In requesting the Fund's support, the authorities stated their beliefs

---

[8] For a study of Colombia's minor exports and how they responded to Colombia's export promotion system, see José D. Teigeiro and R. Anthony Elson, "The Export Promotion System and the Growth of Minor Exports in Colombia," *Staff Papers*, Vol. 20 (1973), pp. 419–70. A discussion of the rationale of Colombia's differentiated rates for exports, and of its experiences with such rates, can also be found in Margaret G. de Vries, "Multiple Exchange Rates: Expectations and Experiences," *Staff Papers*, Vol. 12 (1965), pp. 282–313.

that the exchange reserves, which were very low, were not adequate to guard against unforeseen contingencies, and that such support would provide much-needed flexibility and would strengthen public confidence in the proposed new program.

The Executive Board, noting that the current leadership in Indonesia had demonstrated an ability to pursue stabilizing financial policies and to lay the conditions for new economic growth, believed that the forthcoming program was worthy of support and agreed to the request. Detailed performance criteria and specific objectives in the fields of monetary, fiscal, and exchange policy were written into the stand-by arrangement, and the amounts to be drawn were phased. Throughout the rest of 1968 and in February 1969 Indonesia drew the full amount authorized. Despite some temporary setbacks because a serious scarcity of rice caused sharp increases in consumer prices, the Indonesian authorities managed to achieve a marked deceleration in the rate of price inflation, to balance the budget, and to add to their net exchange reserves. In March 1969 they requested a stand-by arrangement for $70 million, to support a five-year development plan beginning April 1, 1969. This arrangement was approved in April, and Indonesia drew most of the amount authorized before it expired in April 1970.

The year 1969 seemed to be an important turning point for the Indonesian economy. Rapid inflation was effectively brought under control, the exchange rate remained stable, and the Indonesian policymakers were turning their attention to the promotion of economic growth. The financial program for 1970/71 was to include, inter alia, a reform of the exchange system to encourage exports and strict controls on the contracting of short-term and medium-term debt. The stand-by arrangement for $46.3 million, requested and approved in April 1970, was expected to strengthen confidence in the rupiah and to allow flexibility in the management of the external sector. Indonesia drew $38 million under the arrangement.

As Indonesia continued to make progress, a one-year stand-by arrangement for $50 million was approved in April 1971, but no purchases were made under this arrangement. At the end of 1971 the Fund was continuing to keep the Indonesian situation under close surveillance, not only through the annual consultations under Article XIV but also through the quarterly reviews required under the terms of stand-by arrangements.

Brazil

After 1964 Brazil began to experience what some observers labeled an economic miracle. In that year the country was suffering from stagnant output, rampant inflation, and an acute shortage of foreign exchange. The inflation that had plagued the economy since World War II, especially after 1958, had caused prices to rise in 1964 and 1965 by as much as 90 per cent. Recurrent balance of payments deficits had led to the accumulation of commercial and financial arrears, and large foreign indebtedness had resulted in a heavy burden of debt repayment. Upon taking office in April 1964, a new Government introduced, and then continued to apply, economic policies aimed at gradual stabilization of prices, rapid growth, and a strong balance of payments position. By 1971, the end of the period examined here, impressive results had been achieved. For the fourth consecutive year the annual rate of economic growth was more than 9 per cent in real terms and the balance of payments was in surplus by a substantial amount. The 18 per cent rise in the cost of living in Rio de Janeiro was the smallest since the mid-1950s. Automobiles, tractors, cement, drugs and chemicals, nonmetallic minerals, wood and furniture, and paper and printing all had become leading growth industries. Exports of many manufactures expanded and exports as a whole had become quite diversified. (These developments continued after the end of 1971. In fact, in 1973 Brazil's annual exports totaled $6 billion and gross official reserves at the end of that year reached $6.4 billion, by far the highest ever recorded.)

During these years the Fund, through its annual consultations under Article XIV, through participation in the rescheduling of debt repayments, through stand-by arrangements, and through frequent informal contacts and exchanges of visits, kept in close touch with the Brazilian authorities and their economic programs and achievements.

The Fund approved the first in a series of stand-by arrangements for Brazil on January 13, 1965. The amount authorized on that date was $125 million. (The Fund had previously approved stand-by arrangements for Brazil in 1958 and 1961.) The program submitted in support of the January 1965 arrangement placed emphasis, initially, on containing inflation, reducing the imbalances in the economy that were stifling output and exports, and creating an institutional environment appropriate for growth. During the year a central bank was created, credit controls strengthened, public finances revamped, and exchange policies liberalized. By the end of the year, the fiscal and balance of payments positions had improved markedly, the rate of increase in prices had decreased considerably, and some reduction in the rate of monetary expansion had been achieved. There had, however, been a temporary slowdown in economic activity. The authorities drew $75 million of the $125 million authorized by the stand-by arrangement. They planned to exercise continuing restraint over domestic credit expansion and to bring about a further improvement in the Government's financial position, and in February 1966 the Fund approved another stand-by arrangement, again for $125 million. No drawings were made, and Brazil in fact reduced its indebtedness to the Fund. The next stand-by arrangement, authorized in February 1967, was for $30 million.

The year 1967 was the one in which the momentum of the Brazilian inflation was finally broken. The rate of increase in prices slowed appreciably. Although there was a deterioration in the country's net foreign exchange position in 1967, this had been reversed by April 1968, when the Fund approved the fourth in the series of stand-by arrangements, for $87.5 million. The purpose of this arrangement was to enable Brazil to meet its repurchase obligations. The 1967 arrangement had not been used, but drawings under the new arrangement were expected.

In 1968 the authorities turned their attention to accelerating the rate of economic growth. Reform of the tax system had been undertaken in 1967 to assure that rising income and output would generate a steady growth in government revenues and to provide tax incentives for the stimulation of investment and exports, and to encourage the development of a capital market. In August 1968 a flexible exchange rate policy was introduced, which allowed adjustments in the exchange rate by small amounts at frequent, irregular intervals so as to maintain relative parity between the cruzeiro and the currencies of Brazil's major trading partners. This policy aimed at encouraging exports and at rationalizing capital movements by curbing speculative capital flows and stimulating long-term investment.

In 1968 the pace of economic growth did accelerate. A high rate of economic activity induced greater capital inflows, and the capital account of the balance of payments began to show a surplus. Official reserves began to increase. Some problems could, of course, be expected; in particular, prices continued to rise at much the same rate as in 1967. The objective of the Government that took office in 1969 was to achieve a gradual but steady reduction in the rate of inflation. A total of $75 million was drawn under the 1968 stand-by arrangement.

In April 1969 the Fund approved a stand-by arrangement for $50 million. This arrangement was not drawn upon. Nonetheless, the authorities considered stand-by arrangements important to their objectives and stand-by arrangements were approved for Brazil in February 1970 and in February 1971, each for $50 million. In the programs submitted in support of the 1970 and 1971 arrangements, the authorities continued to have as their primary objectives the maintenance of a high rate of economic growth, further gradual reduction in the rate of inflation, and the preservation of a sound balance of payments position. In the financial sphere, three targets continued to be of importance: reducing the cash deficit of the government treasury, slowing down the expansion of domestic credit, and building up foreign exchange reserves. The 1970 and 1971 stand-by arrangements also were not drawn upon.

As 1971 came to a close, production, particularly in the industrial sector, was continuing to rise rapidly and inflation was below 20 per cent a year and continuing to decline. The Fund staff was negotiating with the Brazilian authorities a letter of intent requesting the eighth in the series of stand-by arrangements, again for $50 million.[9] Moreover, serious inflation was gradually

---

[9] The arrangement was approved in March 1972, but through the middle of 1974 no further request was made for a stand-by arrangement in view of the large size of Brazil's external reserves.

developing into a worldwide phenomenon, and Brazil's experiences with anti-inflationary policies were becoming of general interest. In particular, interest began to center on a technique used by the Brazilian authorities that was called "generalized indexing," in which costs and prices were tied closely together.[10]

FINANCIAL PROGRAMMING—A MAJOR ACTIVITY

The particular circumstances that attended each stand-by arrangement differed, but, as we have seen in the foregoing examples, usually a stand-by arrangement was intended to support a member's program to achieve or restore monetary stability in its domestic economy and equilibrium in its balance of payments. In other words, a stand-by arrangement and a stabilization program usually went hand in hand.

The stabilization programs agreed between the Fund and its members customarily consisted of an understanding on the domestic monetary and fiscal policies that would be pursued. By the late 1960s these stabilization programs had come to be referred to rather formally as financial stabilization programs, and they had become very specific. Virtually all the programs submitted to the Fund by members requesting stand-by arrangements in the upper credit tranches contained detailed quantitative ceilings on credit expansion. Most programs contained separate ceilings on the extension of credit by the central bank to the government or to the public sector as a whole. Often credit expansion by the entire banking system was also subject to limits.

Ceilings on domestic credit expansion were emphasized because performance criteria in stand-by arrangements were based on the view of the staff and of the Executive Directors that changes in the supply of money and credit in an economy had a strong impact on aggregate domestic demand and a related effect on the balance of payments. Practical considerations as well led the Fund to the use of credit controls in stabilization programs. Credit policy was an instrument used by the authorities of nearly all members for short-term control of their economies. Moreover, most members kept monetary statistics that were readily available and detailed enough to permit the Fund to follow closely the achievements of the program. Nevertheless, direct fiscal measures— either additional taxes or cuts in aggregate public expenditure or both—were usually also stipulated in members' financial stabilization programs. In effect, the total impact of monetary and fiscal policies was summed up in the form of credit ceilings.

In addition, as we have seen in the examples discussed in the foregoing section, many programs contained exchange rate provisions. Frequently, espe-

---

[10] A brief appraisal of Brazil's experience in using indexing can be found in Jack D. Guenther, " 'Indexing' Versus Discretionary Action—Brazil's Fight Against Inflation," *Finance and Development*, September 1975, pp. 25–29.

cially among developing members with overvalued exchange rates, fluctuating rates were specified as a way to obtain more realistic rates. To ensure that exchange rates would in fact fluctuate freely and that central banks would not intervene in the market, members were committed to acquiring and then maintaining minimum levels of foreign exchange reserves. As another way to ensure that exchange rates were realistic, members were often obligated not to impose restrictions on imports and exchange payments.

Any changes made in the performance criteria during the period that the stand-by arrangement was in existence were subject to review and approval by the Executive Board.

How Programs Were Devised

Helping a member to prepare a comprehensive financial program in support of its request for a stand-by arrangement, and negotiating with the monetary authorities of a member the related credit ceilings and balance of payments goals, had for years played a large part in the Fund's technical work with Latin American members. But as the membership of the Fund grew and as stand-by arrangements became commonly used by members in all regions, the working out of a financial program as a prelude to a stand-by arrangement became almost a standard practice. In addition, as time went by, the staff began to go through essentially the same programming discipline when it held discussions with members for the Article VIII and Article XIV consultations. After 1965 there was a notable decrease in the exchange controls and restrictions and in the bilateral agreements maintained by many of the Fund's members and correspondingly less emphasis in the annual consultations on the nature and purpose of exchange restrictions, which had originally been the *raison d'être* of these consultations. Many of the annual consultations subsequently turned on the question of the financial policies that would best enable members to keep their domestic costs and prices down and their external payments in balance, especially as inflation plagued practically every member.

Financial programming was, in essence, an exercise aimed at determining a set of monetary and fiscal policies for the next 12 to 18 months that would reconcile resource availabilities with resource needs in such a way as to produce minimum strain on the member's domestic price level and a desired balance of payments result. The programs went into ever-greater detail, covering not only the total supply of money but the different sources of expansion of money and quasi-money, the structure of interest rates and interest rate policies, the handling of cash balances, the management of domestic debt, and other subsectors of members' monetary activities.

The greater part of the time and attention of the staff, especially of the five area departments, was increasingly devoted to working with members to devise specific credit ceilings and targets suitable for inclusion in stand-by arrangements and to reviewing members' performances under these arrangements. As stand-by arrangements were initiated with more and more members, as changes in financial programs associated with stand-by arrangements were renegotiated and had to be approved by the Executive Directors, as the financial policies agreed became increasingly specific, and as assistance was requested by members for both the formulation and the execution of their financial policies, the staff's work in this regard became extremely intensive.

The Fund tried to make certain that the programs set up for different members were as consistent and uniform as possible. The Stabilization Policies Division was created in the Exchange and Trade Relations Department in 1965 for just this purpose.

Financial programming also became increasingly subject to quantitative analysis, that is, advanced econometric techniques were applied to working out particular targets of monetary policy. Many of the techniques evolved by the Fund for quantifying monetary targets, as well as the economic concepts and analysis underlying the use of that quantification, had not previously been used by economists. Monetary economists gradually came to refer to the type of analysis that summarized the monetary picture of a country in terms of a few aggregate figures, which in turn were used to estimate the size of a potential balance of payments deficit, as a new "IMF-inspired" monetary approach.

The Fund staff and the officials of a member planning to request a stand-by arrangement often sat down together, in advance of the request, to make quantitative estimates of the total supply of the economy's financial resources (such as bank deposits, government revenues, private savings, loans and credits from abroad) and of the total demand for financial resources (private consumption expenditures, current government expenditures, investment plans of the private and public sectors, and foreign debt repayment). Projections were made of the major flows of funds through the banking system. The projections frequently required a reshuffling of the government's accounts so as to show the prospective effects of the financial operations of the government on the banking system and on the balance of payments. Attempts were often made to extend the analysis of governmental operations to the entire public sector rather than to only that part of it represented by the budget of the national government. The estimates of the demand and supply for financial resources thereby derived were then juxtaposed, to enable a determination of the extent of the possible pressure on a member's internal prices or on its balance of payments. Frequently, this financial programming involved quantifying the effects on prices and on the balance of payments of alternative sets of financial policies. Similarly, a forecast of the consequences of a set of financial policies for the year ahead was often required.

Preliminary calculations were sometimes based on economic models that indicated, if only in an approximate way, the likely relationship between credit creation and the balance of payments. Over time the staff had developed a number of such models. One well-known one was the Polak Model.[11] In 1970 Mr. Polak refined the model, initially developed from 1957 to 1960, so as to incorporate more complex relationships, and he built an alternative model that was more suited to economies with highly developed financial markets, for use in industrial countries.[12] Once estimates of exports and capital movements for the coming year had been made, such economic models permitted calculations of the change in external reserves associated with any assumed amount of domestic credit expansion.

The results obtained by these or other technical methods were, of course, modified by judgment which took into account members' past experiences with various financial policies. Often the computer was used to appraise expected results, using data from past experience. Many further alterations in suggested policies were subsequently worked out in the course of frequent discussions between Fund staff and the authorities of the member concerned. Only then were monetary and fiscal policies agreed upon and aggregate credit ceilings, ceilings for particular parts of the banking system, and targets for reserves determined.

Because financial stabilization programs were worked out with the authorities of numerous countries in which economic circumstances and banking and monetary institutions were widely diverse, the methodology used and the depth of analysis and detail necessarily varied.[13] In effect, there was no standard way in which the quantitative ceilings on credit expansion and the targets for foreign exchange reserves were derived. The ceilings and targets in each stand-by arrangement were adapted to the economic circumstances and the financial institutions of the member concerned and resulted from continuing discussions between the member and the Fund, both at the management and staff level and at the Executive Board level.

PROGRAMMING METHODOLOGY UNDER STUDY

The Executive Directors were very much interested in the general philosophy of the financial programming related to stand-by arrangements and in the models and techniques used. At the time of the general review of the Fund's policy on stand-by arrangements in mid-1968, Mr. Kafka and Mr. Palamenghi-

[11] J. J. Polak, "Monetary Analysis of Income Formation and Payments Problems," *Staff Papers*, Vol. 6 (1957–58), pp. 1–50; and J. J. Polak and Lorette Boissonneault, "Monetary Analysis of Income and Imports and Its Statistical Application," *Staff Papers*, Vol. 7 (1959–60), pp. 349–415.

[12] J. J. Polak and Victor Argy, "Credit Policy and the Balance of Payments," *Staff Papers*, Vol. 18 (1971), pp. 1–24.

[13] For a description of how a stabilization program was formulated and executed, see Rattan J. Bhatia, Gyorgy Szapary, and Brian Quinn, "Stabilization Program in Sierra Leone," *Staff Papers*, Vol. 16 (1969), pp. 504–28.

Crispi urged that the Fund regularly review the methodology of financial programming. Then, and on later occasions, they asked for reviews of, for example, the models used and the Fund's experience with the ceilings imposed under stand-by arrangements.

Consequently, to gain more insight into the efficacy of monetary and fiscal policies, the staff of both the functional departments and the area departments undertook to examine the evidence of the past. This examination was considered more fruitful than earlier examinations because the Fund had built up an accumulated experience with members. Some of the studies looked generally at what could be learned about the demand for money.[14] Others examined the effects of money and monetary policy in developed countries.[15] Conclusions were also drawn concerning the experiences of selected developing members with money supply and with interest rates.[16]

In a study wider in coverage and broader in scope, the balance of payments performance of 23 countries in Latin America and the Caribbean area from 1966 to 1970 was evaluated empirically.[17] The evaluation included examining the relationship between balance of payments performance and governmental policies. A special examination was made of policies of credit restraint and the effects of exchange rate adjustment. Among the conclusions were that the countries that managed demand by restraining credit were, by and large, the smaller ones, while all the larger ones, except Mexico, followed active exchange rate policies.

Early in 1971, Executive Directors began to inquire more closely into the ways in which particular programs had been formulated. For instance, in January, on the occasion of a Board discussion on a stand-by arrangement for Korea, Mr. Palamenghi-Crispi asked several questions: By what analysis and mechanics had the staff estimated the ceiling for the increase in total domestic bank credit for the next 12-month period? What underlying assumptions had been made about the growth in the gross national product, both in real and in money terms? What was the relationship between the financial programs and the growth of the economy? Could not detailed projections be given for the

---

[14] See, for example, Joseph O. Adekunle, "The Demand for Money: Evidence from Developed and Less Developed Economies," *Staff Papers*, Vol. 15 (1968), pp. 220–66; and Yung Chul Park, "The Variability of Velocity: An International Comparison," *Staff Papers*, Vol. 17 (1970), pp. 620–37.

[15] See, for example, Victor Argy, "The Impact of Monetary Policy on Expenditure with Particular Reference to the United Kingdom," *Staff Papers*, Vol. 16 (1969), pp. 436–88, and "The Role of Money in Economic Activity: Some Results for 17 Developed Countries," *Staff Papers*, Vol. 17 (1970), pp. 527–62.

[16] See, for example, Rattan J. Bhatia, "Factors Influencing Changes in Money Supply in BCEAO Countries," *Staff Papers*, Vol. 18 (1971), pp. 389–98; and Anand G. Chandavarkar, "Some Aspects of Interest Rate Policies in Less Developed Economies: The Experience of Selected Asian Countries," *Staff Papers*, Vol. 18 (1971), pp. 48–112.

[17] E. Walter Robichek and Carlos E. Sansón, "The Balance of Payments Performance of Latin America and the Caribbean, 1966–70," *Staff Papers*, Vol. 19 (1972), pp. 286–343.

fiscal, monetary, and reserve accounts? Later, other Executive Directors—among them Mr. Maurice P. Omwony (Kenya) and Mr. Yaméogo—asked for analyses of the degree of success attained with previous financial programs. The Managing Director promised greater quantification in papers relating to stand-by arrangements and a general paper on how credit ceilings were made up.

The paper on credit ceilings was considered by the Executive Board toward the end of 1971. It showed a high positive correlation between members' observance of credit ceilings and their achievement of balance of payments goals. The staff emphasized that credit ceilings reflected the monetary consequences of all financial policies; they did not reflect monetary policy alone. The staff did not believe that monetary policy necessarily must play the prime role in balance of payments adjustment, as the emphasis on credit ceilings seemed to suggest. In most programs the burden of adjustment fell on fiscal policy and, at times, also on incomes policy.

These discussions indicated that, although the Fund's advances in the analysis of monetary policy had been considerable, much remained to be done. Among the questions that needed further consideration were the following: To what extent was a monetarist approach—that is, one based on the assumption that changes in the stock of money are a primary determinant of changes in total spending—valid for all countries? In particular, was a monetarist analysis equally applicable to both developed and developing countries? Were there not important differences between countries in respect of the transmission mechanism explaining how monetary influences affect real output, employment, and the price level? [18] Could monetary variables other than credit ceilings—such as total money supply—be used as an index of financial control? What methods could be devised to adjust credit ceilings more easily? Were not parameters based on past experience given too much weight as against projections of the future? To what degree did programs based on credit ceilings affect domestic employment and the distribution of income? Were aggregative techniques useful for influencing the newly emerging socio-economic objectives of enhancing employment and redistributing income?

EXPEDITING PURCHASES UNDER STAND-BY ARRANGEMENTS

On a number of occasions the question had been raised in connection with purchases under a stand-by arrangement whether the time between the receipt

---

[18] The staff had already begun work on some of these questions. For example, for a review of the divergent views among monetarist and nonmonetarist economists on the transmission process of monetary policy, see Yung Chul Park, "Some Current Issues on the Transmission Process of Monetary Policy," *Staff Papers*, Vol. 19 (1972), pp. 1–45. For a discussion of the efficacy of monetary policy in developing countries, see Deena R. Khatkhate, "Analytic Basis of the Working of Monetary Policy in Less Developed Countries," *Staff Papers*, Vol. 19 (1972), pp. 533–58.

from a member of an authenticated request to draw and the completion of the transaction by the Fund could not be shortened; five business days was the normal interval. There appeared to be no reason why the time required for handling valid requests for purchases under stand-by arrangements needed to be longer than that for gold tranche purchases, for which the procedure had been shortened in September 1969. Therefore, in March 1970 the Executive Board decided that purchases under stand-by arrangements would be handled like gold tranche purchases. This would speed up the procedure by at least two days.[19]

---

[19] E.B. Decision No. 3006-(70/24), March 20, 1970; Vol. II below, p. 198.

CHAPTER

19

Other Developments in the Fund's Finances

𝒥 UST AS THERE WERE IMPORTANT DEVELOPMENTS and changes in the Fund's policies on the use of its resources and with regard to members' quotas in the years 1966–71, so there were a number of interesting developments in the Fund's other financial transactions and operations—viz., in borrowing arrangements, in the charges placed on drawings and stand-by arrangements, in repurchases, in investment of assets, in the budget, and in the distribution to members of net income. These developments in the Fund's other financial operations and transactions are recounted in the present chapter. The sales of gold to replenish currency holdings are discussed in Chapter 20.

GENERAL ARRANGEMENTS TO BORROW RENEWED

The General Arrangements to Borrow became effective on October 24, 1962 for an initial four-year period and were renewed in 1965 for a four-year period ending on October 23, 1970. The ten participants in the Arrangements [1] had consented to the renewal on the understanding that prior to October 24, 1968 the Fund and the participants would initiate and complete a review of the Arrangements. The participants had further agreed that any one of them that wished to withdraw could do so, provided that the notice of withdrawal was given between July 25, 1968 and October 24, 1968. Following the review, the Fund would take a decision not later than October 23, 1969 concerning the renewal.

The process of the Fund's review of the General Arrangements began in mid-1968. The management and staff believed that it would be preferable for the Fund to rely as much as possible on practice to solve any problems that might arise under the Arrangements and not to suggest formal changes.

---

[1] Belgium, Canada, France, the Deutsche Bundesbank, Italy, Japan, the Netherlands, the Sveriges Riksbank, the United Kingdom, and the United States.

Although they considered that a broadening of the Arrangements would be desirable—for example, by raising the ceilings for borrowing or by admitting other members of the Fund as participants—they thought it was unlikely that the ten participants would be receptive to such changes.

One change they considered essential, however. The Fund should be assured of recourse to the General Arrangements not only in connection with drawings in the credit tranches by the participants that were also reserve centers, that is, the United States and the United Kingdom, as had been the original purpose of the General Arrangements to Borrow, but also in connection with gold tranche drawings by the reserve centers and drawings by the other participants. The Fund's holdings of the currencies of the ten participants were down to $745 million. In the opinion of the Managing Director, these low holdings, plus the unsettled situation in world exchange markets, made it appropriate for the Fund to be able to use the General Arrangements in connection with any drawing by any of the ten participants. In fact, Mr. Schweitzer considered such a broadening of the Arrangements necessary to maintain the reserve character of members' gold tranche positions in the Fund, which were then in the process of being made automatically available to members. He feared that otherwise the Fund might find itself short of currencies needed to implement gold tranche purchases.

The existing procedure gave the Deputies of the Group of Ten time to meet in advance of an activation of the General Arrangements to Borrow. This procedure was adequate for requests to the Fund for drawings or stand-by arrangements in the credit tranches. But when the Fund had to deal with a request for a drawing in the gold tranche, there was not time for an advance meeting by the Deputies. In the instance of gold tranche drawings, the Fund itself had no prior discussions with members.

Mr. Schweitzer therefore informed the Executive Directors that he had cabled the chairman of the Deputies of the Group of Ten, Mr. Ossola, to suggest that the Deputies look into a possible adjustment of the existing procedure. The Fund staff suggested two alternatives: (1) an accelerated procedure by which consultations for activation could go through the Executive Directors (rather than the Deputies of the Group of Ten), or (2) a prefinancing of a gold tranche drawing from the Fund's general resources with a subsequent activation of the General Arrangements to Borrow to replenish the Fund's holdings of the currencies drawn.

The Deputies agreed that the Arrangements could be used for drawings, including gold tranche drawings, by all participants. They were opposed, however, to an accelerated procedure for gold tranche drawings—alternative (1) above—preferring to keep the procedures of the Fund and those of the Deputies separate. They accepted instead the prefinancing procedure—alternative (2) above: in effect, any gold tranche drawing prefinanced by the Fund would be refinanced from the General Arrangements to Borrow. Otherwise, the Deputies proposed to their Ministers and Governors that there be no amendments or modifications of the General Arrangements as they had stood since 1962, and Mr. Schweitzer was informed to this effect.

Shortly thereafter, on October 21, 1968, the Executive Board took a decision noting the completion of the required review and concluding that no amendments or modifications of the Arrangements were needed. The Fund's review of the General Arrangements by October 24, 1968 was thus complete.

About one year later, during the 1969 Annual Meeting, the Ministers and Governors of the Group of Ten agreed to renew the Arrangements without modification for a period of five years. Each participant was to have the right, during the six months beginning October 24, 1969, to inform the Fund of its intention to withdraw from the Arrangements as renewed, but it was not expected that any participant would do so. On October 17, 1969, although a few Executive Directors elected by developing members were less than enthusiastic, the Executive Board took a decision renewing the General Arrangements for five years from October 24, 1970.[2] As no participant in the Arrangements had notified the Fund at the end of six months (April 1970) that it intended to withdraw, the period of effectiveness of the Arrangements was thus extended until October 24, 1975 with the continued adherence of all participants.

Since commitments to the Arrangements were expressed in national currency, the commitment of the participants to lend to the Fund gradually became somewhat lower than the original total of $6 billion. With the devaluation of sterling in November 1967, the U.K. commitment fell from $1,000 million to $857 million, and with the devaluation of the franc in August 1969, the French commitment fell from $550 million to $489 million. Although the commitment of the Deutsche Bundesbank rose from $1,000 million to $1,093 million with the revaluation of the deutsche mark in October 1969, the net effect of these changes was to reduce the total commitment of the ten participants from $6,000 million to $5,889 million.

The association of Switzerland with the General Arrangements to Borrow was worked out for the second time in 1967. At that time, the Managing Director discussed with the Swiss authorities the extension of the association of Switzerland, and the Swiss authorities informed him that they were prepared to extend the period of the agreement between Switzerland and the Fund until October 23, 1970, the date on which the first renewal of the Arrangements was to expire. As with the original agreement, the Swiss authorities indicated that they wished the extension to be effected through an exchange of letters between the Ambassador of Switzerland to the United States and the Managing Director of the Fund. After the Executive Board agreed on November 17, 1967, there was an exchange of letters.[3]

---

[2] E.B. Decision No. 2858-(69/96), October 17, 1969; Vol. II below, p. 209.

[3] E.B. Decision No. 2377-(67/85), November 17, 1967; Vol. II below, p. 209.

After the second renewal of the General Arrangements to Borrow, a similar exchange of letters took place extending the period of the agreement between Switzerland and the Fund until April 30, 1974, which was the date of expiration of the Swiss federal decree authorizing the association of Switzerland with the Arrangements.[4]

Some Changes Postponed

During the discussions leading to the amendment of the Articles of Agreement in 1969, several Executive Directors expressed the view that it might be appropriate to effect certain changes in the General Arrangements to Borrow in order to harmonize them with the amended Articles. On the occasion of the second renewal of the Arrangements, the management and staff once more gave some thought to the desirability of introducing such changes. However, they again considered it preferable to wait a bit longer.

In October 1970, one year after the second renewal of the General Arrangements had been agreed, the Executive Directors considered possible changes in them. Two changes—one with respect to a transfer charge and one with respect to the rate of interest—would lower the return on claims under the Arrangements to the level of the remuneration that the Fund, under the amended Articles, paid on super gold tranche positions in the Fund and of the interest paid on holdings of SDRs. A transfer charge of ½ of 1 per cent, together with the interest rate of 1½ per cent per annum, meant that the Fund's payment on claims under the Arrangements exceeded the 1½ per cent per annum remuneration paid on super gold tranche positions and the 1½ per cent per annum paid on holdings of SDRs. A third change would clarify that the meaning of the phrase *currency convertible in fact* as used in the decision on the General Arrangements to Borrow had not been modified by the amendment of the Articles; and a fourth would enable the Fund to use SDRs to pay interest on claims under the General Arrangements and to repay the claims.

Although the majority of the Executive Directors regarded the changes as probably desirable, they saw no need for urgency. In particular, they considered it better not to reopen discussion about the possible elimination of the transfer charge on claims under the Arrangements.

Later on, in March 1971, the Executive Directors considered at length the characteristics of various Fund-related assets, with special reference to the yield received on each by holders of these assets. The staff argued for harmonizing the treatment of the yields on SDRs, super gold tranche positions, and claims under the General Arrangements to Borrow. Most Executive Directors, however, saw considerable differences in the various Fund-related assets and, therefore, thought that some differentiation was necessary.

---

[4] E.B. Decision No. 3363-(71/60), July 7, 1971; Vol. II below, p. 210.

None of these proposed changes in the General Arrangements to Borrow was made.

ACTIVATION OF GENERAL ARRANGEMENTS TO BORROW

After the first two activations of the General Arrangements to Borrow in December 1964 and May 1965 in connection with drawings by the United Kingdom, the Fund made no further calls on the Arrangements until June 1968. Then, to help finance purchases by France and the United Kingdom, $741 million was borrowed from Belgium, the Deutsche Bundesbank, Italy, the Netherlands, and the Sveriges Riksbank (Table 9). The Fund had planned to borrow from France also when it approved the U.K. stand-by arrangement in November 1967, but by June 1968 France's balance of payments position was such that it could not extend credit and was itself drawing from the Fund.

Table 9. Borrowing by Fund Under General Arrangements to Borrow, 1966–71

(In millions of U.S. dollars)

Participant	June 1968	June 1969	Sept. 1969	Feb. 1970
Belgium	70.0	—	—	—
Canada	—	40.0	25.5	24.5
France	—	—	—	—
Deutsche Bundesbank	366.0	90.0	94.0	—
Italy	185.0	20.0	30.5	29.5
Japan	—	40.0	33.0	32.0
Netherlands	75.0	10.0	7.5	7.5
Sveriges Riksbank	45.0	—	—	—
United Kingdom	—	—	—	—
United States	—	—	—	—
Totals	741.0	200.0	190.5	93.5

When France drew from the Fund in June 1968, its claim on the Fund under the General Arrangements, equivalent to $140 million, was transferred to Belgium, the Deutsche Bundesbank, Italy, and the Netherlands. This transfer conformed to a position taken by the Managing Director in October 1966 that a member drawing from the Fund that had a claim on the Fund under the General Arrangements should liquidate its claim on a more or less *pari passu* basis. The rationale was that the Fund should not remain indebted under the General Arrangements any longer than it had to, and the Fund should not continue to pay interest on a claim under the Arrangements if it had ample balances of the lender's currency which it could use without the payment of interest.

The General Arrangements to Borrow were activated twice in 1969, once in June for a purchase by the United Kingdom, when $200 million was borrowed from Canada, the Deutsche Bundesbank, Italy, Japan, and the Netherlands, and again in September, when $190.5 million was borrowed from these same participants for a drawing by France. In February 1970, in connection with a further purchase by France, the Fund borrowed from Canada, Italy, Japan, and the Netherlands. The share for the Deutsche Bundesbank that had been arranged in September 1969, when the stand-by arrangement with France was approved, was omitted from this second borrowing because of the subsequent weakening of the Federal Republic of Germany's balance of payments position.

No further borrowings under the Arrangements took place through the end of 1971. The total borrowed under the General Arrangements to Borrow from 1966 to 1971 was thus $1,225 million.

The drawings involving activation of the General Arrangements to Borrow were financed only in part by the amounts that the Fund borrowed under the Arrangements. Larger amounts came from the Fund's own holdings of currencies. In addition, beginning with the first activations of the General Arrangements to Borrow in 1964 and 1965, it was the Fund's practice on the occasion of each drawing that involved replenishment of the Fund's own currency holdings through the Arrangements also to replenish its currency holdings by sales of gold. No generalized policy had been established providing a link between activation of the General Arrangements and the Fund's sales of gold for currency replenishment. Instead, the proportions of the currencies to come from the Fund's own currency holdings, from borrowings under the General Arrangements, and from the sales of gold were decided for each drawing necessitating activation of the General Arrangements.

Table 10 lists the five large drawings between 1966 and 1971 which entailed activation of the General Arrangements to Borrow, and indicates how the total drawings were financed.

Table 10. Financing of Drawings by France and United Kingdom Involving Activation of General Arrangements to Borrow, 1966–71

(In millions of U.S. dollars)

Date	Purchasing Member	Amount Purchased	Financed by		
			Currency holdings	General Arrangements to Borrow	Gold sales
June 1968	France	745	298	265	182
June 1968	United Kingdom	1,400	559	476	365
June 1969	United Kingdom	500	250	200	50
September 1969	France	500	208	190.5	101.5
February 1970	France	485	293	93.5	98.5

The Fund's first repayments under the General Arrangements to Borrow took place in May 1967. In that month, when the United Kingdom repurchased sterling, the Fund repaid to eight participants the $405 million that it had borrowed in December 1964. From then on the Fund made frequent repayments. Some were made ahead of time, usually when the member was encountering payments difficulties and was drawing from the Fund. In February 1968, for instance, Canada requested a repayment of $35 million. In July 1969, Belgium, when requesting a gold tranche purchase of $46.5 million, asked for repayment of its claim of $70 million. In December 1969, the Deutsche Bundesbank asked for repayment of $340 million and also requested the Fund to transfer the balance of its claim, $210 million, to other participants. The Fund consented and the transfer was made to Canada, Italy, Japan, and the Netherlands. In July 1970, Italy asked the Fund to repay its claims, $330 million, and the Executive Board agreed.

By August 1971 all indebtedness under the General Arrangements to Borrow had been repaid. The attractive gold-colored promissory notes that the Fund had issued to the fiscal agents of the participants in the Arrangements were canceled.

BILATERAL BORROWING

On only one occasion did the Fund engage in bilateral borrowing. In August 1966, when the United States sought to draw $250 million in Italian lire, the Fund's holdings of lire were down to $74 million. The Fund thereupon borrowed the $250 million in lire from Italy under a special arrangement similar to, but outside of, the General Arrangements to Borrow.[5]

In June 1970, when the loan still had a year to run, the Italian authorities, wishing to augment their liquid reserves by acquiring yen from Japan, asked the Fund to transfer its claim to Japan. The Fund agreed, and the transfer was made in two installments of $125 million each, on June 26 and July 10, 1970. Approximately a year later—in April and August 1971—the Fund ended this indebtedness on schedule by repaying Japan, also in two installments, each for $125 million. The repayment was facilitated by the rise in the Fund's holdings of yen as a result of repurchases in that currency by other members and as a result of the increase in Japan's quota late in 1970. This repayment and the final repayments under the General Arrangements to Borrow freed the Fund in August 1971 of all indebtedness for the first time since December 1964.

Although the Fund did not undertake any other bilateral borrowing, thought was given to the possibility. Early in 1968, as crises in foreign exchange markets were becoming more frequent, as the magnitudes involved in international financial transactions were becoming larger, and as drawings from the Fund were expected to be helpful in financing the unusually large

---

[5] E.B. Decision No. 2151-(66/66), August 3, 1966; Vol. II below, p. 211.

flows of capital, the Fund began to look around for additional financial resources. It was thought that still larger drawings could be expected after gold tranche purchases became automatic and after the buffer stock financing facility went into effect. The management and staff, eager to ensure that the Fund's resources would be adequate to meet these potential demands, explored the possibility of instituting some type of standing arrangements by which the Fund might borrow bilaterally from its members.

Such arrangements as were conceived were to be broader than the General Arrangements to Borrow. The Fund would be able to borrow from any member willing to lend if, for whatever reason, it needed to replenish its holdings of that member's currency. Drawings could give rise to a scarcity in the Fund's holdings of particular currencies. Or the Fund might need certain currencies to help finance gold tranche purchases, or to repay an indebtedness to another member from whom the Fund had borrowed. Bilateral borrowing would not be a substitute for increases in quotas. Nor would it be used where resources were available in adequate amounts under the General Arrangements to Borrow. The purpose of bilateral borrowing would be to alleviate temporary shortages in the Fund's liquidity.

At the 1968 Annual Meeting, the Managing Director told the Governors that the time had come to explore the possibilities of general bilateral borrowing arrangements.[6] But the reaction of the Governors of the six EEC countries was negative. They preferred to augment the Fund's resources by a general increase in quotas, by selective increases in their own quotas, and perhaps by a rise in the ceilings under the General Arrangements to Borrow. Similarly, in March 1969 when the Executive Directors discussed their future workload, they gave a much higher priority to other ways of enhancing the Fund's liquidity— the activation of the SDR facility, the fifth general review of quotas, and renewal of the General Arrangements to Borrow—than to the possibility of wider borrowing arrangements.

Because these other prospective ways of expanding the Fund's liquidity had not yet been acted upon, and it appeared that action might not be taken for some time, the management and staff continued to examine all feasible methods of adding to the Fund's liquidity. At their request, an Executive Board discussion of bilateral borrowing was held in May 1969. In general the Executive Directors had no objection in principle to borrowing bilaterally should circumstances justify it, but most of them considered it premature to take any decision on the matter.

At the 1969 Annual Meeting the Governors agreed to activate the SDR facility and to renew the General Arrangements to Borrow, and by February 1970 agreement had been reached on quota increases in connection with the fifth general review of quotas. Consequently, the matter of standing arrangements for bilateral borrowing by the Fund was dropped.

---

[6] Opening Address by the Managing Director, *Summary Proceedings, 1968,* pp. 26–27.

REVIEW OF CHARGES

In the early months of 1966, when the Executive Directors were re-examining many facets of the Fund's policy regarding the use of its resources, it seemed a propitious time to undertake as well a review of the Fund's schedule of charges. The existing schedule had been in effect since May 1, 1963 and had had no more than minor modifications since 1954.

In the paper prepared for the Executive Board's deliberation, the staff did not propose an increase in the level of charges. The staff's analysis was that, despite the continuous inflation and the rise in worldwide interest rates, the prevailing level of the Fund's charges was probably not too low. Charges were meant to be low enough to encourage members in need to make use of the Fund's resources, although not so low as to discourage repurchases. Moreover, inasmuch as the Fund had been running a substantial surplus since the late 1950s, there was no reason to raise charges to enhance the Fund's revenues. Also, there was logic in keeping the Fund's charges below commercial interest rates. A purchase from the Fund involved a repurchase commitment expressed in terms of gold or its equivalent; borrowing in private capital markets did not. It had already been recognized that loans to the Fund by members could justifiably carry an interest rate lower than comparable market rates because of the gold value of the member's claim against the Fund; the same consideration would presumably be valid for members' obligations to repurchase from the Fund.

The staff did recommend, however, that the progression of charges by the tranches in which the Fund held a member's currency be eliminated; instead, there should be a single schedule of charges for all holdings of a member's currency, based only on the time that drawings were outstanding. The progression of charges by tranche position was thought to be much less necessary than when it had last been seriously considered, some 13 years earlier. Since that time, the Fund had instituted a number of other policies that restrained members from drawing excessively. The elimination of this progression would simplify the schedule of charges.

When this subject was discussed in the Board, nearly all the Executive Directors favored retention of the existing schedule, although the discussion revealed the same duality of views as had prevailed in the past—some believing, while others did not, that the Fund's charges could well be set closer to market rates of interest. Mr. Ulrich Beelitz (Federal Republic of Germany), Mr. Eklöf (Sweden), and Mr. Siglienti (Italy), among others, put forward new reasons why the level of charges, especially in the upper credit tranches, should be raised. The Fund should consider as part of its necessary costs the payment of interest or the distribution of a portion of its net income to those members having gold tranche and super gold tranche positions in the Fund. On the other hand, those speaking for developing members—Mr. Arun K. Ghosh

(India, Alternate to Mr. Anjaria), Mr. Mansour, and Mr. Nikoi—reiterated the view that, because of the nature of the Fund and of its objective to help members, the interest rates in private capital markets had no relevance to the charges levied by the Fund.

Most of the Executive Directors were not in favor of the staff's suggestion to abolish the progression of charges by tranches. Mr. Dale regarded progression as a sort of symbolic reward to members that kept their drawings small. Mr. Lieftinck thought that there was still some efficacy in the Board's belief in the incentive and disincentive effects that had been initially responsible for differentiating charges by tranche position.

Accordingly, in April 1966 the Executive Board approved retaining without time limit the existing schedule of charges. The Board provided, however, for a review of the schedule prior to May 1, 1967, when the next fiscal year would begin, and annually thereafter.

The first annual review of the schedule of charges under this decision was carried out in April 1967 using the lapse of time procedure—that is, without a formal meeting or discussion. Once more the Executive Board decided to keep the existing schedule in effect. Similar reviews took place in April 1968, in April 1969, in April 1970, and in April 1971.

Table 11 gives the schedule of charges that thus prevailed. There was also a service charge of ½ of 1 per cent on the amount of the transaction, except for gold tranche purchases, and this charge applied whether or not the purchases were made under a stand-by arrangement. In the instance of a stand-by arrangement, the member paid a commitment charge of ¼ of 1 per cent per annum on the amount that could be purchased under the stand-by arrangement. If the stand-by arrangement was drawn on, the commitment charge was credited against the service charge. There were precise rules for calculating the holdings of a member's currency and the resulting charges; these rules were somewhat liberalized in 1968.[7] Because of the crediting of commitment charges against service charges, a stand-by arrangement involved no cost for the member to the extent that purchases were made under it. If the stand-by arrangement was used in full, it became, retroactively, a free facility.[8]

The reader is also reminded of two other developments regarding the payment of charges mentioned in earlier chapters. In September 1969 the Executive Board decided that no service charge would be payable for gold tranche purchases made after July 27, 1969, and in December 1969 the Executive Board gave members the option of using SDRs to settle charges payable to the General Account. The Board further agreed a few months later that participants obtaining SDRs from the General Account in order to pay charges or assessments did not necessarily have to use gold to obtain those SDRs; if they wished,

---

[7] E.B. Decision No. 1345-(62/23), May 23, 1962, as amended by E.B. Decision No. 2620-(68/141), November 1, 1968; Vol. II below, pp. 197–98.

[8] For details, see Gold, *Stand-By Arrangements*, pp. 127–32.

Table 11. Charges on Fund's Holdings of Member's Currency in
Excess of Member's Quota Resulting from Transactions Effected
from May 1, 1963 to December 31, 1971

	Holdings Equivalent to Following Percentages of Quota		
More than But not more than	100 150	150 200	200
	Charges in Per Cent Per Annum [1]		
Service charge [2]	0.5	0.5	0.5
Duration:			
0–3 months	0.0	0.0	0.0
3–6 "	2.0	2.0	2.0
6–12 "	2.0	2.0	2.5
1–1½ years	2.0	2.5	3.0
1½–2 "	2.5	3.0	3.5
2–2½ "	3.0	3.5	4.0 [3]
2½–3 "	3.5	4.0 [3]	4.5
3–3½ "	4.0 [3]	4.5	5.0
3½–4 "	4.5	5.0	
4–4½ "	5.0		
	Average Effective Rates in Per Cent Per Annum [4]		
Duration:			
3 months	2.00	2.00	2.00
6 "	2.00	2.00	2.00
1 year	2.00	2.00	2.25
1½ years	2.00	2.17	2.50
2 "	2.12	2.38	2.75
2½ "	2.30	2.60	3.00
3 "	2.50	2.83	3.25
3½ "	2.71	3.07	3.50
4 "	2.94	3.31	
4½ "	3.17		

[1] Except for the service charge, which was payable once per transaction and was expressed as a percentage of the amount of the transaction.

[2] No service charge was payable in respect of any gold tranche purchase effected after July 27, 1969.

[3] Point at which consultation between the Fund and the member became obligatory.

[4] Total charges payable by the member over the stated period, expressed as a percentage and divided by the number of years of the period. Includes service charge.

they could use any currency acceptable to the Fund in repurchases, provided that the participant had consulted the Managing Director on the currencies and the amounts of each to be used to acquire the SDRs.[9]

Another development in the fiscal year 1969/70 also affected the payment of charges. As has been noted in Chapter 13, when the amendments to the Articles affecting the Fund's rules and practices went into effect on July 28, 1969 a change was made in the method of calculating a member's monetary

[9] E.B. Decision No. 3010-(70/25) G/S, March 25, 1970; Vol. II below, pp. 219–20.

reserves: currency liabilities were no longer to be deducted from gross reserves. The Articles provided that, if a member's monetary reserves were less than one half of its quota, it might pay some of the charges due to the Fund in its own currency rather than in gold; this change in the method of calculating monetary reserves had repercussions on the media for payment of charges (as well as on the media for repurchase transactions discussed below). Without the deduction of currency liabilities, the size of some members' monetary reserves as officially computed by the Fund became larger, and members that heretofore had paid all of their charges in national currencies, because their currency liabilities exceeded their gold and foreign exchange holdings, were required to pay part or all of their charges in gold.

REPURCHASES

Three important developments in the Fund's policies regarding repurchases during the years 1966–71 have already been discussed—the use of SDRs for repurchases; the recommendations by the Fund to members in connection with repurchases of drawings made under the compensatory financing facility; and the amendments to the Articles of Agreement involving repurchase obligations.[10] But during these years there were also other changes in the policies regarding repurchases. The most important of these changes was contained in a decision of the Executive Board taken in May 1970, a decision to implement the new provisions of the Articles of Agreement regarding repurchases. Basically, the decision enabled members to fulfill their repurchase obligations by substituting currencies for the currencies that the Fund could not accept or could accept only in limited amounts because of the limitation imposed by the Articles on the Fund's holdings of any currency above 75 per cent of the quota of the member concerned.[11]

A related decision speeding up the reporting of monetary reserves data was taken in April 1971. The Executive Board decided to change the previously existing system under which (1) each member whose currency was held by the Fund on any April 30 was required to report provisional monetary reserves data to the Fund not later than the following May 31 and (2) all members had to provide final monetary reserves data by October 31. Rule I-6 of the Fund's Rules and Regulations was amended to provide that not later than June 30 of each year all members must furnish to the Fund the data necessary for the calculation of their monetary reserves as of the previous April 30. The requirement of reporting monetary reserves data on a provisional basis that had been introduced in 1963 was abolished.[12]

---

[10] See above, Chap. 11, pp. 229–30, Chap. 14, pp. 262–63, and Chap. 13, pp. 258–59.

[11] E.B. Decision No. 3049-(70/44), May 20, 1970; Vol. II below, pp. 207–208.

[12] E.B. Decision No. 3314-(71/33), April 21, 1971; Vol. II below, p. 208.

Another problem about repurchases concerned small amounts of repurchase obligations, that is, $500 or less. Since the expense involved in collecting such small amounts often exceeded the amount of the repurchase obligation itself, the Executive Board had decided in 1957 that repurchase obligations of less than $500 should be collected on the next occasion thereafter that a repurchase obligation occurred which, together with the earlier one, would total $500 or more.[13] In the interest of economy of administrative effort and of simplification for both members and the Fund, the staff proposed in 1968 that, if a provisional or final repurchase obligation included an amount of gold or currency equivalent to $500 or less, that amount should be abated. Moreover, should repurchases calculated on the basis of final data for monetary reserves differ from those calculated earlier on the basis of provisional data, the Fund would not refund or collect the difference if the amount involved was $500 or less. This proposal would eliminate repurchase obligations for all members whose currencies were held by the Fund on April 30 at a level of $500 or less above 75 per cent of quota; those members also would not need to make a provisional report on their monetary reserves, as still required at that time. The proposal would also eliminate from currency budgets for repurchases the use of those currencies that were held by the Fund on April 30 at a level of $500 or less below the 75 per cent of a member's quota. The amounts of currency that would not be repurchased would enter into the calculations of subsequent obligations or could be repurchased as part of a voluntary repurchase exceeding $500 made subsequently. The Executive Board agreed to the staff proposal with little discussion.[14]

When in April 1971 the Executive Board agreed to the speeding up of the reporting of monetary reserves data, it was also agreed to round calculations of repurchase obligations to the nearest $1,000. Hence, the 1968 decision on amounts of $500 or less was abrogated.

The Executive Board took two further decisions in 1971 regarding repurchases. These governed the use in repurchase of a currency for which the exchange rates were not maintained on the basis of the member's par value. The Executive Directors elaborated a decision taken in 1954 that governed the use in repurchase of a fluctuating currency.[15]

Total Repurchases

Beginning in 1968 repurchases became very large. For the six years 1966–71 they aggregated $6.7 billion. The United Kingdom repurchased $2.8 billion, India $640 million, and Brazil, Chile, Colombia, France, and the United States $200 million each. In 1968 alone repurchases totaled $1.1 billion, and

---

[13] E.B. Decision No. 705-(57/55), November 7, 1957; *History, 1945–65*, Vol. III, p. 245.

[14] E.B. Decision No. 2499-(68/77), April 19, 1968; Vol. II below, p. 208.

[15] E.B. Decision No. 321-(54/32), June 15, 1954, as amended in 1961 and 1971; Vol. II below, pp. 193–94.

they were $1.5 billion or $1.6 billion in each of the years 1969, 1970, and 1971. In the fiscal year ended April 30, 1971, repurchases exceeded purchases. In the next fiscal year repurchases were by far the largest of any fiscal year since the beginning of the Fund's operations. There also began to be substantial advance repurchases, because members had ample reserves and wished to reduce their indebtedness to the Fund, lest the price of monetary gold be raised.

The total amounts repurchased compared with total purchases for each of the Fund's fiscal years 1965/66–1970/71 are shown in Table 12. The amounts repurchased by each member are given in Table 13 at the end of the chapter.

Table 12. Total Purchases and Repurchases by Members, Fiscal Years Ended April 30, 1966–71

(In millions of U.S. dollars)

	Purchases [1]	Repurchases [2]
1966	2,817.29	406.00
1967	1,061.28	340.12
1968	1,348.25	1,115.51
1969	2,838.85	1,542.33
1970	2,995.65	1,670.69
1971	1,167.41	1,656.86
Total	12,228.73	6,731.51

[1] Includes purchases that raised the Fund's holdings of the drawing members' currencies to no more than 75 per cent of quota. These purchases are not subject to repurchase.

[2] Includes repurchases that reduced the Fund's holdings of members' currencies below the amounts originally paid on subscription account and repurchases of members' currencies paid in settlement of charges. Excludes sales of currencies of members held by the Fund in excess of 75 per cent of quota, as a result of previous purchases, and adjustments due primarily to settlement of accounts with countries that have withdrawn from the Fund; these sales and adjustments have the effect of repurchases.

INVESTMENT OF THE FUND'S ASSETS

As it had since 1956, the Fund continued until early in 1972 to hold short-term securities of the U.S. Treasury as an investment of some of its gold. In earlier years the income from these investments had been used to meet the Fund's administrative deficits, but in the absence of such deficits for several years it had been credited to a Special Reserve as a contingency against possible future deficits.

Until September 1970 the amount so invested remained at $800 million, as authorized by the Executive Board in November 1960 when, at the request of the U.S. authorities, they had raised the amount from $500 million. Beginning early in 1968, however, there were several developments that culminated first in a reduction in the amount of these investments and later, in February 1972, in their termination.

On several occasions when the Executive Board was considering the administrative budget, Mr. Plescoff, Mr. Lieftinck, and others had indicated that the Fund's reserves were reaching a magnitude such that their growth could be slowed. They preferred to see a distribution of some net income rather than continual additions to reserves. Then, in mid-1968, when speculation was rampant that an increase in the official price for gold was imminent, some Executive Directors voiced concern for the safety of the investments themselves. Mr. Lieftinck and Mr. Plescoff inquired closely of the Managing Director about what was being done by the Fund to safeguard the value of these investments of gold.

The Managing Director and some of the senior staff got in touch with the U.S. authorities to ascertain whether the Fund might obtain some kind of gold guarantee or an "instant recall" of its invested gold. The latter would involve an exchange of letters indicating that, in the event of a new par value for the dollar (tantamount to a change in the price of gold), the U.S. authorities would exchange the securities held by the Fund for gold, at the predevaluation price.

When a new U.S. Administration, under President Richard M. Nixon, took office in January 1969, the Managing Director again inquired of the U.S. authorities what action might be taken to help the Fund protect its investments of gold. Mr. Schweitzer explained that the initial reasons for the investments were no longer relevant since the Fund had not had a budgetary deficit for several years. Moreover, the Special Reserve, derived solely from the income from these investments, had grown to $262.9 million at the end of the Fund's last fiscal year, April 30, 1968. The Managing Director pointed out that it was becoming increasingly difficult for him to justify these investments, although he recognized that, since these amounts had been incorporated in the figures for gross U.S. gold reserves, disinvestment now entailed a reduction in the gold reserves of the United States. A decline in U.S. gold reserves, even of such a technical nature, could have adverse effects on the international monetary situation.

Steps Toward Disinvestment

In April 1969, when the administrative budget for the fiscal year 1969/70 was being considered in the Board, the Managing Director promised a review of the Fund's investment program and of the situation regarding the Fund's reserves. The staff had already begun to examine the considerations involved in terminating the investments, and by August 1969 the management had decided that the case for first cutting back and finally eliminating the investments of gold in U.S. securities was overwhelming. All that was needed was to find a proper way to do so.

In September 1969, in the course of the Board's review of the Fund's reserves, most attention centered on the investments of gold. The Executive Directors, while recognizing that it was difficult to judge the adequacy of the Fund's General and Special Reserves, were inclined to think that these reserves were not excessive. But they noted that, under the amended Articles, the Fund could make transfers from the Special Reserve to the General Reserve, and that amounts transferred could be used for operational or administrative deficits. The deficits could include those resulting from the payment of remuneration on members' creditor positions, as required by the amended Articles. However, amounts transferred from the Special Reserve would not be available for distribution of net income to members. The possibility of transfers from the Special Reserve to the General Reserve to cover deficits would probably guarantee, at least for many years, sufficient reserves to cover any operational losses the Fund might incur. Hence, the reasons for creating the Special Reserve had disappeared. Mr. Plescoff, calling the Board's attention to the fact that the Executive Director for France had voted against the investments in the first place, in 1956,[16] regretted that the Fund was not now free to liquidate these investments. Although Mr. Plescoff did not like such a decision, the Executive Board agreed to having annual, rather than quarterly, reviews of the Fund's investment program. It was expected that these annual reviews would be more substantive than the more or less *pro forma* reviews that had been conducted quarterly in the past.[17]

Following further discussions in September 1970 between the Managing Director and the U.S. authorities, covering not only the Fund's investment in U.S. Government securities but also the withdrawal of the gold that the Fund had on general deposit in New York, the Managing Director proposed to the Executive Board that the Fund reduce by one half, to $400 million, the amount of the investment in U.S. Government securities.[18] This was a more substantial and a more immediate reduction than had been envisaged earlier. On September 11, 1970 the Board took a decision approving this disinvestment.[19]

Income from investments for the fiscal year ended April 30, 1971 was $40 million, compared with $57 million for the fiscal year 1969/70. On April 30, 1971 the Fund's Special Reserve totaled $406 million.

THE FUND'S BUDGET

In reviewing developments in the Fund's budget, we first consider the income side. Practically all of the Fund's income in the years 1966–71 was

---

[16] *History, 1945–65*, Vol. I, p. 463.

[17] E.B. Decision No. 488-(56/5), January 25, 1956, as amended by E.B. Decision No. 2844-(69/90), September 19, 1969; Vol. II below, pp. 223–24.

[18] The Fund's general deposits of gold are discussed in Chap. 20.

[19] E.B. Decision No. 3132-(70/87), September 11, 1970; Vol. II below, p. 224.

derived from charges on balances of members' currencies held by the Fund in excess of those members' quotas—the charges that are described above in the section on Review of Charges. On April 30, 1971, 32 members were subject to such charges, and their payments for the fiscal year 1970/71 amounted to $128 million out of total operational income of $136 million. This income from charges was the largest ever in the Fund's history.

From the beginning of the Fund's operations through 1970/71, 60 members had been subject to charges.

Until the fiscal year 1969/70, that part of the Fund's operational income which did not come from the charges on drawings outstanding resulted from service charges payable on all purchases from the Fund and, to a much lesser extent, from charges on stand-by arrangements.[20] Beginning with the fiscal year 1969/70, income received in the General Account included interest payments on the SDRs held in that Account and assessments to cover the expenses of conducting the business of the Special Drawing Account. Assessments were levied on all participants in the Special Drawing Account in proportion to their net cumulative allocation of SDRs, were payable in SDRs to the General Account, and were treated in the General Account as a deduction from expenditure.

On April 30, 1971 the holdings of SDRs in the General Account amounted to $489.8 million, and for the fiscal year 1970/71 interest payments received on those holdings totaled $4 million. These payments exceeded income from service charges, which were only $3 million, compared with $13 million in the preceding fiscal year. The decrease in service charges reflected not only a decline in 1970 and 1971 in drawings from the Fund but also the fact that most of the drawings that did take place were in the gold tranche, and therefore incurred no charge.

Assessments to cover the expenses of the Special Drawing Account amounted to $0.9 million in the fiscal year 1970/71.

As drawings had attained record levels in 1968 and 1969, the Fund's income rose markedly in 1969–71. The total operational income of $136 million in the fiscal year 1970/71, for example, was nearly three times that in the fiscal year ended April 30, 1965.

Turning to the expenditure side of the Fund's accounts, we might note at the outset that for some twenty years the Fund's expenditure was entirely for administration and for the acquisition of fixed property, that is, for buildings and related land costs. In the fiscal year 1964/65 the Fund began to incur expenditure of an operational nature as well. In that year the Fund started to

---

[20] The proceeds of charges from a stand-by arrangement were not considered as income to the Fund until the arrangement expired or was canceled. Under the Fund's procedures, during the life of such an arrangement refunds and other adjustments could occur, depending on the extent to which drawings actually took place under the arrangement and on the changes that occurred in the level of the Fund's holdings of a member's currency while the arrangement existed.

pay interest and charges on its borrowings from members under the General Arrangements to Borrow and, commencing in 1966/67, similar payments and charges in respect of its bilateral borrowing from Italy. These payments were made in gold. In 1970/71 they amounted to $12 million.

In addition, beginning in the fiscal year 1969/70 the Fund was required under the amended Articles of Agreement to pay remuneration to members with creditor positions, that is, to those members that had super gold tranche positions in the Fund. This remuneration, uniform for all members eligible to receive remuneration, was to be at a rate of 1½ per cent per annum. The Fund might increase or reduce this rate, provided that a three-fourths majority of the total voting power had approved an increase above 2 per cent per annum or a reduction below 1 per cent per annum. This remuneration was to be paid in gold or in a member's own currency, as determined by the Fund, but in April 1970 the Executive Board decided that remuneration could also be paid in SDRs at the option of a member.

The Fund paid remuneration amounting to $27 million in the fiscal year 1969/70 and to $37 million in the fiscal year 1970/71. The rate of this remuneration was determined partly by the rate of the distributions of net income that were voted in 1968, 1969, and 1970, discussed in the following section.

In the fiscal years 1969/70 and 1970/71, the Fund's expenditure on operational account was greater than its expenditure on account of administration and property. Since administrative and fixed property expenditure had also been growing, reaching $39.9 million in the fiscal year 1970/71 compared with only $17.6 million six years before, the total of the Fund's expenditure went up faster from 1964/65 to 1970/71 than had the Fund's income. Total administrative and operational expenditure in the fiscal year 1970/71 came to $89.2 million, more than four times the expenditure in 1964/65.

Subtracting expenditure from income, of course, we obtain the resulting "net income." Readers of the earlier history will perhaps recall that, with the exception of the fiscal year 1947/48, the Fund operated with annual losses from the beginning of its activity in 1946 through the fiscal year 1956/57. Losses were charged to the Fund's capital. Starting with the fiscal year 1957/58 and continuing through the fiscal year 1970/71, the Fund consistently had a surplus of income over expenditure, and in many years the surplus itself exceeded total expenditure. In 1968/69 the Fund's net income reached $70.8 million, the highest in its history through fiscal 1970/71.

At the end of each month surpluses were transferred provisionally to the General Reserve, which had been established in April 1958. Final action approving the transfers was taken by the Board of Governors at Annual Meetings. At the end of the fiscal year 1967/68, that is, on April 30, 1968, the General Reserve amounted to $291.3 million. Thereupon, for the first time, the Executive Board recommended to the Board of Governors that there be a distribution of income to members. This distribution of income was approved in October 1968. Similar distributions were made after the close of the fiscal years 1968/69, 1969/70, and 1970/71. Still, on April 30, 1971 the balance in the General Reserve was $378 million.

However, during the five months May–September 1971, the Fund, for the first time since 1956/57, ran a deficit. The cumulative expenditure in the General Account for those five months was in excess of income by about $500,000. The financing of a new building made for unusually large fixed property expenditures. These fixed property expenditures were superimposed on the operational expenditures of remuneration on members' creditor positions and interest and charges on borrowings by the Fund. Nonetheless, in the opinion of the staff this excess of expenditure over income could be regarded as an administrative deficit, and with the agreement of the Executive Board it was charged against the Special Reserve.

Table 14 at the end of the chapter gives details of the Fund's income and expenditure and resulting net income for each of the six fiscal years 1965/66–1970/71.

NET INCOME IS DISTRIBUTED

The amendment of the Articles of Agreement to provide for payment of remuneration on members' creditor positions, to which reference was made in Chapter 13, was preceded by suggestions for several years that the Fund make some payment to these members, that is, to members having super gold tranche positions in the Fund. Indeed, there had been suggestions for payment to members on their gold tranche positions. As early as January 1965 the Managing Director and the Deputy Managing Director discussed the possibility of such payment informally and asked the staff to look into the question. Throughout the next year or so, because of questions that were being asked by members that had elected them, Mr. Saad and Mr. Yaméogo raised the same issue with the management. Some of the Middle Eastern members, not needing to make use of the Fund's resources and in no need of additional reserve positions in the Fund, were reluctant to take up increases in their quotas or to allow their currencies to be used for purchases by other members. Several African members did not like losing interest on the reserves which they had held in French francs until they converted these reserves into gold tranche positions in the Fund.

Early Deliberations

In August 1966, when the staff proposed that the Executive Directors recommend to the Board of Governors that the net income for the fiscal year 1965/66 be allocated to the General Reserve, as had customarily been done, and that this recommendation be agreed, as in the past, through the lapse of time procedure, Mr. Eklöf, supported by Mr. Biron, requested a discussion by the Board. At the Board meeting, Mr. Biron, Mr. Eklöf, Mr. Handfield-Jones (Canada), and Mr. Larre (France) favored payments of some return on members' creditor positions in the Fund. But others—Mr. Anjaria (India), Mr. Lieftinck, and Mr. Saad—wanted a careful examination of the issue of paying "dividends" to members. The Deputy Managing Director, who was Acting Chairman, stressed the need for quick action on the disposition of the net income for the fiscal year 1965/66, and the Executive Board agreed to defer study of the question of payments on creditor positions and to let the net income for 1965/66 be transferred to the General Reserve. Meanwhile, the Deputies of the Group of Ten had also recommended that the Fund study the possibility of paying remuneration on super gold tranche positions.

Although two staff papers on the distribution of net income were circulated to the Executive Directors at the end of 1966, the Board was not ready for formal consideration of the question until the following August. The discussion at that time revealed that, although most of the Directors were prepared to go ahead with some payment on super gold tranche positions, there were important differences of view on amounts and technique. Since the Articles did not provide for regular remuneration, some Executive Directors—including Mr. Handfield-Jones, Mr. Mansour, Mr. Suzuki, and Mr. vom Hofe (Federal Republic of Germany)—wanted the preferential distribution of net income allowed by the Articles of Agreement (2 per cent per annum) to be made retroactive, that is, to be based on the extent to which members had been creditors during the last few years. But others—including Mr. Dale and Mr. Stone—felt strongly that distribution of net income should not be related to the number of years in which a member had had a net creditor position. Distribution should rather be made at a uniform rate to all members that had been net creditors within the fiscal year in question. Otherwise, as Mr. Dale pointed out, members that had been creditors in the distant past might justifiably feel aggrieved. Most Executive Directors realized that the only satisfactory way for the Fund to pay interest or dividends—or whatever it might be called—on creditor positions was to amend the Articles so as to require the payment of remuneration on net creditor positions and to make such remuneration a cost of the Fund's business, deductible from gross income prior to calculating net income.

These differences of opinion prevented the Executive Board from agreeing on a distribution of the net income, even somewhat retroactively, for the fiscal year ended April 30, 1966. Since an allocation of net income to reserves that was only provisional presented legal complications, the following year the Executive Board again agreed to recommend to the Board of Governors that the net income for the fiscal year 1966/67 be allocated to the General Reserve. However, the Executive Directors put the Board of Governors on notice that some recommendation for distribution of net income in the next fiscal year might well be forthcoming and that provision for remuneration was likely to be incorporated in the proposed amendments to the Articles.

By July 1968, when it was time for the Executive Board to agree on a recommendation for the disposition of the net income for 1967/68, the amendments to the Articles had been approved by the Board of Governors (although they had not yet entered into effect). The amendments contained both a provision for remuneration and a change in the provision for distribution of net income in order to assure payment of remuneration up to 2 per cent per annum. The rate of remuneration was to be the same as the return on holdings of SDRs, in order that super gold tranche positions would not receive a rate of interest higher than that paid on SDRs.

Accordingly, the Executive Board recommended that, at the 1968 Annual Meeting, the Board of Governors should approve a distribution to members with net creditor positions of part of the Fund's net income earned during the fiscal year ended April 30, 1968, the distribution to be at a rate of 1½ per cent on the amount by which 75 per cent of the member's quota exceeded the Fund's average holdings of the member's currency during the fiscal year. The Board of Governors approved this action on October 4, 1968, and thereafter distribution of $37.5 million was made to 33 members.

Mr. Mentré had proposed that the whole of the net income for 1967/68 should be transferred to the IDA as a fund for helping to stabilize prices of primary products, but most Executive Directors argued that the Fund had no such power.

In the fiscal year ended April 30, 1969 the Fund's net income rose to a record high figure of $70.8 million, and in July 1969 the Executive Board again recommended a distribution at the rate of 1½ per cent, which came to $31.9 million. Some Executive Directors favored a 2 per cent distribution. However, Messrs. Madan, Mansour, and Williams suggested that any excess funds the Fund might have should be used to assist developing members. Alternatively, the Fund's charges might be reduced.

Discussions Are Widened

The Executive Directors' next discussion of the distribution of income coincided with their first annual review of the Fund's reserves, a review which they had requested in 1969. When they met to consider income distribution in July 1970, they had before them a staff paper which discussed both the distribution of the net income for 1969/70 and the General and Special Reserves. By that time, too, the amendments to the Articles of Agreement, containing, inter alia, the new provisions for remuneration, had become effective and the Fund had paid remuneration at the rate of 1½ per cent per annum for the period July 28, 1969, the date the amendments took effect, through April 30, 1970. The staff proposed a distribution of the income for 1969/70 that would raise the total amount received by members on their net creditor positions during that fiscal year to an amount equivalent to 1½ per cent per annum on those positions, taking into account the remuneration already paid. Such a distribution would amount to $6.3 million and would be consistent with the rate of return of 1½ per cent per annum on net creditor positions, which had been the basis of the distribution of net income for the two previous fiscal years.

A number of members of the Executive Board—Messrs. Johnstone, Plescoff, Stone, Schleiminger, and de Vries—had difficulty with this proposal. They thought that the Fund's total reserves of $700 million and the current net income of $51 million permitted larger payments to members with net creditor positions. Mr. Johnstone said that members were becoming aware of the cost of making their currencies available to the Fund, and suggested that the return on net creditor positions be raised to 2 per cent. Mr. Stone agreed; in fact, he wanted to go even further by having an additional general distribution of net income to all members on the basis of quotas. In the latter idea he was supported by Mr. Mansour.

On the other hand, Messrs. Arriazu, Madan, Phillips O., Plescoff, Williams, and Yaméogo argued for transferring a portion of the Fund's net income to either the IDA or the World Bank. The General Counsel said that he did not believe that making a loan or grant to the IDA could be legally sustained under the Articles of Agreement, but that there might be legal authority for the Fund to invest in World Bank bonds. After discussion, the Executive Board decided to recommend to the Board of Governors a distribution of the net income for the fiscal year 1969/70 that would raise the total return to each member with a net creditor position to 2 per cent. On September 25, 1970 the Board of Governors approved this recommendation and $17.5 million was thereafter distributed to 34 members, 14 of which opted to receive SDRs instead of their own currency.

By mid-1971, when it was time for the next annual discussion of what part of the Fund's net income should be allocated to reserves and what part, if any, should be distributed, the Legal Department had prepared a paper directed to answering the questions whether the Fund had the legal authority (1) to make grants of its income to international development agencies and (2) to invest amounts equivalent to net income in securities issued by such agencies after these amounts had been placed in reserves. The conclusion was that the Fund could not make its assets available to another organization, but that the Fund could invest in the securities of other agencies or of members, subject to certain safeguards.

The staff's recommendation for the disposition of the net income of $46.4 million for the fiscal year 1970/71 took into account the views expressed by the Executive Directors on this subject in the previous year, and was for a distribution to members with net creditor positions that would raise the total amount received by those members from both remuneration and a distribution of net income to 2 per cent. Remuneration for 1970/71 had already been paid at the rate of 1½ per cent, amounting to $37.4 million. Another $12.5 million would be distributed, bringing the total to $49.9 million.

When the Executive Board considered this recommendation in August 1971, there had been a turnabout in the Fund's finances for the first time since 1956/57. A deficit for 1971/72 of about $22 million was envisaged. Most of the Executive Directors were fully in accord with the proposal to distribute net income at a rate of ½ of 1 per cent, so as to raise to 2 per cent the total amount received as remuneration and net income by members with net creditor positions. Mr. Brand (Australia) made a case for a general distribution to all members of $20–25 million, or 0.08 per cent of quotas, but most Executive Directors were reluctant to support such a distribution in view of the contemplated deficit. Mr. Suzuki and Mr. Lieftinck stated explicitly that they did not consider the Fund's reserves too high. As in past discussions of this subject, Mr. Lieftinck was more inclined to put the Fund's net income into reserves than to distribute it.

The Executive Board recommended distribution of net income for 1970/71 at the rate of ½ of 1 per cent.

In addition, the Executive Directors requested that the staff prepare a follow-up paper to the one just mentioned which would clarify the precise policy issues involved in the Fund's investing a portion of its net income in the securities of agencies financing economic development, such as the World Bank. But the Managing Director stressed that the Executive Directors were not asking the staff to make specific proposals; therefore, in the absence of further discussion by the Executive Board, the question about the Fund's investing in World Bank bonds or any similar arrangement would remain unanswered.

The Board of Governors approved the distribution and the Fund distributed $12.5 million to 39 members, of which $8.3 million was paid in SDRs to 21 members.

TURNABOUT IN FINANCIAL OPERATIONS

The seven chapters in this Part give the details of a broad story—that of a sharp U-turn in the Fund's financial operations and transactions. From 1966 to 1969 a number of factors made for an unprecedented use of the Fund's financial resources: a persistent U.S. deficit; a recurrent U.K. deficit; a French deficit in 1968–69; stagnation in the growth of traditional reserves with which to finance these deficits; and unfavorable trade situations for many developing countries. The resulting call on the Fund's resources reached $6 billion in the calendar years 1968 and 1969 as Belgium, Canada, Denmark, France, the Federal Republic of Germany, the United Kingdom, and the United States, among industrial members, all drew on the Fund. Furthermore, because gold tranche drawings had become automatic under the amended Articles of Agreement, because the compensatory financing facility had been extended and liberalized, and because a new buffer stock financing facility had been instituted, expectations were for still greater use of the Fund's financial resources.

In these circumstances, the Executive Directors, the management, and the staff up until 1970, even while proceeding with efforts to introduce and activate SDRs, sought ways in which to augment the Fund's regular financial resources. Additional currencies were made available for purchases. The General Arrangements to Borrow were renewed for a second time and made applicable to drawings for all participants, including any gold tranche drawings. The possibility of more bilateral borrowing from members was explored. Quotas were enlarged by an amount much greater than had been added by previous rounds.

In 1970 and 1971, however, the international financial picture was completely altered. Because of the huge official settlements deficits in the U.S. balance of payments in both years, international reserves had risen by exceptional and disquieting amounts, attaining annual increases unknown since World War II. These reserve increases were additional to the increases in global reserves through the allocations of SDRs at the beginning of 1970, 1971, and 1972 that had been planned earlier. Nearly all countries shared in tremendous increases in world reserves, although by no means evenly.

Consequently, except for drawings in 1971 by the United States, few members had recourse to the Fund after 1970. On the contrary, repurchases began to exceed purchases and the Fund repaid all of its indebtedness.

Until August 1971 the Fund had been able to run surpluses and to add to its reserves. Charges on the very large drawings of 1968 and 1969 had greatly augmented income, so that despite new operational expenditures, including the payment of remuneration on members' creditor positions, income considerably exceeded outgo. Reserves had grown to nearly $800 million by April 30, 1971. This solvent position led to decisions to distribute in 1968, 1969, and 1970 some of the Fund's net income to members with net creditor positions and to disinvest early in 1972 the gold that the Fund had, in more stringent times, placed in interest-bearing U.S. Government securities.

As drawings from the Fund diminished in 1970 and 1971, the Fund's income was reduced. The cash financing of a new building led in August 1971 to a budgetary deficit. At first the deficit seemed temporary. But by the end of 1971 it appeared likely that large deficits might emerge in at least the next two fiscal years, and it was clear that there had been a turnabout in the Fund's financial accounts. The renewed deficits in the Fund's accounts were to elicit some critical comment from monetary officials and the financial press, especially after 1971 when the Fund's deficits coincided with a decrease in its financial operations and its role in exchange rate adjustments, and when discussions about international monetary reform became stalemated. It may, therefore, be worthwhile to put together here the consequences for the Fund's expenditures and its income of a number of decisions taken in the period reviewed in this volume: Apart from the nonrecurrent expenditures in the early 1970s for the acquisition of a new building, higher built-in expenditures by the Fund had resulted from the provision of the amended Articles of Agreement that remuneration be paid to members with net creditor positions regardless of the Fund's current income. Even more crucial for the Fund's budgetary position were several decisions that made for relatively low income, such as decisions to retain the same low charges on purchases, to make gold tranche drawings available automatically and without a service charge, and to forgo the income received from investing gold in U.S. Government securities.

Table 13. Repurchases of Currencies, Fiscal Years Ended
April 30, 1966–71 [1]

(In millions of U.S. dollars)

Member	1966	1967	1968	1969	1970	1971	Total [2]
Afghanistan	1.1	4.4	4.3	2.7	10.2	3.3	26.0
Argentina	52.0	64.0	34.0	7.6	—	—	157.6
Belgium	—	—	—	—	32.9	—	32.9
Bolivia	2.5	2.5	—	8.0	—	1.0	14.0
Brazil	59.0	27.0	7.0	80.0	—	75.2	248.2
Burundi	2.0	3.2	5.2	2.2	0.2	2.2	15.0
Canada	—	—	—	64.8	—	—	64.8
Ceylon	11.2	7.5	—	10.0	20.6	27.2	76.5
Chile	41.5	38.5	26.0	28.0	55.0	31.2	220.2
Colombia	28.0	34.0	35.0	23.2	61.3	35.6	217.1
Costa Rica	2.5	2.5	2.8	9.8	8.8	3.0	29.4
Cyprus	—	1.2	1.2	0.2	0.4	0.8	3.8
Denmark	—	—	—	—	—	25.6	25.6
Dominican Republic	—	—	4.5	7.5	10.5	2.5	25.0
Ecuador	2.0	0.2	3.2	8.2	5.3	6.3	25.2
Egypt	34.5	16.0	53.2	24.0	20.0	7.5	155.2
El Salvador	—	—	5.0	—	15.0	7.3	27.3
Finland	—	—	—	89.7	—	—	89.7
France	—	—	—	—	—	246.3	246.3
Ghana	5.6	4.0	4.6	0.8	18.5	29.0	62.5
Guatemala	—	0.4	0.4	7.2	5.6	8.4	22.0
Guinea	—	—	—	—	0.5	0.5	1.0
Haiti	2.8	3.1	1.6	2.0	2.4	3.2	15.1
Honduras	2.5	5.2	2.2	2.5	—	—	12.4
Iceland	—	—	—	—	—	15.0	15.0
India	75.0	57.5	57.5	128.0	187.0	135.0	640.0
Indonesia	•	—	16.3	27.4	13.4	—	57.1
Iran	3.5	—	14.0	15.3	—	—	32.8
Iraq	—	—	40.0	—	—	—	40.0
Ireland	—	1.3	8.7	—	—	—	10.0
Jamaica	—	—[3]	—	—	—[3]	0.1	0.1
Jordan	—[3]	—[3]	—	0.3	—	—	0.3
Kenya	—	—	—	—	0.9	3.0	3.9
Korea	—	—	—	—	10.7	1.8	12.5
Lesotho	•	•	—	—	0.5	—	0.5
Liberia	—	5.0	3.2	4.4	4.6	4.1	21.3
Malaysia	—[3]	—	—[3]	—	—	—	—[3]
Mali	—	—	3.0	5.0	3.0	3.0	14.0
Mauritius	•	•	—	—	—	4.0	4.0
Morocco	5.9	—	—	4.8	2.4	14.2	27.3
Nepal	—	—	—	1.5	—[3]	—[3]	1.5
New Zealand	—	—	35.0	64.3	20.6	39.2	159.1
Nicaragua	—[3]	5.6	5.6	—	16.3	12.0	39.5
Nigeria	—	—	—	3.1	—	—	3.1
Pakistan	—	1.9	1.9	15.9	32.4	10.9	63.0

Table 13 (concluded). Repurchases of Currencies, Fiscal Years Ended
April 30, 1966–71 [1]

(In millions of U.S. dollars)

Member	1966	1967	1968	1969	1970	1971	Total [2]
Panama	—	—	0.1	0.8	3.2	1.4	5.5
Paraguay	0.4	—	—	—	—	—	0.4
Peru	—	—	—	42.4	11.1	21.3	74.8
Philippines	10.5	10.8	—	—	—	5.5	26.8
Rwanda	—	—	3.0	3.0	—	1.0	7.0
Sierra Leone	—	—	—	—	3.5	3.4	6.9
Somalia	—[3]	—	8.7	8.3	—	1.9	18.9
South Africa	—	—	—	—	50.0	—	50.0
Spain	—	—	—	—	3.7	48.7	52.4
Sudan	2.5	3.1	8.6	6.8	5.6	9.1	35.7
Swaziland	•	•	•	—	1.0	—	1.0
Syrian Arab Republic	7.3	3.2	6.4	12.4	2.5	2.4	34.2
Tanzania	—	—	0.1	0.2	0.1	—	0.4
Trinidad and Tobago	—	—	—	—	1.0	3.8	4.8
Tunisia	0.2	0.5	11.8	6.6	5.8	12.9	37.8
Turkey	21.5	18.0	19.1	−3.1[4]	24.5	24.0	104.0
Uganda	—	—	—	0.4	—	—	0.4
United Kingdom	—	—	654.8	507.5	934.2	684.8	2,781.3
United States	—	—	—	284.2	—	—	284.2
Uruguay	2.0	8.0	5.0	—	14.5	33.3	62.8
Yugoslavia	30.0	11.5	11.5	24.0	47.8	42.8	167.6
Zaïre	—	—	8.1	—	—[3]	—	8.1
Zambia	—	—	3.0	0.2	3.4	2.6	9.2
Total [2]	406.0	340.1	1,115.5	1,542.3	1,670.7	1,656.9	6,731.5

[1] A dot (•) indicates that the country was not a member at the time; a dash (—) indicates that no repurchases were made.

[2] Components may not add to totals because of rounding of figures for individual members.

[3] Less than $50,000.

[4] Reversal of part of the amount repurchased in 1967/68, which was included among repurchase data for that year.

Table 14. Income and Expenditure of Fund, Fiscal Years Ended April 30, 1966–71

(In millions of U.S. dollars)

	1966	1967	1968	1969	1970	1971
Operational income						
Service and stand-by charges, etc.	15.6	7.1	7.4	14.6	13.0	3.2
Charges on balances in excess of quotas	65.7	82.5	82.0	107.4	124.7	128.1
Interest on holdings of SDRs	—	—	—	—	0.4	4.3
Total operational income [1]	81.3	89.6	89.4	122.0	138.1	135.6
Deduct: operational expenditure						
Remuneration	—	—	—	—	27.2	37.4
Other	16.1	17.8	11.9	22.3	19.1	11.8
Net operational income	65.2	71.8	77.5	99.7	91.8	86.3
Budgetary expenditure [2]	15.0	18.1	21.3	24.4	28.6	33.2
Deduct: expenses assessed participants for cost of operating the Special Drawing Account	—	—	—	—	0.9	0.9
Fixed property expenditure (building costs)	5.7	3.3	0.5	4.5	6.5	7.5
Total budgetary and fixed property expenditure	20.7	21.4	21.8	28.9	34.2	39.9
Net income [3]	44.5	50.4	55.7	70.8	57.6	46.4

[1] Excludes income from investments transferred to the Special Reserve.

[2] The composition of the administrative budget can be found in the appendices of the Annual Reports.

[3] Components may not add to totals because of rounding.

PART FOUR

Gold

"Governors are in agreement that
improvement or reform of the
international monetary system will
require the study of all aspects of the
system, including the roles of reserve
currencies, gold, and special drawing
rights."

—PIERRE-PAUL SCHWEITZER, Managing Director,
addressing the Twenty-Sixth Annual Meeting
of the Board of Governors on October 1, 1971.

CHAPTER

20

Gold: New Problems,
New Policies

*I*N A PERIOD OVERFLOWING with international monetary events that
made front-page news, some of the most exciting occurrences involved gold.
For the first time since the founding of the Fund the subject of gold became of
intense interest to monetary officials and even a source of contention among
them. We have already seen in Part One that concern about the position of
gold in the international monetary system delayed the advent of SDRs. After
1967, eruptions in exchange and gold markets began to take place frequently
and discussions about gold became more and more heated. In fact, by the end
of the period covered here, it had become almost impossible to mention gold
without arousing emotion.

This chapter discusses the dramatic developments involving gold that
occurred prior to August 15, 1971. What took place from August 15 to the
end of 1971, including the developments relating to gold, is described in
Chapters 26 and 27.

CALM BEFORE THE STORM: 1965

By 1965 a number of signs of impending trouble over gold already loomed
on the horizon. It was becoming increasingly hard to accommodate the growing
private demand for gold with the desire of national monetary authorities to
build up their official gold holdings. Trends that were to become much more
pronounced could already be discerned. Industrial demand for gold was rising
swiftly because of advances in technology. Defense and aerospace industries
were finding new uses for gold, and so was the medical profession. Higher
incomes throughout the world also increased the demand for gold. The popu-
larity of gold jewelry, for instance, was spreading. In times of inflation, gold
was a relatively cheap metal, its price having remained fixed, for monetary

purposes, at $35 an ounce since the early 1930s.[1] Superimposed on these demands for gold was the traditional hoarding of gold by those who favored keeping their savings in that form. All in all, between 1951 and 1965 private users took some $12 billion of gold off the market.

On the other hand, for several years gold production had not been expanding much, if at all. In 1965 the gold output of the world (excluding that of nonmembers of the Fund) was about $1.45 billion. Although this was the highest annual amount ever recorded, the long-run outlook for increases in the supply of newly mined gold was uncertain. Old mines were being worked out and there were few new gold strikes. In fact, after 1965 the volume of gold production remained relatively stable. The U.S.S.R. at times augmented the gold supplies of the Western world by selling gold to pay for imports, mostly of grain, but these sales did not occur with any regularity.

As a consequence of an expanding private demand impinging on a relatively constant supply, the amount of gold flowing into official reserves was gradually diminishing. As we have seen in Part One, the decline in the gold holdings of national monetary authorities had raised the question whether the U.S. authorities would continue to make the dollar convertible into gold, and monetary officials had begun to fear that the narrowing of the gold base in the total of international reserves might constrict the growth of world liquidity.

The U.S. Treasury, through the Federal Reserve Bank of New York as its fiscal agent, continued to stand ready to buy gold at a price of $34.9125 an ounce and to sell gold for official monetary purposes at $35.0875 an ounce. But this policy was becoming costly. During 1965 the Treasury sold $1.5 billion to foreign countries and international institutions and another $118 million domestically for industrial, professional, and artistic uses. This decrease in the U.S. gold stock was much larger than the decreases of earlier years, and brought U.S. gold reserves down to $14.1 billion.

The Gold Pool, which had been formed in 1961 by the central banks of Belgium, France, the Federal Republic of Germany, Italy, the Netherlands, Switzerland, the United Kingdom, and the United States, continued successfully to intervene in the London gold market to keep the price of gold in that market at the officially fixed level. Because of the operations of the Gold Pool, the London market had become the leading international market for gold bullion. Consequently, prices for gold in other important markets, such as those in Paris and Zürich, or in Beirut, Bombay, or Hong Kong, were kept in line with the fixed price in London as long as there were no restrictions on the import or export of gold between these markets. The official price for gold was thus held fairly constant throughout the world, and without any loss of gold reserves by the countries operating the Gold Pool. On the contrary, on balance the operations involved some acquisition of gold for the reserves of those countries.

---

[1] An ounce of gold, according to the Fund's practice at the end of 1971, meant a troy ounce of 31.1034768 grams of fine gold.

Among private traders, the counterpart of official concerns in the mid-1960s with regard to world liquidity took the form of speculation on the official price of gold. By 1966, traders were beginning to think seriously that the official price of gold might be raised, and private demand for gold, especially for hoarding, started to rise appreciably. On December 23, 1966, the price of gold in the London market, which was quoted in sterling, reached the equivalent of $35.19¾ an ounce, the highest in five years. In January 1967, after some monetary officials had voiced their support for a rise in the official gold price, the demand for gold in the world's main markets became heavy. However, when the U.S. Treasury issued a strong statement rejecting any change in the official price, pressure on gold prices subsided quickly and remained light for several months thereafter.

GOLD POOL ABOLISHED

In mid-October 1967 an intense speculative crisis in gold markets erupted. In effect, a flight into gold took place because of expectations that there would be a change in the exchange rates of major currencies. Then, the actual devaluation of sterling on November 18, 1967 brought about widespread anticipations that the official price for gold would shortly be raised. A virtual gold rush was on.

Through the operations of the Gold Pool the price in the London market was being kept below $35.20 an ounce, but the prevention of premium gold prices through the sale of gold from the reserves of the seven participating countries was becoming extremely costly. (France was not active in the Gold Pool after June 1967.) The official gold stocks of all national authorities declined during 1967 by the equivalent of $1,580 million; the gold losses of the U.S. Treasury alone totaled over $1 billion. The management of the Fund was already cognizant of the fact that a major international crisis concerning gold was likely to develop, and that, within 3 to 12 months, two gold markets might have to be set up.

In the early months of 1968 the private demand for gold became even stronger. To help keep the price down, the members of the Gold Pool sold on a massive scale to the private market. Such sales came to $1.7 billion for the first quarter of 1968 and resulted in a further drop of $1.4 billion in official stocks of monetary gold. The U.S. Treasury alone sold $1.3 billion of gold, surpassing its sales for the entire year of 1967.

The Governors of the central banks of the participants in the Gold Pool, meeting at the BIS in Basle on March 10, 1968, announced that the seven central banks contributing to that Pool would continue their support in the Pool based on the fixed price of $35 an ounce. But this did not allay the demand for gold. On the contrary, it rose to panic proportions, and on March 15, 1968 a decision was made to close the London gold market, thus stopping the drain on official monetary reserves.

In this atmosphere of emergency, the Governors of the central banks of the participants in the Gold Pool examined their operations at a specially called meeting in Washington on March 16 and 17, 1968 and decided to bring the Gold Pool arrangements to an end. In a communiqué following the meeting, they announced that the U.S. Government would continue to buy and sell gold at $35 an ounce but only in transactions with monetary authorities. In effect, there was to be no change in the official price of gold. Furthermore, gold from official reserves would henceforth be used only for transfers among monetary authorities: no longer would gold from official reserves be supplied to the London market or to any other gold market.

The Governors also agreed that, as the existing stock of monetary gold was sufficient in view of the prospective establishment of the Fund's facility for special drawing rights, it was no longer necessary to buy gold from the market. Finally, they agreed that they would not sell gold to monetary authorities to replace any that had been sold in private markets.

The policies of the Fund toward the world's markets for gold had for many years reflected concern about the possible consequences of activity in gold markets on exchange rate stability, one of the Fund's primary objectives. The Fund had sought to proscribe transactions in gold at premium prices because such transactions might undermine official parities. And it had endeavored to channel maximum amounts of gold into members' official reserves; increases in reserves would strengthen members' means of supporting their parities.

On the occasion of the ending of the Gold Pool the Managing Director, who had attended the March meeting in Washington of the Governors of the central banks of the seven participating countries, issued a personal statement expressing his support for their actions and urging other members of the Fund to cooperate with them. He regarded the decision to conserve monetary gold as readily understandable and stressed that the countries that had participated in the Gold Pool were still maintaining the par values of their currencies, a consideration of importance to the Fund.

When Mr. Schweitzer notified the Executive Directors, in advance, of the statement he was planning to make, Mr. Plescoff (France) took some exception to it. He did not want the Fund to appear to be endorsing the operations of the Gold Pool, and, further, he questioned whether the U.S. authorities were any longer fulfilling their obligations under Article IV, Section 4 (b), of the Fund Agreement. The General Counsel replied that the primary obligation of the member under Article IV, Section 4 (b), was that regarding the exchange rate, and that the member could carry out this requirement in either of two ways. The United States was fulfilling that obligation, although it might no longer be fulfilling the obligation specified in the rest of Article IV, Section 4 (b). In any event, the principal obligation concerning exchange rates and gold was under Article VIII, Section 4, which required a member to convert balances of its currency tendered to it by the monetary authorities of other members. The United States was continuing to honor this commitment.

TWO-TIER GOLD MARKET

The immediate effect of the actions of the Governors of the central banks of the participants in the Gold Pool on March 16 and 17, 1968 was the emergence of two markets for gold. The first market was for official transactions only, and the price was to be maintained at $35 an ounce. The second was for private transactions, and the price was to be freely determined by demand and supply. This dual market was a device for permitting the simultaneous retention of an official price for monetary gold and a higher price for nonmonetary gold.

At the outset it was not at all certain how the private market would develop. As the dual market was being announced, the London market remained closed. Preparatory to the latter's reopening, the Bank of England issued revised instructions for gold marketing operations. Forward transactions could take place only with the prior permission of the Bank of England, and authorized banks would not be permitted to finance purchases of gold by nonresidents by lending foreign currency or by accepting gold as collateral for loans in foreign currency. Gold dealers announced that, henceforth, the price of gold in the London market would be fixed twice daily, once at the traditional time of 10:30 A.M. and again at 3:00 P.M., and would be quoted in terms of U.S. dollars.

The U.S. Treasury announced that it would no longer buy gold from any private source nor would it sell gold to licensed domestic industrial and artistic users. These consumers would have to satisfy their requirements at home or abroad at the free market price within the limits of their licenses. A number of banks and commodity firms obtained licenses to acquire gold from private sources for resale to licensed industrial users and for export to foreign buyers. These authorized gold dealers began to quote various competitive daily prices based on the costs involved in obtaining gold.

A number of central banks took actions consonant with the decision of the central banks of the former Gold Pool participants. They announced that they, too, would not buy or sell gold in the free market and began to make changes in their regulations and gold marketing procedures that effectively separated their official gold transactions from other gold transactions.

Prices Up, Then Down

When gold markets reopened, prices in private markets tended to move upward. Initially, in the two weeks from mid-March to April 1, 1968, while the London market was still closed, prices in the private markets in Zürich and

Paris rose to about $40 an ounce. On April 1 the first price fixed by the five bullion brokers in the reopened London market was $38 an ounce, a premium of almost 9 per cent above the official price. By May 21, as both the French franc and sterling came under pressure, the price of gold in the London market reached $42.60 an ounce. As Mr. Schweitzer remarked at the Twenty-Third Annual Meeting, the prices of gold in private markets had since March been consistently higher than the official price, for the most part by 10 to 15 per cent.[2]

After October 1968 prices in private gold markets surged upward even more sharply. Expectations in October–November 1968 and again in February–March 1969 of changes in the exchange rates for the French franc and the deutsche mark produced general activity in the major gold markets. At times the speculative buying of gold was large. By March 1969 the price in London had risen to $43.825 an ounce.

Strong demand was not the only reason for this rise in the free market prices for gold. Supply was unduly low because only a comparatively small amount of newly mined gold was being placed on the private market. South Africa, in the process of negotiations with the U.S. Government and with the Fund about official outlets for its gold (see below), had hung back from supplying the private markets. As a result, demand was being met mainly from stocks that private investors had accumulated during the crises of November 1967 and March 1968. These stocks had been estimated as of mid-March 1968 at almost 90 million ounces—the equivalent of over $3 billion at $35 an ounce and, of course, more than that at free market prices.

In the second half of 1969, however, gold prices in free markets turned around drastically, and in December 1969 prices in London fell back to the official price of $35 an ounce. In January 1970 they dropped even lower but then moved fairly closely around the official price throughout 1970 and the first several months of 1971. Declines in the prices of gold in the London market in the second half of 1969 and the continued low prices through early 1971 were paralleled by corresponding movements in prices in other gold markets.

There were several reasons for the decline in gold prices after the middle of 1969. Although industrial and artistic demand for gold continued to expand rapidly—from about 48 per cent of current production in 1965 to about 63 per cent in 1968—the rate of growth slowed somewhat in 1969. But what was more important was that gold hoarding fell to its lowest point in more than a decade. There had been a change in expectations concerning a possible revaluation of the official price of gold: it appeared possible that monetary authorities could now maintain the official price of $35 an ounce. This change in expectations was, to some extent, a consequence of the greater calm in exchange markets once the exchange rates for the French franc and the deutsche mark had been

---

[2] Opening Address by the Managing Director, *Summary Proceedings, 1968*, p. 20.

altered in August and October 1969. It also reflected the prospective activation of SDRs that had been agreed upon by the Board of Governors in September 1969. The activation of SDRs had dispelled fears of a shortage of world reserves and, it was believed at the time, ensured that any large additions to reserves would be in the form of an asset similar to gold rather than in any national currency. Finally, declines in gold prices reflected the agreement between South Africa and the Fund at the end of 1969 that South Africa would sell gold to the Fund, thus increasing the amount of gold held by monetary authorities.

Consequently, by the end of 1969 it appeared that the agreement made in March 1968 by the participants in the Gold Pool not to sell gold to the private market and to let the price of gold for nonmonetary transactions fluctuate in response to private demand and supply had effectively stopped the drain of gold from monetary stocks and had stabilized the price.

Attitudes Toward the New Arrangements

By the time of the 1968 Annual Meeting, some six months after the two-tier market for gold had been introduced, it was evident that the new procedures had been generally accepted. Canada, for instance, a producer of gold that had not been a participant in the Gold Pool or in the Washington meeting of March 16 and 17 earlier in the year, had associated itself with the arrangements agreed upon at that meeting, and its newly mined gold was being channeled into the private markets. Mr. Edgar J. Benson (Canada) observed that "the two-tier gold system appears to have worked out rather well, and to have introduced a greater degree of realism in attitudes toward gold." [3]

Mr. Fowler, making the last of four appearances at the Annual Meetings as Governor for the United States, stated again the insistence of the U.S. authorities on keeping the official price of gold unchanged. Referring the Governors to a speech that he had made in the previous week, setting forth in detail the gold policies of the United States and their relation to the stability of the international monetary system, Mr. Fowler repeated the salient points. He said, in part:

> The international monetary system has a vital stake in maintaining the value of gold in existing monetary reserves at $35 an ounce—neither less nor more. This provides assurance both to the countries who hold a large proportion of their reserves in gold and to those who hold a small proportion of their reserves in gold. It is clearly within the capabilities of the system to provide such an assurance, and the United States believes it is important to the stability of the system that this be done. [4]

---

[3] Statement by the Governor of the Fund and the World Bank for Canada, *Summary Proceedings, 1968*, p. 44.

[4] Statement by the Governor of the Fund and the World Bank for the United States, *Summary Proceedings, 1968*, p. 53.

Recognizing that certain problems still existed—an obvious reference to the unsettled question of what should be done about South Africa's newly mined gold—Mr. Fowler stressed that any solution should strengthen and not weaken the two-tier system.

Mr. Jenkins (United Kingdom) supported the U.S. position. It was, he said, the firm view of the United Kingdom that the official price of gold should remain unchanged at $35 an ounce. To this end, Mr. Jenkins thought that the two-tier market had "succeeded very well—perhaps surprisingly well" and that the decision bringing about these arrangements had been "a wise one." [5]

Mr. Colombo (Italy) also advocated maintenance of the two-tier gold system as long as the metal remained the main component of reserves. He expressed his reasoning, based on minimizing the impact of speculation on official gold holdings, as follows:

> It has been fully proven that the communication between commercial and monetary sectors is a disequilibrating factor and that free gold markets do not play any useful role in the monetary system. Thus we succeed in avoiding a situation in which conversion of national currencies into gold by private operators reduces existing official gold holdings.[6]

The new arrangements for gold seemed to be a success. These speeches by the Governors strongly suggested that they attached crucial importance to retaining gold as a principal element, if not the fulcrum, of the international monetary system. Gold was not being "demonetized."

Nevertheless, some Governors expressed serious concern about what would happen to gold in the future. Mr. Benito Raúl Losada (Venezuela), addressing the meeting on behalf of Argentina, Bolivia, Brazil, Chile, Colombia, Costa Rica, the Dominican Republic, Ecuador, El Salvador, Guatemala, Haiti, Honduras, Mexico, Nicaragua, Panama, Paraguay, Peru, the Philippines, Uruguay, and Venezuela, as had been prearranged by the Latin American Governors and the Governor for the Philippines in an effort to reduce the number of individual speeches, urged the Fund to study the prospects for gold:

> The abandonment of the policy of supporting the price of gold in the free market and the introduction of the two-tier price system have given rise to fresh apprehension regarding the future role of gold in the functioning of the gold exchange standard system. Our countries believe that, whatever the ultimate fate of gold may be as a monetary standard, it will continue to play an important role for many years to come. We therefore consider it necessary that a study be undertaken in the International Monetary Fund of the collective measures that will prove most effective in maintaining an orderly situation in the gold markets, a primary aim being to obviate speculation in the free market.[7]

---

[5] Statement by the Governor of the Fund for the United Kingdom, *Summary Proceedings, 1968*, pp. 128–29.

[6] Statement by the Governor of the Fund for Italy, *Summary Proceedings, 1968*, p. 85.

[7] Statement by the Governor of the Fund for Venezuela, *Summary Proceedings, 1968*, p. 106.

In addition, as explained in the next section, a number of Governors urged an early solution to the problem of South Africa's gold.

By the Twenty-Fourth Annual Meeting, held from September 29 to October 3, 1969 in Washington, Mr. Schweitzer was able to draw attention to the stability of the gold market even amidst the many exchange crises that occurred between May 1968 and September 1969. The gold arrangements had, he noted, "proved to be workable." [8] But doubts that gold would have a secure role in the international monetary system in the future were being expressed. Mr. Colombo believed that "after the Washington agreement of March 1968—the success of which can hardly be put in doubt today—it is a certainty that in the future gold will play only a limited role in the system." [9]

The Governor who most stressed that the world was continuing "to recognize the pivotal role of gold in the international monetary system" was Mr. Nicolaas Diederichs (South Africa). He pointed not only to the Governors' speeches at the Annual Meeting the previous year but to the subsequent reluctance of monetary authorities to deplete their gold holdings and even their eagerness to augment them. These actions gave eloquent testimony, he thought, to their confidence in gold.[10] Mr. Diederichs spoke as the problem raised by the two-tier gold market for South Africa's gold was just about to be solved. We now turn to a discussion of this problem.

SOUTH AFRICAN GOLD: THE PROBLEM

Following the establishment of a two-tier gold market in March 1968, another chapter was written in the story of the Fund's relations with South Africa in the matter of gold.[11] With two gold markets in existence, there remained unresolved this question: In which of these two markets would newly mined gold be sold?

The answer was vital for South Africa. That member produced over $1 billion of newly mined gold each year, more than two thirds of the Western world's output. The South African authorities, eager to restore the gold component of international liquidity, took the view that there should be a constant channeling of additional gold into official monetary reserves and that therefore they should be able to sell at least some of their gold to monetary authorities. They also took the view that they had a right under the Articles of Agreement to sell gold to the Fund.

---

[8] Opening Address by the Managing Director, *Summary Proceedings, 1969*, p. 9.

[9] Statement by the Governor of the Fund for Italy, *Summary Proceedings, 1969*, p. 65.

[10] Statement by the Governor of the Fund and the World Bank for South Africa, *Summary Proceedings, 1969*, p. 121.

[11] For earlier events, see *History, 1945–65*, Vol. II, Chap. 8.

On June 14, 1968, just three months after the dual market for gold came into being, the South African authorities brought this issue to a test by asking the Fund if they could purchase sterling in the amount of £14.5 million ($34.8 million) in exchange for gold.

The Managing Director took the position that the Fund was legally obliged to comply. The issue proved to be much less simple than that, however. The informal opinions expressed by individual Executive Directors to the Managing Director, the views voiced by the Governors of the central banks at their monthly meetings at the BIS in Basle, any number of bilateral discussions between the monetary authorities of the United States and European countries with the monetary authorities of South Africa, and leaks to the press, all made it clear that there was no meeting of minds about what policy should be followed for purchases of gold from South Africa by central banks.

The U.S. monetary authorities felt strongly that countries should not acquire any more official reserves of gold, at least for the time being. These authorities were eager to maintain the official price of gold at $35 an ounce. To that end, they preferred that additional gold supplies be diverted into the free market to prevent the price there from rising too far above the official price. In fact, the U.S. Treasury refused to buy any gold from South Africa as long as the free market price was above $35 an ounce.

Some of the Governors of European central banks favored augmenting official monetary reserves. But they did not think that individual central banks ought to be buying gold for their own monetary reserves. Therefore, they considered it desirable for the Fund to increase international official holdings of gold by purchasing gold from South Africa.

Because of this lack of agreement, consideration by the Executive Board of South Africa's request to buy sterling in exchange for gold was postponed, despite the appeal of Mr. Stone (Australia) that it be treated with the same speed as any other request to purchase currency. It was of no help to Mr. Stone's position that South Africa had a sizable surplus in its balance of payments at the time. Executive Board consideration was at first postponed for a few days, then for a week. On June 24, 1968 Mr. Stone took the unusual measure of calling for a vote. The Executive Directors cast 177,717 votes (75.41 per cent of the total voting power) in favor of a decision to defer action. On September 6, 1968, just before the Annual Meeting, Mr. Stone again tried to get Executive Board consideration of South Africa's request, but once more most of the Executive Directors favored postponement.

The meeting of the Executive Board early in September revealed some of the emotion engendered by the issue. Mr. Dale (United States) stated the U.S. view that there was no legal obligation for the Fund and that the question whether the Fund should agree to purchase gold offered to it by a member was a matter of policy. The disposition of this request, and of the question in general, involved important and far-reaching implications for the international monetary system. It appeared wise, therefore, to hold quiet and informal discussions to reconcile differing viewpoints. The forthcoming Annual Meeting offered a good opportunity for such discussion. On the other hand, Mr. de Maulde (France), reiterating the views expressed earlier by Mr. Plescoff, insisted that the South African request should immediately be approved for legal reasons. The Articles of Agreement had been openly breached and the proper functioning of the Fund was endangered. Mr. Diz (Argentina) and Mr. Phillips O. (Mexico), observing the importance of any decision for the role of gold in the monetary system, regretted that the decision on South Africa's request was likely to be taken outside the Executive Board.

A few weeks later, during the 1968 Annual Meeting, the Managing Director held a number of informal meetings with Governors to get agreement on what policy the Fund should develop for purchases of gold from members. But no consensus was reached. Meanwhile, Mr. Diederichs appealed publicly to the other Governors not to regard the two-tier system for gold as a rigorous "two-circuit" system. By this he meant a sealing off of the existing stocks of monetary gold from other gold, which encompassed much more than allowing the private market price for gold to rise above the official price. The two-tier system, he said, at least had the advantage of checking the drain on stocks of monetary gold. The two-circuit system, however, stopped new inflows into monetary gold holdings and hence aggravated the world's financial problems.[12]

His plea for some answer to South Africa's question about the sale of its gold was supported by the Governors for Canada and the Federal Republic of Germany,[13] but special support came from Mr. Ortoli (France). He urged the Governors to take action:

> The provisions of the Articles are clear on this point, and I feel that they must be implemented as drafted. . . . In the absence of a jurisdictional institution—I would say even because of that absence—the Board of Executive Directors and the Board of Governors must provide fast, objective, and legally sound interpretation of the Articles, without letting considerations of opportunity or convenience interfere in the application of a text that constitutes an international convention. France's position in this field finds its justification in the role of gold as the basis of the international monetary system.[14]

By the time of the 1969 Annual Meeting a decision had still not been reached. But a solution was imminent. South Africa was more eager than ever for a solution since its imports had gone up sharply and it was incurring fairly severe payments deficits. Lengthy and frequent bilateral discussions between the monetary authorities of South Africa and those of the United States had

---

[12] Statement by the Governor of the Fund and the World Bank for South Africa, *Summary Proceedings, 1968,* pp. 195–200.

[13] Statements by the Governor of the Fund and the World Bank for Canada and the Governor of the World Bank for the Federal Republic of Germany, *Summary Proceedings, 1968,* pp. 44 and 66.

[14] Statement by the Governor of the World Bank for France, *Summary Proceedings, 1968,* p. 73.

provided the ingredients of a compromise. The U.S. authorities were coming around to the view that, if the free market price should fall to $35 an ounce, the Fund, but not the monetary authorities of individual countries, might purchase gold from South Africa. Another part of the emerging U.S. view was that, should South Africa have a balance of payments surplus, the authorities might save current gold production for sale to the Fund at a later time when the country had a deficit. The evolving compromise seemed academic, however: neither member actually expected gold prices in the free market to fall back to $35 an ounce.

Solution Found

Contrary to expectation, at the end of 1969, as we have noted above, free market prices of gold did drop to the official price. Agreement between the United States and South Africa became a reality. Accordingly, Mr. Diederichs, on December 23, 1969, and Mr. Paul A. Volcker, Acting Secretary of the U.S. Treasury, on December 24, 1969, wrote to Mr. Schweitzer indicating the basis of their agreement. South Africa would offer gold to the Fund in certain quantities in specified situations. The United States would support the Fund's purchases of gold offered by South Africa on these terms.

A basis had been laid for a decision by the Fund. On December 30, 1969 the Executive Board took a decision to the effect that, without prejudice to the determination of the legal position under the Articles as to whether South Africa had a right to sell gold to the Fund and whether the Fund was obliged to comply, the Fund would buy gold whenever South Africa offered it to the Fund and indicated that the offer was in accordance with the policy detailed in Mr. Diederichs' letter.[15] This policy specified the following situations in which South Africa might offer gold to the Fund and in what quantities:

First, South Africa might sell gold to the Fund when the market price fell to $35 an ounce or below, in amounts necessary to meet South Africa's current foreign exchange needs for the period involved.

Second, South Africa might offer gold for sale to the Fund regardless of the price in the private market, to the extent that South Africa had a need for foreign exchange over a semiannual period beyond the need that could be satisfied by the sale of all of its current production of newly mined gold in the private market.

Third, South Africa might offer to sell up to $35 million of gold to the Fund in each quarter beginning January 1, 1970 from the stock of gold it had held on March 17, 1968 (with certain specified reductions from that stock). As an implementation of this provision it had been understood, and the Executive Board took a further decision to this effect, that the Fund would agree to

---

[15] E.B. Decision No. 2914-(69/127), December 30, 1969. The decision and the letters from Messrs. Diederichs and Volcker are reproduced in Vol. II below, pp. 203–206.

purchase the gold from South Africa in return for sterling as South Africa had requested in June 1968.

A charge of ¼ of 1 per cent was to be levied by the Fund on its purchases of gold from South Africa, in accordance with the Fund's Rules and Regulations.[16]

The procedure to be followed for these purchases was to be similar to that for gold tranche purchases.

South Africa was to continue to use gold for other Fund transactions— for example, to pay charges, to repurchase Fund holdings of South African rand, or to pay the gold subscription arising from any increase in South Africa's quota. Furthermore, in connection with the newly introduced SDRs, South Africa was to be permitted to sell gold to the Fund to obtain currency when it was designated to receive SDRs from another participant in the Special Drawing Account. In a related Executive Board decision, the handling charges and costs ordinarily collected for a sale of gold to the Fund were waived for sales by a participant designated to receive SDRs that wished to obtain currency to provide to the user of SDRs. Rand drawn from the Fund by other members were also generally to be converted into gold when rand were included in drawings under normal Fund procedures. These Fund-related transactions, which might take place without regard to the market price of gold, were to be reflected in changes in the composition of South Africa's reserves but were not to affect the volume of sales of newly mined gold in the market.

South Africa, in return, agreed to sell its current production of newly mined gold in an orderly manner on the private market to the full extent of its current payments needs. New production in excess of those needs during a semiannual period might be added to South Africa's reserves. The South African authorities also agreed that they would, as a matter of practice, normally offer gold for official reserves only to the Fund, that is, not to central banks.

The letter to Mr. Schweitzer from Mr. Volcker had said that the United States was prepared to support decisions of the Fund to purchase gold from South Africa on these conditions, provided that there was an understanding among the Fund's members generally that they would not initiate official gold purchases directly from South Africa.

The decision authorizing the Fund to buy gold from South Africa was to be reviewed whenever requested because of a major change in circumstances, and in any event after five years. Meanwhile, gold sold to the Fund might be used by it to replenish its holdings of member currencies.

As they took these decisions, the Executive Directors indicated that they welcomed this solution as a pragmatic way to handle the problem of South Africa's newly mined gold within the two-tier gold marketing system, without

---

[16] E.B. Decision No. 2916-(69/127), December 30, 1969; Vol. II below, p. 207.

the need to agree on the much more controversial issue relating to the status of gold in the international monetary system. Elaborating on the views expressed by Mr. Diederichs at the 1968 and 1969 Annual Meetings, Mr. de Kock (South Africa), without mentioning individual country positions, reiterated that there had been divergent interpretations of the two-tier gold marketing arrangement. Some monetary officials, favoring the early if not immediate demonetization of gold, had regarded the two-tier arrangement as a strict two-circuit system that neither provided a floor price for gold nor allowed any newly mined gold to enter official monetary reserves. Diametrically opposed were those monetary authorities who desired an immediate and substantial increase in the price of gold; they viewed the two-tier arrangement as an artificial and temporary gimmick, which could not provide a lasting solution to the problem of gold and which merely reflected the need for an upward adjustment in the official price.

Between these two groups was a growing majority who attached importance to the monetary role of gold at its official price ($35 an ounce at the time). In general they interpreted the two-tier system as a workable one, which promoted international monetary stability without the need to alter the official price of gold but which would not necessitate the sharp division of newly mined gold into two different circuits. This position did not imply the demonetization of gold. Mr. de Kock considered the Fund's decision to be in line with this position: the two-tier system was maintained but the important part played by gold in the monetary system was also reaffirmed.

Mr. Dale emphasized that the U.S. authorities felt strongly about including in the decision a provision that the Fund's members did not intend to initiate official gold purchases directly from South Africa. The Fund was the channel by which South African gold was to enter the monetary holdings of other members. The effect of the decision, Mr. Dale went on, would not be to provide a floor under the private market price for gold directly, although it would serve to provide a floor under the price at which South Africa would sell its new gold production. The institution of the two-tier system had not resolved the question of official purchases of gold from the market if the market price dropped below $35 an ounce. The U.S. authorities favored the abstention of monetary authorities from the market. According to Mr. de Kock, the South African authorities would accept this point, in practice, although they did not agree in principle.

Several Executive Directors expressed the concurrence of their authorities with the understandings on which the decision was based. It was a practical solution to a problem that had existed for a long time. As Mr. Palamenghi-Crispi (Italy) expressed it, the decision was a logical follow-up to the institution of the two-tier market for gold in March 1968. The quasi-monopoly involved for the Fund in respect of gold purchases from South Africa was not only useful but even necessary for the orderly working of the international monetary system.

Mr. Roelandts (Belgium) stressed that the decision would strengthen the role of the Fund in connection with gold transactions and, together with the activation of SDRs that was about to take place, would turn the Fund into a real central bank. Some Executive Directors commented that, as the Fund would be virtually the sole official buyer of gold from South Africa, they wanted to re-examine the Fund's policy with regard to the selling of its own gold stocks to national monetary authorities when it replenished its currency holdings.

FUND GOLD PURCHASES BEGIN

With the agreed arrangements in place, transactions began within a few days. Early in January 1970 the Fund took up the offer South Africa had made a year and a half earlier, and bought $34.8 million of gold in exchange for sterling. Because the price of gold in the London market was fixed at or below $35 an ounce during much of the first half of 1970 and because South Africa had a balance of payments deficit, South Africa in the first six months of 1970 offered to sell to the Fund $272.45 million of gold. The Fund accepted and the currencies sold to South Africa in return included U.S. dollars, pounds sterling, Netherlands guilders, Italian lire, Canadian dollars, and Japanese yen, selected in accordance with the principles of the regular currency budget. Within the Fund, a standing procedure for the selection of the currencies and, as necessary, for their conversion by the member issuing them was arranged to facilitate the technical execution of these gold purchases from South Africa.

In the second half of 1970 South Africa's balance of payments deficit was several times larger than it had been in the first half of 1970 ($333.5 million as against $82.9 million), and South Africa sold $332.5 million of gold to the Fund. South Africa sold even larger amounts of gold (over $900 million) on free markets during the year. These sales, together with relatively small sales of gold to monetary authorities (including Fund-related transactions), exhausted by the end of 1970 the stock of gold South Africa had held on March 17, 1968. Hence, no further sales to the Fund from existing stocks, as authorized by the decision of December 1969, could be made.

During the first six months of 1971 South Africa continued to have a balance of payments deficit and offered gold for sale to the Fund amounting to the equivalent of $102.55 million. The Fund's last purchase of gold from South Africa in 1971 took place in July, for the equivalent of $35 million. South Africa continued to have a sizable payments deficit but financed the portion of that deficit not financed by gold sales to the Fund by drawing down its official exchange reserves, by using its SDRs, and by selling gold on free markets.

The South African authorities seemed satisfied with the arrangements. In August 1970 Mr. T. W. de Jongh, Governor of the South African Reserve

Bank, addressing the annual general meeting of that bank, indicated that the arrangements were working well, and a month later, at the Twenty-Fifth Annual Meetings of the Boards of Governors of the Fund and the World Bank in Copenhagen, Mr. Diederichs, Minister of Finance and Governor of the Fund and the World Bank for South Africa, stated that the agreement of December 1969 represented a "reasonable compromise" and expressed his appreciation of the part played by the Managing Director in making the agreement possible.[17]

Early in 1970 Austria, designated to provide currency to a user of SDRs, also offered gold for sale to the Fund, for $6.26 million, to obtain the necessary currency. The Executive Board agreed.

FUND SELLS GOLD

To Mitigate Impact of Quota Increases

In Chapter 16 it was noted that, in connection both with the fourth quinquennial review of quotas in 1965 and with the fifth general review in 1970, the Fund decided to sell specified amounts of gold to mitigate the secondary impact on the gold holdings of members when other members bought gold from them to pay their increased subscriptions to the Fund. On the occasion of the fourth quinquennial review the amount so authorized was $150 million, and in March and April 1966 five of the special purchases of currencies from the Fund made by members in connection with their quota increases led to corresponding sales of gold by the Fund, for $147.9 million, in exchange for the currencies drawn. Burundi purchased $937,500 of Belgian francs and the Fund sold the same amount of gold to Belgium for Belgian francs. Egypt, Pakistan, the United Kingdom, and Yugoslavia purchased deutsche mark in amounts of $7.5 million, $9.5 million, $122.5 million, and $7.5 million, respectively, and the Fund sold $147.0 million of gold to the Federal Republic of Germany for deutsche mark.

Sales not to exceed $700 million were authorized for the same purpose in connection with the fifth general review of quotas.[18] By April 30, 1971, 75 members had bought $548 million of gold from the United States and $16 million from Austria. The Fund replenished its holdings of U.S. dollars and Austrian schillings by corresponding sales of gold. Some members bought very small amounts of gold, totaling only $95,000, from Italy and South Africa, for which there was no mitigation by the Fund. Later on, one other member bought from the Federal Republic of Germany $7.5 million of gold to pay its

---

[17] Statement by the Governor of the Fund and the World Bank for South Africa, *Summary Proceedings, 1970*, p. 191.

[18] E.B. Decision No. 3150-(70/93), October 23, 1970; Vol. II below, pp. 213–14.

increased gold subscription, and the Fund replenished its holdings of deutsche mark by the sale of the same amount of gold.

To Replenish Currency Holdings

It was the Fund's practice to sell gold whenever the General Arrangements to Borrow were activated, that is, when there were large drawings by countries participating in the Arrangements. On five occasions from June 1968 to February 1970 the Fund sold gold totaling $797 million to replenish currencies needed to help to finance large drawings by France and the United Kingdom.

The arrangements to purchase gold from South Africa beginning in 1970 made essential a review of the Fund's policy governing sales of gold. Not only was the Fund acquiring large amounts of gold from South Africa, but by 1970 sizable repurchases had begun to take place and the proportion of these repurchases made in the form of gold had risen sharply. The Fund's holdings of gold were consequently expanding by more than they ever had before. With members thirsting for gold, it was essential that the Fund reconsider the way in which it distributed its sales of gold among its members.

The Articles of Agreement limited gold sales by the Fund to the Fund's need to replenish its holdings of currencies. Gold sales had, therefore, necessarily been related to the size of the Fund's holdings of particular currencies. Gold sold for individual currencies, as on the occasions of activation of the General Arrangements to Borrow, had thus been allocated among members that had net creditor positions in the Fund, and in proportion to the size of these creditor positions at the time gold sales were made.

Some Executive Directors, Mr. Suzuki (Japan) in particular, regarded this allocation of the Fund's gold sales among members as unfair. Mr. Suzuki contended that members that happened to have large creditor positions when big drawings by Group of Ten countries were made were eligible to buy more gold from the Fund than members whose creditor positions were then small but large at other times. He recalled the remarks at the 1969 Annual Meeting of Mr. Takeo Fukuda (Japan) about the "uneven distribution of monetary gold" in the world and the need for "a happy coexistence of gold with other kinds of liquidity," and the necessity for the Fund to review its gold transactions policy.[19]

In May 1970, when the Executive Board began a review of the Fund's overall policy on gold sales for currency replenishment, they had before them two staff suggestions of methods by which the Fund might do this. Sales of gold might be made at regular intervals, say, twice a year, on the basis of members' net creditor positions in the Fund averaged over the preceding six months. This method, while an improvement over past practice for determining the allocation by country of the Fund's gold sales, provided no guidance for the total amounts

---

[19] Statement by the Governor of the Fund and the World Bank for Japan, *Summary Proceedings, 1969*, pp. 32–33.

of gold that the Fund should sell. A second method might relate sales of gold for replenishment of individual currencies to the extent to which the Fund had increased its use of that currency in its transactions, especially the use of currencies since gold had been acquired from South Africa.

The Executive Board discussion, however, revealed that resolving the question would not be a simple one of choosing techniques. Mr. Suzuki thought that part of the Fund's objective with regard to gold was to help to eliminate the uneven allocation of gold that existed between members. Hence, he wanted the Fund to sell rather considerable amounts of gold, certainly the unexpected and large accruals of gold from South Africa, and he favored a distribution technique that harmonized the ratios between gold and other reserves among the Fund's members.

Most other members of the Executive Board, notably Mr. de Maulde, Mr. Lieftinck (Netherlands), Mr. Stone, and Mr. van Campenhout (Belgium), were worried that the second method was "too automatic," and might lead to gold sales being undertaken when the Fund did not need to replenish its currency holdings. They were emphatic in their belief that the Fund should be most cautious in disposing of its gold. It was, they stressed, the most valuable asset the Fund had. Certainly, any gold that the Fund acquired through quota increases should be relinquished with caution. Even the gold being purchased from South Africa should not be considered as "excess gold." The Fund should sell gold only if absolutely essential for currency replenishment. Thus, a policy for selling the Fund's gold would have to take into account the nature and structure of the Fund's liquidity.

In July 1970, in order to facilitate gold sales, the staff proposed that the Fund sell the equivalent of $250 million in gold to be allocated among members in accordance with the Fund's use of currencies and the average net creditor positions of members for the previous six months. In September the amount proposed to be sold was raised to $325 million, with distribution on the same basis. The Executive Board approved this sale. Several Directors expressed reservations about the techniques used for determining the amounts for individual currencies, however, and accordingly, early in 1971, another effort was made to formulate a general policy for sales of gold for currency replenishment. The staff suggested a number of guidelines to the Executive Board. One policy would apply to sales of the gold acquired by the Fund under Article V, Section 6 (a), that is, basically the gold bought from South Africa, while another policy would apply to general sales of gold. Detailed rules were specified for the distribution of all gold sales among members.

After some relatively minor revisions, the Executive Board agreed that, for gold sales other than those designed to mitigate the effects of quota increases, the Fund should be guided by the following conclusions:

A. With respect to sales of gold acquired under Article V, Section 6 (a):

    1. Such sales should be considered regularly at six-month intervals.

2. Unless there was no case for replenishment, it should be presumed that sales of gold would be justified in amounts roughly corresponding to the amounts acquired under that provision since the last preceding sale.

B. With respect to general sales of gold other than under A:

1. Such sales should be made at times and in amounts determined by the Fund's need for replenishment.

2. In seeking to establish this need, account should be taken inter alia of the Fund's stock of currencies that were currently considered suitable for drawings, relative to the amount of potential drawings on the Fund's resources.

3. Where appropriate and feasible, the Fund should combine with sales of gold replenishment through borrowing.

C. With respect to the currency distribution of gold sales:

1. Sales under both A and B should be distributed among net creditor countries whose currencies were currently considered suitable for drawings, in proportion to their average net creditor positions, provided that the Fund would not purchase any currency beyond the point where its holdings of that currency equaled 75 per cent of quota.

2. For this purpose these averages would be calculated over a period ending at the end of the month preceding the date of the proposal, and beginning either six months before that date, or at the end of the period on which the distribution of gold sales was based on the occasion of the last preceding gold sale, whichever was the earlier.

3. From the amount of gold that would be sold to a member in a gold sale under A according to the calculation under this paragraph, there should be deducted the amount of any gold sold by the Fund to acquire that member's currency in preceding replenishment transactions not made under A or B.

D. Pending the elaboration of a general policy on replenishment with SDRs, the Fund should normally on the occasion of each gold sale under A or B give members the option to have their currencies replenished with SDRs rather than with gold, provided the Fund's holdings of SDRs were considered adequate at the time of such sale.

E. These policies should be reviewed not later than two years after their adoption, without prejudice to earlier reconsideration if that was requested.[20]

The decision to be guided by these conclusions was taken on March 22, 1971. In April the staff, pointing out that during 1970 the Fund had purchased from South Africa $646 million of gold but had sold only $325 million, proposed

---

[20] E.B. Decision No. 3294-(71/22), March 22, 1971; see *Annual Report, 1971*, pp. 210–11.

to sell virtually all the remaining gold that had been so acquired during that year. This gold was to be sold to 14 members (Australia, Austria, Belgium, Brazil, Canada, Finland, the Federal Republic of Germany, Italy, Japan, Kuwait, Mexico, the Netherlands, Norway, and Venezuela), the currencies of which met the definitions listed under C above. The Executive Board agreed. Similarly, in July 1971 the staff recommended, and the Executive Board agreed, that the Fund sell $135 million of gold to the same 14 members. That amount was what had been acquired from South Africa from January 1 to July 2, 1971.

GENERAL DEPOSITS OF GOLD

Beginning in September 1965 the Fund from time to time deposited gold in the accounts opened with the Federal Reserve Bank of New York and the Bank of England. Such deposits, which were not to exceed $250 million in the United States and $100 million in the United Kingdom, had been agreed as part of the arrangements in connection with the fourth quinquennial review of quotas. They were to alleviate the loss of gold stocks by these two large gold-holding members when other members of the Fund purchased gold from them in order to pay gold subscriptions to the Fund. These deposits were to be demand deposits.

The amounts actually deposited were approximately equal to the gold purchased by Fund members from the United States and the United Kingdom to make subscription payments. By October 1, 1967, 62 members had bought gold from the United States and the United Kingdom to make such payments and the Fund's gold on general deposit with the Federal Reserve Bank of New York had reached $233.1 million and that with the Bank of England $44.4 million. By mid-May 1969 gold deposited with the Federal Reserve Bank of New York under these arrangements had attained the maximum permissible total.

Debates on Usage

As gold markets became unsettled in late 1967 and thereafter, and as fears of some change in the status or price of gold grew, several Executive Directors became concerned about the Fund's management of its gold stocks. The steps that the Fund took to disinvest the gold that it had invested in U.S. Government securities have already been spelled out.[21] The considerations that led to that disinvestment applied as well to the gold on general deposit.

Questions about the gold that the Fund held on deposit first arose in December 1967, when the Executive Directors considered the ways in which a possible drawing by the United Kingdom under its stand-by arrangement

---

[21] See Chap. 19 above, pp. 383–85.

of November 1967 might be financed. Mr. Plescoff wanted the Fund, instead of selling gold from its traditional gold holdings, to use the gold on deposit with the United States. The amount involved was small, but Mr. Plescoff objected to having the gold in these deposits, which was the property of the Fund, included in the figures for official reserves of the United States and the United Kingdom.

Mr. Stone agreed that the Fund ought to use the gold it held on general deposit. But other Executive Directors did not agree because of what they considered to be abnormal developments in the world's financial markets following the devaluation of sterling that had taken place only one month before. For this reason, in June 1968, when the United Kingdom drew under the stand-by arrangement and the Fund sold gold to procure the necessary currencies, the Fund did not use gold from its general deposits.

Nevertheless, the Managing Director meanwhile had promised the Executive Directors that these deposits would be utilized more or less *pari passu* with the use of the Fund's other gold holdings whenever the Fund sold gold in the future to replenish its currency holdings, and that the Executive Directors would soon have a chance to re-examine the Fund's policy regarding these deposits. Accordingly, when the Fund sold gold to procure currencies in connection with drawings by France in June and September 1968 and in February 1970, the Fund withdrew gold from the deposits in both New York and London; in June 1969, when the Fund sold gold in connection with a purchase by the United Kingdom, it also withdrew some of the gold in its account in New York. On these occasions the transfers made from the general gold deposits were broadly in the same proportions that these total deposits bore to the total gold holdings of the Fund.

Eliminating the Deposits

Several Executive Directors were concerned that, unless some steps were taken to speed the transfer of gold from these deposits to the Fund's traditional gold bar holdings, the deposits would remain in existence for too long a time. Hence, in April 1970 the staff suggested to the Executive Directors that, when the Fund sold gold for currency replenishment, it should withdraw from the general deposit in New York amounts equal to 10 per cent of the gold sold for replenishment and from the general deposit in London amounts equal to 2 per cent of the gold sold for replenishment. These percentages, 10 per cent and 2 per cent, respectively, were about the proportions of its total gold stocks that the Fund then held in these accounts, but they were well above the proportions that prevailed later in 1970 when the Fund's gold holdings were enlarged following the fifth general review of quotas and the sizable gold purchases from South Africa.

On this basis the deposits, then about $210.5 million with the United States and $38.2 million with the United Kingdom, would be eliminated after the Fund had sold about $2 billion of gold. In order to liquidate these deposits even more quickly, the staff further suggested that any gold sold to the United States or the United Kingdom for currency replenishment that exceeded the amounts calculated by these percentages should also be taken out of the accounts; such gold sales would specifically include those that the Fund would make in connection with the mitigation arrangements for the fifth general review of quotas that had been worked out a few months before.

Mr. Dale objected to these suggestions, especially to the tie-in between the liquidation of the deposits and the gold mitigation operations under the fifth general review of quotas. Mr. Huntrods (United Kingdom), Mr. Lieftinck, and others sympathized with Mr. Dale's position: it would not be correct to undo these features of the quota review that had already been agreed upon as necessary to avoid unduly heavy losses of gold by the United States and the United Kingdom. The Fund also had an obligation to those two members to withdraw gold from the general deposits in "appropriate proportions." Mr. Stone, calling attention to the persistent payments deficits of the United Kingdom and the United States, queried the feasibility of the technique proposed: Was the Fund likely in the near future to be selling much gold to these members for replenishment of its holdings of their currencies?

In July 1970, on the next occasion when the management proposed to the Executive Board that the Fund sell gold to replenish currencies ($250 million, including $101.5 million for U.S. dollars), rules like those above giving percentages by which to draw on the deposits were suggested as a way to bring down the level of the general gold deposits. Gold would be withdrawn from the general deposit in London equivalent to $5 million and from the general deposit in New York equivalent to $101.5 million, and would be transferred to the Fund's gold bar holdings. No action was taken by the Executive Board pending discussions by the Managing Director with the U.S. monetary authorities.

In September 1970 the Managing Director came back to the Executive Board with a package proposal. *One*, the Fund's investment of gold in U.S. securities, four times the size of the gold on deposit in New York, was to be reduced by half. *Two*, the suggested amount of gold sales would be raised from $250 million to $325 million, including $131.89 million for U.S. dollars. *Three*, the Fund's past practice of reducing the general gold deposits would be continued, at least for the time being—that is, whenever gold was sold, gold would be transferred from the two deposits in the same proportions as these deposits bore to the Fund's total gold holdings. At the time, these proportions were about 7.25 per cent and 1.32 per cent for the deposits in New York and London, respectively. The Managing Director's proposal did not preclude the Executive Board from considering a faster rate of reduction of these deposits and of their liquidation at an appropriate future date. The Executive Board, welcoming especially the reduction of the Fund's gold investment, decided to continue the past practice for the general deposits.

In October 1970 this decision was further refined to obviate the necessity for frequent transfers of very small amounts (perhaps less than one gold bar) from these deposits. The transfer of gold from these deposits would take place either on the occasion of the sales of gold or shortly afterward, or when the amount of gold sold by the Fund in replenishment reached at least $100 million.[22]

When the Fund sold gold during 1971 to replenish its currency holdings, gold was transferred from the two general deposits in the proportions that those deposits bore to the Fund's total gold holdings. By the middle of 1971 those proportions were about 3.1 per cent for the deposit in New York and about 0.6 per cent for the deposit in London.

Shortly after the end of 1971, when the U.S. Government requested the Fund to withdraw its gold investment entirely, they made the same request regarding the general deposit of gold. Mr. Dale reported that the initiative for this move came from the U.S. Government. His authorities wanted to "clean up the books" following their decision of August 15, 1971 to discontinue the general convertibility of dollars held by foreign monetary authorities into other reserve assets. At that time the Fund had $144 million of gold on deposit with the Federal Reserve Bank of New York and $26 million on deposit with the Bank of England. The Executive Board decided to close both these accounts. The items "Investments" and "General Deposits" were eliminated from the balance sheet of the Fund, with a consequential increase in gold bars held with depositories.

GOLD SUBSIDIES AND TRANSACTIONS SERVICE

Two other subjects concerned with gold during the period 1966–71 were subsidies to gold producers and the gold transactions service.

Four members (Australia, Canada, the Philippines, and South Africa) continued after 1965 to subsidize gold production under programs that had been introduced between 1947 and 1963 and that the Executive Board had already deemed to be not inconsistent with the objectives of the Fund's statement of December 11, 1947 on gold subsidies.[23]

On several occasions these members asked for approval for the continuation of their programs or modifications in them, or notified the Fund of changes which did not need the approval of the Executive Board. In August 1968, having earlier made minor amendments to its Gold-Mining Industry Assistance Act, Australia proposed that, when a producer sold gold at a price in excess of the official price ($A 31.25 an ounce), he would be required to deduct only 75 per cent of that premium from the subsidy otherwise payable. Previously he had been

---

[22] E.B. Decision No. 3150-(70/93), October 23, 1970; Vol. II below, pp. 213–14.

[23] For the text of this statement, see *History, 1945–65*, Vol. III, pp. 225–26.

required to deduct the whole of such a premium from any subsidy he might receive. The Executive Directors deemed the change to be consistent with the Fund's statement of 1947 on gold subsidies. In July 1970, when the Australian authorities asked for an extension of the Executive Board's approval of its gold subsidy scheme for another period of three years, the Executive Board agreed.

Toward the end of 1967 Canada asked for, and received, the Executive Board's approval for a three-year extension of its gold subsidy arrangement, which was due to expire at the end of the year. Toward the end of 1970, when this approval was about to run out, Canada requested an extension for two and a half years, until June 30, 1973, and the Executive Board agreed.

In March 1967 the Philippines asked for, and received, the Executive Board's approval of an amendment of its Gold Industry Assistance Act. The act, as amended, would provide for increased financial assistance to various categories of gold mines. The amount of the assistance would be related to the productive capacity of each category of gold mine; and where the mine was not producing gold as a by-product, the assistance would be related to the differential between the costs of production and the official price of gold. Further amendments were introduced in September 1971. A subsidy would be given only to gold producers with 70 per cent Filipino ownership and that were mining gold as the principal product. Assistance would be withdrawn from producers that mined gold as a by-product. The amendments also provided that direct assistance would be effective only for the next five years. As it had in the past, the Executive Board deemed these arrangements to be not inconsistent with the objectives of the Fund's statement of 1947 on gold subsidies.

The Executive Board approved the annual extensions of South Africa's governmental assistance to marginal gold mines in the middle of 1966 and again in the middle of 1967. In April 1968 the Fund was advised that the South African Government had decided to continue the program, first introduced in June 1963, of financial assistance to marginal gold mines in connection with the pumping out of water from neighboring mines, but that it would discontinue assistance in the form of unsecured loans to certain mines to cover a proportion of their current working losses and approved capital expenditures. Instead, from April 1, 1968, a new plan to assist certain marginal gold mines would be implemented. In effect, the new scheme was to be based on more scientific principles to assist those mines that were likely to close down within eight years if not assisted. The Executive Board approved.

The gold transactions service, a procedure known within the Fund as "gold marriages," was introduced in 1952. When requested, the staff endeavored, on a confidential basis, to bring governmental buyers and sellers of gold, as well as certain international organizations, into contact with each other. This service, for which the Fund levied a charge of 1/32 of 1 per cent, payable in U.S. dollars, on each partner to a completed transaction, enabled members to effect official gold transactions more economically than they could otherwise do. By the end of 1971 the central banks of 29 members and 5 international organizations had effected purchases or sales of gold with the Fund's assistance. However, after 1965 there had been only two transactions, and the service was eventually ended.

■　■　■　■　■　■

The years 1966–71 were thus witness to the emergence of a number of important problems in the markets for monetary gold and to several changes in the Fund's policies. A single fixed price for gold, one of the cornerstones of the postwar international monetary arrangements designed at Bretton Woods, was abandoned in March 1968 with the introduction of the two-tier system. The Fund radically altered its policies regarding purchases of gold, especially from South Africa, and its policies for selling gold so acquired. Anxiety about the status of gold in the international monetary system was also reflected in a disquietude concerning the Fund's own gold holdings. In 1970 and 1971 steps were taken to reclaim the gold placed on deposit with the United States and the United Kingdom and the gold invested in U.S. Government securities.

As a result of these policy changes, the Fund's transactions and operations in gold in 1970 and 1971 were the largest in its history. There were purchases from South Africa. New subscriptions were received following the fifth general quota review. The gold investments with the United States were reacquired. Deposits with the United Kingdom and the United States were reclaimed. And large amounts were sold for currency replenishment. As an indication of the magnitudes involved, during the fiscal year 1970/71 the Fund received gold equivalent to $2,684 million and disbursed gold equivalent to $1,109 million.

On December 31, 1971 the Fund's holdings of gold, valued at $35 an ounce, were worth $5.3 billion, out of total assets of $29.6 billion. At the end of 1965, by comparison, the Fund's gold holdings totaled just under $2.7 billion, out of aggregate assets of $18.6 billion. In these six years the Fund's gold holdings had nearly doubled.

BASIC QUESTIONS ABOUT GOLD DEVELOP

The period 1966 through 1971 marked the onset of profound questions about gold as the crux of the Bretton Woods system. As the events discussed in this chapter unrolled, concern mounted about the position of gold in the international monetary system, especially once the new reserve asset, the SDR, had been established. Expressions of this concern by some of the Governors at the 1968 and 1969 Annual Meetings have already been mentioned earlier in this chapter.

By the time of the Twenty-Fifth Annual Meeting, held in Copenhagen from September 21 to September 25, 1970, tensions in exchange and gold markets had lessened. Mr. Schweitzer gave credit for this to the successful launching of the SDR, to the substantial increase in Fund quotas, and to the adoption of a policy on purchases of South Africa's gold, as well as to the realignment of the exchange rates for European currencies. Mr. Mario Ferrari-Aggradi, Governor for Italy, specified the same factors.[24] Gold was consequently less of an issue than it had been earlier and certainly much less of an issue than that of exchange rate flexibility, the topic that had been thrust into the forefront by the many exchange rate crises of 1968 and 1969.[25] In these circumstances, Mr. Diederichs cited the agreement between the Fund and South Africa and the subsequent large sale of gold by the Fund as evidence that the world's monetary authorities recognized, and reaffirmed, the key role of gold in the international financial system.[26]

But, in the swift ups and downs of international financial events that characterized these years, calm was once more to be the forerunner of a storm. Important as were the events with respect to gold from 1966 through the early part of 1971, they were suddenly dwarfed by the more drastic changes affecting gold that took place in the last several months of 1971. The Twenty-Sixth Annual Meeting, held from September 27 to October 1, 1971 in Washington, took place just six weeks after the United States had suspended the convertibility of officially held dollars into gold and other reserve assets. Nearly every Governor raised questions or voiced opinions about gold.

The question of most intense and immediate interest was whether, in any realignment of parities, the dollar price of gold would be raised. Such a step was tantamount to devaluation of the dollar. Some of the Governors for the EEC countries, notably Messrs. Ferrari-Aggradi (Italy), Giscard d'Estaing (France), and R. J. Nelissen (Netherlands), hinted at or spoke indirectly of the need for a change of parity of the U.S. dollar as an essential part of any currency realignment.[27] And so did a few of the Governors for developing members, such as Mr. Tan Siew Sin (Malaysia).[28]

But the place of gold in any future international monetary arrangements was also at issue, as Mr. Wardhana (Indonesia) stated early in the session.[29]

---

[24] Opening Address by the Managing Director, *Summary Proceedings, 1970*, p. 21; Statement by the Governor of the Fund for Italy, *ibid.*, pp. 119–20.

[25] The issue of exchange rate flexibility is discussed in Chap. 24.

[26] Statement by the Governor of the Fund and the World Bank for South Africa, *Summary Proceedings, 1970*, p. 191.

[27] Statements by the Governor of the Fund for Italy and the Governors of the World Bank for France and the Netherlands, *Summary Proceedings, 1971*, pp. 37, 41–44, and 156.

[28] Statement by the Governor of the World Bank for Malaysia, *Summary Proceedings, 1971*, pp. 51–52.

[29] Statement by the Governor of the World Bank for Indonesia, *Summary Proceedings, 1971*, p. 21.

Mr. Benson (Canada) likewise observed that modifications in the Fund's practices or Articles of Agreement concerning reserve assets, and in the arrangements governing their interconvertibility, would be needed.[30]

As we have noted in Part Two, some Governors began to recommend a reformed international monetary system built around the SDR, with a reduced emphasis on gold. Mr. Anthony Barber (United Kingdom) outlined at length such a possibility.[31] He saw as one of the advantages of stating all parities in SDRs rather than in gold that the United States would have the same freedom to adjust the parity of its currency as an instrument of economic policy as other members had with regard to their currencies.

The idea of de-emphasizing gold and moving in the direction of an SDR system was supported by Mr. Per Kleppe (Norway) and by a number of Governors for developing members, including Mr. A. A. Ayida (Nigeria), Mr. E. W. Barrow (Barbados), Mr. A. H. Jamal (Tanzania), and Mr. Gregorio S. Licaros (Philippines). Mr. Ayida suggested that "monetarily speaking, gold should now belong in the museum." [32]

The strongest proponent of the opposite position was Mr. Diederichs. He argued not only that the dollar price of gold should be raised but that "gold must continue performing its important international monetary function." [33] But Mr. Connally (United States) believed that a change in the gold price was "of no economic significance and would be patently a retrogressive step in terms of our objective to reduce, if not eliminate, the role of gold in any new monetary system." [34] Mr. B. M. Snedden (Australia) was prepared to look at any schemes, with or without a link to gold, but urged that the present system not be abandoned until there was a better one to take its place.[35]

On December 18, 1971, as we shall read in Part Five, the official price of gold was raised to $38 for a troy ounce of fine gold.

However, the year 1971 closed with the gold story very much unfinished. As we shall also read in Part Five, developments after August 15, 1971 brought to the fore many questions with regard to the entire international monetary system, including fundamental questions about gold: What role should be given

---

[30] Statement by the Governor of the World Bank for Canada, *Summary Proceedings, 1971*, p. 25.

[31] Statement by the Governor of the Fund for the United Kingdom, *Summary Proceedings, 1971*, pp. 32–35.

[32] Statements by the Governors of the World Bank for Norway and Nigeria and the Governors of the Fund for Barbados, Tanzania, and the Philippines, *Summary Proceedings, 1971*, pp. 88, 169, 102, 64–65, and 118.

[33] Statement by the Governor of the Fund and the World Bank for South Africa, *Summary Proceedings, 1971*, p. 84.

[34] Statement by the Governor of the Fund and the World Bank for the United States, *Summary Proceedings, 1971*, pp. 218–19.

[35] Statement by the Governor of the Fund and the World Bank for Australia, *Summary Proceedings, 1971*, pp. 131–33.

to gold in any reformed system? To what extent should gold continue to constitute a principal part of the world's monetary reserves? Should par values be expressed in terms of gold? These and other similar questions centered, in effect, around the issue whether gold should or should not be "monetized," that is, be the primary reserve asset in a reformed international monetary system.

The questions coming into the limelight late in 1971 were to remain unsettled for the next several years as reform of the international monetary system was debated. Meanwhile, the Fund's gold transactions were to decline to negligible amounts as nearly all transactions in monetary gold came to a halt. Speculative demand for gold was to jump tremendously, taking with it the price of gold in private free markets to levels two and three times the official price of gold. The two-tier market was to be disbanded. South Africa, whose balance of payments position had improved markedly, was to begin to acquire in its monetary holdings a substantial part of its new gold production.

Despite the interesting problems about gold in the 1966–71 period, in many respects the most crucial discussions and decisions about gold were just beginning as the period came to a close.

PART FIVE

Exchange Rates in Crisis

"The latter part of the 1960s, it will be
recalled, was a period characterized by
recurrent crises in gold and foreign
exchange markets."

—PIERRE-PAUL SCHWEITZER, Managing Director,
addressing the Twenty-Sixth Annual Meeting of the
Board of Governors on September 27, 1971.

CHAPTER 21

Devaluation of Sterling
(1967)

*A*T THE TIME OF THE ARTICLE VIII CONSULTATION with the United Kingdom in the middle of 1966, there was more pessimism than there had been the year before about the United Kingdom's competitive position. The balance of payments position had not become strong, yet there was not much room in the economy for a release of resources from the domestic sector to the external sector, and costs of production were increasing.

In July 1966, after sterling began to experience pressure in the exchange markets, the U.K. authorities took a number of emergency measures. In the course of the next year the situation improved greatly. Not only was the large speculative capital outflow of the previous year reversed, but the basic balance of payments position was also strengthened. Late in 1966 there was a distinct improvement in the trade balance and a resulting renewed strength of sterling in the world's financial markets. The outflow of private short-term capital was halted. During the first part of 1967 the United Kingdom's external accounts even benefited from inflows of short-term capital. By April 1967 the U.K. authorities had repaid all short-term indebtedness to other central banks, and in May they repurchased almost one half of the 1964 drawing from the Fund, six months ahead of schedule.

PRELUDE TO DEVALUATION

In the second quarter of 1967, however, difficulties did begin to set in. The expected acceleration in the pace of domestic economic activity was not taking place: unemployment was continuing to grow and had reached its highest point since the end of World War II. Likewise, the anticipated improvement in the external trade position was not materializing: imports were high and rising and exports remained sluggish. Consequently, confidence in sterling in world markets was again weakened and the direction of short-term capital flows was once more reversed.

Important developments outside the United Kingdom added to the pressure on sterling in exchange markets. While the United Kingdom was lowering its short-term interest rates to stimulate employment, short-term interest rates in the United States and other financial centers were being raised. The enlarged differential in interest rates stimulated outflows of capital from the United Kingdom. In fact, the main counterpart of capital inflow to the United States in 1967 was a substantial outflow from the United Kingdom. Furthermore, in May and June 1967 the U.K. application for membership in the EEC was rejected, arousing more speculation about the immediate and longer-run prospects for sterling in the world economy. The six-day war in the Middle East in June 1967 also adversely affected the outlook for U.K. trade, owing to the closure of the Suez Canal for an indefinite period. The outflow of funds from London accelerated. There were large and growing losses of external reserves, and the resources that the United Kingdom had received from the other central banks and monetary authorities to help support sterling were being used up.

The management and staff of the Fund were closely in touch with the U.K. authorities and were very much aware that these circumstances could precipitate devaluation. Indeed, as has been noted in Chapter 18, the U.K. authorities, during the 1967 Annual Meeting in Rio de Janeiro, alerted Mr. Schweitzer to the seriousness of the United Kingdom's financial troubles. The staff had already begun to work on calculations of a magnitude of a sterling devaluation and the possible effects on the trade balances of other countries. The previous change in the rate for sterling, a devaluation of 30.5 per cent in September 1949, had been followed immediately by devaluations of the currencies of nearly all sterling area members, of most European countries, and of many other countries.[1] Because of the importance of the United Kingdom in the world economy, because of the intense competition in world markets that had developed by the 1960s, and because sterling was a reserve currency, monetary officials, including those in the Fund, were concerned that a devaluation of sterling might again touch off devaluations of other currencies. And this concern in turn made the U.K. authorities most reluctant to consider devaluation.

In September and October 1967 the U.K. trade deficit widened ominously. With the prolongation of a dock strike, expectations concerning exports sagged, and it appeared that the deficit would continue into 1968. Confidence in sterling ebbed further.

As we have seen in Chapter 18, there were intensive discussions early in November between the Fund management and U.K. officials, and on Novem-

---

[1] *History, 1945–65*, Vol. I, pp. 238–41, and Vol. II, pp. 99–100.

ber 17 the Fund was informed of the United Kingdom's decision to devalue the pound and to request a stand-by arrangement.

NOTIFICATION TO FUND

The message from the Chancellor of the Exchequer that Mr. Maude (United Kingdom) transmitted to the Managing Director on November 17, 1967 sought the Fund's formal concurrence in a change in the par value of the pound sterling. The message stated that the U.K. Government proposed that, with effect from 4:30 P.M., Washington time, on Saturday, November 18, the sterling exchange rate should be altered from 280.000 U.S. cents per pound sterling to 240.000 U.S. cents per pound sterling, a devaluation of 14.3 per cent in the dollar price of sterling.

The Chancellor of the Exchequer explained that the devaluation was necessary to correct a fundamental disequilibrium in the United Kingdom's balance of payments. The persistent deficit, complicated by the outflows of capital in 1967, had resulted in extensive borrowing abroad and had weakened the United Kingdom's reserve position. A point had now been reached beyond which it would be irresponsible for the U.K. authorities to attempt to support the existing rate of exchange by the use of further short-term credits.

The U.K. Government, he continued, had taken all possible steps other than devaluation to restore balance of payments equilibrium. There had been long-term policies to increase productivity throughout the economy and to reform industrial structures and attitudes. Stern measures had reduced domestic demand to such a point that economic growth had been at a subnormal rate since 1964, and abnormally large excess capacity in the economy had developed. Severe price and incomes policies had been applied. Military expenditures abroad had been cut. Restrictions on tourist expenditure and overseas investment had been imposed. These steps had reduced the deficit on current and long-term capital account. But a hoped-for surplus had not materialized.

The failure of the balance of payments to move into surplus despite the low level of domestic economic activity and the restrictions in force, in the U.K. authorities' view, revealed that the balance of payments was in fundamental disequilibrium. Hence, a devaluation was necessary. To delay it any longer would run the risk of having to devalue by a larger amount later, and that in turn might cause a major dislocation in the international monetary system.

The degree of devaluation proposed was, in the opinion of the U.K. authorities, sufficient to establish a strong pound sterling and to enable the United Kingdom to generate a much needed balance of payments surplus. It was not large enough, however, to disrupt world trade and payments or to require changes in the parities of other major currencies. Finally, the message spelled out that additional measures, including severe credit restraints, curtailment of government expenditure, continuation of the price and incomes policies, tightening of hire-purchase restrictions, and increases in taxation in the next budget, would accompany the devaluation.

THE FUND'S DELIBERATIONS

Behind the Scenes

A change in the par value of a major reserve currency had far-reaching repercussions on the work of the staff and of the Executive Directors that were little known outside the closely knit financial circles of the world. Communications via telex, cable, and telephone took place between the Managing Director, Executive Directors, and staff in Washington and monetary officials in member countries all over the globe. Inquiries were made as to what action for its own currency each member intended to take in the light of the change proposed for this major reserve currency. Staff papers were then prepared, usually within a matter of hours, analyzing each proposed par value change, including its justification and adequacy. In order to take decisions while the exchange markets were closed, the Executive Directors met in emergency sessions, often late at night or on weekends. All these activities had of course to take place in the strictest possible secrecy, in order to avoid the speculation in exchange markets that could be extremely costly for a member's exchange reserves. Then, once decisions had been taken by the Executive Board, they had to be communicated to all members so that the new par values and exchange rates for various currencies could go into effect as soon as the exchange markets opened.

On the occasion of the second devaluation of sterling, the operation went unusually smoothly. On instructions of the Managing Director, the Directors or Acting Directors of the five Area Departments were alerted late in the day on Thursday, November 16, 1967, that there was every reason to expect a devaluation of sterling over the weekend and that they should review the situations of all members for which they were responsible in order to sort out those likely to follow suit or to consider doing so. They had, in effect, one business day in which to make this review before reporting back to the Managing Director late on Friday, November 17, 1967. By early Saturday morning, when exchange markets were closed, the staff of the Area Departments was permitted to firm up its information by communicating with Executive Directors, with the monetary officials of member countries, and with staff representatives stationed in a number of countries.

Because of its familiarity with members' circumstances, the staff was able to compile in advance a list of all of the member countries that did in fact devalue following the devaluation of sterling. In addition, during the days just before and after the devaluation of sterling, close contact was maintained with a large number of member countries so that the monetary officials in those countries could be given firsthand reports of what was going on as well as advice on their own situations. This experience was in contrast to that of 1949, when the Fund had been criticized for not playing an effective role.

Staff Paper and Executive Board Discussion

In the paper on the devaluation of sterling, circulated to the Executive Directors at 8:00 A.M. on Saturday, November 18, the staff indicated its agreement with the U.K. authorities that the proposed change in the par value of the pound sterling was necessary to correct a fundamental disequilibrium. The staff cited the cumulative deficit in the United Kingdom's balance of payments of more than £1,300 million over the previous four years, the apparent incompatibility of external equilibrium and satisfactory economic growth, the failure of exports to grow at a rate adequate to meet the import demands of a full-employment economy, and the failure of imports to decrease despite the disinflationary measures that had been imposed. These last two phenomena suggested to the staff the existence of disparities between U.K. prices and costs and those elsewhere. The staff further noted that, although demand pressures at home had been excessive and domestic financial management had been expansionary, an improvement in the balance of payments could have been possible. But that improvement had not developed. Moreover, the reduction in the balance of payments deficit that had taken place in 1966 had rested in part on the use of capital controls.

As far as the magnitude of the proposed devaluation was concerned, the staff had made calculations that showed that, on the basis of reasonable assumptions for trade elasticities, a devaluation of roughly 15 per cent could, after some time, yield an improvement in the U.K. trade balance of more than £500 million a year, provided that the associated rise in domestic prices was kept to a moderate amount and the devaluation of sterling was not accompanied by devaluations of other currencies. Moreover, according to the staff's analysis, an improvement of this magnitude in the U.K. trade balance was unlikely to cut seriously into the export market of any other individual country.

The Executive Directors, meeting three hours after the staff paper was circulated, expressed sympathy with the U.K. authorities in the painful decision that they had had to take, and agreed that the change in the par value of sterling was justified.

Mr. Dale (United States) recognized that determining a new par value involved a very difficult set of judgments, but thought that the U.K. authorities had chosen well in deciding to propose a rate that represented a substantial change but yet would avoid major disruptive effects on the majority of other countries and on the international monetary system itself. He commended the

U.K. authorities for the accompanying measures, which, he thought, generated confidence that the new rate was to be supported with great determination. Mr. González del Valle (Guatemala), Mr. Lieftinck (Netherlands), Mr. Plescoff (France), and Mr. Ungerer (Federal Republic of Germany) underscored the need for strict domestic measures, particularly since the degree of devaluation was modest.

The primary interest of the Executive Directors was to prevent a chain reaction to the devaluation of sterling. They praised the U.K. authorities for proposing a degree of devaluation that should not set off many other devaluations, at least by industrial members. On the occasion of this second devaluation of sterling, the stance of the U.S. authorities in particular was much in contrast to their position at the time of the 1949 currency adjustments. Whereas in 1949 they had been advocating devaluations, they were now eager to prevent devaluations that would worsen the U.S. balance of payments deficits. Mr. Dale said that this was "an historic moment of testing whether the system of par value exchange rates under the Fund's Agreement" could "withstand strain and adversity." He emphasized that the United States did not want other members to respond automatically to the devaluation of sterling by devaluing their own currencies: such devaluations should be limited to those necessary for correcting fundamental disequilibria. Mr. Lieftinck indicated that the major Western European members ought to be able to live with this adjustment of the rate for sterling without devaluing their currencies, although some other members might have to make adjustments. Mr. Suzuki (Japan) confirmed that Japan would not be changing its par value.

As we have seen in Chapter 18, the Managing Director had explored informally the reactions of some of the major countries and again prior to the Saturday morning meeting had been in touch with a number of Executive Directors and with a number of Governors to see whether their governments would or would not devalue. At the Executive Board meeting, Mr. Schweitzer, expressing views which he hoped would prevent a round of devaluations, said that the international payments situation was quite different from that in 1949 and that widespread currency adjustments were not justified at this time. It was, he said, in the interests both of the success of the U.K. action and of the international monetary system in general that this devaluation of sterling not touch off a series of exchange rate changes. He announced that he understood that none of the rest of the countries participating in the General Arrangements to Borrow would be devaluing. Nevertheless, he realized that a number of members whose economies were closely dependent on the U.K. market or who had been contemplating exchange rate changes but had not yet made them might wish to devalue their currencies.

So, on November 18, 1967, the Fund concurred in a change in the par value of the pound sterling to 240.000 U.S. cents per pound sterling (or 2.13281 grams of fine gold per pound sterling) and issued a press release to coincide with the official announcement in London. To help restore confidence in sterling, the Managing Director also gave the press a statement to the effect that the Fund was likely to act favorably within a few days on the United Kingdom's request for a very large stand-by arrangement with the Fund.

On Monday, Mr. Maude brought to the attention of the Executive Directors a number of measures announced by the U.K. Government on Sunday evening. Among these was a rise in the bank rate to 8 per cent, a level which Mr. Maude observed had been exceeded only once in the past fifty years or so.

LIMITED DEVALUATIONS OF OTHER CURRENCIES

The second devaluation of sterling since World War II, unlike the first one, did not precipitate a round of devaluations of other currencies. There were, in fact, only a limited number of immediately subsequent devaluations.

The statements to the Executive Board by Mr. Lieftinck and Mr. Suzuki on November 18, 1967 were taken as official indications that the major Western European members and Japan would not devalue. The U.S. Government issued a public statement to the effect that the par value of the U.S. dollar would be maintained.

Some Executive Directors, including those for Argentina, Australia, Austria, Canada, and South Africa, reported within the next few days that these members would not be changing their par values. Similar communications of decisions to maintain their par values unchanged were received very shortly afterward from Afghanistan, Burma, Ghana, Kenya, Liberia, the Malagasy Republic, Malaysia, Nigeria, Portugal, Singapore, Somalia, Tanzania, Thailand, Uganda, and Zambia.

There were, however, some countries that did devalue. Within ten days of the devaluation of sterling, 13 members altered their par values in agreement with the Fund. These are listed in Table 15. Nine of these changes, those for the currencies of Cyprus, Guyana, Ireland, Israel, Jamaica, Malawi, Sierra Leone, Spain, and Trinidad and Tobago, were of the same degree as the U.K. devaluation, that is, 14.3 per cent. Except for Israel and Spain, the economies of these members were very closely linked with the U.K. economy. The nature of Israel's fundamental disequilibrium was considered to be somewhat long term. Israel had been gaining reserves in recent years but needed to retain its competitive position and was also acting to counter a slowdown in the domestic economy. In the instance of Spain, the devaluation of sterling provided the authorities with an opportunity to correct a previously existing fundamental disequilibrium.

The magnitudes of devaluation by other members were 7.9 per cent for Denmark, 19.45 per cent for New Zealand, 20 per cent for Ceylon, and

Table 15. Changes in Par Values, November 18–27, 1967 [1]

Effective Date	Member	New Par Value in U.S. Cents per Currency Unit	Date Previous Par Value Became Effective
November			
18	United Kingdom	240.000	September 18, 1949
18	Ireland	240.000	May 14, 1958
19	Israel	28.5714	February 9, 1962
20	Cyprus	240.000	July 25, 1962
20	Guyana	50.000	February 13, 1967
20	Malawi	240.000	May 27, 1966
20	New Zealand	112.000	July 10, 1967
20	Spain	1.42857	July 17, 1959
21	Ceylon	16.8000	January 16, 1952
21	Denmark	13.3333	September 18, 1949
21	Jamaica	240.000	March 8, 1963
21	Sierra Leone	120.000	August 6, 1965
22	Trinidad and Tobago	50.000	February 10, 1965
27	Iceland	1.75439	August 4, 1961

[1] Does not include changes in the par values for the separate currencies in the non-metropolitan territories of the United Kingdom; see text, pp. 439–40.

24.6 per cent for Iceland. The last three, it is to be noted, were of greater magnitude than that of sterling. New Zealand was the first member to propose (on November 20, 1967) that it would devalue its currency by more than sterling had been devalued: the par value was to be changed from 139.045 U.S. cents per New Zealand dollar to 112.000 U.S. cents per New Zealand dollar. Initially, this degree of devaluation caused concern to some Executive Directors. After discussion, however, they agreed with Mr. Stone (Australia) that the new rate was needed to eliminate the existing disparity between domestic and external prices and costs. They hoped that the devaluation would lead to a better allocation of resources; improve the competitive position of domestic industry against imports, thereby reducing import demand; encourage tourism; and stimulate the inflow of capital, including the repatriation of capital held abroad by New Zealand residents. Mr. Stone further defended New Zealand's action by noting that the measures previously taken by the authorities during 1967 had had noteworthy effects on the domestic economy; hence, the economic environment was one in which the introduction of a more realistic par value could be expected to yield maximum benefits.

Each member proposing a change in par value customarily explained its action as necessary to correct a fundamental disequilibrium. The Fund, as required by the Articles of Agreement, used the concept of fundamental disequilibrium in examining proposals to change par values. In this context, devaluation of the Ceylon rupee was presented by the member as being necessary to correct a fundamental disequilibrium. Mr. Suzuki explained that the disequilibrium had existed since the time of the devaluation of the Indian rupee in June 1966, but had been intensified by the U.K. devaluation.[2] The Executive Directors agreed that a fundamental disequilibrium existed. But the proposed devaluation raised an old issue that had first come up in 1948, that is, what the Fund should do if it considered that a devaluation proposed by a member might not be adequate to correct the fundamental disequilibrium. The staff had some doubts that a 20 per cent devaluation of the Ceylon rupee was sufficient to encourage new exports, reduce leakages through the exchange controls, or make possible any relaxation of controls. Mr. Saad (Egypt) called attention to a decision by the Executive Board in 1948 to the effect that the Fund would give a member the benefit of any reasonable doubt about the size of its proposed devaluation.[3] Hence, the Fund concurred in Ceylon's proposal to change the par value of the rupee from 21.0000 U.S. cents per rupee to 16.8000 U.S. cents per rupee.

Iceland proposed an even greater degree of devaluation than those proposed by New Zealand and Ceylon. The nature of Iceland's fundamental disequilibrium had been considered by the Executive Directors only two weeks earlier at the conclusion of the 1967 consultation under Article XIV. They had noted that Iceland had high domestic costs and difficult market conditions abroad. At that time, the Icelandic authorities had publicly rejected devaluation on the ground that such a step would be undesirable at a time when the labor market had begun to show an increasing understanding of the need to rationalize production. However, the devaluation of sterling, Mr. Friis (Denmark) stated, had completely changed the situation. The United Kingdom was such an important trading partner that the Icelandic authorities had no choice but to take steps to correct Iceland's fundamental disequilibrium. The Fund concurred in the proposal for a change in the par value of the Icelandic króna from 2.32558 U.S. cents per króna to 1.75439 U.S. cents per króna. Mr. H. M. H. A. van der Valk (Netherlands, Alternate to Mr. Lieftinck), as he had in the past when Iceland had devalued, questioned the extent of the devaluation from the point of view of whether it possibly involved competitive exchange depreciation.

The U.K. Government also proposed changes, in which the Fund concurred, in the par values of most of the separate currencies of nonmetropolitan territories for which the United Kingdom had accepted the Articles of Agreement. The territories for which changes in par value were made were areas in the East Caribbean (Antigua, Dominica, Montserrat, St. Christopher-Nevis-Anguilla, St. Lucia, and St. Vincent), British Honduras, the Federation of South Arabia, Bermuda, the Falkland Islands, Gibraltar, Fiji, Hong Kong, Mauritius,

---

[2] The devaluation of the Indian rupee is discussed in Chap. 23.

[3] See *History, 1945–65*, Vol. II, pp. 93–95.

and Seychelles.[4] The degree of devaluation for the currencies of these territories was 14.3 per cent, the same as that for sterling. A few days later, however, adjustments were made so that the Hong Kong dollar was devalued by only 5.7 per cent and the Fiji pound by 9 per cent. No changes in par values were proposed for the Bahamian dollar, the Bahrain dinar, the Brunei dollar, the Rhodesian pound, and the Tongan pound.

The Gambia, which had not yet established a par value, proposed to the Fund a depreciation of 14.3 per cent in its exchange rate, to which the Fund agreed, effective November 20, 1967. That rate, 240.000 U.S. cents per Gambian pound, was agreed with the Fund as the initial par value for the currency of The Gambia later, on July 8, 1968. The initial par value agreed by Nepal with the Fund on December 11, 1967 represented a devaluation of 24.75 per cent from the previous official exchange rate.

Thus the sterling devaluation of 1967 was carried out with relatively few subsequent devaluations. Including the United Kingdom, the countries devaluing accounted for only 12 per cent of world trade and only 12 per cent of the exports of industrial countries. Excluding the United Kingdom, they accounted for less than 4 per cent of the world's exports and only 2 per cent of the exports of industrial countries, and their share of U.K. exports was only 16.5 per cent. These amounts of trade were very much smaller than those affected by the 1949 devaluations. The countries that devalued at that time accounted for almost half of the world's exports and about 60 per cent of the exports of industrial countries. Excluding the United Kingdom, they accounted for about 40 per cent of the world's exports and about 50 per cent of the exports of industrial countries, and their share of U.K. exports was more than 75 per cent.

U.K. ECONOMY FAILS TO RESPOND

After the sterling devaluation and the stand-by arrangement of November 1967, the Fund kept in close touch with officials of the U.K. Treasury and the Bank of England. In February, July, and November 1968 staff teams returned to London, as agreed under the terms of the stand-by arrangement, to review the domestic economy and the balance of payments. The second and third visits were after the United Kingdom had drawn the full amount of the stand-by arrangement in June 1968. In mid-July the Article VIII consultation became the basis of another discussion of the U.K. economy in the Executive Board, and in January 1969 the Board again reviewed the U.K. economic and financial picture.

---

[4] Mauritius became an independent country on March 12, 1968 and a member of the Fund on September 23, 1968. It had not agreed an initial par value for the Mauritian rupee by the end of 1971.

Improvement in the balance of payments position following the devaluation of November 1967 was disappointingly slow. Because of widespread expectations of price increases and higher indirect taxes in 1968, consumers' expenditures in late 1967 continued upward even after devaluation. Imports increased and inventories of imported goods were drawn down.

In January 1968 the U.K. authorities went ahead with the additional measures to restrain public expenditure that had been planned at the time of devaluation. Cuts in spending on education, health and welfare, housing, and roads for the next two years were announced. Planned expenditure was to be reduced by about £300 million for the financial year 1968/69 and by over £400 million for 1969/70. On March 19, 1968 the Chancellor of the Exchequer, in presenting the 1968/69 budget estimates, announced a still greater tightening of fiscal policy. Higher duties were imposed on alcoholic beverages, tobacco, and mineral oils. Purchase taxes, excise taxes on vehicles, and the rates for the selective employment tax were increased.

Nonetheless, in the second half of 1968 private consumption and imports were still high and rising, and the U.K. authorities took more measures to reduce aggregate demand and to curb imports. A surcharge of 10 per cent was imposed on the purchase tax and on the duties already applied to tobacco, beer, wines, and mineral oils. An import deposit scheme was introduced, under which importers were obliged to deposit with the customs authorities in advance of imports a sum equal to 50 per cent of the value of their imports, such deposits to be refunded after six months. An exchange restriction was also imposed, with the approval of the Fund, on the normal short-term banking and credit facilities in sterling made available by residents to nonresidents to finance trade between nonresidents.

Despite these measures, imports increased by 8 per cent from the second half of 1967 to the second half of 1968. The volume of exports increased by 18.5 per cent, but at the new exchange rate their value as a percentage of world exports declined. The deficit on visible trade account actually worsened by about $200 million. This widening of the trade deficit was largely offset by an increase in the surplus on invisibles, so that the current account worsened only marginally. The long-term capital outflow was reduced, but the short-term capital outflow (including errors and omissions) exceeded $1.8 billion. Consequently, the overall deficit for the calendar year 1968 turned out to be more than twice the 1967 deficit of $1.3 billion.

Some Restrictions Are Approved

A continued lack of confidence in sterling during 1968 was further evidenced when members of the sterling area began to run down balances of sterling accumulated as foreign exchange reserves. Even before the November 1967 devaluation, they had begun to alter the composition of their reserves in

441

order to reduce their relative holdings of sterling. This trend increased significantly in the second quarter of 1968, rendering it necessary for the U.K. authorities to make some arrangements to meet or forestall such diversification of reserves. To help in dealing with this problem, the U.K. authorities announced in July 1968 that provisional agreement had been reached with the BIS and 12 industrial countries—the Basle Group—for a medium-term stand-by credit of $2 billion; by September the facility was established.[5] At the same time, members of the sterling area agreed to keep certain minimum proportions of their reserves in sterling for three (or in some instances for five) years in return for a guarantee of the U.S. dollar value of the bulk of their sterling balances.

The Fund regarded this requirement as a limitation on the use and convertibility of the sterling holdings of sterling area countries, and therefore a requirement of some consequence. There were 64 participants in these sterling agreements, many of which were also members of the Fund. The Fund considered that the United Kingdom was applying a measure subject to the Fund's approval under Article VIII. The Executive Board, recognizing that the Basle facility and the sterling agreements would have a salutary effect on the stability of sterling and on the entire international monetary system, agreed on November 18, 1968 to such features of the agreements as required the Fund's approval.

By September 1971 all but two of the agreements that were to last for three years and were then due to expire had been renegotiated; like the agreements that were originally designed to last for five years, they would continue until September 1973. After September 1971 there was also a reduction in the proportion of sterling that countries in the sterling area agreed to hold as part of their total reserves.

The Fund Urges More Stringent Policies

The Fund's discussions concerning the United Kingdom's situation, both with the U.K. authorities and within the Executive Board, during 1968 centered on the reasons why the member's progress toward external surplus was so slow and on the question whether the domestic policies introduced were adequate. By mid-1968 the staff and several Executive Directors had come to believe that the measures taken were not fully effective and that, while the authorities had imposed strong fiscal measures, they had not made enough use of monetary and credit restraints. Bank credit to the private sector of the economy was growing much more rapidly than had been anticipated and was stimulating a boom in consumer spending, including spending on imports.

The general question of the effectiveness of monetary and credit policy for stabilizing a domestic economy and restoring external equilibrium had for

---

[5] The 12 countries were Austria, Belgium, Canada, Denmark, the Federal Republic of Germany, Italy, Japan, the Netherlands, Norway, Sweden, Switzerland, and the United States.

years been a subject of debate between officials of the U.K. Government and senior members of the Fund staff. Consultations revealed differences of view about the effectiveness of aggregate monetary restraints. To consider these differences at greater length and on a technical level, an informal seminar was held in London in October 1968 between officials and technicians from the Treasury and the Bank of England, and the Economic Counsellor and other members of the Fund staff. The seminar did not entirely resolve these differences of view, but a much greater tightening of U.K. credit policy nevertheless did occur, and as we shall see in the next section of this chapter, the situation of the United Kingdom began to improve.

In presenting the 1969/70 budget on April 15, 1969, the Chancellor of the Exchequer not only announced the imposition of still more taxes but also, significantly, referred to the importance of monetary policy in providing essential support to fiscal policy. He stated that the increase in bank credit in 1968 had been too large, and said that in the coming year the needed balance of payments improvement should be accompanied by restraint on the provision of domestic bank credit to both the public and private sectors of the economy. Steps were then taken to restrict bank credit and to ensure that other financial operations, including debt management, did not make the amount of credit actually extended exceed the intended limitations on credit extension.

EVALUATION OF IMPROVEMENT IN U.K. ECONOMY

Under the terms of the 1969 stand-by arrangement, there were to be quarterly reviews with the Fund. In both the periodic reports of the staff and the Executive Board discussions pertaining to these reviews, efforts were made to pinpoint the reasons for the eventual turnaround in the U.K. balance of payments and why it had been delayed until nearly two years after devaluation.

The evaluation was directed in part to ascertaining the effectiveness of a change in par value and of demand management policies for solving the external financial problems of the United Kingdom. For nearly a decade the United Kingdom's external disequilibrium had been a recurrent theme in international economic discussions, and many economists had come to regard it as basically structural in character. They attributed it to a relative lack of modernization and investment by British industry and, consequently, to an insufficient increase in productivity. It was often said, for instance, that British manufacturing had fallen behind American, European, and Japanese manufacturing, which had made impressive strides since World War II. But it was also important to assess the usefulness of exchange rate, fiscal, credit, and monetary policies in the U.K. economy of the late 1960s. In addition to ascertaining the effectiveness of exchange rate changes and of demand management policies, this evaluation was motivated by the desire to give the Fund management and the Executive

Directors some way to judge how long the U.K. authorities would be advised to continue their stringent domestic policies.

At the time of the 1967 devaluation of sterling it had not been expected that the benefits of the devaluation would be so slow to materialize or that they would come only after the U.K. payments position had worsened. To describe the aftermath of the devaluation, economic journalists in the United Kingdom, as well as economists and government officials, began to use the term J-curve—a shorthand way of denoting that devaluation at first produces a deterioration in the external account (the short downward shaft of the J), and later produces an improvement in the external account that is considerably in excess of the initial deterioration (the long upward shaft of the J). The initial deterioration comes about because the immediate impact of devaluation is a worsening of the country's terms of trade while the effect on trade volumes takes longer to come about. The price effect of devaluation is offset by the quantity effect only after time lags of considerable duration.

Essentially what happens is that, if exporters maintain their prices in terms of local currency, the lower cost to foreign customers in terms of their own currencies should stimulate buying and in time raise the volume of exports enough to produce some increase in export values in terms of foreign currencies and a considerable increase in terms of local currency. On the import side, if foreign exporters hold their export prices in their currencies unchanged, the local currency cost to the customers in the devaluing country rises; eventually the lowering of the volume of purchases will reduce aggregate local currency expenditures on imports. Thus, as current receipts are enlarged and current payments are reduced, the current account position improves.

These effects, however, take some time to materialize. Shifts in demand, both at home and abroad, and changes in resource allocation are required before the quantity of exports of goods and of outgoing services increases and the quantity of imports of goods and of incoming services decreases. Meanwhile, the quantities of exports and imports may well remain substantially unchanged, and the increase in the aggregate local currency value of imports is likely to outweigh any favorable impact on exports. Hence, the current account position worsens immediately following a devaluation.

Increasingly, officials in the United Kingdom and in the Fund took cognizance of the J-curve effects on the United Kingdom's balance of payments after the 1967 devaluation. The United Kingdom's experience, moreover, revealed to many economists who customarily differentiated short-term effects (when price elasticities of demand and supply were small) from long-term effects (when such price elasticities were larger) that for other countries, too, the first effects of devaluation might even be negative and that the long-term effects of changes in exchange rates might take much longer to materialize than had previously been assumed. New interest was generated in both the theory of the effectiveness of exchange rate changes and the empirical study of such changes.[6]

Gradually—by late in 1969—there was sufficient statistical and circumstantial evidence to support the view that strong overall financial policies, persistently applied, were bringing about the necessary shift in resources from the domestic economy to export production and hence were bringing about a marked improvement in the external payments position of the United Kingdom. The U.K. authorities, by applying such policies after the devaluation, had managed in 1969 to bring about a trade and balance of payments surplus, to rebuild foreign exchange reserves, and to repay much short-term indebtedness.

At the same time, the Fund, noting signs of rising labor costs and only small gains in productivity, cautioned against relaxation of stabilizing policies lest an inflationary wage-price spiral ensue. Several Executive Directors, as well as the staff, also drew attention to a number of circumstances that had benefited the U.K. balance of payments in 1969 but that could not be counted on in the future. U.K. imports had fallen and U.K. exports had expanded substantially partly because the growth of the economy had been held down during 1969 to a rate lower than normal while the rest of the world had enjoyed unusually rapid growth. But had demand conditions at home and abroad moved in greater cyclical unison, such a favorable trading situation for the United Kingdom might not have developed. Furthermore, during 1969 the U.K. economy had been able to rely on inventories of imported products; the utilization of such stockpiles could obviously be only temporary. In addition, when the import deposit scheme was removed, the pound sterling would lose an artificial prop. Finally, long-term capital imports might be more difficult to achieve as the interest rate differential between money markets in the United Kingdom and those on the European continent diminished. In any event, it was an anomaly for the United Kingdom to be achieving balance of payments equilibrium by being an importer of long-term capital; one would expect the United Kingdom, a major industrial country, to be an exporter of capital.

In April 1970 in Washington, in a follow-up to the seminar held in London in October 1968, U.K. officials and technicians and members of the Fund staff discussed once more their views about the efficacy of monetary policy. There was a much greater harmony of opinions than at the earlier seminar, and very few areas of difference now remained.

---

[6] Among these studies were several by the staff of the Fund. See, for example, Jacques R. Artus, "The 1967 Devaluation of the Pound Sterling," *Staff Papers*, Vol. 22 (1975), pp. 595–640, and "The Behavior of Export Prices for Manufactures," *ibid.*, Vol. 21 (1974), pp. 583–604; Michael C. Deppler, "Some Evidence on the Effects of Exchange Rate Changes on Trade," *Staff Papers*, Vol. 21 (1974), pp. 605–36; and Avinash Bhagwat and Yusuke Onitsuka, "Export-Import Responses to Devaluation: Experience of the Nonindustrial Countries in the 1960s," *Staff Papers*, Vol. 21 (1974), pp. 414–62. Also see Helen B. Junz and Rudolph R. Rhomberg, "Price Competitiveness in Export Trade Among Industrial Countries," *The American Economic Review* (Papers and Proceedings of the Eighty-Fifth Annual Meeting of the American Economic Association), Vol. 63 (1973), pp. 412–18.

U.K. Surpluses in 1970 and 1971

By July 1970, at the time of the 1970 Article VIII consultation, it was apparent that, after lagging initially, the results of the U.K. devaluation and financial programs had far exceeded expectations. Mr. Derek Mitchell (United Kingdom) reported that the new Government, which had taken office following the general election on June 18, was examining all policies with a view to strengthening the U.K. economy further and especially to curbing inflation. In the opinion of both the U.K. authorities and the Fund, the problem of inflation was becoming critical.

In December 1970 and January 1971, the Fund held consultations with the U.K. authorities in accordance with the provision of the stand-by arrangement that, while any of the Fund's holdings of sterling above the first credit tranche included currency resulting from purchases under the stand-by arrangement, the United Kingdom would consult the Fund from time to time concerning its balance of payments policies. The dramatic improvement in the United Kingdom's external accounts that took place late in 1969 had continued into 1970. The overall balance for 1970 was in surplus by $3 billion, three times the surplus of 1969. Stringent policies had been maintained, dampening any rise in imports and attracting large inflows of short-term capital. The terms of trade had also moved favorably. The potentially serious damage to the United Kingdom's national competitive position that might have resulted from the rapid advances in domestic prices and costs was averted by continuing inflation in other industrial countries.

On the other hand, signs of renewed difficulty were beginning to show. Relatively weak demand in the domestic economy was accompanied by rising unemployment, which by the spring of 1971 had reached the highest level in many years. To stimulate domestic activity, the authorities undertook, in the budget announced at the end of March 1971, to reduce fiscal restraint somewhat and to ease monetary policy. But there was a danger of inflation and of a cost-price spiral, which could have adverse consequences for the competitiveness of British goods in world markets.

Despite these areas of weakness, the United Kingdom had an even larger balance of payments surplus in 1971—$6.5 billion—and the United Kingdom, as well as several other industrial countries, absorbed the counterpart of a U.S. deficit on an official settlements basis that reached $30 billion.

STERLING DEVALUATION AS SEEN AT THE TIME

At the time of the devaluation of sterling in November 1967, it was not expected that this devaluation would be only the first of many alterations in the exchange rates of major currencies to take place over the next several years.

But in fact, by the end of 1971 the par values of the French franc and the deutsche mark had been changed, the dollar had been devalued in terms of gold for the first time since 1934, the exchange rate relationships among all the major currencies had been realigned, and a regime of "central rates" had been introduced as a temporary substitute for the par value system, which had, indeed, collapsed.

Most monetary officials and expert observers did not, in November 1967, regard the collapse of the par value system as imminent. True, they were very well aware that the international monetary system was under severe stress. Disequilibrium in international payments continued to involve deficits for the United States and the United Kingdom and surpluses for the industrial countries of continental Europe as a group. Speculative movements of capital were becoming larger, and harder to counteract by official action. But the elimination of the deficits of the United States and the United Kingdom, on which major emphasis had been placed, seemed to be in process. As far as the United Kingdom was concerned, sterling was being devalued. Although the United States had a large overall deficit in 1967 because of an increase in capital outflows, still it had a sizable current account surplus, and the trade balance was showing improvement. During the first three quarters of 1967, the steep upward trend of Europe's exports to the United States that had taken place in 1965 and 1966 was abruptly reversed. Also, U.S. exports to Europe (to the EEC countries as well as to the United Kingdom) were on the rise. In addition, Japan's exports to the United States had not increased as rapidly in 1966 as they had earlier, and, during the first half of 1967, they actually declined. Japan's overall payments position was close to being in balance.

Moreover, after years of deliberation, an outline for a special drawing rights facility in the Fund had finally been agreed upon less than two months before the devaluation of sterling, and considerable optimism existed that the international monetary system would be bolstered. A new mechanism for reserve creation was anticipated that could substitute for the cessation of reserve increases or for the reserve losses entailed in the elimination of the U.S. and the U.K. deficits.

In these circumstances, the devaluation of sterling was looked upon as a move that would strengthen the international monetary system. This was the view, for instance, of the Managing Director. In a televised interview on Sunday, November 19, the day after sterling was devalued, in response to a direct question about the effect of the devaluation on the U.S. dollar, he replied that the United Kingdom's move should not have an unfavorable impact on the dollar. The situation of the United States was completely different from that of the United Kingdom. The United States had a substantial surplus on current account in its balance of payments. Mr. Schweitzer added that he welcomed President Johnson's statement that there would be no change in the willingness of the United States to continue buying and selling gold freely (that is, without limit) at $35.00 an ounce. Mr. Schweitzer went on to say that, contrary to the belief held by some that devaluation of sterling was harmful to the position of the dollar and indicative of weakness in the monetary system, the devaluation of sterling was "good" both for the dollar and for the monetary system.

CHAPTER 22

Adjustments in Rates for French Franc and Deutsche Mark

(1969)

*H*UGE AMOUNTS OF SHORT-TERM CAPITAL were beginning to flow freely across national boundaries from one monetary center to another by early in 1968.[1] In the course of 1969 these flows of funds, together with other economic circumstances, precipitated changes in the par values of two major currencies—the French franc and the deutsche mark.

PRELUDE TO DEVALUATION OF FRANC

The difficulties that preceded the devaluation of the French franc in August 1969 began late in May 1968. Social unrest, starting among university students, touched off widespread strikes throughout France. At their height these "events," as the French authorities preferred to call them, involved 10 million workers, about half the labor force. They were responsible for a loss of output estimated at 2 per cent of the gross national product for 1968. The potential effects on France's international competitive position of the wage agreement concluded to settle the strikes were of even greater concern, however. This agreement involved an increase in hourly wage rates of over 11 per cent and a shortening of the workweek.

These difficulties, which were compounded by the flight of vast amounts of capital, notably into deutsche mark, prompted the French authorities, in June 1968, to make a gold tranche drawing from the Fund. But if the immediate outlook for the franc was dim, the reverse was true for the deutsche mark. The Federal Republic of Germany had been running surpluses both on trade and on current account since the late 1950s, and many suggestions, including some from highly placed monetary officials in other industrial countries, were

---

[1] The growth of short-term capital movements is described in Chap. 24, pp. 496–500.

being made that the deutsche mark ought to be revalued. Talk of this kind began to produce recurrent rumors, usually near the weekend, that a revaluation was intended. The resulting speculation swelled the capital inflows that were already prompted by the trade surplus. Rumors of an impending revaluation of the deutsche mark persisted throughout most of 1968 despite repeated announcements by the German authorities that the par value of their currency would not be changed.

After settlement of the strikes, the French authorities took steps to minimize the pressure on prices from the loss of output and higher wage costs. Since excess capacity existed in the economy, they hoped to expand output and enhance labor productivity and, therefore, adopted expansionary fiscal and monetary policies. To help control the impact of these policies on the balance of payments, they tightened price controls and introduced temporary restrictions on imports and on certain external payments and subsidies for exports. To curb outbound capital movements, they imposed exchange controls.

Before these policies could be tested, capital flight, especially into deutsche mark, again confronted the French authorities. Beginning late in August 1968 there were, once more, expectations in exchange markets that the franc would be devalued, especially as labor costs in France continued to rise, or that the deutsche mark might be revalued, as the Federal Republic of Germany's trade surplus grew even larger, or that both of these exchange rates might be changed. To revive confidence in the franc, the French authorities, in September 1968, reversed the steps taken earlier. They restricted credit, and in a bold gamble abolished exchange controls. These measures did not work, however, and in November 1968 there was a fresh wave of international currency speculation. With no exchange controls as an impediment, the flow of funds from francs into deutsche mark reached unprecedented proportions. On November 20, 1968 the major European exchange markets were forced to close. By the end of November, France's official exchange reserves had dipped to $4.0 billion, from $6.9 billion at the end of April 1968. This use of $2.9 billion of reserves included the utilization by France of its gold and super gold tranche positions in the Fund. In addition, France drew on the $1.3 billion short-term borrowing facilities that had been made available by foreign monetary authorities.

MEETING AT BONN

Already in September 1968 monetary officials in the United States and in several European countries were finding France's heavy reserve losses worrisome. The large imbalances in the payments positions of France and the Federal Republic of Germany appeared to be chronic, and considerable disagreement and uncertainty existed about how these imbalances would be reduced or eliminated. Monetary officials in the United Kingdom and the United States, fearful of the effects of a devaluation of the franc or of the devaluation of any European currency on the competitive positions of sterling and the dollar, were especially concerned that the franc might be devalued.

Consequently, when the exchange crisis of November 1968 that has been described in the preceding section arose, Mr. Schiller, Minister of the Economy of the Federal Republic of Germany, who was then Chairman of the Ministers and Governors of the Group of Ten, called an emergency meeting of that Group, mainly at the urging of Mr. Fowler, Secretary of the U.S. Treasury, who was in the Federal Republic of Germany at the time. The Ministers and Governors of the Group of Ten met in Bonn on November 20–22, 1968. Mr. Schweitzer, who was traveling in Africa at the time, interrupted his trip and flew from Abidjan to Bonn on November 20. So urgent was the conference that, when Mr. Schweitzer's commercial flight was delayed by bad weather in France, a special plane was chartered for him. He arrived in Bonn very late on the first day of the meeting. Staff representatives had attended the sessions that day.

The Bonn meeting centered primarily on what measures ought to be taken and by whom. Major attention was directed to the need for, and the possibility of, revaluation of the deutsche mark and devaluation of the French franc. At the opening of the meeting, the authorities of the Federal Republic of Germany stated their view that, as appropriate balance of payments measures were being considered, emphasis ought to be placed on basic comparisons of relative prices and costs in different countries and not on speculative activity in currencies. They described a number of measures, mainly changes in the border taxes, which the Federal Republic of Germany had introduced earlier, to reduce the trade surplus and the imposition of restrictions on banking transactions to ward off speculative capital inflows. They also explained that the Cabinet had just agreed upon these measures and was sending them to the Bundestag for approval.

Most other officials of the Group of Ten, including Mr. Fowler, viewing the continuing large overall surpluses of the Federal Republic of Germany as the heart of the problem of international imbalance, took the position that the measures being planned were inadequate and that the deutsche mark ought to be revalued. Many officials were not convinced that the par value of the French franc needed to be changed and were ready to consider financial support for the franc, including aid to France through the Fund without burdensome conditions. In arguing for a revaluation of the deutsche mark, they cited the need for measures that affected all of the Federal Republic of Germany's balance of payments, and not mainly trade, and the need to calm the recurrent speculation that the deutsche mark would be revalued. Some of them argued pointedly that Germany had a "fundamental disequilibrium" and that it ought to be handled by means other than manipulation of border taxes.

451

In reply, the officials of the Federal Republic of Germany strongly defended their measures and opposed revaluation. Border taxes fitted in with the Bretton Woods philosophy of fixed exchange rates. Moreover, they went to the crux of the country's surplus problem because there was a surplus on trade account but a deficit on services. They stressed that the expected reduction of the trade surplus by one third during the course of the next year was a great sacrifice for the country; any further reduction would be intolerable. Revaluation of the deutsche mark alone, in any magnitude considered reasonable, would not, they argued rather pointedly, resolve the payments problems of other countries, a conclusion, they believed, that was warranted by the experience with the revaluation of the deutsche mark in 1961. Instead they suggested that, once the SDR facility had been activated, a conference be called to consider a realignment of all major currencies, "not excluding the dollar." Furthermore, they intimated that much of the speculation against the deutsche mark might be officially inspired.

The discussions were tense. Some officials suggested possible magnitudes for the currency changes they considered necessary. Mention was made of a 4 per cent revaluation of the deutsche mark, since the changes in border taxes were equivalent to about that magnitude of revaluation. A 15 per cent devaluation of the franc was indicated by the French representatives as the amount France would require if the Federal Republic of Germany could not go beyond 4 per cent. Others cautioned against the need for so large a devaluation of the franc.

Mr. Schweitzer counseled against the proposal for a future conference to re-examine currency values. He was apprehensive about the speculation that the prospect of such a conference might provoke. He laid emphasis on the fact that it was the position of only two currencies that raised a problem. Regarding devaluation of the franc, it would be better to delay action until one could estimate the magnitude of any fundamental disequilibrium. A number of Ministers supported Mr. Schweitzer's position on the inadvisability of a future conference to consider a general realignment of currencies.

Mr. Guido Carli, Governor of the Bank of Italy, suggested a recycling of capital flows through the BIS, and the Governors of central banks then met separately to consider a credit package for France and Mr. Carli's proposal. The Ministers of the six EEC countries likewise met separately to consider the exchange rates of their countries.

The conference ended without agreement on adjustment of the exchange rate for either the deutsche mark or the French franc. Instead, it was understood that the Federal Republic of Germany would go ahead with the measures that had been announced. These were a temporary export tax and an import subsidy, which were expected to have effects equivalent to a revaluation of between 3 and 4 per cent. In addition, to forestall capital inflows, certain short-term transactions of domestic banks with nonresidents would be restricted and the reserve requirements in respect of any increases in foreign deposits with domestic banks would be raised to 100 per cent. France would take "appropriate measures" to restore confidence in the franc and could receive short-term credits of up to $2 billion from other central banks and the BIS. The communiqué of the Ministers and Governors of the Group of Ten following their meeting in Bonn further observed that France had nearly another $1 billion of drawing rights in the Fund.

Despite the secrecy of the proceedings, there were many newspaper accounts. In Mr. Schweitzer's oral report to the Executive Board immediately after the meeting, he clarified two points that had been prominently discussed in the press. First, he said that at no time had the French authorities at the meeting announced an intention to devalue; it was always perfectly clear that they reserved for their Government the choice between no devaluation or a devaluation of a very limited amount. Second, he informed the Board that the stand-by credits arranged for France by the central banks of the other countries of the Group of Ten were not subject to conditions.

On November 23, 1968, the day after the Bonn meeting ended, President de Gaulle stated that the par value of the French franc would be maintained unchanged. Having ruled out devaluation, the French Government adopted a number of restrictive economic and financial measures. Government expenditures were reduced and indirect taxes were increased so as to cut the budget deficit for 1969 nearly in half. Ceilings were imposed on commercial bank lending, and interest rates were raised. Exchange controls were reintroduced.

These actions were expected to lead to a reduction in import demand and thereby in the external trade deficit, encouraging, in turn, a reflux of capital. Within days after the Bonn meeting, members of the Fund staff arrived in Paris for discussions in connection with the 1968 Article VIII consultation. In its report of these discussions, the staff stated that the actions taken had had immediate effect. Speculation had been quickly stemmed, the franc's value in exchange markets had been strengthened, and there had been a marked reflux of funds to France.

The favorable effect of the measures taken at the end of 1968 proved, however, to be short-lived. The deficit on the French current account for the first half of 1969 was greater than ever.

DECISION TO DEVALUE THE FRANC

In the first week of May 1969 there were again extremely large flows of funds into the Federal Republic of Germany. Mr. Schweitzer noted that the situation of the French franc had not worsened in the last few weeks—in spite of a referendum that had led to the resignation of President de Gaulle—that the position of sterling had now become favorable, and that the flow of short-term funds into Germany vastly exceeded the aggregate flow out of France and the United Kingdom, and he considered the problem as centering on the Federal Republic of Germany. He cabled the authorities of that member urging them to take "prompt, courageous, and effective action" to avoid serious consequences for the international monetary system and for many other members.

At their regular monthly meeting in Basle, a few days later, the Central Bank Governors of the Group of Ten and Switzerland examined these latest developments. Mr. Blessing, President of the Deutsche Bundesbank, read a message of May 9, 1969 from the Federal Chancellor in which he stated categorically that the decision of the Government to maintain the par value of the deutsche mark would not be altered. The Government took a number of other measures, including several restrictions on foreign deposits, to induce a recycling of speculative capital, and a large proportion of the funds that had come in earlier did leave shortly thereafter.

The French authorities announced another series of monetary restraints. Existing quantitative restrictions on bank credit were extended beyond mid-1969 and tightened, and the minimum requirements for hire purchase were made much stricter. In mid-July the new Government of President Georges Pompidou took more anti-inflationary steps, including freezing the funds previously allocated to a large number of public investment programs. Despite all these measures, the drain on reserves continued. By the end of July they were down to $3.6 billion, barely half of what they had been 16 months earlier, and official short-term debts of some $2.3 billion had been incurred.

In a cable from Mr. Giscard d'Estaing, the Minister of Economy and Finance, to Mr. Schweitzer on Saturday, August 9, 1969, the Government of France requested the Fund's concurrence in a change in the par value of the franc. The par value of the franc was stated in terms of gold and was to be altered from 0.180 gram of fine gold per franc to 0.160 gram, a devaluation of 11.11 per cent. This was the figure that had been calculated earlier by the staff of the Fund and that had been generally accepted at the Bonn meeting as the appropriate magnitude of devaluation for the franc. The new par value was to enter into effect on Sunday, August 10, 1969, at 8:00 P.M., Paris time (3:00 P.M., Washington time). This devaluation, from 4.93706 francs per U.S. dollar to 5.55418 francs per U.S. dollar, was the first change in the par value of the French franc since December 1958, when President de Gaulle, as one of his first acts after taking office, had devalued the franc.

Although France had had balance of payments troubles for at least a year, the decision of the French authorities to devalue the franc took most monetary officials by surprise. Less than nine months before, President de Gaulle had definitively refused to devalue the franc. In the interim, President Pompidou had succeeded President de Gaulle, but the French monetary authorities had continued to rely on internal policies and exchange controls to rectify France's external deficits.

THE FUND'S DELIBERATIONS ON FRANC DEVALUATION

At least from early in 1968 the Fund staff had held the view that, following the remarkable increase in output, productivity, and exports after the devaluation of 1958, there had been, since about 1963, a gradual weakening of France's international competitive position. Admittedly, France's exports were large and had continued to increase. The evidence of a lessening in the country's economic strength lay rather in the reduced rate of growth of the domestic economy, the smaller external surpluses, and the growing penetration of imported goods into domestic markets, especially after the liberalization of trade within the EEC. Mr. Plescoff had taken issue with this assessment, contending that France's economic difficulties were more current and were primarily associated with the events of May–June 1968.

In August 1969, when the staff evaluated the proposed devaluation of the franc, it again cited these longer-run trends. But its explanation of the need for devaluation was based on developments in France's situation in the previous year. In the second half of 1968, domestic costs and prices had risen more than had originally been foreseen, while some of France's main competitors, particularly the Federal Republic of Germany, had succeeded in holding down unit labor costs. Moreover, the cutback in domestic demand required to eliminate the current account deficit in the balance of payments and to restore confidence in the franc at the existing rate of exchange would have to be excessively large and would probably lead to a very substantial increase in unemployment. Devaluation was, therefore, a necessary element in the resolution of this basic conflict between the goals of full employment and external equilibrium.

The Executive Board met on Sunday morning, August 10, 1969. Mr. Plescoff justified the devaluation in terms of the fundamental disequilibrium that had now developed in the French economy. The expansion of costs, prices, and domestic demand in the previous several months had been such that it could no longer be expected that the current account of the balance of payments would soon recover. Continuation of the current account deficit at the level then existing would rapidly deplete France's exchange reserves, increasing the vulnerability of the franc to any fresh waves of currency speculation. The only alternative to devaluation was "ruthless deflation." That policy not only would have grave social consequences but would compromise investment undertakings and efforts to modernize productive capacity. Such investment and modernization were essential to the restoration and maintenance of France's competitive position in foreign markets.

Mr. Plescoff stressed that the degree of the proposed devaluation had been carefully adjusted to what was essential to correct existing disparities between unit production costs in France and those abroad. The proposed devaluation was thus limited strictly to correcting the past. The French authorities were also taking many related measures. Investment spending in the 1969 budget had been frozen at F 4 billion. The budget for 1970 would be balanced. There would be stringently enforced credit ceilings.

The Executive Directors readily agreed that the French balance of payments was experiencing a fundamental disequilibrium. The effects on domestic employment and output of the severe measures that would have been necessary to restore external payments equilibrium at the existing par value would be too adverse. Miss Fuenfgelt (Federal Republic of Germany) reported that the German authorities welcomed the devaluation of the franc as an important step toward a better international equilibrium.

The secrecy and the timing of the French action were, however, the subject of some comment. The authorities had made a quick and unexpected move to devalue over a holiday weekend. They had made a public announcement prior to the Executive Board's formal consideration of the proposed change in par value. The Executive Directors recognized that this timing had avoided any further speculation in exchange markets, but they very much regretted that, prior to the Fund's concurrence, the French Government had already publicly announced the devaluation. Mr. Dale explained that it was only because of the unique circumstances of the French situation that he would not object more formally. Those circumstances, he made clear, were that, after the discussions in Bonn in November 1968 and the international consultative discussions on the French economy since that time, the French authorities rightly had every reason to assume that a devaluation of the amount proposed would be approved by the international community. However, members should not assume that any par value change they might propose would necessarily receive the Fund's concurrence. Mr. Maude, stating that there was a strong presumption that the country in question was best placed to judge the appropriate moment for changing its par value, nonetheless regretted the French authorities' announcement prior to the Fund's concurrence.

The Executive Board then took a decision concurring in the change in the par value of the French franc.

Effective at the same time were corresponding changes in the par values for the separate currencies in France's nonmetropolitan areas. These were the franc of French Guiana, Guadeloupe, and Martinique; the CFA franc of the Comoro Islands, Réunion, and St. Pierre and Miquelon; and the CFP franc of French Polynesia, New Caledonia, and the Wallis and Futuna Islands. The par value of the Djibouti franc of the territory of the Afars and the Issas (formerly French Somaliland) and that of the CFP franc of the New Hebrides remained unchanged.

FRENCH FRANC AREA ALTERS ITS RATES

At the meeting of the Executive Board on Sunday morning, August 10, Mr. Yaméogo (Upper Volta) announced that the countries linked to the French Treasury by an operations account would also wish to change the rates of exchange for their currencies, effective simultaneously with the change in the rate for the French franc, so that trading the next day could take place at the new exchange rates. He was not ready to have the Executive Board consider these currency changes until after the Conference of Ministers of Finance of the Franc Area met in Paris later that afternoon (Washington time).

Accordingly, the Executive Directors reassembled on Sunday evening, August 10, to take action on the changes in the exchange rates for 14 other members: Cameroon, the Central African Republic, Chad, the People's Republic of the Congo, Dahomey, Gabon, Ivory Coast, the Malagasy Republic, Mali, Mauritania, Niger, Senegal, Togo, and Upper Volta. These members had not yet established par values.

Cameroon, the Central African Republic, Chad, the People's Republic of the Congo, and Gabon, all of which used the CFA franc issued by their common central bank, the Central Bank of Equatorial African States and Cameroon (BCEAEC), requested the Fund to agree to a change in the rate of exchange for the CFA franc, from CFAF 246.853 per U.S. dollar to CFAF 277.710 per U.S. dollar. This change represented a devaluation of 11.11 per cent, the same as for the French franc, and kept the relationship between the CFA franc and the French franc at CFAF 1 = F 0.02. Dahomey, Ivory Coast, Mauritania, Niger, Senegal, Togo, and Upper Volta requested the Executive Board's agreement for a similar change in the exchange rate for the CFA franc issued by their common central bank, the Central Bank of West African States (BCEAO).

The Malagasy Republic requested the Executive Board to agree to a change in the official rate of exchange for its currency, the Malagasy franc. The rate of exchange and the change were the same as for the CFA franc, that is, from FMG 246.853 per U.S. dollar to FMG 277.710 per U.S. dollar, a devaluation of 11.11 per cent.

Mali also requested approval of an 11.11 per cent depreciation in the rate for the Mali franc, from MF 493.706 per U.S. dollar to MF 555.419 per U.S. dollar. This depreciation was the second for Mali during the years 1966–71. On May 5, 1967, as part of the process of rejoining the West African Monetary Union and to realign Mali's prices with those of the other countries in the Union, the Malian authorities had, with the Fund's agreement, devalued the Mali franc by 50 per cent.

The staff paper explained that changes in exchange rates for members in the French franc area were necessary to help them avoid serious economic and financial difficulties should their exchange rates deviate from that of the French franc. At the Executive Board meeting, Mr. Yaméogo, on behalf of these members except Mali, and Mr. Omwony (Kenya), on behalf of Mali, elaborated the point, saying that the complete freedom of transfer for both current and capital transactions that existed between countries in the French franc area, and the free interconvertibility of their currencies, had many advantages for the French franc area. Moreover, these countries conducted some 40–60 per cent of their foreign trade with France, and their principal source of foreign aid, both financial and technical and public and private, was France. Any change in the par value of the French franc without a corresponding change in the exchange rates for the CFA, Malagasy, and Mali francs would seriously disrupt external trade and financial transactions. Mr. Plescoff added his support to the proposed changes in these exchange rates.

With relatively little discussion, the Executive Board assented.

Other members in the French franc area, including Algeria, Morocco, and Tunisia, that did not have an operations account with the French Treasury did not devalue their currencies.

SEQUEL TO DEVALUATION OF FRANC

Shortly after the devaluation of the French franc, the Fund approved a one-year stand-by arrangement for France, the details of which, and the subsequent rapid turnaround in France's economy, have been reported in Chapter 18. The economic adjustments in the aftermath of the devaluation took place without much loss of output, and the French authorities maintained a system of surveillance which moderated the rise in prices. France's balance on current account moved from a deficit of $1.7 billion in 1969 to a surplus of $0.5 billion in 1970, and there was an overall balance of payments surplus of $2 billion in 1970, in contrast to a deficit of over $1 billion in 1969. At the end of 1970 net official reserves were about three times as large as at the time of the devaluation.

In 1971 France's balance of payments improved further, showing both current account gains and increases in capital inflows. The surplus on current account reached $1.2 billion; the overall balance showed a surplus of $3.4 billion. In 1971, too, the rate of economic growth continued to be strong. It was well above that of other EEC countries and of the United States and the United Kingdom and, indeed, was matched among major countries only by that of Canada and of Japan.

DEUTSCHE MARK IS REVALUED

Within weeks of the franc devaluation came still another crisis: the future of the deutsche mark had become one of the main issues in the general elections to be held in the Federal Republic of Germany on September 28, 1969. On Monday, September 29, the day after the elections, the German monetary authorities, having closed their exchange markets on the previous Thursday and Friday to halt another rush into deutsche mark, informed the Managing Director that they would not ensure that rates for exchange transactions involving the deutsche mark within their territory would be confined to the limits hitherto observed. This floating of the deutsche mark was intended to ward off further speculative capital inflows.

The Managing Director had been alerted over the weekend that this action was likely. The General Counsel was concerned about the implications for the member's legal position under the Articles of Agreement—specifically, that the member would not be taking appropriate measures to permit within its territory exchange transactions only within the prescribed margins, as required by Article IV, Section 4 (b)—and about the implications for the legal obligations of other members with regard to the exchange rates at which transactions between their respective currencies and the deutsche mark would take place. There had been two precedents for the action now proposed by the Federal Republic of Germany—the action of France in 1948 and that of Canada in 1950. However, the General Counsel stressed that, notwithstanding these precedents, the basic applicable provision was Article IV, Section 4 (a), under which members must "collaborate with the Fund to promote exchange stability, to maintain orderly exchange arrangements with other members, and to avoid competitive exchange alterations." It was for the Fund to specify what it regarded as appropriate collaboration.[2] Because of the General Counsel's concern, precise words were supplied to Mr. Schleiminger (Federal Republic of Germany), who cabled them to his authorities. The communication received by the Fund on Monday morning was in the language suggested. After advising the Managing Director that they had decided that they would not ensure that rates for exchange transactions involving the deutsche mark within their territory would be confined to the limits hitherto observed, the authorities of the Federal Republic of Germany assured him that they would maintain close contact with the Fund and would in the future, as they had in the past, collaborate with it fully in accordance with the Articles of Agreement.

When the notification arrived, Mr. Schweitzer was already on the platform at the Sheraton-Park Hotel ready to deliver his opening address to the Governors at the 1969 Annual Meeting. Because of foreknowledge of the action by the Federal Republic of Germany, the staff was able at the last minute to draft an insert to Mr. Schweitzer's speech. Thus it was Mr. Schweitzer who first informed the world of the floating of the deutsche mark.[3]

---

[2] After August 15, 1971, Article IV, Section 4 (a), became the primary legal basis for the Fund's activities in connection with exchange rates.

[3] Opening Address by the Managing Director, *Summary Proceedings, 1969*, p. 10.

When the Executive Directors met late in the day on September 29 to consider the notification from the member, they expressed anxiety for the par value system. But Mr. Schleiminger stressed the temporary nature of the step, and other Executive Directors recognized that allowing the deutsche mark to float was about the only action that could be taken in the circumstances. The Executive Board's decision noted the intention of the member to collaborate with the Fund and "to resume the maintenance of the limits around par at the earliest opportunity." The Fund was to remain in close consultation with the member for the latter purpose.

When the foreign exchange markets were reopened in the Federal Republic of Germany on September 30, 1969, the Deutsche Bundesbank had suspended its intervention in the exchange market at the former maximum and minimum rates. The spot rate for the deutsche mark against the dollar gradually appreciated.

The floating rate was short-lived, however. Less than four weeks later, on Friday morning, October 24, 1969, in a telex communication from the President of the Deutsche Bundesbank to the Managing Director, the Government of the Federal Republic of Germany requested the Fund's concurrence in a change in the par value of the deutsche mark from 25 U.S. cents per deutsche mark to 27.3224 U.S. cents per deutsche mark, to be effective on Sunday, October 26, 1969, at midnight, Bonn time (6:00 P.M., Washington time). The proposed change represented a revaluation of the deutsche mark of 9.29 per cent and, according to the communication, was needed to correct a fundamental disequilibrium.

Fund's Considerations

The staff and the Executive Directors had been following closely developments in the economy of the Federal Republic of Germany through the various exchange crises of 1968 and 1969, and, in fact, at approximately the time of the May 1969 decision not to revalue, the Executive Directors had been considering the staff's report on the 1968 Article VIII consultation. The report explained that, following a recession in 1966/67, exports had become buoyant and domestic investment had surged, and the resulting economic upswing had been more rapid and comprehensive than either the authorities or the Fund staff had forecast. During 1968 and 1969 the gross national product in real terms had been rising by 7–8 per cent a year, compared with a goal of 4 per cent. By the middle of 1969, unemployment had dropped to 0.7 per cent of the labor force, a postwar minimum. The one major bottleneck that had been feared once full employment had been restored, a general shortage of labor, had not appeared because of an ample supply of foreign labor: of the total labor force of 21.5 million in mid-1969, as many as 1.4 million had been foreign workers, a postwar peak.

The external trade surplus in 1968 had followed an already large surplus in 1967, which had come about because of depressed domestic demand. The monetary authorities had assured the staff that this enlarged surplus had been contrary to their expectations and to their policy. The economic expansion had been achieved with less strain on price stability than they had thought possible. Moreover, the small rise in prices in the Federal Republic of Germany had coincided with large price rises in other industrial countries. The authorities had not welcomed the extraordinary capital inflows, which enhanced bank liquidity and posed a serious threat to domestic stability. They had been trying to reconcile the objectives of full employment with equilibrium in the balance of payments, but had been reluctant to reverse their policy of monetary ease. This policy fitted in with their medium-term objective of promoting greater domestic orientation in the economy and reducing its excessive export orientation.

The Executive Directors had recognized the dilemma confronting the member. As Mr. Palamenghi-Crispi (Italy) had phrased it, the authorities had been "torn between the ghosts of inflation and the unpopularity of revaluation." The Directors had praised the high standards of international monetary cooperation and sense of international responsibility demonstrated by the German authorities in past years, with pointed reference to the fiscal measures taken to dampen the boom, the financing made available to countries that had suffered reserve losses owing to flights into deutsche mark, and the large amounts of development aid.

Against this background, the staff interpreted the decision of October 1969 to revalue as meaning that the authorities of the Federal Republic of Germany regarded the large current account surpluses and the persistent short-term capital inflows of 1968 and the first nine months of 1969 as incompatible with the preservation of internal balance. Production was now close to effective capacity and domestic prices were rising faster than before. Wages were also increasing, and greater proportions of rising incomes were going into consumption. The staff agreed that the events leading to the floating of the deutsche mark on September 29, 1969 had demonstrated that, at the prevailing exchange rate, reasonable price stability and sustainable balance of payments equilibrium, including an appropriate volume of capital exports, could no longer be realized simultaneously.

The Executive Board met on Friday afternoon, October 24, 1969, just hours after the communication was received, to consider the proposed revaluation. Mr. Schleiminger explained that, in determining the new rate for the deutsche mark, the authorities had not only followed the rate in the free market but had aimed at achieving a balance of payments that would, on the one hand, remedy the excessive current surpluses and yet, on the other hand, leave room for long-term capital exports, especially foreign aid. Mr. Plescoff said that he was under personal instructions from the French Minister of Economy and Finance to express the complete support of the French Government for the proposal, and he commended the authorities of the Federal Republic of Germany for their quick response to the wish the Executive Board had expressed on September 29, 1969, when the par value of the deutsche mark had been suspended, that the member revert to a fixed par value as soon as possible.

Mr. Dale expressed his appreciation for the speed, courage, and sense of international responsibility with which the Government had acted. He congratulated the authorities on the farsightedness shown in choosing the new rate; it involved a greater appreciation than had been considered probable by outsiders, at least until very recently. Other Executive Directors also welcomed the proposal. Mr. Kafka (Brazil) congratulated the authorities on being "good citizens of the international financial community." He hoped that the resulting reduction in the payments surplus and therefore in the supply of long-term capital would not lessen the capital flow to developing countries. Mr. Kharmawan (Indonesia) believed that the Executive Directors should be grateful for this bold step; it ought to facilitate international equilibrium. He, too, hoped that the reduction in the outflow of capital would not affect the developing countries. Both Mr. Kafka and Mr. Kharmawan also expressed the thought that the change in par value might provide an opportunity for all aid-giving countries to consider the untying of aid.

After this discussion, the Executive Board took a decision expressing the Fund's concurrence in the new par value of 27.3224 U.S. cents per deutsche mark.

Upon revaluation, the authorities of the Federal Republic of Germany reversed a number of earlier measures to curtail the current account surplus or to fend off excessive inward movements of foreign capital. The previous year's border tax adjustments were suspended, and the special reserve requirements in respect of bank liabilities to foreigners were removed.

Netherlands and Belgian Par Values Unchanged

On Monday morning, October 27, 1969, following the revaluation of the deutsche mark, Mr. de Vries (Netherlands) informed the Executive Board that the Netherlands Government, which had revalued along with the Federal Republic of Germany in 1961, had decided on this occasion to maintain the par value of the guilder unchanged. Mr. Roelandts (Belgium) said that the Belgian authorities would reach a decision on the par value of the Belgian franc following the meeting of the Council of Ministers of the European Communities then going on in Luxembourg. In accordance with that decision, Belgium also maintained its par value unchanged.

DIFFICULTIES AFTER REVALUATION OF DEUTSCHE MARK

When the staff returned to Bonn and Frankfurt some four months later in connection with the 1969 Article VIII consultation, they regarded the decision to revalue the deutsche mark as a material contribution to improving the relationships among the exchange rates of the major currencies. So did the Executive Directors. In the last quarter of 1969, speculative positions had been reversed and large amounts of capital had left the Federal Republic of Germany. As noted in Chapter 17, the member had made a super gold tranche drawing of $540 million from the Fund on November 24, 1969 to meet the capital outflow.

It continued to be difficult and even hazardous to predict the course of the economy of the Federal Republic of Germany. By the beginning of 1970 it was clear that the targets of stabilization policy had been missed by a rather wide margin. Internal inflationary forces had been underestimated and, despite the revaluation, prices and wages continued to rise rapidly. By the end of 1970 domestic prices had risen more sharply than in any year since the Korean war. On the other hand, unusually rapid gains in living standards were taking place, and real wages had increased by 13 per cent.

After revaluation, imports rose sharply. However, the country continued to run a surplus on trade account, which came to about $5.5 billion in 1970. There had been an improvement in the terms of trade. Also, exports were in a very strong competitive position, both because of the substantial investment in industry that had taken place and because consumer prices in the country's main trading partners were rising even more rapidly than they were at home. The current account surplus, nonetheless, declined, from $2.7 billion in 1969 to $1.7 billion in 1970, because the revaluation had a significant effect on the balance of services and transfers. Expenditure on foreign travel, which had increased sharply during the 1950s and 1960s and had become a relatively important component in the overall balance of payments, had a high price elasticity and rose markedly, while receipts from tourism dropped.[4] There was also a sizable increase in the remittances abroad of foreign workers. Accordingly, the deficit on net services and transfers rose from $2.4 billion in 1969 to $4.2 billion in 1970.

In the first quarter of 1970, there began to be very large inflows of foreign funds, including more than $4 billion of short-term borrowing by domestic enterprises and an increase of $2 billion in the liabilities of commercial banks. The net short-term capital inflow of banks and enterprises in 1970 more than accounted for the increase in official reserves, which was in excess of $6 billion.

The authorities, wondering whether their decision to revalue had been "too little and too late" and whether, instead of the usual expansionary measures that accompany revaluation, they should have enacted a stabilization program earlier, took a number of restrictive monetary, fiscal, and incomes policy measures to cool off the overheated economy. They viewed these measures as at least partly self-defeating, however: the tightening of monetary

---

[4] For an econometric analysis of the effect of the revaluation on tourist expenditures, see Jacques R. Artus, "The Effect of Revaluation on the Foreign Travel Balance of Germany," *Staff Papers*, Vol. 17 (1970), pp. 602–19.

policies and the raising of interest rates, which in the past had been effective, now induced domestic enterprises to borrow abroad and foreign depositors to seek haven in domestic banks. Capital inflows became greater than ever. The situation, they thought, showed up the constraints on effective national economic policy that resulted from the growing internationalization of Western economies, including the web of interconnections among financial institutions within Europe and between Europe and North America.

This inflationary domestic situation, together with an external surplus, continued through the first several months of 1971 and, as will be seen in Chapter 25 below, on May 9, 1971, the authorities of the Federal Republic of Germany again informed the Fund that they could not maintain exchange rates within the required margins around the par value of the deutsche mark.[5]

---

[5] See Chap. 25, p. 522.

CHAPTER
23

Other Adjustments in Exchange Rates
(1966–70)

P*AR VALUE ADJUSTMENTS*, especially by the developing countries, were fairly common in the years 1966–71. In addition to the changes in par values by three large industrial countries described in the previous two chapters, there were a number of other par value changes and a suspension of par value by Canada. Moreover, several members, also developing countries, that had not previously done so agreed with the Fund on initial par values. These developments in par values in the years 1966–70 are treated in this chapter. Similar events for 1971 are deferred to Chapters 25 and 26.

INITIAL PAR VALUES

Several members that had joined the Fund in the first half of the 1960s and that had not yet established initial par values—especially former nonmetropolitan territories of the United Kingdom, such as Kenya, Malawi, Tanzania, Uganda, and Zambia—did agree with the Fund on initial par values in the second half of the decade. In 1966 these five countries established initial par values, choosing the same exchange rate relationships with the dollar and with the pound sterling as they had had since 1949, that is, US$2.80 per pound sterling or 14 U.S. cents per shilling. In the course of 1967, 1968, and 1969, The Gambia, Guyana, Malta, and Singapore, which had also been dependencies of the United Kingdom and which had joined the Fund after 1965, established initial par values for their currencies.

Nepal, Rwanda, and Zaïre also agreed on initial par values for their currencies in the period 1966–70. The dollar rate for the Nepalese rupee was fixed so as to maintain its accustomed relationship to the Indian rupee (NRs 135 = Rs 100); most of Nepal's exchange transactions were in terms of Indian rupees. Botswana, Lesotho, and Swaziland notified the Fund in 1968 and 1969 that the South African rand was used as their currency. The par value of the South African rand, established in 1961, became applicable to them.

On September 4, 1970 the Republic of China—having been an original member—paid its gold subscription and set an initial par value. It used the exchange rate relationship between the new Taiwan dollar and the U.S. dollar that had been in effect since 1961. The Republic of China's arrangements with the Fund were thus regularized.

Table 16 lists in chronological order the initial par values established with the Fund from January 1, 1966 to December 31, 1970.

Table 16. Initial Par Values Established, 1966–70

Date [1]	Member and Rate
1966	
March 9	Zambia—280.000 U.S. cents per Zambian pound
April 7	Rwanda—1.000 U.S. cents per Rwanda franc
May 27	Malawi—280.000 U.S. cents per Malawi pound
August 4	Tanzania—14.000 U.S. cents per Tanzania shilling
August 15	Uganda—14.000 U.S. cents per Uganda shilling
September 14	Kenya—14.000 U.S. cents per Kenya shilling
1967	
February 13	Guyana—58.3333 U.S. cents per Guyana dollar
June 12	Singapore—32.6667 U.S. cents per Singapore dollar
December 11	Nepal—9.87654 U.S. cents per Nepalese rupee
1968	
July 8	The Gambia—240.000 U.S. cents per Gambian pound
December 20	Lesotho—140.000 U.S. cents per South African rand
1969	
June 27	Malta—240.000 U.S. cents per Malta pound
August 13	Botswana—140.000 U.S. cents per South African rand
December 22	Swaziland—140.000 U.S. cents per South African rand
1970	
September 2	Zaïre (Democratic Republic of Congo)—200.000 U.S. cents per zaïre
September 4	Republic of China—2.500 U.S. cents per new Taiwan dollar

[1] The date given is that on which the initial par value became effective, which was not necessarily the same date on which the par value was agreed with the Fund; sometimes the Fund had agreed the par value a few days earlier.

As noted in Chapter 21, at the time the pound sterling was devalued in November 1967 there were changes in the initial par values established in May 1966 by Malawi and in February 1967 by Guyana.

CHANGES IN MONETARY UNITS

Many new monetary units were introduced and put into circulation as legal tender during the period 1966–70. A few members replaced currencies that had become excessively depreciated, mainly to reduce the number of digits involved in their monetary accounts. Several members, especially in the sterling area, replaced pounds with dollars as they converted their currencies to the decimal system. Still other members, newly independent politically, put their own currencies into circulation. For the most part, new monetary units did not result in any appreciation or depreciation of exchange rates.

Effective January 1, 1966, Yugoslavia replaced the dinar with a "new dinar" as the legal currency. The new dinar was equivalent to 100 old dinars. The Yugoslav authorities, with the Fund's concurrence, accordingly restated the par value as 8.00000 U.S. cents per new dinar, which was now called simply dinar. On February 14, 1966 Australia replaced the Australian pound with the Australian dollar and established a par value of 112.000 U.S. cents per Australian dollar. On May 25, 1966 the U.K. Government notified the Fund of a change in the currency and the par value of the Bahama Islands, then a nonmetropolitan territory in respect of which the United Kingdom had accepted the Articles of Agreement: the Bahamian dollar replaced the Bahamas pound and a par value of 98.0000 U.S. cents per Bahamian dollar was established. On September 18, 1966 the Sheikdoms of Qatar and Dubai introduced the Qatar/Dubai riyal to replace the Indian rupee. An initial par value of 21.0000 U.S. cents per Qatar/Dubai riyal was established on March 11, 1969, on the proposal of the U.K. Government; this par value was the same as the Indian rupee had had prior to its devaluation on June 6, 1966 (described below).

In 1967 the Government of Brazil notified the Fund that a "new cruzeiro," having a ratio to the old cruzeiro of 1 to 1,000, would be established effective February 13, 1967. (After May 15, 1970 this monetary unit was called merely the cruzeiro.) On February 23, 1967 Ghana introduced a "new cedi," the third monetary unit introduced by Ghana since it had established an initial par value in 1958. The par value, set at 140.000 U.S. cents per new cedi, involved no effective change in the exchange rate. (The new cedi was devalued a few months later, as is discussed below.) Effective June 12, 1967, the Malaysian Government informed the Fund that the name of its currency unit would be changed from Malayan dollar to Malaysian dollar, with no change in par value. Simultaneously, the Singapore Government and the Government of Brunei (the latter a nonmetropolitan territory) replaced the Malayan dollar with the Singapore dollar and the Brunei dollar, respectively, with par values of 32.6667 U.S. cents per Singapore and Brunei dollar, the same as the Malayan dollar had had. Effective June 23, 1967, Zaïre (then the Democratic Republic of Congo), which had not yet established a par value, informed the Fund that a new monetary unit—the zaïre—would replace the Congo franc. A new exchange rate of 200.000 U.S. cents per zaïre was agreed upon. That rate became the initial par value in 1970. New Zealand introduced the New Zealand dollar to replace the New Zealand pound on July 10, 1967 and restated its par value at 139.045 U.S. cents per New Zealand dollar, the par value that was altered in November 1967.[1]

---

[1] See Chap. 21, pp. 437–38.

In 1968, in 1969, and early in 1970 other decimal currencies were introduced and par values accordingly redefined. On January 16, 1968, Zambia introduced the kwacha to replace the Zambian pound and agreed with the Fund on a par value of 140.000 U.S. cents per kwacha. The Fund concurred in a proposal of the U.K. Government for a par value for a new decimal currency, the pa'anga, introduced by Tonga to replace the Tongan pound, effective March 11, 1969. The par value was set at 112.000 U.S. cents per pa'anga, re-establishing the one-for-one relationship between the Tongan and Australian currencies that had existed before the introduction of decimal units. Effective May 14, 1969, the Fund concurred in a proposal of the Government of the United Kingdom that the Fiji dollar, which was replacing the Fiji pound, should have a fixed relationship to sterling of F$2.09 = £1. Jamaica introduced a Jamaica dollar to replace the Jamaica pound on September 8, 1969 and established a par value of 120.000 U.S. cents per Jamaica dollar.

The Government of Argentina notified the Fund that, effective January 1, 1970, a new monetary unit, the "peso," having a ratio to the former "peso moneda nacional" of 1 to 100, would be circulated. On February 6, 1970 the U.K. Government notified the Fund of the introduction by Bermuda of the Bermuda dollar to replace the Bermuda pound, and the Fund concurred in a par value of 100.000 U.S. cents per Bermuda dollar. At the same time the Fund concurred in the proposal of the U.K. Government for a change in the par value of the Bahamian dollar to 100.000 U.S. cents per Bahamian dollar, which involved a slight adjustment in that par value.

DEVALUATION OF INDIAN RUPEE

One of the most interesting developments in members' par values in the years reviewed here was the devaluation of the Indian rupee on June 6, 1966. This devaluation was unusual in several respects. *First*, the change in a par value of any large member was relatively rare at that time: the previous change in the par value of a large member had been more than 5 years before, in March 1961, when the Federal Republic of Germany had revalued the deutsche mark. *Second*, the par value of the Indian rupee had been unaltered for nearly 17 years, that is, since September 1949, when the rupee and many other currencies had been devalued along with the pound sterling. Hence, devaluation of the Indian rupee, unlike devaluation of the currencies of many other developing members, was not something that happened frequently. *Third*, a member of a major currency area, such as the sterling area, had not often undertaken a unilateral devaluation: the currencies of a currency area were usually adjusted together. *Fourth*, in view of the close commercial and economic relationships of India with neighboring countries like Ceylon, Nepal, and Pakistan, a decision by India to devalue the Indian rupee could have repercussions for these other countries.

The decision of the Indian Government to devalue the rupee was taken in the context of India's general economic situation. For the previous ten years India's balance of payments had been under almost continuous strain. In the two years immediately preceding the devaluation, the balance of payments deficits had been enlarged by increased imports, especially of foodgrains, to make up for shortfalls in domestic output. These shortfalls had been caused by the worst drought that India had had in the twentieth century. Because of these difficulties, India had been making substantial use of the Fund's resources since 1964, including the large drawing made without a stand-by arrangement in April 1966, described in Chapter 17.

The Indian authorities had been trying for some years to reduce the balance of payments deficits by the use of selective incentives for exports and severe restrictions on imports. There had been introduced export promotion arrangements which had given rise to different implicit exchange rates—in effect, to multiple currency practices. Import duties and tariffs had been raised to very high levels.

The Fund management and staff and the Indian authorities had been discussing policies to manage India's deficits, and after the drawing of April 1966 these discussions were intensified. It had become increasingly evident that India's balance of payments problem required more fundamental measures than had hitherto been tried and that its economy would benefit greatly from a liberalization of the extremely tight import restrictions. Both the Indian authorities and the Fund management and staff came to the position that if a devaluation of the rupee was undertaken, the degree of devaluation ought to be sizable. It ought to be great enough not only to assist major exports but also to help marginal exports and to provide a safety valve for the future. The Indian authorities were very much concerned about the impact of devaluation on the landed costs of imports. Especially were they concerned that increasing the cost of capital goods imports, which made up a large proportion of the country's total imports, would raise the cost of investment, including the cost of projects already under way.

In the end, the Government did decide on a devaluation, and on June 3, 1966 requested the Fund's concurrence in a change in the par value of the rupee from 21.0000 U.S. cents per rupee to 13.3333 U.S. cents per rupee, a devaluation of 36.5 per cent, to be effective on June 6, 1966 at 2:00 A.M., Indian standard time (June 5, 1966 at 4:30 P.M., Washington time). The particular new par value had been chosen so as to make India's exports more competitive in world markets and, even, to give them a slight edge. Along with the change in par value there were to be major exchange and trade reforms. Quantitative restrictions on a high proportion of imports were to be removed over the next two years, assuming that foreign aid was sufficient to permit such liberalization. In this connection, the Indian authorities were deliberating with the World Bank. Also, a program was worked out in which those quantitative restrictions that were being used for protection of local industry would gradually be phased out in favor of the use of tariffs. Eventually, import liberalization was to be supported by the expected growth of India's exports after devaluation.

In evaluating the proposed change in the par value of the rupee, the staff viewed the devaluation and the accompanying removal of export promotion devices and the liberalization of imports as the most far-reaching changes in economic policy that the Indian Government had made in several years. The staff supported the magnitude involved and thought that the devaluation would make an important contribution to strengthening the Indian economy and accelerating its development along sound lines. When the Executive Directors met to consider the change of par value, the Managing Director told them that the Government had followed fully the advice of the management and staff and that, should the Indian authorities so request, he was prepared to support a sizable stand-by arrangement.

The Executive Directors expressed sympathy with India's overwhelming problems and welcomed "the constructive and courageous" proposal to devalue. They recognized that the new exchange rate was not expected to bring the balance of payments into equilibrium or to permit the removal of all import restrictions. Rather, it was to pave the way for a substantial and beneficial liberalization of imports. Mr. Mansour noted the close relationship between the exchange rate of India and those of neighboring members, such as Ceylon, Nepal, and Pakistan, and hoped that adverse repercussions could be avoided.[2] The Executive Board then concurred in the proposed change of par value.

About a week later the Finance Minister of India, Mr. Sachindra Chaudhuri, cabled Mr. Schweitzer to express his appreciation of the good will shown and the assistance given to India by the Fund.

Aftermath

When the staff went to India several months later in connection with the 1966 consultation under Article XIV, it reported that the Indian authorities had been carrying out a program of import liberalization but that it was too early to assess the beneficial effects therefrom and from the devaluation. In fact, India's balance of payments position had actually deteriorated. When the consultation report was discussed in the Executive Board, Mr. Madan (India) and Mr. Saad stressed the importance of adequate capital inflows to India so as to assist that member with its basic problems of economic development.

At the time of the next Article XIV consultation, late in 1967, although

---

[2] The implication of the devaluation of the Indian rupee on the initial par value of the Nepalese rupee was noted earlier in this chapter; the implication for Ceylon was discussed in Chap. 21 above, pp. 438–39.

exports had not increased very much, India's economic prospects were more favorable, particularly as agricultural growing conditions had improved. When the 1968 consultation was completed, in February 1969, marked improvements had taken place. Agricultural output had increased. Domestic prices had become more stable. Exports had expanded. Balance of payments pressures had eased.

DEVALUATION BY GHANA

In a letter dated July 5, 1967 to Mr. Schweitzer, signed by both the Chairman of the Economic Committee of the National Liberation Council of Ghana, Mr. E. N. Omaboe, and the Governor of the Bank of Ghana, Mr. A. Adomakoh, the Ghanaian authorities requested the Fund's concurrence in a change in the par value of the new cedi. When the new cedi had been introduced in February 1967 there had been no effective change in the par value. The proposal now was to change the par value from 140.000 U.S. cents per new cedi to 98.000 U.S. cents per new cedi, a devaluation of 30 per cent.

A new government had taken over in Ghana early in 1966 and close relations with the Fund had been established. Ghana had been receiving substantial technical assistance from the Fund in the field of tax reform and in the preparation of government budgets, and since July 1966 the Fund had had a resident representative in Accra. Ghana had made several drawings on the Fund and had a stand-by arrangement. The Fund and the World Bank had also been collaborating closely in a number of meetings concerning a possible rearrangement of the payments on Ghana's medium-term external debt.[3]

The Ghanaian authorities had been having extensive informal discussions about Ghana's economic problems with staff of both the World Bank and the Fund and had for some time been considering informally with the Fund the exchange rate for their currency. In the summer of 1967 they suddenly decided to devalue. They proposed a devaluation of 30 per cent and asked for more financial assistance from the Fund. The staff proposed that the latter take the form of a change in the phasing of the amounts available under the stand-by arrangement that had just recently been approved.

The Executive Board concurred in the proposed change in the par value, effective July 8, and agreed to the change in the phasing of drawings under the stand-by arrangement. The Deputy Governor of the Bank of Ghana, Mr. G. H. Frimpong-Ansah, was present at the Board's discussion. Mr. Nikoi (Ghana) explained that the change in par value should be seen in the context of the stabilization efforts that the authorities had embarked upon in May 1966. They believed that the time had come to move to a new and realistic

---

[3] Additional description of the Fund's close relationship with Ghana at this time, including the renegotiation of Ghana's external debt, is contained in Chap. 29 below.

exchange rate which, they thought, would lead to a better allocation of resources and enhance the prospects for long-term growth. Sir John Stevens (United Kingdom) supported the devaluation, which he considered to be of the right magnitude, and the accompanying economic measures. He thought that the devaluation would encourage exports, particularly of timber and gold, but that windfall profits to exporters, especially from cocoa exports, should be recaptured by the Government. Some Executive Directors, believing that producers had to have the necessary incentives to expand production and exports, did not agree about the need to recapture the extra profits of exporters.

Mr. Yaméogo likewise saw the Ghanaian devaluation as part of the stabilization program that had been launched in the early part of 1966 and was still in progress. He believed devaluation would lay the groundwork for the resumption of balanced economic growth. A disparity between domestic and external costs and prices, with a resulting balance of payments deficit, was a legacy of past inflation. Several Executive Directors commented favorably on the substantial liberalization of import and exchange controls that was planned.

Several months thereafter, in February 1968, on the occasion of the 1967 consultation under Article XIV, the economic situation in Ghana seemed to be coming along favorably. The Executive Directors commended the Ghanaian authorities for their achievements in the two years since they had embarked on their stabilization program.

DEVALUATION BY FINLAND

Mr. Klaus Waris, Governor of the Fund for Finland, in a letter dated October 6, 1967, informed Mr. Schweitzer that the Finnish authorities were planning to ask the concurrence of the Fund in a change in the par value of the Finnish markka from 31.25 U.S. cents per markka to 23.8097 U.S. cents per markka, a devaluation of 23.8 per cent. Finland had last devalued the markka in September 1957. (The introduction of a new monetary unit and the establishment of a par value for that unit on January 1, 1963 had not represented an effective change in the par value.)

Mr. Waris explained that Finland's economy was in fundamental disequilibrium. Since 1958 Finnish costs and prices had increased by at least 15 per cent more than the average in the countries with which Finland conducted most of its trade. He added that the Finnish authorities were also taking measures to strengthen investment in, and to enhance the productivity of, export industries.

The official request for the Fund's concurrence in a change of par value was received by the Fund five days later. The Finnish authorities proposed that the devaluation take effect on October 12, 1967 at 9:00 A.M., Finnish time (3:00 A.M., Washington time). The staff supported the devaluation on two main grounds: after 1965 balance of payments considerations had set narrow limits to Finland's growth, and the adjustment in par value ought to help Finland to bring about the structural changes that would enable it to make more productive use of its considerable reserves of skilled manpower.

At the Executive Board meeting, Mr. Jorma Aranko (Finland) explained that since 1965 Finland had given priority in its economic policy to the gradual restoration of balance of payments equilibrium. This had been the goal of monetary policy and, since mid-1966, of fiscal policy as well. In addition, certain more direct measures had been taken to improve the trade balance, and this program had slowly begun to produce results. Exports had become somewhat further diversified and the industrial structure was being rationalized. There had been disappointments, however. It had been more difficult than expected to restrain consumer demand. Even more important, external circumstances had been less favorable than expected, and reserves had diminished. A further tightening of monetary and fiscal policy would lead to unemployment and prejudice new investment. Import restrictions would intensify distortions and lead to higher domestic prices. Hence the decision to devalue had been taken. Mr. Aranko said that the proposed devaluation would be accompanied by taxes on exports, the lifting of tariffs on many imports, and the abolition of several import restrictions.

The Executive Board, recognizing the nature of the fundamental disequilibrium, concurred in the proposed change of par value.

DEVALUATION BY ICELAND

Iceland had devalued its currency four times after the first big wave of devaluations by Fund members in September 1949, changing its par value again in 1950, in 1960, in 1961, and, as described in Chapter 21 above, in 1967.[4] In close consultation with a staff mission that was in Reykjavik at the time, the Icelandic authorities decided in November 1968 once again to devalue the króna. The par value would be changed from 1.75439 U.S. cents per króna to 1.13636 U.S. cents per króna, a devaluation of 35.2 per cent, effective November 12, 1968 at 9:00 A.M., Icelandic time (4:00 A.M., Washington time).

Mr. Asp (Finland) explained to the Executive Directors that Iceland was in an economic crisis. It had suffered a severe decline in export receipts in 1967 and 1968 because the herring catches had greatly diminished and the prices of several important fish products had fallen substantially. In the first nine months of 1968, the herring catch was 78 per cent smaller than in the corresponding period of 1967. At the beginning of the crisis, it had been hoped that the decline in the herring catch would be temporary. When this hope

---

[4] See *History, 1945–65*, Vol. II, pp. 117–18, and Chap. 21 above, pp. 438–39.

was not realized the Government took a series of actions to improve the situation, culminating in the imposition of an import surcharge in September 1968. These actions, together with the lowered income of the fishing industry, had reduced the country's real income. As a result, imports had begun to decrease also. In fact, economic activity generally had started to decline and there were signs of increasing unemployment. A fundamental disequilibrium was evident. Eventually, changes would be made in Iceland's economy, but diversification of its exports was difficult because of limited domestic resources.

The Executive Directors, noting that the gross national income per capita had fallen by 10 per cent in 1968, were very sympathetic. Some drastic changes had to be made, particularly as Iceland did not have a diversified economy. They understood that the authorities preferred the difficult political step of devaluation as a way to cope with export shortfalls rather than resorting to controls and restrictions on imports. Mr. Huntrods (United Kingdom), calling attention to the relative frequency with which the króna had been devalued, supported the staff's call for the most strenuous efforts to prevent excessive increases in monetary incomes after devaluation, since pressures on prices, leading to a wage-price spiral, could be most severe. The Executive Board concurred in the proposed change of par value.

DEVALUATION BY TURKEY

In a communication dated July 31, 1970, the Government of Turkey requested the Fund's concurrence in a change in the par value of the Turkish lira from 11.1111 U.S. cents per lira to 6.66667 U.S. cents per lira, a devaluation of 40 per cent. The new par value was to be effective on August 10, 1970 at 12:01 A.M., Ankara time (August 9, 1970 at 6:01 P.M., Washington time). The existing par value had been in effect since 1960. In addition, the Government requested a stand-by arrangement.

In June 1969, when the Executive Directors had considered Turkey's economic situation, they had commented on the need for an overhaul of the country's trade and exchange arrangements. The Turkish authorities thereafter had committed themselves to a comprehensive review of their exchange practices and had had several discussions with the staff. That review was now completed and had led to a wide-ranging reform.

The change in the par value, which the Turkish authorities stated to be necessary to correct a fundamental disequilibrium, was thus to be accompanied by a general reform of the trade and payments system. This involved a gradual liberalization of quantitative restrictions on imports, the termination of the remaining bilateral payments agreements with Fund members, and a considerable simplification of the various effective exchange rates being applied. Among other exchange rate measures, two of the four multiple rates—resulting from a premium of 33⅓ per cent paid on the amount of specified convertible currencies exchanged by tourists and other nonresidents in Turkey for local currencies and a premium of 25 per cent applied to purchases of convertible currencies acquired by residents in respect of air or road transport—were to be eliminated when the new par value went into effect. Temporarily, a multiple rate, less depreciated than the new rate, would apply to certain traditional exports.

The Executive Directors readily agreed that the Turkish economy was in fundamental disequilibrium. As Mr. de Maulde (France) expressed it, any improvement in Turkey's balance of payments at the existing par value would have been impossible without a marked slowdown in the rate of expansion experienced in recent years and without quantitative controls, which had proved harmful in the past. Mr. Schleiminger, and others, especially commended the comprehensive stabilization program and the general streamlining of the trade and payments system worked out in close cooperation with the staff. The Executive Board welcomed the proposed change of par value and the responsiveness of the Turkish authorities to the Board's views, and approved the related multiple exchange rate.

DEVALUATION BY ECUADOR

In a letter dated August 13, 1970, Mr. Joaquín Zevallós, General Manager of the Central Bank of Ecuador, requested on behalf of the Government that the Fund concur in a proposed change in the par value of the sucre from 5.55556 U.S. cents per sucre to 4.00000 U.S. cents per sucre, a devaluation of 28 per cent, to be effective on August 17, 1970. The existing par value had been in effect since July 1961.

As Mr. Arriazu (Argentina) explained, the Ecuadoran authorities defended the proposed change in par value as necessary to correct a fundamental disequilibrium. They cited the heavy use of multiple currency practices and restrictive measures that had been required to support the existing par value. In spite of these practices, the net international reserves of the Central Bank had declined by over $30 million in the first six months of 1970, leaving reserves equivalent to only two months' imports. The principal reason for Ecuador's balance of payments difficulties had been a rapidly growing deficit in the budget of the Central Government. The budgetary deficit, in turn, had come about because government expenditures had expanded sharply while revenues had expanded slowly.

In July there had been a comprehensive exchange reform aimed at eventually consolidating the official and free markets, which had been long-standing in Ecuador. The proposed change in the par value of the sucre represented achievement of that aim. The official and free market rates were to be replaced by a single fixed rate. Controls would restrict the capital transactions previously assigned to the free market. Tax measures were to be introduced which, together with the profits from the devaluation that would be reaped internally, would enlarge government revenues and reduce the budgetary deficit.

The Ecuadoran authorities asked that a staff mission be sent to Quito immediately both to discuss an overall financial program to follow the change in par value and unification of the exchange system and to negotiate a stand-by arrangement. The Executive Board, pleased to learn of the requested mission, agreed and also concurred in the change of par value. In the course of the discussion, some Executive Directors, notably Mr. Dale and Mr. Lieftinck, commented on the relatively large degree of devaluation, noting that the dangers of competitive devaluation should not be ignored. Nonetheless, they thought that the magnitude of the devaluation was probably not worrisome, considering the levels of the exchange rates effective under the former multiple rate system and the advance import deposits that would be removed.

Following Ecuador's exchange reform, the Ecuadoran authorities were able to notify the Fund that Ecuador accepted the obligations of Article VIII, Sections 2, 3, and 4, of the Fund Agreement with effect from August 31, 1970. On September 11, 1970, when the Executive Board approved a one-year stand-by arrangement for Ecuador, it noted in a further decision that Ecuador had taken this step with regard to Article VIII.

CANADA RETURNS TO A FLOATING RATE

In the first quarter of 1968 Canada had a short-lived crisis and the Canadian dollar came under serious pressure, largely as a result of a succession of external events: the devaluation of sterling in November 1967, the announcement in January 1968 of a new U.S. balance of payments program, and the gold crisis of March 1968. The U.S. payments program had an especially great effect. Because the program involved some mandatory controls ·on the movement of U.S. capital, concerns arose about the continued feasibility of substantial transfers from Canada of funds held there by U.S. corporations.[5] Hence, large amounts of U.S. short-term capital flowed out of Canada in advance. Canada's current account balance was at about the same level as in the first quarter of 1967, but the outflow of short-term capital, combined with a reduced inflow of long-term capital, resulted in an external deficit of $0.7 billion.

A drawing on the Fund in February 1968 equivalent to Canada's gold subscription and the amount of Canadian dollars purchased by other members from the Fund and the repayment by the Fund of loans from Canada under

---

[5] This U.S. payments program is described in Chap. 24 below, pp. 487–88.

the General Arrangements to Borrow, totaling $426 million, together with activation of the swap arrangement with the U.S. Federal Reserve to the extent of $250 million, helped the Canadian dollar through these difficulties. On March 7 Canada was exempted from the U.S. controls on capital outflows. This exemption, together with the March 17 announcement concerning gold market arrangements, helped to restore confidence in the Canadian dollar.

A more serious but different problem arose about two years later. In May 1970, eight years to the month after Canada had set a par value of 92.5 U.S. cents per Canadian dollar following more than a decade with a fluctuating exchange rate, the Government again suspended the par value and returned to a fluctuating exchange rate. On Sunday, May 31, 1970, Mr. Benson, the Minister of Finance, cabled Mr. Schweitzer to let him know that the Government had decided that Canada would not, for the time being, maintain the exchange rate of the Canadian dollar within the present margins, but that it intended to remain in consultation with the Fund and to resume the fulfillment of its obligations under the Articles of Agreement as soon as circumstances permitted. Mr. Benson stated further that he planned to announce this decision publicly at 5:00 P.M. that day.

Precipitating Circumstances and Staff's Reactions

The circumstances that led to the resumption of a floating rate in Canada were similar to those that had caused the member to float its currency in 1950: capital inflows, mainly from the United States, were adding to reserves and hence to the money supply and were making it more difficult to control inflation.[6]

The year 1970 had opened with a dramatic change in Canada's balance of payments position. The current account, which had been in sizable deficit throughout 1969, moved into heavy surplus (seasonally adjusted) in the first quarter of 1970 as merchandise exports rose sharply and imports declined. Added to the upsurge in the current account was a continued heavy inflow of long-term capital.

Since an important element in the export boom was a post-strike recovery in exports of mining products, there was reason to believe that the extraordinary strength shown by the export sector might be short-lived. However, exports continued strong after the first three months of 1970 despite the weakness in 1970 of the U.S. economy, the major external market for Canadian goods, while imports remained weak. Moreover, the rapid easing of financial conditions in the United States and in the Eurodollar market began to manifest itself in a net inflow of short-term capital to Canada. Beginning in March, Canadian monetary policy had become more expansive, and direct steps had also been taken to encourage outflows of short-term funds by the removal of the ceiling on the amounts that banks could receive in the form of swapped deposits. By May 1970 interest rates in Canada were generally well below those prevailing at

---

[6] *History, 1945–65*, Vol. II, pp. 159–65.

the turn of the year, and differentials between Canadian and U.S. interest rates had narrowed appreciably, after more than two years of unusually wide average spreads in favor of Canada.

Nonetheless, the increase in foreign exchange reserves continued at an accelerated pace. In the first four months of 1970, official reserves, including an allocation of SDR 124 million, had risen by more than $700 million, and in May there was a further increase of $260 million. In addition, as a result of official swap and forward transactions, $360 million was acquired by the authorities in May for future delivery.

The accumulation of reserves far in excess of Canada's needs became troublesome. It greatly increased the cash requirements of the Government, and the authorities feared that speculative buying of Canadian dollars might be touched off, with disruptive effects on the entire international monetary system and large windfall profits for speculators.

Concurrent with the decision of the authorities to suspend the par value, the Bank of Canada, in an effort to reduce capital inflows, announced a reduction in the bank rate from 7½ per cent to 7 per cent.

The staff had been in Ottawa the month before, in April 1970, for discussions in connection with the Article VIII consultation, after a two-year interval, and was still writing a report on those discussions. The staff's unfavorable response to the Canadian action in many respects paralleled its views on the floating of the Canadian dollar in 1950. This time, however, remembering the length of that period of floating, the staff placed somewhat less stress on the alternative ways in which the Canadian authorities might deal with capital inflows and much more emphasis on the possible repercussions on the par value system of a prolonged floating of a major currency. The staff suggested to the Executive Board that it adopt a decision noting the Canadian situation but emphasizing the undertaking by members to collaborate with the Fund to promote exchange stability, to maintain orderly exchange arrangements, and to avoid competitive exchange alterations, and requesting the Canadian Government to remain in close consultation with the Fund with a view to a resumption of an effective par value at the earliest possible date.

Executive Directors' Positions

For some months the Executive Directors had been examining, in informal session, the workings of the par value system and the desirability of additional flexibility of exchange rates.[7] Consequently, when they met on Sunday afternoon, May 31, 1970, an hour before Mr. Benson was to broadcast his decision, their positions on the floating of the Canadian rate reflected their differing views on flexible exchange rates. Some of them were eager to preserve fixed rates and

---

[7] See Chap. 24 below.

were concerned lest the introduction of a floating rate in a major country upset the system of par values, while others were more inclined to recognize that certain circumstances might necessitate a floating rate.

Mr. Johnstone (Canada) stressed the promptness with which the Canadian authorities had acted to deal with a situation that was rapidly becoming unmanageable. Their action had been essential. It would avoid, rather than introduce, disruptive pressures on the international monetary system. He objected particularly to the "clearly critical judgment" implied by the Executive Board decision as drafted by the staff.

Mr. Plescoff, noting that the situation in Canada was analogous to that which had caused the Canadian authorities to resort to a fluctuating exchange rate in 1950, and that the fluctuating rate had then persisted for many years, proposed that the Fund place a short time limit on its concurrence, something like two months. Otherwise, more members might act in the same way and destroy the whole international monetary system. He was supported by Mr. Palamenghi-Crispi. Some Executive Directors, however, considered a time limit unwise; such a limit might, inter alia, encourage speculation against the Canadian dollar. Mr. Lieftinck regretted that the Canadian authorities had not allowed time for a genuine debate among the Executive Directors or for them to exercise any influence on the Canadian decision. Nor had the authorities provided the Fund with a clear statement of their policy intentions: Were they planning eventually to alter their par value? Did they consider Canada as having a fundamental disequilibrium? Meanwhile, he shared the staff's concern that continued instability of a major currency could not fail to disturb international economic relations.

Mr. Schleiminger, on the other hand, likened the Canadian situation to that of the Federal Republic of Germany in September 1969 and understood why the Canadian authorities had decided to float the Canadian dollar. Mr. Huntrods, interpreting the Canadian move as temporary and as a way to achieve a more appropriate par value, welcomed it as a useful step away from overly rigid exchange rates.

After several Executive Directors had expressed displeasure that the authorities had not allowed the Fund more time, after Mr. Johnstone had assured the Executive Board that the Canadian Government would cooperate with the Fund, and after the Managing Director had pointed out that the staff would go to Ottawa within a few weeks for discussions with Canadian officials, the Executive Board took a decision along the lines of the staff's suggestion but with adaptations in wording: the Fund noted the situation in Canada, emphasized the undertaking by members to collaborate with the Fund to promote exchange stability, and welcomed the intention of the Canadian authorities to remain in close consultation with the Fund with a view to the resumption of an effective par value at the earliest possible date.

CANADA CONTINUES TO HAVE A FLOATING RATE

In the weeks and months to come the Fund followed intensively the developments pertaining to Canada's exchange rate and general economic situation. Twice in June 1970 Mr. Johnstone reported orally to the Executive Directors, noting that quoted rates for the Canadian dollar were 3.3 to 3.85 per cent above the par value. The highest level reached after the first week was 96.82 U.S. cents per Canadian dollar, some 4.7 per cent above the par value. A staff team visited Ottawa June 15–19, 1970, to resume discussions in connection with the 1970 Article VIII consultation that had begun in April 1970, and conveyed to Canadian officials the views of the Executive Board and of the Managing Director that Canada should move promptly to restore an effective par value. The staff drew attention to the Fund's concern that Canada's suspension of its par value had increased uncertainty over exchange rates in the world and that Canada had acquired for its exchange rate policy a freedom that could not be widely extended to other members without undermining the trade and payments system of the whole world.

For these reasons, the staff urged the Canadian authorities to adopt policies and arrangements that would indicate a well-defined path for a speedy return to the par value system. Specifically, they suggested the pursuit of exchange rate and official reserve management policies that would enable an appropriate exchange rate to be tested in the market.

The staff also questioned the authorities about their stated intention of "maintaining orderly conditions in the market." The authorities explained that their intention was to intervene in the market only to cushion the exchange rate against the effects of especially large transactions and to prevent unduly rapid movements of the exchange rate within a limited period of time. They did not plan to "fix" the rate prevailing in the market.

The Executive Directors supported the staff's position. By the time the report on the 1970 Article VIII consultation was discussed in the Executive Board, on July 31, 1970, the Canadian dollar had appreciated to 97.5 U.S. cents, and the Canadian authorities had been intervening in the market to moderate the upward movement of the rate. Some of the Executive Directors focused on the courses of action that the authorities might take instead of letting the exchange rate float. For example, Mr. Lieftinck asked about the feasibility of (1) restrictions on capital imports, (2) monetary measures, such as raising reserve requirements and imposition of quantitative limits on credit expansion, and (3) the use of open market operations that would neutralize the impact of capital inflows. Messrs. Asp, Carlos Bustelo (Spain), de Kock (South Africa), Kharmawan, Phillips O. (Mexico), van Campenhout (Belgium), and others urged Canada to return to a par value. Mr. Johnstone reiterated that the Canadian authorities had found any alternatives to the floating rate difficult or self-defeating. They, too, wanted to move to a defensible par value as soon as they could. They viewed the floating rate as transitional, and did not expect Canada to be regarded as an exceptional case.

In August 1970 Mr. Louis Rasminsky, Governor of the Bank of Canada and former long-time Executive Director of the Fund, accompanied by Mr. Johnstone, the present Executive Director, called on Mr. Schweitzer and Mr. Southard for informal discussions. In cordial and friendly talks, both sides took the same positions as previously held concerning the best methods of handling the Canadian problem of persistent capital inflows. In other words, Mr. Rasminsky defended the need for a floating rate while the Fund management continued to believe in the usefulness of measures to curb capital inflows and to alleviate their impact on the domestic economy.

Meanwhile, the Canadian authorities began to make weekly reports to the Fund on the U.S. dollar rates for the Canadian dollar and to cable regularly information on the country's official reserves. Toward the end of 1970 the Fund held the first of special quarterly consultations with a member that had suspended transactions at its par value. In this connection a staff team went to Ottawa on October 13–16, 1970. Following the visit, it was the staff's assessment that, although unemployment was high, the balance of payments position and developments in Canada's capital markets had become more normal, improving the climate for re-establishment of an effective par value.

The Executive Directors, meeting in December 1970 to hold these consultations at the Board level, commended the Canadian authorities for their efforts to attain stability. But a consensus existed that Canada, by being the only major country with a floating rate, was in a highly privileged position and that the Fund should press for re-establishment of a par value. A main argument, presented by Messrs. Erik Brofoss (Norway), de Maulde, de Vries, Suzuki, and van Campenhout, was that the existing status of the Canadian dollar created uncertainty for the international monetary system. Mr. de Vries pointed out that the Canadian authorities had set "an extremely bad precedent." Messrs. Dale, Ronald H. Gilchrist (United Kingdom), and Schleiminger commented on the remarkable stability of the exchange rate of the Canadian dollar since September. To them, the calm that prevailed in the Canadian exchange market seemed to have set the stage for a return to a fixed rate. Mr. Madan, while appreciating the dilemma facing the Canadian authorities, thought that the lower current account surplus and reduced volume of capital movements indicated that in the not-too-distant future the Canadian authorities could re-establish a par value. However, at least three members of the Executive Board, Mr. Costa P. Caranicas (Greece), Mr. Eduardo da S. Gomes, Jr. (Brazil), and Mr. Massad (Chile), argued that Canada should be allowed more time.

Mr. Johnstone agreed that the delay in re-establishing a par value had in some degree been a cause of uncertainty for the international monetary system. But he stressed that developments regarding the Canadian dollar had not been the main destabilizing factor in the world monetary system. In the judgment of the Canadian authorities, two conditions should prevail before Canada returned to a fixed rate: one was exchange rate stability, which he acknowledged had already existed for a relatively long period, and the other was the certainty that the balance of forces reflected in the exchange market was "normal." The latter condition had not yet been secured. He reassured the Executive Directors that the Canadian authorities were determined to re-establish an effective par value, but that Canada would set a bad precedent if it chose an exchange rate which, in the short term, proved inappropriate.

At the end of 1970 the Executive Board took a decision to the effect that the Fund had been in consultation with Canada on its exchange system, that it was the Fund's view that Canada should place a high priority on the re-establishment of an effective par value for its currency, and that the Fund would remain in close consultation with Canada for this purpose.

Developments in Canada's fluctuating exchange rate during 1971 and the Fund's continuing relationships with the Canadian authorities form part of Chapter 25.

CHAPTER

24

Examining the
Exchange Rate Mechanism

(1969–70)

*R*EFORM OF THE INTERNATIONAL MONETARY SYSTEM was being advocated as early as the middle of 1968. In particular, proposals were being put forward to alter the par value system so as to permit greater flexibility of exchange rates. Academic economists, for example, were proposing methods by which exchange rates could be adjusted more readily and were suggesting that they have some interchange of ideas with the banking and business world.[1] Those monetary officials who were not yet advocating reform had, as a minimum, become seriously concerned about the functioning of the system. The developments described in the preceding four chapters had made it clear that one crisis quickly followed another. Many officials were worried that these crises, plus the prolonged deficit in the U.S. balance of payments, placed the stability of the international monetary system in jeopardy.[2]

At the 1968 Annual Meeting, even as the accomplishment of amending the Articles of Agreement to incorporate the SDR facility was being hailed, Mr. Schweitzer gave recognition to these developments and concerns. His remarks to the Board of Governors on September 30, 1968 ended on this note:

> I should be the first to recognize that we have much unfinished work on our hands. The world does not stand still and the effort to improve the monetary system which serves it is an unremitting task. Standing as it does at the heart

---

[1] As a result, two conferences, attended by academic economists, private bankers, and businessmen from several different countries, were held in 1969, one in January at Oyster Bay, New York, and one in June at Bürgenstock near Lucerne, Switzerland. The papers that were presented at, or resulted from, the two conferences were published as *Approaches to Greater Flexibility of Exchange Rates: The Bürgenstock Papers*, arranged by C. Fred Bergsten, George N. Halm, Fritz Machlup, and Robert V. Roosa, and edited by George N. Halm (Princeton, 1970).

[2] Developments in the U.S. balance of payments, mentioned only briefly in earlier chapters, are described later in this chapter.

of the system, the Fund is deeply committed to this task. The Fund has given evidence of that commitment in the past through its flexible response to the needs of the times. It will remain alert to those needs and actively explore what contribution it might make to the further strengthening of the world monetary system. Continuing attention will have to be paid to the working of the adjustment process, the long-term structure of reserves, and the role of reserve currencies within that structure. These, Mr. Chairman, are major issues for the Fund in the period ahead.[3]

In the last few months of 1968, attention centered on the probable need for adjusting the exchange rates of the currencies of at least some of the large industrial countries, the Bonn meeting in November being aimed specifically at discussing the rates for the French franc and the deutsche mark. No changes in exchange rates were made, however. As a consequence of this further evidence that par values were exceedingly difficult to change, the feeling was growing that amendment of the Bretton Woods arrangements with respect to the supply of liquidity, which had just been approved, would have to be supplemented by amendment with respect to the process of balance of payments adjustment in general and the exchange rate regime in particular. Recommendations that some kind of meeting or conference be called to reconsider the general system by which exchange rates were altered under the Fund's Articles of Agreement began to be made quite frequently, even by highly placed monetary officials.

These developments prompted the Executive Directors to agree in January 1969 to a thoroughgoing review of the mechanism of exchange rate adjustment, the first such review since the Fund's Articles had entered into effect. After a year and a half of deliberations they produced a report, *The Role of Exchange Rates in the Adjustment of International Payments.*[4] The present chapter gives an account of these deliberations and the resulting report, and explains the lack of action by the Board of Governors at the Annual Meeting in Copenhagen in September 1970.

■ ■ ■ ■ ■ ■

Proposals for improving the adjustment process, especially the exchange rate mechanism, stemmed largely from two problems which, after about 1965, began to disrupt the previously smooth operation of the international monetary system. *One,* the imbalance that had plagued international payments for ten years seemed to be perpetual; and its prolongation implied that the process of balance of payments adjustment was not working properly. *Two,* short-term capital movements, which had become of unprecedented dimensions, were seriously adding to the difficulties of attaining payments equilibrium or of preserving exchange rate stability.

---

[3] Opening Address by the Managing Director, *Summary Proceedings, 1968,* p. 29.
[4] Reproduced in Vol. II below, pp. 273–330.

U.S. DEFICIT

The imbalance in world payments consisted principally of the coexistence of a large deficit in the balance of payments of the United States and sizable surpluses in the balance of payments of a number of other industrial countries. The U.S. deficit, which when it first emerged in the late 1950s had been welcomed as a way to redress the chronic world dollar shortage of the early postwar period, and which had been considered temporary, persisted into the late 1960s, becoming especially large after 1965. This deficit had been a source of concern even before apprehensions about the working of the balance of payments adjustment process became serious in 1968. The reader of Part One will recall these concerns and that periodic improvements and deterioration in the U.S. external payments position had profoundly affected the discussions on the need for a new reserve asset in the monetary system.[5] The reader of Part One will recall mention also of a number of steps taken by the U.S. authorities to reduce external deficits. Among the measures taken were extraordinary ones aimed at curbing the outflow of private long-term capital, particularly of direct investment in Europe: an interest equalization tax had been introduced in 1963 and extended in 1965, and a voluntary foreign credit restraint program providing guidelines to banks and other financial institutions for the reduction of their dollar outflows had been introduced in 1965.

Measures to restrain capital outflows had been emphasized in a context in which huge long-term capital transfers, both private and official, were the primary cause of the U.S. payments deficit. In 1965, for instance, the United States had had a surplus on current account (defined here as in the Fund's Annual Reports for these years as the balance on goods, services, and private transfers) of $6.0 billion. This surplus, while sharply lower (by $1.6 billion) than the current account surplus in 1964, had been, nonetheless, much higher than those in most previous years except 1964.[6] There was, however, a large deficit on capital account because U.S. long-term private investment continued to be very large—about $4.5 billion a year—as the United States had for many years been the main exporter of funds for direct investment and, in addition, capital payments and transfers abroad by the U.S. Government had remained substantial, more than $3 billion a year. Together with short-term capital flows, the deficit on capital account in 1965 had been $7.5 billion. The overall deficit, as measured on the official settlements basis, had thus been $1.5 billion.

Year-by-year developments in the U.S. balance of payments position in the next few years indicate the complex of factors underlying the U.S. external

---

[5] Chap. 3, pp. 52–53 and 63–64; Chap. 4, pp. 74–75; and Chap. 7, p. 171.

[6] The data used here for the U.S. balance of payments and reserve positions were, for the most part, taken from the Fund's Annual Reports, which in turn were based on data of the U.S. Department of Commerce. Although balance of payments figures are often subsequently revised from those available currently, the views expressed and decisions taken at the time, which form the subject of this history, are usually based on the initial data.

deficits and the attempts to deal with these deficits. In 1966 the voluntary foreign credit restraint program continued to operate under guidelines that were increasingly restrictive, and there was a decline in the net outflow of private long-term capital that outweighed increases in the outflow of government payments. A tightening of general credit conditions in the United States to curb growing inflationary pressures led also to a considerable inflow of short-term banking funds. The capital account deficit was accordingly reduced to $4.3 billion. However, the slack that had been prevalent in the U.S. economy was ending, and as domestic activity expanded to close to capacity and U.S. prices began to rise, imports rose considerably. As a result, a marked deterioration of the U.S. current account took place; the surplus was only $4.1 billion. Thus in 1966 the United States still had an overall deficit—of about $200 million.

To contain inflation and to dampen imports, the U.S. Administration in January 1967 announced its intention to propose certain tax measures to take effect at mid-year, including a 6 per cent surcharge on the income tax liabilities of individuals and corporations. In August, when the expected budget deficit had become much larger than that initially forecast, the Administration proposed that the surcharge be at the rate of 10 per cent and requested that the planned reductions in certain excise duties be postponed. These proposals remained under consideration in the Congress for many months. Also during 1967 the voluntary foreign credit restraint program continued to apply, the interest equalization tax was amended and extended for two years beyond July 31, 1967, and the Administration was given discretionary power to vary the effective rate of the interest equalization tax within a specified range, actually applying new effective rates in August.

In 1967 the balance of payments deficit worsened considerably. Aggregate domestic demand expanded rapidly, the rise in prices accelerated, imports again surged upward, and the current account surplus deteriorated further, to $4.0 billion. At the same time, net capital outflows once more increased, and the capital account deficit reached $7.4 billion. Official transactions accounted for most of the increase in capital outflows: there were virtually no advance debt repayments to the United States by foreign governments in 1967, as there had been in 1966, and loans by the Export-Import Bank rose sharply. The private long-term capital position showed a much smaller deterioration. The voluntary foreign credit restraint program, together with rising interest rates in the United States, had induced U.S. corporations to borrow abroad for their overseas operations in amounts greater than ever before; and there had been large placements of bonds and other securities in the U.S. securities market not only by Canada, which customarily borrowed large amounts in U.S. markets, but also by many developing countries. The overall U.S. deficit reached $3.4 billion, the highest since 1960 and considered at the time to be a large sum. Foreign reserves of the United States at the end of 1967 had declined to $14.8 billion, from $19.4 billion at the end of 1960, and liabilities to foreign official agencies in these seven years had risen from $11.9 billion to $19.3 billion.

TIGHTER U.S. MEASURES IN 1968

It was evident that inflation in the United States had been accelerating since the latter part of 1965, when military expenditures associated with the war in Viet-Nam had increased. Hence, on January 1, 1968, President Johnson, in a special New Year's Day message, announced a new, comprehensive program both to slow down inflationary pressures at home and to improve the balance of payments. He again urged the Congress to enact a 10 per cent surcharge on individual and corporate income taxes, and leaders of business and labor were asked to make more effective the existing voluntary program of wage and price restraint. On the external side, mandatory controls on direct investment abroad were introduced. New outflows on account of direct investment to countries in continental Western Europe and other developed nations not heavily dependent on U.S. capital were to be stopped altogether in 1968. Net new investments in other developed countries would be limited to 65 per cent of the 1965–66 average, and such outlays in developing countries would be limited to 110 per cent of the 1965–66 average. The program also required that businesses continue to repatriate foreign earnings in line with their 1964–66 practices. The voluntary program for banks and other financial institutions was also tightened, with the restraints now to be formulated in such a way that there would be a net repatriation of funds from continental Western Europe.

In addition to the measures controlling capital outflows, the new program included a proposal for congressional action to reduce the balance of payments impact of foreign travel by U.S. residents; reductions in net government expenditures abroad, partly through negotiations with other countries designed to minimize the foreign exchange costs of maintaining U.S. troops in Europe; consideration of possible legislative measures in the area of tax rebates on exports and special border tax charges, depending on the outcome of negotiations with other countries aimed at reducing the international trade impact of differences among national tax systems; more intensive efforts to promote exports; and the development of new incentives for foreign investment and travel in the United States.

For the calendar year 1968, the U.S. authorities expected the new program to yield balance of payments "savings" of $3 billion, of which $1 billion was to result from the measures to curb direct investment outflow and $0.5 billion from the tightening of the voluntary program for banks and other financial institutions. The U.S. balance of payments would, accordingly, be brought back to equilibrium, or close to equilibrium.

During the course of 1968, because the economy continued to be over-heated, further measures were taken. On the fiscal side, the tax increase proposed to the Congress by the Administration in 1967, including the 10 per cent income tax surcharge, was enacted in June 1968, and was accompanied by substantial cuts in government expenditures. On the monetary side, the discount rate was twice raised, reserve requirements against demand deposits at large banks were increased, and open market operations were directed toward a tighter monetary policy.

Primarily as a result of the measures taken, but also because purchases by countries abroad of existing U.S. corporate securities on U.S. markets doubled, there was an exceedingly large turnaround in the U.S. capital account in 1968. It improved by $7.5 billion. The overall payments position on an official settlements basis moved from a deficit of $3.4 billion in 1967 to a surplus of $1.6 billion in 1968—a favorable swing of $5.0 billion. These surpluses imparted to the dollar a new and timely strength in foreign exchange markets after the middle of 1968 and through most of 1969, and thus it was not seriously affected by the crises of 1968 and 1969 that disturbed European currencies (described in Chapter 22). Nevertheless, the current account in 1968 worsened further, by some $2.6 billion, and the surplus was only $1.4 billion.

DISCUSSIONS OF U.S. DEFICIT

The management and staff and the Executive Directors had been following these developments in the U.S. economy and balance of payments position very closely, especially through the Article VIII consultations. Assessing the situation at the beginning of 1969, the Fund staff believed that, despite the surpluses of 1968 and the renewed strength of the dollar in exchange markets, the U.S. external accounts had a very unbalanced structure. Traditionally, the United States had had a large trade surplus, and a resulting large current account surplus that had helped to finance long-term capital outflows. The trade surplus, however, had gradually dwindled from $6.8 billion in 1964 to $3.9 billion in 1967 and to only about $0.6 billion in 1968. The staff believed that the crux of the U.S. payments problem was that the loss of a trade surplus yielded a current account surplus much too small to cover the substantial outflows of private long-term capital and government expenditures abroad.

At about this time a new Administration, which took office in January 1969 under President Richard M. Nixon, introduced additional measures to deal with the domestic inflation and the external deficit. For the fiscal year 1969/70 there were to be downward adjustments in expenditures, repeal of the tax credit for investment, and extension of the surcharge on individual and corporate income tax at the prevailing rate of 10 per cent during the second half of the calendar year 1969 and at 5 per cent during the first half of 1970. The budget was expected to yield a surplus in the fiscal year 1969/70 of $6 billion. (The fiscal year 1968/69 had ended with a surplus of $3 billion, compared with a deficit of $25 billion in the fiscal year 1967/68.) In addition, the Federal Reserve Board once again raised the discount rate and the reserve requirements on demand deposits. Policy measures addressed specifically to the balance of payments, such as mandatory controls on U.S. direct investment abroad and the voluntary restraints on bank lending to foreign borrowers, were not substantially altered.

The tighter financial restraints produced a marked slowdown of economic activity in the United States in 1969. Prices, however, continued to rise rapidly and the strength of inflationary forces was manifested in the largest increases in prices and unit labor costs in almost two decades. The restrictive financial policies combined with the persisting inflationary momentum of the economy produced a striking mixture of balance of payments results—generally disappointing in the current account but favorable in the capital account. The trade surplus was less than $0.7 billion and the current account surplus was only $0.8 billion. On the other hand, a heavy influx of banking funds made for an inflow of foreign capital to the United States which, as in 1968, offset a moderate increase in the outflow of U.S. capital to other countries. Thus, in 1969 the overall surplus on an official settlements basis reached a record high figure of $2.9 billion.

Executive Directors' Positions

As expressed in their Annual Report for 1970, the Executive Directors considered that neither of the two bases commonly used for measurement, the official settlements basis or the liquidity basis, represented a valid gauge of the external payments position of the United States. They regarded as a preferable guide the basic balance, a concept developed within the Fund, as a better measurement of members' payments positions. Basic balance was defined as the balance on goods, services, and private transfers (that is, the current account) plus net long-term capital. The basic balance of the United States showed a deficit in 1969 of about $2.5 billion.

In 1970 the U.S. economy continued to be sluggish and unemployment rose, but the inflationary forces built up over several years continued to exert strong upward pressure on costs and prices. Because exports increased considerably, the U.S. surplus on current account rose to $2.1 billion. However, U.S. banks liquidated the large volume of Eurodollar liabilities that they had acquired during the period of credit stringency in 1969, and an outflow of liquid banking funds reversed the surplus on an official settlements basis to an unprecedented deficit of $9.8 billion. The basic balance was again in deficit by about $2.5 billion. By the end of 1970 the official reserves of the United States were down to $14.5 billion, the lowest they had been in the postwar period. Moreover, U.S. liabilities to foreign official agencies had risen to $24.4 billion, much higher than they had ever been, exceeding U.S. official reserves by close to $10 billion.

In July 1969, and again in April 1970 and in January 1971—that is, three times within a year and a half—the Executive Directors considered the domestic and external economic and financial problems of the United States. The occasions were the 1968, 1969, and 1970 Article VIII consultations. The views expressed by the Executive Directors as they considered the U.S. position in these years are indicative of the views on the U.S. balance of payments that were being expressed by other monetary officials, privately and publicly, both at the time and later.

Of primary concern to most of the Directors were the implications of the continued U.S. deficit for the international monetary system. They had just finished introducing SDRs into the system to improve the mechanism for creating liquidity, and now they were worried about the mechanism for balance of payments adjustment. They were especially mindful that, as the staff had stressed in its reports, the strengthening of the U.S. balance of payments was a basic prerequisite to improving the adjustment process and restoring confidence in the soundness and effectiveness of the international monetary system. Whatever the Fund might do in the foreseeable future to bolster the system, a better U.S. balance of payments position was vital to a successful outcome of the Fund's efforts. Against this background, the Executive Directors were therefore eager that the U.S. authorities should be successful in their endeavors to cool off the inflation in the domestic economy and to bring about "an impressive improvement" in the balance of payments, whatever definition of "deficit" was used.

At their meeting in July 1969, the Executive Directors recognized the difficulties of being a high official in the U.S. Government: his actions and decisions, or absence thereof, had not only a national but a worldwide impact. By contrast, the Executive Directors' own positions were relatively easy. Nevertheless, they tried to come up with specific suggestions, some believing, for example, that the U.S. authorities put undue weight on monetary policy instead of fiscal policy, and some regretting the lack of an incomes policy. Most were concerned lest the deteriorating U.S. trade situation provoke greater protectionist sentiment and practices in the United States.

Several Executive Directors, notably Messrs. Johnstone, Lieftinck, Plescoff, Schleiminger, and Stone, stated forcibly that the U.S. authorities had to deal decisively with inflation and the inflationary psychology that had taken hold in the United States, stressing that the world economy could not function successfully so long as rapid inflation continued in the United States. Mr. Stone said that he had examined the U.S. national accounts in detail and had concluded that there was not much evidence that the anti-inflationary policies were working. Data showed that the growth of the gross national product at constant prices had slowed down; but he was less interested in slowing down output than in slowing down expenditure. Lower output aggravated inflation. Expenditure itself had actually been rising, causing higher prices and higher costs. Productivity had been increasing, but at slower rates than before. In addition, the U.S. balance of payments position, in Mr. Stone's view, was now worse and showed no sign of improvement.

At their meeting in April 1970, the Executive Directors were more critical of U.S. endeavors "to curb inflationary pressures by a gradual adjustment process that would slow down the rise of demand without inducing an undue rise of unemployment." In the opinion of Mr. Palamenghi-Crispi, for instance, "even-handedness," "fine-tuning," "jaw-boning," "gradualism," and other terms used to denote the U.S. domestic economic policies of the last several years ought to be replaced by a policy of "firm-handedness." In contrast, some members of the Executive Board, including Mr. Nguyên Huu Hanh (Viet-Nam) and Mr. Plescoff, observed that the U.S. domestic economy was much healthier in April 1970 than it had been in the previous July. In their view, the U.S. authorities had been exerting strenuous efforts to bring inflation under control.

The Fund's Annual Report for 1970 termed the need to rectify the U.S. payments position the most urgent remaining task in the field of international payments, a view reiterated by the Managing Director at the Twenty-Fifth Annual Meeting in Copenhagen.[7] Noting that the U.S. basic balance was currently in deficit by $3–4 billion at an annual rate, he stressed that improvement in the U.S. payments position depended greatly on the current program of the authorities to stabilize the domestic economy.

Moreover, Mr. Schweitzer believed that "until the payments position of the United States [was] brought into balance, it [was] important that the deficit should be financed by the use of U.S. reserve assets to the extent necessary to avoid an excessive expansion of official holdings of dollars by other countries."[8] He went on to say that such a policy was necessary if control over the issuance of SDRs was to provide the means of regulating the aggregate volume of world reserves. In effect, contrary to U.S. practice, the United States would have to use its gold or SDRs for international payments rather than let U.S. dollar liabilities increase.

This statement was the first mention of what later was to become known as "asset settlement," that is, the idea that all countries should settle their payments deficits and surpluses by the transfer or receipt of gold, SDRs, or any other reserve asset that might be agreed upon. This idea contrasted with the Bretton Woods system of "on demand" convertibility, under which a reserve center might finance its deficits by the building up of liabilities subject to conversion at any time, and which meant that a reserve center might lose

---

[7] Opening Address by the Managing Director, *Summary Proceedings, 1970*, p. 22.

[8] *Ibid.*, p. 18.

reserves by conversion in amounts greater or less than its deficit. Asset settlement was to become one of the issues heatedly debated after 1971 when discussions on international monetary reform intensified.

On January 8, 1971 the Executive Directors, in taking up the staff's report for the 1970 Article VIII consultation, again reviewed the U.S. economy. The U.S. authorities, in a two-year anti-inflationary program, had succeeded in slowing down the economy. In fact, virtual recession was at hand as employment had been sacrificed in an attempt to halt and reverse inflation. Nevertheless, despite the decline in employment, prices and wages had not fallen and the goal of price stability had been illusive.

Noting these developments, the Executive Directors, especially Mr. Lieftinck, commented that the United States had paid a heavy price—a stagnating economy, mounting unemployment, and decreasing levels of productivity—for its efforts to combat inflation. The poor results were, for that reason, all the more depressing. From the experience of the United States, as well as from the experiences of other countries, they concluded that it was extraordinarily difficult to stem a strongly entrenched inflation.

Mr. Viénot (France) and Mr. Brofoss brought out other aspects of the U.S. payments deficit which were becoming sources of increased concern, and even agitation, to some officials abroad. Mr. Viénot inquired, rhetorically, whether the introduction of SDRs had, in fact, eliminated the generation of deficits in the U.S. external accounts. His question had reference to the argument that many monetary officials had advanced earlier in supporting the establishment of SDRs and their later activation: the SDR facility would enable reserve creation to take place under controlled regulation and thereby eliminate the need for the United States to run deficits as a way to add to the supply of world reserves. Citing the continuing U.S. deficits and the resultant accumulation of reserves abroad, Mr. Viénot, as Mr. Giscard d'Estaing had done at the 1970 Annual Meeting, asked the Fund to re-evaluate the foreseeable needs of the world economy for liquidity.

Mr. Brofoss was concerned about the massive acquisition by both the private and public sectors of the United States of foreign physical assets and claims, which he estimated at more than $70 billion from 1960 to 1969. The export performance of the U.S. economy, he stressed, had to be considered in the context of the tremendous expansion of production by U.S.-owned enterprises in European and other foreign countries. Goods which had previously been recorded in the export statistics of the United States itself were now recorded in the trade returns of countries where subsidiaries of U.S. companies were operating. U.S. receipts, which had once appeared under the heading "merchandise exports," were now reflected in the statistics as "earnings from direct investments"; the latter had been increasing by about $0.5 billion a year. Even these figures did not reveal the full story. The net income of U.S. subsidiaries operating in countries abroad was much higher. The major part of their profits, together with amortization funds, was plowed back in the form of new equipment. Consequently, these companies had established and consolidated an even firmer grip on some of the most rapidly growing fields of production in the world.

COUNTRIES IN SURPLUS

The counterpart of the dwindling U.S. current account surplus and the large U.S. capital deficit was current account surpluses for many other industrial countries significantly larger than what might be considered "normal," and vast capital flows into many of these countries. In addition to the current account surpluses and capital inflows of Canada, France, the Federal Republic of Germany, and the United Kingdom (noted in earlier chapters), Belgium-Luxembourg, Italy, Japan, the Netherlands, Norway, and Switzerland also had sizable trade or current account surpluses, or both, in varying degrees, for at least some of the years 1968–70. The figures for 1970 illustrate the pattern and relative size of surpluses. Current account surpluses were recorded by Japan ($2.1 billion), the United Kingdom ($1.9 billion, the highest it had yet reached), the Federal Republic of Germany ($1.7 billion, much below its current account surpluses of 1968 and 1969), Canada ($1.4 billion, the largest ever experienced by that member), Italy ($1.3 billion, less than half its surpluses in 1968 and 1969), and Belgium-Luxembourg ($0.9 billion, much above the surpluses of 1968 and 1969). Overall balance of payments surpluses, including all capital movements, were registered by the Federal Republic of Germany ($6.2 billion), the United Kingdom ($3.0 billion), France ($2.0 billion), Canada ($1.6 billion), Japan ($1.1 billion), the Netherlands ($0.7 billion), and Belgium-Luxembourg ($0.5 billion).

Japan's Surplus

The situation of Japan, which has not been commented upon previously in this volume, merits some description here.

Late in 1965, under the stimulus of a sharp increase in exports and of expansionary monetary and fiscal policies, Japan's economy began a period of rapid growth, which was also to be the longest period of uninterrupted expansion in the country's recent economic history. The gross national product in real terms increased at an average annual rate of more than 13 per cent from 1967 to 1969 and by 11 per cent in 1970.

Recessionary conditions in Japan's major trading partners in 1966 and 1967, however, meant that the current account position did not become very strong until early in 1968. In fact, in 1967 there was a large current account deficit after sizable surpluses in the preceding two years. By 1968 the economic upswing in other industrial countries, especially in the United States, began to bring about increases in Japanese exports. These increases reached nearly 25 per cent in 1968, 23 per cent in 1969, and 21 per cent in 1970. Hence, Japan's high and sustained rate of economic growth was now accompanied by large and expanding current account surpluses that were only partially offset by net capital outflows. In 1968 there was a current account surplus of $1.0 billion and an overall balance of payments surplus of $1.1 billion. In 1969 the trade surplus reached an unprecedented $3.7 billion, the current account surplus was $2.1 billion, and the overall surplus was $2.3 billion. Accordingly, Japan's foreign exchange reserves, which were about $2.0 billion at the end of 1967, had doubled by March 1970.

Japanese imports increased sharply during most of 1970. The trade surplus in that year thus rose only moderately, to $4.0 billion. The current account surplus declined slightly, to $2.0 billion, and the overall surplus fell to $1.4 billion.

The economy of Japan, like that of other members, was regularly examined by the Executive Directors. In January 1969, on the occasion of the 1968 Article VIII consultation, they praised the Japanese authorities for the remarkable rate of growth of Japan's economy and for the spectacular reversal during 1968 from economic slack to economic boom and from external deficit to surplus. They commented that Japan's economy compared with that of other countries seemed unusually flexible and unusually responsive to monetary policy measures. Messrs. Plescoff and Stone doubted that the Fund should offer advice to the Japanese authorities, who were doing extremely well on their own. Most of the Executive Directors did, however, recommend that consideration be given to liberalizing the remaining impediments to imports, invisibles, and capital transfers.

In February 1970, in the course of the 1969 Article VIII consultation, the Japanese authorities stated their belief that the monetary measures which they had been taking would keep the domestic economy on an even keel, while a slowing down of foreign demand, coupled with a rising rate of imports, would keep the balance of payments surplus within bounds. However, the staff foresaw possible threats by 1970 or later to domestic stability from the strong balance of payments position. The extremely favorable competitive position of Japanese exports in world markets might, the staff thought, be underestimated by the authorities.

At the Executive Board meeting, Mr. Suzuki elaborated the balance of payments aim of the Japanese authorities: a current account surplus, offset for the most part by aid to developing countries and other long-term capital exports, and only a gradual increase in official reserves. Since the deficit on invisibles tended to increase with economic growth, the trade surplus would have to be big enough to cover the deficits both on invisible account and on capital account.

The Executive Directors again commended the Japanese authorities for their continuing success, Miss Fuenfgelt pointing out some parallels with the economic situation of the Federal Republic of Germany: rapid increases in exports, large trade surpluses, and offsetting capital exports. She drew attention to the freedom of trade and capital movements in Germany, however, and like other members of the Executive Board, including Mr. Dale, said that there was considerable scope for the Japanese authorities to liberalize restrictions on imports and similar impediments, both to trade and to capital transfers abroad, and to give up export incentives. Many Executive Directors queried whether the removal of limitations on trade or capital outflow would, in fact, increase Japanese payments abroad to any appreciable extent.

By January 1971, in the course of the 1970 Article VIII consultation, the staff was able to report to the Executive Directors that in 1970 the Japanese authorities had resolved the conflict posed by domestic inflationary pressures and a strong balance of payments position and had made substantial adjustments in their balance of payments policies. Measures to promote exports had been de-emphasized. Import restrictions had been liberalized. Tariffs had been changed to permit more imports. A program to increase foreign aid by considerable amounts had been instituted. Other measures to liberalize capital flows, both inward and outward, had been taken. Finally, accumulation of official reserves had been moderated, partly by encouraging private commercial banks to strengthen their net asset positions. As a result, wholesale prices were stable, the current account surplus was smaller, and the increase in official reserves had been sharply reduced.

Once more the Executive Directors noted the competent management of the economy by the Japanese authorities and, in the words of Mr. Schleiminger, characterized "the dynamism of the Japanese economy as breathtaking." Nonetheless, they noted that the growth of Japan's economy had not been entirely balanced and advised that the time had come for the authorities to pay greater heed to investment in infrastructure, to domestic shortages of foodstuffs, to the effects of economic growth on the environment, to the problems associated with very rapid urbanization and industrialization, to housing, to education, and, more generally, to the well-being of the people. Mr. Suzuki assured the Executive Directors that the Japanese authorities were well aware of these requirements of economic policy.

THE PROBLEM OF ADJUSTMENT

That the pattern of deficits and surpluses in world payments during the late 1960s persisted and even worsened in 1970 and 1971 gave rise to what monetary experts labeled "the problem of adjustment," as distinct from "the problem of liquidity" discussed in Part One. "Adjustment" of international imbalance was considered a "problem" because neither of the traditional ways of correcting balance of payments disequilibria—changes in internal monetary and financial policies or changes in par values—seemed to be available. A number of factors made changes in internal policies less effective than they had been in the 1950s. Not least among these factors were the acute difficulties many countries were experiencing in halting or reversing inflation, however much they shifted their internal policies, and the likelihood that changes in such policies might touch off heavy flows of banking funds.

Consequently, interest was focused on adjustments of par values, one of the primary instruments of the Bretton Woods system for correcting a "fundamental disequilibrium." In practice, however, changes in par values also seemed to be ruled out. For most of the large industrial countries, a change in par value had major political repercussions. As a result, needed changes were being delayed too long. For some years the difficulties of par value changes by the United Kingdom and the United States, whose currencies were held by others as reserves, had been recognized: changes in the rates for reserve currencies altered the value of reserves held by other countries. Devaluation of the dollar was tantamount to an increase in the dollar price of gold and hence involved the further complication that devaluation of the dollar would reward those who had been converting their dollar holdings into gold and penalize those who had been willing to augment their holdings of dollars. Now, in addition, political leaders feared the consequences of downward changes in their par values on the inflationary pressures in their economies or of upward changes in their par values on the competitive positions of their exports and on domestic employment. Therefore, it was also becoming increasingly awkward politically for the authorities of France, the Federal Republic of Germany, and Japan, for example, to propose changes in their par values.

It was to solve this problem of adjustment that proposals for altering the par value system were being made. All such proposals had in common the objective of making exchange rate changes easier or more automatic.

INCREASINGLY DISRUPTIVE CAPITAL FLOWS

The second major problem facing the international monetary system in the late 1960s was that large flows of short-term capital now took place and radically transformed the environment in which international financial relations were conducted.

Greater Size and Mobility

During the decade of the 1960s, short-term capital grew by what seemed at the time to be astronomical amounts and became much more likely to move from one money center to another.

A number of factors underlay the phenomenal build-up of short-term capital and its increasing shiftability between major currencies. For one thing, there was a large growth of liquid liabilities in U.S. dollars. These were, of course, the counterpart of much of the U.S. payments deficit, which was financed heavily by the accumulation of dollars by foreign official and private entities. For a long time after World War II, the U.S. dollar had been the strongest currency in the world, and it had become the "intervention currency" (the currency used by central bankers to intervene in their exchange markets to keep exchange rates within the prescribed margins around their par values), the most widely used "vehicle currency" (the currency used by traders and investors to make international payments), and the principal "reserve currency" (the currency in which central banks kept their reserves). Hence, official and private holders of liquid assets had been willing to augment their holdings of dollars almost without limit.

A factor contributing initially to the mobility of these funds was the convertibility of Western European currencies in the late 1950s and the achievement by these currencies of a strength that they had not enjoyed since before World War I. Holders of dollars became much more prone than before to switch into other currencies.

The broadening and growth of the Eurocurrency market was still another factor facilitating short-term capital transactions. Already by 1966 what was originally the Eurodollar market, because the market was in Europe and because most transactions were in dollars, had broadened into a Eurocurrency market, in which operations in an increasing number of currencies other than the dollar—especially the deutsche mark and the Swiss franc—were carried out.[9] Even in its first few years the market experienced a rapid growth. By 1966 it had already become one of the world's largest markets for short-term funds: within eight years after its beginnings in 1958 its net size had grown to more than $10 billion and its gross size to over $20 billion. But this amount was small compared with the manifold increases of the next few years. After some expansion in 1967, the Eurocurrency market in 1968 experienced its largest growth so far, reaching an estimated $30 billion, on a gross basis, by the end of that year. During 1969 its further expansion was estimated at 50 per cent, to about $45 billion, and by the end of 1970 it had expanded by another 30 per cent, to an estimated $57 billion.[10]

---

[9] The origin of the Eurocurrency market and developments in its early years were described by Oscar L. Altman in "Foreign Markets for Dollars, Sterling, and Other Currencies," *Staff Papers*, Vol. 8 (1960–61), pp. 313–52; "Recent Developments in Foreign Markets for Dollars and Other Currencies," *Staff Papers*, Vol. 10 (1963), pp. 48–96; and "Euro-Dollars: Some Further Comments," *Staff Papers*, Vol. 12 (1965), pp. 1–16.

[10] *Annual Report, 1969*, pp. 84–86, *Annual Report, 1970*, pp. 92–96, and *Annual Report, 1971*, pp. 103–10, contain details on the expansion of the Eurocurrency market in the years 1968 through 1970. Estimates of the size of the Eurocurrency market were published by the Morgan Guaranty Trust Company in its *World Financial Markets*, and by the Bank for International Settlements in its *Annual Reports*. A description of the structure of the market

Furthermore, international financial integration accompanied the worldwide economic integration that was a dominant feature of the decade of the 1960s. U.S. banks, for instance, opened many overseas branches. The number of international banks in London—the center for handling Eurocurrency funds—and the size of their deposits swelled appreciably. Bankers of various countries developed intimate working relationships with one another. In effect, a progressive internationalization of banking operations developed. The customers of commercial banks, such as resident companies in good standing, could, for example, borrow as readily from foreign as from domestic banks, should the divergence in interest rates make such a change profitable.

The elimination of exchange and capital controls, along with the competitive edge enjoyed by banks operating in Europe over banks operating in the United States, were important factors in the emergence and expansion of the Eurocurrency market itself. For example, banks operating in the United Kingdom, unlike banks operating in the United States, were not subject to legal reserve requirements or to official interest rate ceilings in respect of their dollar transactions. The absence of such regulations enabled banks based in London to pay higher deposit rates and to operate with narrower margins than banks based in New York. Such differential treatment of national and offshore banking operations was typical not only for the United Kingdom but also for most other countries where important offshore banking centers developed.

Another factor that stimulated the rapid growth of the Eurocurrency market, particularly in the late 1960s and early 1970s, was the action taken by the U.S. authorities, as part of the balance of payments program, to restrict the flow of funds from the United States. The mandatory controls over U.S. direct investment abroad that were introduced in January 1968 were especially relevant in this regard. U.S. companies wishing to finance new or additional foreign investment had to rely more on funds raised outside the United States, and U.S. banks, constrained in lending to residents abroad, including foreign branches of U.S. companies, had to raise funds outside the United States if they wanted to avoid losing out in the growing international loan business. They therefore established branches in London and elsewhere, thus shifting a large part of their international business from New York to offshore banking centers. The much more restrictive monetary policy on which the U.S. authorities embarked in 1969 likewise stimulated the growth of the Eurocurrency market. There was a substantial drain of funds from the United States to more profitable investment outlets; in addition, U.S. banks relied heavily on their London branches for borrowing.[11]

---

and of the institutional mechanics can be found in Geoffrey Bell, *The Euro-Dollar Market and the International Financial System* (London, 1973), and in Andrew Shonfield, ed., *International Economic Relations of the Western World, 1959–1971*, Vol. 2—*International Monetary Relations*, by Susan Strange (London, 1976), Chap. 6.

[11] Fuller explanations of the rapid growth of the Eurocurrency market in the late 1960s and early 1970s are given in Eisuke Sakakibara, "The Euro-Currency Market in

There was still another factor that brought about the growth of large and mobile short-term funds. As the world economy became more integrated, ties between and within business enterprises (apart from banks) were getting larger and were increasingly extending beyond national boundaries. The close connections between businesses based in different countries and the growth of giant multinational corporations meant that there existed on the world scene companies with sizable balances of working capital that had ready access to borrowing facilities in many countries and that had the ability and know-how to take advantage of interest rate spreads or crises in confidence in currencies in the countries where they operated. A telephone call enabled these companies, within minutes, to switch their excess balances, or even their working funds, from one currency to another. In fact, it became a matter of good management by the executives of these companies to make such shifts of short-term capital so as to safeguard their liquid balances, especially against losses from currency depreciations.

In the late 1960s, the inducement for interest arbitrage also became greater than it perhaps had ever been. There were marked variations among the major countries in the phase of the business cycle through which they were passing, and important differences in the intensity of their rates of inflation. Also, for the first time since the 1930s monetary policy, in contrast to fiscal policy, became a principal instrument of domestic economic management in nearly all the industrial countries. These factors combined to give rise to wider and more persistent differentials in interest rates between the industrial countries than had existed earlier.

For all these reasons, movements of short-term capital had by 1968 become enormously large, swift, and volatile.[12]

Restrictions Reimposed

By the mid-1960s there was another facet to the problem of short-term capital. The scale and speed of capital movements meant that the instruments used in the late 1950s and the first half of the 1960s to cope with these movements—the drawing down by a country of its exchange reserves, the international network of swap arrangements, the extension to a country under pressure of short-term credits by other countries or by the Fund, and the countering of capital flows by shifts in interest rates by national monetary authorities—were no longer adequate to the task. Even acting in unison, the monetary authorities of the main industrial countries were less able to counter

Perspective," and in Paul de Grauwe, "The Development of the Euro-Currency Market," in *Finance and Development*, Vol. 12, September 1975, pp. 11–13 and 14–16, respectively.

[12] There was renewed interest in the theory of international short-term capital movements and in empirical investigation of such movements. For a survey of the studies made, see Zoran Hodjera, "International Short-Term Capital Movements: A Survey of Theory and Empirical Analysis," *Staff Papers*, Vol. 20 (1973), pp. 683–740.

the effects of short-term capital outflows on the reserve positions of countries subjected to unexpected capital flight or the repercussions on the domestic monetary positions of countries experiencing sudden capital inflows. Accordingly, monetary authorities were put in the position of repeatedly having to deny that they were contemplating par value changes, and then, suddenly, changes in par values were forced upon them by the pressure of capital movements. Moreover, when speculators profited from the changes in exchange rates wrought by their own movements of capital, they were encouraged to act again.

Because of the continuous imbalance in world payments and because of the risk of sudden pressure on the exchange rate of any major currency, restrictions on trade and capital movements were reimposed. The liberalization of trade in manufactures, which had been the great accomplishment of the 1950s, had been well maintained, and the Kennedy Round of tariff cuts of 1967 carried still further the liberalization of such trade from tariff barriers. But measures indirectly restricting or distorting international trade, in the form of nontariff restrictions, aid-tying, and a strong preference for domestic production in the granting of government contracts, had been retained or were imposed by many countries. Most notably, measures to control capital flows were being intensified.

Moreover, many officials had begun to worry that the harmonious and cooperative economic relationships which had prevailed since the late 1940s, and which had even been strengthened in the early 1960s, might come to an end. There was danger that the world's main trading and investing nations would regress into a vicious spiral of restrictions and retaliations.

INITIAL REVIEW OF EXCHANGE RATE MECHANISM

These were the circumstances which caused the Executive Directors to agree in January 1969 to examine the mechanism of exchange rate adjustment as set out in the Fund's Articles. They were prompted also to undertake such a review because they were concerned that decisions regarding the exchange rates of major currencies, like other key decisions in the Fund's field of interest, were increasingly being taken outside the Fund and that the initiative for any serious consideration of whether, and how, the par value system should be altered might fall to bodies other than themselves.

These concerns had been sharpened by events in the latter part of 1968. The Bonn meeting in 1968 had brought home clearly the distinct possibility that the Ministers and Governors of the Group of Ten might assume a leading role in discussions about changes in par values. And Mr. Roy Jenkins, the Chancellor of the Exchequer of the United Kingdom, in a speech to the House of Commons upon his return from the Bonn meeting had urged that a "new international monetary conference," like the one at Bretton Woods, be assembled. His remarks were reminiscent of those of Mr. Henry H. Fowler, Secretary of the U.S. Treasury, some years before in connection with questions of international liquidity. Doubts had been raised before about the appropriateness of the par value system, but these had been raised primarily by academic economists in the United States and the United Kingdom, where there had always been many detractors of the par value system and supporters of freely fluctuating rates. Now the calls for reform of the par value system had spread from the universities to official circles and were being taken up by leading newspapers and public personalities throughout the world.

Hence, when Mr. Schweitzer told the Executive Directors that he believed it preferable to use the existing machinery for international consultation, and suggested that they begin in mid-January 1969 to exchange views, in a preliminary way, about the need for greater flexibility in the exchange rate system, they welcomed the idea. Most of them did not favor an "international monetary conference."

Opinions Expressed

From January 15 to March 10, 1969 the Executive Directors held ten discussions covering a broad range of topics relating to the need for, and possible techniques of, greater flexibility of exchange rates. So sensitive were the discussions, or even the fact that discussions were in process, that they were not held in the Executive Board room nor in the usual seating arrangement around the Board table. Instead, the sessions were held in a large conference room on another floor of the Fund's building, with the chairs arranged as for a seminar. Thus, there was no suggestion of any kind that the Board was deliberating, even informally, on the par value system.

In this setting, referred to as "fourth floor meetings," the Executive Directors discussed a number of papers on the exchange rate mechanism prepared by the staff. They considered, for instance, general guidelines that might be used to adjust balances of payments.[13] They debated particular techniques for altering the par value system through the use of slightly wider margins around par values, through the use of small changes in exchange rates or par values, and through the use of what were being referred to by economists as gliding parities or crawling pegs, that is, changes in par values at specified intervals. They discussed as well the merits and demerits of a dual exchange rate system, that is, one with a separate exchange rate for capital transactions. Pointedly, they did not discuss regimes that were inconsistent with the par value system—a general

---

[13] See J. Marcus Fleming, *Guidelines for Balance-of-Payments Adjustment Under the Par-Value System*, Essays in International Finance, No. 67 (Princeton, 1968), 31 pp.; reprinted in his *Essays in International Economics* (London and Cambridge, Massachusetts, 1971), pp. 268–95.

system of freely floating exchange rates, substantially wider margins around par values, or automatic adjustment of par values in accordance with selected indicators.

The Executive Directors did not come to any specific conclusions as to whether the par value system could be improved. They reviewed the original rationale of the par value system and the assumptions on which it had been based, and reiterated views about the par value system similar to those that had been expressed formally by the Executive Board in the past.

They did distinguish stability of exchange rates from rigidity of exchange rates, emphasizing that changes in par values had been contemplated as one of the means of balance of payments adjustment and that certainly par values were supposed to be altered from time to time. Nonetheless, they recognized that the enormous expansion in the volume of short-term funds that could potentially move from currency to currency in response to expectations regarding rates of exchange had vastly changed the framework in which countries operated from that envisaged at the Bretton Woods Conference and that had been reflected in the Articles of Agreement. The drafters of the Articles, as the Executive Directors pointed out in their Annual Report for 1969, had been well aware that a country might have to alter its exchange rate because of changes in its relative real economic position. But these architects of the par value system had not envisaged that a country would have to be so much concerned about the public's views on the strength of its currency. Also, speculative capital movements had been expected to be suppressed rather than financed; in fact, limitations had been put on members' access to the Fund to finance capital outflows, and the Fund was empowered to request a member to impose capital controls as a condition for the use of the Fund's resources.

The Executive Directors, nevertheless, announced their intention to continue their study of the subject of exchange rates. Their further study would investigate whether a limited increase in flexibility of exchange rate variation would be desirable and attainable with the necessary safeguards, and the means by which any such increased flexibility might be achieved. There was stress on the word "limited." Further flexibility of exchange rates might involve some "limited" change in the par value system, but, conceivably, it might involve only a more active use of the existing system. Commenting that other economists and exchange rate practitioners were vigorously studying the exchange rate mechanism, they emphasized that any changes that might be made in the mechanism ought to preserve the essential characteristics of the par value system—stability of rates and rates that were internationally agreed. The stability of exchange rates at realistic levels had made a key contribution to the balanced expansion of international trade, and the determination of the rate of exchange for each currency was a matter of international concern. Those characteristics were, they believed, as beneficial for the world as they were twenty-five years before when the Articles had been written.

The Conclusions in Context

These conclusions concerning the exchange rate mechanism were reached at the same time—in the first nine months of 1969—that the Executive Directors were deliberating on the first allocation of SDRs and the substantial increases in quotas that were to follow the fifth general review of quotas. For some years, as we have seen in Part One, they had taken the position that easing the supply of world reserves was closely connected with the balance of payments adjustment process. Consequently, before committing themselves to changes in the system of par values, they wished to see the effects on the monetary system of supplementing the supply of liquidity.

GOVERNORS' POSITIONS

The preference of the Executive Directors for caution in changing the par value system was representative of the thinking at the time of the highest financial authorities in their countries. As a way of gauging international financial opinion on the topic of exchange rate flexibility, the Managing Director, at the 1969 Annual Meeting, encouraged the Governors to express their thoughts. The Governors who responded all praised the contribution of the par value system to the expansion of international trade since World War II and categorically rejected the replacement of that system by any general system of fluctuating rates. But they had divergent views about the value of proposals for "limited" flexibility of exchange rates.

One position was expressed by Mr. Giscard d'Estaing (France) and Mr. Blessing (Federal Republic of Germany). Their views reflected mutual distaste for any greater flexibility of exchange rates. Mr. Giscard d'Estaing, explaining that the Common Market could not "survive daily fluctuations or 'crawling' uncertainty," said that France would not refuse to participate in such studies of exchange rate flexibility as might be undertaken, but he warned that introducing flexibility into exchange rates was not an easy way out of international monetary difficulties—"a sort of monetary LSD." [14] Mr. Blessing, noting that the floating rate just introduced for the deutsche mark was temporary, said that he very much preferred to see more flexible monetary, fiscal, and economic policies pursued in various countries rather than making exchange rates more flexible. "The fundamental problems of our time," he said, "cannot be solved by technical devices but only by greater monetary discipline and by better coordination of the economic and fiscal policies of the various countries." [15]

---

[14] Statement by the Governor of the World Bank for France, *Summary Proceedings, 1969*, p. 60.

[15] Statement by the Governor of the Fund for the Federal Republic of Germany, *Summary Proceedings, 1969*, p. 202.

Mr. Fukuda (Japan) agreed with this position, saying that "the question of changing the exchange rate system can and should be resolved within the framework of the present system through improvement in management and operations."[16]

Mr. David Kennedy (United States), in some contrast, supported the further study of proposals for "limited flexibility," which "need not be looked upon as radical new departures from the mainstream of developments in the monetary area." He called attention to several characteristics of the existing situation, and in particular expressed two views that were reflected in Mr. Dale's position in the deliberations of the Executive Directors in the coming year. *One*, given the pivotal role of the dollar in the international monetary system, the initiative for even limited exchange rate adjustments would continue to lie with countries other than the United States. *Two*, the possibility of encouraging a bias toward currency devaluations, in contrast to revaluations, ought to be guarded against.[17]

Some of the Governors were much more eager for the study of exchange rate flexibility to continue. Mr. Jenkins (United Kingdom), who reminded the Governors that in November 1968 he had told the House of Commons that the time had come to consider both the objectives of international monetary arrangements and the institutions for implementing them, very much welcomed debates on and studies of methods to introduce flexibility into the exchange rate system. He elaborated his views about these methods, stating his preference for a very slight widening of the margins, perhaps to 2 per cent above and below par.[18] Mr. Colombo (Italy) spoke favorably of the crawling peg.[19]

The Managing Director and the Executive Directors concluded that they had sufficient support to proceed with their study of exchange rate flexibility.

CONTINUED REVIEW BY EXECUTIVE DIRECTORS

By the time the Executive Directors again took up the subject of exchange rate flexibility, late in 1969, the November 1967 devaluation of sterling had begun to show results and changes had been made in the par values for the French franc and the deutsche mark. The position of the U.S. dollar in exchange markets was strong, with an inflow of funds and overall surpluses in 1968 and 1969 as noted above. The world's exchange markets were again calm, and

---

[16] Statement by the Governor of the Fund and the World Bank for Japan, *Summary Proceedings, 1969*, p. 32.

[17] Statement by the Governor of the Fund and the World Bank for the United States, *Summary Proceedings, 1969*, p. 55.

[18] Statement by the Governor of the Fund for the United Kingdom, *Summary Proceedings, 1969*, pp. 36–40.

[19] Statement by the Governor of the Fund for Italy, *Summary Proceedings, 1969*, p. 68.

international payments seemed less unbalanced. Hence, there was less of a sense of urgency about finding a way to induce more frequent changes in par values. Nonetheless, the problem of adjustment had replaced the problem of liquidity as the prime topic of international monetary discussions, and monetary experts everywhere were continuing to discuss techniques for introducing greater flexibility and automaticity into the exchange rate mechanism.

Difficulties of Agreement

In December 1969 the Executive Directors agreed to hold informal sessions to discuss exchange rate adjustment, on the basis of an agenda proposed by the staff. Many of the Directors, notably Messrs. Johnstone, Lieftinck, and Stone, wanted to broaden the study beyond the particular techniques for adjusting exchange rates, to an examination of the whole adjustment process. The latter would have included, for example, a review of the concept of fundamental disequilibrium, consideration of the special role, if any, of reserve currency centers in the adjustment process, the nature of the disturbances to the adjustment process in recent years, and the contribution that exchange rate changes might make to mitigating these disturbances. A compromise was agreed: the main focus of the informal sessions would be on the techniques for adjusting exchange rates, but there would also be some examination of the balance of payments adjustment process.

The year 1970 thus commenced with a series of informal sessions of the Executive Directors on the mechanism of exchange rate adjustment that were carried on intensively for the next eight months. As a starting point the Executive Directors had before them a number of technical staff papers, all of which dealt with what was called "limited flexibility of exchange rates," as opposed to more generally flexible rates. One staff paper, for instance, compared the method of changing par values under the Bretton Woods system with a number of alternatives, all of which provided for adjustments in par values by a series of small changes regularly over time. Another paper set out some reflections on the procedure for changing par values based on the experience with the deutsche mark in September and October 1969. The conclusion was that a fluctuating exchange rate as a transition to a fixed par value might help to make the best of a temporary absence of the conditions needed for a successful instantaneous change of par value, but that a continued absence of such conditions would cause major problems for an exchange rate regime based on effective par values. A third paper assessed the main economic consequences that might be expected from a modest widening of the effective margins of fluctuation in spot exchange rates around a par value beyond the maximum 1 per cent laid down in the Articles. The conclusion was that the advantages of slightly wider margins might not outweigh the disadvantages for countries such as those in the EEC that wanted to keep their rates in line with each other or for countries that could not hope, through slight exchange rate variations, to achieve any significant equilibrating flows of short-term capital. The Executive Directors had before them, as well, technical papers prepared by the U.S. authorities and by several other monetary experts.

It proved difficult for the Executive Directors to arrive at a common view, even on exchange rate flexibility of a limited nature. Several of the Executive Directors for developing members, as well as some of those for industrial members, remained unconvinced of the need for any change in the par value system, while those who favored introducing flexibility could not agree on a method. Given these divergences, it was problematic for some months whether they would submit any conclusions or recommendations to the Board of Governors.

There was another complication. As the General Counsel pointed out, any of the possible techniques even for limited exchange rate flexibility—such as widening the margins slightly or using a sliding parity or a crawling peg— required amendment of the Articles of Agreement. As a result of the meeting of the Deputies of the Group of Ten in April 1970, it seemed unlikely that the countries of the Group of Ten would be willing to consider fresh amendments to the Articles at that time.

Arguments Against Exchange Rate Flexibility

The developing countries, like the industrial ones, did not have a unified position on the subject of exchange rate flexibility. Arguments against flexibility were put forward by Mr. Madan and Mr. Kharmawan. Mr. Madan explained that greater exchange rate flexibility in the system in general meant for the developing members that the prices of their export products, and correspondingly their terms of trade, would be even more unpredictable and more variable than at present. Furthermore, the developing countries had probably changed their par values under the existing par value system more often than had the industrial countries; hence, they were less interested in finding an alternative system.

Mr. Kharmawan outlined the positions of the developing countries that had elected him. For years the Fund had been advising them to create conditions of internal and external stability as a prerequisite for a balanced and sustained growth of their economies and as a means of achieving stable exchange rates. In the Fund's philosophy, exchange rate stability and fiscal and monetary discipline were interlinked. What, then, were the implications of the interest some developed countries now showed in studying the possibility of introducing flexibility into the exchange rate system? Would the introduction of such flexibility, consciously or unconsciously, lead to a postponement of the measures to be taken in the monetary and fiscal fields?

The authorities of the members that had elected him, Mr. Kharmawan continued, doubted that this inquiry into exchange rate flexibility was necessary. Their view was that, if the tools available in the framework of the Bretton

Woods system, including the possibility of changing a par value in the event of fundamental disequilibrium, had been correctly used at the right time, distortions and disequilibria might not have occurred and speculative short-term capital movements might have been averted. As long as there were no convincing arguments for introducing exchange rate flexibility, their preference was for making use of the existing tools, and perhaps for redefining the concept of fundamental disequilibrium in order to make the Bretton Woods system easier to implement.

Mr. Kharmawan added to his argument by referring to the Fund's rather grudging acceptance of flexible exchange rates in the past for members with weaker economies than those of the industrial members. Why was it that flexibility was now being considered to give leeway to members with major currencies widely used in international trade? Mr. Williams (Trinidad and Tobago) supported the views expressed by Mr. Kharmawan and asked for the staff to study the likely effects of exchange rate flexibility on the developing members.

Messrs. Lieftinck, Plescoff, Stone, Suzuki, and van Campenhout, all appointed or elected by industrial or other developed countries, were also disinclined to change the par value system. Together with some other Executive Directors, they particularly rejected any purely automatic version of the crawling peg, or any system under which exchange rates would change week by week by minute fractions of 1 per cent.

Mr. Lieftinck, although willing to consider an upward crawling peg, regarded exchange rate policy as too important to be left to purely automatic arrangements. He favored retaining the par value system, but instituting greater enforcement of the Fund's rules against a member maintaining or imposing balance of payments restrictions and extending less short-term balance of payments credit to a member in trouble. Members in disequilibrium would then have to adjust their par values more frequently.

Mr. Plescoff underscored the remarks of Mr. Giscard d'Estaing at the 1969 Annual Meeting to the effect that nobody wanted lasting floating rates and that the crawling peg would cause problems. Perhaps margins of about 2–2½ per cent on either side of parity could be considered because they might provide for better management of reserves. To authorize governments to make small changes in par values would not overcome the political difficulties of par value adjustment. Indeed, the situation would be worse in that small changes in par values would not enable governments to justify orthodox economic stabilization programs that might be unpopular.

Against the background of his strongly held views about the dangers inherent in the world inflationary situation that was developing, Mr. Stone strongly opposed the crawling peg in all its variants because it would lead to a weakening of countries' determination to pursue policies that would keep inflation firmly under control.

Mr. Suzuki stated that the Japanese authorities had a negative attitude toward greater exchange rate flexibility. By increasing the chances of combining continued inflation with successive depreciations of the currency, exchange rate flexibility would lead to a further loosening of discipline in economic management. The Executive Directors, he said, had no actual experience with the application of a more flexible exchange rate system and did not seem to be moving toward a consensus on the proper direction to take to obtain greater flexibility. Was it not better to maintain the present system with some improvement in its management?

Mr. van Campenhout believed that none of the techniques proposed for exchange rate flexibility—crawling pegs, fluctuating rates, wider margins—was sufficiently attractive to be introduced as a permanent legal feature of the international monetary system. If some rate flexibility was considered necessary, any measures that deviated from those prescribed by the Fund's Articles of Agreement could be approved on an ad hoc basis. This procedure would have the advantage that the deviating measures would be subject to international surveillance, through consultations or even through the imposition of sanctions, by an international organization that was already well established. Therefore, the Executive Directors should explore the additional authority that could be given to the Fund to permit members to use unorthodox techniques in certain defined circumstances, or possibly to authorize a temporary departure from the par value system for the entire membership. Were this line of thought to be pursued, one question that would have to be considered was whether such broad powers for the Fund would weaken the present system of par values or reinforce it. Another was whether the Fund could take the initiative in assuming such powers: member governments might regard any suggestion by the Fund that it acquire this much authority in the exchange rate field as a violation of their sovereignty.

Arguments for Exchange Rate Flexibility

The need for examining techniques to increase flexibility of exchange rates nonetheless received the support of several Executive Directors. These Directors thought that, even if the Executive Board did not formally agree on a particular technique, the Executive Directors ought to give serious consideration to ways in which par values could be more readily altered.

In Mr. Dale's opinion, the Board could take either of two general attitudes. It could take the view that, because there was now calm in exchange markets after the par value changes of the last five months of 1969, there was no need to proceed with any urgency. Or it could take the position that, although the existing quiet in the exchange markets lessened the immediate significance of the discussions, every effort should be made to prevent the kind of crisis that had occurred in the past year.

Mr. Schleiminger emphasized the experience of the recent past, which showed that it was the countries that had applied financial and monetary restraint that had been most pinched by the existing system of par values and that had encountered difficulties which had even led them into clashes with the letter of the Fund's Articles of Agreement. That was the reason why the Board of Governors had endorsed the intention of the Executive Directors to proceed with their study. The role of the Executive Directors was to present a range of solutions, perhaps eliminating those that would have no chance of being seriously considered. The Executive Directors should now, therefore, offer a spectrum of possible methods for achieving better balance of payments adjustment, including adjustment through the exchange rate system, rather than limit themselves to a mere statement of policy objectives. The intention at this stage was not to find a common denominator but to stake out the area within which greater exchange rate flexibility might be possible, thus preparing policymakers to make the choice, which would inevitably be a political one.

Mr. Johnstone likewise favored a review of the techniques for achieving exchange rate flexibility. He took the position that there were causes other than lack of financial discipline, such as structural changes in the world economy and shifts in international demand, that could lead to inappropriate exchange rates.

Mr. Mitchell, too, argued for a full-scale review of schemes for exchange rate flexibility and for a report to the Board of Governors. The public, he stated, had been encouraged to believe that the mechanism of exchange rate adjustment was a principal topic for discussion by the Fund in the year 1970, and it was important for the world's image of the Fund that some positive step be taken at the Annual Meeting in September. He argued further that the more the subject of adjustment of exchange rates was aired, the more the political inhibitions that obstructed adjustment would be undermined. It was, he went on, these political inhibitions, more than imperfections in the Fund's Articles of Agreement, that were delaying needed changes in the exchange rates of the major currencies.

Debate on Techniques

Examination of the possible techniques for introducing some limited exchange rate flexibility into the par value system also revealed divergent viewpoints.

Several Executive Directors had already been vocal in their distaste for crawling pegs or sliding parities. The main objection of the Executive Directors for the EEC countries to the crawling peg was its upsetting consequences for the harmonization of their exchange rates. Therefore, interest centered on wider margins. But here there were debates about the extent to which wider margins would, or would not, lessen speculative capital flows. Mr. Palamenghi-Crispi and Mr. Bustelo defended wider margins as helpful in restraining speculative capital movements, against the doubts of Mr. Omwony and Mr. Suzuki. Mr. Dale and Mr. Huntrods especially liked wider margins, noting that they would be optional for all members, which should make it possible for members of the EEC, who were trying to keep the relations between the exchange rates for their six currencies fairly fixed, to have smaller margins among themselves.

Mr. Dale further argued for the use of "presumptive criteria" that might serve as "indicators" to signal the need for a change in par value. Mr. Kafka and others, however, had grave doubts whether the Fund ought to be involved in the formulation of "presumptive indicators." Mr. Suzuki contended that there could be no meaningful presumptive criteria applicable to all members because the economic situation of every member was different. Moreover, should presumptive criteria be used, speculation against a currency could occur if the public knew what the criteria were and which countries were not living up to them.

A few Executive Directors, including Mr. Kafka and Mr. Schleiminger, recalling the successful transition by the Federal Republic of Germany to a new par value through use of a short-lived floating rate, suggested as a possible solution that the Fund be able legally to approve or concur in justified deviations from the par value system in exceptional situations for individual countries. It had been awkward in the past for the Fund not to be able legally to permit such situations. The subsequent discussion, however, revealed the difficulties of developing suitable codes of approval for the wide variety of members' situations that would arise in practice. Should there be a time limit to the Fund's approval? Should there be a suspension of margins or of par values? How would the Fund concur in the effective changes of par values being made? What, if any, conditions should be attached?

Positions of Deputies of Group of Ten

While these informal sessions were in progress, the Deputies of the Group of Ten met in Paris on April 23, 1970. According to the report of the Economic Counsellor, who attended that meeting, there was a unanimous view that the issue of greater exchange rate flexibility ought to be kept within the confines of the range of limited possibilities that the Fund had been considering. There was a strong endorsement of the basic elements of the Bretton Woods system and agreement not to change the fundamentals of that system. There appeared also to be a strong general desire to do as much as possible without amending the Articles of Agreement. This desire to work within the existing Articles had two implications: the existing Articles ought to be applied as broadly as possible, and acquiescence by the Fund could be resorted to where formal approval was not possible.

The majority of the Deputies of the Group of Ten thought that the most important way in which to achieve greater flexibility of exchange rates was to facilitate small adjustments in par values. Most of the Deputies also expressed a preference for maintaining the need for the Fund to concur in such small adjustments. There was a marked decline from their previous position in respect to the importance the Deputies attached to slightly wider margins. They realized that wider margins could not be achieved without amendment of the Articles of Agreement. Indeed, many Deputies believed that the case for wider margins as an antispeculation device had not been proved. There was general sympathy for a fluctuating exchange rate for a short period, but belief that it would not be desirable to legalize long-term deviations from the par value system.

Attempts at Consensus

These positions of the Deputies of the Group of Ten placed the Executive Directors in somewhat of a quandary. How far should they go along the "stretch-the-Articles" road? Some of them indicated that, from the reports they had from the representatives of their countries to the Deputies' meeting, the United States, Italy, and the Federal Republic of Germany had by no means ruled out amendment of the Articles of Agreement. Mr. Lieftinck objected to the "policy of acquiescence." The Articles, he said, constituted an international treaty, and the agreement entered into by countries when they became members of the Fund should be carried out in good faith. Furthermore, the present international monetary system could be weakened step by step if the rules of the game were no longer observed. Mr. Palamenghi-Crispi and Mr. van Campenhout also warned against acquiescence by the Fund to situations that it could not approve formally; a practice developed for marginal situations could easily turn into a major *modus operandi*, and the Bretton Woods system could be undermined.

Both to help the Executive Directors find common ground and to try to formulate a report that the Executive Directors might submit to the Board of Governors, the staff in March and April 1970 had been drafting possible outlines of a report and revising them as the discussions went along. By the middle of May the staff had drafted a long Part I, tentatively entitled "Description and Analysis," and at the end of June the staff circulated a draft of Part II, entitled "Implications for Policy."

Part I of the draft found general acceptance among the Executive Directors; but Part II, which contained possible recommendations by the Executive Board, encountered new objections. Three Directors, Mr. Dale, Mr. Palamenghi-Crispi, and Mr. Schleiminger, were now favoring something like a crawling peg and seemed to be willing to amend the Articles of Agreement accordingly. However, in line with his previously expressed views, Mr. Stone was especially resistant to "U.S.-German-Italian proposals" for small and frequent changes in par values. The Australian authorities, and probably the South African and New Zealand authorities, would, he thought, simply not be prepared to agree to amendments to the Articles that would open the door to easy changes in par values, floating rates, or crawling pegs. In addition, reflecting the recent agreement of the EEC countries to coordinate their exchange rate policies and to arrive at a common position on whatever changes were to be made in the exchange rate mechanism, many of the Executive Directors for the EEC countries wanted to minimize any emphasis on exchange rate flexibility. They argued for an "open document" that reflected the dissenting or minority opinions as well as the majority opinions.

AGREEMENT BY EXECUTIVE DIRECTORS

Toward the end of July 1970 the discussions became intensive as the Executive Directors held informal sessions in both the morning and the afternoon on July 22, 27, 29, and 31 to consider the draft report. Most Directors favored sending Part I to the Board of Governors as indicative of their efforts and discussions of some eighteen months and to supply supporting material for Part II. They differed, however, on whether the report should be the responsibility of the Executive Directors, if they could agree, or of the staff, in which case it would be an annex to a report of the Executive Directors. Part II was amended to include the possibility of a crawling peg, with an indication that different views existed about it.

In August, after several more informal sessions and further revisions of Part II, the Executive Directors began to meet in formal session to take final action on the draft report, on which near agreement had been reached. After half a dozen formal meetings, at which the substance of the final report as well as its format and transmittal were discussed, the Executive Board took a decision on August 12, 1970 approving the report, entitled *The Role of Exchange Rates in the Adjustment of International Payments*, for publication and transmittal to the Board of Governors. The status agreed upon for the report was that Part II, entitled "Implications for Policy," gave the views of the Executive Directors with respect to the policy aspects of the subject and Part I, entitled "Review and Analysis," contained the descriptive and analytical material on which their views were based.[20]

The Executive Directors had spent some one hundred hours in the preparation of the report. The number of hours spent by the staff in preparing drafts under high pressure had been far greater, and the Executive Directors expressed warmest thanks to the staff for its contribution to the study.

The main elements of Part II were, briefly, as follows:

One: The par value system, based on stable but adjustable par values at realistic levels, remained the most appropriate general regime to govern exchange

---

[20] The report was released on September 13, 1970. It is reproduced in Vol. II, below, pp. 273–330.

rates in a world of managed national economies. Any particular regime of exchange rate adjustment had both advantages and disadvantages when compared with other possible arrangements. Technical or organizational arrangements could never serve as substitutes for correct policy decisions. Judgment on the advisability of instituting any change in existing arrangements or in their implementation involved a weighing of the balance between potential benefits and potential costs. The risks that would be involved in any general departure from the par value system would not be justified by such special benefits as could be foreseen therefrom.

Two: The par value system was based on *stability* of exchange rates but not *rigidity*. Changes in par values were to be related to the correction of fundamental disequilibrium. The Executive Directors had discussed proposals to get members to make a quicker response to an emerging or imminent fundamental disequilibrium by changing their par values, but they had not reached an agreed conclusion. The term "fundamental disequilibrium" had never been defined, but the Fund would continue to study the elements to be taken into account in judging its presence and magnitude.

Three: Under the par value system, a change in the par value of a member's currency might be made only on the proposal of the member. This provision remained appropriate, although the expressions of views by the Fund at any time under established procedures should not be precluded.

Four: The Executive Directors rejected three alternative exchange rate regimes that had been proposed, viz., (*a*) a regime of fluctuating exchange rates, (*b*) a regime based on par values agreed with the Fund but allowing substantially wider margins, and (*c*) a regime under which par values would be adjusted at fixed intervals on the basis of some predetermined formula to be applied automatically. They recognized that any one of these regimes could in some respects and on certain assumptions perform more satisfactorily than the existing par value system, with not inconsequential benefits. But the disadvantages would clearly outweigh the potential advantages.

Five: The Executive Directors had considered three ways in which additional flexibility might be introduced into the par value system, all of which would require amendment of the Articles of Agreement. These were (*a*) prompt and small adjustments in par values in appropriate cases, say, 3 per cent in any 12-month period, or a cumulative amount of 10 per cent in any 5-year period, without the concurrence of the Fund; (*b*) a slight widening of the margins around par values from 1 per cent to 2 per cent or, at most, 3 per cent; and (*c*) temporary deviations from par value obligations. Some of the issues involved in these techniques, such as the necessary amendments to the Articles, were still open. They would continue their study of these issues in the period ahead.

In sum, the report of the Executive Directors, while supporting the par value system and rejecting widely different exchange rate arrangements, set out for the Board of Governors the ways in which the par value system might be made more flexible and the issues involved in introducing such techniques. In effect it invited the Governors, as the world's monetary authorities, to indicate what future course of action they might desire. In particular, did they wish the Fund's Articles of Agreement to be amended to provide for greater flexibility of exchange rates, and if so, how?

REACTIONS OF GOVERNORS

To proceed with their consideration of these proposals, the Executive Directors looked to the Governors at the Twenty-Fifth Annual Meeting, held in Copenhagen from September 21 to 25, 1970. But at that meeting the Governors made it very clear that they did not want to pursue the subject of exchange rate flexibility much further, certainly not if it involved amending the Fund's Articles of Agreement.

Mr. Barber (United Kingdom) and Mr. Fukuda urged that, since frequent changes in exchange rates might enhance capital speculation, attention should be given instead to an analysis of capital movements.[21] The speeches of the Governors for the countries of the EEC reflected their recent decision at The Hague to create, in the course of the 1970s, an economic and monetary union among themselves. Mr. Schiller (Federal Republic of Germany) referred to the intended harmonization of their exchange rate policies.[22] Mr. Witteveen (Netherlands) described at some length the possibilities for adjusting par values under the existing Articles and recommended that the Articles not be changed for that purpose.[23]

Italy, a member that had previously been in favor of introducing a moderate degree of flexibility into the international monetary system with regard to par values, exchange rates, and transitional regimes, took the position, in the words of Mr. Ferrari-Aggradi (Italy), that exchange rate flexibility had become an issue "strictly connected with that of the future monetary arrangements within the European Economic Community." He explained that the EEC countries would have to formulate a common policy on this subject. Meanwhile, it was necessary for the proper functioning of the EEC that, once agreement on common economic policies had been attained, the margins of the currencies of the countries involved should be progressively reduced and ultimately eliminated. In effect, the Euro-

---

[21] Statements by the Governor of the Fund for the United Kingdom and the Governor of the Fund and the World Bank for Japan, *Summary Proceedings, 1970*, pp. 67–69 and 73–74.

[22] Statement by the Governor of the World Bank for the Federal Republic of Germany, *Summary Proceedings, 1970*, p. 37.

[23] Statement by the Governor of the World Bank for the Netherlands, *Summary Proceedings, 1970*, p. 97.

pean currencies would have to move together vis-à-vis the dollar within a wider band, while oscillating within a smaller band against each other or not fluctuating at all.[24]

After the devaluation of the franc in August 1969, France had recovered from the severe economic difficulties which it had faced at the time of the previous Annual Meeting, and it was Mr. Giscard d'Estaing who most adamantly opposed any change in the "Bretton Woods charter, which aimed at putting an end to a quarter of a century of frequent parity changes and the general practice of competitive devaluations. Greater flexibility would weaken the will to protect currencies against inflation." [25]

Referring to the possibility of wider margins around par values, Mr. Giscard d'Estaing, too, stressed the agreement of the EEC countries to work out a plan, by stages, for creation of an economic and monetary union, and the implications of this union for exchange rates: the less flexibility, the better. "They cannot but realize what consequences a widening of the fluctuation bands would have for their own organization." They had already agreed "not to use, among themselves, the facilities that would be introduced at the world level." Accordingly, he summed up his position as "minimum flexibility and maximum stability." [26]

Mr. Kennedy was thus virtually alone in being receptive to the idea that the Executive Directors might examine more precisely the forms an amendment to the Articles of Agreement might take. But even he phrased this suggestion very cautiously as being conditional on "the evolving situation" and on whether "our objectives and experience subsequently make it desirable to move in that direction." [27]

AFTER COPENHAGEN

After studying the statements made by the Governors at the 1970 Annual Meeting, the staff concluded that it would not be profitable for the Fund at this stage to resume a discussion of the economic merits and demerits of various suggestions for greater exchange rate flexibility. However, the General Counsel believed that some additional light might be thrown on some of these issues by a study of the manner in which the Articles of Agreement could be amended,

---

[24] Statement by the Governor of the Fund for Italy, *Summary Proceedings, 1970,* pp. 123–24.

[25] Statement by the Governor of the World Bank for France, *Summary Proceedings, 1970,* p. 83.

[26] *Ibid.,* p. 86.

[27] Statement by the Governor of the Fund and the World Bank for the United States, *Summary Proceedings, 1970,* p. 92.

and the Legal Department worked in the latter part of 1970 and early in 1971 to draft possible amendments to the Articles. When the Deputies of the Group of Ten met in Paris in March 1971, the only topic on their agenda was exchange rate flexibility. They recognized that the Fund would not be able to permit wider margins without amendment of the Articles, and they were not inclined to such action.

CHAPTER 25

*Collapse of the
Par Value System*
(January 1–August 15, 1971)

*E*XCHANGE RATES became the Fund's paramount problem in 1971. The
Board of Governors had failed to act on the par value system in Copenhagen in September 1970 mainly because, in the year preceding that meeting,
the world's exchange markets had remained calm. The succession of crises
that had marked 1968 and most of 1969 had ended. Within eight months after
the 1970 Annual Meeting, however, this calm in exchange markets disappeared.
In May 1971 six European countries took exchange rate action, including resort
to floating rates by the Federal Republic of Germany and the Netherlands.
On August 15, 1971 the largest convulsion of all shook the international monetary system: the U.S. authorities suspended the convertibility into gold or other
reserve assets of dollars held by the monetary authorities of other countries.
Both the par value system and the convertibility of dollars into gold—two pillars
of the monetary system designed at Bretton Woods—thereby collapsed.

This chapter relates these reverberating events. But first, the other, relatively minor, changes in par values and other adjustments that were made
between January 1 and August 15, 1971 are discussed. (Similar changes that
were made in the years 1966 through 1970 were covered in Chapter 23.)

PAR VALUE AND OTHER ADJUSTMENTS

Yugoslavia

Effective on January 24, 1971 at 12:01 A.M., Belgrade time (January 23, 1971
at 6:01 P.M., Washington time), the par value of the Yugoslav dinar was changed
from 8.0000 U.S. cents per dinar to 6.66667 U.S. cents per dinar, a devaluation

of 16.7 per cent. This was the first effective change in Yugoslavia's par value since July 1965, when multiple currency practices were abolished. To give the Fund time for consideration, the National Bank of Yugoslavia alerted Mr. Schweitzer several days in advance of the intention to devalue.

The staff—a mission had been in Belgrade a few weeks before, in December 1970, in connection with a requested stand-by arrangement—supported the member's proposed devaluation. The increase in domestic costs had eroded the competitive position, and there had been speculation against the dinar. The authorities were in the process of taking a number of financial policy measures to support the proposed par value and bring about the desired shift of resources from the internal to the external sector.

Mr. Ivo Perisin, Governor for Yugoslavia, came to Washington to attend the Executive Board meeting held on Saturday, January 23, 1971. At that meeting Mr. Lieftinck explained that the deterioration in the balance of payments had been due mainly to an increase in imports that was much too rapid. These larger imports had resulted from an excessive rise in personal incomes. The fundamental disequilibrium that had developed could no longer be remedied by measures of domestic restraint alone.

The Executive Board agreed that fundamental disequilibrium existed and concurred in the change of par value.

New Monetary Units

On February 15, 1971 the United Kingdom and the Republic of Ireland adopted decimal systems for the pound sterling and the Irish pound, actions that did not involve any change of par value. In both cases the denominations for the new currencies were to be the pound and the new penny (1/100 of a pound), which was to replace the former system of pounds, shillings, and pence (sterling or Irish). The new penny was to be equal to 2.4 old pence. The new system was also to be adopted in the Falkland Islands and dependencies and in Gibraltar.

On the same day the Government of Malawi replaced the Malawi pound with a new currency, the kwacha, equivalent to 10 Malawi shillings. With the Fund's concurrence, a par value of 120.000 U.S. cents per kwacha was established, but no appreciation or depreciation was involved.

Effective July 1 the Fund concurred in a proposed par value for a new monetary unit, the dalasi, introduced by The Gambia to replace the Gambian pound. The new unit was equivalent to 4 Gambian shillings. The par value was set at 48 U.S. cents per dalasi, which did not involve any appreciation or depreciation.

On August 9 the Fund agreed to a proposal by Barbados for an initial par value of 2 East Caribbean dollars per U.S. dollar.

Canada Retains a Floating Rate

During the period January 1–August 15, 1971 the exchange rate for the Canadian dollar continued to float, with quoted rates averaging 6–7 per cent above the par value.

Under the Fund's evolving policy for quarterly consultations with members having floating exchange rates, the Fund held consultations with the Canadian Government in January, April, and July. Unemployment had become Canada's most serious economic problem. With more than 6 per cent of the labor force unemployed, the Canadian authorities were trying to reactivate the economy without sparking a return to higher rates of price increase. They continued to be reluctant to set a par value. The Executive Directors, as well as the staff, continued to argue that it was preferable for Canada to return to the par value system: that system was in jeopardy and the continued floating of the Canadian dollar certainly did not help to bolster it.

After May, when the currencies of the Federal Republic of Germany and the Netherlands were also floating, and especially after August 15, when the official convertibility for the U.S. dollar was suspended, the Fund's arguments concerning the need for a par value for the Canadian dollar necessarily became much weaker. The report of the staff's visit to Ottawa on July 26–29 was not circulated to the Executive Directors until after August 15, when, following the suspension of official convertibility by the United States, exchange markets everywhere were disrupted. The Executive Directors began to center their attention on the exchange rate situations of all the major industrial countries and on the prospects for a general realignment of currencies. (These developments are discussed later in this chapter and in Chapter 26.) In these circumstances, the floating of the Canadian dollar was obviously less of an aberration from the system of par values, and the Executive Directors did not discuss the staff's report.

FRESH DISTURBANCES IN EUROPEAN MARKETS

Although the renewed disturbances that afflicted European exchange markets in the first week of May 1971 were the sixth or seventh exchange crisis within three years, no one seemed quite prepared. It was only afterward that particular causes were sought for the onset in the first few months of 1971 of voluminous outflows of privately held foreign capital from the United States. Increasing alarm about the size of the U.S. balance of payments deficit had been evident in January 1971 in the Executive Directors' comments during the 1970 Article VIII consultation with the United States, but no great change had occurred in 1970 and the first quarter of 1971 in the trade balances of the major industrial countries, nor in their "basic balances," that would explain a sudden reversal of capital flows.

In their Annual Report for 1971, the Executive Directors attributed the shift in capital flows to the opening of an unusually wide gap between credit conditions and interest rates in the United States and in continental European countries.[1] This gap had opened because both the United States and continental European countries were opting in favor of monetary policy, as against other anti-inflationary measures, to regulate their domestic economies and because, at the time, their cyclical positions and the ways in which they applied monetary policy diverged. Most relevant was the easing of monetary conditions in the United States while those in the Federal Republic of Germany were being made stringent. This explanation for the sudden outflows of yield-sensitive capital from the United States was also the one subscribed to by Mr. Arthur F. Burns, Chairman of the Board of Governors of the Federal Reserve System, speaking in Munich on May 28 at the 1971 International Banking Conference of the American Bankers Association.

The monetary authorities in the United States and Europe had already taken steps by April to bring their short-term interest rates closer together. Interest-induced capital movements were, however, overtaken by speculative capital movements. Many officials and academic economists had been making public references to "overvaluation of the dollar," and speculators anticipated changes in the exchange rates of major currencies, including the dollar.

In the first few days of May the rush of funds into European markets took on gigantic proportions. The outflow of funds from the United States not only once again severely aggravated the balance of payments and reserve positions of that country, but the inflows made it virtually impossible for the authorities of the recipient countries to cope with the consequent inflationary threats to their domestic economies. These inflationary pressures worsened when countries bought dollars so as to keep the exchange rates for their currencies in terms of dollars stable and were then confronted with greatly augmented monetary reserves and enhanced bank liquidity. On Wednesday, May 5, the central banking authorities of Austria, Belgium and Luxembourg, the Federal Republic of Germany, the Netherlands, Portugal, and Switzerland closed their official exchange markets, and those of Finland, Greece, Norway, Singapore, and South Africa withdrew their support for the U.S. dollar and suspended dealings in deutsche mark, Netherlands guilders, and Swiss francs.

Managing Director Suggests a Technique

As European Cabinets and the Finance Ministers of the EEC countries were assembling to decide what to do, the Executive Directors, although they had no specific proposals before them, met twice in formal meetings on May 5 and again in informal session on May 7. It was already evident that a new realignment of the par values of the major currencies was most unlikely. Mr. John B.

---

[1] *Annual Report, 1971*, pp. 9–11.

Connally, appointed by President Nixon as Secretary of the Treasury in March 1971, had emphasized once more in a press release issued by the U.S. Treasury on May 4 the official view of the U.S. Government that no change in the present structure of parities was necessary or anticipated.

In an attempt to be helpful in this latest crisis, the Managing Director circulated to the Executive Directors first a statement, and then an aide-mémoire, which they could pass on to their authorities. He stressed that it was important for the Fund, in these difficult circumstances, to try to maintain the system of par values, if that was at all possible. Nonetheless, at least until the current uncertainties had been dispelled, some additional flexibility of exchange rates might be required to permit European authorities to reopen their exchange markets on Monday, May 10. To avoid floating rates for the deutsche mark and other currencies, which might do permanent damage to the system of par values, he suggested a widening of the upward margins, say, to 5 or 6 per cent from par in relation to the dollar. These wider margins would prevail only for a limited time, at most a few months, to test what if any changes of par value were needed.

Two ways might be used, Mr. Schweitzer suggested, to effect a temporary widening of the margins under the existing Articles. Under Article XVI, Section 1, the Fund could, in the event of an emergency or the development of unforeseen circumstances threatening the operations of the Fund, temporarily suspend the margin provisions. The Executive Board could, by unanimous vote, suspend these provisions for 120 days and the Board of Governors could, by a four-fifths majority of the total voting power, extend any suspension for a further 240 days. In deciding on such a suspension, the Executive Board could as a condition of the suspension determine the widened margins around parity that members would have to observe for the period of the suspension. During this period, active consideration would be given to amending the Articles.

Alternatively, the Fund could call on members to collaborate with it, under the provisions of Article IV, Section 4 (a), to observe the same specified wider margins in those cases where they felt unable to observe the 1 per cent margins.

Most of the Executive Directors expressed appreciation for the leadership shown by Mr. Schweitzer, and several of them, including Messrs. Dale, de Kock, Johnstone, Lieftinck, Palamenghi-Crispi, and Schleiminger, supported his suggestion for wider margins. Nevertheless, this suggestion was not implemented. Mr. Dale and Mr. Schleiminger wanted any widening of the margins to be made symmetrical, downward as well as upward. Mr. Lieftinck and Mr. Palamenghi-Crispi doubted that margins of 5–6 per cent were wide enough, while Mr. Gilchrist considered them excessive. Mr. Palamenghi-Crispi said that the Italian authorities favored a number of measures to control capital movements: controlling the supplies of money; freezing foreign deposits and placing charges on their unfreezing; instituting restrictions on nonbank borrowing abroad; and introducing controls on movements of capital. Mr. Koichi Satow

(Japan) reported that the Japanese authorities were opposed to wider margins even temporarily, and Mr. Viénot called the Managing Director's suggestion "premature," inasmuch as EEC members had not yet discussed widening the margins to deal with the current crisis, and "extremely dangerous," since it provided an opportunity for a substantial change in the way the international monetary system operated.

NEW MEASURES BY EUROPEAN COUNTRIES

On Sunday, May 9, 1971, five European members of the Fund and Switzerland took steps preparatory to reopening their exchange markets the next morning.

Federal Republic of Germany, Netherlands, Belgium, and Luxembourg

The Federal Republic of Germany informed the Fund that, for the time being, it would not maintain the exchange rates for its currency within the established margins. The Netherlands informed the Fund that it had found it necessary to take similar action, both because of the recent developments in foreign exchange markets and because of the action of the German authorities, since commercial transactions between the two countries were sizable. In other words, the exchange rates for both the deutsche mark and the Netherlands guilder would float. Both members gave assurances to the Fund that they would remain in close consultation with the Fund, that they would collaborate fully with the Fund in accordance with the Articles of Agreement, and that they would resume maintenance of the limits around their par values as soon as circumstances permitted.

Belgium and Luxembourg notified the Fund that the Belgian-Luxembourg Economic Union was changing the regulations concerning its free market for capital transactions with a view to stemming any large inflows of capital. Previously, the free market had been used as an instrument for containing excessive capital outflows; the rate in the free market could depreciate but not appreciate relative to the rate in the official market, as currencies acquired in the free market could be sold in the official market. Now the dual market system would be altered so that capital inflows could not be channeled through the official market. This and other changes affecting the scope and structure of the free market would make it possible for the rate in the free market to appreciate above that in the official market. Thus, the free market would be useful in discouraging large-scale inflows of capital.

As they had often done in the past few crises, the Executive Directors met on a Sunday evening (May 9, 1971). Mr. Schleiminger, Mr. Lieftinck, and

Mr. van Campenhout all reported that the authorities of their countries saw no reason, either currently or in the foreseeable future, to change the par values of their currencies. In particular, the authorities of the Federal Republic of Germany had ruled out another revaluation: costs and prices were rising sharply, even relative to those in other countries, and the basic balance of payments was in deficit. Floating the deutsche mark would insulate the economy and buy time for a restrictive monetary policy to take effect. Restrictions were also being placed on capital transactions. These included the abolition of interest on nonresidents' deposits and the requirement that residents obtain official authorization to sell domestic securities to nonresidents. Mr. Schleiminger pointed out that the authorities of the Federal Republic of Germany had few other options. The German public wanted some response. No suitable machinery existed for implementing administrative controls quickly and effectively. And agreement by the members of the EEC on widening the margins of fluctuation for their currencies for a limited period had not been found feasible.

Although most of the Executive Directors understood the actions of the authorities of the Federal Republic of Germany, the Netherlands, and Belgium and Luxembourg, several of them were disturbed by the situation that was developing and expressed their deep concern for the par value system. Their decisions for the Federal Republic of Germany and the Netherlands, which in the customary way for such decisions noted the circumstances and called for close consultation with the Fund, went further than usual. Authority was specifically conferred on the Managing Director to initiate consultations between the member and the Fund. The intent was to help to keep the Fund involved in the exchange rate discussions of major countries to a greater extent and at an earlier stage by explicitly enabling the Managing Director to have informal communication with the authorities of members on their exchange rate policies. He could then use his discretion in deciding when consultations of a formal nature, culminating in a formal discussion and possibly a decision by the Executive Board, would be most useful.

Mr. Brofoss, insisting that much tighter restrictions on capital movements should be instituted on a worldwide basis to stop speculators from destroying the international monetary system, dissociated himself from the decisions.

In July, in the course of the next Article VIII consultation with Belgium and Luxembourg, the Fund approved the changes in the exchange regulations of those members.

Because of the concern of some Executive Directors about the threat to the par value system, because most of them again urged that the Fund have a more active role in exchange rate decisions that were increasingly being taken outside the Fund, and because the Managing Director had, at the outset of the latest crisis, come up with positive suggestions for handling that crisis, the press release issued by the Fund on May 9, 1971 in regard to the measures being taken by the Federal Republic of Germany, the Netherlands, and Belgium and Luxembourg included the following paragraph:

> The Fund has given consideration to various ways of coping with the diffi-culties presently facing its members. In its consultations with members, and in its continuing work, the Fund will seek to maintain and strengthen the basic principles of the Bretton Woods system. The recent disturbances demonstrate the need to improve the international adjustment process and to bring about a better coordination among members with respect to their internal and external policies.

The Executive Board could not agree, however, that the Fund should expedite its study of limited exchange rate flexibility.

Austrian Schilling

Also on May 9, 1971, Austria informed the Fund that, effective on that day at 7:00 P.M., Washington time, it proposed to change the par value of the schilling from S 26 to S 24.75 per U.S. dollar, a revaluation of 5.05 per cent. The staff's assessment justified this revaluation, partly because of a fundamental disequilibrium but mainly as a protective move following the floating of the deutsche mark. Given Austria's strong external position and its close relations with the Federal Republic of Germany, the action by the latter might otherwise stimulate an unwanted inflow of speculative capital from that country and other countries. Inasmuch as the change in par value for the schilling, together with all previous changes, did not exceed 10 per cent of the initial par value set by Austria in May 1953, the change fell within the provisions of Article IV, Section 5 (c) (i), and the Fund therefore merely noted the new par value.

Swiss Franc

The Swiss authorities on May 9, 1971 announced a revaluation of the Swiss franc from a parity equivalent to Sw F 4.37282 per U.S. dollar to Sw F 4.08415 per U.S. dollar, effective from May 10, 1971. In making the announcement, the Minister of Finance said that the revaluation was necessary to prevent an excessive flow of funds into Switzerland.

DIFFICULT ISSUES ARISE

By mid-1971 the problems of the international monetary system were being aired everywhere. Three major currencies—the Canadian dollar, the deutsche mark, and the Netherlands guilder—were now floating. The disequi-librium in international payments seemed greater than ever. There was much talk, especially among economists, that the U.S. dollar was overvalued relative to the currencies of some other industrial countries and that there ought to be a moderate change in the exchange rate relationships between the dollar and the other currencies. But official spokesmen for the United States and for other countries held disparate views about whether it should be the United States or those nations that had persistent surpluses which should take the initiative in correcting the disequilibrium by a change of par value. Should the dollar be devalued or should other currencies be revalued? In the meantime, the formation of exchange rate policy was being heavily dominated by short-term capital movements. Moreover, the likelihood was increasing that an otherwise minor political or financial crisis would unhinge the entire international monetary system or precipitate a general resurgence of protectionism.

The questions being raised by monetary officials paralleled those coming up in Executive Board discussions during these months—for example, in the Board's informal sessions on the world economic outlook, in the 1971 Article VIII consultation with the Federal Republic of Germany, and in the Board's continuing discussions about techniques for enhancing exchange rate flexibility. These questions were directed in the first instance to the immediate future. Need the floating rate for the deutsche mark continue for long? Within two months the Federal Republic of Germany had regained a measure of control over the liquidity of its banking system, with a moderate appreciation in the rate for the deutsche mark of 4 per cent, to DM 3.50–3.56 per U.S. dollar. Therefore, should not that country resume the maintenance of regular margins around its par value, especially since the floating rate for the deutsche mark was creating uncertainties and difficulties for transactions among members of the EEC? Mr. Lieftinck had already confirmed that some of these difficulties existed for the Netherlands.

Other questions were directed to the longer run, but with the realization that the longer run was not so far in the future any more. Could the present floating of three major currencies be regarded as a test of how a general system of floating rates would work? To what extent had short-term capital movements been fostered because the mix of domestic policies that countries had been using to check inflation had relied excessively on monetary policy and insufficiently on fiscal and wage-price, that is, incomes, policies? Would capital flows be reduced sufficiently by better coordination of monetary policy among countries aimed at preventing very high interest rates and interest-rate differentials among countries? How could such international policy coordination be implemented? To what extent, and how, should capital transactions be made subject to restrictions? Was it even possible to place controls on capital movements between free economies that had become closely integrated economically and financially? How should the basic imbalances in international payments be rectified? And, lastly, in what forum should these and related questions be answered?

There were, of course, difficulties of a technical nature involved in answering these perplexing economic questions. But from discussions that had already taken place among international monetary authorities—and from statements that high monetary officials were increasingly making to the press, debating in public, as it were, their positions on international monetary questions—it was evident that sharp differences of opinion that were really political in character would have to be resolved as well.

Managing Director's Initiative

Immediately after the events of the first ten days of May (described above), Mr. Schweitzer, seeking to give the Fund a more active, effective, and visible role in the solution of these problems, suggested to the Executive Directors a three-pronged program.

First, and most urgently, they should submit a final report on the question of exchange rate flexibility to the Board of Governors, preferably before the Annual Meeting in September; such a report should include specific recommendations for amending the Articles of Agreement. Mr. Schweitzer continued to believe that the fact that the Fund's views on the exchange rate system remained unsettled could potentially disturb the world's exchange markets.

Second, they should examine the ways in which the adjustment process might be improved and in which domestic economic and financial policies of nations might be better coordinated.

Third, they should study means of preventing short-term capital flows, including the use of more generally applied restrictions on such transactions.

The Executive Directors all welcomed the Managing Director's initiative, although many had some difficulty with setting a deadline for a report on exchange rate flexibility. Mr. Suzuki and Mr. Viénot wanted assurances (*a*) that priority would not be assigned to the study of exchange rate flexibility at the expense of the other topics, and (*b*) that the possible final recommendation could be "no change in the par value system."

United States Shapes Its Views

Before the Executive Directors had had time to act on the program suggested by the Managing Director, some issues that were even more controversial than those listed at the beginning of this section were brought forward. The Secretary of the U.S. Treasury, Mr. Connally, in a speech on May 28, 1971 at the International Banking Conference of the American Bankers Association in Munich that was praised by some as "telling it as it is" and "forthright" and criticized by others as "tough" and "unconciliatory," brought into the open two very sensitive issues that until that time had been submerged in international discussions of the U.S. balance of payments deficit, namely, the cost of military defense and international trade policy.

Reciting the history of the United States in the field of international monetary cooperation since World War II, Mr. Connally pointed out that, despite its chronic payments deficits, the United States nonetheless had remained a major exporter of capital, had continued to make substantial outlays for defense costs abroad, had maintained a large foreign aid program, and had not heavily protected its domestic markets. Neither the U.S. deficit nor the enormous short-term money flows were "uniquely American" problems, and joint responsibility for their solution should be accepted. The responsibility of the United States was to bring inflation in its domestic economy under control; to that end, it had implemented stern fiscal and monetary policies, with considerable domestic tolls in terms of unutilized economic capacity, low profits, and unemployment.

Mr. Connally stated explicitly that the burden of defense costs had to be shared more fully among the allies of the free world and that action must be taken to make trading arrangements more equitable and to permit freer entry of imports into European and Japanese markets. The United States, he said emphatically, was not going to devalue the dollar and was not going to change the price of gold.

UNITED STATES SUSPENDS CONVERTIBILITY

During the course of 1971 the U.S. balance of payments situation deteriorated more and more. In the first quarter the balance on the official settlements basis, seasonally adjusted, was in deficit by $5,506 million ($5,686 million excluding allocations of SDRs), a deterioration of $2.2 billion from the fourth quarter of 1970.[2] In the second quarter there was a trade deficit, the first such quarterly deficit since 1935, and it appeared that for the year as a whole the first trade deficit since 1893 might develop. Contributing to the trade deficit was a strengthening of demand in the United States, as the authorities took stimulative monetary measures to combat the 1969–70 recession, and a slowing down of economic activity in Western Europe and Japan, where anti-inflationary measures still prevailed. As a result, the underlying downward trend in the U.S. trade balance was compounded by a cyclical situation less favorable than that in the preceding year. In addition, prolonged dock strikes reduced exports more than imports, and strikes or threats of strikes in several major industries also had an adverse effect on the trade balance. There may have been, as well, an acceleration of imports into the United States in anticipation of exchange

---

[2] U.S. Department of Commerce, *News*, May 17, 1971, p. 1.

rate changes or import restrictions. But apart from cyclical influences and special situations, the continuous upsurge in U.S. imports reflected a persistent growth in U.S. consumers' preferences for imported products.

By far the largest factor responsible for the sharply deteriorating balance of payments position, however, was an enormous increase in short-term capital outflows. These, plus the trade deficit and a larger outflow on long-term capital account, gave rise to a U.S. deficit (official settlements basis) for the first half of 1971 of more than $22 billion at an annual rate.

The outward movement of capital was in part the response of participants in financial markets to the shift in comparative monetary conditions and interest rate levels. However, the deteriorating U.S. trade position was being accompanied by a huge advance in the trade surplus of Japan, suggesting a sharply growing imbalance in the global payments structure. Hence, large shifts of capital that were clearly speculative—in anticipation of, or hedging against, possible changes in exchange rates for major currencies—began to take place. A contributing factor to speculative capital movements was the spreading realization that the modest improvement of the U.S. current account in 1970 had been a temporary manifestation of a favorable combination of circumstances, and that the tapering off of the European boom, together with the commencement of a domestic economic upswing in the United States itself, was again exposing the fundamental weakness of the U.S. current account.

There was evidence of further large deficits to come. No early correction was in sight. Consequently, in July and early August another and even more massive flow of funds into foreign currencies got under way. A number of countries began to present more of their dollar holdings to the U.S. Treasury for conversion into gold. By August 15, the net U.S. reserve position—already weak at the beginning of the year—had deteriorated to the point where liabilities to foreign official authorities exceeded U.S. official reserves by almost $30 billion. The deficit on an official settlements basis for the third quarter alone would amount to nearly $13 billion.

Furthermore, public concern with the U.S. economic situation had deepened. Domestically, rising prices coexisted with unemployment. On the external side, a report issued on August 6 by the U.S. Congress recommended action in respect of the dollar and explained that a change in the exchange rate could probably come only by breaking the link with gold.[3] It was argued that merely increasing the dollar price of gold not only had the unfortunate side effects of yielding windfall profits to gold producing countries and to those who had been accumu-

---

[3] U.S. Congress, Joint Economic Committee, *Action Now to Strengthen the U.S. Dollar: Report of the Subcommittee on International Exchange and Payments*, 92nd Cong., 1st Sess. (Washington, 1971). This subcommittee was often referred to as the Reuss committee because it was chaired by Mr. Henry S. Reuss, Congressman from Wisconsin. (Mr. William Proxmire, Senator from Wisconsin, was the chairman of the Joint Economic Committee.)

lating gold, but held no assurance that exchange rates in terms of dollars would change: other countries might correspondingly alter the gold value of their currencies, leaving no change in the position of the dollar. A second possibility of effecting a change in the value of the dollar was impracticable because other countries were reluctant to revalue their currencies vis-à-vis the dollar.

On Sunday evening, August 15, 1971, President Nixon, in an address on radio and television, announced a far-ranging New Economic Program for the United States.[4] The program reflected in part the findings of the Commission on International Trade and Investment Policy, which he had appointed in May 1970 "to examine the principal problems in the field of U.S. foreign trade and investment, and to produce recommendations designed to meet the challenges of the changing world economy during the present decade." That Commission had given the President its report in July 1971.[5] The program included measures to improve both the domestic economy and the balance of payments position.

In the domestic field, there were tax cuts to stimulate employment, but in order to achieve price stability more quickly, there were also reductions in budgetary expenditures and, in a sharp reversal of governmental policy, a 90-day freeze on prices and wages.

On the external side, a series of actions restricted the conversion into gold or other reserve assets of dollars held by monetary authorities abroad. *First*, the U.S. authorities notified the Fund that, with effect from August 15, 1971, the United States no longer, for the settlement of international transactions, in fact freely bought and sold gold under the second sentence of Article IV, Section 4 (*b*), of the Articles of Agreement. *Second*, further use of U.S. international reserve assets (gold, SDRs, drawing rights in the Fund, and foreign exchange holdings) was "strictly limited" to "settlement of outstanding obligations and, in cooperation with the Fund, to other situations that may arise in which such use can contribute to international monetary stability and the interests of the United States." *Third*, the Secretary of the Treasury requested the Board of Governors of the Federal Reserve System to suspend the virtually automatic use of its swap network for the purpose of converting dollars into other currencies. Thus, what had earlier been referred to informally by financiers and bankers as a prospective "closing of the gold window" by the United States became a formal reality. *Fourth*, President Nixon announced that the United States was imposing, effective immediately, a temporary surcharge of 10 per cent on all dutiable imports not already subject to quantitative limitation. (In effect, the only exemptions to the surcharge were imports of raw materials and imports of a few manufactured commodities that were already subject to import quotas.)

---

[4] Reproduced in Supplement to *International Financial News Survey*, Vol. 23 (1971), pp. 257–60.

[5] U.S. Commission on International Trade and Investment Policy, *United States International Economic Policy in an Interdependent World: Report to the President* (Washington, 1971); released to the public in September 1971.

IMPLICATIONS FOR THE FUND

The U.S. actions had profound implications for the international monetary system and for the Fund. Under the par value system, the members of the Fund were obliged to maintain the exchange rates for their currencies within prescribed margins around agreed par values. In general, members other than the United States had chosen to fulfill this obligation by intervening in their exchange markets so as to peg the rates for their currencies, usually to the dollar. They bought dollars when the rate for dollars was depreciating in terms of their currencies and sold dollars when the dollar rate in terms of their currencies was appreciating. The United States, for its part, had opted to carry out its exchange rate obligations by being willing to buy and sell gold for dollars freely—that is, without limit—from and to the monetary authorities of other members, at the official price plus or minus the margin prescribed by the Fund. Thus, the monetary authorities of other members could, if they wished, exchange for gold any dollars they acquired.

The assumption of the obligation by the United States with respect to buying and selling gold for dollars, which had been spelled out in a letter of May 20, 1949 from the Secretary of the Treasury to the Managing Director, was rescinded by the letter to the Managing Director of August 15, 1971. One of the foundation stones of the international monetary system as it had operated since World War II under the Bretton Woods agreements—the convertibility of officially held dollar balances into gold—had crumbled. In the President's statement, the United States also gave up the obligation of conversion through the Fund under Article VIII, Section 4, thereby further limiting the convertibility envisaged under the Bretton Woods system. Following the U.S. actions, the par value system, too, was formally in abeyance: other members of the Fund, which had to decide whether to continue to accumulate dollars or to let their exchange rates fluctuate, could no longer assure that they would intervene in exchange markets in such a way that transactions between their currencies and the U.S. dollar would take place within prescribed limits around par values.

CHAPTER
26

Road to the
Smithsonian Agreement
(August 16–December 18, 1971)

MONETARY AFFAIRS WERE IN A CRITICAL STATE following the U.S. announcement of August 15, 1971. On Monday morning, August 16, most of the world's exchange markets were closed: it was unclear what exchange rates would prevail or how they would be determined. There was an urgent need for monetary officials to decide what to do in the new circumstances.

FUND'S IMMEDIATE RESPONSE TO U.S. ANNOUNCEMENT

The Managing Director had been invited to come to the U.S. Treasury on Sunday evening, August 15. He was accompanied by the Deputy Managing Director, Mr. Southard. They were informed by the Under Secretary for Monetary Affairs, Mr. Paul Volcker, of the actions that President Nixon would be announcing from the White House on radio and television in less than an hour. The Secretary of the Treasury, Mr. Connally, was at the White House. The U.S. monetary authorities told the Fund's management that no one else had been given advance notice of the U.S. actions, and that they did not have in mind a package of proposals, including exchange rate adjustments, to be discussed with officials of other countries. They had acted on the belief that they could not negotiate a new structure of exchange rates while they were maintaining gold sales against officially held dollars.

Mr. Schweitzer and Mr. Southard commented that the 10 per cent import surcharge was likely to cause consternation among the officials of other countries and that a realignment of exchange rates could be anticipated but would be a complicated negotiation. They also explained that the staff of the Fund had done some work on exchange rate relationships among the major currencies.

As was their custom during the last two weeks of August, the Executive Directors were in informal recess. Nonetheless, a Board meeting was called for Monday morning, August 16, and on that day there were both morning and afternoon sessions; several of the Executive Directors were on vacation and were represented by their Alternates. The Managing Director pointed out that the U.S. announcement raised two issues. The first concerned the action that the Fund should take with respect to the communication sent by the U.S. Secretary of the Treasury. The second issue was a broader one. It had been evident for some time that the prevailing pattern of parities was a major cause of the persistent imbalances in international payments. The actions of the U.S. authorities opened up the possibility of dealing in a fundamental way with the pattern of exchange rates and thus of attacking one of the basic causes of the disequilibrium in international payments. Mr. Schweitzer believed that a new pattern of parities was required and that it should be agreed on quickly, and he reported that the staff had been giving consideration to the changes in exchange rates that would permit a better balance in international payments. He added that, while the central focus would be on a new structure of parities, consideration might also be given to the question whether somewhat wider margins might be permitted temporarily.

Mr. Schweitzer believed that it was necessary that early decisions be taken on rates of exchange for currencies in terms of each other and in terms of gold, if for no other reason, because new agreed rates were needed to permit the effective functioning of the Fund's General Account and Special Drawing Account. While the present uncertainty prevailed, transactions in both Accounts might have to be halted, a situation that could not be allowed to continue for any length of time.

The problems for the Fund's transactions to which Mr. Schweitzer referred have already been described in Chapters 12 and 17. In brief, the Fund's financial transactions and operations were being hampered by three circumstances. *One,* the widespread expectation that the future price of gold and of SDRs in terms of currencies might increase was inducing members to reduce their liabilities to the Fund and to avoid any decrease in their SDR holdings and their reserve positions in the Fund. *Two,* the exchange rates for almost all of the currencies that the Fund would use in drawings and repurchases and other transactions under its regular procedures were not being effectively maintained within the margins around par values established under the Articles or decisions of the Fund, and the decision on fluctuating currencies had been applied only to the three currencies that were floating before August 15, 1971. As a result, purchases and repurchases through the General Account could not be effected in the usual way on the basis of agreed par values or of provisionally agreed exchange rates, and transactions in the Special Drawing Account could not be conducted on the basis of representative exchange rates.[1] *Three,* in the absence of agreed arrangements for convertibility, difficulties might be encountered by members in using currencies which they held in their reserves, but which could not be accepted by the Fund, in the acquisition of other currencies that were needed for their transactions with the Fund. In addition, without agreement on the values to be used for currencies and gold, there was a problem concerning the valuation of the Fund's assets.

The reactions to the U.S. actions expressed by the Executive Directors on August 16 exemplified the initial reactions of most monetary officials. There was, in effect, an atmosphere of crisis. Many Executive Directors pressed Mr. Dale about the intentions of the U.S. authorities, especially in regard to the exchange rate situation that was likely to arise immediately, and regarding the import surcharge. Several believed that new par values would have to be negotiated urgently, that is, within the next few days. When the Executive Directors took up a draft decision containing the Fund's reply to the U.S. communication, Mr. Dale explained that the U.S. authorities believed that the U.S. action was essential in order to induce momentum among industrial countries on exchange and trade measures that were basic to correcting the imbalance in world payments. Hence, they preferred that the Fund not take any decision at this time. Mr. Viénot had an opposite view, expressing surprise that in the draft decision the Fund only "took note" of the U.S. actions; he preferred the Fund to express its disagreement with the U.S. action, which, he contended, constituted "a clear deviation from the Articles of Agreement."

It was not until Friday, August 20, after considerable discussion during the week, that the Executive Directors, including Mr. Dale, were able to agree on a decision. The text of the decision, which was cabled to all members was as follows (the decision was also made public in Press Release No. 853):

1. The United States authorities, in a letter from the Secretary of the Treasury to the Managing Director, have notified the International Monetary Fund "that, with effect August 15, 1971, the United States no longer, for the settlement of international transactions, in fact, freely buys and sells gold under the second sentence of Article IV, Section 4 (*b*). The United States will continue to collaborate with the Fund to promote exchange stability, to maintain orderly exchange arrangements with other members, and to avoid competitive exchange alterations." The Fund notes that exchange transactions in the territories of the United States have been occurring outside the limits prescribed by Article IV, Section 3, and the actions taken by the United States authorities do not at the present time ensure that transactions between their currency and the currencies of other members take place within their territories only within the limits prescribed by Article IV, Section 3.

---

[1] The breakdown of the par value system eventually caused a number of difficulties with respect to the valuation of currencies, both in terms of gold and in terms of other currencies. These difficulties became pronounced when the rates for several currencies began to float early in 1973. For a discussion of these problems, see Joseph Gold, *Floating Currencies, Gold, and SDRs: Some Recent Legal Developments,* IMF Pamphlet Series, No. 19 (Washington, 1976).

2. The Fund notes the circumstances which have led the United States authorities to take the actions described above. The Fund emphasizes the undertaking of members to collaborate with it to promote exchange stability, to maintain orderly exchange arrangements with other members, and to avoid competitive exchange alterations, and therefore welcomes the intention of the United States authorities to act in accordance with this undertaking.

3. The Fund will remain in close consultation with the authorities of the United States and of the other members with a view to the prompt achievement of a viable structure of exchange rates on the basis of parities established and maintained in accordance with the Articles of Agreement. The Managing Director will take appropriate initiatives to this end.

EXCHANGE RATE REALIGNMENT—A SENSITIVE ISSUE

The second issue to which the Managing Director referred in the Executive Board meeting of August 16—that of realignment of the exchange rates of the major industrial nations—was an extremely sensitive one. There were many officials and economists who regarded the U.S. dollar as overvalued, at least in relation to some of the currencies of the EEC countries—such as the deutsche mark, the Netherlands guilder, and the Belgian franc—and in relation to the Japanese yen. At a minimum it was now generally recognized that a realignment of the par values of the industrial countries had somehow to be achieved. Just how the readjustment of exchange rates was to be effected, however, was not so clear. Although there had been informal hints at least as far back as 1968 that countries with surpluses should revalue their currencies vis-à-vis the dollar, the authorities of the countries experiencing the most protracted surpluses—the Federal Republic of Germany and Japan—fearing that reduced levels of exports might endanger their rates of economic growth, continued to be very reluctant to do so. Moreover, monetary officials of most of the EEC countries, centering attention on the prolonged balance of payments deficit of the United States, had for some time considered a change in exchange rates through an increase in the dollar price of gold to be essential. Because of the severe aggravation of inflationary pressures in the United States and the substantial enlargement of the U.S. balance of payments deficit following a sizable expansion of U.S. military expenditures in Viet-Nam, European officials believed more strongly than ever that corrective action was up to the United States.

U.S. Position on Dollar Devaluation

The management of the Fund had been in touch informally with the U.S. authorities throughout the first seven months of 1971, especially after the first week of May, and knew the position of the U.S. authorities to be sharply different from that being expressed by European officials. Moreover, as the speeches reported in the preceding chapter indicate, the U.S. authorities had begun openly to state their views. They took the position that the responsibility for correcting the chronic imbalances in international payments—the U.S. deficit on the one side and the surpluses of several other industrial countries on the other side— ought to be shared. More explicitly, they believed that the U.S. payments deficit resulted at least partly because the United States for many years had been shouldering a very heavy share of the defense costs of Western Europe, Japan, and other militarily allied countries, and because the trading arrangements of the EEC and of Japan did not permit the liberal entry of U.S. goods. Therefore, countries with surpluses ought to revalue their currencies and some concessions ought to be made in respect of military burden-sharing and trading arrangements. Especially was it imperative that changes be made in the common agricultural policy of the EEC, which was hampering U.S. exports of agricultural goods to European countries, and in restrictions on imports by Japan, which were preventing a correction of the large U.S. trade deficit with that country.

In addition to wanting action on these broad fronts, the U.S. monetary authorities had another problem—how to attain a realignment of the exchange rates for the major currencies without changing the dollar price of gold. They had stated on a number of occasions, and again on August 15, 1971, that they would not devalue the dollar. (*De facto* depreciation of the dollar vis-à-vis other major currencies that might take place in exchange markets following the suspension of official convertibility was not, of course, devaluation in terms of gold. Indeed, market depreciation of the dollar against other currencies could be construed as tantamount, economically, to appreciation of other currencies in terms of the dollar.)

The way in which the par value system had been implemented since its establishment made it difficult for the United States to take action on the exchange rate for the dollar. Market intervention was the main technique by which members of the Fund ensured that spot rates between their currencies and the currencies of other members stayed within prescribed margins around par values. Thus an intervention currency was necessary, and margins came to be defined in terms of the intervention currency. As the strongest convertible currency after World War II, the dollar rapidly became the principal intervention currency and the currency in terms of which most margins were stated. The United States, for its part, fulfilled its exchange rate obligations by opting to buy and sell gold freely—that is, without limit—for the settlement of international payments. In these circumstances, the United States assumed a basically passive role in the exchange market: exchange rates of other currencies vis-à-vis the dollar were determined not by U.S. actions but by actions of the central banks of other countries.

Because of this operation of the par value system, there was a belief on the part of some officials that there was no method by which the United States could actually devalue the dollar. In fact, some knowledgeable monetary officials believed that the par value system had to function in this way under the Fund's

Articles of Agreement and that in effect the Articles of Agreement, which contained a definition of the dollar in terms of gold, even precluded a change in the dollar price of gold.

But, more importantly, there were a number of basic economic reasons why devaluation of the dollar by raising the price of gold was being avoided. For one thing, it was considered possible that other countries would also raise the price of gold in terms of their currencies, thereby undoing the desired effect of realigning the dollar vis-à-vis these other currencies. Moreover, the dollar was the major reserve currency of the world. For a number of reasons, many countries had accumulated large holdings of dollars since World War II. To avoid jeopardizing the stability of the dollar, several countries, especially after 1965, had refrained from exercising their right to convert these holdings into gold. Devaluation of the dollar would have an adverse effect on the value of countries' reserves of dollars.

There was another consideration governing the attitudes of the U.S. monetary authorities toward devaluation of the dollar—that an appropriate realignment of the dollar vis-à-vis the currencies of other industrial nations might well have to be considerably larger than those countries were prepared to accept. In their view, it was imperative that the U.S. deficit be converted into a surplus, at least for a few years. Should the dollar be devalued in 1971 and the size of the devaluation prove to be too small, perhaps because other countries would not initially be prepared to agree to a large enough change, it would be extremely awkward, and would shake confidence in the dollar, to devalue it in terms of gold again later.

The adverse reactions in the United States to the possibility of a formal devaluation of the dollar were strengthened by still another factor. There were many U.S. officials and economists who firmly opposed any action that might enhance the role of gold in the international monetary system; hence there was concern, and even anxiety, that an increase in the official dollar price of gold incidental to a devaluation of the dollar in terms of other currencies might have such an effect. The risk of enhancing the status of gold in the monetary system was believed to be especially great if there should have to be a second devaluation of the dollar.

Over time, the conviction had grown in U.S. Government circles that the only way in which the United States could take action on the rates of exchange between the dollar and other currencies was to break the link between the dollar and gold. For instance, the report of the President's Commission on International Trade and Investment Policy, submitted to the President in July 1971, pointed out that the problems of the deteriorating trade balance were compounded by the dollar's pivotal role in the monetary system as an intervention currency and a reserve currency; therefore, the United States did not have ready recourse to the remedy of a change in its exchange rate. The report of the Subcommittee on International Exchange and Payments of the Joint Economic

Committee of Congress likewise emphasized that the legal link between the dollar and the price of gold and the role of the dollar as the chief intervention currency effectively limited any U.S. initiative to alter dollar exchange rates, and, in effect, suggested the need to break that link.[2]

The Staff's Calculations

For some years the staff of the Research Department of the Fund had been developing a multilateral exchange rate model (MERM) designed to analyze the effects of changes in exchange rates on foreign trade flows.[3] Early in 1971 the staff began to use the model to examine the implications for international payments imbalance of realignments in the exchange rates of the major currencies and made calculations for changes in the exchange rates of the 11 currencies of the countries of the Group of Ten and Switzerland that would correct existing imbalances on current account.

At the afternoon session of the Executive Board on August 16, the Economic Counsellor presented the staff's thinking on the relative exchange rates of the currencies of the major industrial nations. He divided the subject into two parts: (1) the determination of the relative exchange rates of the major currencies, a determination that affected the competitiveness of countries in international transactions and the relative value of reserves held in various currencies; and (2) the link between the pattern of exchange rates and gold, a link determined by specifying the price of gold in terms of one of the currencies involved, presumably the dollar. This second part affected the value of gold, SDRs, and reserve positions in the Fund that were in the form of currencies. The Economic Counsellor said that, although he was addressing himself only to the question of relative exchange rates, he considered it more likely that agreement could be reached if the questions concerning relative exchange rates and gold were settled at the same time.

The Economic Counsellor stressed that, in his view, a "satisfactory new pattern of exchange rates could not be found by letting all currencies float for a certain period." A regime of many floating currencies could not "even in theory be expected to lead to a viable system of rates." Floating rates were, inter alia, too much affected by the extent to which countries imposed controls on capital movements and intervened in exchange markets, and by anticipations of official actions. It was necessary, therefore, to derive a new pattern of exchange

---

[2] The reports of the President's Commission and the Congressional subcommittee were cited in Chap. 25 above, footnotes 3 and 5.

[3] See the following articles in *Staff Papers*: Paul S. Armington, "A Theory of Demand for Products Distinguished by Place of Production," Vol. 16 (1969), pp. 159–78, "The Geographic Pattern of Trade and the Effects of Price Changes," Vol. 16 (1969), pp. 179–201, and "Adjustment of Trade Balances: Some Experiments with a Model of Trade Among Many Countries," Vol. 17 (1970), pp. 488–526; and, for a later and fuller description of this model, Jacques R. Artus and Rudolf R. Rhomberg, "A Multilateral Exchange Rate Model," Vol. 20 (1973), pp. 591–611.

rates on the basis of analysis. Here, he emphasized that to create a sufficiently large current account surplus in the U.S. balance of payments would require an adequate average depreciation of the U.S. dollar against other currencies. The staff's analysis suggested, he said, that a decline in the value of the U.S. dollar in terms of other currencies on the average of approximately 10 per cent would be sufficient for this purpose. It would not be appropriate, however, to adjust the rates of the U.S. dollar in terms of all currencies by the same percentage. For some currencies, the relative appreciation in terms of the dollar should be less than 10 per cent; for others, an appreciation somewhat in excess of 10 per cent would appear appropriate.

Although secret, some of the figures in the staff's calculations appeared on the wire services the following week and were cited in the press as the exchange rate changes that the Fund believed were necessary. Because of the sharply differing points of view on the part of monetary officials concerning the exchange rate action they believed desirable, the revelation of these figures caused considerable repercussions in the press and reportedly affected trading on exchange markets. The Managing Director publicly denied that these calculations had any authenticity, explaining that they were only working calculations of the staff. A subsequent investigation by Mr. Schweitzer did not reveal the source of the leak.

MR. SCHWEITZER'S CONCERNS AND RESPONSES

At a meeting in Brussels on August 19, 1971, the Finance Ministers of the EEC decided that a reform of the international monetary system, including a restructuring of par values, was necessary, and that to this end they would take "a common initiative" within the appropriate international institutions, naming the Fund in particular. Meanwhile, to enable exchange markets to reopen on Monday, August 23, they agreed that the rates between the U.S. dollar and five of the six currencies of the EEC countries—the Belgian franc, the deutsche mark, the Italian lira, the Luxembourg franc, and the Netherlands guilder—would be freely determined in exchange markets; there was to be a dual market for the French franc (see the following section). They further agreed that the EEC countries would work out among themselves techniques for market intervention in order to minimize the degree of rate fluctuation among their own currencies. They emphasized that it was important for the operation of EEC agricultural policy that fluctuation among the rates for their own currencies be limited. The common agricultural policy, in turn, was indispensable for the achievement of greater economic and monetary union among the six countries of the EEC.

The Managing Director was apprehensive lest, in the existing circumstances, the international monetary situation deteriorate beyond repair. If exchange markets reopened on August 23 on their own terms, there was not the slightest chance, he thought, that the rates quoted would bear any resemblance to an appropriate pattern of exchange rates. Morever, if the U.S. import surcharge was retained for long, it would distort trade and make the achievement of a satisfactory pattern of rates difficult, if not impossible. There was, he believed, a real danger that countries might resort to restrictions on trade, exchange controls, and multiple exchange rates, such as had prevailed in the late 1940s and early 1950s, and which would be very hard to remove. Yet, as he remarked to the Executive Directors on Thursday, August 19, the U.S. authorities did not appear to be in a hurry to bring the existing difficulties to an end, nor did the EEC countries seem to have agreed on a solution.

The situation presented serious problems not only for the industrial countries but also for the developing and other primary producing members, which were worried about the adverse effects of exchange rate fluctuations, the accompanying uncertainties, and the U.S. import surcharge. Many of them were unsure what exchange rate policies to pursue and were asking for advice from the management and staff of the Fund. Mr. Schweitzer was also concerned that the vast majority of countries would not have a chance to participate in any solution.

Keeping in close communication with the Executive Directors and with the top officials of the EEC, the BIS, and the Group of Ten, the Managing Director in consultation with the senior staff formulated his positions. The staff of the Research Department had already been working not only on a possible new pattern of exchange rates but also on ways in which the operation of the international monetary system might be improved. The staff of the Legal Department had been working on draft amendments to the Articles of Agreement governing changes in exchange rates and margin requirements, as was described at the end of Chapter 24, and on other possible changes in the Articles. The General Counsel proposed a program of work that would encompass the study by the Executive Directors of all alternatives for a reformed international monetary system, including proposals that would involve the broadest kinds of amendments to the Articles of Agreement. The Economic Counsellor presented the calculations discussed above and put forward for consideration by the Executive Directors a paper outlining a new framework for the monetary system. The Area Departments examined the implications for all members of a realignment of the currencies of the major industrial members. The Treasurer's Department and the Legal Department suggested ways to adjust the Fund's holdings of currencies and to continue operations in the General Account and the Special Drawing Account.

Several Initiatives

Thus, when Mr. Schweitzer addressed the Executive Board on August 19, he stressed that the whole of the international monetary system was at stake and that he thought the Fund could, and should, take the initiative. The Fund was in a unique position, he said, to propose a comprehensive and impartial solution to both the procedural and the substantive problems that had been raised.

As for procedure, Mr. Schweitzer regarded agreement by the major industrial countries as the first essential step. He was convinced that the Finance Ministers and Central Bank Governors of the countries of the Group of Ten should not wait until their scheduled meeting in Washington on September 26—the Sunday before the opening of the Annual Meeting of the Fund's Board of Governors. That would be too late, he thought, for the Fund, acting through the Governors of all member countries, to take suitable action. Therefore, he would press for an earlier meeting of the Group of Ten. The question of when the Group of Ten would meet was not one which the Fund could decide, but Mr. Schweitzer told the Executive Directors that he had informed the Minister of Finance of Canada, Mr. Benson, then chairman of the Group of Ten, of his strong belief in the need for Mr. Benson to call such a meeting.

As the best possible way to coordinate the interests of the countries of the Group of Ten with those of the rest of the Fund's members, the Fund, Mr. Schweitzer said, was prepared to invite the Group of Ten to meet at the Fund's headquarters. He assured the Executive Directors that the Fund could present concrete proposals, which would include proposals for new relative exchange rates, the price of gold in terms of currencies, temporary wider margins, a transitional regime for convertibility, and the removal of the U.S. import surcharge.

With the Executive Board's concurrence, the Managing Director sent a message to all Governors of the Fund on August 19. Recent developments, he cabled, gave great cause for concern but at the same time created the opportunity for strengthening the system. Unless prompt action was taken, the prospect was for disorder and discrimination in currency and trade relationships, which would seriously disrupt trade and undermine the system that had served the world well and had been the basis for effective collaboration for a quarter of a century. Piecemeal approaches to change were not likely to yield beneficial results even for a single country, much less for the whole community of countries represented in the Fund, and he considered it vitally important that action be "prompt, collective, and collaborative." This action was the assigned task of the Fund, and the Fund was in a position to make a contribution of great importance to the establishment of a better monetary system. He intended to press for rapid progress toward agreement on appropriate exchange rates and other measures that would restore the monetary system to effective and lasting operation.

In the next few days, many of the Governors, especially those for the developing members, cabled their support of the Managing Director's efforts.

It became evident almost at once, however, that the Group of Ten was not yet ready to proceed. On Friday, August 20, Mr. Benson advised Mr. Schweitzer that there was insufficient support among the Group of Ten for an immediate ministerial meeting; he had therefore requested Mr. Ossola, then chairman of the Deputies of the Group of Ten, to convene a meeting of the Deputies "at the earliest possible date."

Mr. Schweitzer's grave concern about the monetary situation was revealed to the world when, in the following week, he appeared twice on television. In an interview on Monday morning, August 23—as exchange markets were reopened and a variety of exchange rates prevailed, many involving fluctuations in the rates for the U.S. dollar—Mr. Schweitzer was asked for his view about a change in the dollar price of gold as a way to improve the situation. He replied that a whole new pattern of exchange rates was necessary, and that "in my opinion it would be normal for the U.S. to make a contribution." The next day, August 24, he was asked whether a change in the price of gold in terms of the U.S. dollar would be a major contribution to solving the international imbalance problem. He again replied in such a way as to suggest that, in a new pattern of exchange rates, the dollar might have to be redefined in terms of gold.

Mr. Schweitzer's statements on this subject reflected his interest in currency realignment as the first essential step to improving the world monetary situation. In this regard he was especially mindful of the problems that would confront the United States if it decided to devalue. In his opinion, the view that dollar devaluation was not possible deprived the United States, alone among nations, of the use of a vital instrument of balance of payments adjustment, namely, a change in the exchange rate for its currency. Given these circumstances, Mr. Schweitzer acted on his belief that public statements by the Managing Director of the Fund could help to prepare the way for dollar devaluation and for a quick realignment of exchange rates. But there were press reports that the U.S. monetary authorities, believing that the time was not ripe for action, did not welcome public expression of views about dollar devaluation.

VARIETY OF EXCHANGE RATES INTRODUCED

In the week after the U.S. suspension of official convertibility, the Managing Director also asked the Executive Directors to communicate to all member countries a statement in which the Fund called attention to the undertaking of each member under Article IV, Section 4 (*a*), "to collaborate with the Fund to promote exchange stability, to maintain orderly exchange arrangements with other members, and to avoid competitive exchange alterations," and in which each member was requested to advise the Fund promptly and in detail of the exchange measures and practices applied in its territories.

It was evident from the replies that members were resorting to a number of exchange rate expedients. Several members advised the Fund that, notwithstanding their desire to maintain orderly exchange rates, they no longer found it possible to observe margins around their par values. Most of the industrial members in Europe (Austria, Belgium, Denmark, the Federal Republic of Germany, Italy, Luxembourg, the Netherlands, Norway, Sweden, and the United Kingdom) and Japan were letting the exchange rates for their currencies float. The rate for the Canadian dollar also continued to float.

The exchange rates of some European currencies and of the Japanese yen were under strong upward pressure, but the monetary authorities of these countries were intervening in the markets so as to limit upward movements.

The currencies of Australia, Burma, Iraq, Ireland, Malaysia, New Zealand, Singapore, and a number of other sterling area members were pegged to sterling, and so they too were, in effect, floating against the dollar. Several developing countries—including the Khmer Republic, the Libyan Arab Republic, Portugal, Somalia, and Viet-Nam—likewise introduced floating rates for their currencies. The rates for the currencies of Afghanistan, Brazil, Colombia, Korea, Lebanon, the Philippines, and the Yemen Arab Republic continued to fluctuate, as they had prior to August 15.

A few members introduced dual exchange markets. For example, France did so with effect from August 23, 1971. The official market was reserved for transactions for trade and trade-related items and for government exchange dealings; these transactions were to take place at rates based on the par value. A separate market—the financial market—was established for all other authorized transactions, primarily capital transactions; these were to take place at freely fluctuating rates. Capital flows into France from the end of 1970 to the end of July 1971 had totaled close to $1.5 billion. To discourage such inflows, the French authorities had already taken a variety of domestic measures, including the introduction of exchange controls over some capital transactions and the elimination of interest on short-term deposits of nonresidents. Fourteen members of the Fund that were members of the French franc area and maintained operations accounts with the French Treasury instituted dual exchange markets comparable to those in France. Other countries, too—such as Argentina, Ecuador, and the Netherlands—set up secondary markets for capital transactions in which exchange rates were to be determined by supply and demand.

Many members of the Fund, however, continued to apply the same fixed U.S. dollar rates for their currencies, although some of them widened the margins around their par values within which the dollar rates could fluctuate. Members that kept the same fixed dollar rates included most of those in Latin America, African members other than those in the French franc area, and several members in Asia, Europe, and the Middle East. Several members, including Ceylon, Ghana, India, Kenya, Nigeria, Pakistan, South Africa, the Sudan, Tanzania, and Uganda, changed the peg for their currencies from sterling to the dollar.

The French dual market was a multiple currency practice and thus, unlike a single fluctuating exchange rate, produced exchange rates in a form that the Fund could approve under the Articles. The Executive Board approved this practice until the end of 1971. Toward the end of the year, they extended that approval until the next Article VIII consultation with France.

Apart from approval of the dual market in France, the Fund was called upon to take little formal action between August 15 and mid-December 1971 with respect to individual exchange rates. Only one par value was changed: with the Fund's concurrence, Israel devalued the pound on August 21 from 3.50 Israel pounds per U.S. dollar to 4.20 Israel pounds per U.S. dollar, a depreciation of 16.7 per cent. On September 1 the Libyan pound was replaced by the Libyan dinar, but no appreciation or depreciation was involved.

GROUP OF TEN MEETINGS

Mr. Schweitzer was informed by Mr. Benson on August 25 that a meeting of the Finance Ministers and Central Bank Governors of the Group of Ten was being called for September 15 and 16 in London, and he was invited to attend. The ministerial meeting was preceded by a meeting of the Deputies of the Group of Ten in the Fund's Paris Office on September 3 and 4. The Economic Counsellor attended the Deputies' meeting and reported to the Executive Directors that the Deputies had considered the views of the Under Secretary for Monetary Affairs in the U.S. Treasury, Mr. Volcker, on the outlook for the U.S. balance of payments and the aims of the U.S. authorities. These aims included the restoration of a basic position of long-term equilibrium, together with a modest surplus at least for a few years in order to restore confidence in the U.S. dollar. Much attention was directed to the magnitude of the improvement needed in the U.S. balance of payments. Any lessening of the U.S. deficit necessarily had counterparts in reduced surpluses by other countries, and the implication of surpluses by the United States was deficits by other countries. Some countries now in surplus saw in any reduction of these surpluses the specter of recession. Obviously, the greater the improvement expected in the U.S. position and the more rapidly it was to be achieved, the stronger the actions that were required. Hence, important negotiations hinged on estimates of the magnitude of the turnaround to be attained in the U.S. payments position and when it was to be achieved.

Mr. Dale spelled out the details to the Executive Directors. The U.S. authorities believed that the U.S. overall balance had to be improved by at least $13 billion. The projections of the U.S. Government for 1972, in the absence of corrective measures, was for a trade deficit of about $5 billion and a deficit on basic balance, that is, a current account and long-term capital deficit, of about $10 billion. The authorities considered a $13 billion turnaround to be a minimum. It did not allow for the momentum which the pace of deterioration had gained nor for the lag which would occur before the effects of new measures, including exchange rate changes, took place. Furthermore, such a figure provided for only modest capital outflow to developing countries and for virtually no net long-term capital flow to the rest of the developed world. In particular, it assumed that Canada would not resort to the New York bond market for any great amounts and that European and other developed countries would not make much use of the New York securities market on a net basis.

On September 13, 1971, just before the ministerial meeting of the Group of Ten, the Finance Ministers of the EEC countries reached agreement on the common position that they would take at the meeting. That position included, inter alia, the need for realignment against gold of the currencies of all industrial countries, including the dollar, and the removal of the U.S. import surcharge. The differences between the positions of the industrial countries meant that when the Finance Ministers and Central Bank Governors of the Group of Ten met on September 15 and 16 very little could be agreed except generalities. The Ministers and Governors agreed only that a very substantial adjustment was required to redress the position of the United States, with corresponding adjustments in the positions of other countries; that a large part of this adjustment would have to come about by selective currency realignment; and that "fair world trading arrangements and [military] burden-sharing" would have to be considered. Differences in view continued on the key issues: exchange rates, the approximate magnitude of the necessary improvement to be achieved in the U.S. position, and the timing of the removal of the U.S. import surcharge. It was evident that multilateral negotiations of a major and complex nature lay ahead.

In the course of the London meeting, Mr. Schweitzer put forward a list of the substantive problems requiring discussion, including fundamental monetary reform, and expressed his concern about the continuation of the disarray in exchange rates. He stressed to the Ministers and Governors, as he had to the Executive Directors, his view that the pattern of exchange rates which was emerging did not provide a satisfactory basis for a more permanent pattern. He pointed out that many countries had already made contributions toward the needed currency realignment, noting that the currencies of Canada, the Federal Republic of Germany, and the Netherlands had floated upward vis-à-vis the dollar even before August 15 and that the currencies of Belgium, Italy, Japan, Sweden, and the United Kingdom had been floating upward since that date. So far, there had been no contribution from the United States, and he considered it unlikely that a solution could be found to the realignment problem if one major country refused to accept its share of adjustment. After an adequate move by the United States, the remainder of the realignment would have to be brought about by changes in the rates of the other currencies.

The Finance Ministers and Central Bank Governors of the Group of Ten met again, less than two weeks later, in Washington, on September 26, 1971, the day before the opening of the Annual Meeting, but again no agreement was reached. What talks about trade might take place, whether the United States would remove the surcharge before new parities were negotiated, and what new parities would be agreed were issues that were still being hotly debated. European officials were pressing hard for new parities. The monetary authorities of France, in particular, were insisting on a change in the dollar price of gold. That the United States had a different view was evident in the remarks of Mr. Connally (United States) at a press conference after the Group of Ten meeting on September 26. In accordance with the established procedures of that Group for rotating the chairmanship, Mr. Connally had just succeeded Mr. Benson as chairman for the coming year. He characterized "the gold question" as primarily "a political problem, not an economic one," and rather than a "premature decision regarding parities," he proposed a "general clean float" of major exchange rates (*clean* referring to the absence of official intervention in exchange markets).

1971 ANNUAL MEETING

The Governors assembled in Washington for their Twenty-Sixth Annual Meeting, held from September 27 to October 1, 1971, amid talk of a "collision course" and of the possibility of a "trade war."

Mr. Schweitzer, in his opening address, repeated his views about the urgent need for a collaborative international approach to the situation and the need for currency realignment, including a change in the rate for the dollar. Real dangers, he stressed again, were inherent in any prolongation of the present impasse, with the possibility of serious disarray in international monetary and trade affairs and an abandonment of the rules of law providing for just and orderly international economic relations. While many had reservations about the precise content of the existing rules, there was universal acceptance of the need for agreed rules for the conduct of international economic intercourse. The Fund itself was an expression of that need. Mr. Schweitzer went on to note that some multiple currency practices had been adopted, but exchange restrictions had so far been avoided. He believed, however, that the longer the necessary international action was delayed, the greater was the prospect of serious disorder and discrimination in currency and trade relationships.

He called upon all countries to cooperate with the United States in improving its balance of payments position, and stated his conviction that the current situation afforded a unique opportunity to strengthen the international monetary system. Some issues might be handled more urgently than others, and of first priority was the "establishment for the major currencies of an appropriate new structure of parities or official exchange rates, together with the abolition of the temporary import surcharge imposed by the United States."

Regarding currency realignment, he thought that it would be desirable "if all the major countries involved were to make a contribution to the realignment of currencies, not only for reasons of equity, but also for achievement of an appropriate relationship of currencies to gold and, what is perhaps more important, to SDRs and reserve positions in the Fund." Mr. Schweitzer was concerned, among other things, that the SDR should not depreciate with the dollar, that is, that its value in terms of gold should be maintained.[4]

Conflicting Views Persist

The speeches of the Governors revealed little if any change in the divergent positions of the EEC countries on the one hand and the United States on the other hand. The authorities of the EEC countries believed, as Mr. Ferrari-Aggradi (Italy) said, that it was politically important for the success of the negotiations that all countries take part in any currency realignment. Mr. Giscard d'Estaing (France), Mr. Nelissen (Netherlands), and Baron Snoy et d'Oppuers (Belgium) joined Mr. Ferrari-Aggradi in calling for a change in the par value of the U.S. dollar.[5] Many pressed for the removal of the U.S. surcharge as a *prelude* to negotiations.

Mr. Connally (United States) explained that the United States fully appreciated the concerns expressed by other countries. The officials of some countries, he realized, considered the turnaround in the U.S. payments position sought by the U.S. officials to be too large and too rapid. Some thought that a quick, albeit partial, solution ought to be accepted, lest restrictions and even retaliation begin and economic recession set in. Some thought that the quick and partial solution must entail a change in the official dollar price of gold. Some wanted the surcharge taken off before exchange rates were readjusted. He emphasized too that the U.S. authorities fully understood that the surcharge, while applied in a nondiscriminatory way, affected products and countries unevenly, and they were conscious of the political sensitivities of decisions on exchange rates.

Mr. Connally elaborated on the position of the U.S. authorities regarding the immediate future. Exchange markets should operate freely for a transitional period as a way to determine the size and distribution of the needed exchange rate realignment. In order that exchange rates should reflect market realities, other governments should, in the coming weeks, dismantle specific barriers to trade and not influence floating exchange rates by market intervention or by

---

[4] Opening Address by the Managing Director, *Summary Proceedings, 1971*, pp. 8–15. The quotations are on pp. 12 and 13–14, respectively.

[5] Statements by the Governor of the Fund for Italy and the Governors of the World Bank for France, the Netherlands, and Belgium, *Summary Proceedings 1971*, pp. 37, 43, 156, and 152.

exchange controls. Then, the United States would be prepared to remove the surcharge.[6]

Governors' Resolution

Early in September Mr. Lieftinck had suggested to the Executive Board that it present to the Board of Governors a resolution, or a set of resolutions, for consideration and adoption during the Annual Meeting. He thought that a Governors' resolution could aim at giving "a proper role" to the Fund and additional authority to the Executive Directors. The Board of Governors could, for example, urge the governments of members with a fundamental disequilibrium to realign the exchange rates of their currencies. The Governors could strengthen the position of the Executive Board by explicitly asking it to take whatever measures might be necessary to continue the Fund's operations under the prevailing circumstances, to submit proposals for greater flexibility of exchange rates, and to study monetary reform for the longer run. A few Executive Directors had responded positively to Mr. Lieftinck's suggestion. Several of them, however, believing that there was inadequate time in which to agree on a draft resolution or that the meetings of the Group of Ten that were to take place before the Annual Meeting would obviate the need for a Governors' resolution, had not been favorably disposed to the idea. There had also been a reluctance on the part of the U.S. authorities to have the Fund take any such action in connection with monetary reform as would be stated in a Governors' resolution.

After the ministerial meeting of the Group of Ten failed to produce results, Mr. Schweitzer, on the weekend before the Annual Meeting, circulated to the Executive Directors a proposed draft resolution for presentation to the Board of Governors. The Executive Directors, in unusual sessions of the Executive Board during the week of the Annual Meeting, considered the draft resolution on Monday and Tuesday afternoons, September 27 and 28. Most of them supported the Managing Director's attempt at a Governors' resolution. But precise language proved elusive and controversial. Mr. Dale submitted a draft which avoided any implication that the difficult monetary situation had been brought about by actions of the U.S. monetary authorities and in which there was no reference to the possibility that currency convertibility might be restored once exchange rate realignment was effected. The Executive Board agreed on a revised draft resolution, which was adopted by the Board of Governors on Friday, October 1, 1971, the last day of the Annual Meeting.[7]

The resolution pointed out the dangers of instability and disorder in currency and trade relationships in the situation then existing, and emphasized

---

[6] Statement by the Governor of the Fund and the World Bank for the United States, *Summary Proceedings, 1971*, pp. 218–19.

[7] Resolution No. 26-9; Vol. II below, pp. 331–32.

the need to avoid these dangers and to assure continuance of the progress that had been made in national and international well-being in the previous quarter of a century. It further stressed that, in the interest of all of the Fund's members, the orderly conduct of the operations of the Fund should be resumed as promptly as possible. To achieve these objectives, the resolution called upon members to collaborate with the Fund and with each other to bring about a reversal of the tendency to maintain and extend restrictive trade and exchange practices, and to establish, as promptly as possible, a satisfactory structure of exchange rates, maintained within appropriate margins, for their currencies, together with the reduction of restrictive trade and exchange practices.

The resolution was also designed to ensure the Fund's role in the forthcoming discussions on monetary reform. The Executive Directors were requested to make reports to the Governors without delay on the measures necessary or desirable for the improvement or reform of the international monetary system. For this purpose, the Executive Directors were specifically requested to study all aspects of the international monetary system, including the role of reserve currencies, gold, and SDRs, convertibility, the provisions of the Articles with respect to exchange rates, and the problems caused by destabilizing capital movements. They were further requested, when reporting, to include if possible the texts of any amendments to the Articles of Agreement which they considered necessary to give effect to their recommendations.

AFTER THE 1971 ANNUAL MEETING

During the months of October and November there were discussions in many forums. Officials of the U.S. Treasury went to Canada, to Europe, and to Japan to discuss specific actions on trade and defense. Mr. Schweitzer held informal conversations with U.S. monetary officials and traveled to Europe to talk with monetary officials there. The Executive Directors resumed their discussions of the magnitude of the change needed in the U.S. balance of payments and, in line with the Governors' resolution, undertook to examine measures to continue the Fund's operations and to improve the monetary system.

With regard to the first of these topics—the change necessary in the U.S. balance of payments—the calculations of the staff of the Research Department had put the size of the correction in the current account of the U.S. balance of payments and of corresponding changes in the payments positions of other countries that ought to be effected by exchange rate adjustments at $8 billion. This figure was considerably lower than the $13 billion estimated by the U.S. monetary authorities, and, although there were differences in the bases of the two calculations, they were concerned that the estimate of $8 billion, together with the estimated depreciation of the dollar against other currencies of 10 per cent, would hamper them in negotiating measures that they considered essential for a sufficiently large improvement in the U.S. balance of payments. When the Executive Directors considered the debated figures in detail, including differences in the technical methodology underlying the estimates, Mr. Dale reiterated the U.S. view that the figure of $13 billion was an essential and conservative one and not "a negotiating one." In addition, Mr. Viénot had difficulty in accepting the staff's target for France's current account.

The size of the improvement needed in the U.S. balance of payments was also discussed by the Deputies of the Group of Ten at a meeting in Paris on October 19 and 20, immediately after Working Party 3 of the OECD had considered this question. Reporting on the latter meeting, the Economic Counsellor said that the results of the calculations of the staff of the OECD were not far from those of the Fund staff in regard to the main components, such as the size of the change in the U.S. current account (the OECD staff had estimated a change of the magnitude of $8 billion or $8.5 billion), and the matching swings for other areas, such as the EEC countries and Japan. The positions presented by individual countries, however, were far from consistent. For example, while the United States indicated that it needed a swing of $13 billion, the net amount of the swings offered by all other countries amounted to only $2–3 billion.

Discussions on Resuming the Fund's Operations

As mentioned above, in October and November the Executive Directors also discussed measures to resolve the practical difficulties that the Fund faced in carrying out its financial operations and transactions. Since August 15 operations had been based on the provisional valuation of the Fund's assets in U.S. dollars at the old par value for the dollar and a turnstile technique under which repurchases were accommodated to the extent that drawings were made on the Fund. The need for a better method became more urgent as hopes for a quick realignment of exchange rates began to fade. The questions that needed answers fell into two categories: (1) the exchange rates at which the Fund would hold, and conduct transactions in, currencies, gold, and SDRs; and (2) the currencies to be used in drawings and repurchases and similar operations and arrangements for conversion.

When the Executive Directors considered these questions at the end of October, it quickly became apparent that much more was involved than the technical questions affecting the Fund's operations. Any decision that the Fund might take carried with it implications about the price of gold (and hence the exchange rate of the dollar), implications as to whether the price of gold was to be defined in terms of dollars or in some other way, and implications about the role of gold in future monetary arrangements. In effect, the Fund could be breaking new ground with respect to the price of gold, and, as Mr. Dale reiterated, the U.S. authorities had firm views about any change in the price of gold. Mr. Schleiminger argued that it would be inadvisable to make any radical changes in the Fund's procedures, and suggested that the interim arrangements that the staff had been using should be continued until currency realignment could be achieved.[8] He was supported by Messrs. Mitchell, Palamenghi-Crispi, Suzuki, and Viénot, and by several of the Executive Directors or Alternate Executive Directors for developing members, notably Mr. Arriazu, Mr. Guillermo González (Costa Rica), Mr. Kafka, and Mr. Prasad. Mr. Arriazu explained that access to the Fund's resources was frequently crucial for developing countries and that any basic changes in procedures should first be thoroughly examined and discussed. Therefore, further discussion about normalizing the Fund's operations was temporarily suspended.

Discussions on Prospects for Dollar Convertibility

When the Executive Directors turned to measures for improving or reforming the monetary system, their discussions indicated that some interim arrangements might have to prevail in the period after exchange rates had been realigned but before proposals for fundamental reforms, such as reliance on an international reserve asset and the elimination of reserve currencies, could be considered. Since officials of many members were particularly interested in the early resumption of convertibility of the U.S. dollar, much attention centered on the future position of the dollar in the monetary system and on what arrangements for convertibility might apply in any interim period. At the meeting of the Deputies of the Group of Ten on October 19 and 20, the U.S. representative had made it clear that, given the unfavorable indications with respect to the adjustment in payments balances that other countries were willing to make, it would be unwise for the United States to undertake convertibility commitments which it might not be able to keep. He had suggested, therefore, that the question of convertibility was one for long-term reform.

In October and November the Executive Directors considered the subject of dollar convertibility. For their discussion the Economic Counsellor set forth two phases of limited convertibility that might be introduced in the period after currency realignment had occurred and before some ultimate phase when long-term reform had been achieved. Phase A would be a regime of very limited convertibility of the dollar, which would start immediately upon realignment but before conditions had been met, or arrangements made, for the type of convertibility that would prevail in Phase B. The view of the General Counsel, who was concerned that the violation by the United States of the convertibility provisions of the Articles of Agreement might go on for an unduly long time, was that some such arrangement as the enlargement of the General Arrangements to Borrow might be used to permit the United States to convert dollars during Phase A. However, the prospects for any degree of convertibility of the

---

[8] These interim arrangements were described in Chap. 17 above, p. 328.

dollar depended entirely on developments in the U.S. balance of payments and reserves, and when the Executive Directors discussed these phases of limited convertibility, Mr. Dale emphasized the reluctance of the U.S. authorities to undertake obligations that might prove hopelessly unrealistic. They believed that a return to a strong U.S. balance of payments position depended on actions to be taken by other countries, and international discussions concerning those actions and even about the size of the adjustment problem had not given them "confidence to leap into assuming obligations to pay out reserves." Mr. Viénot, too, had a number of doubts about the desirability of the system envisaged by the staff with respect to the future convertibility of the dollar. That system was one, he said, in which the U.S. dollar continued to have "a privileged position," since other countries would have to intervene in their own markets to support the dollar while the United States would not have a legal obligation to maintain a stable exchange rate.

As the Executive Directors' discussion continued, it became evident (1) that the U.S. authorities were determined not to undertake commitments to convert dollars or to defend a given exchange rate until the U.S. balance of payments position was substantially improved, or, at a minimum, that mutual measures for an adequate improvement had been agreed; (2) that discussions concerning future convertibility really involved basic decisions as to what part the U.S. dollar would play as a reserve currency and as an intervention currency in a reformed monetary system; and (3) that, because of these two factors, inconvertibility of the dollar into gold or SDRs would continue to exist even after exchange rates were realigned, and might exist for a long period.

GROUP OF TEN MEETS AGAIN

By the middle of November, prospects for agreement on currency realignment among the countries of the Group of Ten were brighter. The U.S. authorities had worked out arrangements for trade with Canada and with Japan that they considered satisfactory. Moreover, as Mr. Schweitzer had emphasized to the U.S. authorities, other countries of the Group of Ten (that is, all except the United States) favored a change in the dollar price of gold at least partly to enhance SDRs as an international reserve asset. In addition, the countries that were not in the Group of Ten were becoming increasingly restless about the prolongation of the existing situation, and the UN General Assembly had passed a resolution calling for some action to ease the international monetary situation.

It now appeared that the U.S. authorities were more inclined toward participation in a currency realignment that included a devaluation of the dollar, even though they regarded the realignment likely to be attained as inadequate.

In return, European authorities would take some measures regarding trade, and the nine other countries composing the Group of Ten would make a credible commitment on sharing the military burden. There was also what amounted to another condition to the U.S. willingness to devalue the dollar: convertibility of the dollar would not be re-established at this time but would await improvement of the world payments situation following the new measures agreed upon and discussions regarding reform of the monetary system.

On November 30 and December 1, the Group of Ten met again at the ministerial level under the chairmanship of Mr. Connally, this time in Rome. Unusually frank negotiations were carried on in executive session: specific percentages and figures for the exchange rates of the currencies of the ten countries involved were discussed. The negotiations also focused for a long time on trade matters, specifically the agricultural problems of the EEC, and the EEC countries twice went into caucus to discuss these problems among themselves. That progress had been made was apparent from the remarks of Mr. Connally to the press after the meeting: "We did not reach a decision; we did not solve the problem, but we most certainly did discuss the various elements of that problem."

Another ministerial meeting of the Group of Ten was planned for December 17 and 18, in Washington.

On December 14, President Nixon flew to the Azores for a meeting with President Pompidou of France. The two heads of state agreed on devaluation of the dollar and, in the words of the communiqué issued after their meeting, on the "contribution that vigorous implementation by the United States of measures to restore domestic wage-price stability and productivity would make toward international equilibrium and the defense of the new dollar exchange rate." This renewed public recognition by the United States of the need to restore internal cost and price stability helped further to pave the way for agreement on a realignment of exchange rates.

DEVELOPING COUNTRIES PRESENT THEIR VIEWS

The nine Executive Directors for the developing members of the Fund—Messrs. Nazih Deif (Egypt), Peh Yuan Hsu (Republic of China), Kafka, Kharmawan, Massad, Omwony, Prasad, Luis Ugueto (Venezuela), and Yaméogo—had, as we have seen in earlier chapters, been meeting regularly as a "G-9 Caucus," or Group of Nine. During the latter part of 1971 this group repeatedly pressed Mr. Schweitzer to set up a procedure by which officials of the developing countries, in one way or another, could formally express their views—not only on the longer-run issues of reform but also on the immediate question of currency realignment. Currency realignment might necessitate changes in their par values, and most certainly would affect their exchange rates. The issue of convertibility of the dollar, moreover, was of great importance to the developing members because it was linked with the normalization of the Fund's operations.

When it appeared, late in November, that the countries of the Group of Ten were coming close to agreement on currency realignment, the Executive Directors for the developing members wrote formally to Mr. Schweitzer insisting that some broader meeting than that of the Executive Board be called. Therefore, a fifth joint meeting of Executive Directors and the Deputies of the Group of Ten (the previous four were held between November 1966 and June 1967 and were described in Part One above) was held in Washington on December 16, 1971, the day before the Group of Ten was to meet at the ministerial level. The meeting was attended also by representatives of the Swiss National Bank, the OECD, the BIS, and the EEC.

At this fifth joint meeting, the Executive Directors for developing members set forth those members' aspirations regarding any agreement the industrial nations might work out among themselves. They urged that the size and structure of any exchange rate realignment be such as to permit an expansion of world trade and avoid adverse effects on the international flow of capital. They urged further that all restrictions on international transactions that had been imposed because of the latest crisis be removed without delay. With regard to a change in the dollar price of gold, they drew attention to the adverse effects which this could have on the reserve situation of the countries in question, particularly if it led to a reduction in the amount of SDRs allocated. These effects might be expected because of the relatively low share of developing countries in world gold reserves and their relatively higher share in the allocation of SDRs, and because a substantial proportion of the indebtedness of these countries, such as their indebtedness to the Fund, was expressed in terms of gold. They also urged that the Fund be the forum of discussion for reform of the international system.

SMITHSONIAN AGREEMENT

Four months of negotiations came to fruition on December 17 and 18, 1971, when the Finance Ministers and Central Bank Governors of the Group of Ten, under the chairmanship of Mr. Connally, met in Washington in the Commons Room of the Smithsonian Institution's Old Red Castle. Mr. Schweitzer took part in the meeting and, among other things, reported the views of the Executive Directors for the countries that were not in the Group of Ten.

Almost the whole of the meeting took place in executive session, as the Ministers and Governors reached agreement on a pattern of exchange rate relationships among their currencies.

The United States agreed "to propose to Congress a suitable means for devaluing the dollar in terms of gold to $38.00 an ounce as soon as the related set of short-term measures [relating to trade arrangements] is available for Congressional scrutiny. Upon passage of required legislative authority in this framework, the United States will propose the corresponding new par value of the dollar to the International Monetary Fund." [9] In other words, the U.S. Administration committed itself to seek—following negotiations on certain short-term issues relating to trade arrangements—legislative approval of a 7.89 per cent devaluation of the dollar against gold. It was understood that formal action establishing a new par value for the U.S. dollar would take some time.

Despite the delay in establishing a new par value for the U.S. dollar, the changes agreed in the rates for other currencies were to become effective in the markets at once. In return, the United States agreed to suppress the U.S. import surcharge immediately. Each Minister was to announce the exchange rate for the currency of his country in the way he saw fit. The Fund would inform its member countries of all the new exchange rates.

The United Kingdom and France agreed not to change their par values in terms of gold, which would thus represent a revaluation against the new par value for the dollar of 8.57 per cent. The effective parity relationship between sterling and the dollar was to become £1 = US$2.60571. The effective parity relationship between the French franc and the dollar in France's official exchange market, previously F 5.55419 = US$1, was to become F 5.11570 = US$1.

The other countries, with the exception of Canada, agreed to establish central rates for their currencies for the time being. A central rate was one that could be communicated to the Fund by any member that did not maintain rates for spot exchange transactions based on a par value, but declared its intention to maintain rates for these transactions within maximum margins from a central rate communicated to the Fund. [10]

The central rate communicated by Japan, ¥ 308.00 = US$1, meant a revaluation of the yen in terms of gold of 7.66 per cent, and therefore a revaluation of the yen in terms of the dollar of 16.88 per cent. The central rate communicated by the Federal Republic of Germany, DM 3.225 = US$1, was a revaluation of the deutsche mark in terms of gold of 4.61 per cent and of the deutsche mark in terms of the dollar of 13.58 per cent. The central rates communicated for the Belgian franc and the Netherlands guilder represented a revaluation in terms of gold of 2.76 per cent and in terms of the dollar of 11.57 per cent. The central rates communicated for the Italian lira and the Swedish krona represented slight devaluations in terms of gold—1.00 per cent;

---

[9] Par. 5 of Communique of Ministers and Governors of the "Group of Ten" issued on December 18, 1971, *International Financial News Survey*, Vol. 23 (1971), p. 418.

[10] For further elaboration, see Chap. 27.

in terms of the dollar, therefore, the lira was revalued by 7.48 per cent and the Swedish krona by 7.49 per cent.

All these new relationships became effective within the week following the Smithsonian agreement. The Canadian dollar continued to float. The agreed exchange rate relationships are summarized in Table 17.

Table 17. Exchange Rate Relationships Resulting from Smithsonian Agreement, December 18, 1971

Member	Percentage Change in Terms of Par Value	Percentage Change in Terms of U.S. Dollar	Exchange Rate Action	Effective Date
Belgium	+2.76 [1]	+11.57	central rate [2]	Dec. 21, 1971
Canada			floating rate continued	
France	—	+8.57	par value maintained	
Germany, Federal Republic of	+4.61	+13.58 [3]	central rate [2]	Dec. 21, 1971
Italy	−1.00	+7.48	central rate [2]	Dec. 20, 1971
Japan	+7.66	+16.88	central rate [2]	Dec. 20, 1971
Netherlands	+2.76	+11.57 [3]	central rate [2]	Dec. 21, 1971
Sweden	−1.00	+7.49	central rate [2]	Dec. 21, 1971
United Kingdom	—	+8.57	par value maintained	
United States	−7.89	—	new par value	May 8, 1972

[1] A plus sign (+) indicates a revaluation and a minus sign (−) a devaluation.

[2] See Chap. 27 for an explanation of a central rate.

[3] Based on the par value that was in effect prior to May 9, 1971.

In addition to the currency realignment, the Finance Ministers and Central Bank Governors of the Group of Ten agreed as part of the Smithsonian accord that, pending agreement on longer-term monetary reforms, provision should be made for 2¼ per cent margins of exchange rate fluctuation above and below the new parity relationships. The Ministers and Governors further agreed that discussions should be started promptly, particularly in what they called the framework of the Fund, to consider reform of the international monetary system. Explicit attention was to be directed to the appropriate means and division of responsibilities for defending stable exchange rates and for insuring convertibility of currencies; to the proper role of gold, of reserve currencies, and of SDRs in the system; to the appropriate volume of liquidity; to a re-examination of the permissible margins of fluctuation around established parities and other means of achieving exchange rate flexibility; and to measures to deal with volatile capital movements.

At the time it was negotiated, some observers regarded the Smithsonian agreement as a landmark in international monetary diplomacy. The response of many monetary experts, however, was cautious: they were concerned that the partial shoring up of the par value system, without any safeguards, did not provide a lasting solution. The particular exchange rates agreed were in fact to last for less than 14 months. Nonetheless, the agreement had significance in that it represented the first time in international monetary history that the exchange rates of the large industrial nations were negotiated around a conference table.

The impasse that had existed since August 15, 1971 had finally been broken.

■   ■   ■   ■   ■   ■

But the international monetary system was not again to be the same. Moreover, discussions of international monetary reform would be shifted from the Group of Ten to the ad hoc Committee of Twenty. And talk would become common about the possibility of changes in the "structure of the Fund."

CHAPTER

27

A Temporary Regime Established
(December 18–31, 1971)

*I*MMEDIATELY AFTER THE SMITHSONIAN AGREEMENT, the Managing Director cabled all the Fund's members (1) to let them know the new exchange rates for the currencies of the ten countries participating in the agreement, (2) to inform them that the United States was expected in the next few months to propose to the Fund a new par value for the dollar, based on a price for gold of $38 per troy ounce of fine gold, and (3) to alert them to a forthcoming decision by the Executive Board regarding exchange rates.

CONSIDERATION OF CENTRAL RATES

The last point had reference to action that had been in preparation for some weeks. The Executive Directors had begun in the first part of November 1971 to consider the immediate impact that a new series of exchange rates for the major industrial countries would have on the par value system. It appeared probable that, whatever realignment of rates was eventually worked out, monetary officials would agree, for the time being, on the use of margins somewhat wider than the existing maximum limits of 1 per cent on either side of par. In addition, since the United States could not propose a change in par value until after the Congress had acted, and since some other countries also needed legislation in order to establish new par values, there would be an interval in which several members might wish to communicate to the Fund *central rates* of exchange around which margins would be maintained, rather than new par values.

The Executive Directors had addressed themselves to the two questions of wider margins and central rates as part of a temporary regime that would come into effect after a currency realignment had taken place. They had been considering the possibility that a central rate of exchange could be communicated to the Fund by any member that did not maintain rates for spot exchange transactions based on a par value, but declared its intention to maintain rates for these transactions within maximum margins from a communicated central rate for its currency expressed in terms of the U.S. dollar.

Central rate was not a term used in the Articles of Agreement. Moreover, under the existing Articles, the Fund lacked the authority to substitute wider margins for those specified in Article IV, Section 3. However, the legal basis for a temporary regime of wider margins and central rates, according to the General Counsel, was Article I (iii) and Article IV, Section 4 (a), relating to the basic purposes of the Fund and to members' obligations to collaborate with the Fund in order to promote exchange stability, to maintain orderly exchange arrangements, and to avoid competitive exchange alterations. According to the General Counsel, in situations in which members did not observe Sections 3 and 4 (b) of Article IV, it was Section 4 (a) of Article IV that was the main provision under which the Fund and members could collaborate in order to do their utmost to preserve the objectives of the Articles. Collaboration under Section 4 (a) would minimize the harm that might flow from the breach of obligation, but it would not mend the breach.

When the Executive Directors first discussed the possibility of such a regime, in mid-November 1971, some members of the Board had difficulty with the idea of central rates rather than par values. Mr. de Vries, for example, indicated that the Netherlands authorities had difficulties with the suggestion that after realignment had taken place central rates rather than par values would be established: central rates might be too flexible. Mr. Viénot argued that dollar convertibility ought to be re-established and objected to central rates on the grounds that they would pave the way for a general floating of exchange rates. He insisted also that margins should not exceed 2½ per cent. Mr. Suzuki, too, stated that the Japanese authorities favored an early return to a system of par values. The central rate regime might be a prelude to a more permanent departure from the par value system. Much discussion turned on what rules would apply for a member's intervention in the exchange markets within its territories.

Further revisions by the staff and discussion in the Board clarified the character of a regime that could be introduced as a temporary one and led to an understanding of the conditions and safeguards that would apply. Central rates were to be rates regulated by the Fund in order to ensure that the purposes of the Fund were protected to the maximum extent possible in conditions of nonobservance of other exchange rate provisions of the Articles. The gold equivalent of a central rate was to be regarded as if it were a par value for certain purposes without, however, having the legal validity of a par value.

DECISION ADOPTED

By December 18, 1971, the date of the Smithsonian agreement, the Executive Directors were ready to go ahead with a decision. They met that Saturday evening and took a decision entitled "Central Rates and Wider Margins—A Temporary Regime." [1] The decision was intended to enable members to comply with the Fund's primary objectives "to the maximum extent possible during the temporary period preceding the resumption of effective par values with appropriate margins in accordance with the Articles." Practices that members could follow that would be consistent with the obligation of Article IV, Section 4 (*a*), as well as with Resolution No. 26-9 adopted by the Board of Governors at the 1971 Annual Meeting, were specified in some detail. [2]

Under the decision, a member was deemed to be acting in accordance with Article IV, Section 4 (*a*), and Resolution No. 26-9 if it took appropriate measures "to permit spot exchange transactions between its currency and the currencies of other members taking place within its territories only at rates within 2¼ per cent from the effective parity relationship among currencies as determined by the Fund, provided that these margins may be within 4½ per cent from the said relationship if they result from the maintenance by the member of rates within margins of 2¼ per cent from the said relationship for spot exchange transactions between its currency and its intervention currency." An *intervention currency* was defined as the currency that a member indicated to the Fund that it stood ready to buy and sell in order to perform its obligations regarding exchange stability. A member that availed itself of wider margins was to notify the Fund and would then be subject to certain rules regarding multiple currency practices and discriminatory currency arrangements and regarding intervention in the exchange markets within its territories.

A member that was temporarily not maintaining rates based on a par value for its currency but was maintaining a stable rate as the basis for exchange transactions in its territories could communicate that rate to the Fund. If the Fund found that this rate was not unsatisfactory, the rate was referred to as a *central rate*. The member could then maintain margins around that central rate. A central rate for a member's currency could be communicated to the Fund in gold, units of SDRs, or another member's currency.

RATES COMMUNICATED

In the weeks that followed, members began to notify the Fund of their actions, and the Fund acted on these notifications as necessary.

---

[1] E.B. Decision No. 3463-(71/126), December 18, 1971; Vol. II below, pp. 195–96.

[2] The resolution is reproduced in Vol. II below, pp. 331–32.

Par Values Unchanged

By December 31, 1971, 24 members and 1 nonmetropolitan territory had decided to maintain unchanged the par values of their currencies; such action meant that the currencies of these members were appreciated vis-à-vis the dollar by 8.57 per cent from the par values existing on May 1, 1971. These countries included France and Spain as well as the United Kingdom and most members of the sterling area, such as Australia, Iraq, Ireland, Jamaica, Malaysia, New Zealand, and Nigeria.

The complete list and the par values maintained are given in Table 18.

Table 18. Par Values Maintained Unchanged as of December 31, 1971

Member	Par Value in U.S. Dollars per Currency Unit [1]
Australia [2]	1.21600
Barbados	0.542857
Cyprus [2]	2.60571
Ethiopia [2]	0.434285
France [2]	0.195477
Gambia, The	0.521143
Iraq [2]	3.04000
Ireland [2]	2.60571
Jamaica [2]	1.30286
Kuwait	3.04000
Libyan Arab Republic [2]	3.04000
Malawi	1.30286
Malaysia	0.354666
Morocco [2]	0.214547
New Zealand [2]	1.21600
Nigeria [2]	3.04000
Rwanda [2]	0.010857
Saudi Arabia	0.241269
Sierra Leone	1.30286
Singapore [2]	0.354666
Somalia	0.152000
Spain [2]	0.0155102
Tunisia [2]	2.06803
United Kingdom [2]	2.60571
United Kingdom: Hong Kong	0.179143

[1] Represented an appreciation of 8.57 per cent in terms of the U.S. dollar from the rates in effect on May 1, 1971.

[2] Member availed itself of the wider margins of up to 2¼ per cent.

Par Values Changed

Changes were made in the par values for the currencies of 10 members and 2 nonmetropolitan territories. The par values for the shillings of Kenya, Tanzania, and Uganda and for the Zambian kwacha were altered so that they all remained in line with the U.S. dollar. In terms of the U.S. dollar, the South African rand, also used by Botswana, Lesotho, and Swaziland, was devalued by 4.76 per cent, the Yugoslav dinar by 11.76 per cent, and the Ghanaian new cedi by 43.88 per cent. Revaluations occurred for the Surinam guilder and for the Bahamian dollar.

Details are given in Table 19.

Table 19. Par Values Changed, December 18–31, 1971

Member	New Par Value in U.S. Dollars per Currency Unit	Percentage Change in Terms of U.S. Dollars [1]
Botswana	1.33333	−4.76
Ghana [2]	0.550000	−43.88
Kenya [2]	0.140000	0.00
Lesotho	1.33333	−4.76
South Africa	1.33333	−4.76
Swaziland	1.33333	−4.76
Tanzania [2]	0.140000	0.00
Uganda [2]	0.140000	0.00
Yugoslavia [2]	0.0588235	−11.76
Zambia [2]	1.40000	0.00
Netherlands:		
Surinam [2]	0.559047	+5.43
United Kingdom:		
Bahama Islands	1.03093	+3.09

[1] The percentage change in the amount of U.S. dollars required to purchase a unit of national currency, calculated on the basis of the par values in effect on May 1, 1971.

[2] Member availed itself of the wider margins of up to 2¼ per cent.

Central Rates Established

Central rates were established for the currencies of 28 members and of 1 nonmetropolitan territory. The majority also availed themselves of the wider margins. Members that set central rates included Belgium, the Federal Republic of Germany, Italy, Japan, the Netherlands, and Sweden.

Details of the central rates established are given in Table 20.

Rates of Other Members

The overwhelming majority of the Fund's members kept their exchange rates unchanged in terms of their intervention currency, and did not avail themselves of the wider margins. Many such members used the French franc as their intervention currency and kept their rates fixed in terms of French francs. Thus, Cameroon, the Central African Republic, Chad, the People's Republic of the Congo, Dahomey, Gabon, Ivory Coast, the Malagasy Republic, Mauritania, Niger, Senegal, Togo, and Upper Volta retained the relationship between the CFA franc and the French franc at 50 to 1, yielding an appreciation

Table 20. Central Rates Established, December 18–31, 1971

Member	Central Rate Expressed in U.S. Dollars per Currency Unit [1]	Percentage Change in Terms of U.S. Dollars [2]
Austria [3]	0.0429185	+11.59 [4]
Belgium [3]	0.0223135	+11.57
Burma [3]	0.186961	−10.97
Denmark [3]	0.143266	+7.45
Dominican Republic	1.000000	0.00
Finland [3]	0.243902	+2.44
Germany, Federal Republic of [3]	0.310318	+13.58
Greece [3]	0.0333333	0.00
Guyana [3]	0.500000	0.00
Haiti	0.200000	0.00
Honduras	0.500000	0.00
Iceland	0.0113636	0.00
India [3]	0.137376	+3.03
Israel [3]	0.238095	−16.67 [4]
Italy [3]	0.00171969	+7.48
Japan [3]	0.00324675	+16.88
Jordan [3]	2.80000	0.00
Luxembourg [3]	0.0223135	+11.57
Malta [3]	2.67086	+11.29
Mexico	0.0800000	0.00
Netherlands [3]	0.308195	+11.57
Nicaragua	0.142857	0.00
Norway [3]	0.150480	+7.49
Panama	1.00000	0.00
Portugal [3]	0.0366972	+5.50
Sweden [3]	0.207775	+7.49
Turkey [3]	0.0714286	+7.14
Zäire [3]	2.00000	0.00
Netherlands:		
Netherlands Antilles	0.558659	+5.35

[1] Central rates are here expressed in U.S. dollars even though some members communicated them to the Fund in other terms.

[2] The percentage change in the amount of U.S. dollars required to purchase a unit of national currency, calculated on the basis of the par values in effect on May 1, 1971.

[3] Member availed itself of the wider margins of up to 2¼ per cent.

[4] Includes the changes in par values between May 1, 1971 and December 18, 1971.

in terms of dollars from 277.710 CFA francs per U.S. dollar to 255.785 CFA francs per U.S. dollar, the same appreciation as that of the French franc in terms of the dollar. Algeria similarly maintained its exchange rate fixed in terms of French francs, thus also appreciating its currency by 8.57 per cent in terms of the dollar.

The Republic of China, El Salvador, Iran, Liberia, Nepal, and Thailand all had had effective par values prior to August 15, 1971, and they continued to keep their exchange rates unchanged in terms of dollars. This meant that they devalued in terms of gold to the same extent as the United States was expected to do. Many other members that did not have effective par values prior to

August 15, 1971 likewise kept their exchange rates unaltered in terms of the U.S. dollar. Some of these members had free exchange markets for at least part of their transactions, where exchange rates might change according to the new realignments. These members included Argentina, Brazil, Chile, Costa Rica, Ecuador, Egypt, Indonesia, Korea, Lebanon, Pakistan, Paraguay, Peru, the Philippines, the Sudan, the Syrian Arab Republic, Viet-Nam, and the Yemen Arab Republic.

The Executive Board took a blanket decision on December 23, 1971 affecting primarily the members mentioned in the preceding paragraph. The Board agreed to the changes in exchange rates that they had made and approved the multiple currency practices involved. The countries concerned all had membership resolutions, or exchange rates already approved by the Fund as pre-par value rates, that specified as fixed the number of currency units to be maintained per U.S. dollar. Hence, their rates in terms of dollars had already been approved by the Fund. The Fund now deemed to be approved any change in the gold equivalents of such exchange rates that resulted from the country's continuing to maintain the same number of currency units per U.S. dollar.[3] This decision meant that these members did not individually have to seek the Fund's approval for the changes in their exchange rates, which, while unchanged in terms of dollars, were necessarily depreciated in terms of gold.

THE FUND'S OPERATIONS RESTORED

To facilitate the resumption of the orderly conduct of the Fund's operations after the decision taken on December 18, 1971, the staff submitted to the Executive Directors, on December 22, some proposals for valuing the Fund's holdings of currencies and for determining the exchange rates that would be applicable in the Fund's operations. There was preliminary discussion of these proposals by the Executive Directors at two informal sessions on December 23, which led to further refinements of technical points by the staff. Then, on January 4, 1972, the Executive Board took a decision that would apply until the new par value for the U.S. dollar became effective.

There were several elements to the decision. Within a reasonable period after a member established a central rate for its currency, the Fund would adjust its holdings of the member's currency in accordance with the central rate. If the member was availing itself of wider margins, the adjustment of the Fund's holdings of a currency that was involved in a transaction with the Fund was to be based on the ratio of the representative rate for the member's currency in the exchange market to the effective parity relationship between that currency and the member's intervention currency. And participants in the Special Draw-

---

[3] E.B. Decision No. 3504-(71/134), December 23, 1971; Vol. II below, p. 215.

ing Account that used SDRs were enabled to obtain against them amounts of foreign exchange that corresponded to the prospective par value of the U.S. dollar based on a price for gold of $38 an ounce, rather than on the par value of the U.S. dollar based on a gold price of $35 an ounce.[4]

WORLD PAYMENTS SITUATION AT THE END OF 1971

As 1971 drew to a close, it was uncertain whether, and to what extent, the new exchange rates would redress the imbalance in world payments. That imbalance had not only persisted but had become much worse. The overall U.S. balance of payments deficit on official settlements for the year had come to $30 billion, three times the size of that of 1970. The trade surplus of 1970 had turned into a $3 billion deficit, and the current account had now also shifted into a deficit of somewhat less than $1 billion. The 1971 U.S. basic balance was in deficit by $9.3 billion, compared with the $2.5–3 billion of the preceding few years.

In contrast, Japan had an overall balance of payments surplus in 1971 of more than $7 billion and a current account surplus of $5.8 billion, unprecedented in that country's postwar history. The overall surplus of the United Kingdom had also shown a tremendous rise, second only to that of Japan, reaching $6.5 billion, which was $3.5 billion larger than it had been in 1970. The Federal Republic of Germany's overall surplus had declined from that of 1970 but was still $4.5 billion, and France also had a large surplus, of $3.5 billion.

INTERNATIONAL MONETARY REFORM—THE NEXT STEP

The system of par values had been suspended. The U.S. authorities were not converting foreign official holdings of U.S. dollars into gold or other reserve assets. Thus, two key features of the international monetary system that had been designed at Bretton Woods a quarter of a century earlier no longer existed. The need for international monetary reform, or, as a minimum, measures to improve vastly the functioning of the international monetary system, were on everyone's mind. The resolution taken by the Board of Governors at the 1971 Annual Meeting had provided the official blessing for a study of monetary reform, and the Executive Directors had begun consideration of many issues.

The spectrum of topics to be considered in discussions about monetary reform had already become wide. Should greater flexibility of exchange rates be

---

[4] E.B. Decision No. 3537-(72/3)G/S, January 4, 1972; see *Annual Report, 1972*, pp. 87–88. When the United States established a new par value, on May 8, 1972, this decision was replaced.

provided for, and, if so, how great and by what techniques? How should the relative responsibilities for correcting future imbalances be apportioned between deficit and surplus countries? What measures should be used to reduce disequilibrating capital flows, and, in particular, to what extent should resort be made to capital controls? Should the substantial amounts of dollars held in foreign official reserves be converted into some other form of international reserve asset, such as the SDR? What should be the position of gold in any future monetary system? These were fundamental questions, and it was likely that some years would pass before international monetary reform would be achieved.

A BACKWARD GLANCE

Although what is commonly called the Bretton Woods system did not collapse entirely until the early months of 1973, at the end of 1971 it was already evident that the regime of par values was in jeopardy. Economists, financial officials, and monetary historians looked backward, as well as forward, endeavoring to seek explanations for the breakdown of the system that had served so well at least until 1965, if not a year or two longer.

In retrospect, it is clear that the developments in the international monetary field and in the world's exchange markets that placed the par value system under stress were a direct reflection of the basic changes in the world economy that had been gradually evolving since the end of World War II. Over time the world had become integrated, economically and financially, and a true "world economy" had developed. Not only had international trade expanded to unprecedented levels but production, too, had become international: giant multinational corporations could shift production from country to country, depending on changes in costs or other circumstances. A progressive internationalization of banking operations had taken place, making it possible, among other things, for large and potentially disruptive short-term capital movements suddenly to cross national boundaries.

There had been other changes in the world economy as well. Instead of the widespread unemployment that had been feared when the Fund was created, inflation had persisted as the key problem for nearly all countries and had eventually reached historically high rates; to make matters worse, inflation coexisted with unemployment and danger of recession. World economic circumstances became subject to frequent changes, making economic forecasting very difficult. World economic power had become distributed among a number of countries. And as shortages of natural resources began to make themselves felt, an awareness developed that there could be limits to economic growth.

These changes in the world economy made it much more difficult for central bankers and economic policymakers, including those in the international economic institutions established after World War II, to achieve the four principal objectives of economic policy that, for the previous twenty-five years, had been their goal: full employment, price stability, economic growth, and balance of payments equilibrium. And the international monetary system that had been designed to help achieve those objectives inevitably broke down.

PART SIX

The Fund as an Institution

"Close relations with members and
understanding of their points of view . . .
have been the basis of the Fund's
policies in many areas . . . and have led
to new activities."

—PIERRE-PAUL SCHWEITZER, Managing Director,
addressing the Economic and Social Council of the
United Nations on November 12, 1970.

CHAPTER
28

Growth of Responsibilities

$\mathcal{G}$OLD, EXCHANGE RATES, SDRs, and use of the Fund's resources constituted the glamorous activities of the Fund during the period of this
history. They were the events that captured headlines. Their importance notwithstanding, the major part of the Fund's day-to-day work in the years 1966–71
was of a more routine nature. Regular contacts with members, technical assistance, the gathering and dispensing of information, and cooperating with other
agencies in the solution of financial and economic problems, although less publicized than the Fund's other endeavors, took up much of the time and effort
of the Executive Directors, the management, and the staff. The Fund's work
and responsibilities in these fields so expanded after 1965 that, in effect, a quiet
revolution took place.

Sheer expansion of membership alone brought with it an increase in the
volume of regular activities. The number of annual consultations with members,
for example, expanded *pari passu* with membership. By the late 1960s the
impact of the sharp spurt in membership brought about by the admission of
many newly independent African countries in 1963 had begun to make itself
felt. But a more significant factor in the expansion of and change in the
activities of the Fund was the greater complexity and interdependence of the
world economy. Changes in the ways in which the Fund conducted its traditional
activities and extensions into new fields could be expected, particularly since
the Fund, as a relatively large organization operating on a global scale, could
readily make use of the advances being made in communication, transportation,
economic theory and methodology, and computer technology, and of the explosion of information that was taking place. Indeed, in the several fields of
international economics, international financial statistics, and international law,
the Fund was expanding the boundaries of knowledge and developing new
techniques.

INCREASES IN MEMBERSHIP

Basic to the expansion and evolving character of the activities of the Fund
described in this chapter was the changing nature of the membership. The

17 countries that became members from 1966 to 1971 were, like most of the new members after 1960, if not earlier, developing countries. Hence, at the end of 1971 by far the greater part of the Fund's membership of 120 countries was in this category. (The 17 new members and the dates on which they became members are indicated in Chapter 16 in connection with their initial quotas; see also Table 5, pages 306–308.

Many of the Fund's newer members, like the African countries, had only recently become politically independent. Nearly all nonmetropolitan territories, as one of their first acts upon acquiring independence, became separate members of the Fund. For some the motive was that membership in the Fund was a precondition for membership in the World Bank, and they were especially eager for development aid. Several of the newer members were very small. These were referred to in UN discussions as ministates, and their applications had, in fact, raised the question whether a nation had to be of a certain minimum size in order to be admitted to international organizations. In 1966 the management of the Fund, recognizing the significance of membership to the countries concerned, settled on the proposition that the Fund should consider the application of any independent country, regardless of size, but this proposition was subject to review should the United Nations refuse membership to a ministate on grounds of size.

So many newly independent, developing, and small members inevitably meant a broadening of consultation discussions and an increase in technical assistance and in the training of members' officials.

Although as 1971 came to a close it seemed unlikely that the membership would increase much further, six countries did in fact join shortly thereafter: the Bahamas, Bahrain, Bangladesh, Qatar, Romania, and the United Arab Emirates.

CONTINUED IMPORTANCE OF ANNUAL CONSULTATIONS

After 1967 there was an increase in the number of special consultations between the Fund and members. Usually these special consultations were in connection with stand-by arrangements, although later on, after 1970, special consultations also began to be held with members with fluctuating exchange rates. Nevertheless, the process of holding an annual consultation with each member continued through 1971 to be the primary vehicle by which both the Executive Directors and the staff kept intimately in touch with the members' economic and financial situations. Annual consultations were the principal way in which the Fund stayed equipped to handle members' external payments emergencies. They provided the Fund with the background necessary to enable it to evaluate quickly, for instance, proposals for adjustments in par values or exchange rates, or requests for financial support. They were also the instrument by which the Fund reviewed members' economic and financial policies with them and pointed out to them the international implications of their policies.

Examples of the role of annual consultations were given in Chapters 18 and 21 in connection with the stand-by arrangements for the United Kingdom and France in the late 1960s. Similarly, we have seen the part played by annual consultations in the Fund's discussions with a number of members, including Canada, the Federal Republic of Germany, Ghana, and India, as they changed the par values for their currencies in the years covered here. Annual consultations also provided the mechanism by which the Fund was able to review the external economic situations of two members, Japan and the United States, crucial to the international monetary scene, which might not otherwise have come under the Fund's purview. Neither of these members requested a stand-by arrangement during the period reviewed here nor, until after the Smithsonian agreement in December 1971, did they change their par values. Hence, without the annual consultation procedure, the Fund would not have had a way to hold formal discussions with these members.

For members under Article XIV, the Article which in effect permitted the temporary retention of certain restrictions without the Fund's explicit approval, consultations were mandatory. Through 1971 the great majority of members remained under this Article. As of April 30, 1971 only 35 members had assumed the obligations of Article VIII, Sections 2, 3, and 4, of which 8 (Argentina, Bolivia, Denmark, Ecuador, Guyana, Malaysia, Norway, and Singapore) had done so after 1965.[1] No additional member countries accepted the obligations of Article VIII, Sections 2, 3, and 4, during the remainder of 1971. Annual consultations with members that had accepted the obligations of Article VIII, similar in scope to consultations under Article XIV, although not required by the Articles, were instituted in 1960 and subsequently continued.

As both the Fund and members grew accustomed to having annual consultations, the usefulness of consultations increased. The habit grew, even in the largest industrial members, of using the occasion of a consultation with the Fund for a general internal review of policy by government officials. In the newer developing members, consultations were often also used not only to serve their principal purpose of a thoroughgoing review of monetary and financial policies but also to explore requests for technical assistance. Thus, in addition to the usual staff from the relevant Area Department to consider general economic policy and from the Exchange and Trade Relations Department to consider exchange restrictions and stabilization policies, missions also frequently

---

[1] El Salvador, Guatemala, Mexico, Panama, and the United States assumed the obligations of Article VIII, Sections 2, 3, and 4, shortly after the Fund came into existence, and Canada, the Dominican Republic, Haiti, and Honduras did so in the early 1950s. In 1961–62 Austria, Belgium, France, the Federal Republic of Germany, Ireland, Italy, Luxembourg, the Netherlands, Peru, Saudi Arabia, Sweden, and the United Kingdom took up Article VIII obligations, followed in 1963–65 by Australia, Costa Rica, Jamaica, Japan, Kuwait, and Nicaragua.

included a staff member from one of the functional departments responsible for technical assistance, such as the Fiscal Affairs Department, to help to determine the details of a technical assistance request by a member and the kind of expertise required. Sometimes technical assistance, such as with problems of economic data and analysis, was provided then and there, when the staff was able to provide advice based on the experience of other countries facing similar problems.

Because of their usefulness, the Fund had as its aim to conduct the consultations in connection with Article VIII or Article XIV annually with all members. As a result, consultations constituted both for the Executive Directors and for the staff by far the major, and certainly the most time-consuming, of the Fund's endeavors. Especially was this true for the staff of the five Area Departments, which had the primary responsibility for relations with members and, insofar as consultations were concerned, the major responsibility for preparing the staff papers and carrying out the review of policies with officials of member governments. Tedious as are long lists of countries, it is perhaps instructive for the reader to realize that during the calendar year 1971 the Fund held consultations at the Executive Board level with 78 members and 2 nonmetropolitan territories.[2] The members with which consultations were held included the largest industrial ones (Belgium, Canada, France, the Federal Republic of Germany, Italy, Japan, the Netherlands, Sweden, the United Kingdom, and the United States) as well as 10 other industrial or developed members (Australia, Austria, Denmark, Iceland, Ireland, New Zealand, Portugal, South Africa, Turkey, and Yugoslavia). Consultations were also held with 13 members in Latin America and the Caribbean area (Chile, Colombia, the Dominican Republic, Ecuador, El Salvador, Guyana, Haiti, Honduras, Panama, Paraguay, Peru, Trinidad and Tobago, and Venezuela), with 13 members in Asia (Afghanistan, Burma, Ceylon, the Republic of China, India, Indonesia, Korea, Laos, Malaysia, Nepal, the Philippines, Singapore, and Thailand), with 7 members in the Middle East (Egypt, Iran, Iraq, Israel, Jordan, the Yemen Arab Republic, and the People's Democratic Republic of Yemen), and with 25 members in Africa (Algeria, Botswana, Burundi, Cameroon, the Central African Republic, Dahomey, Ethiopia, Gabon, The Gambia, Ghana, Guinea, Ivory Coast, Kenya, Liberia, Mauritius, Niger, Nigeria, Rwanda, Senegal, Sierra Leone, the Sudan, Swaziland, Togo, Tunisia, and Zambia). Consultations with the Netherlands were extended to the Netherlands Antilles and Surinam.

A total of 89 professional staff members, primarily from the Area Departments, participated in the missions connected with the consultations listed above.

---

[2] Following the pattern that began on April 1, 1952, the Fund's "consultation year" continued to run from April 1 to March 31 of each year until March 31, 1972, when it was then decided that confusion between the calendar year and the consultation year should be avoided by making the two coincide. The consultation year 1973 was accordingly made "a nine-month year" to end on December 31, 1973, so that the 1974 consultation year could start on January 1, 1974.

Most missions consisted of 4 or 5 professionals and a secretary; they worked with the officials of members for periods of time ranging from a few days to two weeks before returning to headquarters to write their reports.

Achievement of the goal of holding an annual consultation with each member was not possible for a variety of reasons. The timing of members' elections and of their budget preparations and presentations, and the availability of their senior monetary officials for discussions with the Fund staff, all influenced the scheduling of missions. Moreover, when special problems with individual members arose claiming priority on the staff's time, the interval for regular consultations with other members was sometimes lengthened. Thus, in a fair number of instances the period between two regular consultations worked out to be as long as 18 months.

The Executive Directors' reviews of country situations were anything but cursory. Fourteen of their consultation discussions in 1971 lasted for two hours or more each. In the last half of 1971 the Executive Directors spent an increasing number of hours deliberating on the fundamental problems facing the international monetary system, but consultations and discussions about individual country situations still, as in previous years, took up nearly 40 per cent of their time.

TRENDS IN EXCHANGE RESTRICTIONS

Because under the Articles of Agreement the Fund has special responsibilities for exchange restrictions, consultations with members continued to be addressed first to that subject. However, the industrial members had all formally accepted the obligations of Article VIII, Sections 2, 3, and 4, before 1965, and until the disruptions of August 15, 1971 they lived up to these obligations, maintaining no restrictions on current payments or on transfers for invisibles. Indeed, not only did industrial and most developed members virtually eliminate exchange restrictions during the 1960s but, following the Kennedy Round of trade and tariff negotiations completed in mid-1967 in Geneva under the auspices of the GATT, they also greatly reduced quantitative restrictions on imports and tariffs. Concern by international and national officials about restrictions still maintained by industrial countries turned to nontariff barriers to trade.

Even the minor exchange restrictions that the Fund's industrial members applied from time to time between 1966 and 1971 were not long-lasting. For example, as we have read in earlier chapters, the United Kingdom in 1966 and France in 1968 and 1969 reacted to their balance of payments deficits partly by reinstituting restrictions on exchange allocations for travel. But in 1970 the United Kingdom lifted these restrictions, and France, twice in 1970 and again early in 1971, increased the allocations that it made available for tourism. In 1969 Japan ceased to restrict exchange for travel, and in 1971 increased further the automatic allocations, that is, allocations without license, which authorized banks might make available to tourists.

Advance deposits on imports, to which some industrial members had turned in the late 1960s, similarly were later abolished. Japan suspended the requirement of advance deposits in May 1970; and the United Kingdom, which introduced an import deposit scheme in 1968, gradually reduced the rate of deposit in several steps from 50 per cent to 20 per cent, and then, in December 1970, terminated the scheme.

It is worthy of mention that the turbulence in exchange markets in 1971 did not lead to any significant increase in quantitative restrictions on imports or to an intensification of exchange restrictions. On the contrary, most developed members took further measures to liberalize trade, and following the December 1971 currency realignment, the member countries of the EEC and the United States pursued their discussions regarding immediate and longer-term trade arrangements. The United States, the EEC countries, and Japan also agreed to have a multilateral review of trade matters within the framework of the GATT.

As 1971 ended, the six EEC countries, together with Denmark, Finland, Japan, New Zealand, Norway, Sweden, and the United Kingdom, were starting a system of generalized tariff preferences on selected commodities (primarily manufactures and semimanufactures) originating in developing countries. Industrial countries were also liberalizing imports from countries belonging to the Council for Mutual Economic Assistance (CMEA or COMECON). That Council consisted in 1971 of Bulgaria, Cuba, Czechoslovakia, the German Democratic Republic, Hungary, Mongolia, Poland, Romania, and the U.S.S.R.

The use of restrictions on current transactions and of multiple exchange rates by the Fund's developing members, on balance, also showed a marked tendency to decline after 1965. By early 1971 there were fewer than ten members whose restrictive systems could be characterized as extensive or complex. Those members, including Ecuador, Indonesia, the Philippines, Turkey, Viet-Nam, and Yugoslavia, that had continued to have substantial restrictions or multiple currency practices in the late 1960s, or had reintroduced them, simplified their rate structures and liberalized their restrictions. Continuing an earlier trend, developing members increased their use of export promotion measures, government participation in export financing was enhanced, and there was a tendency toward greater state trading in the purchase of imports.

In contrast to the continued liberalization of trade and current transactions, industrial members, especially in 1971, introduced dual exchange markets, primarily to discourage excessive capital flows, and took steps to control destabilizing capital flows. The two separate exchange markets, one for current and one for capital transactions, that existed in Belgium in the 1950s and 1960s continued into 1970 and 1971. There was the introduction in August 1971 by France as well of two exchange markets, together with similar action by the operations account countries of the French franc area that the reader will recall from

Chapter 26. In September 1971 the Netherlands created a security currency market by prescribing that nonresidents could acquire listed guilder bonds only with the proceeds from the sale of such bonds by nonresidents to residents. This mechanism was to prevent net new investment by nonresidents in officially listed guilder bonds. What was called the "O-guilder" in this bond circuit went to a small premium. The investment currency market in the United Kingdom remained in operation and, indeed, was considerably enlarged after the end of 1971 as a result of portfolio investment in securities of the overseas sterling area being channeled into it.

After 1965, tighter direct measures to stem capital flows were also applied. A variety of controls designed to curb outflows were put into effect in the late 1960s and early 1970s. In 1971 these controls were supplemented by measures aimed at reducing inflows. Many of the measures taken were of a monetary nature, intended to decrease capital flows indirectly by influencing the operations of the banking system. Increasingly, however, direct controls limiting, or prohibiting outright, certain capital transactions were adopted.

Like developed members, developing members took steps against capital flows. Mainly, measures were enacted to control inward capital movements. These measures were motivated not so much by the immediate monetary and balance of payments consequences of capital inflows, the motivating factor in industrial countries, as by concern by developing members over the extent of foreign ownership in their economies.[3]

DEVELOPMENTS IN ANNUAL CONSULTATIONS

Broadening of Discussions

Annual consultations necessarily continued to include reviews of existing exchange restrictions. Especially were consultations with developing members often the occasion for working out exchange reforms, for examining reversals of liberal exchange policies, or for discussing changes in the form of restrictions and exchange practices.

In general, however, in the period reviewed here, the Fund's annual consultations with members began to shift away from the subject of restrictions, and an ever-widening range of financial and economic topics became primary. Increasingly, consultations aimed at assessing members' monetary and fiscal policies and the effects of those policies on the member's own balance of payments position and on the world's financial situation. After 1967, when

---

[3] This description of trends in members' restrictions is necessarily very brief. Since 1952 the Fund has published an Annual Report on Exchange Restrictions describing in detail the exchange system of each member and containing several pages summarizing the main developments in restrictions for the year. For the situation at the end of 1971, see *Twenty-Third Annual Report on Exchange Restrictions* (1972).

the international monetary system started to malfunction seriously, consultations with industrial members included in particular detailed discussions about the causes of recurrent exchange crises. Furthermore, as inflation became of paramount concern to all members, as it proved to be exceedingly difficult to restrain, and as the anomaly of the coexistence of rising prices and increasing unemployment baffled monetary officials and economists everywhere, consultations centered more and more on ascertaining the effectiveness of different techniques and policies for combating inflation.

Consultations with developing members were also extended. They began to cover more fully the consequences of economic development efforts, both in the short run and in the somewhat longer run, for prices, production, monetary and fiscal policies, and the balance of payments; problems of joblessness and measures to increase employment opportunities; the size and servicing of external indebtedness; and members' relationships with regional organizations, as the latter multiplied in number and strength (the last two topics are discussed at some length in the following chapter). In addition, we have already noted in Chapter 18 that consultation discussions with developing members were increasingly devoted to obtaining the background information and appraisal essential for deriving the monetary, fiscal, and other targets included in the financial programs associated with stand-by arrangements.

Changes in the Process

The process by which the Fund's consultations were conducted remained much the same during the years 1966–71 as that which had evolved by the end of 1965.[4] However, to relieve the expanding workload of consultations on the staff and the management, on the Executive Directors, and on the officials of member countries, some important changes were introduced. More extensive preparatory work was done by the staff at headquarters, and junior staff usually arrived in the field in advance to assemble factual data before senior staff arrived to conduct policy talks. To facilitate the consideration of consultation reports by the Executive Board, the basic staff reports on the policy discussions, formerly called Part I, were shortened to a maximum of 20 pages. These reports were redesigned so as to put less emphasis on the reporting of factual information and more on the assessment of both the member's current economic situation and the policies it was pursuing or formulating.

The title of the economic background report, formerly called Part II, was altered to "Recent Economic Developments," and the paper was issued separately from the basic staff report on the policy discussions. Much greater use was made of graphs, charts, and other visual aids, both to improve the quality of the reports and to stimulate the younger economists who were involved in

---

[4] The consultations process as of the end of 1965 and its evolution until then were described in *History, 1945–65*, Vol. II, Chap. 11.

the long and painstaking work of preparing such reports. More econometric techniques were used to quantify the relationships between economic variables. In some instances, notably in reports on industrial countries, the quantitative techniques used included new analytical methods developed by academic economists or other experts outside the Fund. The Executive Board, regarding the consultations as an extremely useful and major part of the Fund's activities, approved all these changes in scope and procedure.

Despite the broadening of consultations, the economies of members had become so interrelated and so subject to abrupt change that by the beginning of 1971 thought was being given by the Executive Directors, the management, and the staff to ways in which the annual consultations might be supplemented. It was evident that many of the problems faced by members were problems they had in common. All of them had, for example, cost-push inflation coexisting with unemployment, a novel economic phenomenon. Among industrial members, balance of payments emergencies for any one of them were much more likely to arise from shifts of capital than from changes in trade balances. The problems of developing members were closely related to what happened in the industrial members. As the latter tightened their monetary policies, raising their interest rates, the cost of borrowing by developing members went up. As industrial members faced balance of payments deficits, the outflow of capital to developing members went down. Hence, among developing members the usual problems of development financing became more and more aggravated by the upheavals in international money markets, by relative declines in the receipt of foreign capital, and by the heavier burden of servicing foreign debt.

It was evident, too, that no adequate solutions to common problems were being found. There were more questions than answers. How useful were monetary and fiscal policies for restraining inflation? Were incomes policies workable? And it had become clear also that the solution of most problems plaguing the international monetary system would require joint action by several members.

In these circumstances, the Executive Directors began to seek ways to supplement the bilateral "micro-approach" of an annual consultation with each member. To obtain broader views of the international monetary situation, the Executive Directors began, in January 1971, to hold informal sessions at least once a year, usually just after the turn of the year, on the world economic outlook. They hoped that, as a minimum, broad discussions would point to solutions to some of the common economic problems, and would enhance the consistency of the recommendations on economic policy made to individual members. Possibly, too, the Fund might find a way to help in resolving problems that were of an international nature, as distinct from those of individual countries.

To widen the view obtained by consultations between the Fund and each individual member, the staff by 1971 was experimentally introducing multinational analysis and forecasting into the consultations process. Nonetheless, it appeared that before long the Fund might have to supplement its bilateral consultations, that is, between the Fund and a member country, with some kind of wider consultations. It was not yet clear what form such wider consultations might take. Possibly, they might be multilateral in character, that is, conducted with a small group of countries that had similar economic concerns. Alternatively, a series of relatively brief bilateral consultations might be held with a number of countries, either at the same time or in close succession to one another.

In addition, the Fund began to give more attention than previously to the role of fiscal policy in promoting internal and external stability. Traditionally, the Fund had been cautious in examining fiscal policies because they involved the social objectives of members. However, at the Annual Meeting in Copenhagen in 1970, Mr. Witteveen (Netherlands) explicitly urged that the Fund pay greater heed to fiscal policy. He said:

> Regarding monetary policy, I have great appreciation for the work done by the Fund in recent years in explaining its importance and introducing quantitative targets for domestic credit creation, though this has been limited to an ad hoc basis.
>
> In the field of public finance we are unfortunately less advanced. It would be a contribution toward more internal stability in the world at large if here too the Fund would be able to elaborate some concepts with operational value which would come to be accepted by member countries as part of their internal policy considerations regarding acceptable expansion of demand even if the balance of payments does not pose an immediate problem.[5]

Subsequently, Mr. Lieftinck (Netherlands), referring to this statement, urged that the Fund add to its work program a special study of the role of public finance and of fiscal policy in the fight against inflation.

TECHNICAL ASSISTANCE EVOLVES INTO A LARGE PROGRAM

Since the Fund's earliest days, members requested and received technical advice on banking, finance, taxation, and other monetary and fiscal matters.[6] After 1965 the technical assistance provided by the Fund grew rapidly and became one of the Fund's primary endeavors. More complete and regular reporting and evaluating procedures had to be introduced as part of the Fund's internal procedures. Whereas the names and functions of outside experts on duty in member countries had previously been circulated to the Executive Directors periodically, usually once a year as an annex to the administrative budget, beginning in March 1967 detailed lists of both staff and outside experts

---

[5] Statement by the Governor of the World Bank for the Netherlands, *Summary Proceedings, 1970,* pp. 97–98.

[6] See *History, 1945–65,* Vol. I, pp. 185–86, 286–87, 391–94, 428, 545, and 551–54.

were circulated twice each year; a list covering assignments for the six months from March 1 to August 31 was distributed in mid-September, just prior to the Annual Meeting; and another list, covering the whole year from March 1 to the end of February, was distributed in late March, just before the Executive Directors considered the Fund's administrative budget. In addition, beginning in March 1968 the staff made an annual report to the Executive Directors describing and evaluating the technical assistance activities undertaken in certain specialized fields.

As has been mentioned above, some technical assistance occurred rather routinely in the course of annual consultations. Consultation missions were often the occasion for the staff to advise officials of member countries on particular problems, usually relating to economic data or analysis. Consultations also gave members an opportunity to discuss their financial and economic problems with international officials familiar with the experiences of many other countries, and to gain information helpful for assessing alternative policies. In addition, resident representatives whom the Fund frequently assigned to members that were implementing Fund-approved stabilization programs in connection with stand-by arrangements often gave technical advice along with their other duties.

Important as were these types of technical advice, what the Fund customarily called technical assistance was something more specialized: (1) the assignment for extended periods of personnel, either staff members or outside experts specially recruited by the Fund, to governments or central banks in advisory, executive, or operational positions; and (2) staff missions of shorter durations to advise members on specific problems in particular fields. It was the growth of this specialized technical assistance that gained great momentum in the late 1960s and early 1970s.

TECHNICAL ASSISTANCE IN CENTRAL BANKING

Within a few years after its establishment at the end of 1963, the Central Banking Service became the principal source in the world for meeting the needs of numerous developing countries for technical assistance in all matters pertaining to central banks—their organization, their administration, and their operation. In the earlier phases of its activities, and continuing through the first part of 1968, members mainly requested assistance in setting up central banks. They wanted legislation drafted and senior officials supplied as managers. Many of the newly independent countries that joined the Fund in the late 1950s and in the 1960s had no central banks of their own. Some maintained joint central banks with other countries (that is, multinational banks) but desired separate ones. Several older members wanted to revise their central banking laws. Thus, in 1966 and 1967, the Central Banking Service sent advisory missions composed of its own staff and some staff from the Legal Department to 18 members, primarily to help draft central banking legislation, and also supplied to 31 members 48 outside experts, most of whom served for a year or longer as central bank governors, deputy governors, or general managers. By the end of 1967 the Fund had helped to establish central banks in Burundi (May 19, 1964), Rwanda (May 19, 1964), Tanzania (June 14, 1966), Uganda (August 15, 1966), and Kenya (September 14, 1966); and Cyprus, the Democratic Republic of Congo (known as Zaïre from October 27, 1971), Guinea, Guyana, Iraq, Jordan, Malta, Nepal, Sierra Leone, the Sudan, Trinidad and Tobago, and Viet-Nam had received technical assistance in the form of drafting central banking legislation or of managing central banks.

Local personnel were trained as quickly as possible to take over the top positions in new central banks, and by 1968 requests for officers to fill senior management posts had begun to taper off. Nevertheless, as members' economies became increasingly monetized and as the newly formed central banks took on greater responsibility for monetary policy, requests were made for technicians to assist with a number of specialized tasks: to help in setting up facilities for recruiting and training personnel, to evolve or strengthen research capabilities, to improve the managerial and administrative structures of new central banks, and to demonstrate how to prepare financial accounts and how to conduct foreign exchange operations. As a result, requests for outside experts did not abate and even increased.

Most advisory missions, composed of staff as distinct from outside experts, still devoted themselves to drafting central banking legislation for, and setting up, new central banks, but they also began to deal with more complex topics. Members sought advice on how central banks could best apply the various instruments of monetary policy, such as interest rates and reserve requirements; on how they might mobilize financial savings; and on how they might regulate the expansion of bank credit. Assistance was also sought in drafting legislation for general banking systems, in reforming whole banking structures, and in working out appropriate relations between the central bank and commercial banks. Also, advice was sought concerning dealings between central banks in the same geographic area.

There was a growing tendency for members to request more than one staff member or outside expert and more than one advisory mission. As the number of advisory missions expanded, the Central Banking Service drew primarily from its own staff but, more and more, staff of the Area Departments, the Legal Department, and the Treasurer's Department also participated in these missions or worked in Washington on members' requests. At times, outside experts were added to the missions. Several central banks had as many as three outside experts at a given time.

A few statistics suggest the magnitudes of the Central Banking Service's technical assistance from 1968 to 1971. In 1968, assistance was received by

32 members, 7 (Indonesia, the Malagasy Republic, Mauritius, Pakistan, Panama, Tunisia, and Zambia) for the first time: there were 6 advisory missions; 58 experts served in 27 member countries, of which 18 were receiving experts for the first time; and a new central bank was established in Malta (April 17, 1968). In 1970, 13 members received advisory missions, 2 more than in 1969, and the number of experts serving during the year rose to 80, in 36 member countries. The Republic of China, Nicaragua, Nigeria, the Yemen Arab Republic, and the People's Democratic Republic of Yemen received central banking experts for the first time, and other members, not previously mentioned, that received central banking assistance included The Gambia, Laos, Malawi, Malaysia, Sierra Leone, Singapore, Somalia, and the Sudan. New central banks were established, with the Fund's assistance, in Equatorial Guinea (October 9, 1969) and Guyana (October 16, 1969).

In 1971 there were further interesting developments. The Central Banking Service continued to help in establishing new central banks, which were inaugurated in Singapore (January 1), The Gambia (March 1), the People's Democratic Republic of Yemen (July 14), and the Yemen Arab Republic (July 26). Requests increased for reorganizing existing central banks so as to make them more effective in formulating and implementing monetary policy. Especially were members eager for help in selecting and training staff for their banks. In 1971, for instance, the Central Banking Service set up a training institute in Djakarta, Indonesia, to retrain staff for both the central bank and the commercial banking community. More members began to ask for appraisals of their entire financial systems.

One innovation during 1971 was the provision of technical assistance by the Central Banking Service to a regional monetary institution. An expert in national accounts was assigned to the Executive Secretariat of the Central American Monetary Council, a council serving Costa Rica, El Salvador, Guatemala, Honduras, and Nicaragua, which had as one of its primary functions the standardization of the statistical data of these countries. Also for the first time, a staff member from the Central Banking Service accompanied a mission of the International Finance Corporation in 1971 to study possible improvements in the structure of a member's capital market.

In 1971 the number of members to which advisory missions were sent was 15, and the number of experts 81. Several experts still served as heads or senior officials of central banks, although the number in such capacities had declined. For example, from 1968 to 1971 a Cypriot served as manager of the Central Bank of Kenya; experts from Denmark and New Zealand served, successively, as Director-General of the Bank of Tanzania; and a staff member from the Fund was Director-General of the Bank of Zaïre. When the Central Bank of The Gambia was opened, a Burmese expert who had helped in the planning stayed on as its general manager. The Central Banking Service developed a series of ways to monitor the progress of these experts: correspondence, information gathered by staff missions from other departments of the Fund, formal and informal contacts with the authorities of the members in which the experts served, and, most importantly, inspection visits by the staff of the Central Banking Service, generally at the time of an advisory mission to a nearby country, and often jointly with staff from the Administration Department.

The names of the member countries given above indicate that most of the recipients of the Fund's technical assistance in the field of central banking were in Africa. In the eight years from the establishment of the Central Banking Service to the end of 1971, a total of 177 experts served in 56 member countries and one regional organization. Of these, 92 served in Africa, 31 in Asia, 26 in the Western Hemisphere, 19 in the Middle East, and 9 in Europe.

Two other aspects of the technical assistance provided by the Central Banking Service are especially worthy of note. *One*, the aid rendered was purely technical. The purpose was to assist members in organizing or reorganizing their financial institutions or systems so that these could function more effectively in the national environments of the members concerned. In other words, the aim was to enable members better to develop and implement "sound monetary and financial policies" by advising them on how to improve their institutional framework. The choice between particular monetary and financial policies was regarded as being outside the scope of the Central Banking Service.

Two, there was broad participation not only by recipient countries but also by the countries that furnished experts. Experts were recruited from developing countries as well as from developed ones. In addition to the examples of experts from Burma and Cyprus already cited, central banking experts were drawn from Egypt, Guatemala, India, the Khmer Republic, Pakistan, Peru, the Syrian Arab Republic, and the Sudan. Moreover, the extent to which experts came from developing members was increasing. In the first year of the program, 1964–65, two thirds of the 19 experts were provided by European countries, whereas, of the 81 experts in 1971, 36 came from Europe, 20 from the Western Hemisphere, 17 from Asia, 4 from the Middle East, 2 from Africa, and 2 from other regions.

TECHNICAL ASSISTANCE IN FISCAL AFFAIRS

The specialized technical assistance rendered by the Fiscal Affairs Department, which was established on May 1, 1964, expanded rapidly both in dimension and complexity. From the beginning, this program utilized both staff members of the department and experts drawn from a fiscal panel made up of senior officials in government service, retired officials, and economists from the academic world specializing in public finance. The subjects on which assistance was provided were far ranging: the preparation of budgets and their execution; particular forms of taxation; tax administration, including customs administration; general taxation policy and the prospects for raising revenue; budgetary classifications; and accounting and reporting systems.

There was a marked growth of the program in 1967, when 16 new assignments were undertaken. Of all the assignments operating in that year, 23 were for six months or more and were undertaken in 14 member countries—Costa Rica, Indonesia (2), Iran, Liberia (2), Morocco, Pakistan (2), Peru (5), Rwanda, Sierra Leone (2), Somalia, the Sudan (2), Tanzania, Tunisia, and Zaïre. In March 1968, when the report on technical assistance for the year ended February 29, 1968 was circulated, 25 members had received technical assistance in the fiscal field. Of these, 15 were in Africa, 5 in the Western Hemisphere, 3 in Asia, and 2 in the Middle East; 7 members—Ghana, Indonesia, Liberia, Pakistan, Peru, Sierra Leone, and the Sudan—had received intensified assistance.

The program gradually grew, both in the number of members served and in the topics covered. In the year ended March 15, 1969, the Fiscal Affairs Department gave technical assistance to 21 members; in the calendar year 1969, to 23 members; in the calendar year 1970, to 20 members and 1 regional organization, the East African Community; and in the calendar year 1971, to 24 members and the same regional organization. In terms of manpower, the program grew from 105 man-months in 1966 to 191 in 1971.

The majority of the recipients were in Africa. But a number of members in Asia and Latin America also received technical assistance in fiscal affairs. Several members wanted assistance on more than one subject. From early 1967 onward, a group of fiscal experts operated in Indonesia, and by 1971, teams of two advisors each were operating in several countries.

While general fiscal advisors concerned with the day-to-day problems of finance ministries were provided, requests were also received for advice in specific areas. Short-term missions were requested to advise on reforming tax structures, especially in countries that had inherited tax systems from pre-independence days. Advice was often requested in setting up specific taxes, such as sales, corporation, or property taxes, whether the country was introducing new taxes or developing and modernizing existing taxes. Rate structures were also reviewed, for example, where members wished to make the burden of individual taxation more progressive or to make sure that similarly situated persons were treated uniformly; customs tariffs were revised, to remove rate inconsistencies or to reclassify tariff schedules in accordance with the more customarily used tariff classification. Assistance was also often given for the improvement of tax administration, for the reorganization of tax departments, and for the improvement of procedures for assessment and collection of taxes. Help was given in implementing new taxes, including drafting legislation, recruiting and training staff, and preparing instruction manuals and information for the public.

In regard to budgetary matters, the Fund's technical assistance in fiscal affairs ranged from providing high-level advisors in financial management who considered the major policy questions facing finance ministers in developing countries, to supplying specialists in government accounting. The latter helped, for example, with the mechanization of accounts and the use of electronic data processing equipment. In between were subjects of budget preparation and expenditure control. Technical assistance in fiscal matters was also extended to financial problems of local governments.

By the end of 1970, the number of staff and the number of panel experts engaged in technical assistance in fiscal affairs were about equal, though panel experts had spent three times as long in the field. Employment of staff members on technical assistance duties enabled the Fund to respond more promptly to member governments' requests than would ordinarily have been possible if only panel experts had been recruited, and the accumulation of experience so gained enhanced the staff's capacity to deal with problems presented. However, in 1971 the number of staff employed in the field fell to 15, compared with 26 panel experts, and in total length of assignments to 26 man-months, compared with 165 for panel experts. Nevertheless, by reason of the increased volume of technical assistance work, the staff of the Fiscal Affairs Department devoted a substantial amount of time at headquarters on correspondence with field experts and on support and supervision of their work.

The Area Departments were consulted both in regard to the initiation of technical assistance in their areas and in the assignments. The Legal Department collaborated with the Fiscal Affairs Department in reviewing the increased volume of draft legislation. Moreover, to avoid duplication with other agencies providing technical assistance in fiscal affairs, regular exchanges of information and discussions took place with representatives of the United Nations and of the Organization of American States and the Inter-American Development Bank. Informal discussions were also carried on with the World Bank staff in respect of activities in countries in which the World Bank was particularly interested, and contacts were maintained with some of the national agencies promoting technical assistance in fiscal affairs on a bilateral basis.

As 1971 came to a close, the Fund's programs of technical assistance in fiscal affairs were increasing sharply.

TECHNICAL ASSISTANCE IN STATISTICS

For some years the Balance of Payments Division of the Research Department had assisted members in compiling balance of payments statistics. Some of this assistance was discharged in connection with regular missions of the

Fund, such as those connected with consultations or with stand-by arrangements, but there were also special missions to help members with balance of payments data and methodology. In the calendar years 1966–68 staff members were stationed in Jamaica and in Malaysia for a year, in Chad for two months, and in Indonesia for three weeks, and there were missions not formally designated as technical assistance missions but actually for that purpose to 5 French-speaking members in Africa—Chad, the Democratic Republic of Congo (Zaïre), the People's Republic of the Congo, Mali, and Tunisia. In the internal reporting year ended in March 1970, technicians from the Balance of Payments Division undertook short-term assignments ranging up to a month's duration in 11 countries in Africa and the Middle East.

In much the same way, that is, in association with the Fund's regular missions or through special missions, the Statistics Division of the Research and Statistics Department had for years provided technical assistance in financial statistics. Although this technical assistance was directed primarily to obtaining the data which the Fund needed for its own work, advice was often given to local officials about their statistical problems.

Technical assistance in financial statistics intensified after 1965. In 1966 and 1967 the Statistics Division sent special missions to Indonesia and to the Syrian Arab Republic. In 1968 the Bureau of Statistics [7] sent missions to Colombia, East Africa (Kenya, Tanzania, and Uganda), Indonesia, Iran, Mali, Mauritania, Portugal, and the Syrian Arab Republic, four of which were labeled as technical assistance missions and lasted from two weeks to two months. Later on, assistance for financial statistics was usually rendered as part of the Fund's regular missions. In 1970, for instance, statistical assistance was given in this way to Afghanistan, Algeria, Costa Rica, Malta, the Syrian Arab Republic, the Yemen Arab Republic, and the People's Democratic Republic of Yemen. In 1971 similar assistance was given to Oman and again to the Yemen Arab Republic, and at the request of the Bank of Spain there was a special visit to Spain to discuss statistical concepts, electronic data processing, and other statistical matters.

New Program for Central Bank Bulletins

After 1968, what is described above was only a relatively small part of the Fund's technical assistance in financial statistics. After a year of planning, the Bureau of Statistics in February 1969 launched a special program to help members to establish or improve their central bank bulletins, or similar bulletins containing basic financial and general economic statistics. This program was set up on the premises (1) that there is a body of interrelated statistics, including data on international reserves, money and banking, government finance, bal-

---

[7] The Statistics Division was separated from the Research and Statistics Department and became the Bureau of Statistics on May 1, 1968.

ances of trade and payments, prices, production, and the national accounts, that are relevant to the analysis of problems of inflation or deflation and the balance of payments deficit and surplus and are very useful for the formulation of financial and monetary policies; and (2) that the assembly and the publication in one place of such statistics are helpful for the authorities of the member concerned, the Fund, and others interested in monetary and payments problems. By concentrating on the publication of bulletins, the Fund's technical assistance work, it was believed, would have continuity and be more assured of success. A bulletin, once established, would be a "living medium."

The program was designed to make use of the staff of the Bureau of Statistics rather than of outside experts. It represented an extension of the regular work of the Bureau in reviewing national bulletins and in sharing with the technicians of member governments the experience of the Bureau's staff in organizing statistics so that data could be made useful for analyzing monetary problems. Over a 12-month period, participating central banks received four staff visits of 2 weeks' duration each; two visits were concerned with money and banking statistics, one with government finance statistics, and one with general statistics. About 20 central banks a year could be assisted, of which 15 would be central banks for which aid was initiated during the year and 5 would be central banks for which assistance had been previously begun.

In the first year of the program, ended early in 1970, 94 visits were made to 26 central banks. In the second year, roughly comparable to the calendar year 1970, 13 staff members from the Bureau of Statistics and, by special arrangement, 2 staff members from the Western Hemisphere Department made a total of 57 visits to 15 central banks. During 1971 the program involved 74 visits to 21 central banks. These visits involved intensive evaluation of existing statistical bulletins and examination of ways in which available data could be improved or new statistics assembled.

From the start of the program early in 1969 until the end of 1971, 48 members received assistance in the compilation and presentation of statistics for central bank bulletins. Several central banks were publishing bulletins where none had existed before, and several were bringing out substantially improved bulletins more frequently than they had before.

The scope of the technical assistance work of the Bureau of Statistics was being broadened as 1971 came to a close. The Bureau of Statistics, in cooperation with the Fiscal Affairs Department, was inaugurating a project for the assembly and eventual publication of government finance statistics, and a Government Finance Statistics Division was being set up in the Bureau of Statistics. The project reflected an increasing concern of the Fund both with government finance statistics and with members' fiscal, as distinct from monetary, policies and was aimed at establishing standard formats designed to produce greater uniformity in the ways in which national government finance statistics could be presented.

GENERAL TECHNICAL ASSISTANCE

Specialized help in central banking, fiscal affairs, and statistics made up what might be termed the Fund's systematic programs of technical assistance: requests were received and filled more or less on a regular basis. In addition, the Fund over the years gave assistance to members asking for help on an ad hoc basis. In 1966–71 members asked and obtained technical assistance from the Fund, for example, to reform exchange rate systems; to simplify exchange control or customs duty procedures; to reduce or eliminate exchange restrictions; to alter interest rate structures; to revise interest rate policies; to evaluate current economic and financial conditions; to revamp monetary policies; to consider national debt problems; to implement stabilization programs; and even to prepare for membership in the Fund. One member requested that a study be made of the feasibility of establishing a local bond market. Another wanted assistance in setting up a small library of the best materials on money and finance.

In response to members' requests, staff personnel frequently made short visits, that is, for a few days, a few weeks, or at most a few months, to give technical advice. In addition, as part of a complex of arrangements between some members and the Fund, usually involving stand-by arrangements, staff representatives were stationed for at least six months but more commonly for a year or two in many member countries as resident representatives or as advisors in other capacities. Many of the long-term residency assignments were carried forward after the lapse of the period originally agreed upon, and the staff representatives initially assigned were replaced by others. Depending on the nature of the request and on the current availability of staff, these short-term technical assistance and long-term residency assignments were filled by staff from the Fund's five Area Departments, the Exchange and Trade Relations Department, the Joint Bank-Fund Library, the Legal Department, and the Research Department. Occasionally, the Administration Department and the Treasurer's Department also provided staff for technical assistance assignments.

Like the Fund's programs of specialized technical assistance, these other forms of technical aid expanded after mid-1960 as did the number of staff representatives stationed in member countries. During the years 1966 through 1971 the countries in which long-term staff representatives resided included many Latin American members (Argentina, Bolivia, Costa Rica, Ecuador, El Salvador, Guatemala, Haiti, Honduras, Nicaragua, Panama, Paraguay, Peru, and Uruguay), several African members (Ghana, Liberia, Mali, Sierra Leone, Somalia, and the Sudan), and several Asian members (Afghanistan, Indonesia, Korea, Laos, and the Philippines). The members receiving short-term technical assistance, other than that described in previous sections of this chapter, included Costa Rica, El Salvador, Ethiopia, Indonesia, Kenya, the Khmer Republic, Laos, Malaysia, Morocco, Nicaragua, Peru, Singapore, Togo, Trinidad and Tobago, and Viet-Nam. Aid was also given to the nonmetropolitan territories of British Honduras and the Netherlands Antilles.

SPECIAL PROGRAM FOR ZAÏRE ENDED

The special program of technical assistance to Zaïre (formerly the Democratic Republic of Congo) with which the Fund had been preoccupied since June 1960 was phased out in 1967 and 1968.[8] Six experts were on duty under this program in the course of 1966, but four of the appointments involved were allowed to expire during the year. Of the remaining two experts under the program, one completed his assignment in June 1967 and the other in February 1968. The Fund then supplied several experts through the Central Banking Service. Experts under the auspices of the Central Banking Service were still on duty in Zaïre at the end of 1971.

GROWTH OF IMF INSTITUTE

The training of officials was another important and growing part of the Fund's assistance to its members in the years 1966–71. This training was carried out through the IMF Institute, with the object of enabling participants in the training programs of the Institute to discharge their responsibilities more effectively after they returned to their home countries.[9] Although the great majority of participants in the Institute's training courses were from developing members, there were also some from industrial members.

As more space in the Fund's headquarters became available to the Institute, it was able to add to the courses offered, to lengthen the duration of courses offered, and to enroll more participants. As the period here reviewed came to a close, the five courses offered each year had been increased to seven, and the number of participants had risen to about 175 a year.

At the end of 1971 the main course offered continued to be that on Financial Analysis and Policy. It was conducted each year for 20 weeks in English, French, and Spanish, in effect constituting three courses. The principal aims of the course were to examine the modern tools used in economic analysis and how they were applied to policy problems; to survey the instruments of monetary, fiscal, and balance of payments policies; and to assess their effectiveness in achieving given policy objectives in various economic circumstances.

---

[8] See *History, 1945–65*, Vol. I, pp. 551–52.

[9] The origin of the IMF Institute in 1964 and the evolution of its program through the fiscal year 1969/70 were described in *History, 1945–65*, Vol. I, pp. 554–55 and 604.

The course was progressively reoriented so as to place more emphasis on experience and practice, particularly on the experience accumulated by the Fund in dealing with developing countries.

The Institute continued also to provide two shorter courses. An 8-week course on Balance of Payments Methodology was held in collaboration with the Balance of Payments Division of the Research Department in English, French, and Spanish, but in only two of the languages in each year. This course concentrated on the balance of payments concepts and definitions used in the Fund's *Balance of Payments Manual* and aimed at assisting members to improve their balance of payments statistics. The sessions took up such questions as the coverage of real and financial assets, the double-entry accounting system, and such fundamentals of balance of payments recording as valuation, timing, and the choice of a unit of account.

The other, a 10-week course on Public Finance, first offered in English in 1967, repeated in 1969 and 1970, and offered in French in 1971, was organized in cooperation with the Fiscal Affairs Department and covered the objectives, instruments, and procedures of public finance, with special attention to the fiscal problems of developing countries. It covered, for instance, the requirements that a tax system should meet; tax administration; the procedures and techniques of budget formulation, execution, and control; and the role of fiscal policy in relation to economic development and stability.

By the end of the fiscal year 1971/72 the IMF Institute, since its inception in 1964, had conducted 40 courses, which were attended by 906 participants from 111 member countries.

During 1971 the Fund purchased outright two apartment buildings adjacent to one another and about half a mile from the headquarters building. The Fund had previously rented one of these buildings on behalf of both the Fund and the World Bank to house participants of the IMF Institute and the Bank's Economic Development Institute. The expanded facilities could house 80 instead of 50 participants. The World Bank continued to rent part of the space from the Fund. Toward the end of 1971 it was decided to renovate the older of the two apartment buildings. The larger instructional space in the Fund's new headquarters, to be opened in a year or two, and the additional housing space would enable the Institute, for the first time, to hold three courses simultaneously. Thus eight courses for approximately 200 participants could be conducted during a given year.

In addition to its regular courses, the Institute provided lectures to other training institutes from time to time. In the years 1966–71 staff members gave lectures, for example, in the training program of the Center for Latin American Monetary Studies (CEMLA) in Mexico City and arranged a program of lectures for CEMLA participants during their visit to Washington. Several staff members gave lectures at the Latin American Institute for Economic and Social Planning in Santiago, Chile; at the African Institute for Economic Development and Planning in courses held in Abidjan, Ivory Coast; Cairo, Egypt; Lomé, Togo; and other African countries; and at the Asian Institute for Economic Development and Planning in Bangkok, Thailand. During the years reviewed here, the IMF Institute also received groups of officials, bankers, professors, and students from member countries, and provided them with lectures and source material.

CHAPTER
29

Further Expansion of Activities

CONSULTATIONS AND TECHNICAL ASSISTANCE were not the only
fields where the Fund's responsibilities and functions grew in 1966–71.
The Fund also became more active with regard to members' payments arrears
and their external indebtedness. In addition, its information activities were
expanded and it extended its relations with other international agencies.

PAYMENTS ARREARS DEFINED AS RESTRICTIONS

Since the days of the Fund's first operations, one of the problems in international finance was that of payments arrears. Such arrears arose from time to
time in a number of member countries as a result of undue delays in payments
and transfers for current international transactions. Some of the delays in
payments which resulted in accumulated arrears were formal ones, specified in
circulars or exchange control regulations. Members faced with weak balance of
payments and reserve positions often introduced, for example, explicit compulsory waiting periods for foreign exchange or let *de facto* waiting periods
develop by failing to make adequate amounts of foreign exchange available.
There were also informal or ad hoc practices that gave rise to payments arrears.
Applicants for exchange might, for instance, be "queued up," with applications
being processed on a first in, first out basis as exchange became available.

For many years the Fund had been concerned with payments arrears,
viewing them as damaging to a member's international financial relations and
creditworthiness, as causing distortions in exchange and trade systems, and as
likely to undermine prevailing exchange rates. The Fund also regarded undue
delay by a member in making foreign exchange available for payments or
transfers for current international transactions as a restriction under Article VIII,
Section 2 (*a*), and under Article XIV, Section 2, of the Articles of Agreement,
and thereby subject to the Fund's review or approval.

591

Nevertheless, in practice, until late in 1970 the emphasis and treatment which payments arrears received in staff reports and in Executive Board decisions varied considerably between members. An Executive Board decision in respect of an Article XIV consultation included a reference to a member's payments arrears if sufficient facts were available. Usually, payments arrears were not treated separately in the decision as a particular restriction, but were approved collectively with other restrictions for a temporary period. Only at times did decisions adopted at the conclusion of Article VIII consultations include payments arrears as one of the practices requiring the Fund's approval. In other instances, no action was taken on payments arrears that were known to exist, with the result that the practice remained unapproved. There were also differences in the Fund's treatment of payments arrears in connection with stand-by arrangements. Some stand-by arrangement documents included specific lines of action for the reduction or elimination of arrears; others referred to arrears but contained no specific performance criteria or policies about them. Differences in the treatment accorded payments arrears in consultation reports and stand-by arrangement documents stemmed partly from insufficient information about the practices in force and partly from doubt about whether particular arrears did in fact result from governmental limitations.

In order to make more uniform the Fund's policies concerning payments arrears, the staff initiated a review in the second half of 1970. The staff believed that the Fund ought to give arrears greater attention. Not only did arrears have a destructive effect on confidence in international payments, but there was also a close interrelation between payments arrears and stand-by arrangements with the Fund. One interrelation with stand-by arrangements was that the Fund made its resources available to strengthen a member's ability to meet its payments obligations, thus enabling the member to avoid arrears. Another interrelation between arrears and stand-by arrangements was that a stand-by arrangement aimed at creating confidence in a member's situation and at quickly restoring new credits by trading partners. Confidence was likely to return more rapidly, thought the staff, if the Fund paid greater attention to the problem of arrears and worked out with members schedules for repayment of arrears.

In October 1970, with Mr. Southard as Acting Chairman, the Executive Board considered specific suggestions made by the staff for payments arrears, whether arising from formal or informal practices, to be treated consistently among members. Most of the Executive Directors supported the codification of rules concerning payments arrears that the staff suggested. However, some members of the Board, including Mr. Escobar (Chile), Mr. Phillips O. (Mexico), Mr. Rajaobelina (Malagasy Republic), and Mr. Williams (Trinidad and Tobago), had certain misgivings. They feared that the policy envisaged would involve some tightening of the Fund's attitude on the use of its resources, particularly in the first credit tranche, the tranche which developing members used heavily after the general decision on stand-by arrangements of September 1968, discussed in Chapter 18. They were, however, assured that the elimination of arrears was not to be made a prerequisite for use of the Fund's resources.

Following this consideration, the Executive Board adopted a decision on October 26, 1970. Undue delays in making foreign exchange available for the settlement of international transactions that gave rise to payments arrears were to be regarded as payments restrictions under Article VIII, Section 2 (*a*), and Article XIV, Section 2, whether the limitations on exchange were formal or informal.[1] Attention was drawn to the harm that these restrictions caused to a country's international financial relationships, and general guidelines for their treatment by the Fund were set forth. These guidelines allowed for the possibility of the Fund's approval of the restriction involved, provided that the member presented a satisfactory program for its elimination. Similarly, when a member having payments arrears requested the Fund's financial assistance, such assistance might be granted if the member's financial program, inter alia, envisaged a phasing out of the arrears.

GREATER CONCERN WITH EXTERNAL DEBT SERVICE

In the mid-1960s the staff began to attend a number of meetings between creditor and debtor countries, especially as the World Bank stepped up its efforts to arrange formal meetings of this type. The Annual Reports for 1964 and 1965 also contained passages dealing with external indebtedness.[2] After 1965 the subject of the external debt of developing members received much more of the Fund's attention.

Governors' Interest

Increasing recognition of the problem of servicing of external debt by developing countries was reflected in the speeches at the Twenty-First Annual Meeting, held in Washington in September 1966. Mr. Jamshid Amouzegar (Iran), the Chairman, observed that more than half the inflow of development finance was being offset by debt servicing, and Mr. Schweitzer similarly noted that the debt servicing burden of developing countries had grown heavier.[3] The problem was emphasized as well by Mr. Se Ryun Kim (Korea), Mr. Antonio Ortiz Mena (Mexico), Mr. Tan (Malaysia), and Mr. Abdullah Yaftaly (Afghanistan).[4]

---

[1] E.B. Decision No. 3153-(70/95), October 26, 1970; Vol. II below, pp. 214–15.

[2] See *History, 1945–65*, Vol. I, pp. 553–54.

[3] Address by the Chairman of the Boards of Governors and Opening Address by the Managing Director, *Summary Proceedings, 1966*, pp. 5 and 17.

[4] Statements by the Alternate Governor of the Fund and the World Bank for Korea, the Governors of the Fund and the World Bank for Mexico and Malaysia, and the Governor of the World Bank for Afghanistan, *Summary Proceedings, 1966*, pp. 76, 125–26, 26, and 66–67.

By the time of the Twenty-Second Annual Meeting, in September 1967 in Rio de Janeiro, the problem had become "critical—even dangerous," according to Mr. Kåre Willoch (Norway), Chairman of the opening session.[5] Mr. Smole (Yugoslavia) stressed that the debt repayment problems threatened to nullify the net transfer of capital to the affected countries, and Mr. A. A. Atta (Nigeria), Mr. Abdalla Siddig Ghandour (Sudan), Mr. Abdul Rahman Al Habeeb (Iraq), Mr. N. M. Uquaili (Pakistan), and Mr. J. Milton Weeks (Liberia), among others, also addressed themselves to the problem.[6] Mr. Horowitz (Israel) was concerned, for example, that what he called the "zero hour of equilibrium between capital flow and redemption" was only a few years away.[7]

That the creditor nations recognized the seriousness of the situation was apparent in the remarks of some Governors at the next Annual Meeting, the Twenty-Third, held in Washington from September 30 to October 4, 1968. Both Mr. Gunnar Sträng (Sweden) and Mr. Witteveen (Netherlands) made suggestions for dealing with debt servicing.[8]

Many references to debt burden and servicing problems were made at the 1969 Annual Meeting. The fifth general review of quotas was then under way, and Mr. Zeev Sharef (Israel) went so far as to suggest that the increasing influence of debt service, including retirement of debt, on the balance of payments of developing countries ought to be taken into account in fixing quotas of developing members. His reasoning was that, because developing countries had to devote an increasing share of their export earnings and capital imports to foreign debt service, the part of their reserves which could be used for financing cyclical or temporary contractions in their export earnings was limited.[9]

New Efforts by the Fund

It was in this environment that the Fund intensified its efforts to help developing members with problems associated with their external indebtedness.

In October and November 1967, in order to assess what more the Fund might do in the field of external debt, the Executive Board reviewed the problems of managing external debt that members had been encountering. This review

---

[5] Address by the Chairman of the Boards of Governors of the World Bank, IFC, and IDA, *Summary Proceedings, 1967*, p. 6.

[6] Statements by the Governors of the World Bank for Yugoslavia, Nigeria, the Sudan, Iraq, and Pakistan, and the Governor of the Fund and the World Bank for Liberia, *Summary Proceedings, 1967*, pp. 76, 192–93, 206, 87, 202, and 200.

[7] Statement by the Governor of the World Bank for Israel, *Summary Proceedings, 1967*, p. 105.

[8] Statements by the Governors of the World Bank for Sweden and the Netherlands, *Summary Proceedings, 1968*, pp. 169 and 187.

[9] Statement by the Governor of the Fund for Israel, *Summary Proceedings, 1969*, pp. 243–44.

included examination of the Fund's experience with limitations on external indebtedness that had been incorporated into a number of the stabilization programs associated with stand-by arrangements approved by the Fund. The Executive Directors, as well as the management and the staff, considered external indebtedness to be one of the most sensitive areas of international finance, and were therefore resolved to proceed with the utmost caution. After its review, the Board agreed that discussions pursuant to annual consultations should cover external debt positions and policies and that the information obtained should be included in the staff's reports. It further agreed that the Fund should continue its past collaboration with other international agencies, such as the World Bank, the Development Assistance Committee of the OECD, the UNCTAD, and the Committee on the Alliance for Progress of the Organization of American States (CIAP), that were also concerning themselves with problems of foreign indebtedness.

In the next several years these policies were implemented. In its consultations the Fund indicated to members the usefulness of central registration of their external indebtedness and of careful assessment of the effects of different levels of external debt on their balances of payments. Many members evolved policies for managing their external debt. In consultations with those members having potentially serious debt problems, the Fund cautioned against the incurrence of further net foreign indebtedness.

At the request of the creditor and debtor countries involved, the staff continued, as it had since 1959, also to participate in multilateral debt renegotiation meetings. These were meetings with creditors on behalf of certain debtor members called under the auspices of ad hoc groupings and usually chaired by representatives of one of the main creditor governments. The negotiations aimed at rearranging the terms of repayment for certain categories of external debt or at refinancing or consolidating some of the external debt involved.

By the end of 1971 there had been 17 multilateral debt renegotiations on behalf of eight countries. Seven renegotiations on behalf of four countries— Argentina, Brazil, Chile, and Turkey—had transpired before the end of 1965. In the six years 1966–71 there were a further 10 debt renegotiations on behalf of another four countries. There were 3 renegotiations, in 1966, 1968, and 1970, on behalf of Ghana; 4 in 1966, 1967, 1968, and 1970, on behalf of Indonesia; 1 in 1968, on behalf of India; and 2 in 1968 and 1969, on behalf of Peru. As these figures indicate, the external debts of most of these eight debtor nations were renegotiated a number of times.

The Fund staff participated as observers and advisors in all of the multilateral debt renegotiations. A principal task of the staff was to prepare an analysis of the economic position and prospects of the debtor country. In some instances, the staff was requested to assess the economic consequences of various renegotiation proposals submitted to a meeting by the creditors and the debtor;

and, when agreed by the creditors and the debtor, the staff at times prepared reports on the status of the various bilateral debt agreements and the evolution of the country's debt position.

Another important part of the Fund's action in regard to external indebtedness was the working out with several developing members of provisions in their financial stabilization programs dealing with indebtedness. Limits on medium-term external indebtedness were included in many financial stabilization programs, either as performance criteria or as statements of policy.

Review of Policies

After three years of implementing these policies, the Fund in the course of 1971 undertook to review its experience in working with members on the management of their external indebtedness and with multilateral debt renegotiations. The timing of this review was geared in part to a request by the CIAP that the Fund join with other international institutions in a program of debt service studies.

The review included an assessment in April of the use of limitations on foreign debt as performance criteria in stand-by arrangements. The staff concluded that such limitations had been useful, but that they had to be precisely defined and easy to control. The staff further concluded that just how restrictive limitations on debt specified in stand-by arrangements should be should depend very much on the particular situation of the member: only in the most serious situations should it be necessary to ask a member to prohibit the authorization of a given category of new indebtedness.

The Executive Directors generally concurred with the staff's conclusions, but they debated the guidelines that the Fund ought to use in setting debt limits. The existing practice was that debt limitations were set in terms of the amounts of new debt obligations of specified maturities that could be incurred. They considered whether limitations should be set instead in terms of maximum annual debt service payments. And they discussed the length of maturities that should be restricted. Mr. Massad (Chile) pleaded for flexibility in the Fund's policies in regard to external indebtedness, saying that the Fund had to heed the close relationship between the contracting of foreign debt and the rate of economic development. In general, it was agreed that the existing policies would be continued.

In August 1971, just before the Annual Meeting, the staff appraised the experience of the Fund's members with multilateral debt renegotiations, in conjunction with a study by the World Bank on the same subject, also done at the request of the CIAP. In November, after the Annual Meeting, the Executive Directors discussed the staff's study. They agreed with the conclusion that the debt renegotiation exercises had achieved the desired objectives of providing a substantial amount of balance of payments relief to the debtor countries concerned and of helping to prevent an undue retardation of capital flows from developed to developing countries. The direct balance of payments impact of debt renegotiations had been significant, and multilateral debt renegotiations had helped debtor countries to reorient their economic policies.

The general staff study on multilateral debt renegotiations was sent to the CIAP and to the World Bank and the OECD, along with special studies that the staff prepared on the debt service of ten members (Argentina, Brazil, Chile, Colombia, Ghana, India, Indonesia, Korea, Peru, and Turkey).

EXTERNAL DEBT OF GHANA

Inasmuch as the external debt renegotiation exercises represented a major effort by the Fund staff (as well as by the staff of the World Bank) over a number of years, it is worthwhile to elaborate on what was involved and what was accomplished. Ghana has been selected as illustrative.

On February 24, 1966 a new Government superseded the Government of Kwame Nkrumah, which had been in power since Ghana gained its independence in March 1957. The new Government faced a number of difficult problems that had resulted from the development strategy of the Nkrumah Government combined with a gradual decline after mid-1958 in world prices for cocoa, Ghana's main export. Development policy from 1960 to 1966 had focused on the simultaneous achievement of rapid industrialization, increased agricultural productivity, and higher employment. The economic policies pursued, plus the low prices for cocoa, found Ghana at the end of 1965 with a declining rate of growth of real gross domestic product, sizable investments in numerous large projects of questionable economic merit and with long gestation periods, a depletion of Ghana's once-large foreign exchange reserves, and an external indebtedness far in excess of what Ghana's economic size or structure warranted. Debt service payments were putting a severe strain on the balance of payments, and certain payments were already in arrears. Confidence both at home and abroad had been seriously undermined.

Almost immediately the new Government embarked on a fundamental reorientation of economic policy and began to introduce economic reforms. Many of the monetary and financial measures taken were worked out closely with the Fund, and in May 1966 the Fund approved a stand-by arrangement for Ghana and in July 1966 assigned a resident representative.[10]

---

[10] Among the economic reforms that the new Government effected were the introduction in February 1967 of a new cedi and a devaluation of that cedi in July 1967, actions that have already been described in Chap. 23.

Meetings on External Debt

Among other measures, the new Government that took power in February 1966 announced that it would honor Ghana's obligations with regard to external debt. However, in June 1966 debt repayments were temporarily suspended after the Government asked for a rescheduling of payments on Ghana's medium-term debt. Responding to this request, representatives of several major Western creditor countries met with representatives of Ghana in four meetings held in London between June and December 1966, under the chairmanship of the United Kingdom. These creditor countries were Australia, Belgium, Canada, France, the Federal Republic of Germany, Israel, Italy, Japan, the Netherlands, Norway, Spain, Switzerland, the United Kingdom, and the United States. Members of the Fund staff were present at these meetings, as were members of the staff of the World Bank. The Fund staff assisted in the preparation of documents for the meetings.

The discussions were confined to a rescheduling of repayments on credits or loans provided by the Governments of the creditor countries to the Government of Ghana or to persons or corporations resident in Ghana; only credits granted or insured by the Governments or the competent institutions of the creditor countries were under consideration. Debt relief was limited to credits with an original maturity of more than 1 year but not exceeding 12 years and arising under, or relating to, contracts for the supply of goods or services, or both, from outside Ghana, concluded before February 24, 1966. The terms of this first rescheduling, which covered 80 per cent of the payments for interest and principal due during the consolidation period on insured suppliers' credits, included a consolidation period of $2\frac{1}{2}$ years (until December 31, 1968), a grace period following the consolidation period of $2\frac{1}{2}$ years, and a repayment period of 8 years. In other words, there was a "stretch-out" of 13 years. Interest rates during the moratorium, averaging 6 per cent, were comparable to interest rates prevailing commercially at the time.

In accordance with what was also agreed in the 1966 meetings, the Government of Ghana requested the Government of the United Kingdom to convene another meeting in 1968 to consider a further rearrangement of Ghana's external debt. Two meetings held in London in July and October 1968 under the chairmanship of the United Kingdom focused on a rearrangement of service payments on suppliers' credits due after December 31, 1968, the end of the 1966 consolidation period. The terms and the coverage of the 1968 rescheduling were, with some exceptions, similar to those of the 1966 arrangement.

The result of the two reschedulings was to reduce debt service on suppliers' credits in the years 1967 through 1970 to about one third of the amounts due under the original schedules and to avert the possibility of technical default. Relief was extended only for a rather limited period of time, however; substantial payments would still fall due in the early 1970s. The short-term nature of the arrangement was justified on the grounds that it would give the creditors an early opportunity to re-examine Ghana's performance. Creditor countries wished to be assured that Ghana would pursue policies compatible with the objective of restoring internal and external economic stability.

Ghana's stand-by arrangements with the Fund, involving among other things limitations on new borrowing, provided the basis for such assurances. But the Fund did more than authorize stand-by arrangements and participate in the debt renegotiation meetings. In order to help to increase the flow of resources to Ghana, the Fund in 1967 began to sponsor meetings, the basic purpose of which was to provide a multilateral framework for extending balance of payments assistance to Ghana. Because these aid meetings were an innovation for the Fund, they are described in a separate subsection below.

The debt relief that was arranged was an essential element in Ghana's stabilization efforts from 1967 through 1969. Progress toward financial and economic stability slowed the rate of increase in domestic prices and the balance of payments developed favorably, partly because the inflow of grants and long-term official capital recovered. Economic growth in real terms was resumed, although at a rather slow rate. Very few new suppliers' credits were contracted and arrears of profits and dividends were systematically reduced.

Nevertheless, by early 1970 projections of Ghana's debt service showed that repayments of principal and interest on suppliers' credits were likely to reach a peak in 1972 and would continue to be fairly large through 1978. The Ghanaian authorities believed that the earlier debt rearrangements, while affording immediate and sizable relief, had the defect of not being based on a realistic appreciation of Ghana's balance of payments problem, and of providing a short-term solution to a long-term problem. In their opinion, the burden of debt repayment presented an insuperable obstacle to the economic development of the country; there was talk among some economists and experts that, perhaps, the Government of Ghana should not have announced that it would honor the debt that had accumulated before 1966. The Government requested that another meeting between creditor nations and Ghana be convened, possibly to arrange a long-term refinancing loan at a low interest rate from the creditor nations.

Accordingly, a Ghana debt conference was held in London, again under the chairmanship of the United Kingdom, in May and July 1970. Relief equivalent to half the principal and interest falling due in the two years from July 1970 to July 1972 was worked out. Thus, as 1971 ended, the Ghanaian authorities were still struggling with large external debt problems. But it had been agreed that a further review of the situation in the longer term should be undertaken before mid-1972 to consider, in the light of the circumstances then prevailing, what additional measures might be required. The Fund and the World Bank were to be invited to assist countries participating in this further conference and to prepare documentation for it.

The Fund Chairs Ghana Aid Meetings

During the meetings on external debt in 1966, Ghana's representatives raised the question of whether the external debt problems ought not to be considered in conjunction with what other external aid Ghana might receive, particularly financial assistance for balance of payments support. Representatives of creditor countries had accepted the view that debt consolidation could meet only part of Ghana's balance of payments problem; hence, Ghana had a balance of payments problem wider than that of debt servicing.

Early in 1967 Ghana submitted an aide-mémoire to the representatives in Accra of potential donor countries, proposing a meeting under the chairmanship of the Fund to discuss Ghana's aid requirements for 1967, and requested the Fund to have such a meeting. After having ascertained that such a role for the Fund would be agreeable to the countries concerned, the Fund issued invitations for a meeting in Paris in April 1967. Fund staff chaired the meeting and assisted in preparing documents. World Bank staff participated in the meeting and collaborated in the preparations for it.

The meeting was considered satisfactory, and a follow-up meeting was held in Accra in September 1967, again convened and chaired by the Fund with the collaboration of the World Bank. A third meeting was held in Paris in February 1968, and a fourth, also in Paris, in May 1969. Participating in these meetings, in addition to the Fund, the World Bank, and Ghana, were Canada, Denmark, France, the Federal Republic of Germany, Italy, Japan, the Netherlands, Norway, Switzerland, the United Kingdom, the United States, the Development Assistance Committee of the OECD, and the United Nations Development Program.

The underlying assumption of the meetings was that a continuing dialogue among countries, both aid-giving and aid-receiving, and international institutions, which served them both, were beneficial to all concerned. The Fund, for the first time, provided the forum and the facilities for carrying out such a dialogue. Subsequently, the World Bank took over this responsibility, organizing a Consultative Group for Ghana, which held its first meeting in London in mid-1970, and Ghana pursued bilateral discussions with donor countries concerning its aid requirements.

EXTERNAL DEBT: A LONG-TERM PROBLEM

The external indebtedness of developing members remained a long-run and basic problem. Mr. Morales Bermúdez (Peru) observed at the Twenty-Fifth Annual Meeting, held in Copenhagen in September 1970, that debt refinancing had brought his country only temporary respite. He considered the difficulty of external debt of developing countries a basic one stemming from the way in which international economic relations were conducted. He stated that "commercial relations, the process of investment and loans, and the application of orthodox rules of economic policy are continuing to cause our countries serious harm through 'external dependence,' converting us into net exporters of capital." He foresaw as the result the destruction of most of the Latin American monetary systems.[11]

As interest rates and the cost of borrowing rose still further, countries that had not previously encountered serious debt servicing problems were beginning to fear them, a point brought out also at the 1970 Annual Meeting by Mr. Kibaki (Kenya).[12]

The problems of developing countries, including the problems of debt servicing, were of major concern to Mr. Schweitzer. At the 1971 Annual Meeting he drew special attention to the consequences for developing countries of the crisis in international monetary affairs that had occurred after the suspension of official convertibility by the United States six weeks before. He used these words to sum up the several problems facing developing countries:

> Inflation and balance of payments difficulties in the industrial world during recent years led to higher costs and restricted availability of international credit and to sluggishness in the flow of official capital and aid at a time when developing countries were faced with a rising burden of external debt. The present exchange rate uncertainties add a new and serious impediment to the development efforts of these countries, which also must contend with the effects of the U.S. import surcharge and the cuts in U.S. aid. All this is not an auspicious beginning for the Second Development Decade, when developing countries have the task of finding new avenues of productive employment for their growing populations.[13]

THE FUND AS A CENTER FOR INFORMATION

During the years described in this history there was also an expansion of the Fund's activities in the fields of information and publication.

Information to Members

In this regard, the Fund's primary responsibility continued to be to report to its members on a wide range of economic and financial topics. The Fund supplied members, for example, with information relevant to all its decisions and operations. The information given to members took the form mainly of

---

[11] Statement by the Governor of the World Bank for Peru, *Summary Proceedings, 1970*, pp. 111–12.

[12] Statement by the Governor of the Fund and the World Bank for Kenya, *Summary Proceedings, 1970*, p. 140.

[13] Opening Address by the Managing Director, *Summary Proceedings, 1971*, p. 13.

detailed minutes of meetings of the Executive Board, of hundreds of reports and studies prepared by the staff, and of a great deal of statistical and factual material gathered from member governments. This information was necessarily confidential and was customarily dispatched by the Executive Directors to the authorities in the countries that elected or appointed them.

In the years 1966–71 there was a very marked increase in the flow of documents to member governments. In part, the increase was a reflection of the growth of membership and of the expansion of the whole range of the Fund's activities. But in addition, the Fund had become a central source of information on economic and financial conditions in member countries. For their assessments of the economic situations in different countries, member governments relied more than ever on the Fund's consultation reports, particularly the background reports for the annual consultations, entitled "Recent Economic Developments" and referred to informally as RED reports.[14] Usually over 100 pages long, these reports contained considerable information that members found useful in connection with their foreign aid programs, their studies of commodities, and their work on debt relief. By 1971, Executive Directors were requesting as many as 500 copies of RED reports for transmittal to member governments. As we shall see in the next two sections, requests from international organizations for these reports also increased.

Publications

From the inception of the Fund, the Executive Board emphasized the need for confidentiality of the Fund's consultations with members and of the Fund's documents as a prime requirement of good relations with member governments. At the same time, they recognized that the general public was entitled to a regular accounting of the Fund's resources and their use, and they placed emphasis on the desirability of a better understanding of the Fund's activities among government officials, bankers, businessmen, professors, students, and others. Therefore, under policies and procedures developed by the Executive Board and the management, the Fund made public over the years a great deal of information about what it was doing and about subjects closely related to its work.

Press releases were issued following the Fund's transactions and other important decisions of the Executive Board. A monthly newsletter called the "IMF Memorandum," in English, French, German, and Spanish, was distributed to financial writers throughout the Fund's membership. A broad range of publications (formal reports and documents, proceedings of meetings, staff studies, periodicals, books, pamphlets, and leaflets) explaining the Fund's actions was made available. Some of these publications, such as *International Financial Statistics* (*IFS*), were the by-products of the Fund's regular work. In other

---

[14] See Chap. 28 above, pp. 576–77.

instances, as with the *Annual Report on Exchange Restrictions*, the Fund chose to publish information that the Articles of Agreement required it to report on to members in one or another form.

A list of the publications that the Fund had made available from its inception through December 31, 1968 was given in the earlier history.[15] Several of the Fund's publications—such as the Annual Reports of the Executive Directors, the Summary Proceedings of the Annual Meetings, the Annual Reports on Exchange Restrictions, reports of the Executive Board on primary product prices and on exchange rates, and an amended Articles of Agreement—have been mentioned in previous chapters. Some are reproduced, in whole or in part, in Volume II of this history. In 1972, for the first time, the Fund published a *Catalogue of Publications, 1946–71*.[16]

During the years reviewed here there was also an interesting change in the techniques used for preparing publications, especially those of a statistical nature. Following the establishment by the Fund and the World Bank of a Joint Computer Center in 1968, the Bureau of Statistics built up a Data Fund, an electronically operated data bank system. Thousands of statistical time series for international trade, prices, reserves, banking, and money supply—the data used in *IFS* and *Direction of Trade* (*DOT*)—were transcribed onto magnetic tapes which were stored for use on high-speed computers. The Data Fund, of course, facilitated the Fund's research, as it became possible to rearrange the large mass of *IFS* data easily and neatly in alternative forms, such as ratios, percentages, indices, or charts, and to make comparisons of different economic indicators, either within a country or between countries, quickly and accurately. But it also transformed the publication of *IFS* and *DOT* because the copying and reconciling of figures previously done by hand were eliminated.

In order to report on its activities more fully, especially in the context of other international monetary developments, the Fund during 1971 planned a new publication, a semimonthly, to be called the *IMF Survey* to replace the *International Financial News Survey* (*IFNS*).[17]

Increased Flow of Information

The discussions that culminated in the creation of SDRs and recurrent crises in exchange and gold markets led to an intensified interest in all phases of the Fund's work. According to a UN report, the Fund was mentioned more frequently in the late 1960s in the daily press than were most other international organizations. At the 1971 Annual Meeting, more than 640 financial writers, newsmen, and television commentators covered the proceedings.

---

[15] *History, 1945–65*, Vol. I, pp. 555–57, and Vol. III, pp. 545–59.

[16] Vol. II of this history also contains a list of the publications of the Fund for the years 1966–71; see pp. 335–39 of that volume.

[17] *IFNS* ceased publication in June 1972 and the first issue of the *IMF Survey* appeared in August 1972.

As a consequence of these developments, the Fund stepped up appreciably its informational activities and other public contacts. In the six years ended December 31, 1971, the number of press releases issued averaged more than one a week, double the rate in the preceding two decades. The Fund continued all of its series of publications, published several books, reports, and pamphlets, and published more of them in French, German, and Spanish. Material contained in the Fund's publications was cited, or even reproduced, more and more frequently as the Fund became the authoritative source of information on international financial and monetary topics.

Personal appearances became another regular part of the Fund's activities. In the years described in this volume, Mr. Schweitzer became a familiar figure as he traveled to all regions of the globe, representing the Fund at numerous financial meetings and accepting many speaking engagements. He also maintained communication with the press through numerous off-the-record interviews and general press conferences, and made several televised appearances. Mr. Southard and senior staff officials likewise undertook many speaking engagements and represented the Fund at international meetings. Information through personal contact was increased in other ways as well. A number of seminars were organized for university professors and outside economists. And the Information Office kept its doors open to outside inquiries and nonofficial visitors, often informally briefing newsmen and representatives of other communications media about the Fund.

Not only was the Fund to an increasing extent a center for dispensing information to the outside world, as it were, but the need for the Executive Directors and the staff to keep closely informed of important new developments taking place externally and of trends of opinion in the Fund's fields of interest also became much greater than in earlier years. For this purpose, periodicals from all over the world were sifted and reports from news-gathering associations were rapidly disseminated throughout the Fund.

As the year 1971 came to a close, interest in the Fund's affairs was being stimulated even further by the start of discussions, at the highest political levels, to reform the world monetary system. Moreover, the topics being discussed were becoming increasingly technical. It was evident, therefore, that the Fund's informational activities would continue to expand.

RELATIONS WITH UN, GATT, AND OECD

At several points in previous chapters, mention has been made of the Fund's relations with special groups that were working on international monetary issues, such as the Group of Ten and the Group of Seventy-Seven, and with global, regional, and subregional organizations in the economic and financial field, such as the World Bank, the OECD, the UNCTAD, the CIAP, and the

FAO. As the world became more closely knit, liaison with other groups and organizations in the economic field became an essential part of the Fund's work. The Fund enhanced its cooperation with other groups partly in the belief that its competence in areas where it had primary concern or jurisdiction could help to serve the broader informational needs of many organizations, and partly because the Fund, in return, would gain greater insight into members' interests and problems. This cooperation also sought to avoid duplication of effort on the part both of organizations and of government officials.

The Fund's representatives participated in meetings at all levels—plenary sessions, committee meetings, and working groups—of a growing number of organizations, and representatives of more organizations came to the Annual Meetings of the Board of Governors, which continued to be held jointly with the Board of Governors of the World Bank. In addition, the exchange of documents and information between the Fund and other organizations and the number of informal staff contacts expanded steadily.

UN Family

As a specialized agency of the United Nations, the Fund had always had close relations with that body and a staff member served as Special Representative to the United Nations. The Managing Director continued to make his annual address to the Economic and Social Council (Ecosoc), presenting the Fund's Annual Report. It was usual for a number of Executive Directors and senior staff to attend plenary sessions of the Ecosoc. The Managing Director or the Deputy Managing Director participated in meetings of the Administrative Committee on Coordination (ACC). In 1966 Mr. Schweitzer also attended the first session of the Interagency Consultative Board of the newly established United Nations Development Program (UNDP), which was held in New York, and in July 1968 he went to the first joint meeting of the ACC and the Committee for Program and Coordination, in Bucharest. In 1969, 1970, and 1971 he also attended such joint meetings. Mr. Southard represented the Fund at the twenty-fifth anniversary meeting of the United Nations in New York on October 24, 1970.

Other staff members represented the Fund in preliminary meetings and subcommittee activities of the ACC; at the General Assembly; at the Committee for Development Planning of the Ecosoc; at the first session of the Industrial Development Board; and at the Governing Council of the UNDP, including the special meetings in 1969 to consider the report by Sir Robert Jackson on the capacity of the development system of the United Nations.[18]

The Fund staff continued to attend the meetings of the various regional economic commissions of the United Nations—the Economic Commissions for Africa (ECA), Asia and the Far East (ECAFE), Europe (ECE), and Latin America

---

[18] United Nations, *A Study of the Capacity of the United Nations Development System* (Geneva, 1969), 2 vols.

(ECLA)—and to go to working party and committee meetings of these commissions. A few details illustrate the extent to which the Fund participated. In the fiscal year 1966/67, for example, observers were sent to the Sub-Regional Meeting on Economic Cooperation in West Africa at Niamey, and to the Tenth Session of the Working Party on Economic Development Planning and its Fourth Workshop on Problems of Budget Classification and Management in Countries of the ECAFE Region, both of which were held in Bangkok. In the fiscal year 1969/70, the Fund was represented at meetings of the Committee on the Development of Trade of the ECE, the Committee of Trade of the ECAFE, and the Committee of the Whole of the ECLA, and at an informal meeting of the ECAFE on regional payments and trade liberalization. In 1970/71 Fund representatives participated in two Extraordinary Meetings of the Committee of the Whole of the ECLA, held in New York, the first to review the work of the ECLA and the second to review the situation in Peru following a disastrous earthquake. In that year, too, staff members attended the meeting of Government and Central Bank Officials on Regional Trade and Monetary Cooperation of the ECAFE, in Bangkok, and the Ad Hoc Meeting on Methods for International Trade Projections of the ECE, in Geneva.

From time to time the staff attended meetings of ad hoc groups that were assembled by the United Nations to consider specialized topics. These meetings included, for instance, those of a Committee of Experts on Development Planning, an Inter-Regional Seminar on the Planning of the Foreign Trade Sector, an expert group on the measurement of capital flow to the developing countries, an Inter-Regional Seminar on Government Accounting and Financial Management, and a Round Table on Export Credits. The staff also participated in the Fourth Session of the Commission on International Trade Law, held in Geneva.

The agency of the United Nations with which the Fund has had a virtually continuous relationship was the UNCTAD. In fact, it was primarily in order to maintain close relations with the UNCTAD and with the GATT that an office was set up in Geneva in 1965.[19] Thereafter, the Fund was represented at numerous meetings of the regular committees and of special groups of the UNCTAD, both in Geneva and in New York. Of particular interest to the Fund was the Committee on Invisibles and Financing Related to Trade, the Expert Group on International Monetary Issues (discussed above in Chapter 4), the Intergovernmental Group on Supplementary Financing, the Special Committee on Preferences, and the UNCTAD Intergovernmental Group on Trade Expansion, Economic Cooperation, and Regional Integration Among Developing Countries. By 1971, keeping in touch with the work of the UNCTAD absorbed the full-time services of one staff member of the Fund's Office in Geneva.

The Fund sent staff not only from its Geneva office but also from headquarters to sessions in 1967 and 1969 of the United Nations Trade and Develop-

---

[19] *History, 1945–65,* Vol. I, pp. 559–60.

ment Board (the permanent organ of the UNCTAD), and to the Second Session of the UNCTAD in New Delhi in February and March 1968. In addition, prior to the 1968 UNCTAD Conference, a mission representing a group of developing countries (the Group of Seventy-Seven) met with the Managing Director and members of the staff in Washington in December 1967 and presented for information the "Charter of Algiers," which contained the developing countries' program for action at the forthcoming Conference. Later on, in response to Decision 29 (II) adopted by the UNCTAD at its Second Session, the staff prepared a study entitled "The Use of Commercial Credits by Developing Countries for Financing Imports of Capital Goods," which was transmitted to the Secretary-General of the UNCTAD on January 16, 1970.[20]

GATT and OECD

During the years reviewed here the Fund continued to have close relations both with the CONTRACTING PARTIES to the General Agreement on Tariffs and Trade (GATT) in Geneva and with the Organization for Economic Cooperation and Development (OECD) in Paris.[21]

As in the past, the Fund's representatives attended the General Sessions of the GATT, as well as the consultations held by the Committee on Balance of Payments Restrictions with regard to import restrictions, import deposit requirements, and import surcharges imposed for balance of payments reasons. In the six years ended 1971 the Fund was represented at GATT consultations with many countries, including Brazil, Ceylon, Chile, Ghana, Finland, Greece, Iceland, India, Indonesia, Israel, Korea, New Zealand, Pakistan, Peru, South Africa, Spain, Tunisia, Turkey, the United Arab Republic, Uruguay, and Yugoslavia. And the Fund staff participated in a working party on the United Kingdom's import deposit scheme.

For countries consulting with the GATT on restrictions imposed for balance of payments reasons, in accordance with arrangements that had been worked out years before, the Fund supplied the GATT with copies of the Fund's consultation reports (not only the RED reports but also the staff's report on its discussions with member officials). It also sent to the GATT the decisions reached by the Executive Board at the conclusion of Article XIV consultations.

The staff attended a number of other meetings of subsidiary bodies of the GATT, such as those of the Council of Representatives and the Committees on

---

[20] In 1972 the Fund's relations with the UNCTAD became closer still. The Group of Twenty-Four had emerged as the "financial arm" of the Group of Seventy-Seven, and Mr. Schweitzer participated in the ministerial meeting of the Group of Twenty-Four in Caracas on April 6 and 7, 1972. In addition, Mr. Schweitzer addressed the Third UNCTAD Conference in Santiago on April 25, 1972.

[21] For background on the Fund's relations with these organizations, see *History, 1945–65*, Vol. II, Chaps. 15 and 16. For further discussion of the Fund's relations with the GATT, see Edgar Jones, "The Fund and the GATT," *Finance and Development*, Vol. 9, September 1972, pp. 30–33.

Trade in Industrial Products and Agriculture, and the Working Party on Border Tax Adjustments. Most of the meetings of the GATT were attended by the staff of the Fund's Office in Geneva; GATT affairs came to absorb the full-time services of one staff member in that office. At times, staff members from headquarters went to Geneva to attend particular meetings of the GATT.

The Fund had active working relations with the OECD, mainly through its Office in Europe (Paris). In addition to joint activities mentioned elsewhere in this volume, the Fund was invited to attend the annual meetings of the Ministerial Council and the meetings of the Executive Committee in special session. Mr. Schweitzer attended meetings at the ministerial level. Staff members, designated as representatives of the Managing Director rather than of the Fund, attended the meetings of a number of the committees of the OECD. Most notable were the Economic Policy Committee and its Working Party 3 (discussed in particular in Part One above), the Economic and Development Review Committee, the Board of Management of the European Monetary Agreement, and the Development Assistance Committee (DAC) including its several working parties.

During the years reviewed here the Fund continued to supply the OECD with copies of its consultation reports, including the staff reports (formerly called Part I), on countries that were members of the OECD. The staff attended meetings of a Special Group on Trade with Developing Countries set up by the DAC to consider the special tariff treatment that developing countries might receive in the markets of developed countries, and participated for several years with the OECD in a study on the improvement of capital markets and a study on a code of liberalization for capital movements.

RELATIONS WITH OTHER ORGANIZATIONS

The Fund maintained close ties with the Bank for International Settlements (BIS), in Basle, principally by means of frequent informal discussions between the Managing Director and BIS officials.

The Fund's Office in Europe (Paris) maintained close contacts with the European Economic Community in Brussels, the European Investment Bank in Luxembourg, and the Council of Europe in Strasbourg, and with some nongovernmental organizations, such as the International Chamber of Commerce and the International Confederation of Free Trade Unions.

Among the organizations composed of Caribbean and Latin American countries, the Fund's relations with the Organization of American States (OAS) and its Committee on the Alliance for Progress (CIAP) were probably the most continuous. During the years reviewed here the Fund's representatives, for example, in 1966 went to the fourth annual meetings of the Inter-American

Economic and Social Council (IA-Ecosoc) in Buenos Aires at the expert and the ministerial levels, as well as the seventh meeting of the CIAP that preceded them. In February 1967 members of the staff attended the Third Special Inter-American Conference of the OAS, also in Buenos Aires, which was preceded by an extraordinary meeting of the IA-Ecosoc at the ministerial level. In June 1967 staff representatives went to the fifth annual IA-Ecosoc meeting in Viña del Mar, Chile, and in June 1969 and February 1970, to the next annual meetings of the IA-Ecosoc at the expert and ministerial levels. The Fund's representatives also regularly attended special meetings of the CIAP. Among other activities, they, as in previous years, participated informally in an advisory capacity in a series of interagency meetings arranged by the CIAP secretariat. And, of course, the external debt studies discussed above were at the request of the CIAP.

There were any number of contacts between the staff and other Latin American organizations. The Fund customarily sent representatives, for example, to the annual meetings of the Board of Governors of the Inter-American Development Bank (IDB), to meetings of Central Banking Experts of the American Continent, to meetings of the Central American Monetary Council, and to meetings of the Center for Latin American Monetary Studies (CEMLA). The Fund was represented at the inaugural meeting of the Caribbean Development Bank in January 1970. Fund staff went to the First Subregional (Andean Area) Meeting of the Latin American Association of Development Financing Institutions, in Lima, and then to the first and second meetings of Central Banks of Signatory States of the Andean Subregional Integration Agreement, in Quito in June 1970 and in La Paz in November 1971. On March 1, 1971 the Managing Director attended a special meeting in Buenos Aires of the IDB on the occasion of the installation of a new president of that organization.

In 1969 and 1970 the staff went to meetings of the Inter-American Center of Tax Administrators (CIAT), and participated in a CIAT workshop on the use of automatic data processing in tax administration. A joint study by the Fund staff and the executive secretariat of the Central American Monetary Council on the state of economic integration within the Central American Common Market was undertaken as well.

There was a growing participation with organizations in other geographic regions, especially the regional development banks. Staff members attended, for instance, the inaugural meeting of the Asian Development Bank in Tokyo in November 1966 and, thereafter, its annual meetings. The Fund was represented at a special meeting in July–August 1969 of experts on economic growth in Southeast Asia, organized by the Asian Development Bank. The Fund continued to be represented at the annual meetings of the African Development Bank, and in September 1971 staff went to the inaugural meeting in Rabat of the Association of African Central Banks. Reflecting its interest in commercial credits, the Fund began in June 1968 to send representatives to the meetings of the Union d'Assureurs des Crédits Internationaux (Berne Union).

In addition to participation in meetings, the Fund's cooperation with other organizations took the form of an exchange of documents. More and more organizations made requests for the Fund's consultation reports on countries that were common members. For some years, as we have seen above, the Fund had been regularly making available copies of its consultation reports to the OECD and to the GATT on countries that were members of these organizations. In 1964 a procedure had been set up by which other organizations, upon request, might receive copies of Part II of consultation reports (later the RED report) on common members, provided that the Executive Director elected or appointed by the country which was the subject of the report had no objection.

The organizations subsequently requesting and receiving RED reports on this ad hoc basis included the Asian Development Bank, the Caribbean Development Bank, the Caribbean Free Trade Association, the European Free Trade Association, the Food and Agriculture Organization, the Inter-American Development Bank, the World Bank on behalf of the Morocco Consultative Group and on behalf of the Tunisia Consultative Group, the International Coffee Organization, the International Labor Organization, the Inter-American Committee on the Alliance for Progress of the Organization of American States, and a number of agencies of the United Nations, such as the Development Program, the Economic and Social Office in Beirut, the Economic Commission for Africa, the Economic Commission for Asia and the Far East, the Economic and Social Council, and the United Nations Conference on Trade and Development.[22]

COOPERATION WITH THE WORLD BANK

The Fund has always had a special relationship with the World Bank, frequently called its sister organization because both institutions were born at the same time at Bretton Woods and, from the beginning have lived side by side in Washington. Many Executive Directors have served simultaneously on the Boards of both organizations in what were called interlocking directorates, and over the years there has been a great deal of informal interchange at the management and staff levels. The nature and degree of informal contacts and of the exchange of information and documents have varied, depending, among other things, on the type of problem concerned, on the jurisdiction and interest of each institution in a given problem or member country, and even on the particular Fund and Bank staff involved. Informal collaboration has inevitably been more regular and closer on some subjects and on some member countries than on other topics and members. Fund-Bank cooperation in the study of the stabilization of primary product prices, in multilateral debt renegotiations, and in work on some member countries has been cited in previous

---

[22] Shortly after the close of 1971, arrangements similar to those with the OECD for receiving the Fund's consultation reports were agreed with the EEC.

chapters. Mention also has been made of a Joint Computer Center, of publications issued jointly, and of coordination in the housing of participants in training programs.

Fresh Arrangements in 1966

In January and February of 1966, further steps were taken to achieve systematic coordination between the Fund and the Bank, particularly in their mutual dealings with member governments, and to define their spheres of primary responsibility. The idea was to assure, to the fullest extent feasible, a consistent view at the staff level by both organizations on economic policy matters relating to individual members and to avoid unintended conflict or overlapping that might lead to contradictory or inconsistent advice to members. Because the professional staffs of the two institutions were greatly enlarged, more formal arrangements for the exchange of factual information, of plans for sending missions, and of views on countries seemed necessary to provide guidance to the staff involved. Previously, when the conduct of their respective affairs was in fewer hands, the senior officials of the two organizations could handle these matters more informally.

It was agreed that the Fund had primary responsibility for exchange rates and restrictive systems, for adjustment of temporary balance of payments disequilibria, and for evaluating and assisting members to work out financial stabilization programs. On the matters thus identified, the staff of the Bank, particularly those on field missions, were to inform themselves of the established views and positions of the Fund and adopt these as a working basis for their own activities. On the other hand, the Bank was recognized as having primary responsibility for the composition and appropriateness of development programs and project evaluation, including development priorities. On these matters, the Fund staff, particularly those on field missions, were to adopt the views of the Bank. This division of responsibility meant that each institution, including missions, undertook not to engage with member countries in critical reviews of matters that were within the jurisdiction of the sister institution. In spheres which were not the primary responsibility of either institution, such as the structure and functioning of capital markets, the capacity of a member to generate domestic savings, the financial implications of economic development programs, and foreign debt problems, the staff of the Fund was to acquaint itself, before visiting a member country, with the views of the Bank, and vice versa.

Arrangements were also set out for collaboration in the field. Each institution agreed to be receptive to a request from the other to have a staff member accompany a mission as an observer, subject to the approval of the member government concerned; formulas were devised to preserve the autonomy of the observer. It was agreed that in appropriate situations it was desirable to have parallel missions, i.e., with both institutions visiting the same member at the same time and working closely together. In lieu of parallel missions, on occasion a staff member from the sister institution might work on certain subjects of the mission of the other institution, or even be completely integrated into the mission of the other institution.

Fund Participation in Aid-Coordinating Groups

Another important part of collaboration with the World Bank concerned the participation of Fund staff in consortia and consultative groups sponsored by the Bank. In July 1965, as the World Bank was planning to intensify its efforts to improve the coordination of development assistance provided by donor countries and intergovernmental institutions, Mr. George D. Woods, President of the World Bank, invited Mr. Schweitzer to send representatives to the consortia and consultative groups that the Bank would be arranging. Previously, the Bank had organized consortia for India and Pakistan and consultative groups for Colombia, Nigeria, the Sudan, and Turkey, in which Fund staff had participated on an informal basis. Now the Bank was expecting not only to strengthen the existing consortia and consultative groups but also to initiate new coordinating arrangements where it seemed likely that such arrangements could significantly improve the prospects for development. During the 1965 Annual Meetings, a general meeting of interested donor governments and intergovernmental organizations was to be convened under the World Bank's auspices, and immediately after the Annual Meetings there were to be separate meetings pertinent to particular recipient countries. The Executive Board approved participation in these meetings for the next 12 to 18 months, and Mr. Schweitzer so informed Mr. Woods.

Thereafter, the number of meetings for aid coordination arranged by the World Bank increased substantially. In the course of the next year the Bank convened nine meetings, some in Washington and some outside the United States, concerning nine developing countries. Several were meetings of already established consultative groups, including recently established groups for Malaysia and Thailand; others, such as the meetings on Korea and Peru, were preliminary, to discuss the need for, or appropriate timing of, the establishment of more regular consultative machinery. As we have seen in the foregoing section, copies of the Fund's RED reports were supplied where appropriate and under agreed procedures. At the various meetings, the Fund staff made brief factual statements describing in general terms the country's relations with the Fund and its economic situation, and answered questions raised by capital exporting countries.

The pattern thus established continued. During the 1966 Annual Meetings the World Bank again convened a general meeting on aid coordination to which the Fund was invited. The Executive Board approved, and Fund staff, along with representatives of 18 donor countries, the DAC, the IDB, the African Development Bank, and the UNDP, joined the staff of the World Bank in the meeting.

In the 12 months after September 1966 Fund representatives attended meetings of the consortium on India and the consortium on Pakistan, as well as several other meetings on coordination of aid to Ceylon, Colombia, Ghana, Korea, Malaysia, Morocco, and Tunisia.

At the third general meeting on coordination of aid programs, which was held during the 1967 Annual Meetings in Rio de Janeiro, the consensus was that the program had been useful and that it should be carried on in the future very much as it had been during the previous 12 months. The authorization of the Executive Board for the staff to attend these meetings, which was expiring, was extended. The staff continued to participate closely in many of these groups. From the end of 1967 through the end of 1971 there were meetings of the consortium on India, the consortium on Pakistan, the consultative groups on development assistance to East Africa, Korea, the Philippines, and Tunisia, and meetings on aid to Ceylon and Ghana.

In a similar way in the years reviewed in this volume the Fund staff participated in a consortium on Turkey sponsored by the OECD and in meetings of an intergovernmental group convened by the Netherlands Government to coordinate aid to Indonesia.

Further Steps Toward Fund-Bank Collaboration

In the latter part of 1969 and early in 1970, the Fund and the Bank reviewed their experience of collaboration, with the purpose of finding ways to work together still more closely. Several factors prompted this review. Executive Directors of each institution had been asking for greater cooperation to make the fullest possible use of the expertise and information of the other, to minimize the duplication of requests to member governments for information, and to reduce to a minimum the risk of inconsistent policy advice. Moreover, the Fund was planning to increase its activity in the area of consultations and the World Bank under President Robert S. McNamara (who had taken office on April 1, 1968) was embarking on a substantially enlarged program of economic analyses of member countries. The report of the Pearson Commission, which was published in 1969, recommended that "the World Bank and the IMF, in countries where both operate, adopt procedures for preparing unified country assessments and assuring consistent policy advice." [23]

After intensive conversations at various levels, the two organizations agreed that the practices that had been evolving since the 1966 understanding ought to be generalized and more uniformly observed. There were to be mutual briefings before Fund missions or Bank economic missions departed and debriefings after their return. There were to be increased efforts by the two institutions to use the same basic data, and common statistical definitions and series. Drafts

---

[23] *Partners in Development*, Report of the Commission on International Development (New York, 1969), p. 220.

as well as final documents were to be exchanged. To take advantage of the specialization of each institution, there was to be an experimental program in which there would be incorporated into one another's economic reports sections drafted by staff of the other institution.

The Executive Board approved these broad procedures in April 1970 and authorized a general invitation to the Bank to send a staff member as an observer to attend the Fund's Executive Board discussions on members in connection with Article VIII and Article XIV consultations and in connection with requests to use the Fund's resources; Mr. Schweitzer so informed Mr. McNamara.

These procedures were subsequently implemented. As far as missions were concerned, for instance, in the fiscal year 1969/70 there were 5 cases of parallel missions and there was 1 case of overlapping missions (that is, a mission from each organization was in the field simultaneously for at least a few days). Apart from meetings of aid-coordinating groups, staff of the Fund joined 10 missions of the Bank; staff of the Bank participated in 2 of the Fund's missions; and the Fund sent missions to a member especially to coordinate with a resident Bank mission. In the fiscal year 1970/71 there was even greater interrelation between missions of the two institutions. There were 10 cases of parallel missions and 4 cases of overlapping missions; staff of the Fund joined 16 Bank missions, apart from aid-coordinating meetings; and staff of the Bank joined 6 Fund missions. Likewise, after these new efforts at collaboration in 1969/70, informal interchange at the management and staff levels accelerated.

Fund-Bank Relations in Sum

The history of Fund-Bank relations from 1966 to 1971 clearly reflected the efforts of the two institutions to work more closely together. Both organizations, recognizing the wide and growing range of their common interests and the mutual advantages of working together to the maximum extent feasible, began to seek more ways to cooperate. Closer collaboration was not always feasible because of differences in the areas of responsibility of the two institutions, in the nature of the tasks they performed, in their objectives, and in their methods of working. Complicating factors on the Fund side included, for instance, the need for strict secrecy and urgent decision concerning certain actions of member governments, such as in connection with stand-by arrangements or changes in exchange rates. Another complicating factor was the Fund's primary concern with relatively short-run economic circumstances and their balance of payments implications, whereas the World Bank directed its efforts mainly to long-term resource allocation and economic development. Nonetheless, as of the end of 1971, the management of each institution was taking steps to ensure that there was minimum duplication of effort, that the advice given to members was consistent, and that cooperation did not depend on the particular staff involved. Coordination of mission activity, of technical assistance provided to members, and of work on broad economic problems and policies was increasing.[24]

In addition to the interrelationships outlined above, the Fund and the Bank had for many years sought to harmonize their policies with regard to internal administrative matters, including staff policies and benefits. In the six years 1966–71 there were new and major efforts to coordinate the administrative policies of the two institutions.

---

[24] The Bank's relations with the Fund have also been described at some length in the World Bank's history. See *The World Bank Since Bretton Woods*, by Edward S. Mason and Robert E. Asher (Washington, 1973), Chap. 16, especially pp. 544–58.

CHAPTER

30

Complexities in the Process of Policymaking

*T*HE BASIC STRUCTURE OF THE FUND underwent little change in the six years 1966–71. The process of policymaking continued to involve the same institutional framework as that established when the Fund was created. Policymaking was carried out through five major instruments—member governments, the Board of Governors, the Executive Board, the Managing Director, and the staff.[1] Even the organization of the staff remained roughly the same. There were, however, very important developments in the functioning of each of the five instruments, and the relationships between them became more complex. In addition, new trends emerged that were harbingers of major changes to be made in the Fund's process of policymaking after 1971. Also, with the growth of the Fund's activities there was an increase in the size of the staff.

MEMBERSHIP: FORMATION OF GROUPS

The addition of 17 members from the end of 1965 to the end of 1971, noted in Chapter 28, brought the total to 120 at the end of 1971, four times the original membership (30 countries at the end of 1945). Since most of the independent nations of the world had joined the Fund, only a few countries were still not members.

The most significant development among the Fund's member governments in the period reviewed here was undoubtedly the extent to which they organized themselves into rather formal groups outside the Fund to discuss, and even to agree on, their mutual positions on international monetary issues.

---

[1] For a brief description of the Fund's policymaking process as of the end of 1965, see *History, 1945–65,* Vol. II, Chap. 1. A more detailed account of the process as of September 1972 can be found in Joseph Gold, *Voting and Decisions in the International Monetary Fund: An Essay on the Law and Practice of the Fund* (Washington, 1972). (Hereinafter cited as Gold, *Voting and Decisions.*)

Of these groups, probably the most attention centered on the Group of Ten. Beginning in about 1963 the Finance Ministers and the Central Bank Governors of the ten main industrial members of the Fund—Belgium, Canada, France, the Federal Republic of Germany, Italy, Japan, the Netherlands, Sweden, the United Kingdom, and the United States—began to meet frequently as the Group of Ten. Their objective at the time was to examine the prospective need for additional liquidity in the international monetary system. When the problems involved became technical, requiring deeper study, they designated Deputies, who also began to meet regularly.[2] Gradually the Group of Ten, both at the ministerial level and at the deputy level, undertook also to consider other problems basic to the international monetary system. The Group of Ten discussed, for example, increases in Fund quotas and realignment of the par values of the currencies of their own countries, subjects which went well beyond the questions arising in connection with the General Arrangements to Borrow, which had been the origin of the Group of Ten.[3]

Similarly, after the establishment on January 1, 1958 of the European Economic Community, the six countries comprising it—Belgium, France, the Federal Republic of Germany, Italy, Luxembourg, and the Netherlands—met from time to time in formal sessions and eventually began also to consult each other concerning their external monetary and economic positions, and to coordinate their positions on the international monetary questions being discussed in the Executive Board of the Fund.

The developing countries, too, began to set up separate forums in which to consider their common economic problems. When the UNCTAD was being formed and planning to hold its first session in Geneva in 1964, the developing countries joined together, on June 15, 1964, into the Group of Seventy-Seven.[4] Some seven years later, in November 1971, at the ministerial meeting of the Group in Lima, in a desire to have a body parallel to the Group of Ten, especially in anticipation of discussions on reforming the international monetary system which were beginning to take place, the developing countries set up an Intergovernmental Group of Twenty-Four on International Monetary Affairs. This Group was to consist of 24 Finance Ministers or senior monetary or financial authorities, 8 appointed by each of the African, Asian, and Latin American contingents of the Group of Seventy-Seven. However, any member of the Group of Seventy-Seven might participate in all meetings and deliberations and, just as the Group of Seventy-Seven gradually increased to 96 countries, nearly all of which were represented at meetings, so were the meetings of the Group of Twenty-Four usually attended by representatives from more than 24 countries.

---

[2] The regular meetings of the Group of Ten on the questions concerning international liquidity and the establishment of SDRs in the Fund have been described in detail in Parts One and Two.

[3] See Chaps. 16 and 26.

[4] *Proceedings of the United Nations Conference on Trade and Development, Volume I: Final Act and Report* (New York, 1964), pp. 66–68.

As part of its functions, the Group of Twenty-Four was to review the progress of the international monetary system, take cognizance of studies by the International Monetary Fund, keep the members of the Group of Seventy-Seven informed, "evaluate events in the monetary field, as well as any decisions which might be taken by a single country or group of countries within the framework of the International Monetary Fund, relating to the interests of the developing countries," and recommend coordinated positions in international bodies.[5] The Group of Twenty-Four was modeled to some extent on the Group of Ten. Hence, there were to be Deputies; these would consist of the Deputies of the Group of Twenty-Four plus those Executive Directors of the Fund who were appointed or elected exclusively by developing members.

These Executive Directors, nine in all, in effect constituted still another, less formal, group. The "G-9 Caucus," or Group of Nine, which started to meet in 1966, continued to meet, usually monthly, even after the creation of the Group of Twenty-Four.

Reasons for Groups

The trend toward separate groupings in which members met outside the Fund's mechanism to deliberate and discuss their positions on international monetary questions reflected partly the greater interdependence in economic and financial affairs among particular groupings of countries that had come about by the mid-1960s. Among the industrial countries, for example, economic and financial developments in one country now affected directly and almost instantaneously the financial and economic conditions of others. As was seen in Chapter 1, cooperation between the central banks of the industrial countries, in the form of swap and other lending arrangements, had become imperative as early as 1961. Growing economic and financial interdependence also meant that official decisions in the monetary field taken by one country could immediately undo the policies of others. Also contributing to the formation of groups were the recurrent disruptions that began to occur after 1967 in the previously smooth functioning of the international monetary system. As was described in Chapters 22 and 26, urgent decisions were required that had to be taken at the ministerial level. The Group of Ten, therefore, seemed to its members to be a natural successor to the previous ad hoc meetings and contacts of central bankers of the large industrial nations: informal inter-central-bank cooperation was made more formal and was broadened.

Just as the Group of Ten broadened its concerns, so did the EEC countries: the extension of their consultations to international financial subjects seemed

---

[5] *The Declaration and Principles of the Action Programme of Lima*, adopted by the Group of Seventy-Seven at the Second Ministerial Meeting on November 7, 1971, MM/77/II/11, November 9, 1971, Part Three, Section A (I), pars. 13 and 14 (b). This document was also circulated by the United Nations Conference on Trade and Development as TD/143, November 12, 1971, and by the UN General Assembly as A/C.2/270, November 15, 1971.

a logical outgrowth of their consultations on domestic economic policies. In the same way, the developing countries gradually came to the view that, by meeting separately from the industrial and the more developed countries, they could better study and examine their own particular needs in the international economic and monetary fields.

Compelling as these reasons were for the formation of these groups, yet another circumstance explained their existence, a circumstance which was indicative of what began to happen in the area of international economic and monetary relations after about 1965. Acting in unison, groups of countries could do what one or two countries could no longer do. Countries had become economically, and perhaps politically as well, so coequal and interdependent that no longer could one country, the United States included, or even two or three countries together, dominate decisions relating to international monetary affairs. The creation of the Fund itself, for instance, had been the result of decisions taken in 1943 and 1944 primarily by the United Kingdom and the United States; other countries joined on the terms that were for the most part specified by these two powers. Moreover, during the Fund's first two decades, the views of the United States, virtually the sole source of large amounts of investment capital, advanced technology, and the latest managerial and marketing techniques, dominated the international rules and institutions governing world economic relations. In general, in the Fund's decisions, the views of the United States prevailed. By the mid-1960s, however, the interests of a much wider range of countries had to be fully considered, and their agreement secured, before decisions relating to the international monetary system could be taken. In this circumstance, groups of countries, certainly when acting together, could be assured that their opinions were articulated and respected.

In short, they could exert more influence as a unit. By the latter part of 1971 groups had an especially strong motive for presenting their views in this way: the issues to be resolved encompassed the whole of the international monetary mechanism, and were soon to encompass virtually all international economic transactions—trade, investment, and capital—as well as the monetary system.

Implications for the Fund

Because members discussed within groups the leading questions on which the Fund was working toward decisions, and the positions that they would take in the Board of Governors or in the Executive Board, the existence of groups began to have great effect on the decision-making process of the Fund. The influence of the Group of Ten and of the EEC on the Fund's actions has been visible at a number of points in the foregoing chapters, especially in the chapters on SDRs. While the Fund's membership by and large accepted the existence of groups, the influence of some groups, most notably the Group of Ten, which had a majority of the total voting power in the Fund, caused considerable concern within the Fund during the years reviewed here, as the reader will recall from Parts One and Two. In fact, it was the existence of the Group of Ten that impelled the formation of some other groups, especially the Group of Twenty-Four.

Not only did these various groups exist, and not only were they increasingly active, but they also began to take somewhat conflicting positions. In fact, by 1971 the crystallization of the membership into groups holding somewhat diverse positions on major international monetary questions had become a trend. By then the major industrial countries no longer saw their interests as identical with each other, and the positions of some were often diametrically opposed to the positions of others. In addition, there had emerged an increasing conscious-ness of the differing interests as between developed and developing members; and after a generation of political independence, growth, and development, with heavy emphasis on education, the developing members had produced leaders in the science of economic theory and policy who were able to formulate and articulate the views of the developing members. Thus, by the end of the period reviewed in this volume positions on international monetary matters tended to be more polarized than before. The international monetary cooperation that had characterized the Fund's first twenty years had become increasingly more elusive. As a result, the agreement of the Fund's membership in 1969 on the creation of an SDR facility and on its activation in 1970 seemed, in retrospect, to represent the zenith of international cooperation in the monetary field for the next several years.

BOARD OF GOVERNORS: GROWTH IN SIZE AND POWERS

The Board of Governors was affected by two changes of note in the years 1966–71. The first change related to size. As countries joined the Fund and the World Bank, the increasing number of Governors and Alternate Governors became particularly apparent when, accompanied by expanding delegations and greater numbers of advisors, they gathered for their Annual Meetings. The Annual Meetings became massive affairs. Not only were there more and larger delegations from member countries; representatives of a lengthening list of international organizations also attended. More and more bankers and economic experts were invited as special guests, and hundreds of press officers came to cover the deliberations. By way of illustration, it may be noted that the 1971 Annual Meeting, held in Washington, was attended by 3,175 persons, exclusive of Bank and Fund staff; of this number, members' delegations made up about 1,800.

The growing size of the Board of Governors prompted the taking of further informal measures to enable the work conducted at an Annual Meeting to

Joint session of Boards of Governors of Fund and World Bank at an Annual Meeting

be completed within the customary five days.[6] Attempts were made, for instance, to avoid two speeches being given by the same delegation, that is, one by the Governor of the Fund and one by the Governor of the World Bank; the member was to select which Governor would speak on its behalf. This limitation was particularly relevant to the bigger members. Governors from groups of smaller members were encouraged to select one of their number to be spokesman.

The size of the plenary sessions, together with the desire of Governors from some countries to take advantage of the occasion to hold meetings among themselves, led to an increasing number of meetings or caucuses in addition to the Annual Meeting itself. Governors from regions with similar interests wished to meet separately in smaller groupings. Some of the groups mentioned above, such as the Group of Ten, met immediately before or at the time of an Annual Meeting. Meetings of Governors for Latin American and for African members at the time of the Annual Meeting became traditional and fairly formalized: the Managing Director attended the meetings both to address these groups of Governors and to answer their questions. Gradually, too, the presence of high-level and well-known monetary officials from all over the world led to contemporaneous seminars, conferences, and lectures, such as the lectures sponsored by the Per Jacobsson Foundation. All in all, already by 1968 the number of ancillary meetings had reached a total of 35 and, for the staff of the Secretary's Department, the time and effort involved in arranging and servicing ancillary meetings were about equal to the time and effort spent on the Governors' plenary sessions.

The second noteworthy change in the Board of Governors in the years 1966 through 1971 was in the growth of its powers. The amendments to the Articles of Agreement that became effective on July 28, 1969 added to the powers that were expressly reserved to the Board of Governors, that is, the powers that could not be delegated to the Executive Directors. Many of the newly reserved powers dealt with SDRs: only the Governors could, for example, allocate or cancel SDRs, provide that the duration of a basic period for allocation should be other than five years, change the rates of allocation, or modify the rules for reconstitution. In addition, power was reserved to the Governors, inter alia, to decide on the mitigation of the effects of payment of increases in quotas following a general review of quotas, to revise the provisions on repurchases, and to make transfers to the Fund's General Reserve from any special reserve.[7]

The augmented decision-making power of the Board of Governors—both legally under the amended Articles of Agreement and effectively because only the highest-ranking monetary officials could take decisions on the perplexing

---

[6] For a description of earlier measures, introduced in 1963, see *History, 1945–65*, Vol. I, p. 500.

[7] For a fuller discussion of the powers reserved to the Board of Governors, see Gold, *Voting and Decisions*, pp. 9–15.

questions confronting the international monetary system—meant that by the late 1960s the Annual Meeting of the Board of Governors was increasingly the focal point for international monetary decisions and was being regarded more and more as the occasion when decisions that had not been possible earlier might be taken. Between Annual Meetings, technical studies might be made and preliminary reports written, even reports containing recommendations by the Executive Board. But the hard political decisions necessary to resolve the questions outstanding had to await the gathering of the Ministers of Finance and Governors of central banks that composed the Fund's Board of Governors. Key decisions might not be taken in full plenary sessions—most often they were not. Instead, they were taken in committee or in ancillary meetings. All in all, the Annual Meeting became an important decision-taking event.

EXECUTIVE BOARD: INCREASING FUNCTIONS

As had been the situation since the origin of the Fund, so during the years reviewed here, the Executive Directors were the organ of the Fund that was in continuous session and was responsible for the conduct of the general operations of the Fund. It was through the Executive Directors that members continued to exercise a close control over the Fund's day-to-day activities.[8]

In the early part of the period covered in this volume, the Executive Board exercised its responsibilities in the main by administering the international monetary system set up at Bretton Woods in 1944 and by ensuring that the Fund developed ways and means to keep its Articles of Agreement relevant to the demands made upon the Fund by the changing circumstances of the world economy. Its primary responsibilities, as in the past, reflected the Fund's three principal functions: regulatory, financial, and consultative.

In its regulatory role, the Executive Board, through the consultation procedures and moral suasion, sought to ensure that members adhered to the general principles of conduct with respect to exchange rates and international payments laid down in the Articles. The Board served also as custodian of certain widely accepted, but purely informal, propositions with respect to the appropriate methods of balance of payments adjustment and of international monetary policy and behavior. The Executive Board of the Fund was, in effect, an international conscience.

The Executive Board spent more time in its financial role than in its regulatory role, however. *First*, it was responsible for the basic policies and

---

[8] Article XII, Sections 3 (*a*) and (*g*) and 4 (*b*). Although the organ was referred to in the Articles of Agreement as *the Executive Directors*, it became more common in the Fund to refer to the organ as *the Executive Board* and to the members of that Board as the Executive Directors (or Alternate Executive Directors). The latter practice has been followed in this history.

techniques for the use by members of the Fund's financial resources. For instance, in the years 1966–71 the Board liberalized the compensatory financing facility; introduced a new buffer stock financing facility; implemented a general increase in quotas and various selective quota increases; reviewed the conditions under which members might use the Fund's resources through stand-by arrangements; assumed responsibility for further evolution in the Fund's policies with regard to the selection of currencies used in drawings and repurchases, charges for the use of the Fund's resources, and repurchases; and took a number of decisions with regard to the Fund's assets, including its policies on replenishment of currencies and on sales of gold. *Second*, it applied established policies and techniques to specific members' requests for purchases and stand-by arrangements and to members' proposals for scheduling and rescheduling repurchases.

As a consultative body, the Executive Board served as the central forum in which the monetary and payments problems of the world in general and of individual countries in particular were discussed. Members' economic situations and prospects were reviewed at length in connection with the Article VIII and Article XIV consultations. These consultations, often accompanied by requests for financial aid, constituted much of the Board's work. The Board also undertook a similar review when a member proposed a change in its exchange rate or par value, or when a member requested a stand-by arrangement or a drawing. Indeed, the Fund was the instrument of multilateral cooperation in international finance because the Executive Board constituted the only effective forum in the field in which the views of over a hundred countries of all sizes and in all stages of economic development could be taken into account on a continuous basis.

Although the regulatory, financial, and consultative functions occupied a great deal of the Board's time, an increasing proportion of its efforts during the years 1966–71 was devoted to the establishment of new policies, either directly or through recommendations to the Board of Governors. When in the second half of the 1960s it became apparent that the Articles of Agreement required revision, the Executive Board was called upon to serve as an innovative force in adapting the Fund to changed circumstances. Its role in connection with the establishment, use, and development of the SDR facility has been described in Parts One and Two. Its consideration and approval of complementary changes in the By-Laws for submission to the Board of Governors, and the working out of changes in the Rules and Regulations, have been described in Chapter 13.

An especially vital role of the Executive Board with regard to SDRs came after the facility was incorporated into the Articles of Agreement. In order to make the new facility operational, much pathbreaking had to be done. As was described in Chapters 10 and 11, in the latter part of 1969 considerable attention was devoted to discussing and agreeing on features of the SDR arrangements that had to be worked out before SDRs could actually be allocated. Also, the

Board was charged with the continuing responsibility for deciding upon quarterly designation plans and their application; its decisions in these matters had a major bearing on the channeling of SDRs among participants.

In the latter part of the period reviewed here, when the international monetary system was subjected to mounting pressures, the Executive Board had to concern itself with even more fundamental questions. In Part Five have been described, for example, its examination of the exchange rate adjustment mechanism in 1969 and 1970 and its adoption of a temporary regime of central rates and wider margins in December 1971. Also described have been the attempts to alleviate the problems involved in conducting the Fund's financial operations in the circumstances that prevailed after August 15, 1971. Finally, as 1971 came to a close, the Board was starting to consider intensively many of the issues involved in a comprehensive reform of the monetary system.

Of the other responsibilities and functions, one in particular should be noted. The Executive Directors were required by the By-Laws to prepare for the Board of Governors an Annual Report discussing the operations and policies of the Fund and making recommendations to the Board of Governors on the problems confronting the Fund. As part of the Annual Report, the Executive Directors were to review the operation of the Special Drawing Account and the adequacy of global reserves; this requirement was, of course, added after the amendment of the Articles of Agreement in July 1969.[9] The Annual Reports of the Executive Directors to the Board of Governors for the fiscal years 1965/66 through 1970/71 were, like those for earlier years, valuable sources of information to member governments and others on, among other things, the international economic and monetary situation, and they served as a guide to Governors in preparing for their participation in Annual Meetings. The Executive Directors devoted much time and attention to reviewing and approving the content of their Annual Reports.

Illustrative of the work of Executive Directors are some figures for the hours devoted to meetings in the calendar year 1971. In that year they held 138 formal and 19 informal sessions, for a cumulative total of 288 hours, of which 129 hours were devoted to policy matters (including floating exchange rates, currency realignment, the mechanism of exchange rate adjustment, and SDRs), 111 hours to more than two hundred country subjects, 29 hours to the Annual Report, and 20 hours to administrative matters. The Board took a total of 553 decisions, a record high number and 184 more than in 1965. For these decisions, careful preparatory work was, of course, necessary. Executive Directors also served on several standing and ad hoc committees.

In addition to the above workload, Executive Directors traveled frequently to the countries that appointed or elected them in order to attend discussions between the staff and the officials of member countries in connection with

---

[9] By-Laws, Sec. 10; Vol. II below, p. 161.

Article VIII and Article XIV consultations, to confer with their authorities, and to report to their Governors on developments in the Fund.

EXECUTIVE BOARD: CHANGES IN COMPOSITION

After the tenth biennial election of Executive Directors in 1964, the Executive Board consisted of 20 Executive Directors. The five members with the largest quotas appointed one Director each; the remaining 15 Directors were elected for two-year terms by the other members.[10]

Until November 1, 1970, the five members that appointed Directors were the United States, the United Kingdom, France, India, and the Federal Republic of Germany. After the fifth general review of quotas, Japan became the member with the fifth largest quota and was therefore entitled to appoint an Executive Director, and India ceased to be in that position. As has been mentioned in Chapter 16, the Board of Governors adopted a resolution agreeing to the proposed rules for the conduct of the 1970 regular election of Executive Directors, the implications of which were that India would continue to appoint a Director until the next regular election of Executive Directors in 1972, and that, with effect from November 1, 1970, Japan would also appoint a Director, instead of electing one as in the past.[11] There were thus, in the two-year interim from 1970 to 1972, 6 appointed Directors; the total number of Executive Directors remained at 20, however. In the 1970 regular election of Executive Directors, Burma, Ceylon, Laos, Malaysia, Nepal, Singapore, and Thailand did not cast votes for any of the Executive Directors that were elected, and they designated the Executive Director appointed by Japan to look after their interests in the Fund until the 1972 election.

Several changes in the composition of the Executive Board took place in the six years described in this volume, especially after the biennial elections of 1966, 1968, and 1970, and as countries appointing Executive Directors, with the exception of the United States, continued to change their appointees with a regular periodicity. The changes in the composition of the Executive Board—both Executive Directors and Alternates—are listed in Appendices A–1, A–2, and A–3 to this volume. But a few highlights may be noted. Several Directors served for most of the period covered in this history: Messrs. Dale, Kafka, Lieftinck, Saad, Suzuki, Tann, van Campenhout, and Yaméogo. Some Directors returned to the Board for a second time, having served earlier: Messrs. Asp,

---

[10] The provisions of the Articles of Agreement concerning the appointment and election of Executive Directors, how these provisions were implemented from 1946 through 1970, the voting strength of individual Directors, and how this strength was determined and exercised have been described in Gold, *Voting and Decisions.*

[11] Resolution No. 25-5, adopted by the Board of Governors effective September 10, 1970, *Summary Proceedings, 1970,* p. 262. For the rules for the conduct of the election and the results of the 1970 regular election, see *ibid.,* pp. 243–49 and 249–53.

Escobar, Friis, Madan, and Prasad. Two Directors, Messrs. Saad and Tann, retired, after more than two decades on the Executive Board.

Mr. Saad's retirement, at the age of 70, came after more than 24 consecutive years as an Executive Director. His departure meant that there were no longer on the Board any of the Directors who had served on the first Board. From the time he was elected to the first Board of Executive Directors in March 1946 until he retired from the Board on October 31, 1970, not only did Mr. Saad look after the interests of the Middle Eastern members that elected him, but he was also known for his persistent efforts first to establish and later to uphold the Fund's authority in international finance and monetary affairs. A lawyer by training, he played a prominent part in Executive Board decisions involving the Fund's jurisdiction. He served for many years as chairman of the Executive Board Committee on Interpretation (of the Articles of Agreement). He headed the Fund's delegations to conferences to design a proposed International Trade Organization and later to meetings of the GATT. These activities were described in the earlier history.[12] In the years reviewed here he continued to be a zealous guardian of the authority of the Fund and of the Executive Board. For instance, in the course of the discussions leading to the establishment of SDRs, he felt so strongly that the Group of Ten should not involve itself in the Fund's business that he refused to attend the Joint Meetings of Executive Directors and the Deputies of the Group of Ten.

After leaving the Executive Board, Mr. Saad remained the Governor of the Fund for Saudi Arabia and was named Principal Resident Representative of Saudi Arabia to the International Monetary Fund, with the rank of Ambassador, and continued to have an office at the headquarters of the Fund. He was succeeded on the Executive Board with effect from November 1, 1970 by Mr. Deif (Egypt).

Mr. Tann's retirement in 1970 was after 20 years as an Executive Director. He had been the Executive Director appointed by the Republic of China from July 11, 1950 to October 31, 1960, at which time the Federal Republic of Germany had replaced the Republic of China as one of the members with the five largest quotas. Mr. Tann then became the Executive Director elected by the Republic of China, Korea, Viet-Nam, and the Philippines. He served in this capacity for another 10 years before retiring on October 31, 1970. He was succeeded, with effect from November 1, 1970, by Mr. Peh Yuan Hsu.

During the period reviewed in this volume there were three Alternate Executive Directors who left the Board after more than, or close to, two decades of service: Mr. H. M. H. A. van der Valk (Netherlands), Mr. John S. Hooker (United States), and Mr. Albert Mansour (Egypt). Mr. van der Valk joined the staff of the Fund in December 1946 as a Division Chief in the Research Department. In May 1949 he was appointed by Mr. J. W. Beyen as his Alternate on

---

[12] See *History, 1945–65*, Vol. I, pp. 165–66, 173–75, 198, 224, 246, 251, 269–70, 310–12, 370, 376, 390, 404, 420, 506, 529, 566, and 577; and Vol. II, pp. 94–95, 334, 337, and 340.

the Executive Board, and he was subsequently reappointed by Mr. D. Crena de Iongh and by Mr. Lieftinck. Mr. van der Valk remained as Alternate Executive Director until his retirement from the Board on November 30, 1968, after 22 years in the Fund.

Mr. Hooker was appointed by Mr. Southard as his Alternate in January 1950. In 1962, when Mr. Dale succeeded Mr. Southard, Mr. Hooker became Alternate Executive Director to Mr. Dale, and remained as Alternate Executive Director until his retirement on March 31, 1970.

Mr. Mansour became Alternate Executive Director to Mr. Saad in November 1951, and continued in that capacity until he retired, on October 31, 1970, when Mr. Saad retired.

EXECUTIVE BOARD: COMPOSITION AT END OF 1971

As a result of the changes in the composition of the Executive Board in the six years 1966–71, the Board was considerably different on December 31, 1971 than it was on January 1, 1966. There had, nevertheless, been some continuity and several of the Executive Directors had served for long periods of time. Senior in length of service were Mr. van Campenhout, who at the end of 1971 had been on the Board for 17 years; Mr. Lieftinck, who had served for 16 years; and Mr. Dale, who had served for 9 years. By then, Mr. Kafka, Mr. Suzuki, and Mr. Yaméogo had also already been Executive Directors for 5 years, Mr. Palamenghi-Crispi for 4, and Mr. Schleiminger and Mr. Kharmawan for 3. Of the remaining members of the Executive Board, Mr. Mitchell was appointed in 1969 and Mr. Brand and Mr. Viénot in 1970, Messrs. Brofoss, Deif, Hsu, Massad, Omwony, and Ugueto were elected in 1970, and Messrs. Prasad and Bryce came to the Board in 1971.

The Executive Directors serving at the end of 1971 possessed individual qualifications covering a wide spectrum of economic and financial experience, and several had held very high posts in their countries before joining the Executive Board. Nearly all had been closely associated with the work of the Fund, several having previously been Governors, Executive Directors, Alternate Executive Directors, or members of the staff.

Mr. van Campenhout had been head of the Belgian Economic Mission in London during World War II. He was appointed as the Fund's first General Counsel in 1946, in which capacity he served for 8 years before becoming an Executive Director. After 1960 he was also an Executive Director of the World Bank.

Mr. Lieftinck had been the Minister of Finance of the Netherlands during the critical period immediately following World War II and had been responsible for the monetary and financial policies that shaped the Netherlands' post-war recovery. He was also Executive Director of the World Bank.

Mr. Dale had been Deputy Assistant Secretary for International Affairs in the U.S. Department of Commerce, Program Manager for International Research of the Stanford Research Institute in Washington, and U.S. Treasury Representative in the Middle East.

Mr. Kafka had been Director of the Brazilian Institute of Economics and later Advisor to the Superintendency of Money and Credit, the predecessor of the Central Bank of Brazil, and then Advisor to the Minister of Finance; earlier, he had been an Alternate Executive Director and a member of the staff of the Fund.

Mr. Suzuki had been Special Advisor to the Minister of Finance of Japan and Special Assistant to the Minister of Foreign Affairs; he had also been a Deputy of the Group of Ten and a member of Working Party 3 of the OECD. For the 5 years 1966–70 he was an Executive Director of the World Bank as well as of the Fund.

Mr. Yaméogo had been an Alternate Executive Director before becoming Executive Director, and he had also been a member of the staff of the Fund; previously, he had been Director of the Treasury and, later, Minister of National Economy, in Upper Volta.

Mr. Palamenghi-Crispi (Italy) had been Managing Director and Deputy President of the Somali National Bank and a Director of the Bank of Italy; for 5 years he had been Alternate Governor of the World Bank for Somalia.

Mr. Schleiminger had been Deputy Head of the Department of International Organizations of the Deutsche Bundesbank for 10 years; he had previously been on the German Delegation to the OEEC and Chairman of the Alternate Members of the Managing Board of the EPU.

Mr. Kharmawan had been Chief Economic Advisor of the Central Bank of Indonesia and, later, an Executive Director of the Asian Development Bank.

Mr. Mitchell had been Deputy Under Secretary of State for the Department of Economic Affairs dealing with External Economic Affairs and, later, Deputy Secretary of the Ministry of Agriculture, Fisheries and Food, of the United Kingdom. He was also Executive Director of the World Bank.

Mr. Brand, as an official of the Australian Treasury for many years, had been the First Assistant Secretary of the Revenue Loans and Investment Division.

Mr. Viénot, long with the Ministry of Finance of France, had more recently been Deputy Director of the Direction du Trésor, and had also been Chairman of the Economic and Development Review Committee of the OECD; he, too, was an Executive Director of the World Bank at the same time that he was Executive Director of the Fund.

Mr. Brofoss had been the Minister of Finance and the Minister of Commerce of Norway and, later, the Governor of the Bank of Norway; in the last capacity he had also been the Governor of the Fund for Norway for 16 years.

Mr. Deif had been Minister of the Treasury of Egypt and, in that capacity, had also been Governor of the Fund for Egypt.

Mr. Hsu had been the Minister of Finance and, later, the Governor of the Central Bank of China; in these capacities he had been the Governor of the Fund and the World Bank for the Republic of China for 4 years and the Governor of the Fund for another 5 years.

Mr. Massad had been Vice President and then President of the Central Bank of Chile and Chairman of the Board of Governors of the Center for Latin American Monetary Studies; he had been the Governor of the Fund and the World Bank for Chile for 5 years.

Mr. Omwony (Kenya) had been Personnel Manager of the East African Posts and Telecommunications Corporation before his appointment as Alternate Executive Director.

Mr. Ugueto had been Director General of the Ministry of Finance of Venezuela and, in the Finance Minister's absence, Acting Minister; he had also been Secretary to the Caucus of the Fund and World Bank Governors for the Latin American members and for the Philippines, and Deputy Chief of Mission in the Embassy of Venezuela in Washington.

Mr. Prasad had been Economic Advisor of the Reserve Bank of India before his first term as Executive Director of the Fund, and had then been Assistant Director of the Economic Staff of the World Bank, Economic Advisor to the Prime Minister of Nigeria, and Director of the Asian Institute for Economic Development Planning of the United Nations.

Mr. Bryce had been Deputy Minister of Finance and Economic Advisor to the Prime Minister of Canada and an Executive Director of the World Bank.

The Alternate Executive Directors generally had fewer years of service on the Executive Board, but they, too, had had varying experience in monetary and financial matters, including the work of the Fund. They are listed here in alphabetical order.

Mr. Al-Atrash had been Director of the Credit Department in the Central Bank of Syria, and for some years had been Advisor to the Syrian delegation to the Annual Meetings of the Board of Governors.

Mr. Arriazu (Argentina) had been Technical Assistant to the Executive Director before being appointed Alternate Executive Director in 1968.

Mr. Beaurain had been Chargé de mission au Cabinet of the Ministry of Finance of France.

Mr. Bustelo had been Chief of the Balance of Payments Division of the Ministry of Commerce of Spain.

Mr. Caranicas, from 1952 to 1968, had served as Alternate Executive Director to the Executive Director elected by Italy, Greece, Spain, and Portugal, and then returned in 1970 as Alternate Executive Director to Mr. Kharmawan; before becoming an Alternate Executive Director, Mr. Caranicas had been

Secretary General of the Ministry of National Economy and the Ministry of Agriculture of Greece.

Mr. de Vries (Netherlands) had, for 5 years, been Director for Monetary Affairs of the EEC and a member of the Monetary Committee of the EEC.

Miss Fuenfgelt had been with the Ministry of Economics of the Federal Republic of Germany for 8 years and a member of the Fund staff for 2 years; she had also been an Alternate Deputy in the Group of Ten.

Mr. Gilchrist, long with the Bank of England, had been Assistant to the Chief of the Overseas Department.

Mr. González, for 20 years with the Central Bank of Costa Rica, had been Director of the Department of Economic Studies.

Mr. Hanh had been Governor of the National Bank of Viet-Nam and Minister of Finance and Minister of National Economy.

Mr. Harley had been Director of the Office of International Financial Policy Coordination and Operations in the U.S. Treasury.

Mr. Jónsson had been Economic Advisor to the Central Bank of Iceland.

Mr. Marathe, for 13 years with the Ministry of Finance of India, had been Economic Advisor to the Indian Government.

Mr. Martins had been Chief of the Economics Department of the Central Bank of Brazil.

Mr. Mills had been Director of the Central Planning Unit in Jamaica and had been Deputy Director of Statistics in the Central Bureau of Statistics.

Mr. Nicol-Cole had been first Deputy Governor and then Governor of the Bank of Sierra Leone, and had been Alternate Governor and Governor of the Fund and the World Bank for Sierra Leone.

Mr. Rajaobelina, serving with the Ministry of Finance of the Malagasy Republic, had been Financial Advisor to the Secretary of State.

Mr. Satow had been Senior Advisor for International Affairs in the Bank of Japan and had been on the Fund staff.

Mr. Schneider had been Deputy Head of the Foreign Section of the Economic Research Department of the Austrian National Bank and, earlier, Technical Assistant to the Executive Director.

Mr. Smit had been Deputy Secretary for Finance in the South African Treasury and Head of the Foreign Trade Relations Division of the Department of Commerce and Industries.

EXECUTIVE BOARD: SIZE AND STRUCTURE

In the course of the preparation of the rules for the conduct of the 1970 regular election of Executive Directors, questions were raised about the size and structure of the Executive Board.[13] One of the questions related to the optimal size of the Board. At issue was whether the number of Executive Directors should be increased from 20 to 21, by adding to the number of elected Directors. Under Article XII, Section 3 (*b*), of the Articles of Agreement, when countries not listed in Schedule A entered the Fund, the Board of Governors, by a four-fifths majority of the total voting power, might increase the number of Executive Directors to be elected. In the course of the Board's discussion in 1970, it was observed that each increase in the number of Executive Directors to be elected in the past had been based on the acceptance of membership by countries that had, as a minimum, the number of votes considered appropriate for an increase in the circumstances then prevailing. In 1970 the application of that test did not justify an increase. It was also pointed out, however, that the approach followed in the past was not mandatory under the Articles, and that it was proper to take into account other factors, including the effect of the size of the Board on the dispatch of its business, in establishing the number of Executive Directors to be elected.

Another question that was considered stemmed from a request that the rules of election be arranged so as to assure two seats for the African members. The two additions, in 1963 and 1964, to the number of elected Executive Directors had been based principally on the entry into the Fund during the early 1960s of a large number of countries in Africa. Under the present rules, however, it was conceivable that, in an election, groupings of members could be such that the African members would no longer have two representatives on the Executive Board. Moreover, even the present groupings meant that the Executive Directors elected by African members had a large number of members to take care of, Mr. Omwony with 15 constituents and Mr. Yaméogo with 18. Mr. Deif was another Executive Director with a large constituency: he was elected by 13 members, including three in Africa, and he looked after the interests of another country that was in the process of joining the Fund.

During the discussion in the Executive Board, there was broad support for the view that, if the large number of African countries were able to elect only one Executive Director, the burden on him would be excessive, and the efficient conduct of the business of the Executive Directors as a group, particularly when the interests of the African members were involved, would be hindered. There was widespread support among the Executive Directors for the view that African members should have the opportunity to elect two Executive Directors. The Executive Directors strongly preferred as a matter of principle to keep the existing number of Directors at 20. They noted that even increasing the membership of the Board from 20 to 21 by introducing into the Articles provisions like Article XII, Section 3 (*b*) (iv), would not necessarily ensure a solution to the African problem: other new regional groups might be formed that could compete

---

[13] These rules can be found in Gold, *Voting and Decisions*, pp. 243–48, and in *Summary Proceedings, 1970*, pp. 243–49.

in elections. Were "Africa" to receive the same special treatment as the "Latin American Republics," with separate provisions in the Articles assuring them of seats on the Executive Board, there might be requests for similar treatment for "Asia," or "Southeast Asia," or the "Middle East," or even "Europe."

The Executive Directors did not propose to reach any conclusions on these questions before the 1970 election. They believed that these and other questions related to the size and structure of the Executive Board deserved further study. Accordingly, paragraph 7 of the report of the Executive Directors to the Board of Governors on the rules for the 1970 election stated that

> the Executive Directors consider it desirable to continue to give attention to the problems of the size and structure of the Executive Board. They intend to complete a study of these matters within 2 years, bearing in mind the recurrent need to prepare for the biennial elections of Executive Directors.

After the 1970 election, the Executive Directors discussed a number of topics connected with the size and structure of the Executive Board. They considered the consequences for the Executive Board of the potential membership in the Fund of numerous small states. They discussed the implications of distributing directorships on the basis of geographical or other patterns. They debated two fundamental questions concerning the existing distribution of voting power: Should voting power in the Fund continue to vary according to the size of a member's quota? Should the number of basic votes which each member received regardless of the size of its quota continue to be 250? They considered what additional assistance might be given to Executive Directors with ever-heavier workloads. And they discussed the possibility of new rules of election favoring large groups of members.

These basic questions concerning the size and structure of the Executive Board were still unanswered as 1971 closed. One consequence of the discussions during 1971 was that the Executive Board changed the Fund's administrative rules to provide for the appointment of an "Advisor to Executive Director" to assist each Executive Director who was elected by more than 10 members. Advisors to Executive Directors were subject in most respects to the same terms and conditions of service as were the Executive Directors and their Alternates. At the end of 1971, three Executive Directors had Advisors. In addition, after June 1969 each Executive Director was entitled to four assistants, no more than two of whom might be technical assistants.

MANAGING DIRECTOR

The work and decisions of the Fund are the fruits of a rich interchange of views and ideas among the Executive Directors, the management, and the staff, in a process that has been described in the earlier history and elsewhere.[14]

---

[14] *History, 1945–65*, Vol. II, pp. 10–17, and Gold, *Voting and Decisions*, pp. 171–80.

Hence, it is difficult to single out the contribution of any individual. However, the position and influence of the Managing Director are of such moment that much that the Fund accomplishes during his time in office reflects his leadership.

Mr. Pierre-Paul Schweitzer was the Managing Director and the Chairman of the Executive Directors during the six years reviewed in this volume. Of the four Managing Directors that had served since the Fund's inception, he was the youngest and the only one to be appointed to and to serve a full second term. His first term began on September 1, 1963 and his second term ended on August 31, 1973.[15] Inasmuch as he was still Managing Director after 1971, a summing up of Mr. Schweitzer's leadership of the Fund might better await an account of the Fund's history that includes 1972 and 1973. Nonetheless, the years related here were definitely "Schweitzer years," and this narration would be incomplete without an attempt to describe his imprint on the policies and activities of the Fund that have been recounted in the foregoing chapters.

Almost immediately upon taking office, Mr. Schweitzer became known as the first Managing Director of the Fund to be particularly concerned about the developing countries, and as one who was eager to see that solutions to the world's monetary problems were truly international, reflecting the interests of the developing, as well as of the industrialized, nations. The prime illustration of Mr. Schweitzer's concern for the developing countries is, of course, his effort on their behalf in the formation of the SDR facility. We have seen in Part One how, in the protracted deliberations concerning international liquidity from 1963 through 1967, he stressed time and time again, publicly, that techniques for adding to the world's liquidity should include all countries, rich and poor alike, on an equal basis. This position was contrary to the then fashionable views in industrial countries. We have further seen that, in order to bring about such a solution, he worked quietly behind the scenes, putting forward his own proposal for a universal scheme operated through an international body, the Fund, or an affiliate thereof. And we have noted that these and other private initiatives by Mr. Schweitzer were immensely instrumental in shaping the character of the arrangement to create liquidity that was finally agreed upon—special drawing rights created by the Fund for all its members in proportion to their quotas.

Economists and laymen outside the inner official circles of those involved in the negotiations have often expressed regret that no link between liquidity creation and development finance was set up on the occasion of the initial agreement on the SDR facility. It is, therefore, to be emphasized that the scheme established represented, in the circumstances of the mid-1960s, a signal victory for the Fund and most especially for Mr. Schweitzer. The greatness of his achievement is likely to become even more apparent should SDRs take on a central role in a reformed international monetary system.

---

[15] The period from 1963 through the end of 1965 was covered in *History, 1945–65.*

Undoubtedly the SDRs were the apogee of Mr. Schweitzer's achievements during his tenure in the Fund. But a number of other developments in the Fund's policies and activities related in this volume were also a reflection of his understanding of, and close attention to, the problems of developing countries: the liberalization and extension of the compensatory financing facility; the introduction of the buffer stock financing facility; and—a development in which Mr. Schweitzer took particular pride—the large growth in the Fund's technical assistance programs after he became Managing Director. From Part Five the reader will recall, too, that when the par value system came apart in 1971, and many were concerned about the adverse consequences for the major industrial nations, it was Mr. Schweitzer who pointed out the painful implications for the developing countries.

The developing nations were very responsive to what they recognized to be a shift in the Fund's attitudes. Especially among the Latin American countries, which had been sharply critical of many of the Fund's policies during the 1950s, was Mr. Schweitzer able to reverse the image of the Fund.

While it was a fortunate circumstance that Mr. Schweitzer was Managing Director when so many newly emerging countries were becoming members of the Fund, he did not confine his efforts to developing members. Presiding over the Fund during the worst international monetary crises by far since the Fund was created in 1944, he participated in the negotiations that led, among other things, to a two-tier market for gold, to devaluation of the pound sterling and the French franc, to large stand-by arrangements for the United Kingdom and France, to revaluation of the deutsche mark, to the currency realignments of the Smithsonian agreement, to the establishment in the Fund of a temporary regime of central rates and wider margins, and to the formation of a Committee of Twenty, representing all the Fund's members, to consider monetary reform.[16] In these negotiations, which involved monetary officials of the highest rank from the largest member countries, who oftentimes held conflicting positions, Mr. Schweitzer usually maintained a "low profile," working quietly and diplomatically to see what consensus might be possible. During his years in office, international monetary and financial problems became more complex and the danger of conflicting national interests increased. Working closely with the senior staff of the Fund, as was his custom, he sought solutions that would not damage the economies of other countries and that would be in the best interests of the international community at large. A dedicated internationalist, Mr. Schweitzer sought to preserve, in a period of turmoil, the harmonious cooperation that had gradually been built up among the Fund's members in less troublesome times.

Much of his work was necessarily outside the limelight, but he often spoke out on leading questions and made public pronouncements when he

---

[16] The formal name of the Committee of Twenty was Committee of the Board of Governors on Reform of the International Monetary System and Related Issues.

believed they would be useful. In addition, he traveled extensively throughout the world to promote international monetary cooperation and to strengthen member relations. He became a prominent world figure in monetary affairs. He was called upon to make speeches before banking groups, international commissions and conferences, and the like; he appeared on a number of occasions before the press and on television; he was awarded honorary degrees by the Universities of Leeds and Wales and by Harvard, Yale, George Washington, and New York Universities.

A man of unusual charm, warmth, and modesty, the officials with whom he dealt became his friends, and he was admired, respected, and held in great affection by his staff.

DEPUTY MANAGING DIRECTOR

Mr. Frank A. Southard, Jr., became the Deputy Managing Director on October 31, 1962 (while Mr. Per Jacobsson was the Managing Director) and was reappointed to a second five-year term beginning November 1, 1967. He was in that post during all of Mr. Schweitzer's tenure.[17]

In the complex of relationships, many of which are informal, between the Managing Director and the Deputy Managing Director, between them (as the management) and the Executive Directors, and between the management and the staff, it is even more difficult than in the instance of the Managing Director to disentangle the contribution of the Deputy Managing Director. Nonetheless, it is important to note here that Mr. Southard worked very closely and harmoniously with Mr. Schweitzer as a management team. To that team, Mr. Southard, who from February 1949 to November 1962 had been the Executive Director for the United States, brought his intimate familiarity with the Fund's policies and their origin and evolution; his widespread acquaintance with the financial officials of member countries, the Executive Directors, and the Fund staff; and his eminent qualifications as an economist. Mr. Southard was very much involved in the development of the Fund's policies and activities described in this history, participating in informal discussions on a number of levels—including discussions by the Managing Director with officials of member countries, consulting the Executive Directors, and offering his advice and judgment to the Managing Director. With a keen sense of the historical significance of the events taking place, Mr. Southard made concise but complete summary accounts of many of these informal discussions.

---

[17] Mr. Southard's second term, which would have ended on November 1, 1972, was extended. He resigned as the Deputy Managing Director on March 1, 1974, which was the twenty-fifth anniversary of his arrival in the Fund, and retired on April 30, 1974. In September 1973, Mr. H. Johannes Witteveen had succeeded Mr. Schweitzer as the Managing Director.

The Deputy Managing Director also had the primary responsibility for the administration of the staff. This function included not only organizing the staff and preparing the budget but also playing a major role in planning, with the senior staff, the studies undertaken, the assignments given, and the composition of missions sent to member countries, and seeing final reports through to completion. The meticulous care, conscientiousness, and industry with which Mr. Southard carried out these responsibilities, his prodigious output, and his sensitive concern for the staff were often a source of marvel to those with whom he worked.

Mr. Southard was identified with certain projects in which he had keen personal interest. He was instrumental, for example, in establishing the IMF Institute and the programs of technical assistance in central banking, fiscal affairs, and statistics, and he followed these activities closely. He also initiated several of the Fund's publications, such as the periodical *Finance and Development*, the histories of the Fund, and the Pamphlet Series.

In sum, Mr. Southard, serving in two capacities for 25 years, with all five Managing Directors, provided the Fund's policymaking process and its management and administration with continuity, and facilitated the transitions from one Managing Director to another.

STAFF: ORGANIZATION AND EXPANSION

Organization

In the first few years after Mr. Schweitzer became Managing Director and Mr. Southard became Deputy Managing Director, several changes had been made in the organization of the staff.[18] The Central Banking Service, the Fiscal Affairs Department, and the IMF Institute had been established; the Exchange Restrictions Department had been converted, with newly defined functions, into the Exchange and Trade Relations Department; and the Office of Administration, the Secretary's Office, and the Treasurer's Office had been elevated to departments and given additional responsibilities. In 1968, the Bureau of Statistics was formed as an entity separate from the Research and Statistics Department, and the latter was renamed the Research Department. Thereafter, the basic organization of the staff remained unaltered.

The staff continued to be organized into 14 departments plus the Bureau of Statistics and certain other units in the Office of the Managing Director. The departments were, in alphabetical order, the Administration Department,

---

[18] The reader interested in tracing the origins of the various departments and their functions is referred to *History, 1945–65*, Vol. I; see the listing under Staff, Organization of, in Index A, p. 648. A brief description of the organization of the staff as of the end of 1965 may be found in *History, 1945–65*, Vol. II, p. 10.

Frank A. Southard, Jr., Deputy Managing Director,
November 1, 1962–February 28, 1974

the African Department, the Asian Department, the Central Banking Service, the European Department, the Exchange and Trade Relations Department, the Fiscal Affairs Department, the IMF Institute, the Legal Department, the Middle Eastern Department, the Research Department, the Secretary's Department, the Treasurer's Department, and the Western Hemisphere Department. There were also the Office in Europe (Paris), the Office in Geneva, the Special Representative to the United Nations, the Information Office, and the Internal Auditor, all of which were, in the organizational structure, a part of the Managing Director's Office. Appendix C to this volume provides an organizational chart.

Rapid Expansion

Within the organizational structure described above, the number of staff from April 30, 1966 (the end of the fiscal year) to April 30, 1972 rose from 750 to 1,175 in what was by far the largest expansion in any six-year interval so far in the Fund's history, including even the first years. By the standards of most international organizations, however, the Fund was still relatively small.

The expansion took place in all departments and offices. There was an impressive growth in the five Area Departments because concentrated work on the problems of individual member countries continued to be the main task. The four functional departments, the IMF Institute, and the Bureau of Statistics added considerably to their staffs because of heavier responsibilities for the development of the Fund's general policies dealing with exchange rates, monetary stabilization, and fiscal affairs, because of the growth of technical assistance and training, and because of the impact on the research programs of larger and more numerous operations.

There were repercussions of the Fund's greater activity in the Administration Department, the Secretary's Department, and the Treasurer's Department. The increased demands on these departments were partly of an internal nature. Personnel recruitment, in-service training, general office services, and administrative payments, for example, all increased, not only because of the enlargement of the staff but also because of the engagement of numerous outside technical experts. But the demands made on these departments may have reflected even more the provision of greater services to member countries. For instance, in the Secretary's Department some of the staff began to work on a year-round basis to arrange the Annual Meetings. The flow of documentation and communications between the Fund and member countries accelerated to a point where additional staff were engaged in record-keeping, communications, mailing, and the like.

A dramatic increase in the Secretary's Department was in the staff involved in "language services." At the request of member countries, more and more of the Fund's documents were translated from English (the official language of the Fund) into other languages, especially French; publications were put out in more languages; and increasing use was made of simultaneous interpretation at meetings, lectures, and conferences. It followed that the staff employed in language work quadrupled. Fifty of the additional staff members taken on after the fiscal year 1965/66 were accounted for by the Language Services Division, and by 1971/72 this Division alone accounted for 6 per cent of the total staff.[19]

Also especially marked was the growth of the Treasurer's Department, which became the third largest department. Not only were administrative functions of the Treasurer's Department enlarged as transactions reached record high levels, but its operational duties were also greatly augmented. And there was now both a General Account and a Special Drawing Account to be operated. Many more reports on developments in the financial accounts of the Fund and in gold markets also had to be issued. Beginning in 1966, moreover, as a matter of deliberate management decision, the Treasurer's Department was charged, in conjunction with the Legal and Research Departments, with greater responsibility for the formulation of the Fund's financial policies, such as those in connection with general quota reviews, the formula for calculating quotas, and the designation plans for SDRs. As a result of all of these factors, the staff of the Treasurer's Department increased and in the fiscal year 1971/72 was more than two and a half times its size six years earlier.

The greater volume of the Fund's activities was reflected in the expansion of the other departments and offices as well. The Legal Department, occupied with amending the Articles of Agreement, with examining the legal implications of the actions members were taking to cope with recurrent international monetary crises, and with considering the possibilities of further amendments to the Articles, added somewhat to the number of lawyers employed. The staff of the Joint Bank-Fund Library likewise increased; with the continued growth of its collection to over 110,000 volumes and nearly 3,000 journals and 150 newspapers in 36 languages, it had become a world-renowned collection of materials on monetary and financial affairs and economic development. The Library, too, engaged in more technical assistance, by assembling and distributing lists of books and articles on economic development, money and banking, and public finance to central banks, government agencies, and faculties of economics in member countries. As their functions expanded, the Information Office, the Office of the Internal Auditor, and the Offices in Paris and Geneva also acquired additional personnel.

The increase in staff could be absorbed without creating additional departments because the existing departments included some, such as the Central Banking Service, the Fiscal Affairs Department, and the IMF Institute, that were relatively new and still in the process of staffing. A related factor was that several more divisions within each department were established. The division became the principal organizational unit, and the Division Chief was given enlarged duties and responsibilities.

---

[19] In 1972 a separate Bureau of Language Services was formed under Mr. J. S. Haszard.

Greater Use of Electronic Data Processing

Another aspect of the work of the staff was the increasing use of electronic data processing. The Joint Computer Center went into operation in 1968, when the Fund and the World Bank purchased a large general purpose computer. Jobs which in the past had been done with computer facilities outside the organizations were quickly adapted for operation on the jointly owned computer, and new programs and systems began to be devised. Reference was made in Chapter 29 to the Data Fund organized and operated by the Bureau of Statistics, a system which some of the Area Departments began to use to examine quantitatively the relationships between economic variables in member countries. The Research Department, which had been using computers in its studies for many years, adapted its existing programs to the new computer, and undertook a number of further econometric studies relating, for example, to financial programming, exchange rates, and export performance. The Research Department continued its participation with outside groups of econometricians in Project Link, a project aimed at developing a world trade model. The Treasurer's Department used the computer for operations in the General Account and, after the allocation of SDRs, in the Special Drawing Account; for calculations relating to quotas and to data on monetary reserves; and for disbursements of payroll and pension payments.

The staff of most departments included increasing numbers of young economists trained in modern statistical and econometric methods, and personnel specially trained in electronic data processing (such as systems analysts, programmers, and keypunch operators) were assigned to the Research Department, the Treasurer's Department, and the Bureau of Statistics. A Data Processing Division was set up in the Administration Department to act as liaison with the World Bank and to provide assistance to those departments or divisions that did not have specially trained personnel.

In addition to processing data by electronic means, the staff made use of the latest equipment for typing and reproducing an ever-expanding flow of documents.

Geographic Distribution

The Fund had always taken particular pride in the diverse national origins of its staff. That this diversity had widened considerably by 1971 is suggested by a few facts and figures. The staff at the end of the fiscal year 1970/71 (1,106 people) was drawn from 82 countries. The largest numbers were, as in the past, from the United States and the United Kingdom, but in 1971 these countries accounted for only about 28 per cent and 10 per cent, respectively, of the total staff. The next largest numbers, in absolute terms, came from 9 countries; these were, in descending order of the number therefrom, France, Canada, India, Australia, the Philippines, the Federal Republic of Germany, Italy, the

Netherlands, and Japan; the numbers of staff members from each of these countries ranged from 60 to 20. In addition, between 20 and 10 staff members came from each of 15 countries, which, in descending order of the number therefrom, were Chile, Jamaica, Korea, Haiti, Peru, Spain, Belgium, Bolivia, the Republic of China, Norway, Greece, Egypt, Brazil, Finland, and Trinidad and Tobago. And at least 5 staff members came from each of the following countries: Argentina, Austria, Burma, Ceylon, Colombia, Denmark, Ecuador, Guyana, Iran, Ireland, Mexico, New Zealand, Nicaragua, Nigeria, Pakistan, Panama, Portugal, Sweden, Thailand, and Turkey.

Worldwide recruitment efforts were a significant factor in explaining the diversity achieved. In the years 1966–71 there was a 60 per cent expansion of staff, but only 15 per cent of the additional staff came from the United States and 10 per cent from the United Kingdom. Instead, they came from a wide range of member countries, with the largest absolute numbers from, in descending order, France, India, Canada, Italy, Australia, the Philippines, Jamaica, Peru, Spain, Bolivia, Chile, Korea, the Federal Republic of Germany, Haiti, Japan, Finland, Norway, and Iceland. Furthermore, staff was recruited for the first time from Algeria, the Khmer Republic (Cambodia), Cameroon, Dahomey, Guyana, Israel, Kenya, Malaysia, Mali, Mauritania, Morocco, Singapore, Tunisia, Uganda, Upper Volta, and Zambia.

A wide diversity of nationality was also to be found among the senior officials. The 150 staff members at the level of Division Chief or above on February 28, 1971 were from 35 countries.

The staff was international in another, and more important, respect. Regardless of nationality, the staff worked together as a body of international civil servants, in the interests of the Fund, and did not try to represent, or lobby for, the national interests of particular member governments.

STAFF: TEAMWORK, ANONYMITY, AND LONG SERVICE

A brief description of how the work of the staff was carried out in the twenty years from 1945 to 1965 was given in the earlier history.[20] The same description applied to the six years from 1966 to 1971. As the size of the staff increased, two points of emphasis became especially important: teamwork and general anonymity.

The end product of virtually all of the work done by the staff in the period described here was the result of the combined efforts of many people. There were divisions of responsibility, of course, but in carrying out their responsibilities, staff from the various departments continuously pooled and shared their information and ideas and their specialized knowledge and experi-

---

[20] *History, 1945–65*, Vol. II, pp. 12–14 and 16–17.

ence. Although differing opinions among the staff might well have been aired and considered prior to the formulation of "a staff view," what was presented to the Executive Directors was a consensus. For example, a staff team undertaking a mission to a member country to conduct discussions in connection with a consultation conferred with the senior staff of a number of departments, both in advance of departure and upon return to headquarters. The subsequent report on the discussions was drafted by the mission team and, after approval by the departments concerned, was sent to the Executive Directors as a Staff Memorandum (SM series) prepared "by the staff representatives" who were on the mission. General policy papers evolved gradually through a process in which the personnel of several departments consulted and coordinated very closely. These papers, too, were sent to the Executive Directors as Staff Memoranda without specifying the names of the individuals concerned; they contained an identification only of the departments that had major responsibility for their preparation.

This collaboration meant that the papers sent to the Executive Directors reflected the combined views of the staff. Then, having received the approval of the Managing Director or of the Deputy Managing Director or, often, of both, these papers had the support of the management. The collaboration among the staff also meant that it was almost never possible to separate from the final product the contribution of an individual. Furthermore, much of the work of the Fund involved confidential information and discussions that could not be revealed except to "insiders." Hence, while the work of individual staff members was well known within the organization and among colleagues, and often among the monetary and financial officials of member countries, most of the members of the staff, like civil servants throughout the world, remained anonymous to all but a very limited number of people.

These factors explain the absence in this narrative of staff names, except for the few mentioned in the chapters on SDRs; those staff members were in a unique capacity, representing the Managing Director and speaking on his behalf in forums outside the Fund. The Fund's history, nevertheless, involves not only events and issues in the economic and financial fields and the formation of related policies; it also involves people. Indeed, the foregoing chapters are filled with names of many of the monetary officials involved in the history of the Fund in these years. To personalize further the account contained in this history, and particularly to give identity to the often-used term "the Fund staff," we now mention a number of staff members who, by virtue of their seniority and their long service, were in a special category: all Directors of Departments, of Offices, and of one Bureau, plus those with the rank of Division Chief or above who had served for more than 20 years by the end of 1971. The listing of names is in line with the trend of recent years toward reducing, at least to some extent, the anonymity of the staff. For example, names appeared on RED reports, in the *Annual Report on Exchange Restrictions,* and on the volumes of the earlier history. At times the staff on missions in member countries were identified in the local press. Signed articles (as in the past) appeared in *Staff Papers* and *Finance and Development*.

Because the staff, regardless of nationality, worked as a cohesive body of international civil servants, the nationalities of individual staff members are not indicated below.

In order of length of service, the Directors of Departments and Offices and of the Bureau of Statistics at the end of 1971 were as follows:

Mr. Jan V. Mládek, the Director of the Central Banking Service, was elected by Czechoslovakia in March 1946 to be on the first Board of Executive Directors. After serving as an Executive Director for two years, Mr. Mládek joined the staff. In 1953 he became the Director of the Paris Office, a position he held for nearly 8 years, and in 1961 he was placed temporarily in charge of the newly created African Department, pending the appointment of an African. When the Central Banking Service was formed in 1964, Mr. Mládek became the Director.

Mr. Phillip Thorson, the Director of the Administration Department, was one of the "oldest" staff members, in terms of length of service. Mr. Thorson was one of the very few original members of the staff when the staff was established on April 8, 1946. He held a senior post in the Secretary's Office for 8 years and in May 1954 was appointed Director of what was then the Office of Administration and later became the Administration Department. Thus, at the end of 1971, Mr. Thorson had been the Director of Administration for over 17 years.

Three other Directors of Departments, the Director of the Bureau of Statistics, and the Director of the Office in Europe (Paris) also came to the staff in 1946, and one came in January 1947. They too had had 25 or more years of continuous service on the staff at the end of 1971:

Mr. Earl Hicks began his career in the Fund in July 1946, undertaking the amassing of the financial statistics that culminated shortly thereafter in the monthly bulletin, *International Financial Statistics*. From then on, Mr. Hicks was continuously identified with the responsibility for the Fund's financial statistics. When the Bureau of Statistics was set up in 1968, he became the Director.

Mr. Ernest Sturc joined the Research Department as a Division Chief in September 1946. Subsequently he served for a number of years as Deputy Director in the European Department. In January 1965 he was appointed Director of the Exchange Restrictions Department. In May 1965 that department became the Exchange and Trade Relations Department, with new responsibilities. Mr. Sturc continued as the Director, in which capacity he was serving at the end of 1971.

Mr. Jorge Del Canto was also among the Fund's earliest staff members, joining the staff in September 1946. From the outset and continuously thereafter, Mr. Del Canto was closely associated with the Fund's work with its Latin American members, and in May 1957 he became the Director of the Western Hemisphere Department, which was composed of Latin America, Canada, and the United States. At the end of 1971 Mr. Del Canto had been involved in the Fund's Latin American work for more than 25 years and in charge of the Western Hemisphere Department for over 14 years.

Mr. Joseph Gold came to the staff in October 1946. After several years as a senior lawyer in the Legal Department, he became the head of that department (which carried the title General Counsel) in 1960. Mr. Gold was made The General Counsel in May 1966. This was a new position in the Fund, even though it carried the former title, because the former position was changed to Director, in which position Mr. Gold also continued to serve.

Mr. Jean-Paul Sallé, who in 1963 was made the Director of the Office in Europe (Paris), joined the staff in December 1946. Mr. Sallé had already been with the Paris Office for many years before becoming the Director, and earlier had worked at headquarters on the Fund's relations with its European members.

Mr. J. J. Polak joined the staff of the Research Department in January 1947. Initially responsible for formulating and directing the Fund's quantitative and econometric research, Mr. Polak's responsibilities were gradually enlarged. After several years as Deputy Director in the Research and Statistics Department he became the Director in 1958. He was appointed The Economic Counsellor, the first such post in the Fund, in May 1966, and continued to serve also as the Director of the Research Department.

The Directors of three departments and the Director of the IMF Institute had been with the Fund since the early 1950s:

Mr. F. A. G. Keesing joined the staff of the Exchange Restrictions Department in 1951 as an Advisor and remained with that department until May 1964. With the creation of the IMF Institute, Mr. Keesing became its first Director.[21]

Mr. Richard Goode joined the staff in 1951 and for the next 8 years held senior posts successively in the Research Department and the Asian Department. In 1959 he left the Fund to go to the Brookings Institution. In 1965 Mr. Goode returned to head the newly established Fiscal Affairs Department.

The Middle Eastern Department was headed by staff who had been with the Fund for over 15 years. Mr. Anwar Ali became the Director in October 1954. However, in 1958 he went on a special assignment as Governor of the Saudi Arabian Monetary Agency (central bank), and Mr. John W. Gunter, who had joined the staff of the Middle Eastern Department in 1953, acted as

---

[21] Mr. Keesing died in September 1972 and was succeeded by Mr. Gérard M. Teyssier, who had been Deputy Director of the IMF Institute since 1967. From 1964 to 1967 Mr. Teyssier had been an Alternate Executive Director.

Director. After 1965, when Mr. Anwar Ali continued in Saudi Arabia, on leave of absence from the Fund, Mr. Gunter became officially the Acting Director.

Mr. W. Lawrence Hebbard had been on the staff for more than 12 years when he was appointed Secretary of the Fund in January 1967. He came to the Fund in 1954 as a Division Chief in the Exchange Restrictions Department, and later became an Assistant Director in that department. Upon the retirement of Mr. Roman L. Horne in December 1966, Mr. Hebbard became the Secretary of the Fund. (The Secretary is also the administrative head of the Secretary's Department.)

At the time of his retirement at the end of 1966, Mr. Horne had been on the staff for more than 20 years and had been Secretary since January 1, 1953.

The periods of service of the Directors of the four remaining departments were relatively shorter, but they too had been with the Fund for several years:

Mr. D. S. Savkar joined the staff in June 1959 as the Director of the Asian Department. Having been an Alternate Executive Director from 1948 to 1951, Mr. Savkar was familiar with the work of the Fund.[22]

Mr. L. A. Whittome joined the staff as the Director of the European Department in August 1964. Mr. Whittome had previously had a 14-year career with the Bank of England, where, since 1962, he had held the post of Deputy Chief Cashier.

Mr. Walter O. Habermeier was an Alternate Executive Director from 1962 to 1965 and became a member of the staff of the Treasurer's Department in 1966. The Treasurer of the Fund, Mr. Oscar L. Altman, died in December 1968, and Mr. Habermeier was appointed Treasurer in February 1969. (The Treasurer of the Fund is also the administrative head of the Treasurer's Department.)

At the time of his death, Mr. Altman had been on the staff for more than 20 years. He joined the staff as an Assistant to the Managing Director with general responsibility for administration and then became the first Director of Administration. In 1956 he moved to the Research and Statistics Department as Advisor, and he was subsequently promoted to Deputy Director of that department. In May 1966 the Treasurer's Department acquired expanded responsibilities and functions and Mr. Altman was appointed Treasurer.

Mr. Mamoudou Touré joined the staff as the Director of the African Department in April 1967. Mr. Touré had previously held a variety of positions. Just prior to his appointment to the Fund staff, he had been Director of the UN African Institute for Economic Development and Planning in Dakar.

Mr. Edgar Jones, who was appointed in 1967 as the Director of the Office in Geneva, had been with the Fund since 1953. Before moving to Geneva to

---

[22] When Mr. Savkar retired in 1972, he was succeeded by Mr. Tun Thin. Mr. Tun Thin had been an Alternate Executive Director from 1957 to 1959, when he joined the staff of the Asian Department.

take charge of the office in October 1965 (when it was established on a provisional basis), Mr. Jones was Deputy Director of the Exchange Restrictions Department, and had been in that department for 12 years.

By the end of 1971 dozens of other senior staff members had also accumulated 20 to 25 years of experience in the Fund. In the following paragraphs they are listed by department, taking the departments in alphabetical order and the staff within the departments in order of length of service.

In the Administration Department, Mr. Walter H. Windsor, senior Assistant Director, came to the staff on the very first day the staff was established, and, beginning with the organization of the Fund's first offices in temporary quarters in the Washington Hotel, he was subsequently involved, with other staff, in providing the Fund with office space. This involvement included the construction of the new headquarters described in the following section. Mr. William M. Avery, Assistant Director, was similarly a member of the administrative staff from June 1946, and was responsible for, among other things, overseeing services and supplies, transportation, and graphic arts. Mr. Martin L. Loftus, the Librarian of the Joint Bank-Fund Library, came to the Fund in September 1946, as the staff was just being organized, to establish the Library and to begin assembling volumes, acquiring back publications, and the like. Thereafter, he continued in charge of the growing collection. Mr. Kenneth N. Clark, appointed Deputy Director of the department in 1966, joined the staff in 1947 and in subsequent years worked at a senior level on a variety of administrative and personnel matters. Mr. Henri H. P. King, Assistant Director, in charge of preparing the administrative budget, joined the staff in 1948; for several years, Mr. King performed a variety of administrative and personnel tasks.

In the African Department, Mr. Charles L. Merwin, Deputy Director from 1964 onward, had come to the Fund in 1946. He was in the Research Department from 1946 to 1952, and helped to start the collection and statistical presentation of balance of payments data; then he worked in the European Department from 1952 to 1964. Mr. Ali R. Bengur, Senior Advisor, had been on the staff since 1947 and had been associated with the Fund's work on some of its European member countries and on Middle Eastern member countries before he undertook assignments on African member countries. Likewise, Messrs. D. Boushehri and Alberto S. Foz were staff in the African Department who joined the Fund in the early years, and who worked previously on member countries in other geographic regions, Mr. Boushehri in the Middle East and Mr. Foz in Latin America.

The Asian Department, too, had three staff members whose periods of service began before 1950. Mr. W. John R. Woodley, Deputy Director, had been with the Fund, except for a 3-year interval, since July 1948, working on problems of exchange restrictions and multiple exchange rates prior to moving to the Asian Department, where he became Deputy Director in 1966.

Mr. Andreas Abadjis, Senior Advisor, had been on the staff since September 1948 and had been with the Research Department and with the European Department before beginning work on Asian member countries. Mr. Albert A. Mattera, Senior Advisor, came to the Fund in 1949 and dealt with matters of exchange control and multiple exchange rates prior to taking up assignments on the Asian member countries.

Besides the Director, the Central Banking Service had three senior people with long experience in the Fund. Mr. Marcin R. Wyczalkowski joined the staff in 1946 as an economist in the Research Department and later was in the European Department before becoming Senior Advisor in the Central Banking Service in 1967. Mr. Rudolf Kroc, Senior Advisor, joined what was then the Operations Department in 1947; subsequently he took on a number of special assignments, particularly in regard to technical assistance, and was a senior officer in the Treasurer's Department before joining the Central Banking Service. Mr. Graeme S. Dorrance joined the staff in 1951 and was a Senior Economist and a Division Chief in the Research Department before going to the Central Banking Service.

In the European Department, both of the Deputy Directors and the three Senior Advisors had had more than 20 years of experience on the staff in 1971. Mr. Albin Pfeifer, who came to the staff in October 1946, had long been working on European problems and had been with the Paris Office and with the African Department before becoming Deputy Director in the European Department in 1966. Mr. Poul Høst-Madsen came to the Fund in November 1946 and had been in the Research Department before becoming Deputy Director in the European Department in 1966. Mr. Rolf Evensen, who became a Senior Advisor in 1970, had been on the staff since 1947, working continuously with European member countries. Mr. Brian Rose, appointed a Senior Advisor in 1966, had been on the staff also since 1947, dealing primarily with European member countries. Mr. H. Ponsen, appointed a Senior Advisor in 1966, had been on the staff since 1950, also dealing with European member countries.

In the Exchange and Trade Relations Department, four senior staff members had had at least two decades of experience with the Fund by the end of 1971. Mr. Erik Elmholt, Advisor, and participant in any number of annual consultation missions, joined the staff in 1949. Mr. C. David Finch, appointed Deputy Director in 1966, joined the staff in 1950 and was previously with the Research Department and the Western Hemisphere Department. Mr. J. H. C. de Looper, Advisor, who was primarily responsible for the *Annual Report on Exchange Restrictions*, also joined the staff in 1950. Mr. Timothy Sweeney, who became a Senior Advisor in 1966, had come to the Fund in 1951 and had served with the Research Department, the Western Hemisphere Department, and the Fiscal Affairs Department.

In the Fiscal Affairs Department, Mr. Jakob Saper, appointed Deputy

Director when the department was established in 1964, had been with the staff since 1947, working on a range of administrative and accounting matters.

In the IMF Institute, Mr. Herbert K. Zassenhaus, Deputy Director, had been on the staff since 1951 and had had a varied career in the Research Department, the Exchange and Trade Relations Department, and the Western Hemisphere Department.

Other than The General Counsel, three members of the senior legal staff had been handling a variety of legal problems continuously for more than 20 years. Ms. Philine R. Lachman, a Senior Counsellor since 1969, joined the Legal Department in 1947. Mr. Albert S. Gerstein, who became a Deputy General Counsel in 1964, joined the Fund's corps of lawyers in 1948. Mr. George P. Nicoletopoulos, who likewise became a Deputy General Counsel in 1964, came to the legal staff in 1950.

In the Middle Eastern Department, Mr. M. M. Hassanein, Advisor, joined the staff in 1950. Mr. A. S. Ray, Deputy Director since 1967, had been with that department since 1951. Mr. A. K. El Selehdar, Chief of the Arabian Peninsula Division, also joined the staff in 1951. These staff members all participated in a variety of assignments on the Middle Eastern member countries.

In the Research Department none of the senior staff, apart from The Economic Counsellor, had, by the end of 1971, served on the staff for a full two decades. However, many members of the long-standing staff of other departments—including several Directors and Deputy Directors of Departments and Senior Advisors mentioned elsewhere in this account—had started their careers in the Fund as economists in the Research Department.

The Secretary's Department had a number of long-standing senior staff members. Mrs. Katherine F. Magurn joined the staff in September 1946 and had been in charge of language services before becoming an Assistant Secretary in 1970. Mr. Roger V. Anderson, the Deputy Secretary and the Chief Editor since 1967, joined the staff in October 1946 and worked in the Research Department and then for many years in the Exchange Restrictions Department, where, among other things, he dealt with the Fund's relations with the GATT. Mr. George E. Bishop, managing the Fund's official communications with members and Governors, had been handling that assignment since 1947. Miss Marie C. Stark, appointed Archivist in 1951, had been in charge of the Fund's records, documents, and archives since 1947. Mr. D. E. Brantley, appointed in 1970 as Assistant Secretary for Annual Meetings, headed a joint Fund-Bank office charged with arranging Annual Meetings, work which he had already been doing for some years; joining the Fund in 1949, he previously had been with the administrative staff, where he was instrumental in launching the first training programs.

The Treasurer's Department similarly had several senior staff members who had been with the Fund for more than 20 years and who had been dealing continuously with the Fund's operational and administrative accounts: Mr. Carl B. Fink came in 1947, Mr. Walter T. Powers in 1948, and Mr. Charles E. Jones in 1949. Mr. Frederick C. Dirks, who was transferred as Senior Advisor to the Treasurer's Department in 1968, had joined the staff in 1950, and had been in the Western Hemisphere Department and the IMF Institute.

In the Western Hemisphere Department, both Deputy Directors and three additional senior staff members had not only been with the Fund for nearly 25 years but, except for one, their careers in the Fund had been devoted entirely to Latin America. Mr. Edison V. Zayas, Chief of the Grancolombian Division, joined the staff in 1946 and for the next 25 years worked on a number of Latin American member countries. Mr. E. Walter Robichek joined the staff in February 1947 and thereafter worked continuously and intensively with many of the Latin American member countries, serving in a number of departments as the staff's structure was reorganized; Mr. Robichek became Deputy Director of the Western Hemisphere Department in 1961. Mr. Richard A. Radford, Advisor, who at the end of 1971 had been working with Latin American member countries for several years, joined the staff in June 1947 and had previously worked in several other departments. Mr. Paul J. Brand, Senior Advisor as of the end of 1971, joined the staff in August 1947 and thereafter had a 24-year career of dealing with the Latin American member countries. Mr. Fernando A. Vera, appointed Deputy Director in 1966, joined the staff in 1948, and subsequently dealt continuously with Latin American member countries.

In the Bureau of Statistics were five senior staff members who came to the Fund before 1950 and who subsequently spent all, or practically all, of their careers in the Fund handling the financial statistics of member countries. Messrs. Akira P. Nose, Advisor, and Robert L. Praetorius, Chief of the General Statistics Division, joined the staff in 1946, Messrs. Leonello Boccia, Advisor, and José C. Sánchiz, Chief of the Financial Statistics Division (B), in 1947, and Mr. Dan R. Silling, Chief of the Financial Statistics Division (A), in 1949. Hence, by the end of 1971 they had intimate familiarity with the collecting, compiling, and publishing of the Fund's financial data.

Some of the senior staff in the Office of the Managing Director also had had more than two decades of experience in the Fund. Mr. Gordon Williams, the Special Representative to the United Nations, joined the staff in 1946, and for most of his career in the Fund he had been responsible for overseeing the complex of relationships between the Fund and the UN family. Mr. J. William Lowe, the Internal Auditor, joined the staff early in 1947, so that by the end of 1971 he had worked on the Fund's accounting controls and procedures for many years. Mr. Jay H. Reid, Chief Information Officer, joined the staff in 1948 to be in charge of the Fund's information and public relations activities. As time went on these activities expanded and Mr. Reid's responsibilities increased.

Three staff members who retired before the end of 1971 had joined the Fund staff in the early years and served for more than 20 years before retiring, attaining ranks equivalent to those mentioned above. Mr. Eduardo Laso, who joined the staff in 1946, was an economist and Division Chief in the Western Hemisphere Department before he moved, in 1967, to the IMF Institute where he became an Advisor and later an Assistant Director. Mr. C. C. Liang, who also joined the staff in 1946, was Chief of the Far Eastern Division in the Research Department and in the Asian Department, and later became an Advisor. Mr. Henry C. Murphy, who joined the staff in 1949, was Chief of the Finance Division in the Research Department before becoming Deputy Director in the Asian Department and, later, Senior Advisor in the Fiscal Affairs Department.

Young when they joined the Fund's staff—most being in their early or mid-thirties and some in their twenties—the afore-mentioned staff members by the mid-1960s were, together with the Governors, the Executive Directors, and the management, among the Fund's top policymakers.

Other staff members with fewer years of service also had a major role in the formulation and implementation of several of the policies described in this narrative, or in the research underlying those policies. There were some 70 additional members of the staff, most of whom came to the Fund either in the late 1950s or in the 1960s, who by 1971 had attained Division Chief status or higher. Three among them, all being Deputy Directors during the years reviewed here, should be mentioned in particular. Mr. J. Marcus Fleming, who was appointed Deputy Director of the Research Department in 1964, joined the Research Department's staff in 1954 as Chief of the Special Studies Division. Mr. Charles F. Schwartz, appointed Deputy Director of the Research Department in 1966, joined the staff of the Western Hemisphere Department in 1959 as Chief of the North American Division. Mr. Jacques Waïtzenegger, who was appointed Deputy Director of the African Department in 1964, had been an Alternate Executive Director from 1960 to 1964.

As the Fund celebrated its twenty-fifth anniversary in 1971, there were many other individuals among the supporting staff who had served for over two decades and, indeed, several who had served for a quarter of a century. Surely, one of the salient features of the staff was its long experience in the Fund. Appendix B lists the names of all staff members who held the rank of Division Chief or above at the end of 1971.

NEW HEADQUARTERS BUILDING

The building referred to in Chapter 19 in the discussion of the budget was under construction by late in 1970. The Fund and the World Bank were already occupying the block between 18th and 19th Streets, bounded by

G Street on the south and H Street on the north.[23] Forecasts of the growth of personnel suggested that the Fund would be out of space in its existing headquarters by the middle of 1970. With a view to expansion, the Fund had started in 1966 to acquire property on the west side of 19th Street.

Because of complications with land acquisition, it was decided to construct a building in three phases. Initially, Phase I was to involve the construction of additional office space, and not a new headquarters building. But by mid-1969 enough land had been acquired to permit a substantial broadening of Phase I, and the Executive Board, after considerable deliberation, in December 1969 approved a revised plan under which the Fund would build a new headquarters building and sell the buildings it now owned to the World Bank. A tunnel would be constructed under 19th Street to provide an all-weather passage for pedestrians between the new Fund building and the World Bank. Construction of the new headquarters proceeded beyond 1971 into 1972 and early 1973.[24]

In the spring of 1970 the World Bank completed construction of a new building in Paris at 66 Avenue d'Iena to house its European Office, and also to house the Fund's Office in Europe, for which the Fund rented space from the Bank.

THE FUND AS 1971 ENDED

When 1971 came to a close, the international monetary system that had been designed a little more than a quarter of a century earlier with the Fund as the institutional center had been disrupted, and discussions and negotiations on measures to improve, overhaul, or reform it were under way. In these circumstances, the Fund was suspended between the collapse of the old order and the initiation of a new one the features of which would take some years to work out.

As the issues involved in working out an improved or reformed system began to be debated, it quickly became apparent that opposing views might be very difficult to reconcile. Hence, the period of transition through which the Fund had been passing in the previous six years, the period in which the par value system had come under severe stress and had eventually collapsed, seemed

---

[23] The construction of the Fund's headquarters in 1958 and its extension in 1966 were described in *History, 1945–65*, Vol. I, p. 560.

[24] The first occupants moved into the building in February 1973. The new headquarters was officially opened on August 17, 1973. The 13-story structure, between 19th and 20th Streets, bounded by G Street on the south and H Street on the north, was the result of close teamwork between the responsible Fund officers, the designers, and the contractor. Vincent G. Kling & Partners were the architects and interior designers, Clas, Riggs, Owens & Ramos the consulting architects, and the Charles H. Tompkins Company the contractor. What was now called Phase II was delayed pending the Fund's acquisition of the remaining land in the block.

Interior court

Exterior view

Headquarters, Washington, 1973

likely to extend for however long it might take to negotiate and complete the reform of the international monetary system.

The precise character that the Fund might develop in the future looked uncertain. A few even went so far as to intimate that the Fund had outlived its usefulness. They suggested, for example, that in a world of massive capital flows, giant multinational corporations, and private banking operations on a huge and global scale, the international consultative and regulatory techniques exemplified by the Fund were slow, cumbersome, and inadequate. Reliance would have to be placed virtually entirely on market mechanisms.

Such pessimistic views about the Fund were extreme, however, even at the time. A number of countertrends suggested that the Fund in the future could, quite conceivably, be given even greater responsibilities in the international monetary system. Several economists and monetary experts were advocating that the Fund become "truly an international central bank," in which all monetary reserves would be deposited. Some monetary officials in key government posts were suggesting that the Fund's new reserve asset, the SDR, should be made the primary reserve for international transactions. Others were recommending that the Fund be given somewhat greater functions in the field of international trade, in addition to those it already had in the monetary and exchange fields. Most important of all, perhaps, was that nations meeting in smaller groups were having increasing difficulties among themselves in agreeing not only on international monetary arrangements but also on a number of other economic and political issues.

It was in this spirit of optimism about the Fund that Mr. Schweitzer addressed the Governors at the 1971 Annual Meeting:

> What is at stake is the question of consolidating the achievements of a quarter of a century—or of jeopardizing those achievements. In trade and payments, we seek to preserve a liberal regime governed by international rules. In the aid field, the continuing goal is effective action in recognition of common interests and responsibilities. With respect to exchange rates, the pressing need is to improve upon established procedures for maintaining exchange stability and allowing for necessary adjustments in a way that avoids conflict. In the sphere of international liquidity, the challenge is to utilize the instrument of SDRs and other facilities of the Fund as a means of assuring effective control of the world's reserves.
>
> On all these fronts, we must now move forward with enthusiasm and high purpose.[25]

---

[25] Opening Address by the Managing Director, *Summary Proceedings, 1971*, p. 15.

Appendices

Appendix A–1. Appointed Executive Directors and Their Alternates
Article XII, Section 3 (b) (i)
1966–71

Countries Represented		Representation		Executive Director and Alternate [1]	Dates [2] of Service	
Name	Date [2] Became Member	Began	Ended	Name	Began	Ended
United States	12/27/45	1946		William B. Dale	11/1/62	
				John S. Hooker	1/3/50	3/31/70
				Charles R. Harley	9/17/70	
United Kingdom	12/27/45	1946		Sir John Stevens	1/15/65	8/8/67
				Douglas W. G. Wass	6/3/65	
				Evan W. Maude	8/9/67	10/21/69
				Douglas W. G. Wass		10/27/67
				Guy Huntrods	10/28/67	
				Derek Mitchell	11/7/69	
				Guy Huntrods		7/19/70
				Ronald H. Gilchrist	7/20/70	
France	12/27/45	1946		René Larre	6/6/64	8/31/67
				Gérard M. Teyssier	6/1/64	7/30/67
				Paul Mentré	7/31/67	
				Georges Plescoff	9/1/67	10/31/70
				Paul Mentré		8/15/68
				Bruno de Maulde	8/16/68	
				Marc Viénot	11/1/70	
				Bruno de Maulde		12/31/70
				Claude Beaurain	1/1/71	

Appendix A–1 (concluded). Appointed Executive Directors and Their Alternates
Article XII, Section 3 (b) (i)
1966–71

Countries Represented		Representation		Executive Director and Alternate[1]	Dates[2] of Service	
Name	Date[2] Became Member	Began	Ended	Name	Began	Ended
India[3]	12/27/45	1946		J. J. Anjaria	8/1/61	1/31/67
				Arun K. Ghosh	*7/1/64*	*6/30/66*
				Arun K. Banerji	*7/1/66*	
				B. K. Madan	2/1/67	6/4/71
				Arun K. Banerji		*1/31/69*
				Sharad S. Marathe	*2/1/69*	
				P. S. N. Prasad	6/5/71	
Germany, Federal Republic of[4]	8/14/52	1960		Ulrich Beelitz	4/1/64	5/31/66
				Horst Ungerer	*11/1/65*	
				Ernst vom Hofe	6/1/66	4/30/68
				Guenther Schleiminger	5/1/68	
				Horst Ungerer		*8/25/68*
				Lore Fuenfgelt	*8/26/68*	
Japan[3]	8/13/52	1970		Hideo Suzuki	11/1/70	
				Koichi Satow	*11/1/70*	

[1] Alternate Executive Directors, always appointed by the Executive Director, are indicated by italic type.

[2] Dates are given in the following order: month/day/year.

[3] On November 1, 1970, Japan replaced India as one of the five members having the largest quotas and therefore qualified to appoint an Executive Director in accordance with Article XII, Section 3 (b) (i). India continued, however, to be entitled to appoint an Executive Director until the next regular election of Executive Directors in 1972, pursuant to Board of Governors Resolution No. IM-7.

[4] On November 1, 1960, the Federal Republic of Germany replaced the Republic of China as one of the five members having the largest quotas and therefore qualified to appoint an Executive Director in accordance with Article XII, Section 3 (b) (i).

Appendix A–2. Elected Executive Directors and Their Alternates
Article XII, Section 3 (b) (iii)
1966–71

Countries Represented — Name	Date[2] Became Member	Representation Began	Representation Ended	Executive Director and Alternate[1] — Name	Dates[2] of Service Began	Dates[2] of Service Ended
China, Republic of[3]	12/27/45	1960		Beue Tann (Republic of China)	11/1/60	10/31/70
Korea	8/26/55	1966		Chi-Ling Chow (Republic of China)	10/5/65	10/31/68
Viet-Nam	9/21/56	1966		Nguyên Huu Hanh (Viet-Nam)	11/1/68	
Philippines	12/27/45	1970		Peh Yuan Hsu (Republic of China)	11/1/70	
Canada	12/27/45	1946		S. J. Handfield-Jones (Canada)	5/1/65	10/31/68
Ireland	8/8/57	1960		Patrick M. Reid (Canada)	7/1/65	10/31/68
Jamaica	2/21/63	1964		Robert Johnstone (Canada)	11/1/68	9/30/71
Guyana	9/26/66	1966	1970	Maurice Horgan (Ireland)	11/1/68	12/31/70
Barbados[4]	12/29/70	—		Donald Owen Mills (Jamaica)	1/1/71	
				Robert Bryce (Canada)	10/1/71	
Netherlands	12/27/45	1946		Pieter Lieftinck (Netherlands)	10/1/55	
Israel	7/12/54	1954		H. M. H. A. van der Valk (Netherlands)	5/23/49	11/30/68
Yugoslavia	12/27/45	1954		Pieter C. Timmerman (Netherlands)	12/1/68	1/14/69
Cyprus	12/21/61	1962		Tom de Vries (Netherlands)	1/15/69	
Ceylon[5]	8/29/50	1950	1970	Gengo Suzuki (Japan)	11/1/60	10/31/66
Thailand[5]	5/3/49	1950	1970	Eiji Ozaki (Japan)	7/1/65	
Burma[5]	1/3/52	1952	1970	Hideo Suzuki (Japan)	11/1/66	10/31/70
Japan[6]	8/13/52	1952	1970	Eiji Ozaki (Japan)		4/26/68
Nepal[5]	9/6/61	1962	1970	Seitaro Hattori (Japan)	4/27/68	6/15/70
				Koichi Satow (Japan)	6/16/70	10/31/70
Egypt	12/27/45	1946		Ahmed Zaki Saad (Egypt)	5/6/46	10/31/70
Ethiopia	12/27/45	1946	1970	Albert Mansour (Egypt)	11/16/51	7/31/68
Iran	12/29/45	1946		Albert Mansour (Egypt)	12/26/68	10/31/70
Iraq	12/27/45	1946		Nazih Deif (Egypt)	11/1/70	
Philippines	12/27/45	1946	1970	Muhammad Al-Atrash (Syrian Arab Republic)	12/1/70	
Lebanon	4/14/47	1948				

Appendix A–2 (continued). Elected Executive Directors and Their Alternates
Article XII, Section 3 (b) (iii)
1966–71

| Countries Represented | Date[2] Became Member | Representation | | Executive Director and Alternate[1] | Dates[2] of Service | |
Name		Began	Ended	Name	Began	Ended
Syrian Arab Republic	4/10/47	1948				
Pakistan	7/11/50	1950				
Jordan	8/29/52	1952				
Afghanistan	7/14/55	1956				
Saudi Arabia	8/26/57	1958				
Kuwait	9/13/62	1962				
Somalia	8/31/62	1964				
Yemen Arab Republic	5/22/70	1970				
Yemen, People's Democratic Republic of	9/29/69	1970				
Oman[4]	12/23/71	—				
Belgium	12/27/45	1946		André van Campenhout (Belgium)	12/1/54	
Luxembourg	12/27/45	1946		Herman Biron (Belgium)	11/24/65	11/15/68
Austria	8/27/48	1954		Jacques Roelandts (Belgium)	11/16/68	11/30/70
Turkey	3/11/47	1954		Heinrich G. Schneider (Austria)	12/1/70	
Italy	3/27/47	[1947][7]		Sergio Siglienti (Italy)	11/1/60	11/30/67
Greece[8]	12/27/45	1948	1970	Costa P. Caranicas (Greece)	11/1/52	
Spain[8]	9/15/58	1958		Francesco Palamenghi-Crispi (Italy)[9]	12/1/67	
Portugal[8]	3/29/61	1962		Costa P. Caranicas (Greece)		10/31/68
Malta[8]	9/11/68	1970		Carlos Bustelo (Spain)	11/1/68	
Australia	8/5/47	[1948][7]		J. M. Garland (Australia)	11/11/59	1/17/66
South Africa	12/27/45	1948		Roy Daniel (Australia)	1/10/64	
Viet-Nam	9/21/56	1956	1966	M. W. O'Donnell (Australia)	1/18/66	2/1/67
New Zealand	8/31/61	1962		Roy Daniel (Australia)		2/1/66
Lesotho	7/25/68	1968		A. M. de Villiers (South Africa)	2/2/66	

Member countries

Country	Date	Year	
Swaziland	9/22/69	1970	
Western Samoa [4]	12/28/71	—	
Denmark	3/30/46	1952	
Finland	1/14/48	1952	
Iceland	12/27/45	1952	
Norway	12/27/45	1952	
Sweden	8/31/51	1952	
Ghana	9/20/57	1958	
Libyan Arab Republic	9/17/58	1958	
Malaysia [5]	3/7/58	1958	1970
Morocco	4/25/58	1958	
Tunisia	4/14/58	1958	
Laos [5]	7/5/61	1962	1970
Algeria	9/26/63	1964	
Singapore [5]	8/3/66	1966	1970
Indonesia [10]	2/21/67	1968	
Greece	12/27/45	1970	
Khmer Republic	12/31/69	1970	
Fiji [4]	5/28/71	—	
Cameroon	7/10/63	[1963] [7]	
Central African Republic	7/10/63	[1963] [7]	
Chad	7/10/63	[1963] [7]	
Congo, People's Republic of the	7/10/63	[1963] [7]	
Dahomey	7/10/63	[1963] [7]	
Gabon	9/10/63	[1963] [7]	
Ivory Coast	3/11/63	[1963] [7]	

Executive Directors and Alternates

Director / Alternate		
J. O. Stone (Australia)	2/2/67	12/23/70
A. M. de Villiers (South Africa)		8/31/68
G. P. C. de Kock (South Africa)	9/1/68	
Lindsay B. Brand (Australia)	12/24/70	6/4/71
G. P. C. de Kock (South Africa)	6/5/71	
Robert van S. Smit (South Africa)		
Kurt Eklöf (Sweden)	11/1/64	10/31/66
Otto Schelin (Denmark)	11/2/64	10/31/66
Torben Friis (Denmark)	11/1/66	10/31/68
Jorma Aranko (Finland)	11/1/66	
Eero Asp (Finland)	11/1/68	10/31/70
Jorma Aranko (Finland)		12/12/68
Sigurgeir Jónsson (Iceland)	12/13/68	
Erik Brofoss (Norway)	11/1/70	
Amon Nikoi (Ghana)	6/15/65	10/31/68
Muhamad Barmawie Alwie (Indonesia)	1/16/67	2/16/68
Byanti Kharmawan (Indonesia)	11/1/68	
Abdoel Hamid (Indonesia)	11/1/68	12/4/68
Malek Ali Merican (Malaysia)	12/5/68	10/30/70
Costa P. Caranicas (Greece)	11/1/70	
Louis Kandé (Senegal)	10/3/63	
Antoine W. Yaméogo (Upper Volta)	11/1/64	10/31/66
Antoine W. Yaméogo (Upper Volta)	11/1/66	10/31/66
Léon M. Rajaobelina (Malagasy Republic)	11/1/66	

Appendix A–2 (concluded). Elected Executive Directors and Their Alternates
Article XII, Section 3 (b) (iii)
1966–71

Countries Represented				Executive Director and Alternate [1]		
Name	Date [2] Became Member	Representation Began	Representation Ended	Name	Dates [2] of Service Began	Ended
Malagasy Republic	9/25/63	[1963] [7]				
Mauritania	9/10/63	[1963] [7]				
Niger	4/24/63	[1963] [7]				
Rwanda	9/30/63	[1963] [7]				
Senegal	8/31/62	[1963] [7]				
Togo	8/1/62	[1963] [7]				
Upper Volta	5/2/63	[1963] [7]				
Congo, Democratic Republic of (Zaïre)	9/28/63	1966				
Mauritius	9/23/68	1968				
Equatorial Guinea	12/22/69	1970				
Mali	9/27/63	1970				
Burundi	9/28/63	1964		Semyano Kiingi (Uganda)	11/1/64	10/31/66
				Paul L. Faber (Guinea)	*11/1/64*	*10/31/66*
Congo, Democratic Republic of (Zaïre)	9/28/63	1964	1966	Paul L. Faber (Guinea)	11/1/66	10/31/68
Guinea	9/28/63	1964		*Leonard A. Williams (Trinidad and Tobago)*	*11/1/66*	*10/31/68*
Kenya	2/3/64	1964		Leonard A. Williams (Trinidad and Tobago)	11/1/68	10/31/70
Liberia	3/28/62	1964		*Maurice P. Omwony (Kenya)*	*11/1/68*	*10/31/70*
Mali	9/27/63	1964	1970	Maurice P. Omwony (Kenya)	11/1/70	
Nigeria	3/30/61	1964		*S. B. Nicol-Cole (Sierra Leone)*	*11/1/70*	
Sierra Leone	9/10/62	1964				
Sudan	9/5/57	1964				
Tanzania	9/10/62	1964				
Trinidad and Tobago	9/16/63	1964				
Uganda	9/27/63	1964				
Malawi	7/19/65	1966				
Zambia	9/23/65	1966				

Botswana	7/24/68	1968
Gambia, The	9/21/67	1968
Ethiopia	12/27/45	1970

[1] Alternate Executive Directors, always appointed by the Executive Director, are indicated by italic type.

[2] Dates are given in the following order: month/day/year.

[3] Executive Directors were appointed by the Republic of China in accordance with Article XII, Section 3 (b) (i), until 1960, when the Federal Republic of Germany replaced the Republic of China as a member having one of the five largest quotas.

[4] Barbados, Fiji, Oman, and Western Samoa joined the Fund after the 1970 regular election of Executive Directors. Barbados designated the Executive Director elected by Canada, Ireland, and Jamaica to look after its interests in the Fund until the next regular election of Executive Directors; Fiji, the Executive Director elected by Algeria, Ghana, Greece, Indonesia, the Khmer Republic, the Libyan Arab Republic, Morocco, and Tunisia; Oman, the Executive Director elected by the Middle Eastern countries; and Western Samoa, the Executive Director elected by Australia, Lesotho, New Zealand, South Africa, and Swaziland.

[5] Burma, Ceylon, Laos, Malaysia, Nepal, Singapore, and Thailand, whose votes were not cast for any of the Executive Directors elected in the 1970 regular election of Executive Directors, designated the Executive Director appointed by Japan to look after their interests in the Fund until the next regular election of Executive Directors.

[6] With effect from November 1, 1970, Mr. Hideo Suzuki was appointed as Executive Director for Japan in accordance with Article XII, Section 3 (b) (i).

[7] Interim elections, pursuant to Board of Governors Resolutions Nos. IM-10, 2-8, and 17-5, as amended by Resolution No. 18-7, respectively.

[8] Greece, Malta, Portugal, and Spain, which were eligible to vote in the 1968 regular election of Executive Directors, abstained. These countries designated the Executive Director appointed by Italy to look after their interests in the Fund until the next regular election of Executive Directors in 1970.

[9] For the term November 1, 1968–October 31, 1970, Mr. Palamenghi-Crispi was appointed by Italy in accordance with Article XII, Section 3 (c). He was elected at the 1970 regular election of Executive Directors in accordance with Article XII, Section 3 (b) (iii).

[10] Indonesia withdrew from the Fund, effective August 17, 1965, and rejoined on February 21, 1967.

Appendix A–3. Elected Executive Directors and Their Alternates
Article XII, Section 3 (b) (iv)
1966–71

Countries Represented				Executive Director and Alternate [1]		
		Representation			Dates [2] of Service	
Name	Date [2] Became Member	Began	Ended	Name	Began	Ended
Brazil	1/14/46	1946		Maurício Chagas Bicalho (Brazil)	11/1/60	10/31/66
Peru	12/31/45	1946		*Antonio de Abreu Coutinho (Brazil)*	*11/1/62*	*4/18/66*
Dominican Republic	12/28/45	1948		*Alexandre Kafka (Brazil)*	*6/5/66*	*10/31/66*
Panama	3/14/46	1952		Alexandre Kafka (Brazil)	11/1/66	
Haiti	9/8/53	1954		*Paulo H. Pereira Lira (Brazil)*	*11/13/66*	*3/4/68*
Colombia	12/27/45	1956		*Eduardo da S. Gomes, Jr. (Brazil)*	*3/29/68*	
Guyana	9/26/66	1970		*Basilio Martins (Brazil)*	*10/2/71*	*10/1/71*
Costa Rica	1/8/46	1946		Enrique Tejera-París (Venezuela)	3/2/65	10/31/66
El Salvador	3/14/46	1946		*Jorge Gonzáles del Valle (Guatemala)*	*11/1/64*	*10/31/66*
Guatemala	12/28/45	1946		Jorge González del Valle (Guatemala)	11/1/66	10/31/68
Mexico	12/31/45	1946		*Alfredo Phillips O. (Mexico)*	*11/1/66*	*10/31/68*
Venezuela	12/30/46	1948		Alfredo Phillips O. (Mexico)	11/1/68	10/31/70
Honduras	12/27/45	1952		*Marcos A. Sandoval (Venezuela)*	*11/1/68*	*10/31/70*
Nicaragua	3/14/46	1952		Luis Ugueto (Venezuela)	11/1/70	
				Guillermo González (Costa Rica)	*11/25/70*	
Argentina	9/20/56	1956		Luis Escobar (Chile)	11/1/64	10/31/66
Bolivia	12/27/45	1956		*Enrique Domenech (Argentina)*	*11/1/64*	*10/31/66*
Chile	12/31/45	1956		Adolfo C. Diz (Argentina)	11/1/66	10/31/68
Ecuador	12/28/45	1956		*Yamandú S. Patrón (Uruguay)*	*11/1/66*	*10/31/68*
Paraguay	12/28/45	1956		Luis Escobar (Chile)	11/1/68	10/31/70
Uruguay	3/11/46	1956		*Ricardo H. Arriazu (Argentina)*	*11/1/68*	
				Carlos Massad A. (Chile)	11/1/70	

[1] Alternate Executive Directors, always appointed by the Executive Director, are indicated by italic type.

[2] All dates are given in the following order: month/day/year.

662

Appendix B. Management and Senior Staff
as of December 31, 1971

The Managing Director	Pierre-Paul Schweitzer
The Deputy Managing Director	Frank A. Southard, Jr.

The General Counsel	Joseph Gold
The Economic Counsellor	J. J. Polak

Department or Office	**Head of Department or Office**	**Other Senior Staff** [1]
Administration	Phillip Thorson	Kenneth N. Clark
		William M. Avery
		Robert Harris
		P. N. Kaul
		Henri H. P. King
		Martin L. Loftus
		Walter H. Windsor
African	Mamoudou Touré	Ali R. Bengur
		Lamberto Dini
		Charles L. Merwin
		U Tun Wai
		Jacques Waïtzenegger
		R. J. Bhatia
		Edwin L. Bornemann
		D. Boushehri
		Francis d'A. Collings
		Alberto S. Foz
		Kwame Kwateng
Asian	D. S. Savkar	Andreas Abadjis
		Albert A. Mattera
		Koji Suzuki
		Tun Thin
		W. John R. Woodley
		Joachim Ahrensdorf
		A. G. Chandavarkar
		S. Kanesa-Thasan
		Prabhakar Narvekar
		Douglas A. Scott
Central Banking Service	Jan V. Mládek	Rudolf Kroc
		San Lin
		Marcin R. Wyczalkowski
		Graeme S. Dorrance
		D. R. Khatkhate
		James K. Nettles
		Roland Tenconi
European	L. A. Whittome	Rolf Evensen
		Poul Høst-Madsen
		Albin Pfeifer
		H. Ponsen
		Brian Rose

663

Appendix B (*continued*). Management and Senior Staff
as of December 31, 1971

Department or Office	Head of Department or Office	Other Senior Staff [1]
		Ekhard O. C. Brehmer B. S. Karlstroem Geoffrey Tyler Horst Ungerer Leo M. J. Van Houtven A. Charles Woodward
Exchange and Trade Relations	Ernest Sturc	C. David Finch Subimal Mookerjee Donald K. Palmer Timothy Sweeney Michael Dakolias J. H. C. de Looper Erik Elmholt Hans W. Gerhard W. F. Hughes Azizali Mohammed Kemal Siber
Fiscal Affairs	Richard Goode	W. A. Beveridge Leif Mutén Jakob Saper William M. Wedderspoon Raja J. Chelliah Rasheed O. Khalid Richard S. Latham George E. Lent Jonathan Levin G. W. van der Feltz
IMF Institute	F. A. G. Keesing	Gérard M. Teyssier Herbert K. Zassenhaus Orlando H. Lobo Ciro Tognetti Jean O. van der Mensbrugghe
Legal	Joseph Gold	Albert S. Gerstein George P. Nicoletopoulos Robert C. Effros James G. Evans, Jr. Philine R. Lachman N. S. Narayana Chari Olav C. A. Snellingen
Middle Eastern	Anwar Ali (on leave) John W. Gunter (Acting)	A. S. Ray A. K. El Selehdar Andreas S. Gerakis M. M. Hassanein A. S. Shaalan

Appendix B (*continued*). Management and Senior Staff
as of December 31, 1971

Department or Office	Head of Department or Office	Other Senior Staff [1]
Research	J. J. Polak	J. Marcus Fleming Fred Hirsch Charles F. Schwartz Victor Argy Carl P. Blackwell Arie C. Bouter Rudolph R. Rhomberg Duncan Ridler John S. Smith
Secretary's	W. Lawrence Hebbard	Roger V. Anderson J. D. Scott [2] George E. Bishop D. E. Brantley Norman K. Humphreys Joseph W. Lang, Jr. Katherine F. Magurn Marie C. Stark
Treasurer's	Walter O. Habermeier	Frederick C. Dirks Robert J. Familton Carl B. Fink Charles E. Jones Richard H. Miller Walter T. Powers David Williams
Western Hemisphere	Jorge Del Canto	Sterie T. Beza Paul J. Brand E. Walter Robichek Carlos E. Sansón Fernando A. Vera Jack P. Barnouin Marcello Caiola Joseph Chatelain John W. Crow Joaquín Ferrán Fernando Gaviria Julio E. González Jack Guenther Richard A. Radford Edison V. Zayas
Bureau of Statistics	Earl Hicks	Leonello Boccia Werner Dannemann Jai B. Gupta Akira P. Nose Robert L. Praetorius José C. Sánchiz Dan R. Silling

Appendix B (*concluded*). Management and Senior Staff
as of December 31, 1971

Department or Office	Head of Department or Office	Other Senior Staff [1]
Office in Europe (Paris)	Jean-Paul Sallé	Aldo Guetta
Office in Geneva	Edgar Jones	
Chief Information Officer		Jay H. Reid
Internal Auditor		J. William Lowe
Special Representative to the United Nations		Gordon Williams
Personal Assistant to the Managing Director		L. F. T. Smith

[1] In each department or office the first grouping lists, in alphabetical order, Deputy Directors and Senior Advisors or the equivalent; the second grouping lists, in alphabetical order, all other senior staff.

[2] Editor, *Finance and Development.*

Appendix C. Organizational Chart
as of December 31, 1971

MANAGING DIRECTOR
DEPUTY MANAGING DIRECTOR

INFORMATION OFFICE

INTERNAL AUDITOR

OFFICE IN EUROPE

OFFICE IN GENEVA

SPECIAL REPRESENTATIVE TO THE UNITED NATIONS

BUREAU OF STATISTICS

ADMINISTRATION DEPARTMENT

ASIAN DEPARTMENT

EUROPEAN DEPARTMENT

FISCAL AFFAIRS DEPARTMENT

LEGAL DEPARTMENT

RESEARCH DEPARTMENT

TREASURER'S DEPARTMENT

AFRICAN DEPARTMENT

CENTRAL BANKING SERVICE

EXCHANGE AND TRADE RELATIONS DEPARTMENT

IMF INSTITUTE

MIDDLE EASTERN DEPARTMENT

SECRETARY'S DEPARTMENT

WESTERN HEMISPHERE DEPARTMENT

Index

References are to pages; page numbers marked with an asterisk (*) refer to tables in the text, and those marked with the letter n refer to footnotes. The appendices have not been included in this index

A

ABADJIS, ANDREAS, 646

ACC. *See* UNITED NATIONS ADMINISTRATIVE COMMITTEE ON COORDINATION

ADJUSTMENT PROCESS. *See* BALANCE OF PAYMENTS ADJUSTMENT PROCESS

ADOMAKOH, A., 471

AFGHANISTAN
Drawings (purchases) and repurchases from Fund: purchases, 264, 268*, 312, 321, 330*; repurchases, 268*, 395*; under compensatory financing facility, 264, 268*
Exchange rate and par value, 437, 542
Quota in Fund, 306*
SDR allocations, 248*
Stand-by arrangements with Fund, 321, 333*
Technical assistance from Fund, 585

AFRICA
Drawings (purchases) from Fund, 312, 316
Export earnings, decline in, 269–70
Fund consultations, 572
Representation on Executive Board, 631–32
Stabilization of primary product prices, interest expressed in, 270–71, 282
Technical assistance from Fund, 582, 583, 585

AFRICAN DEVELOPMENT BANK, 609

AFRICAN INSTITUTE FOR ECONOMIC DEVELOPMENT AND PLANNING, 590

AHMAD, ALI BIN HAJI, 220, 281

AL-ATRASH, MUHAMMAD
Background, 629

ALGERIA
Exchange rate, 562
Quota in Fund, 296, 301, 306*
SDR allocations, 248*
Technical assistance from Fund, 585

AL HABEEB, ABDUL RAHMAN, 594

ALKHIMOV, V. S., 83n

ALLOCATIONS OF SDRs. *See* SPECIAL DRAWING RIGHTS

ALTMAN, OSCAR L., 22, 644

ALWIE, MUHAMAD BARMAWIE, 162*

ANDEAN SUBREGIONAL INTEGRATION AGREEMENT, 609

ANDERSON, ROGER V., 647

ANJARIA, J. J., 88, 89, 109, 121, 134*, 379, 389

ANNUAL MEETINGS, 5, 387, 605, 620–22, 624, 637, 647
12th (1957), 12
15th (1960), 15, 16, 191
16th (1961, Vienna), 15, 16, 192
17th (1962), 23–24, 193
18th (1963), 26, 27–31, 193, 194
19th (1964, Tokyo), 33, 38–42, 43, 195, 255
20th (1965), 58, 63, 68–73, 75, 81, 86, 97, 99, 196–97, 255, 261, 612
21st (1966), 102–103, 200, 593, 612

22nd (1967, Rio de Janeiro), 104–105, 130–31, 138, 159, 173, 201, 204, 255, 270–72, 273, 339, 432, 594, 613
23rd (1968), 175, 176, 272, 273, 277–78, 285, 348, 377, 390, 407–409, 411, 414, 483–84, 594
24th (1969), 176–77, 187, 188–89, 205, 211–12, 214, 218, 219–20, 267, 281–82, 285, 294, 303–304, 352, 372, 377, 409, 411, 414, 417, 459, 503–504, 507, 594
25th (1970, Copenhagen), 245, 267, 282, 298–99, 416, 426, 484, 491, 509, 514–15, 517, 578, 600–601
26th (1971), 244, 246, 267, 282, 426, 545–48, 559, 564, 601, 603, 620, 651
27th (1972), 299

ANNUAL REPORTS OF EXECUTIVE DIRECTORS
Contents of, 177, 200, 204, 624
See also Publications Cited (under International Monetary Fund, p. 697 of this volume)

ANSIAUX, HUBERT, 255

ANWAR ALI, 643, 644

AQUINO h., FRANCISCO, 41

ARANKO, JORMA, 134*, 162*, 473

ARGENTINA
Art. VIII, Secs. 2, 3, and 4, acceptance of obligations of, 571
Currency: new unit, 468; used in Fund transactions, 337*
Debt renegotiation, 595
Drawings (purchases) and repurchases from Fund: purchases, 268*, 311, 316, 317, 321, 330*; repurchases, 395*; under compensatory financing facility, 268*
Exchange market for capital transactions, 542
Exchange rate and par value, 437, 563
Quota in Fund, 296, 306*
SDR allocations, 248*
Stand-by arrangements with Fund, 321, 333*

ARRIAZU, RICARDO H., 391, 475, 550
Background, 629
Suggestion for new quota formula, 304–305

ARTICLES OF AGREEMENT
Amended to establish SDR facility, xix, xx, 166–76, 188, 204, 205, 253
Amended to modify rules and practices of Fund, xix, xx, 155, 159, 166, 173–75, 188, 203, 253–60, 289n
Amendments considered in reserve creation discussions, 28, 93, 152, 160, 204
Amendments on exchange rate provisions discussed, 484, 506, 511, 513, 514, 515, 521, 558
Art. VIII, Secs. 2, 3, and 4, acceptance of obligations of, 571
EEC suggestions for changes, 131–33, 202
Executive Directors' report on first amendment, 175, 204
Provisions on exchange rate margins, 521
Provisions on gold sales, 417

ASIA
Drawings (purchases) from Fund, 312, 316
Fund consultations, 572
Technical assistance from Fund, 582, 583

ASIAN DEVELOPMENT BANK, 609, 610

ASIAN INSTITUTE FOR ECONOMIC DEVELOPMENT AND PLANNING, 590

ASP, EERO, 295, 473, 480, 625

ASSET SETTLEMENT, 491–92

ASSETS OF FUND. *See* HOLDINGS OF FUND *and* RESOURCES OF FUND—NATURE AND SIZE

ASSOCIATION OF AFRICAN CENTRAL BANKS, 609

ATTA, A. A., 594

AUSTRALIA
Art. VIII, Secs. 2, 3, and 4, acceptance of obligations of, 571*n*
Currency: new unit, 467; used in Fund transactions, 337*
Exchange rate and par value, 437, 467, 542, 560*
Gold production subsidies, 423–24
Quota in Fund, 296, 306*
SDR allocations, 248*

AUSTRIA
Art. VIII, Secs. 2, 3, and 4, acceptance of obligations of, 571*n*
Basle Group, 442*n*
Currency used in Fund transactions, 337*
Exchange rate: central, 562*; floating, 542
Gold sales to Fund, 416
Par value, xxii, 437, 524
Quota in Fund, 296, 306*
SDR allocations, 248*

AVERY, WILLIAM M., 645

AYIDA, A. A., 427

B

BAHAMAS
Currency unit, new, 467
Membership in Fund, 570
Par value, 467, 468, 561*

BAHRAIN
Membership in Fund, 570

BALANCE OF PAYMENTS
Basic balance defined, 489, 543
Need test required: for buffer stock drawings, 283, 284; for SDR use, 149, 151, 160, 182, 183, 242–43
Of debtor countries, impact of debt renegotiations on, 597
Positions: EEC countries, 52, 69–70, 211–12; industrial countries (surpluses as counterpart of U.S. deficits), 493; primary producing countries, 82, 264–65, 269–70; reserve currency countries, 26, 30, 52, 63, 70, 75, 119–20, 171–72, 194; world, 564
See also FUNDAMENTAL DISEQUILIBRIUM; TRADE, INTERNATIONAL; *and* individual countries

BALANCE OF PAYMENTS ADJUSTMENT PROCESS
Emphasis on in liquidity debates, 29–30, 39, 69–70, 119–20, 141, 171, 193
Inadequacy for first SDR allocation, 218
Multilateral surveillance, 35–36, 40, 69–71, 78, 96–97, 100, 195
OECD Working Party 3 studies, 36, 38, 96, 98
Priority assessed, 30–31, 65–66, 96–97, 120, 142, 214
Problems, 484, 490, 495–96, 505; of short-term capital flows, 496–99; of world imbalances, 485–88, 493–94
Proposals for improving, 483, 484, 490, 509, 526
Reserve creation tied to, 97, 98, 100, 113, 172, 180, 221
See also EXCHANGE RATE MECHANISM *and* PAR VALUE SYSTEM

BANCOR, 19, 143

BANERJI, ARUN K., 134*, 162*

BANGLADESH
Membership in Fund, 570

BANK FOR INTERNATIONAL SETTLEMENTS (BIS), 14, 36, 452, 453
As other holder of SDRs, 173

Attendance at meetings on reserve creation, 71, **106**, 553
Basle Agreement, 14, 192
Basle Group, 442
Fund's relations with, 608

BANZA, ALEXANDRE, 271

BARBADOS
Par value, 518, 560*
Quota in Fund, 302, 306*
SDR allocations, 248*
Special Drawing Account, participation in, 232

BARBER, ANTHONY, 427, 514

BARCOURGNE, COURMO, 271

BARROW, E. W., 427

BASLE AGREEMENT, 14, 192

BASLE GROUP, 442

BCEAEC. *See* CENTRAL BANK OF EQUATORIAL AFRICAN STATES AND CAMEROON

BCEAO. *See* CENTRAL BANK OF WEST AFRICAN STATES

BEAURAIN, CLAUDE
Background, 629

BEELITZ, ULRICH, 378

BELGIAN-LUXEMBOURG ECONOMIC UNION, 522

BELGIUM
Art. VIII consultations, 523
Art. VIII, Secs. 2, 3, and 4, acceptance of obligations of, 571*n*
Balance of payments surplus, 493
Basle Agreement, 14, 192
Basle Group, 442*n*
Borrowing by Fund under GAB, 374*; repayment, 376
Currency: declared convertible in fact, 225, 226; swap arrangements, 314–15; used in Fund transactions, 313, 314, 315, 337*
Drawings (purchases) and repurchases from Fund, 311, 315, 330*, 395*
Exchange markets, dual, xxii, 522–24, 574
Exchange rate: central, 554, 555*, 562*; floating, 542, 544
Gold tranche, views on, 255
Par value, 462, 522–23
Quota in Fund, 296, 306*
Reserve creation, views on, 79, 111–12, 120
SDRs: allocations, 248*; excess holdings, 240; transactions, 240, 243, 314

BELGO-LUXEMBOURG EXCHANGE INSTITUTE, xxii

BENGUR, ALI R., 645

BENSON, EDGAR J., 477, 478, 540, 541, 543, 545

BERMUDA. *See* UNITED KINGDOM: Nonmetropolitan territories

BERNE UNION. *See* UNION d'ASSUREURS DES CREDITS INTERNATIONAUX

BERNSTEIN, EDWARD M., 20
Collective reserve unit (CRU) plan, 53–54, 55–56, 111, 194
Multiple reserve currency plan, 20, 191

BEYEN, J. W., 626

BICALHO, MAURICIO CHAGAS, 89

BIDIAS A NGON, BERNARD, 267

BIRON, HERMAN, 134*, 148, 152, 162*, 345, 389

BIS. *See* BANK FOR INTERNATIONAL SETTLEMENTS

BISHOP, GEORGE E., 647

BLESSING, KARL, 39, 69, 72, 73, 454, 503

BOARD OF GOVERNORS
Annual Meetings, 620–22
Committees: on interpretation of Articles, 178, 259; on reform of monetary system (Committee of Twenty), 556; to study reserve creation, 67, 68, 101, 102, 197
Growth in size and powers, 620–22

Resolutions: on amendment to Articles, xix, 104–105, 175, 201; on buffer stock financing, xviii, 271, 272, 278; on outline for SDR facility, xviii, 158–59; on reform of monetary system, 547–48; on SDR allocations, xx, 219
Voting, 155, 156, 158, 161, 203

BOCCIA, LEONELLO, 648

BOLIVIA
Art. VIII, Secs. 2, 3, and 4, acceptance of obligations of, 571
Drawings (purchases) and repurchases from Fund: purchases, xxii, 283–84, 311, 321, 330*; repurchases, 395*; under buffer stock facility, xxii, 283–84
Quota in Fund, 306*
SDR allocations, 248*
Stand-by arrangements with Fund, 321, 333*

BONN MEETING OF GROUP OF TEN, 450–53

BORROWING BY FUND (BILATERAL), 376–77, 387. And see GENERAL ARRANGEMENTS TO BORROW

BOTSWANA
Currency unit, 465
Membership in Fund, 289
Par value, 465, 466*, 561*
Quota in Fund, 302, 303, 306*
SDR allocations, 248*

BOUSHEHRI, D., 645

BRAND, LINDSAY B., 242, 392
Background and length of service, 627, 628

BRAND, PAUL J., 648

BRANTLEY, D. E., 647

BRAZIL
Capital flows, 362
Currency: new unit, 467; used in Fund transactions, 324, 337*
Debt renegotiation, 361, 595
Drawings (purchases) and repurchases from Fund: purchases, 263, 268*, 311, 322, 330*, 361, 362; repurchases, 268*, 395*; under compensatory financing facility, 263, 268*
Exchange rate, 362, 542, 563
Financial stabilization programs, 360–63
Inflation, 360–63; indexing, 363
Payments arrears, 360–61
Proposal at Bretton Woods for stabilization of primary product prices, 273
Quota in Fund, 296, 306*
SDR allocations, 248*
Stand-by arrangements with Fund, 320, 333*, 360–63

BRETTON WOODS SYSTEM. See INTERNATIONAL MONETARY SYSTEM

BROFOSS, ERIK, 481, 492–93, 523
Background and length of service, 627, 628

BRYCE, ROBERT
Background and length of service, 627, 629

BUDGET OF FUND, 383–88, 392–94, 397*

BUFFER STOCK FINANCING
African Governors' request for study, 270–71
Brazilian proposal at Bretton Woods, 273
Cocoa, 274, 286n
Commodities included in consultations, 275, 284–86
Executive Board decisions, xx, xxi, 279–83
Executive Board discussions, 276–79
Governors' resolutions, xviii, 271, 272, 278
Governors' views, 271, 277, 278, 279, 281
Joint ceiling with compensatory financing drawings, 263, 276, 280
Liberalization suggested, 282
Study by Fund and Bank, 269, 271, 272–82
Study of possible Fund arrangements, 275–76
Tin, xxi, 274, 282–84
Transactions: drawings (purchases), xxii, 283–84, 316; for contributions under International Tin

Agreement, xxi, 282–84; relation to gold tranche drawings, 280–81; repurchase provisions, 276, 281
See also COMMODITIES

BURMA
Drawings (purchases) and repurchases from Fund: purchases, 264, 265, 266, 312, 321, 330*; repurchases, 268*; under compensatory financing facility, 264, 265, 266, 268*; waiver, 322
Exchange rate and par value, 437, 542, 562*
Quota in Fund, 289, 306*
SDR allocations, 248*
Stand-by arrangements with Fund, 320, 321, 333*

BURNS, ARTHUR F., 520

BURUNDI
Drawings (purchases) and repurchases from Fund: purchases, 265, 268*, 310, 312, 321, 330*; repurchases, 268*, 395*; under compensatory financing facility, 265, 268*
Quota in Fund, 306*
SDR allocations, 248*
Stand-by arrangements with Fund, 321, 333*
Technical assistance from Fund, 580

BURY, LESLIE H. E., 285

BUSTELO, CARLOS, 480, 509–10
Background, 629

BY-LAWS
Amendments, 166, 177–78, 205
Sec. 23 on Committee on Interpretation not yet adopted, 178

C

CALLAGHAN, JAMES, 70, 71, 73, 126, 155, 159, 339

CAMBODIA. See KHMER REPUBLIC

CAMEROON
Exchange rate, 457–58, 561
Quota in Fund, 296, 302, 306*
SDR allocations, 248*

CANADA
Art. VIII consultations, 478, 480, 571
Art. VIII, Secs. 2, 3, and 4, acceptance of obligations of, 571n
Balance of payments, 476, 493
Basle Group, 442n
Borrowing by Fund under GAB, 374*, 375, 376; repayment, 376, 476–77
Capital flows, 476–78, 493
Currency: swap arrangements, 477, 478; use of in Fund transactions, 312, 328, 337*
Drawings (purchases) and repurchases from Fund: purchases, 311, 315, 330*, 476; repurchases, 395*
Exchange rate: consultations with Fund on, 519; factors governing, 476–82, 519; floating, xxi, 3, 327–28, 476–82, 519, 542, 544, 555*. See also Par value, below
Gold production subsidies, 423, 424
Interest rates, 477, 478
Par value, 437, 477; re-establishment urged by Fund, 478, 480–82, 519
Quota in Fund, 13, 296
Reserve creation: proposals, 59, 79, 81, 197; views, 111–12, 120
SDRs: allocations, 248*; excess holdings, 240; receipts, 236, 240
Trade arrangements with U.S., 551

CAPITAL MOVEMENTS
Factor undermining par values, 350, 449, 476, 499–500, 502, 525
Liberalization suggested for Japan, 494–95
Long-term to developing countries, 82, 470, 544, 601
Measures to control, 221, 499–500, 574–75; Belgium and Luxembourg, 522; France, 450; Fed. Rep. of Germany, 451, 452–53, 523; studies, 66, 196, 521, 523, 525, 526, 565; U.S., 63, 64, 74, 210, 484, 487, 489

Short-term, growth of, 66, 196; in aftermath of convertibility, 13–15, 191–92; reasons for, 496–99
Short-term, to and from: Brazil, 302; Canada, 476, 477; France, 352, 449, 450, 453, 542; Fed. Rep. of Germany, 212, 461, 463, 464; Switzerland, 524; U.K., 350; U.S., 485, 486, 488, 489, 519–20, 528

CARANICAS, COSTA P., 134*, 162*, 481
  Background, 629–30

CARIBBEAN DEVELOPMENT BANK, 609, 610

CARIBBEAN FREE TRADE ASSOCIATION, 610

CARLI, GUIDO, 452

CARNEIRO, OCTAVIO A. DIAS, 83n

"CATCHING UP" FORMULA, 239

CENTER FOR LATIN AMERICAN MONETARY STUDIES (CEMLA), 589, 609

CENTRAL AFRICAN CUSTOMS AND ECONOMIC UNION (UDEAC), 271

CENTRAL AFRICAN REPUBLIC
  Drawings from Fund, 312, 316, 330*
  Exchange rate, 457–58, 561
  Quota in Fund, 302, 306*
  SDR allocations, 248*

CENTRAL AMERICAN COMMON MARKET, 609

CENTRAL AMERICAN MONETARY COUNCIL, 581, 609

CENTRAL BANK OF EQUATORIAL AFRICAN STATES AND CAMEROON (BCEAEC), 457

CENTRAL BANK OF WEST AFRICAN STATES (BCEAO), 457

CENTRAL BANKING EXPERTS OF THE AMERICAN CONTINENT, 609

CENTRAL BANKING, TECHNICAL ASSISTANCE IN; See TECHNICAL ASSISTANCE

CENTRAL BANKS
  Currency swap arrangements, 14–15, 192, 499; repayments by U.S., 315; use by Canada, 477
  Fund technical assistance, 579–82, 585–86
  In Southeast Asia, 278–79
  Loans: to France, 452–53; to U.K., 442
  Suggestions for extending cooperation among, 20

CENTRAL RATES. See EXCHANGE RATES

CEYLON
  Drawings (purchases) and repurchases from Fund: purchases, 264, 266, 268*, 310, 312, 316, 321, 330*; repurchases, 268*, 395*; under compensatory financing facility, 264, 266, 268*; waiver, 322
  Exchange rate, 542
  Par value, xviii–xix, 437, 438*, 439
  Quota in Fund, 306*
  SDR allocations, 248*
  Stand-by arrangements with Fund, 321, 333*

CFA FRANC AREA, 357, 457

CHAD
  Drawings from Fund, 312, 318, 330*
  Exchange rate, 457–58, 561
  Quota in Fund, 301, 306*
  SDR allocations, 248*
  Technical assistance from Fund, 585

CHARGES ON USE OF FUND'S RESOURCES
  Commitment and service charges, 256, 379
  Description and schedule, 378–81
  Income from, 386, 397*
  On gold tranche purchases, 256, 379
  Payable in gold, 379, 380, 381
  Payable in SDRs, 173, 229–30, 234–35, 243, 379

CHARTER OF ALGIERS (UNCTAD), 607

CHAUDHURI, SACHINDRA, 470

CHAVAN, Y. B., 245n

CHILE
  Debt renegotiation, 595
  Drawings (purchases) and repurchases from Fund: purchases, 265–66, 268*, 311, 316, 321, 330*; re-

purchases, 395*; under compensatory financing facility, 265–66, 268*
  Exchange rate, 563
  Quota in Fund, 306*
  SDR allocations, 248*
  Stand-by arrangements with Fund, 321, 333*

CHINA, REPUBLIC OF
  Drawings (purchases) from Fund, 312, 316, 330*
  Exchange rate and par value, 466*, 562
  Quota in Fund, 288–89, 293, 295, 306*
  SDR allocations, opting out of, 232, 233, 244
  Technical assistance from Fund, 581

CHOW, CHI-LING, 134*, 162*

CIAP. See INTER-AMERICAN COMMITTEE ON THE ALLIANCE FOR PROGRESS

CIAT. See INTER-AMERICAN CENTER OF TAX ADMINISTRATORS

CLAPPIER, B., 135*, 163*

CLARK, KENNETH N., 645

CLEARING UNION, 19

CMEA. See COUNCIL FOR MUTUAL ECONOMIC ASSISTANCE

COLLECTIVE RESERVE UNIT (CRU). See RESERVE CREATION PLANS

COLOMBIA
  Drawings (purchases) and repurchases from Fund: purchases, 264, 266, 268*, 310, 311, 316, 321, 330*, 358–59; repurchases, 268*; under compensatory financing facility, 264, 266, 268*
  Exchange markets, dual, 358
  Exchange rates, 358, 542
  Financial stabilization programs, 358–59
  Payments arrears, 358
  Quota in Fund, 306*
  SDR allocations, 248*
  Stand-by arrangements with Fund, 320, 333*, 358–59
  Technical assistance from Fund, 359, 585

COLOMBO, EMILIO, 39, 41, 69, 72, 132n, 408, 409, 504
  Views and comments on: harmonization, 156; SDR–development finance link, 219–20

COMECON. See COUNCIL FOR MUTUAL ECONOMIC ASSISTANCE

COMMITTEE ON REFORM OF THE INTERNATIONAL MONETARY SYSTEM AND RELATED ISSUES (COMMITTEE OF TWENTY), 68, 556, 634n
  U.S. proposal, 67, 101, 102

COMMODITIES
  Fund involvement: buffer stock facility introduced, 269–86; Commodities Division established, 286; compensatory financing facility extended and liberalized, 261–68; discussions of commodities included in consultations, 275, 284–86; increased concern with commodity problems, 261, 267, 282, 284, 286; review of outlook suggested, 275
  Prices, 358–59; as factor in buffer stock and compensatory financing facilities, 261, 263–65, 266–67, 269
  See also individual commodity organizations

COMMON MARKET. See CENTRAL AMERICAN COMMON MARKET and EUROPEAN ECONOMIC COMMUNITY

COMMONWEALTH FINANCE MINISTERS' MEETING, 245

COMPENSATORY FINANCING OF EXPORT FLUCTUATIONS
  Calculations: of "export excesses" for repurchase obligations, 262–63, 266; of export shortfalls, 262; to avoid "double compensation," 263
  Floating character, 256, 262
  Joint ceiling with buffer stock drawings, 263, 276, 280
  Liberalization of facility, xviii, 261–63; suggestions for, 80, 81, 84, 197, 200, 261, 267, 278–79

Limits on outstanding purchases, 262, 265
Quota increases under compensatory financing decision, 288, 289, 296, 301
Transactions: by copper exporting countries, 265–66; purchases, 263–64, 265–66, 268*, 316, 319; reclassification, 262, 263, 265; repurchases, 266, 268*; rules for repurchase, 262–63

COMPETITIVE DEPRECIATION
Concern expressed, 439, 476

COMPOSITE RESERVE UNIT (CRU). *See* RESERVE CREATION PLANS

CONGO, DEMOCRATIC REPUBLIC OF. *See* ZAIRE

CONGO, PEOPLE'S REPUBLIC OF THE
Exchange rate, 457–58, 561
Quota in Fund, 301, 306*
SDR allocations, 248*
Technical assistance from Fund, 585

CONNALLY, JOHN B., 315, 427, 520–21, 526–27, 531, 545, 546–47, 552, 553

CONSULTATIONS
By Managing Director on allocation of SDRs, 214–17
Changes in, 575–78; commodities added, 275, 284–86; external debt added, 595; payments arrears added, xxi, 592–93
"Consultation year," 572n
Importance of, 570–73; number held, 572; participation by staff, 571, 572–73; time spent by Executive Directors, 573
Reports made available to international organizations, 607, 610
Special, 570
Supplementation needed, 577–78
With individual countries: Belgium and Luxembourg, 523; Canada, 478, 480, 571; France, 353, 453; Fed. Rep. of Germany, 460–61, 462–63, 525, 571; Ghana, 472, 571, 572; Iceland, 439; India, 470, 571; Japan, 494, 495, 571; U.K., 218, 349, 431, 440, 446; U.S., 218–19, 488, 490, 492, 519, 571

CONVERTIBILITY
Of European currencies, 11, 13, 190; factor in capital movements, 13, 497
Of U.S. dollar, 131; official suspended, xxii, 3, 241–42, 327–29, 517, 527–30, 531–33; prospects for resumption discussed, 540, 550–51, 552, 553
Reference to asset settlement, 491–92

COREA, GAMANI, 83n

COSTA RICA
Art. VIII, Secs. 2, 3, and 4, acceptance of obligations of, 571n
Drawings (purchases) and repurchases from Fund, 311, 316, 330*, 395*; waiver, 322
Exchange rate, 563
Quota in Fund, 306*
SDR allocations, 248*
Stand-by arrangements with Fund, 321, 333*
Technical assistance from Fund, 583, 585

COTTIER, JEAN, 137*, 165*

COUNCIL FOR MUTUAL ECONOMIC ASSISTANCE (CMEA/COMECON), 574

COUNCIL OF EUROPE, 608

COUTINHO, ANTONIO DE ABREU, 89

CRAWLING PEG. *See* EXCHANGE RATE MECHANISM

CREDIT CONTROLS. *See* MONETARY POLICY

CREDIT TRANCHES. *See* RESOURCES OF FUND—NATURE AND SIZE *and* RESOURCES OF FUND—USE

CRENA DE IONGH, D., 627

CRU. *See* RESERVE CREATION PLANS

CURRENCIES
Definitions: intervention currency, 497, 559; reserve currency, 497; vehicle currency, 497
In exchange for SDRs: convertible, 145, 148, 149, 160; methods of conversion, 169–70, 178, 184, 225–26, 244

New units, 466–68, 518, 543
Use in Fund transactions, 172, 173, 337*, 381; for U.S. drawings, 313, 314, 315; in 1971, special arrangements for, 328; of currencies with fluctuating rates, 327–28
See also CONVERTIBILITY; CURRENCY CONVERTIBLE IN FACT; HOLDINGS OF FUND; SELECTION OF CURRENCIES IN FUND TRANSACTIONS; *and* individual countries

CURRENCY BUDGET. *See* SELECTION OF CURRENCIES IN FUND TRANSACTIONS

CURRENCY CONVERTIBLE IN FACT
Concept used in GAB, 168, 373
Defined in amended Articles, 167, 168–70, 183, 184
Interconvertibility, 169, 170, 223
Obligation to provide, 179, 184
Particular currencies specified, 178, 184, 222, 223–26
Related to "principle of equal value," 169, 170, 184
SDRs encashed for, 183, 243, 244

CURRENCY SWAP ARRANGEMENTS. *See* CENTRAL BANKS

CYPRUS
Drawings (purchases) and repurchases from Fund, 312, 316, 330*, 395*
Par value, xviii–xix, 437, 438*, 560*
Quota in Fund, 289, 306*
SDR allocations, 248*
Technical assistance from Fund, 580

D

DAANE, J. DEWEY, 120, 137*, 165*

DAHOMEY
Exchange rate, 457–58, 561
Quota in Fund, 301, 306*
SDR allocations, 248*

DALE, WILLIAM B., 32, 134*, 162*, 174–75, 547
Background and length of service, 625, 627, 628
Comments and views on: buffer stock financing, 277, 279; Canadian exchange rate, 481; charges by tranche position, 379; currency conversion procedures, 223; deutsche mark revaluation, 462; differentiation among Fund members, 293; distribution of Fund's net income, 389; Ecuadoran devaluation, 476; exchange rate flexibility and wider margins, 504, 508, 510, 511, 521; French franc devaluation (1969), 456; gold deposits, general, 422, 423; gold purchases from South Africa, 410–11, 414; Japanese surplus, 495; reconstitution of credit tranche positions, 114; reserve creation, 88, 128, 147, 149, 157; reserve creation-development finance link, 110; SDR allocations and use, 215, 240; stand-by arrangements, 345, 349; sterling devaluation (1967), 435–36; U.S. balance of payments, 543–44, 551; U.S. dollar convertibility, 533, 549–50; use of Fund's resources and stand-by arrangements, 345

DAY, A. C. L. (Day Plan), 20

DEBRE, MICHEL, 132n, 156, 159, 171–72, 173, 271

DEBT, EXTERNAL, OF DEVELOPING COUNTRIES, 577
Fund involvement: appraised, 596–97; increased, 533, 594–96; jointly with World Bank, 471, 595; subject of consultations and stand-by arrangements, 576, 595, 596
Fund studies made available to other agencies, 597
Ghana as example of Fund's experience, 597–600
Long-term nature, 600–601
Particular countries, 359, 361, 471, 597–600

DE GAULLE, CHARLES, 61, 62, 63, 195, 453, 454

DEGUEN, DANIEL, 135*, 163*

DEIF, NAZIH AHMED, 552, 626, 631
Background and length of service, 627, 629

DE JONGH, T. W., 415–16

DE KOCK, G. P. C., 231, 414, 480, 521

INDEX

DE LATTRE, ANDRE, 36

DEL CANTO, JORGE, 643

DE LOOPER, J. H. C., 646

DE MAULDE, BRUNO, 224, 228, 235, 279, 286, 293, 357, 411, 418, 475, 481

DEMING, FREDERICK L., 97, 120, 137*, 143, 165*

DENMARK
Art. VIII, Secs. 2, 3, and 4, acceptance of obligations of, 571
Basle Group, 442n
Currency used in Fund transactions, 337*
Drawings (purchases) and repurchases from Fund, 311, 315, 330*, 395*
Exchange rate: central, 562*; floating, 542
Par value, xix, 437, 438*
Quota in Fund, 296, 306*
SDR allocations, 248*

DEPUTY MANAGING DIRECTOR (Frank A. Southard, Jr.), 134*, 162*, 276, 339, 481, 592, 636
Meetings and speaking engagements, 44, 604, 605
Resumé of Fund service, 635–36
Views, comments, explanations: distribution of Fund's net income, 388, 389; remuneration on gold tranche positions, 388; reserve creation, 44, 95; U.S. import surcharge, 531

DE STRYCKER, CECIL, 120, 135*, 163*, 255

DEVELOPING COUNTRIES
Exchange rates, 465–66, 542, 552–53, 560–63
Exchange restrictions, 553, 574, 575, 591–93
Fund consultations, 572, 576
Fund resources and, 261, 267, 269, 311–12, 320–21, 378–79
Groups. See GROUP OF NINE; GROUP OF SEVENTY-SEVEN; GROUP OF THIRTY-ONE; and GROUP OF TWENTY-FOUR
Interdependence with industrial countries, 269, 270, 577
Managing Director's concern for, 601, 633–34
Membership in Fund, 569–71
Problems: capital inflow, 82, 577; debt, 577, 594; exports, 269, 274, 601; interest rates, 349; output, 270; restrictions by developed countries, 284–86
Quotas in Fund, 291, 294
Stand-by arrangements with Fund, 358–63; financial programs, 367–68
Technical assistance, 578–88; training of officials, 588–90
Views: articulation, 620; exchange rate system, 506–507, 552–53; Fund quotas, 215–16, 291–92, 303–305; gold price, 553; reserve creation, 82–85, 88–89, 99, 110, 174, 215–16, 219, 245; stand-by arrangements, 342–43, 345–46
See also DEBT, EXTERNAL, OF DEVELOPING COUNTRIES; EXPORTS; and PRIMARY PRODUCING COUNTRIES

DEVELOPMENT FINANCE
Fund participation in meetings, 600, 609, 612–13
Transfer of Fund net income considered, 390, 391, 392
See also RESERVE CREATION: Link with development finance

DE VILLIERS, A. M., 134*, 162*

DE VRIES, TOM, 286, 293, 391, 462, 481, 558
Background, 630

D'HAEZE, MARCEL, 135*, 163*

DIEDERICHS, NICOLAAS, 409, 411, 412, 414, 416, 426, 427

DILLON, C. DOUGLAS, 30, 41

DIRKS, FREDERICK C., 648

DIZ, ADOLFO C., 110, 134*, 141, 148, 162*, 174, 273, 277, 342, 343, 345, 346, 411

DOCUMENTS AND INFORMATION
Exchange with other organizations, 605, 610

DOMINICAN REPUBLIC
Art. VIII, Secs. 2, 3, and 4, acceptance of obligations of, 571n
Drawings (purchases) and repurchases from Fund: purchases, 264, 268*, 311, 317, 330*; repurchases, 268*, 395*; under compensatory financing facility, 264, 268*
Exchange rate, central, 562*
Quota in Fund, 306*
SDR allocations, 248*

DORRANCE, GRAEME S., 646

DOW, J. C. R., 165*

DRAWING RIGHTS IN FUND, PROPOSED NEW. See RESERVE CREATION PLANS and SPECIAL DRAWING RIGHTS

DRAWING UNIT RESERVE ASSET (DURA), 143

DRAWINGS (PURCHASES) FROM FUND. See RESOURCES OF FUND—USE and individual countries

DUBAI
Currency unit and par value, 467

DURA, 143

E

EAST AFRICAN COMMUNITY, 583

ECONOMIC COMMISSION FOR AFRICA (ECA), 605, 610

ECONOMIC COMMISSION FOR ASIA AND THE FAR EAST (ECAFE), 605, 606

ECONOMIC COMMISSION FOR EUROPE (ECE), 605, 606

ECONOMIC COMMISSION FOR LATIN AMERICA (ECLA), 605, 606

ECONOMIC COUNSELLOR (J. J. Polak), 36, 113, 135*, 163*, 245
Appointment, 77
Economic models, 366
Reports on Group of Ten Deputies' meetings, 95, 100, 295, 510
Resumé of Fund service, 643
Staff positions and explanations: exchange rates, 537–38; international monetary reform, 539; reserve creation, 86, 111–12, 117, 121, 130; U.S. dollar convertibility, 550

ECONOMIC DEVELOPMENT
Development Decade, 270; second, 601
Discussed in Fund consultations, 576
In particular countries, 361, 470, 493–95
Related to export earnings, 273
Related to reserve creation, 110
See also DEVELOPING COUNTRIES and DEVELOPMENT FINANCE

ECOSOC. See UNITED NATIONS ECONOMIC AND SOCIAL COUNCIL

ECUADOR
Art. VIII, Secs. 2, 3, and 4, acceptance of obligations of, 476, 571
Drawings (purchases) and repurchases from Fund: purchases, 265, 268*, 311, 316, 321, 330*; repurchases, 268*, 395*; under compensatory financing facility, 265, 268*
Exchange markets, 475, 542
Exchange rate and par value, xxi, 475–76, 563
Exchange reform, 475–76
Quota in Fund, 306*
SDR allocations, 248*
Stand-by arrangements with Fund, 321, 333*, 476

EEC. See EUROPEAN ECONOMIC COMMUNITY

EGYPT
Drawings (purchases) and repurchases from Fund: purchases, 263, 264, 268*, 312, 316, 318, 319, 330*; repurchases, 268*, 395*; under compensatory financing facility, 263, 264, 268*; waiver, 322

Exchange rate, 563
Quota in Fund, 306*
SDR allocations, 248*

EKLÖF, KURT, 112, 378, 389

ELECTRONIC DATA PROCESSING IN FUND, 603, 639

ELMHOLT, ERIK, 646

EL SALVADOR
Art. VIII, Secs. 2, 3, and 4, acceptance of obligations of, 571*n*
Drawings (purchases) and repurchases from Fund: purchases, 265, 268*, 310, 311, 321, 330*; repurchases, 268*, 395*; under compensatory financing facility, 265, 268*
Exchange rate, 562
Quota in Fund, 306*
SDR allocations, 248*
Stand-by arrangements with Fund, 321, 333*

EL SELEHDAR, A. K., 647

EMMINGER, OTMAR, 36, 59–60, 76, 102, 106, 107, 120, 121, 130, 136*, 144, 153, 164*
Reserve creation plans, 79–82, 150*n*, 197, 202

EQUAL VALUE PRINCIPLE, 169, 170, 184

EQUATORIAL GUINEA
Quota in Fund, 301, 303, 306*
SDR allocations, 248*
Technical assistance from Fund, 581

ESCOBAR, LUIS, 88, 101, 216, 291, 304, 592, 626

ESTEVA, PIERRE, 135*

ETHIOPIA
Par value, 560*
Quota in Fund, 306*

EUROCURRENCY MARKET, 497–98

EUROPE
Technical assistance from Fund, 582

EUROPEAN ECONOMIC COMMUNITY (EEC)
Attendance at joint meetings of Executive Directors and Group of Ten Deputies, 553
Balance of payments, 52, 69–70, 211–12
Common market policy, 455, 514, 515, 535, 538
Currencies used in Fund transactions, 254, 337*
Finance Ministers' meetings, 104, 127, 132, 133, 155, 200, 202, 452, 538; communiqué at Munich, 133, 202
Fund Articles of Agreement, recommendations for changes in, 132, 133, 138, 155, 173, 200–201, 202
Fund quotas, 131, 290, 306*–308*
Fund relations with, 254, 539, 608, 610*n*
Fund voting power, 123, 131, 151, 254
Separate group outside Fund, 608, 617, 618–19
Views on exchange rates: dollar devaluation urged, 534, 546; flexible rates and wider margins opposed, 503, 514, 515, 522, 538; for franc and deutsche mark, 452–54, 538
Views on reserve creation: emphasis on limited schemes, 82, 100; emphasis on payments adjustment, 70; preference for drawing rights, 127, 130, 148, 200–201; rejection of reserve asset concept, 107, 127; ultimate acceptance of SDR facility and activation, 104, 127, 130, 132, 133, 138, 143, 148, 155, 166, 173, 202, 211–12

EUROPEAN FREE TRADE ASSOCIATION, 610

EVENSEN, ROLF, 646

EXCHANGE MARGINS. *See* EXCHANGE RATE MECHANISM: Wider margins

EXCHANGE MARKETS
Crises, 212, 450, 459, 517, 519, 520, 522–24, 531; discussed in Fund consultations, 576; role of Fund, 523–24, 526
Dual, xxii, 358, 522, 542–43, 574–75
Forward, 15
In securities, 575
Intervention in, 15, 546
Year of calm, 517

EXCHANGE RATE MECHANISM
Calls for review of, 483, 484, 501–502
Crawling peg: amendment of Fund Articles required, 506; defined, 501; favored, 504, 510–11; opposed, 503, 507, 508, 509, 511–12
Dual rate systems considered, 501
Executive Directors' report: discussions, 500–502, 504–10, 511–14; drafted, xxi, 511–15; Governors' reactions, xxi, 503–504, 514–15; sequel to, 515–16, 523–24
Flexibility of exchange rates: arguments against, 506–508; arguments for, 508–509; discussion of greater, 501–504, 526; discussion of limited, 504, 505–506, 508, 509–10; views of developing versus industrial countries, 506–508; views of Governors, 503–504; views of Group of Ten Deputies, 510–11
Fluctuating rates considered, 503, 505, 508, 511, 513
Fund's role in decisions on, 523–24, 526
Gliding par values. *See* Crawling peg, *above*
Wider margins: considered, 501, 505, 506, 511, 513, 521–22, 532, 540, 557–58; favored, 504, 507, 509–10; opposed, 508, 515, 516; temporary regime established, xxii, 4, 555, 557–59, 560*, 561*, 562*
See also BALANCE OF PAYMENTS ADJUSTMENT PROCESS; INTERNATIONAL MONETARY SYSTEM; *and* PAR VALUE SYSTEM

EXCHANGE RATES
Central rates: communicated to Fund, 554, 555*, 561, 562*; decision on regime, xxii, 4, 447, 557–59; defined, 554, 558, 559
Changes: after sterling devaluation, 437–440; in French franc area, 457–58. *See also* PAR VALUES
Competitive depreciation, concern about, 439, 476
Fixed rates assumed in liquidity studies, 29, 31, 194
Forward rates, 15
Fund decisions, 226, 327–28, 512–14, 559, 563–64
Fund studies, 537–38. *See also* EXCHANGE RATE MECHANISM: Executive Directors' report
In Fund operations: for currencies in SDR transactions, 167, 169, 170, 172, 178, 184, 226; in financial programs, 363–64; special problems, 327–29, 531–33, 563–64
Managing Director's views on: Canadian dollar, 481; deutsche mark, 453–54, 458–59; exchange rate system, 504, 521–23; French franc, 452, 453–54; Indian rupee, 470; realignment, 452, 531, 532, 538–41, 544, 557; sterling, 447–48, 454; U.S. dollar, 448, 541, 545–46
Realignment: needed, 450–53, 520, 524–25, 528, 531–34; negotiated, 534–41, 543–49, 551–52; related to price of gold, 535, 536, 537, 541, 546, 549, 554; ultimately agreed, xxii, 4, 553–56, 557–63
Reform in Ecuador, 475–76
Representative rates, 226
Smithsonian agreement, xxii, 4, 553–56, 557–63
Wider margins. *See* EXCHANGE RATE MECHANISM
See also individual countries

EXCHANGE RATES, FLOATING
Brazil, 362, 364
Canada, xxi, 327–28, 476–79, 480–82, 519
Colombia, 358
Fed. Rep. of Germany: in 1969, xx, 3, 212, 328, 459–60; in 1971, 3, 517, 522, 525, 542, 544
In Fund operations, 327–29
Introduced after August 15, 1971, xxii, 541–43
Netherlands, xxii, 3, 328, 517, 522, 525, 542, 544
Views: as alternative to reserve creation, 21; disruptive to monetary system, 478–79; unsatisfactory for new pattern of par values, 537–38
See also EXCHANGE RATE MECHANISM *and* individual countries

EXCHANGE RATES, MULTIPLE
Belgium and Luxembourg, 522
Colombia, 358
Ecuador, 475–76
France, 543
Fund decisions on, 559, 563
India, 469
Trends, 539, 545, 574–75

Turkey, 474–75
Yugoslavia, 518
EXCHANGE RESTRICTIONS
Annual reports on by Fund, 575n
Developed countries, 573, 574; France, 356–57, 450, 453, 573; Japan, 494, 573; U.K., 441, 573
Developing countries, 574; Ceylon, 439; CFA franc area, 357; Colombia, 358
Fund decisions on, 357, 441–42, 591–93
Increased reliance on, 221, 539–40, 545
On capital movements, 13, 526, 575
Payments arrears defined as, xxi, 591–93
Subject of Fund consultations, 573–75
See also CAPITAL MOVEMENTS; EXCHANGE RATES, MULTIPLE; IMPORTS; and TARIFFS
EXECUTIVE DIRECTORS/EXECUTIVE BOARD
Alternate Directors, 629–30
Annual Reports, 177, 200, 204, 624
Appointment of Advisors, 632
Articles of Agreement, report on proposed first amendment to, 175, 204
Assistants, 632
CIAP, suggested discussions with, 106
Composition, 298–300, 625–30
Decisions. See specific subjects
Elections, 298, 625, 631–32
Functions, 622–25
Group of Nine ("G-9 Caucus"), 107, 552, 618
Group of Ten Deputies: closer liaison with, 76–77, 101, 197; joint meeting on currency realignment, 553; joint meetings on reserve creation, 101–103, 104, 105–108, 119–21, 126–27, 130, 134*–37*, 141–43, 150–53, 162*–65*, 200, 201, 202, 203; reports of Managing Director's representatives on Deputies' meetings, 76–77, 95, 197
Meetings, number of and time spent in, 624
Reports. See specific subjects
Retirement, 626–27
Size and structure, 625–32
Travel to constituent countries, 624–25
UNCTAD: seminar with secretariat members, 104; suggested joint discussions with, 106, 110
Vote, formal, 410
Voting power, discussion of distribution of, 632
World Bank representative at meeting, 276
See also Appendices A–1, A–2, A–3 (pp. 655–62 of this volume) and individual members of Executive Board
EXPORTS
Developed countries: France, 455; Fed. Rep. of Germany, 451, 452, 460, 462, 463; Iceland, 473; Japan, 493, 494, 495; U.S., 492, 527
Developing countries: earnings from, 264–65, 269–70, 271–72, 275–76; experiences with, 358, 361, 471, 472; measures to promote, 450, 469, 470, 574

F

FABER, PAUL L., 88, 89, 110, 134*, 146, 148, 162*, 174, 273, 345, 346
FAO. See FOOD AND AGRICULTURE ORGANIZATION
FERNANDEZ, DIOGENES H., 267
FERRARI-AGGRADI, MARIO, 426, 514, 546
FIJI
Currency unit and par value, 468
Participation in Special Drawing Account, 233
Quota in Fund, 302, 306*
FINANCIAL PROGRAMMING
Definition, 364
Discussed in consultations, 576
In individual countries: Colombia, 358; Ghana, 471, 472; Indonesia, 359, 360; Turkey, 475
Major Fund activity, 363–68
Methodology, 364–68; evaluated, 366–68
Provisions regarding indebtedness, 596
Stabilization Policies Division created in Fund, 365

FINCH, DAVID C., 646
FINK, CARL B., 648
FINLAND
Currency: unit, new, 472; used in Fund transactions, 324, 337*
Drawings (purchases) and repurchases from Fund, 311, 315, 321, 330*, 395*
Exchange rate and par value, xviii, 472–73, 562*
Quota in Fund, 296, 306*
SDR allocations, 248*
Stand-by arrangements with Fund, 320, 333*
FISCAL AFFAIRS, TECHNICAL ASSISTANCE IN. See TECHNICAL ASSISTANCE
FISCAL POLICY
Discussed in consultations, 575–76
Greater Fund attention urged, 578
Measures taken: Brazil, 361–62; Colombia, 358; Ecuador, 476; France, 353, 354, 450, 453; Fed. Rep. of Germany, 451, 452, 463; Indonesia, 359–60; U.K., 340, 350, 351, 441; U.S., 486–89, 490
Use: as criteria in stand-by arrangements, 344–45, 346; compared with monetary policy, 354, 356, 490, 578; in financial programs, 363, 364
See also MONETARY POLICY
FLANDORFFER, W., 164*
FLEMING, J. MARCUS, 52, 77, 115–16, 135*, 163*, 649
FOOD AND AGRICULTURE ORGANIZATION (FAO), 272, 274, 285, 286, 610
Committees and study groups, 286
FOREIGN EXCHANGE RESERVES. See RESERVES
FORWARD EXCHANGE MARKETS, 15
FOWLER, HENRY H., 71, 501
Proposal for monetary conference, 63, 67, 196
Views and comments on: deutsche mark revaluation, 451; gold price, 407–408; reconstitution of SDRs, 156; reserve creation, 73, 131, 201; U.S. balance of payments, 70, 172
FOZ, ALBERTO S., 645
FRANCE
Amendment to Articles of Agreement: acceptance of, 176; position on, 171–73, 175, 204
Art. VIII consultations, 353, 354, 355, 453
Art. VIII, Secs. 2, 3, and 4, acceptance of obligations of, 571n
Balance of payments: deficits, 209, 211; surpluses, 355–56, 458, 493, 564. See also Capital flows, below
Basle Agreement, 14, 192
Capital flows, 449–50, 453–54, 542
Currency: declared convertible in fact, 225–26; Fund holdings, 352, 355, 356; used in Fund transactions, 337*
Drawing rights in Fund, 453
Drawings (purchases) and repurchases from Fund: purchases, 311, 330*; purchases in gold and super gold tranche, xix, 315, 352, 449, 450; purchases under stand-by arrangement, xx, 212, 321, 355; repurchases, 356, 395*
Economic situation and policies, 211, 352–57, 449–56, 458
Exchange and trade controls: abolished, 450; imposed, 356–57, 450
Exchange markets, dual, 542, 543, 574
Financial stabilization program, 352–57
Gold Pool, 403
Gold, views on role of, 40, 61–63, 132, 171–72, 195
Nonmetropolitan territories, par value changes in, 456
Par value: discussion, xix, 451–56; 1969 devaluation, xx, 454–56; unchanged, 554, 555*, 560*
Quota in Fund, 296, 306*, 356
Reserve creation: proposals, 54, 55, 63, 131–32, 196; views, 79, 107, 112–13, 119–20, 124–25, 188–89
Reserves. See Balance of payments and Capital flows, above
SDRs: allocations, 248*; views on reconstitution, 158
Seminar with Fund staff, 356
Special Drawing Account, participation in, 215, 218

Stabilization of primary product prices, views on, 279
Stand-by arrangement with Fund, xx, 212, 320, 334*, 352–57, 458

FRENCH FRANC AREA
Exchange markets, dual, 542, 574
Exchange rates and par values, 456–58
Exchange restrictions in CFA franc countries, 357

FRIEDMAN, MILTON, 21, 191
FRIIS, TORBEN, 129, 134*, 162*, 439, 626
FRIMPONG-ANSAH, G. H., 471
FRONZONI, L., 136*, 164*
FUENFGELT, LORE, 136*, 164*, 292, 456, 495
Background, 630
FUKUDA, TAKEO, 417, 504, 514

FUND
Accounts. *See* GENERAL ACCOUNT *and* SPECIAL DRAWING ACCOUNT
Affiliate proposed, 112, 126, 129, 144, 150–51, 202–203; International Reserve Fund (IRF), 92, 152, 198; International Reserve Organization, 128, 146; International Reserve Union, 146, 152; proposal given up, 152, 155, 157, 160, 203; voting provisions, 122, 125
Assets. *See* GOLD TRANSACTIONS AND OPERATIONS OF FUND *and* HOLDINGS OF FUND
Borrowing: bilateral, 376–77, 387; under GAB, *see* GENERAL ARRANGEMENTS TO BORROW
Budget, 383–88, 392–94, 397*
Buildings, 589, 649–50
Chairmanship of Ghana aid meetings, 600
General Reserve, 385
Implications for Fund of: change in par value of major currency, 434; formation of outside groups, 619–20; suspension of convertibility by U.S., 530
Income and expenditure, 385–88, 397*; distribution of net income, 235–36, 244, 388–92, 393
Office in Europe (Paris), 77, 608, 637, 643, 650
Office in Geneva, 608, 637, 644–45
Organization, 77n, 556, 616; Executive Board, 622–32; IMF Institute, 588–90; new bureaus, 585n, 638n; new divisions, 286, 365; staff, 636–37
Policymaking process, 616–49
Resources. *See* QUOTAS IN FUND *and* RESOURCES OF FUND . . .
Rules and practices, changes in, 253–60
Special Reserve, 383, 385, 388
Transactions. *See* RESOURCES OF FUND—USE *and* REPURCHASES
See also ARTICLES OF AGREEMENT; BOARD OF GOVERNORS; DEPUTY MANAGING DIRECTOR; EXECUTIVE DIRECTORS/EXECUTIVE BOARD; MANAGING DIRECTOR; MEMBERSHIP; STAFF; *and* specific functions and activities, *e.g.*, TECHNICAL ASSISTANCE

FUNDAMENTAL DISEQUILIBRIUM
Cited as reason for change in par value: Austria, 524; Canada, 479; Ceylon, 439; Ecuador, 475; Finland, 472, 473; France, 452, 455, 456; Fed. Rep. of Germany, 451, 460; Iceland, 474; Israel, 437; New Zealand, 438; Spain, 439; Turkey, 474, 475; U.K., 433, 435, 443; Yugoslavia, 518
Noted as important in Fund Articles, 507, 514

G

G-9 CAUCUS (GROUP OF NINE), 107, 552, 618
GAB. *See* GENERAL ARRANGEMENTS TO BORROW
GABON
Exchange rate, 457–58, 561
Quota in Fund, 302, 306*
SDR allocations, 248*
GAMBIA, THE
Currency unit, new, 518
Exchange rate and par value, xix, 440, 465, 466*, 518, 560*

Quota in Fund, 289, 302, 303, 306*
SDR allocations, 248*
Technical assistance from Fund, 581

GARANGO, TIEMOKO MARC, 304
GARLAND, J. M., 32
GATT. *See* GENERAL AGREEMENT ON TARIFFS AND TRADE

GENERAL ACCOUNT
Contrasted with Special Drawing Account, 179
Establishment, 146, 152, 167
Payments for expenses of Special Drawing Account, 179, 229, 386
SDR transactions, 172, 173, 229–30, 234–37, 241, 243, 325, 337*, 379–80
Voting, 254–55
See also RESOURCES OF FUND—USE

GENERAL AGREEMENT ON TARIFFS AND TRADE (GATT)
Fund relations with, 284, 607–608, 610
Kennedy Round of negotiations, 573
Trade restrictions prerogative of, 284
Work on commodities, 274

GENERAL ARRANGEMENTS TO BORROW (GAB)
Activation, 313, 339, 340, 352, 374–76, 374*
Association of Switzerland, 372–73
Borrowing under, 374*–76
Claims under: consideration of in liquidity discussions, 47, 49, 50, 123; yield on, 246, 373
Establishment, 17, 21, 22, 192, 193, 370
Fund repayments, 375–76, 387, 476–77
Modifications discussed, 370–74
Participants, 370n, 372
Renewals, xx, 37, 195, 370–73
Use of term "currency convertible in fact," 168

GENERAL COUNSEL (Joseph Gold), 135*, 163*, 166, 253, 647
Appointment, 77
Resumé of Fund service, 643
Staff positions and explanations: central rates and wider margins, 558; deutsche mark revaluation, 459; distribution of Fund's net income, 391; exchange rates, 506, 515–16; international monetary reform, 539; obligations under Art. IV, Sec. 4(b), 404–405, 459; reconstitution of SDRs, 158; reserve creation, 86, 130, 152, 154; U.S. dollar convertibility, 550
Uniqueness of SDRs noted, 187–88

GENERAL RESERVE, 385

GENERALIZED SYSTEM OF TARIFF PREFERENCES (EEC), 574

GERMANY, FEDERAL REPUBLIC OF
Art. VIII consultations, 460–61, 462–64, 525, 571
Art. VIII, Secs. 2, 3, and 4, acceptance of obligations of, 571n
Balance of payments surplus, 449–52, 460–64, 493, 564
Basle Agreement, 14, 192
Basle Group, 442n
Border taxes, 451, 452, 462
Borrowing by Fund under GAB, 374*; repayment, 376
Capital flows and measures to control, 212, 352, 449–51, 453–54, 461, 463, 464, 523
Currency: declared convertible in fact, 225–26; used in Fund transactions, 312, 313–14, 327–28, 337*
Drawings (purchases) from Fund, 311, 315, 330*, 463
Economic situation and policies, 460–64
Exchange markets, 212, 459–60
Exchange rate: central, 554, 555*, 562*; floating (1969), xx, 212, 459–60; floating (1971), xxii, 327–28, 517, 522, 525, 542, 544
Par value: change, xx, 3, 458–62; discussion, xix, 449–52, 454, 522–23
Quota in Fund, 13, 296, 306*
Reserve creation, views on, 79
SDRs: allocations, 248*; receipt, 236, 243

GERSTEIN, ALBERT S., 647

GHANA
Aid, multilateral, 599, 600
Art. XIV consultations, 472, 571, 572
Currency unit, new, 467, 597n
Debt renegotiations, 471, 595, 597–600
Drawings from Fund. See Transactions . . . purchases, below
Exchange rate and par value, xviii, 437, 467, 471–72, 542, 561*, 597n
Financial stabilization program, 471–72, 597
Payments arrears, 597
Quota in Fund, 306*
SDR allocations, 248*
Stand-by arrangements with Fund, 320, 321, 334*, 471, 597, 599; phasing of drawings under, 471
Technical assistance from Fund, 471
Transactions with Fund: purchases, 264, 268*, 312, 321, 330*, 471; repurchases, 268*, 395*; under compensatory financing facility, 264, 268*; waiver, 322

GHANDOUR, ABDALLA SIDDIG, 594

GHOSH, ARUN K., 378–79

GILBERT, MILTON, 137*, 165*

GILCHRIST, RONALD H., 481, 521
Background, 630

GISCARD D'ESTAING, VALERY, 37, 54, 188–89, 196, 281, 353, 454, 492
Views and comments on: exchange rates, 426, 503, 507, 515, 546; gold, 39–40, 61, 62–63, 195; international liquidity, 29–30, 69–70, 75, 193

GLIDING PAR VALUES. See EXCHANGE RATE MECHANISM: Crawling peg

GOCHT, ROLF, 136*

GOLD AND FOREIGN EXCHANGE RESERVES. See RESERVES

GOLD EXCHANGE STANDARD. See INTERNATIONAL MONETARY SYSTEM

GOLD, JOSEPH. See GENERAL COUNSEL

GOLD MARKETS
Fund policy, 404
Two-tier market, xix, 3, 171, 405–409, 411, 414, 425

"GOLD MARRIAGES," 424–25

GOLD POOL, 15, 171, 192, 403–405

GOLD PRICE
Free market, 405–407, 412, 428
Official, xix, 401–402, 427; assumed fixed in liquidity studies, 29, 194; pressure on, 401–404; proposals to change, 21, 118, 172, 534, 540, 545, 551; proposals to change rejected, 66, 196, 403, 536; raised, 554
Relation to dollar devaluation, 426–27, 534, 536, 540, 545, 551, 553
Relation to Fund operations, 327, 328, 549–50
Speculation, 15, 403

GOLD PRODUCTION. See GOLD, ROLE OF: Demand and supply

GOLD RESERVES. See RESERVES

GOLD, ROLE OF
Demand and supply, 18, 25, 401–402, 403, 406
In dollar devaluation, 528–29, 530, 534, 536–37, 541, 545
In monetary system, 140; emphasized, 40, 61, 62–63, 195, 427; questioned, 408–409, 427, 428, 536, 537, 565; suggested changes in Fund's Articles, 132; working party to study, 115n
In reserve creation plans, 46–47, 60, 115, 116, 118, 120, 129, 196

GOLD STANDARD. See INTERNATIONAL MONETARY SYSTEM

GOLD TRANCHE. See RESOURCES OF FUND—NATURE AND SIZE and RESOURCES OF FUND—USE

GOLD TRANSACTIONS AND OPERATIONS OF FUND
Decisions: general deposits, 420–23, 425; production subsidies, 423–24; purchases from South Africa, xxi, 409–14; sales, 417–20

Holdings, 16, 300, 328, 425; investment in U.S. securities, 383–85; on general deposit, 420–23, 425, 426
Purchases: from Austria, 416; from South Africa, 409–16, 425
Relation to price expectations, 327, 328, 549–50
Repurchases, 327, 337*
Sales: allocation among members, 417–20; to mitigate impact of quota increases, 254, 297–98, 300, 416–17; to replenish currency holdings, 236, 298, 301, 417–20
SDRs, gold value of guaranteed, 186–87, 327
SDRs in lieu of gold: accepted by Fund, 47, 112, 172, 173, 297, 298; accepted by members, 236, 244; as basis for par values, 427
Subscriptions, 254, 297–98, 300, 301, 356; mitigation of impact of payment of, see Sales, above; payment of, 47, 112, 172, 173, 297, 298
Transactions service, 424–25

GOMES, EDUARDO DA S., JR., 481

GONZALEZ DEL VALLE, JORGE, 83n, 109–10, 134*, 141, 149, 153, 162*, 174, 273, 343, 345–46, 436

GONZALEZ, GUILLERMO, 550
Background, 630

GOODE, RICHARD, 643

GORDON, WALTER L., 71

GOVERNORS OF FUND. See BOARD OF GOVERNORS

GRADI, FLORIO, 136*

GREECE
Exchange rate, 562*
Quota in Fund, 296, 306*
SDR allocations, 248*

GROUP OF NINE (G–9 CAUCUS), 107, 552, 618

GROUP OF SEVENTY-SEVEN, 245, 617–18
Charter of Algiers, 607

GROUP OF TEN
Acceptance of SDR facility and amended Articles, 99, 155–58, 166, 170–76, 204
Deputies: meetings, 35–37, 76–81, 86, 95, 100, 157, 158, 166, 203, 216, 295, 506, 510, 516, 543, 549, 550; other references to, 29, 52, 59, 69, 95, 102, 111, 113, 115, 130, 144, 156–57, 195, 197, 198, 216, 292, 295, 510–11; reports, 35–37, 59–61, 95–98, 109, 194–95. See also Joint meetings, below
Finance Ministers and Central Bank Governors: communiqués, 70–74, 96n, 98n, 174, 196, 199, 453, 554; meetings, xxii, 4, 28–29, 36–37, 96n, 98, 105, 155–56, 158, 166, 170–75, 203–204, 253, 450–53, 500, 540, 543–45, 552–56
International liquidity studies, 28–29, 35–38, 194
Joint meetings of Deputies with Fund Executive Directors: arranged, 101–103, 104–108, 153, 200; on reserve creation, 119–21, 126–27, 130, 141–43, 150–53, 200, 201, 202, 203; participants' names, 134*–37*, 162*–65*; prior to Smithsonian agreement, 553
Relations with Fund, 29, 71, 76–77, 130, 194, 197, 198, 201, 290, 617–18
Separate group outside Fund, 290, 617–18
Views on: change in gold price, 551; exchange rate flexibility, 510–11; harmonization of reserve ratios, 97, 109; multilateral surveillance, 35–36, 40, 69, 70–71, 100, 195; quotas in Fund, 290, 292, 295; reserve creation, 28, 70–73, 76–78, 79–81, 95–99, 199; SDR allocations, 216; U.S. balance of payments, 69–70, 544–45, 549, 552–56
Working parties: on acceptability of new reserve asset, 115; to study role of gold in monetary system, 115n
See also OSSOLA GROUP and individual countries

GROUP OF THIRTY-ONE, 85, 199

GROUP OF TWENTY-FOUR (INTERGOVERNMENTAL GROUP OF TWENTY-FOUR ON INTERNATIONAL MONETARY AFFAIRS), 607n, 617–18

GUATEMALA
  Art. VIII, Secs. 2, 3, and 4, acceptance of obligations
    of, 571n
  Drawings (purchases) and repurchases from Fund:
    purchases, 264, 268*, 311, 321, 330*; repurchases,
    268*, 395*; under compensatory financing facility,
    264, 268*
  Quota in Fund, 306*
  SDR allocations, 248*
  Stand-by arrangements with Fund, 321, 334*

GUINEA
  Drawings (purchases) and repurchases from Fund,
    312, 316–18, 330*, 395*
  Quota in Fund, 306*
  SDR allocations, 248*
  Technical assistance from Fund, 580

GUNTER, JOHN W., 643–44

GUYANA
  Art. VIII, Secs. 2, 3, and 4, acceptance of obliga-
    tions of, 571
  Drawings (purchases) from Fund, 310–11, 316, 322,
    330*
  Exchange rate, 562*
  Par value, xviii, 437, 438*, 465, 466
  Quota in Fund, 288, 306*
  SDR allocations, 248*
  Stand-by arrangements with Fund, 320–21, 334*
  Technical assistance from Fund, 580–81

H

HABERER, JEAN-YVES, 163*

HABERMEIER, WALTER O., 644

HAITI
  Art. VIII, Secs. 2, 3, and 4, acceptance of obliga-
    tions of, 571n
  Drawings (purchases) and repurchases from Fund:
    purchases, 264, 266, 268*, 311, 316, 318, 330*;
    repurchases, 268*, 395*; under compensatory
    financing facility, 264, 266, 268*
  Exchange rate, 562*
  Quota in Fund, 306*
  SDR allocations, 248*
  Stand-by arrangements with Fund, 34, 334*

HAJEK, JULIUS, 83n

HALL, F. L., 163*

HANDFIELD-JONES, S. J., 112, 121, 123, 128–29, 134*,
  141, 147, 149, 152, 162*, 345, 389

HANH, NGUYEN HUU, 491
  Background, 630

HARLEY, CHARLES R.
  Background, 630

HARMONIZATION. See SPECIAL DRAWING
  RIGHTS

HARROD, SIR ROY, 21

HASSANEIN, M. M., 647

HASZARD, J. S., 638n

HATTORI, SEITARO, 224, 293, 345

HEBBARD, W. LAWRENCE, 135*, 163*, 644

HEILPERIN, MICHAEL, 21

HENRION, ROBERT, 132n

HICKS, EARL, 642

HOCKIN, A. B., 135*, 163*

HOLDINGS OF FUND
  Currencies: French franc, 352, 355, 356; pound ster-
    ling, 351; replenishment, 236, 244, 298, 301, 417–
    20; valuation, 328, 539, 563
  Gold, 16, 300, 328, 420–23, 425; investment of, 383–85
  See also RESOURCES OF FUND—NATURE AND
    SIZE

HOLT, HAROLD, 81, 189

HOLTROP, M. W., 16, 38–39, 40, 41

HONDURAS
  Art. VIII, Secs. 2, 3, and 4, acceptance of obliga-
    tions of, 571n
  Drawings (purchases) and repurchases from Fund,
    311, 316, 330*, 395*
  Exchange rate, 562*
  Quota in Fund, 306*
  SDR allocations, 248*
  Stand-by arrangements with Fund, 321, 334*

HONG KONG. See UNITED KINGDOM: Nonmetropolitan territories

HOOD, W. C., 135*, 163*

HOOKER, JOHN S., 134*, 162*
  Length of service, 626, 627

HORNE, ROMAN L., 135*, 644

HOROWITZ, DAVID, 245n, 246, 594

HOSHINO, DAIZO, 136*, 164*

HØST-MADSEN, POUL, 646

HSU, PEH YUAN, 552
  Background and length of service, 626, 627, 629

HUBBACK, D. F., 136*, 164*

HUNTRODS, GUY, 345, 422, 474, 479, 510

I

IA-ECOSOC. See INTER-AMERICAN ECONOMIC
  AND SOCIAL COUNCIL

IBRD. See WORLD BANK

ICELAND
  Art. XIV consultation, 439
  Drawings (purchases) and repurchases from Fund:
    purchases, 264, 265, 266, 268*, 311, 321, 330*;
    repurchases, 268*, 395*; under compensatory
    financing facility, 264, 265, 266, 268*; waiver, 322
  Economic situation, 439, 473–74
  Exchange rate, 562*
  Par value, xviii, xix, 438*, 439, 473–74
  Quota in Fund, 296, 306*
  SDR allocations, 248*

IDA. See INTERNATIONAL DEVELOPMENT ASSO-
  CIATION

IDB. See INTER-AMERICAN DEVELOPMENT BANK

IFC. See INTERNATIONAL FINANCE CORPORA-
  TION

IKLE, M., 137*, 165*

IMF INSTITUTE, 588–90

IMPORTS
  Deposits, 441, 574
  Japan, 494
  Restrictions: increased, 221, 500; liberalized, 574;
    particular countries, 441, 451, 452, 469–70, 474, 495;
    tightening feared, 221, 539–40, 545
  Subsidies, 452
  U.S., 528; imposition of surcharge, 529; reactions to
    surcharge, 531, 533, 539, 544, 546; removal of sur-
    charge, 544, 545, 546, 554
  Yugoslavia, 518

INCOME AND EXPENDITURE OF FUND, 385–88,
  397*
  Distribution of net income, 388–92, 393; alternatives,
    390–92; use of SDRs, 235–36, 244

INCOMES POLICY, 463, 490

INDIA
  Art. XIV consultations, 470–71, 571
  Debt renegotiation, 595
  Drawings (purchases) and repurchases from Fund:
    purchases, 264, 268*, 312, 316, 318–19, 331*, 469;
    repurchases, 268*, 395*; under compensatory
    financing facility, 264, 268*
  Economic situation and policies, 469–71
  Exchange rate, 542, 562*
  Executive Director no longer appointed, 299–300, 625
  Par value, xviii, 468–71

Quota in Fund, 296, 307*
SDR allocations, 248*; use, 234

INDONESIA
Debt rescheduling and renegotiation, 359, 595
Drawings (purchases) and repurchases from Fund: purchases, xxii, 283–84, 312, 331*; repurchases, 395*; under buffer stock facility, xxii, 283–84
Exchange rate, 563
Financial stabilization programs, 359–60
Quota in Fund, 288, 307*
SDR allocations, 248*
Stand-by arrangements with Fund, 320, 321, 334*, 359–60
Technical assistance from Fund, 581, 583, 585

INDUSTRIAL COUNTRIES
Art. VIII, Secs. 2, 3, and 4, acceptance of obligations of, 573
Balance of payments surpluses, 493
Classification in Fund statistics, 82n
Exchange and trade restrictions, 274, 276, 285, 573, 574
Exchange rates, 537–38, 542, 574
Fund consultations, 572
Interdependence with developing countries, 269, 270, 577
Output, 269, 460, 490, 493
Participation in limited reserve creation plans, 53–58, 72–73, 78–79, 81–82, 99–100. See also RESERVE CREATION PLANS: Limited schemes
Use of Fund resources, 310, 311, 312, 315, 320
Views on: exchange rate system, 507–508; quotas in Fund, 290–92, 294, 295; SDR-development finance link, 110–11, 196, 219, 220; use of Fund resources, 261, 345, 378
See also individual countries

INFLATION
Co-existing with unemployment, 576, 577
Commodity purchases as hedge against, 266
Discussed in Fund consultations, 576
Factor in Fund quotas, 291
Feared as result of reserve creation, 39, 45, 69, 97, 98, 118, 124, 125, 212
From capital inflows, 463–64, 520
In individual countries: Brazil, 360, 361, 362–63; Colombia, 359; France, 354, 356, 449–50, 455; Fed. Rep. of Germany, 461, 463, 464; Ghana, 472; India, 471; Indonesia, 359, 360; U.K., 354, 445, 446; U.S., 218, 221, 354, 486–92, 527–28, 534
Measures to control: Brazil, 363; France, 354, 450, 454; U.K., 354, 442–43; U.S., 354, 486, 487, 488–89, 491, 492
Worldwide problem, 565, 576, 577
See also FISCAL POLICY; MONETARY POLICY; and individual countries

INFORMATION AND PUBLICATIONS, 601–604
Made available to other organizations, 597, 605, 607, 610
On SDR transactions, 231, 233

INSTITUTE, IMF, 588–90

INTER-AMERICAN CENTER OF TAX ADMINISTRATORS (CIAT), 609

INTER-AMERICAN COMMITTEE ON THE ALLIANCE FOR PROGRESS (CIAP)
Fund's relations with: on external debt, 595, 597, 608, 609; on reports, 597, 610; on reserve creation, 106
Report on international monetary reform, 84–85, 198

INTER-AMERICAN DEVELOPMENT BANK (IDB), 609, 610

INTER-AMERICAN ECONOMIC AND SOCIAL COUNCIL (IA-ECOSOC), 85, 608–609

INTER-CENTRAL-BANK COOPERATION. See CENTRAL BANKS

INTERCONVERTIBILITY. See CURRENCY CONVERTIBLE IN FACT

INTEREST RATES. See MONETARY POLICY

INTERGOVERNMENTAL GROUP OF TWENTY-FOUR ON INTERNATIONAL MONETARY AFFAIRS (GROUP OF TWENTY-FOUR), 607n, 617–18

INTERNATIONAL BANK FOR RECONSTRUCTION AND DEVELOPMENT (IBRD). See WORLD BANK

INTERNATIONAL CHAMBER OF COMMERCE, 608

INTERNATIONAL COCOA AGREEMENT, 274, 286n

INTERNATIONAL COFFEE COUNCIL, 286

INTERNATIONAL COFFEE ORGANIZATION, 286, 610

INTERNATIONAL CONFEDERATION OF FREE TRADE UNIONS, 608

INTERNATIONAL COTTON ADVISORY COMMITTEE, 286

INTERNATIONAL DEVELOPMENT ASSOCIATION (IDA), 19, 111, 219, 390, 391

INTERNATIONAL FINANCE CORPORATION (IFC), 92, 581

INTERNATIONAL GRAINS AGREEMENT, 286

INTERNATIONAL LABOR ORGANIZATION, 610

INTERNATIONAL MONETARY FUND. See FUND

INTERNATIONAL MONETARY SYSTEM
Bretton Woods system, 501; collapse of, 3–4, 517, 564, 565; defense of, 510, 511, 515, 524, 525; operation of, 484, 496, 502, 506–507, 511. See also Gold exchange standard, below
Collapse: danger of, 171, 172, 341, 490, 523, 524–25, 538–39; following suspension of U.S. convertibility, 3–4, 517, 530, 564, 565–66, 601, 650
Considered in liquidity discussions: by CIAP, 84–85; by Fund, 27–28, 31–32, 44–45, 64–67; by Group of Ten, 28–29, 73, 119; by UN, 83, 84, 197
Exchange rate conference suggested, 484, 500–501
Gold exchange standard: calls for change, 18, 20, 53, 61–62, 65–66, 171–72; implications of SDRs for, 246; provision for liquidity under, 36–37
Gold standard: advocated, 61–63, 195; rejected, 65
Liquidity conference: proposed by U.S., 63, 73; reactions of Fund, 67–68, 196, 197
Outlook, 189, 247, 446–48
Reform: Governors' resolution, xxii, 547–48; role of Fund, 547, 548, 553, 555; suggestions by Fund, 539, 564–65
See also BALANCE OF PAYMENTS ADJUSTMENT PROCESS; EXCHANGE RATE MECHANISM; LIQUIDITY, INTERNATIONAL; and PAR VALUE SYSTEM

INTERNATIONAL ORGANIZATIONS
Fund relations with, 595, 604–15
See also individual organizations

INTERNATIONAL RESERVE FUND (IRF), 92–95, 152, 198

INTERNATIONAL RESERVE ORGANIZATION, 128, 146

INTERNATIONAL RESERVE UNION (IRU), 146, 152

INTERNATIONAL TIN AGREEMENT, 269, 274, 282–84, 286

INTERNATIONAL TIN COUNCIL, 283, 286

INTERNATIONAL WHEAT AGREEMENT, 286

INTERVENTION CURRENCY, 497, 559

INVESTMENT OF FUND'S ASSETS, 383–85

IRAN
Drawings (purchases) and repurchases from Fund, 312, 316, 331*, 395*
Exchange rate, 562
Quota in Fund, 296, 307*
SDR allocations, 249*
Technical assistance from Fund, 583

IRAQ
Drawings (purchases) and repurchases from Fund: purchases, 264, 268*, 312, 316, 331*; repurchases, 268*, 395*; under compensatory financing facility, 264, 268*; waiver, 322
Exchange rate and par value, 542, 560*

Quota in Fund, 296, 307*
SDR allocations, 249*
Special Drawing Account, participation in, 232
Technical assistance from Fund, 580, 585

IRELAND
Art. VIII, Secs. 2, 3, and 4, acceptance of obligations of, 571*n*
Currency: decimal system, 518; used in Fund transactions, 324, 337*
Drawings (purchases) and repurchases from Fund, 311, 315, 317, 331*, 395*
Exchange rate and par value, xviii–xix, 437, 438*, 542, 560*
Quota in Fund, 296, 307*
SDR allocations, 249*

IRF. *See* INTERNATIONAL RESERVE FUND

IRU. *See* INTERNATIONAL RESERVE UNION

ISMAIL BIN MOHAMED ALI, 277–78

ISRAEL
Drawings (purchases) from Fund, 312, 316, 318, 331*
Exchange rate, central, 562*
Par value, xviii–xix, 437, 438*, 543
Quota in Fund, 296, 307*
SDR allocations, 249*

ITALY
Acceptance of amendment to Articles of Agreement, 176
Art. VIII, Secs. 2, 3, and 4, acceptance of obligations of, 571*n*
Balance of payments surplus, 493
Basle Agreement, 14, 192
Basle Group, 442*n*
Borrowing by Fund: bilateral, 376, 387; repayment, 376; under GAB, 374*, 376
Currency: declared convertible in fact, 225–26; used in Fund transactions, 313–14, 337*, 376
Drawings (purchases) from Fund, 311, 315, 331*
Exchange rate: central, 554, 555*, 562*; floating, 542, 544
Quota in Fund, 296, 307*
Reserve creation, views on, 79, 120
SDRs: allocations, 249*; receipt, 236

IVORY COAST
Exchange rate, 457–58, 561
Quota in Fund, 296, 301, 307*
SDR allocations, 249*

J

J-CURVE, 444

JACKSON, SIR ROBERT, 605

JACOBSSON, PER. *See* MANAGING DIRECTOR (Per Jacobsson)

JAMAICA
Art. VIII, Secs. 2, 3, and 4, acceptance of obligations of, 571*n*
Currency unit, new, 468
Drawings (purchases) and repurchases from Fund, 311, 316, 331*, 395*
Par value, xix, 437, 438*, 468, 560*
Quota in Fund, 288, 296, 301, 307*
SDR allocations, 249*
Technical assistance from Fund, 585

JAMAICA DECLARATION, 85, 109, 198

JAMAL, A. H., 427

JAPAN
Art. VIII consultations, 494, 495, 571
Art. VIII, Secs. 2, 3, and 4, acceptance of obligations of, 571*n*
Balance of payments surplus, 493–95, 528, 564
Basle Group, 442*n*
Borrowing by Fund: bilateral, 376; under GAB, 374*, 375, 376
Currency used in Fund transactions, 337*
Economic situation and policies, 493–95
Exchange and trade controls, 494, 495, 574

Exchange rate: central, 554, 555*, 562*; floating, 542–44
Executive Director appointed, 299, 625
Quota in Fund, 13, 296, 307*
Reserve creation, views on, 111, 120
SDRs: allocations, 249*; receipt, 236
Trade: arrangements with U.S., 551; surpluses, 494, 528

JENKINS, ROY, 220, 408, 500, 504

JHA, L. K., 219, 304

JOGE, SVEN F., 136*, 143, 151, 164*

JOHNSON, LYNDON B., 63, 176, 187, 210, 447, 487

JOHNSTONE, ROBERT, 224, 279, 292, 295, 349, 354, 391, 490, 505, 509, 521
Explanation of Canadian floating rate, 479–82

JOINT COMPUTER CENTER, 603, 639

JONES, CHARLES E., 648

JONES, EDGAR, 644–45

JONSSON, SIGURGEIR
Background, 630

JORDAN
Drawings (purchases) and repurchases from Fund, 265, 312, 331*, 395*; under compensatory financing facility, 265, 268*
Exchange rate, central, 562*
Quota in Fund, 307*
SDR allocations, 249*
Technical assistance from Fund, 580

K

KAFKA, ALEXANDRE, 85*n*, 134*, 153, 162*, 174, 349, 462, 550, 552
Background and length of service, 625, 627, 628
Comments and views on: buffer stock financing, 273, 277, 279; exchange rate mechanism, 510; financial programming, 366–67; quota formula, 304; quota review, 216, 291, 293–94, 296; reserve creation, 109, 117–18, 125, 129, 149, 151, 152; SDR designation plan, 242; stand-by arrangements, 342–43, 345–46, 354

KAHN, LORD, 83*n*

KASHIWAGI, YUSUKE, 136*, 164*

KEESING, F. A. G., 643

KENNEDY, DAVID, 504, 515

KENNEDY, JOHN F., 26, 92

KENNEDY ROUND, 573

KENNETT, W. A., 135*, 163*

KENYA
Exchange rate, 542
Par value, 437, 465, 466*, 560, 561*
Quota in Fund, 296, 307*
Repurchases from Fund, 395*
SDR allocations, 249*
Technical assistance from Fund, 580, 585

KESSLER, G. A., 115*n*, 120, 136*, 164*

KEYNES PLAN, 19

KHARMAWAN, BYANTI, 216, 278, 279, 298, 462, 480, 506–507, 552
Background and length of service, 627, 628

KHMER REPUBLIC
Drawings (purchases) from Fund, 268*, 312, 316, 331*; under compensatory financing facility, 268*
Exchange rate, floating, 542
Quota in Fund, 301, 307*
SDR allocations, 249*

KIBAKI, MWAI, 245*n*, 601

KIM, SE RYUN, 593

KING, HENRI H. P., 645

KLACKENBERG, L., 136*, 164*

KLEPPE, PER, 427

KONAN BEDIE, HENRI, 282

KOREA
Drawings (purchases) and repurchases from Fund, 312, 316, 321, 331*, 395*
Exchange rate, 542, 563
Quota in Fund, 289, 296, 307*
SDR allocations, 249*
Stand-by arrangements with Fund, 320, 334*

KROC, RUDOLF, 646

KUWAIT
Art. VIII, Secs. 2, 3, and 4, acceptance of obligations of, 571n
Currency used in Fund transactions, 324, 337*
Par value, 560*
Quota in Fund, 296, 307*

L

LACHMAN, PHILINE R., 647

LADEMANN, J., 137*, 165*

LAMANA, ABDOULAYE, 282

LAOS
Drawings (purchases) from Fund, 312, 316, 331*
Quota in Fund, 301, 307*
SDR allocations, 249*
Technical assistance from Fund, 581

LARRE, RENE, 101, 134*, 155, 158, 162*
Comments and views: balance of payments need for SDR use, 149; distribution of Fund's net income, 389; reserve creation, 110, 112–13, 118, 124–25, 127, 128, 144, 147, 148

LASO, EDUARDO, 649

LATIN AMERICA AND CARIBBEAN
Declaration of Jamaica issued by central bank governors, 85, 109, 198
Drawings (purchases) from Fund, 311, 316
Fund consultations, 572
Report on monetary reform, 84–85
Technical assistance from Fund, 582, 583

LATIN AMERICAN ASSOCIATION OF DEVELOPMENT FINANCING INSTITUTIONS, 609

LATIN AMERICAN INSTITUTE FOR ECONOMIC AND SOCIAL PLANNING, 589

LAWSON, R. W., 135*, 163*

LEBANON
Exchange rate, 542, 563
Quota in Fund, 296, 307*

LESOTHO
Currency unit, 465
Drawings (purchases) and repurchases from Fund, 312, 316, 331*, 395*
Membership in Fund, 289
Par value, 465, 466*, 561*
Quota in Fund, 302, 303, 307*
SDR allocations, 249*

LIANG, C. C., 649

LIBERIA
Drawings (purchases) and repurchases from Fund, 310, 312, 316, 321, 331*, 395*
Exchange rate and par value, 437, 562
Quota in Fund, 307*
SDR allocations, 249*
Stand-by arrangements with Fund, 321, 334*
Technical assistance from Fund, 583

LIBYAN ARAB REPUBLIC
Currency unit, new, 543
Exchange rate and par value, 542, 560*
Quota in Fund, 296, 307*

LICAROS, GREGORIO S., 427

LIEFTINCK, PIETER, 134*, 155, 162*, 286, 349, 384, 422, 436, 437, 439, 578
Background and length of service, 625, 627
Comments and views on: buffer stock financing, 277, 279, 283; Canadian dollar, 479, 480; currency convertible in fact, 224; distribution of Fund's net income, 389, 392; Ecuadoran devaluation, 476;

exchange rate flexibility and crises, 505, 507, 511, 521, 522–23, 525, 547; gold sales for currency replenishment, 418; quota reviews, 290, 292, 295; reserve creation, 27, 109, 112, 114, 116, 120, 124, 127, 149, 150, 152; SDRs, use of, 228, 231, 235, 242; stand-by arrangement, French, 354; use of Fund's resources and stand-by arrangements, 318, 319, 345, 379; U.S. inflation, 490, 492; Yugoslav par value, 518

LINDÅ, A., 136*, 164*

LINK BETWEEN RESERVE CREATION AND DEVELOPMENT FINANCE. See RESERVE CREATION: Link with development finance

LIQUIDITY, INTERNATIONAL
Adequacy: studied in 1950s, 11–13, 87–88, 190; views on, 15, 16, 27, 34–35, 39, 193, 194, 195
Conditional versus unconditional, 38; defined, 23, 194; preference for conditional, 26–27, 33, 109–10; relationship, 34, 43, 91, 109–10, 119, 129; techniques for expanding unconditional, 47–49
Conference suggested by U.S., 63, 67, 196
Defined to include positions in Fund, 26
Dependence on gold and reserve currencies, 25–26, 39, 40, 52
Expansion: Fund policies, 15, 26, 32–34, 194; Fund reactions to early proposals, 17–24
Fund as administering agency: advocated by Managing Director, 41–42, 46, 66–68, 73, 89, 100, 193, 195, 196, 197; advocated by others, 17–19, 40–41, 85
Fund role discussed by Group of Ten, 60, 89
Relation to balance of payments adjustment, 29–31, 96, 193
Studies: by academic economists, 17–19, 20, 21, 29, 38, 195; by Fund, 23, 26–28, 31–32, 34–35, 42, 68–69, 190, 193; by Group of Ten, 28–29, 35–38, 194
See also RESERVE ASSETS; RESERVE CREATION; RESERVE CREATION PLANS; RESERVES; and RESERVE UNITS

LOFTUS, MARTIN L., 645

LOSADA, BENITO RAUL, 408

LOWE, J. WILLIAM, 648

LUXEMBOURG
Art. VIII consultations, 523
Art. VIII, Secs. 2, 3, and 4, acceptance of obligations of, 571n
Balance of payments surplus, 493
Exchange markets, dual, xxii, 522–24
Exchange rate: central, 562*; floating, 542
Par value, 522–23
Quota in Fund, 301, 307*
SDR allocations, 249*
See also BELGIUM

M

MACKAY, BARON A. W. R., 136*, 164*

MADAN, B. K., 162*, 291, 345, 346, 349, 470, 481, 626
Comments and views on: distribution of Fund's net income, 390, 391; exchange rate flexibility, 506; reserve creation, 128, 141–42, 148, 152, 157; SDR allocation, link with quota increases, 215–16; SDR facility, activation of, 174; stabilization of commodity prices, 273, 277

MAGURN, KATHERINE F., 647

MALAGASY REPUBLIC
Exchange rate and par value, 437, 457–58, 561
Quota in Fund, 307*
SDR allocations, 249*
Technical assistance from Fund, 581

MALAWI
Currency unit, new, 518
Drawing (purchase) from Fund, 312, 331*
Par value, xviii–xix, 437, 438*, 465, 466*, 518, 560*
Quota in Fund, 307*
SDR allocations, 249*
Technical assistance from Fund, 581

MALAYSIA
Art. VIII, Secs. 2, 3, and 4, acceptance of obligations of, 571
Buffer stock financing, views on, 271–72
Currency: new unit, 467; used in Fund transactions, 324, 337*
Drawings (purchases) and repurchases from Fund: purchases, xxii, 284, 312, 316, 331*; repurchases, 395*; under buffer stock facility, xxii, 284
Exchange rate and par value, 437, 542
Quota in Fund, 288, 296, 301, 307*
SDR allocations, 249*
Technical assistance from Fund, 581, 585

MALI
Drawings (purchases) and repurchases from Fund, 310, 312, 316, 321, 331*, 395*
Exchange rate, 457–58
Quota in Fund, 307*
SDR allocations, 249*
Stand-by arrangements with Fund, 321, 334*
Technical assistance from Fund, 585

MALTA
Exchange rate, central, 562*
Membership in Fund, 289
Par value, 465, 466*
Quota in Fund, 307*
SDR allocations, 249*
Technical assistance from Fund, 580, 581, 585

MANAGING DIRECTOR (Per Jacobsson), 12, 16, 21–22, 24, 191, 192, 193, 621, 635

MANAGING DIRECTOR (Pierre-Paul Schweitzer), 84, 134*, 162*, 368, 454, 470–72, 518, 636
Appointment and resumé of service, 27, 632–35
Chronology of actions on liquidity, 193–203
Consultations with Secretary-General of UNCTAD, 104
Cooperation with World Bank, 612, 614
Meetings and speaking engagements, 45, 46, 64, 90, 91, 404, 604, 605, 607, 621
Positions, comments, explanations: borrowing, bilateral, 377; borrowing, GAB, 371–72; buffer stock financing, 270, 272, 278; Canadian dollar float, 477, 479, 481; deutsche mark float, 459–60; developing countries' debt service, 593, 601; distribution of Fund's net income, 388, 392; exchange rate mechanism and crises (1970 and 1971), 426, 501, 503–504, 521, 523, 526, 531–32, 538–41, 545–48, 551–53; gold deposits, general, 421, 422; gold, disinvestment of, 384–85; Gold Pool, 404; gold prices, 406; gold purchases from South Africa, 409–13; quotas, 292; reserve creation and liquidity—debates, studies, and joint meetings on, 27–28, 29–32, 36, 41–42, 44–46, 58, 64–69, 86–95, 99–103, 105–107, 125–26, 130, 142, 144, 151, 153, 159, 171, 193–203, 451–53, 543–44, 553; role of Fund, future, 651; split voting, 173; stand-by arrangement, U.K., 341, 348; sterling devaluation (1967), 339, 436–37, 447–48; U.S. balance of payments, 491
SDRs: actions and views, 176–77, 187; allocations, 181–82, 214–21; designation plan, 228–29; link with development finance, 245

MANAGING DIRECTOR (H. Johannes Witteveen), 635n

MANAGING DIRECTOR, DEPUTY. See DEPUTY MANAGING DIRECTOR

MANSOUR, ALBERT, 137n, 165n, 343, 379, 389, 390, 391, 470
Length of service, 626, 627

MARATHE, SHARAD S.
Background, 630

MARQUEZ, JAVIER, 85n

MARRIS, S., 137*

MARTINS, BASILIO
Background, 630

MASSAD A., CARLOS, 219, 304, 481, 552, 596
Background and length of service, 627, 629

MATTERA, ALBERT A., 646

MAUDE, EVAN W., 279, 292, 339, 341–42, 345, 349, 433, 437, 456

MAUDLING, REGINALD, 30–31, 40, 41
Mutual currency account plan, 24, 59, 60, 193

MAURITANIA
Drawings (purchases) from Fund, 312, 316, 331*
Exchange rate, 457–58, 561
Quota in Fund, 301, 307*
SDR allocations, 249*
Technical assistance from Fund, 585

MAURITIUS
Drawings (purchases) and repurchases from Fund, 312, 331*, 395*
Membership in Fund, 289, 440n
Quota in Fund, 307*
SDR allocations, 249*
Technical assistance from Fund, 581

MAYEKAWA, HARUO, 136*, 164*

MAYNARD, GEOFFREY, 85n

McMAHON, C. W., 136*, 164*

McNAMARA, ROBERT S., 613, 614

MEMBERSHIP
As of selected dates, 306*–308*
Changing nature of, 569–70; developing countries, 570; ministates, 302–303, 570, 632
Classification in Fund statistics, 82n
Formation of groups outside Fund, 576, 616–20
New members, 232–33, 289, 301, 302, 303, 570
See also NONMETROPOLITAN TERRITORIES OF MEMBERS

MENTRE, PAUL, 158, 169, 345, 390

MERM (Multilateral Exchange Rate Model), 537

MERTENS DE WILMARS, JACQUES, 135*, 163*

MERWIN, CHARLES L., 645

MEXICO
Art. VIII, Secs. 2, 3, and 4, acceptance of obligations of, 571n
Currency: declared convertible in fact, 225, 226; used in Fund transactions, 337*
Exchange rate, central, 562*
Quota in Fund, 296, 305, 307*
SDR allocations, 249*

MIDDLE EAST
Drawings (purchases) from Fund, 312, 316
Fund consultations, 572
Technical assistance from Fund, 582, 583, 585

MILLS, DONALD OWEN
Background, 630

MINISTATES. See STATES, SMALL

MITCHELL, DEREK, 446, 509, 550
Background and length of service, 627, 628

M'KHAITIRAT, MOHAMED SALEM OULD, 271

MLADEK, JAN V., 642

MONETARY POLICY
Coordination of, 14–15, 192, 520, 525, 618
Credit controls in financial programs, 340, 342, 344, 348, 353, 361–68
Criteria used in stand-by arrangements: in general, 343–48, 363–68; in individual countries, 342–43, 348, 353–54, 359–60, 361–62
Discussed in consultations, 575–76
Interest rates as factor in capital movements, 13–14, 499, 520
Seminars of Fund staff: and French officials, 356; and U.K. officials, 443, 445
Use: Brazil, 361, 362; Canada, 478; France, 353–54, 450, 453–54; Fed. Rep. of Germany, 463–64; Indonesia, 360; Japan, 494; U.K., 441–45; U.S., 74, 488, 490
See also FINANCIAL PROGRAMMING and FISCAL POLICY

MONETARY UNITS, NEW, 466–68, 518, 543

MONTANARO, SILVANO, 136*, 164*

MORALES BERMUDEZ, FRANCISCO, 245n, 600–601

MOROCCO
Drawings (purchases) and repurchases from Fund, 310, 312, 321, 331*, 395*
Par value, 560*
Quota in Fund, 301, 307*
SDR allocations, 249*
Stand-by arrangements with Fund, 321, 335*
Technical assistance from Fund, 583

MORSE, C. J., 136*, 164*

MUDENDA, E. H. K., 282

MULDOON, R. D., 277–78, 282, 285

MULTILATERAL EXCHANGE RATE MODEL (MERM), 537

MULTILATERAL SURVEILLANCE
Emphasized by Group of Ten, 35–36, 40, 69, 70–71, 100, 195
Interpretations of, 40, 78, 96–97

MULTINATIONAL CORPORATIONS, 499, 565

MULTIPLE CURRENCY PRACTICES. See EXCHANGE RATES, MULTIPLE

MULTIPLE RESERVE CURRENCY PLANS, 20, 191

MURPHY, HENRY C., 649

MUTUAL CURRENCY ACCOUNT PLAN. See MAUDLING, REGINALD

N

NELISSEN, R. J., 426, 546

NEPAL
Exchange rate and par value, 440, 465, 466*, 562
Quota in Fund, 300, 307*
Repurchases from Fund, 395*
SDR allocations, 249*
Special Drawing Account, participation in, 232
Technical assistance from Fund, 580

NETHERLANDS
Art. VIII, Secs. 2, 3, and 4, acceptance of obligations of, 571n
Balance of payments surplus, 493
Basle Agreement, 14, 192
Basle Group, 442n
Borrowing by Fund under GAB, 374*, 375, 376
Currency: declared convertible in fact, 226; swap arrangements, 314–15; used in Fund transactions, 314–15, 328, 337*
Exchange markets, dual, 542, 575
Exchange rate: central, 554, 555*, 562*; floating, xxii, 3, 327–28, 517, 522, 525, 542, 544
Nonmetropolitan territories: exchange rate, 562*; par value, 561*
Par value, 462
Quota in Fund, 307*
Reserve creation, views on, 79, 120
SDRs: allocations, 249*; excess holdings, 240; receipt, 236, 240, 243, 314–15

NETHERLANDS ANTILLES. See NETHERLANDS: Nonmetropolitan territories

NEW ZEALAND
Currency unit, new, 467
Drawings (purchases) and repurchases from Fund: purchases, 264, 268*, 311, 316, 321, 331*; repurchases, 268*, 395*; under compensatory financing facility, 264, 268*
Exchange rate, floating, 542
Par value, xviii–xix, 437, 438*, 467, 560*
Quota in Fund, 307*
SDR allocations, 249*
Stand-by arrangement with Fund, 320, 335*

NGUYEN HUU HANH. See HANH, NGUYEN HUU

NICARAGUA
Art. VIII, Secs. 2, 3, and 4, acceptance of obligations of, 571n
Drawings (purchases) and repurchases from Fund, 310, 311, 321, 331*, 395*

Exchange rate, central, 562*
Quota in Fund, 288, 307*
SDR allocations, 249*
Stand-by arrangements with Fund, 321, 335*
Technical assistance from Fund, 581

NICOL-COLE, S. B.
Background, 630

NICOLETOPOULOS, GEORGE, 77, 135*, 163*, 647

NIGER
Exchange rate, 457, 561
Quota in Fund, 301, 307*
SDR allocations, 249*

NIGERIA
Drawings (purchases) and repurchases from Fund: purchases, 284, 312, 316, 331*; repurchases, 395*; under buffer stock facility, 284
Exchange rate and par value, 437, 542, 560*
Quota in Fund, 289, 296, 307*
SDR allocations, 249*
Technical assistance from Fund, 581

NIKOI, AMON, 83n, 89, 101, 125, 134*, 162*, 174, 273, 277, 345, 346, 379, 471

NIPSTAD, J., 164*

NIXON, RICHARD M., 384, 488, 521, 529, 531, 552

NKRUMAH, KWAME, 597

NONMETROPOLITAN TERRITORIES OF MEMBERS
Currency units: decimal system, 518; new, 467, 468
Exchange rates, 562*
Par values, 439–40, 456, 467, 468, 560, 561

NORWAY
Art. VIII, Secs. 2, 3, and 4, acceptance of obligations of, 571
Balance of payments surplus, 493
Basle Group, 442n
Currency used in Fund transactions, 324, 337*
Exchange rate: central, 562*; floating, 542
Quota in Fund, 296, 307*
SDR allocations, 249*

NOSE, AKIRA P., 648

NOUIRA, HEDI, xxi, 282

O

OAS. See ORGANIZATION OF AMERICAN STATES

O'BRIEN, SIR LESLIE, 339

O'DONNELL, M. W., 89, 94–95, 101, 118, 125, 126, 134*

OECD. See ORGANIZATION FOR ECONOMIC CO-OPERATION AND DEVELOPMENT

OMABOE, E. N., 471

OMAN
Quota in Fund, 302, 303, 307*
SDR allocations, 249*
Special Drawing Account, participation in, 232
Technical assistance from Fund, 585

OMWONY, MAURICE P., 368, 510, 552, 631
Background and length of service, 627, 629

ORGANIZATION FOR ECONOMIC COOPERATION AND DEVELOPMENT (OECD)
Development Assistance Committee (DAC), 595
Fund's relations with, 595, 597, 608, 610
Participation in reserve creation discussions, 71, 76, 106, 137*, 165*, 553
U.S. balance of payments estimates, 549
Working Party 3 of Economic Policy Committee, 76, 98, 199, 212, 549; multilateral surveillance, 78, 96–97, 195; study of adjustment process, 3, 36, 38, 194–95

ORGANIZATION OF AMERICAN STATES (OAS), 608–609

ORTIZ MENA, ANTONIO, 593

ORTOLI, FRANÇOIS-XAVIER, 277–78, 411

OSSOLA GROUP, 36–37, 195
  Exploration of reserve creation methods, 52
  Report, 58–61, 71, 196
OSSOLA, RINALDO, 37, 52, 115, 120, 136*, 156, 157,
  164*, 166, 195, 292, 371, 541
OUTLINE OF A FACILITY BASED ON SPECIAL
  DRAWING RIGHTS IN THE FUND
  Approved, xviii, 104–105, 155–59, 175, 204
  Drafted, 104, 143–47, 153–55, 203
  Features, 160–61
  Incorporated in Articles of Agreement, 166–70, 172,
  175
  See also SPECIAL DRAWING RIGHTS
OZAKI, EIJI, 134*, 162*

P

PAKISTAN
  Drawings (purchases) and repurchases from Fund,
  312, 316, 331*, 395*
  Exchange rate, 542, 563
  Quota in Fund, 307*
  SDR allocations, 249*
  Stand-by arrangements with Fund, 321, 335*
  Technical assistance from Fund, 581, 583
PALAMENGHI-CRISPI, FRANCESCO, 224, 228, 279,
  286, 354, 414, 479, 550
  Background and length of service, 627, 628
  Comments and views on: deutsche mark revalua-
  tion, 461; exchange rate flexibility and wider
  margins, 509–10, 511, 521; financial programming,
  366–67; quota review, 292–93, 295; SDRs, use of,
  236, 240, 241; U.S. economy, 491
PANAMA
  Art. VIII, Secs. 2, 3, and 4, acceptance of obliga-
  tions of, 571n
  Drawings (purchases) and repurchases from Fund,
  311, 321, 331*, 396*
  Exchange rate, central, 562*
  Quota in Fund, 289, 307*
  SDR allocations, 249*
  Stand-by arrangements with Fund, 321, 335*
  Technical assistance from Fund, 581
PANT, YADAV PRASAD, 220
PAR VALUE SYSTEM
  Calls for review, 21, 452, 483, 484, 501–502, 521, 526
  Collapse, 3–4, 517, 519–30, 531, 555–56, 564, 565
  Functioning: concerns, 447–48, 450–51, 478, 479, 481,
  514–15, 519, 521, 523; difficulties, 496, 502; nature
  of implementation, 514, 535–36
  Governors' views, 500–501, 503–504, 514–15
  Managing Director's views, 447–48, 483–84, 501
  Special position of U.S. dollar, 535
  Suggestions for change: numeraire in SDRs rather
  than gold, 427; "presumptive indicators," 510
  Techniques for change studied by Executive Direc-
  tors, 501–503, 504–10, 511–14
  Temporary regime of central rates, 557–62
  See also BALANCE OF PAYMENTS ADJUSTMENT
  PROCESS *and* EXCHANGE RATE MECHANISM
PAR VALUES
  Central rates in lieu of, 557–59, 561, 562*
  Changes: by individual countries, xviii–xxii, 433–40,
  438*, 453–56, 460–62, 468–70, 471–81, 517–18, 522–24,
  560–61; responsibility for initiative, 525; small,
  discussions and studies of, 501, 505, 507, 511, 513;
  voting majority required for uniform change, 254
  Competitive depreciation, concern about, 439, 476
  Currency/monetary units changed, 466–68, 518, 543
  Exchange rate model (MERM), 537
  Initial, 465–66*
  Maintained after devaluations by other countries,
  437, 560*
  Realignment (1971), xxii, 4, 531–56
  See also EXCHANGE RATES; FUNDAMENTAL
  DISEQUILIBRIUM; *and* individual countries

PARAGUAY
  Exchange rate, 563
  Quota in Fund, 307*
  Repurchases from Fund, 396*
  SDR allocations, 249*
  Stand-by arrangements with Fund, 321, 335*
PATEL, I. G., 83n
PATRON, YAMANDU S., 134*, 162*
PAYMENTS ARREARS
  Fund decision on, xxi, 591–93
  Fund treatment of, 592, 593
  In individual countries, 358, 360–61, 597
PER JACOBSSON FOUNDATION LECTURES, 621
PEREIRA LIRA, PAULO H., 134*, 162*
PERERA, N. M., 245n
PEREZ GUERRERO, MANUEL, 245
PERISIN, IVO, 518
PEROUSE, MAURICE, 119–20, 126, 127, 135*, 141, 163*
PERSONNEL. *See* STAFF
PERU
  Art. VIII, Secs. 2, 3, and 4, acceptance of obliga-
  tions of, 571n
  Debt renegotiations, 595
  Drawings (purchases) and repurchases from Fund:
  purchases, 265, 310, 311, 321, 331*; repurchases,
  396*; under compensatory financing facility, 265,
  266n
  Exchange rate, 563
  Quota in Fund, 289, 296, 307*
  SDR allocations, 249*
  Stand-by arrangements with Fund, 321, 335*
  Technical assistance from Fund, 583
PFEIFER, ALBIN, 646
PHILIPPINES
  Drawings (purchases) and repurchases from Fund:
  purchases, 265, 310, 312, 316, 321, 331*; repur-
  chases, 396*; under compensatory financing fa-
  cility, 265, 266n
  Exchange rate, 542, 563
  Gold production subsidies, 423, 424
  Quota in Fund, 296, 307*
  SDR allocations, 249*
  Stand-by arrangements with Fund, 321, 335*
PHILLIPS O., ALFREDO, 134*, 162*
  Comments and views on: Canadian exchange rate,
  480; distribution of Fund's net income, 391; gold
  purchases from South Africa, 411; payments
  arrears, 592; quota, Mexican, 305; quotas, general
  increase in, 291, 293, 296; reserve assets, 149; SDR
  allocation–quota increase link, 216; stand-by arrangements, 343, 345, 354
PLESCOFF, GEORGES, 215, 218, 223, 224, 295, 345, 349,
  357, 404, 411, 436, 455, 458, 479, 490, 491, 494
  Comments and views on: buffer stock financing, 273,
  277, 279; deutsche mark revaluation, 461–62; dis-
  tribution of Fund's net income, 391; exchange rate
  flexibility, 507; French franc devaluation (1969),
  455–56; gold deposits, general, 421; investment of
  Fund assets, 384, 385; stand-by arrangement,
  French, 353; stand-by arrangement, U.K. (1967),
  342
PLUMPTRE, A. F. W., 32
POLAK, J. J. *See* ECONOMIC COUNSELLOR
POMPIDOU, GEORGES, 454
PONSEN, H., 646
PORTUGAL
  Exchange rate: central, 562*; floating, 542
  Par value, 437
  Quota in Fund, 307*
  Technical assistance from Fund, 585
POSTHUMA, S., 53
POWERS, WALTER T., 648
PRAETORIUS, ROBERT L., 648

PRASAD, P. S. N., 550, 552, 626
  Background and length of service, 627, 629
PREBISCH, RAUL, 104, 245, 278
PRIMARY PRODUCING COUNTRIES
  Classification in Fund statistics, 82*n*
  Exports, 264–65, 269–70, 275–76
  Payments situation, 82, 269–70
  Use of Fund resources, 311–12, 315–16, 320–21
  See also DEVELOPING COUNTRIES
PROXMIRE, WILLIAM, 528*n*
PUBLICATIONS CITED IN THIS VOLUME, 695–99
PUBLICATIONS OF FUND, 602–603, 604
PURCHASES (DRAWINGS) FROM FUND. *See* RE-
  SOURCES OF FUND—USE *and* individual coun-
  tries

Q

QATAR
  Currency unit and par value, 467
  Membership in Fund, 570
QIZILBASH, NAWAB MOZAFFAR ALI KHAN, 220,
  281
QUOTAS IN FUND
  As basis of reserve unit or SDR allocations, 48, 49,
    86–87, 122, 181, 217, 232, 287
  As conditional liquidity, 32, 43, 287, 291
  Considered in reserve creation discussions, 32, 43,
    109–10, 112, 127, 194
  Drawings to finance increases in, 257, 297, 316
  Fifth general review (1969–70), xxi, 222, 289–300;
    relation to SDR allocation, 215–16, 217, 289–90,
    292
  Formula for calculating, 290, 291*n*, 303–305
  Fourth quinquennial review (1964–67), xviii, 33, 37,
    41, 42, 194, 195, 196, 198, 288–89
  Gold subscriptions, 47, 112, 172, 173, 297–98, 300,
    356, 416–17
  Increases not taken, 288–89, 293, 295, 301
  Increases under compensatory financing decision,
    288, 289, 296, 301
  Of new members, 289, 301, 302, 303
  Selective increases, 288, 290, 291, 292, 293, 294, 295
  Small, 302–303
  Total, 16, 287–89, 295–96, 300, 302, 306*–308*
  Voting majorities for changes in, 133, 174, 202, 254,
    255
  See also RESOURCES OF FUND—NATURE AND
    SIZE

R

RADCLIFFE COMMITTEE, 20
RADFORD, RICHARD A., 648
RAJ, K. N., 83*n*
RAJAOBELINA, LEON M., 135*, 163*, 216, 276, 277,
  298, 345, 346, 592
  Background, 630
RASMINSKY, LOUIS, 481
RAY, A. S., 647
RECONSTITUTION. *See* SPECIAL DRAWING RIGHTS
REID, JAY H., 648
REID, PATRICK M., 134*, 162*, 345
REMUNERATION ON NET CREDITOR POSITIONS,
  236, 244, 256, 373, 387, 388
REPRESENTATIVE EXCHANGE RATES, 226
REPURCHASES
  Abatement, 258–59
  Amounts, 268*, 282–83, 382–83, 383*, 395*–96*
  By individual countries, 314, 319, 351, 356, 382
  Calculations concerning, 230–31, 282, 381
  Currencies used in, 17, 325, 326, 337*, 395*–96*
  Gold used in, 337*

  Of buffer stock drawings, 276, 281
  Of compensatory financing drawings, 262–63, 266,
    268*
  Problems: fluctuating rates, 382; inability to use U.S.
    dollars, 312–13, 327; small amounts, 282; substitu-
    tion of currencies, 381; suspension of U.S. con-
    vertibility, 328, 532
  Rules for, 258–59, 322–24, 325–26, 381–82
  SDRs used in, 229–30, 325, 337*
  Special arrangements (1971), 326–29
  See also individual countries
REQUIREMENT OF NEED: for drawings under buffer
  stock facility, 283, 284; for use of SDRs, 149, 151,
  160, 182, 183, 242–43
RESERVE ASSETS
  Distribution: criteria, 77, 89, 119, 120, 142, 200;
    debates on limited group, 78–81, 86–87, 117; re-
    lated to Fund quotas, 122, 146–47, 151, 160
  Features: basic, 37, 60, 79, 94, 119, 120, 128, 144–46;
    relation to existing assets, including gold, 60, 78,
    115–16, 118, 196
  Ossola study groups: 1964 group, 37, 52, 58–61, 71,
    195, 196; 1966 working party, 115–16
  Rules for use and transfer: Fund guidance, 94, 115,
    147; general questions, 115, 142, 143, 147–50, 200;
    gradually determined, 151, 202, 203
  Term: avoided, 107–108, 153–55; broadly used, 80,
    143; compromise, 145; drawing unit reserve asset
    (Dura), 143; reserve asset concept accepted, 188
  Transfer of real resources involved, 57
  See also RESERVE CREATION; RESERVE CREA-
    TION PLANS; *and* RESERVE UNITS
RESERVE CREATION
  Agreement: facilitated by economic circumstances,
    74–75, 209–11; on basic principles by Group of
    Ten, 95–96, 99–100, 111, 199; on global need for
    reserves as criterion, 108–109; on need to study
    new techniques, 39, 195
  Alternative ways of meeting liquidity deficiency, 21,
    191
  Compulsory reconstitution of credit tranche posi-
    tions in Fund, 113–14, 119
  Concern of Executive Directors outside Group of
    Ten, 105–106
  Defined, 43, 108
  Distribution. *See* RESERVE ASSETS: Distribution
  Financing: discussed, 117–19, 142, 143, 146, 202;
    resolved, 145, 146, 160, 203
  Form of, 111–13, 119, 147, 160, 200
  Inflation feared, 39, 45, 69, 97, 98, 118, 124, 125, 212
  Link with development finance, 61, 72, 84, 85, 110–
    11, 197, 219, 220, 245–46
  Purpose, 107, 108–11, 119, 200
  Related to balance of payments equilibrium and
    adjustment process, 97, 98, 113, 119, 120, 141, 172,
    180, 214, 218, 221
  Related to gold subscriptions in Fund, 112
  Techniques examined: by Fund, 44–53, 57, 59, 68,
    77, 195; by Ossola Group, 59, 196
  Timing, 110, 120, 123
  See also LIQUIDITY, INTERNATIONAL; RESERVE
    ASSETS; RESERVE CREATION PLANS; RESERVE
    UNITS; *and* SPECIAL DRAWING RIGHTS
RESERVE CREATION PLANS
  Bernstein plans, 20, 53–54, 55–56, 111, 191, 194
  Contingency plan: agreement to draft, 69–73, 76;
    distinct from activation, 97–99, 199; push toward
    agreement on, 130–33, 201; search for, 74–103;
    specifying conditions for activation, 119, 120, 124,
    125, 126, 199
  Contingency planning: first phase of discussions,
    70–72, 196; second phase of discussions, 72–73,
    100, 101, 104, 110–11, 196–97
  CRU proposals, 52, 53–58, 59, 60, 63, 111, 189, 191,
    194, 196
  Day Plan, 20
  Decision-making and voting arrangements: consider-
    ations involved, 78, 96, 121, 127, 146, 173, 199, 201;
    difficult issue, 55, 121, 126, 142, 150, 151–52, 167,

196, 200, 203; procedures for, 56, 122–26, 131, 133, 143, 144, 155, 156, 160, 177, 179, 202, 203

Drawing rights versus reserve units, 119, 128, 143, 201; drawing rights preferred, 111–12, 127, 128, 142, 150; drawing rights recommended by EEC, 132, 133, 202; reserve units preferred, 112–13, 142; two concepts converge, 144–45, 146–47, 150, 203

"Dual approach": arguments for, 78, 79, 81; characteristics of, 80, 81, 197; criticisms of, 81, 88, 89, 90, 91, 95, 98, 198, 199; given up, 99, 199. *See also* Universal plan, *below*

EEC recommendations on amendment of Articles of Agreement, 132–33

Fund plans: early plans, 46–51, 195; Group of Ten's discussion, 59, 60, 77, 89; joint meeting discussions, 141–43, 201, 202; Managing Director's proposals (1966), 86–95, 100, 198, 200; outlines (February 1967), 127–30, 201; outlines (May–June 1967), 144–53, 202–203; outline (final) drafted, 153–55, 203

Limited schemes: preference for, 56–57, 73, 77, 78–82, 95, 99; response of developing countries, 82–85; size of group to be included, 55, 56–57, 60, 77, 196, 197. *See also* "Dual approach," *above, and* Universal plan, *below*

Liquidation, provision for, 145

Maudling plan, 24, 59, 60, 193

Opting out. *See* SPECIAL DRAWING RIGHTS: Allocations, opting out of

Ossola Group report, 58–61, 71, 196

Outlines. *See* Fund plans, *above*

Parallel schemes. *See* "Dual approach," *above*

Plans submitted to Group of Ten: Canadian, 79–81, 197; Otmar Emminger's, 79–81, 197; U.K., 79–80, 197; U.S., 79–80, 143, 197, 202

Reconstitution, provision for, 142, 143, 147, 149, 150, 151, 152, 153, 156–58, 202

Separate or merged resources, 143, 146

Stamp Plan, 19, 22, 191

Suggestions for extension of mutual assistance among central banks, 20–21

Triffin Plan, 17–19, 22, 191; Fund's reactions to, 22

Universal plan: accepted, 95–100, 199; emphasized, 45–46, 67, 89–91, 196, 197, 199

Zolotas Plan, 23, 193

See also LIQUIDITY, INTERNATIONAL; RESERVE ASSETS; RESERVE CREATION; RESERVE UNITS; *and* SPECIAL DRAWING RIGHTS

RESERVE CURRENCY COUNTRIES

Balance of payments improvement: noted, 26, 52, 63, 70, 75; urged, 30, 171–72, 194

Difficulties of devaluing: U.K., 432; U.S., 535–36

Reserve policies, 140, 204, 209–10

Special needs of U.S. in currencies selected in drawings, 314

See also UNITED KINGDOM *and* UNITED STATES

RESERVE POSITIONS IN FUND

Definition, 323

Included in supply of liquidity, 15–16, 26

Increases in, 140, 141, 204

Scheme for converting currency balances into, 60

Taken into account in policy on selection of currencies, 323, 324, 326

RESERVE UNITS

Distinct from reserve assets, 80, 107–108

Distribution. *See* RESERVE ASSETS: Distribution

Features of: general, 120–21, 126, 128–29, 142–45; relation to traditional reserves, 115, 116, 118, 120, 129

Proposals for: by E. M. Bernstein, 53–54, 55–56, 111, 194; by Fund, 92–95, 127–30, 141–43, 144–47, 150–53, 198, 199, 200, 201, 202, 203; by Group of Ten, 79–81

Rules for use and transfer, 114–17, 119, 128–30, 142–43, 147–48. *See also* RESERVE ASSETS: Rules for use and transfer

Versus drawing rights: both considered, 111–12, 119, 127–28, 142, 146, 150, 202–203; differences, 112–13, 128–29, 201; drawing rights preferred, 111, 147, 150;

preference for units, 112, 120, 147; ultimate convergence, 131, 144, 145, 151

See also RESERVE ASSETS; RESERVE CREATION; *and* RESERVE CREATION PLANS

RESERVES

Calculations for Fund operations: Articles amended, 258–59; concept changed from net to gross, 258–59, 380–81; data to be supplied to Fund, 381; exclusion of SDRs, 230–31; in selection of currencies, 323–24, 326

Definitions, 49; adequacy, 12–13, 190; "official holdings" in first designation plan, 227, 229; positions in Fund included, 16, 26, 49, 191, 192; SDRs included, 159

Developments: Canada, 478; developing countries, 90; France, 209, 450, 454, 458; Fed. Rep. of Germany, 463; Japan, 494; primary producing countries, 82; U.K., 433; U.S., 15, 486–87, 489–90, 528

Global need: difficulties of estimating, 37, 44, 87–88, 90, 141–42, 213–14, 216; requirement for SDR allocations, 154, 172, 180; seminar of Fund staff with specialists, 213–14, 221

Gold, 25; debate on augmenting official holdings, 410–11; low share of developing countries, 553

"Owned" as distinguished from "borrowed," 37, 38, 40, 41

Relation to new reserve assets, 37, 49, 78

Studies: by Fund, 87–88, 139–41; by U.S., 141

World: composition of, 25, 139–40, 204, 209–10, 211, 212, 215; developments in, 75, 139–41, 204, 215; term as used by Fund, 25n, 138n; U.S. as supplier of, 25–26, 193

See also RESERVE POSITIONS IN FUND

RESOURCES OF FUND—NATURE AND SIZE

Access to: by France, 453; expansion of, 16–17, 192, 198

Adequacy, 12–13, 16

Conditionality, 257

Credit tranche positions: definition, 26; included in reserves, 26, 33; role in reserve creation, 113–14, 119

Gold tranche positions: definition, 25n; included in reserves, 26, 32, 191; payment of interest on, 246

Replenishment of currencies, 298, 301; policies on, 417–20; use of SDRs in, 236

Super gold tranche positions: definition, 47n; payment of remuneration on, 236, 244, 256, 373, 387, 388

Total quotas, 16, 287–89, 295–96, 300, 302, 306*–308*

See also QUOTAS IN FUND

RESOURCES OF FUND—USE

Amendment of Articles on, 253, 255–57

Credit tranche drawings (purchases), 33, 316–19

Currencies selected: 236–37, 241, 254, 313–14, 315. *See also* SELECTION OF CURRENCIES IN FUND TRANSACTIONS

Gold tranche drawings (purchases): amounts of, 310, 312–16; by France, xix, 315, 352–53, 449–50; by U.S., 310, 312–15; changes in procedures for, 32–33, 309; definition of, 255, 309; discussed in plans for reserve creation, 80; excluded from stand-by arrangements, 256; liberalization of, 32–33, 127, 194; made legally automatic, 33, 255–56; relation to GAB, 371

In crises of 1950s, 13

Magnitudes, xx, xxi, 310–12, 330*–32*, 337*, 383*, 393; under stand-by arrangements, 320–22

Policies: adjusted in early 1960s, 15–17, 32–34, 192; for credit tranche drawings, 317–19, 593; for gold tranche drawings, 32–33, 127, 194, 255–56; on stand-by arrangements, 338, 341–42, 343–48, 352–54, 363–69; under amended Articles, 255–57; vis-à-vis U.S., 312–14

Quota increases financed by drawings, 257, 297, 316

Special problems after August 15, 1971, 532–33, 549–50, 563–64

Super gold tranche drawings (purchases), 310, 312, 314, 315, 450, 463

Temporary in character, 256
U.S. technical drawings, 312–13
Waivers, 26n, 322
See also BUFFER STOCK FINANCING; CHARGES
ON USE OF FUND RESOURCES; COMPENSA-
TORY FINANCING OF EXPORT FLUCTUA-
TIONS; REPURCHASES; RESOURCES OF FUND—
NATURE AND SIZE; and STAND-BY ARRANGE-
MENTS

REUSS, HENRY S., 38, 528n

RICKETT, SIR DENIS, 136*, 164*

RIEKE, WOLFGANG, 136*, 164*

ROBICHEK, E. WALTER, 648

ROELANDTS, JACQUES, 292–93, 415, 462

ROMANIA
Membership in Fund, 570

ROOSA, ROBERT V., 14–15, 36, 54, 56, 191, 196

ROSE, BRIAN, 646

ROTA, GIORGIO, 136*, 164*

RUEFF, JACQUES, 21, 191

RULES AND REGULATIONS OF FUND, 158, 166,
177–78, 205, 256, 381

RWANDA
Drawings (purchases) and repurchases from Fund,
312, 321, 331*, 396*
Par value, 465, 466*, 560*
Quota in Fund, 307*
SDR allocations, 249*
Stand-by arrangements with Fund, 320, 321, 335*
Technical assistance from Fund, 580, 583

S

SAAD, AHMED ZAKI, 343, 625, 626
Fund's authority stressed, 89, 137n, 165n, 626
Views and comments on: individual countries, 317,
439, 470; remuneration to creditors, 388, 389; SDRs,
125, 129, 158, 229

SALLE, JEAN-PAUL, 77, 135*, 163*, 643

SAN LIN, 663

SANCHIZ, JOSE C., 648

SANNER, PIERRE, 83n

SAPER, JAKOB, 646

SATOW, KOICHI, 521–22
Background, 630

SAUDI ARABIA
Art. VIII, Secs. 2, 3, and 4, acceptance of obligations
of, 571n
Par value, 560*
Quota in Fund, 296, 308*

SAVKAR, D. S., 644

SCHELIN, OTTO, 112

SCHILLER, KARL, 159, 451, 514

SCHLEIMINGER, GUENTHER, 216, 224, 293, 295, 349,
391, 459, 495, 522–23, 550
Background and length of service, 627, 628
Comments and views on: buffer stock financing, 279,
283; Canadian dollar, 479, 481; deutsche mark
float, 460; deutsche mark revaluation, 461; exchange rate flexibility and wider margins, 509,
510, 511, 521; SDRs, use of, 235, 240; stand-by
arrangement, French (1969), 354; Turkish stabilization program, 475; use of Fund resources and
stand-by arrangements, 345; U.S. inflation, 490

SCHNEIDER, HEINRICH G.
Background, 630

SCHOELLHORN, J., 132n

SCHWARTZ, CHARLES F., 649

SCHWEITZER, PIERRE-PAUL. See MANAGING
DIRECTOR (Pierre-Paul Schweitzer)

SCITOVSKY, TIBOR, 83n

SDRs. See SPECIAL DRAWING RIGHTS

SELECTION OF CURRENCIES IN FUND TRANS-
ACTIONS
Currencies used, 337*
Currency budget, 323–35
Discussed in reserve creation plans, 129, 150, 160
Fund decision (1962), 17, 192, 322–24, 325
In drawings by U.S., 313–14, 315
See also RESOURCES OF FUND—USE: Currencies
selected

SENEGAL
Exchange rate, 457, 561
Quota in Fund, 289–90, 308*
SDR allocations, 249*

SHAREF, ZEEV, 594

SIERRA LEONE
Drawings (purchases) and repurchases from Fund,
312, 322, 332*, 396*
Par value, xix, 437, 438*, 560*
Quota in Fund, 296, 308*
SDR allocations, 249*
Stand-by arrangements with Fund, 320, 321, 335*
Technical assistance from Fund, 580, 581, 583

SIGLIENTI, SERGIO, 101, 112, 118, 124, 125, 129, 134*,
148, 152, 155, 162*, 378

SILLING, DAN R., 648

SINGAPORE
Art. VIII, Secs. 2, 3, and 4, acceptance of obligations
of, 571
Currency unit, new, 467
Exchange rate, 542
Par value, 437, 465, 466*, 467, 560*
Quota in Fund, 288, 308*
Technical assistance from Fund, 581

SMIT, ROBERT VAN S.
Background, 630

SMITHSONIAN AGREEMENT, xxii, 329, 553–56

SMOLE, JANKO, 220, 245n, 594

SNEDDEN, B. M., 427

SNOY ET D'OPPUERS, BARON, 546

SOLOMON, ROBERT, 137*, 165*

SOMALIA
Drawings (purchases) and repurchases from Fund,
312, 316, 322, 332*, 396*
Exchange rate and par value, 437, 542, 560*
Quota in Fund, 308*
SDR allocations, 249*
Stand-by arrangements with Fund, 321, 335*
Technical assistance from Fund, 581, 583

SOUTH AFRICA
Balance of payments deficit, 415
Currency: monetary unit of Botswana, Lesotho, and
Swaziland, 465, 466*; used in Fund transactions,
324, 337*
Drawings (purchases) and repurchases from Fund,
311, 315, 332*, 396*
Exchange rate and par value, 437, 465, 542, 561*
Gold production subsidies, 423, 424
Gold sales to Fund, xxi, 409–16, 425
Quota in Fund, 296, 308*
Request for Fund study of international liquidity, 12
SDR allocations, 249*

SOUTHARD, FRANK A., JR., 627. See also DEPUTY
MANAGING DIRECTOR

SOUTHEAST ASIAN CENTRAL BANKS, 278–79

SOUTHERN YEMEN. See YEMEN, PEOPLE'S DEMO-
CRATIC REPUBLIC OF

SPAIN
Currency used in Fund transactions, 337*
Drawings (purchases) and repurchases from Fund,
311, 315, 332*, 396*
Par value, xviii-xix, 437, 438*, 560*
Quota in Fund, 296, 308*
SDR allocations, 249*
Technical assistance from Fund, 585

SPECIAL DRAWING ACCOUNT

Description, 178–79

Establishment, xx, 167, 176, 205; requirements for, 175, 205, 214

Financing, 177, 179, 229, 286

Genesis, 128, 130, 146–47, 152, 154

Obligations of participants, 179, 182–85, 242; failure to fulfill, 178, 183, 185; reconstitution of SDR holdings, 167, 178, 185, 186

Operations after 1971 crises, 241–42, 244

Participation, 176, 179; France, 176, 218; Italy, 176; new members of Fund, 232–33; total, 176, 220, 232–33, 244; U.S., 176

Voting, 177, 179; majority required for allocations and cancellations, 155, 156, 158, 160, 203

SPECIAL DRAWING RIGHTS (SDRs)

Allocations for first basic period, xxi, xxii, 232, 233, 248*–50*; Managing Director's consultations and proposal, Governors' approval, and Executive Board's concurrence, xx, 181–82, 203, 214–21; prerequisites for decision, 172, 180–82, 214, 220; principles and techniques, 180–81; reservations of some Executive Directors, 218–19; views of Group of Ten Deputies, 216

Allocations, opting out of: by China, 232, 244; implications for total allocations, 217; provisions for discussed, 117, 122, 124–25, 127, 146–47, 152–53; provisions for resolved, 157, 172, 173, 181

Allocations to be excluded from members' reserves in determining repurchase obligations, 230–31

Cancellation, 154, 180–82

Characteristics, 160–61, 172–73, 178–86, 188

Designation of participants to provide currency for SDRs: plans, 185, 226–29, 237, 241–42; principles and procedures, 227–28, 235, 238–40; specified in Articles, 167, 178, 183, 184–85, 186

Evolution, 190–205

Executive Board's special role, 222, 623–24

Facility based on SDRs: activation, 212–31, 492; entry into force, xx, 173–75, 176, 177, 204, 205, 253

Gold-value guarantee, 186–87

Harmonization of ratios between holdings of SDRs and other reserves: desired objective, 109, 151, 156–58, 228; techniques for achieving, 156–58, 185, 234–35, 237–41

Information published on, 233

Interest on, 182, 246, 373, 386

Link with development finance. *See* RESERVE CREATION: Link with development finance

Manual of Procedures, 231

Other holders, 172, 173, 181

Outline of facility. *See* OUTLINE OF A FACILITY BASED ON SPECIAL DRAWING RIGHTS IN THE FUND

Reconstitution of holdings: difficult issues, 142, 143, 147, 149, 150, 151, 152, 153, 202; issues gradually settled, 154, 155, 157, 158, 160–61, 167, 178, 203; nature of provisions, 183, 185, 186; study of implementation, 246, 247

Requirement of need, 149, 151, 160, 182, 183, 242–43; not subject to challenge, 183

Significance, 187–89; an accepted reserve, 244–45; zenith of international cooperation, 3, 620

Terminology, 80, 128, 143, 145, 150–55 *passim*, 157, 197

Transactions, 234–37, 240–41, 243–44, 314–15; representative exchange rates for, 226

Uses vis-à-vis Fund: for payment of charges and repurchases, 173, 229–30, 234–35, 243, 325, 337*, 379; for payments to members and in currency budgets, 235–36, 244, 325; not for payment of gold subscriptions, 173, 297, 298; reluctance of members to use after suspension of dollar convertibility, 243–44

Widened use suggested: as means of development finance, 245–46; as numeraire for monetary system, 244, 427; as primary reserve, 244, 551, 651; as technique for "asset settlement," 491; questions studied, 246–47

See also LIQUIDITY, INTERNATIONAL; RESERVE ASSETS; RESERVE CREATION; RESERVE CREATION PLANS; RESERVE UNITS; *and* SPECIAL DRAWING ACCOUNT

SPECIAL RESERVE, 383, 385, 388

SPECIAL RESERVE DRAWING RIGHTS (SRDR), 80, 153, 154, 197

SRI LANKA. *See* CEYLON

STABILIZATION OF PRICES OF PRIMARY PRODUCTS. *See* BUFFER STOCK FINANCING

STABILIZATION PROGRAMS. *See* FINANCIAL PROGRAMMING

STAFF

Expansion, 637–38

Geographic distribution, 639–40

Identification, 640–49

Lectures, 589–90

Organization, 77n, 636–37

Seminars: on reserve needs and availabilities, 213–14, 221; with French officials, 356; with U.K. officials, 443, 445

Use of electronic data processing, 603, 639

STAMP, ARTHUR MAXWELL (Stamp Plan), 19, 22, 110, 191

STAND-BY ARRANGEMENTS

Approved, 320–22, 333*–36*; for developing countries, 358–63; for France, 352–56; for U.K., 338–43, 348–49

Charges, 379

Decision on repurchases in SDRs, 230

Discussed with U.S., 313

Drawings: Brazil, 361, 362; Colombia, 310, 321, 358, 359; expedited, 368–69; France, xx, xxi, 321, 355; gold tranche excluded, 256, 309; Indonesia, 321, 360; total, 309, 310, 320–22; U.K., xix, 310, 321, 349, 350, 351

Policies, 338, 341–42, 343–48, 352–54, 363–69

Terms, 343–49, 353–54, 358–62, 363–64, 592, 596; Executive Board's review of, xix, 343–48

Waivers granted, 322

See also FINANCIAL PROGRAMMING *and* individual countries

STARK, MARIE C., 647

STATES, SMALL, 302–303, 570, 632

STERLING AGREEMENTS. *See* UNITED KINGDOM

STEVENS, SIR JOHN (formerly J. M. Stevens), 112, 116, 125, 128, 134*, 162*, 472

STOFFERS, ERICH, 164

STONE, JOHN O., 134*, 141, 152, 153, 157, 162*, 216, 231, 326, 342, 349, 418, 438, 494

Comments and views on: distribution of Fund's net income, 389, 391; exchange rate adjustment, 505, 507, 511; gold deposits, general, 421, 422; gold purchases from South Africa, 410; quota review, 291–92, 293, 295, 298; SDR designation plans, 237, 239–40; SDR facility, activation of, 218–19; SDRs, use of, 236; stabilization of commodity prices, 276–77; U.S. inflation, 490–91

STRÄNG, GUNNER, 594

STRAUSS, FRANZ JOSEF, 132n

STUDY GROUP ON CREATION OF RESERVE ASSETS. *See* OSSOLA GROUP

STURC, ERNEST, 642

SUBSCRIPTIONS. *See* GOLD TRANSACTIONS AND OPERATIONS OF FUND *and* QUOTAS IN FUND: Gold subscriptions

SUDAN

Drawings (purchases) and repurchases from Fund: purchases, 263, 268*, 312, 316, 321, 332*; repurchases, 268*, 396*; under compensatory financing facility, 263, 268*

Exchange rate, 542, 563

Quota in Fund, 308*

SDR allocations, 249*

Stand-by arrangements with Fund, 320, 321, 335*
Technical assistance from Fund, 580, 581, 583

SUPER GOLD TRANCHE. *See* RESOURCES OF FUND—NATURE AND SIZE *and* RESOURCES OF FUND—USE

SURINAM. *See* NETHERLANDS: Nonmetropolitan territories

SUZUKI, HIDEO, 134*, 162*, 216, 228, 392, 439, 481, 495, 550, 558
  Background and length of service, 625, 627, 628
  Comments and views on: distribution of Fund's net income, 389; exchange rate flexibility, 507, 508, 510, 526; gold sales for currency replenishment, 417, 418; Japanese balance of payments, 494; Japanese par value, 436, 437; quota review, 292; reserve creation, 128, 147

SWAN, T. W., 83n

SWAP ARRANGEMENTS. *See* CENTRAL BANKS

SWAZILAND
  Currency unit, 465
  Drawing (purchase) and repurchase from Fund, 312, 316, 332*, 396*
  Par value, 465, 466*, 561*
  Quota in Fund, 301, 303, 308*
  SDR allocations, 250*

SWEDEN
  Art. VIII, Secs. 2, 3, and 4, acceptance of obligations of, 571n
  Basle Agreement, 14, 192
  Basle Group, 442n
  Borrowing by Fund under GAB, 374*
  Currency used in Fund transactions, 337*
  Exchange rate: central, 554, 555*, 562*; floating, 542, 544
  Quota in Fund, 308*
  SDR allocations, 250*

SWEENEY, TIMOTHY, 646

SWITZERLAND
  Association with GAB, 372–73
  Attendance at joint meetings of Fund Executive Directors and Group of Ten Deputies, 106, 137*, 165*, 553
  Balance of payments surplus, 493
  Basle Group, 442n
  Capital inflows, 524
  Exchange rate, 524
  Participation in CRU plan proposed, 53, 55, 194

SYRIAN ARAB REPUBLIC
  Drawings (purchases) and repurchases from Fund: purchases, 264, 268*, 312, 316, 332*; repurchases, 268*, 396*; under compensatory financing facility, 264, 268*
  Exchange rate, 563
  Quota in Fund, 288, 308*
  SDR allocations, 250*
  Technical assistance from Fund, 585

T

TAN SIEW SIN, 267, 271–72, 282, 426, 593

TANAKA, KEIJIRO, 136*, 164*

TANN, BEUE, 134*, 162*, 295
  Length of service, 625, 626

TANZANIA
  Exchange rate, 542
  Par value, 437, 465, 466*, 560, 561*
  Quota in Fund, 308*
  Repurchases from Fund, 396*
  SDR allocations, 250*
  Technical assistance from Fund, 580, 583, 585

TARIFFS
  Generalized system of preferences (EEC, Denmark, Finland, Japan, New Zealand, Norway, Sweden, U.K.), 574
  In Japan, 495
  Kennedy round of negotiations, 573

TECHNICAL ASSISTANCE
  Carried out through: consultations, 572, 579; outside experts, 580, 582, 584, 588; resident representatives, 471, 579, 587–88; staff, 580, 582, 584
  Definition, 579
  Fields of assistance: balance of payments statistics, 584–85; central banking, 579–82; financial statistics, 585–86; fiscal affairs, 582–84; general, 587–88
  Growth, 578, 583, 585, 587
  Information exchanged with other international organizations to avoid duplication, 584
  Recipients: countries, 580–81, 582, 583, 585, 587–88; regional organizations, 581, 583; special program for Zaïre ended, 588
  Reports to Executive Board, 578–79
  See also individual countries

TEJERA-PARIS, ENRIQUE, 89, 101

TEYSSIER, GERARD M., 134*, 162*, 643n

THAILAND
  Drawings (purchases) from Fund under buffer stock facility, 284
  Exchange rate and par value, 437, 562
  Quota in Fund, 296, 308*
  SDR allocations, 250*
  Special Drawing Account, participation in, 232

THOMPSON-McCAUSLAND, L. P., 136*, 164*

THORSON, PHILLIP, 642

TIN. *See* BUFFER STOCK FINANCING and INTERNATIONAL TIN AGREEMENT

TOGO
  Exchange rate, 457, 561
  Quota in Fund, 289–90, 308*
  SDR allocations, 250*

TONGA. *See* UNITED KINGDOM: Nonmetropolitan territories

TOURE, MAMOUDOU, 644

TRADE, INTERNATIONAL
  Magnitudes, 25, 565; affected by sterling devaluation, 440; and need for reserves, 18, 75; in French franc area, 458
  Measures related to 1971 currency realignment, 535, 551, 574
  Restrictions on, 221, 500, 539, 546
  Study of commodity trade by Fund and World Bank, 272–75
  Surpluses: Fed. Rep. of Germany, 449–52, 463; Japan, 494, 528; U.S., 488, 494
  See also EXPORTS; IMPORTS; *and* TARIFFS

TRIFFIN, ROBERT (Triffin Plan), 17–19, 22, 191

TRINIDAD AND TOBAGO
  Drawings (purchases) and repurchases from Fund, 311, 316, 332*, 396*
  Par value, xviii–xix, 437, 438*
  Quota in Fund, 289, 296, 308*
  SDR allocations, 250*
  Technical assistance from Fund, 580

TUN THIN, 644n

TUNISIA
  Drawings (purchases) and repurchases from Fund, 310, 312, 316, 332*, 396*; waiver, 322
  Par value, 560*
  Quota in Fund, 288, 296, 308*
  SDR allocations, 250*
  Stand-by arrangements with Fund, 321, 336*
  Technical assistance from Fund, 581, 583, 585

TURKEY
  Debt renegotiation, 595
  Drawings (purchases) and repurchases from Fund, 310, 311, 321, 332*, 396*
  Exchange and trade reform, 474–75
  Exchange rate, central, 562*
  Financial stabilization program, 474–75
  Multiple exchange practice, 475
  Par value, xxi, 474–75
  Payments agreements, bilateral, 474

Quota in Fund, 296, 308*
SDR allocations, 250*
Stand-by arrangements with Fund, 320, 336*, 474

U

UDEAC. *See* CENTRAL AFRICAN CUSTOMS AND ECONOMIC UNION

UGANDA
Drawings (purchases) and repurchases from Fund, 310, 312, 316, 332*, 396*
Exchange rate, 542
Par value, 437, 465, 466*, 560, 561*
Quota in Fund, 308*
SDR allocations, 250*
Stand-by arrangement with Fund, 320, 321, 336*
Technical assistance from Fund, 580

UGUETO, LUIS, 552
Background and length of service, 627, 629

UMOA. *See* WEST AFRICAN MONETARY UNION

UNCTAD. *See* UNITED NATIONS CONFERENCE ON TRADE AND DEVELOPMENT

UNDP. *See* UNITED NATIONS DEVELOPMENT PROGRAM

UNGERER, HORST, 102, 135*, 163*, 436

UNION D'ASSUREURS DES CREDITS INTERNA-TIONAUX (Berne Union), 609

UNION OF SOVIET SOCIALIST REPUBLICS, 402

UNITAS, 143

UNITED ARAB EMIRATES
Membership in Fund, 570

UNITED KINGDOM
Art. VIII consultations, 218, 349, 431, 440, 446
Art. VIII, Secs. 2, 3, and 4, acceptance of obligations of, 571n
Balance of payments: correction of deficit advocated, 66, 196; deficit, 14, 29, 171, 212, 221, 339, 432–33, 435, 441, 447; improvement, 74–75, 115, 186, 209–10, 218, 349, 350, 351, 431; surplus, 350, 446, 493, 564
Basle Agreement, 14, 192
Basle Group, 442
Credit, stand-by, from Basle Group, 442
Credit from Group of Ten, 339, 340
Currency: decimal system, 518; declared convertible in fact, 225–26; Fund holdings, 351; used in Fund transactions, 337*
Debt repayment, 351
Drawings from Fund. *See* Transactions . . . purchases, *below*
Economic situation and policies, 140, 141, 339–42, 348–51, 431–36, 440–46
Exchange and trade controls, 441–42; import deposits, 441, 574
Exchange markets, dual, 575
Exchange rate, floating, 542, 544
Nonmetropolitan territories: decimal system for currencies, 518; new currency units, 467, 468; par values, 439–40, 467, 468, 560*, 561
Parliament, 38
Par value: 1967 devaluation, xviii, 339, 433–37, 438*; unchanged, 554, 555*, 560*
Quota in Fund, 296, 308*
Reserve creation: proposal, 79–80, 197; views, 111, 112, 120. *See also* MAUDLING, REGINALD
SDRs: allocations, 250*; use, 234, 243
Seminars with Fund staff on credit policy, 443, 445
Stand-by arrangements with Fund, xix, xx, 320, 336*, 338–43, 345, 348–51
Sterling agreements, 441–42
Transactions with Fund: purchases, 311, 315, 316, 332*; purchases under stand-by arrangements, xix, 321, 349, 350, 351; repurchases, 348, 351, 396*

UNITED NATIONS
Development Decades, 270, 601
Fund relations with, 286, 605–607

General Assembly: position on SDR-development finance link, 245; resolution on monetary reform, 84
See also respective ECONOMIC COMMISSIONS *and* various subagencies and committees

UNITED NATIONS ADMINISTRATIVE COMMITTEE ON COORDINATION (ACC), 605

UNITED NATIONS CONFERENCE ON TRADE AND DEVELOPMENT (UNCTAD)
Commodity problems, 261, 272, 273, 278, 285
Fund's relations with, 606–607, 610; on commodity problems, 261, 273, 278, 286; on debt problems, 595; on reserve creation, 104, 106, 110
Meetings, 270, 286
Reserve creation studied, 83–85, 99, 197, 198, 199, 219
See also GROUP OF SEVENTY-SEVEN *and* GROUP OF TWENTY-FOUR

UNITED NATIONS DEVELOPMENT PROGRAM (UNDP), 605, 610

UNITED NATIONS ECONOMIC AND SOCIAL COUNCIL (ECOSOC), 11, 190, 605, 610

UNITED STATES
Acceptance of amendment to Articles of Agreement, 176; legislation, 187
Art. IV and Art. VIII, obligations under, 404–405
Art. VIII consultations, 218–19, 488, 490, 492, 519, 571
Art. VIII, Secs. 2, 3, and 4, acceptance of obligations of, 571n
As supplier of world reserves, 25–26, 193
Asset settlement suggested by Fund, 491–92
Balance of payments: bases defined, 211n; correction of deficit advocated, 66, 196; deficits, 14, 25–26, 29, 31, 171–72, 212, 221, 310, 313, 447, 485–93, 519–20, 527–28, 534, 564; estimate of improvement needed, 543–44, 548–49; improvement, 74–75, 209, 210–11, 218–19; measures to improve, 52, 63–64, 70, 210, 221, 485–93 *passim*
Basle Group, 442n
Capital movements, 485, 486, 488, 489, 519–20, 528
Capital outflows, measures to stem, 63, 74, 210, 485, 487
Congress, 26, 38, 63, 110, 159, 536–37
Convertibility of dollar suspended, xxii, 3, 241–42, 517, 527–30, 531–33. *See also* CONVERTIBILITY
Currency: as intervention currency, 497, 535, 536; as reserve currency, 497, 536; as vehicle currency, 497; declared convertible in fact, 223–24, 225–26; role of in monetary system, 20; swap arrangements, 14–15, 192, 314–15, 477; used in Fund transactions, 327, 337*. *See also* Exchange rate devaluation *and* Par value, *below*
Dollar shortage ended, 485
Drawings from Fund. *See* Transactions . . . purchases, *below*
Economic situation and policies, 140, 141, 485–93
EEC agricultural policy, views on, 535
European exchange markets, arrangements to operate in, 15
Exchange rate devaluation: agreed, 554; difficulties, 535–36; relation of to gold price, 528–29, 530, 534, 536–37, 540–41, 545; urged, 525, 534, 546; U.S. views on, 527, 528–29, 531, 534–37, 551–52
Fiscal and monetary policies, 488, 490
Foreign credit restraint program, 63–64, 210, 485, 486, 489
Fund Board of Governors Committee of Twenty proposed, 67, 101, 102
Fund credit tranche positions, views on compulsory reconstitution of, 114
Fund investment and disinvestment of gold in U.S. securities, 383–85
Gold sales at official price, 402, 404
Impact on dollar of French franc devaluation, 451; of sterling devaluation, 437, 447–48
Import surcharge, 529, 531, 532, 539, 544, 545, 546, 547; imposed, 529; lifted, 554
Income tax surcharge, 487

Inflation, 218, 489–92, 527–28, 534
Interest equalization tax, 63, 210, 485, 486
Interest rates, 74
International monetary conference suggested, 63, 67, 196
International monetary cooperation, 526–27
Investment abroad, 492; controls on, 210, 487, 489, 498
New Economic Program, 529
Par value: effect of French franc devaluation, 451; effect of sterling devaluation, 437, 447–48; 1971 adjustment, 554, 563–64, 564*n*
Quota in Fund, 295–96, 308*
Reserve creation: position on link with development finance, 110–11; proposals, 54, 79, 80, 141, 143, 151, 196, 197, 202; views, 112, 120, 131, 201
Reserves, 486–87, 489–90, 528
SDRs: allocations, 250*; receipt, 236; use, 240, 243, 314–15
Stand-by arrangement with Fund suggested, 313
Swap facilities, 14–15, 192, 314–15, 477
Trade arrangements with Canada and Japan, 551
Transactions with Fund: purchases, 311, 312–15, 332*; repurchases, 314, 396*
Unemployment, 489, 492, 528
Voting power in Fund, 254
Wage and price restraint program, 487

UPPER VOLTA
Drawings (purchases) from Fund, 312, 316, 332*
Exchange rate, 457–58, 561–62
Quota in Fund, 301, 308*
SDR allocations, 250*

UQUAILI, N. M., 594

URQUIDI, VICTOR L., 85*n*

URUGUAY
Drawings (purchases) and repurchases from Fund: purchases, 264, 268*, 310, 311, 316, 321, 332*; repurchases, 268*, 396*; under compensatory financing facility, 264, 268*
Quota in Fund, 289, 308*
SDR allocations, 250*
Stand-by arrangements with Fund, 321, 336*

U.S.S.R., 402

V

VALESCHI, ATHOS, 132*n*

VALLE, E., 136*, 164*

VAN CAMPENHOUT, ANDRE, 134*, 148, 155, 162*, 231, 292, 295, 523
Background and length of service, 625, 627
Comments and views on: buffer stock financing facility, 279, 283, 286; Canadian dollar, 480, 481; exchange rate flexibility, 507, 508, 511; gold sales for currency replenishment, 418; reserve creation, 112, 114, 124, 127, 129

VAN DER BRANDEN, R., 135*

VAN DER VALK, H. M. H. A., 134*, 162*, 439
Length of service, 626–27

VAN LENNEP, EMILE, 36, 120, 136*, 164*

VAN WENSVEEN, D. M. N., 136*, 164*

VEHICLE CURRENCY, 497

VENEZUELA
Currency used in Fund transactions, 324, 337*
Quota in Fund, 296, 308*
SDR allocations, 250*

VERA, FERNANDO A., 648

VIENOT, MARC, 357, 492, 522, 526, 533, 549, 550, 551, 558
Background and length of service, 627, 628

VIET-NAM
Exchange rate, 563; floating, 542
Quota in Fund, 289, 308*

SDR allocations, 250*
Technical assistance from Fund, 580

VOLCKER, PAUL A., 412, 413, 531, 543

VOM HOFE, ERNST, 102, 112, 114, 116, 135*, 146, 147, 151–52, 155, 163*, 389

VOTING
Distribution among members, 105, 254, 632; adjustment discussed, 121–23, 125, 127, 151, 632
Provisions proposed in reserve creation plans, 55–56, 78, 121–27, 131–33, 143, 144, 146, 147, 150, 151–52, 155, 156, 158, 160, 161, 167, 202, 203; bloc voting accepted, 173; split voting considered, 123–24, 151–52
Special majorities required: in respect of General Account, 254–55; in respect of quotas, 133, 174, 202, 254, 255; in respect of SDRs, 173, 177, 179, 181, 182; in respect of uniform change of par values, 254

W

WAITZENEGGER, JACQUES, 649

WAIVERS OF CONDITIONS FOR DRAWINGS AND STAND-BY ARRANGEMENTS, 26*n*, 322

WARDHANA, ALI, 267, 281, 426

WARIS, KLAUS, 472

WASS, DOUGLAS W. G., 128, 134*, 152, 162*

WEEKS, J. MILTON, 594

WERNER, PIERRE, 132*n*

WEST AFRICAN MONETARY UNION (UMOA), 271, 304, 457

WESTERN HEMISPHERE. See LATIN AMERICA AND CARIBBEAN

WESTERN SAMOA
Quota in Fund, 302, 303, 308*
SDR allocations, 250*
Special Drawing Account, participation in, 232

WHITTOME, L. A., 644

WICKMAN, KRISTER, 171

WIDER MARGINS. See EXCHANGE RATE MECHANISM

WILLIAMS, GORDON, 648

WILLIAMS, LEONARD A., 162*, 174, 343, 349, 390, 391, 507, 592

WILLIS, GEORGE H., 137*, 165*

WILLOCH, KÅRE, 594

WINDSOR, WALTER H., 645

WITTEVEEN, H. JOHANNES, 132*n*, 514, 578, 594, 635*n*

WOODLEY, W. JOHN R., 645

WOODS, GEORGE D., 612

WORKING PARTY ON PROVISIONS TO ENSURE ACCEPTABILITY OF A NEW RESERVE ASSET, 115–16

WORLD BANK
Building arrangements, 589, 650
Economic Development Institute, 589
Fund-Bank office for Annual Meetings, 647
Fund-Bank study on primary products, 269, 271, 272–82; Bank attendance at Fund Board meetings on, 276; Fund attendance at Bank seminar on, 278
Fund collaboration with, 469–70, 471, 581, 595, 610–15, 650
Fund contribution to development finance proposed through, 119, 246, 391, 392
Fund participation in debt meetings of, 471, 593, 595–97, 598
International Development Association (IDA), 19, 111, 219, 390, 391
International Finance Corporation (IFC), 92, 581
Joint Computer Center, 603, 639
Participation in Ghana aid meetings, 600

WORLD ECONOMIC OUTLOOK, 577
WYCZALKOWSKI, MARCIN R., 646

Y

YAFTALY, ABDULLAH, 593
YAMEOGO, ANTOINE W., 135*, 163*, 174, 216, 219, 345, 368, 457, 458, 552, 631
  Background and length of service, 625, 627, 628
  Comments and views on: devaluation by Ghana, 472; distribution of Fund's net income, 388, 391; split voting, 152; stabilization of commodity prices, 273, 279; stand-by arrangement, French (1969), 354

YEMEN ARAB REPUBLIC
  Drawing (purchase) from Fund, 312, 316, 332*
  Exchange rate, 542, 563
  Membership in Fund, 312
  Quota in Fund, 302, 303, 308*
  SDR allocations, 250*
  Special Drawing Account, participation in, 222
  Technical assistance from Fund, 581, 585

YEMEN, PEOPLE'S DEMOCRATIC REPUBLIC OF
  Quota in Fund, 301, 308*
  SDR allocations, 250*
  Technical assistance from Fund, 581, 585

YU, KUO-HWA, 267

YUGOSLAVIA
  Currency unit, new, 467
  Drawings (purchases) and repurchases from Fund, 310, 311, 315, 316, 321, 332*, 396*
  Par value, xxii, 467, 517–18, 561*

Quota in Fund, 296, 308*
SDR allocations, 250*
Stand-by arrangements with Fund, 320, 336*

Z

ZAIRE
  Currency unit, new, 467
  Drawing (purchase) from Fund under compensatory financing facility and repurchases, 266n, 396*
  Exchange rate, central, 562*
  Par value, 455, 466*, 467
  Quota in Fund, 301, 308*
  SDR allocations, 250*
  Stand-by arrangement with Fund, 320, 321, 336*
  Technical assistance from Fund, 580, 583, 585

ZAKI, HASSAN ABBAS, 267

ZAMBIA
  Currency unit, new, 468
  Drawings (purchases) and repurchases from Fund: purchases, 265–66, 268*, 312, 332*; repurchases, 396*; under compensatory financing facility, 265–66, 268*
  Par value, 437, 465, 466*, 468, 560, 561*
  Quota in Fund, 308*
  SDR allocations, 250*
  Technical assistance from Fund, 581

ZASSENHAUS, HERBERT K., 647

ZAYAS, EDISON V., 648

ZEVALLOS, JOAQUIN, 475

ZOLOTAS, XENOPHON (Zolotas Plan), 23, 193

Publications Cited

Numbers refer to pages. The publication is usually cited in a footnote. The list is also intended to serve as a guide to the short titles that have been used in this history for publications frequently cited. For a complete listing of the publications issued by the Fund in the years 1966–71, see Volume II of this history, pages 335–39.

A

Adekunle, Joseph O. "The Demand for Money: Evidence from Developed and Less Developed Economies," *Staff Papers*, Vol. 15 (1968), pp. 220–66: 367

Altman, Oscar L. "Euro-Dollars: Some Further Comments," *Staff Papers*, Vol. 12 (1965), pp. 1–16: 497

———. "Foreign Markets for Dollars, Sterling, and Other Currencies," *Staff Papers*, Vol. 8 (1960–61), pp. 313–52: 497

———. "The Management of International Liquidity," *Staff Papers*, Vol. 11 (1964), pp. 216–47: 34

———. "Professor Triffin on International Liquidity and the Role of the Fund," *Staff Papers*, Vol. 8 (1960–61), pp. 151–91: 22

———. "Quotas in the International Monetary Fund," *Staff Papers*, Vol. 5 (1956–57), pp. 129–50: 291

———. "Recent Developments in Foreign Markets for Dollars and Other Currencies," *Staff Papers*, Vol. 10 (1963), pp. 48–96: 497

Annual Report, 19—: see International Monetary Fund. *Annual Report of the Executive Directors . . .*

Annual Report on Exchange Restrictions: see International Monetary Fund

Approaches to Greater Flexibility of Exchange Rates: The Bürgenstock Papers, arranged by C. Fred Bergsten, George N. Halm, Fritz Machlup, and Robert V. Roosa, and edited by George N. Halm (Princeton, 1970): 483

Argy, Victor. "The Impact of Monetary Policy on Expenditure with Particular Reference to the United Kingdom," *Staff Papers*, Vol. 16 (1969), pp. 436–88: 367

———. "The Role of Money in Economic Activity: Some Results for 17 Developed Countries," *Staff Papers*, Vol. 17 (1970), pp. 527–62: 367

See also Polak, J. J., and Victor Argy

Armington, Paul S. "Adjustment of Trade Balances: Some Experiments with a Model of Trade Among Many Countries," *Staff Papers*, Vol. 17 (1970), pp. 488–526: 537

———. "The Geographic Pattern of Trade and the Effects of Price Changes," *Staff Papers*, Vol. 16 (1969), pp. 179–201: 537

———. "A Theory of Demand for Products Distinguished by Place of Production," *Staff Papers*, Vol. 16 (1969), pp. 159–78: 537

Artus, Jacques R. "The Behavior of Export Prices for Manufactures," *Staff Papers*, Vol. 21 (1974), pp. 583–604: 445

———. "The Effect of Revaluation on the Foreign Travel Balance of Germany," *Staff Papers*, Vol. 17 (1970), pp. 602–19: 463

———. "The 1967 Devaluation of the Pound Sterling," *Staff Papers*, Vol. 22 (1975), pp. 595–640: 445

———, and Rudolf R. Rhomberg. "A Multilateral Exchange Rate Model," *Staff Papers*, Vol. 20 (1973), pp. 591–611: 537

B

Bank for International Settlements. *Annual Reports*: 497

Bell, Geoffrey. *The Euro-Dollar Market and the International Financial System* (London, 1973): 498

Bernstein, Edward M. "The Adequacy of United States Gold Reserves," *American Economic Review* (Papers and Proceedings of the Seventy-Third Annual Meeting of the American Economic Association), Vol. 51 (1961), pp. 439–46: 20

———. "The Dollar Is the Problem of the International Monetary System," *Quarterly Review and Investment Survey*, Model, Roland & Co. (New York), Second Quarter, 1971, pp. 1–12: 246

———. "Further Evolution of the International Monetary System," *Moorgate and Wall Street* (London), Summer 1965, pp. 51–70: 54

———. "International Effects of U.S. Economic Policy," in *Employment, Growth and Price Levels*, U.S. Congress, Joint Economic Committee (Study Paper No. 16), 86th Cong., 2nd sess. (Washington, 1960): 20

———. "A Practical Program for International Monetary Reserves," *Quarterly Review and Investment Survey*, Model, Roland & Co. (New York), Fourth Quarter, 1963, pp. 1–8: 53

———. "Statement: The Problem of International Monetary Reserves," in *International Payments Imbalances and Need for Strengthening International Financial Arrangements*, U.S. Congress, Joint Economic Committee, Hearings Before the Subcommittee on International Exchange and Payments, 87th Cong., 1st sess., May 16–June 21, 1961 (Washington, 1961), pp. 107–37: 20

———. "The U.S. Balance of Payments and International Liquidity" (June 18, 1965), "Changes in the International Monetary System" (October 27, 1964), "Two Reports on International Liquidity" (August 19, 1964), and "The Underdeveloped Countries and Monetary Reserves" (March 24, 1965), in *Guidelines for International Monetary Reform*, U.S. Congress, Joint Economic Committee, Hearings Before the Subcommittee on International Exchange and Payments, 89th Cong., 1st sess. (Washington, 1965), Part 2, Supplement, pp. 230–81: 54

Bhagwat, Avinash, and Yusuke Onitsuka. "Export-Import Responses to Devaluation: Experience of the Nonindustrial Countries in the 1960s," *Staff Papers*, Vol. 21 (1974), pp. 414–62: 445

Bhatia, Rattan J. "Factors Influencing Changes in Money Supply in BCEAO Countries," *Staff Papers*, Vol. 18 (1971), pp. 389–98: 367

———, Gyorgy Szapary, and Brian Quinn. "Stabilization Program in Sierra Leone," *Staff Papers*, Vol. 16 (1969), pp. 504–28: 366

Boissonneault, Lorette. *See* Polak, J. J., and Lorette Boissonneault

Bürgenstock Papers: see Approaches to Greater Flexibility of Exchange Rates

PUBLICATIONS CITED

C

Chandavarkar, Anand G. "Some Aspects of Interest Rate Policies in Less Developed Economies: The Experience of Selected Asian Countries," *Staff Papers*, Vol. 18 (1971), pp. 48–112: 367

CIAP. *See International Monetary Reform and Latin America*

D

Day, A. C. L. "Memorandum of Evidence," in *Principal Memoranda of Evidence*, [Radcliffe] Committee on the Working of the Monetary System, Vol. 3 (London, 1960): 20

————. "The World's Payments System," in *International Payments Imbalances and Need for Strengthening International Financial Arrangements*, U.S. Congress, Joint Economic Committee, Hearings Before the Subcommittee on International Exchange and Payments, 87th Cong., 1st sess., May 16–June 21, 1961 (Washington, 1961), pp. 325–30: 20

Deming, Frederick L. Remarks at the Third International Investment Symposium, U.S. Treasury Department, Press Release, July 14, 1966: 97

Deppler, Michael C. "Some Evidence on the Effects of Exchange Rate Changes on Trade," *Staff Papers*, Vol. 21 (1974), pp. 605–36: 445

de Grauwe, Paul. "The Development of the Euro-Currency Market," *Finance and Development*, September 1975, pp. 14–16: 499

de Vries, Margaret G. "Exchange Depreciation in Developing Countries," *Staff Papers*, Vol. 15 (1968), pp. 560–78: 305

————. "Multiple Exchange Rates: Expectations and Experiences," *Staff Papers*, Vol. 12 (1965), pp. 282–313: 359

E

Elson, R. Anthony. *See* Teigeiro, José D., and R. Anthony Elson

Expert Group on International Monetary Issues (Unctad). *International Monetary Issues and the Developing Countries* (New York, 1965, UN document TD/B/32 and TD/B/C.3/6): 83, 197

F

Fleming, J. Marcus. "Effects of Various Types of Fund Reserve Creation on Fund Liquidity," *Staff Papers*, Vol. 12 (1965), pp. 163–88: 51

————. "The Fund and International Liquidity," *Staff Papers*, Vol. 11 (1964), pp. 177–215: 34

————. *Guidelines for Balance-of-Payments Adjustment Under the Par-Value System*, Essays in International Finance, No. 67 (Princeton, 1968); reprinted in his *Essays in International Economics* (London and Cambridge, Massachusetts, 1971), pp. 268–95: 501

————. "International Liquidity: Ends and Means," *Staff Papers*, Vol. 8 (1960–61), pp. 439–63: 23

————. "The SDR: Some Problems and Possibilities," *Staff Papers*, Vol. 18 (1971), pp. 25–47: 246

————. "Use and Acceptance of Reserve Claims," *Staff Papers*, Vol. 13 (1966), pp. 443–52: 94

Fowler, Henry H. Speech to Virginia State Bar Association, July 10, 1965, U.S. Treasury Department, Press Release, July 11, 1965, and *International Financial News Survey*, Vol. 17 (1965), p. 251: 63

G

Giscard d'Estaing, Valéry. "La politique monétaire internationale de la France," in *Exposés de M. Valéry Giscard d'Estaing, Ministre des Finances et des Affaires Economiques, sur les problèmes monétaires internationaux* (Paris, 1965), in *Les problèmes monétaires internationaux* (Paris, 1965), and in *Problèmes Economiques*, August 1965: 54

Gold, Joseph. "The Amendments," in *History, 1945–1965*, Vol. II, Chap. 27: 166

————. *Floating Currencies, Gold, and SDRs: Some Recent Legal Developments*, IMF Pamphlet Series, No. 19 (Washington, 1976): 533

————. *The Fund's Concepts of Convertibility*, IMF Pamphlet Series, No. 14 (Washington, 1971): 168

————. "Legal Technique in the Creation of a New International Reserve Asset: Special Drawing Rights and the Amendment of the Articles of Agreement of the International Monetary Fund," *Case Western Reserve Journal of International Law*, Vol. 1 (Cleveland, 1969), pp. 105–23: 152

————. "The Next Stage in the Development of International Monetary Law: The Deliberate Control of Liquidity," *American Journal of International Law*, Vol. 62 (Washington, 1968), pp. 365–402: 161, 166

————. *The Reform of the Fund*, IMF Pamphlet Series, No. 12 (Washington, 1969): 166, 253

————. *Special Drawing Rights: Character and Use*, IMF Pamphlet Series, No. 13, 2nd ed. (Washington, 1970): 166, 178, 188

————. *Special Drawing Rights: The Role of Language*, IMF Pamphlet Series, No. 15 (Washington, 1971): 153, 154, 166

————. *Stand-By Arrangements*
The Stand-By Arrangements of the International Monetary Fund: A Commentary on Their Formal, Legal, and Financial Aspects (Washington, 1970): 25, 263, 317, 347, 379

————. *Voting and Decisions*
Voting and Decisions in the International Monetary Fund: An Essay on the Law and Practice of the Fund (Washington, 1972): 616, 621, 625, 631, 632

Group of Seventy-Seven. *The Declaration and Principles of the Action Programme of Lima*, adopted by the Group of Seventy-Seven at the Second Ministerial Meeting on November 7, 1971: 618

Group of Ten. Communiqué of the Ministers and Governors of the "Group of Ten." Issued on September 28, 1965, *Summary Proceedings, 1965*, p. 281: 72

————. *Communiqué of Ministers and Governors and Report of Deputies* ([Frankfurt], 1966): 96, 98

————. Communiqué of the Ministers and Central Bank Governors of the Group of Ten, July 18, 1967, *International Financial News Survey*, Vol. 19 (1967), p. 229: 157

————. Communiqué of the Ministers and Central Bank Governors of the Group of Ten, December 18, 1971, *International Financial News Survey*, Vol. 23 (1971), pp. 417–18: 554

————. *Ministerial Statement of the Group of Ten and Annex Prepared by Deputies* ([Washington], 1964): 36

————. *Report of the Study Group on the Creation of Reserve Assets* (Washington, 1965): 59

————. Statement Issued on October 2, 1963 by the Secretary of the Treasury of the United States on Behalf of the "Group of 10" Members of the Fund, *Summary Proceedings, 1963*, pp. 285–86: 29

Guenther, Jack D. " 'Indexing' Versus Discretionary Action—Brazil's Fight Against Inflation," *Finance and Development*, September 1975, pp. 25–29: 363

H

Habermeier, Walter. *Operations and Transactions in SDRs: The First Basic Period*, IMF Pamphlet Series, No. 17 (Washington, 1973): 244

Hirsch, Fred. "SDRs and the Working of the Gold Exchange Standard," *Staff Papers*, Vol. 18 (1971), pp. 221–53: 246

Hodjera, Zoran. "International Short-Term Capital Movements: A Survey of Theory and Empirical Analysis," *Staff Papers*, Vol. 20 (1973), pp. 683–740: 499

History, 1945–65
The International Monetary Fund, 1945–1965: Twenty Years of International Monetary Cooperation (Washington, 1969). **Vol. I,** *Chronicle*, by J. Keith Horsefield: 4, 11, 12, 14, 15, 17, 21, 33, 143, 168, 313, 343, 385, 432, 578, 588, 593, 603, 606, 621, 626, 633, 636, 650; **Vol. II,** *Analysis*, by Margaret G. de Vries and J. Keith Horsefield with the collaboration of Joseph Gold, Mary H. Gumbart, Gertrud Lovasy, and Emil G. Spitzer and edited by J. Keith Horsefield: 4, 166, 167, 168, 253, 262, 284, 313, 317, 343, 409, 432, 439, 473, 477, 576, 607, 616, 626, 632, 636, 640; **Vol. III,** *Documents*, edited by J. Keith Horsefield: 4, 11, 12, 19, 33, 188, 262, 313, 382, 423, 603

I

An International Development Strategy for the Second United Nations Development Decade (New York, 1970, UN document A/C.2/L.1104/Rev. 1): 245

International Monetary Fund. "The Adequacy of Monetary Reserves," *Staff Papers*, Vol. III (1953–54), pp. 181–227, and *History, 1945–65*, Vol. III, pp. 311–48: 11

——. *Annual Report of the Executive Directors for the Fiscal Year Ended April 30, 1961–1972* (Washington, 1961–1972): **1961,** 16; **1963,** 26, 27; **1964,** 34, 35, 41, 46; **1965,** 43, 46, 53, 72; **1966,** 82, 88, 95; **1967,** 139, 204; **1969,** 220, 497; **1970,** 491, 497; **1971,** 419, 497, 520; **1972,** 564

——. *Annual Report on Exchange Restrictions, 1972* (Washington, 1972): 575

——. *International Financial News Survey:* 96, 153, 529, 603

See also references listed by author

——. *Establishment of a Facility Based on Special Drawing Rights in the International Monetary Fund and Modifications in the Rules and Practices of the Fund: A Report by the Executive Directors to the Board of Governors Proposing Amendment of the Articles of Agreement* (Washington, April 1968): 175, 204

——. *International Reserves and Liquidity* (Washington, 1958): 12

——. *Press Release No. 853*, August 20, 1971: 533

——. *The Problem of Stabilization of Prices of Primary Products: A Joint Staff Study (Part I)*, International Monetary Fund and International Bank for Reconstruction and Development; *Report of the Executive Directors [and] Scope for Action by the Fund (Part II of a Staff Study)*, International Monetary Fund (Washington, 1969, 2 vols.): 273, 274, 279, 280

——. *A Report to the Board of Governors of the International Monetary Fund Containing the Managing Director's Proposal on the Allocation of Special Drawing Rights for the First Basic Period* (Washington, 1969): 220

——. *The Role of Exchange Rates in the Adjustment of International Payments* (Washington, 1970): 484, 512

——. *Special Drawing Account: Manual of Procedures [for] Operations and Transactions in Special Drawing Rights* (Washington, 1970); and Supplement No. 1, *Principles and Procedures for Reconstitution* (Washington, 1971); and Revised Supplement No. 1, *Principles and Procedures for Reconstitution* (Washington, 1973): 231

——. *Staff Papers: see* various articles listed by author

——. *Summary Proceedings of the . . . Annual Meeting of the Board of Governors, 19—* (Washington, 19—): **1960,** 16; **1961,** 16, 21; **1962,** 22, 23, 24; **1963,** 26, 28, 29, 30, 31; **1964,** 38, 39, 40, 41, 42, 255; **1965,** 68, 69, 70, 71, 72, 73, 81, 255; **1966,** 102, 103, 271, 593; **1967,** 159, 173, 270, 271, 272, 273, 594; **1968,** 175, 176, 278, 285, 348, 377, 406, 407, 408, 411, 484, 594; **1969,** 177, 178, 187, 189, 212, 219, 220, 267, 281, 282, 285, 294, 304, 409, 417, 459, 503, 504, 594; **1970,** 245, 267, 282, 416, 426, 491, 514, 515, 578, 601, 625, 631; **1971,** 244, 246, 267, 426, 427, 546, 547, 601, 651

International Reserves: Needs and Availability, Papers and Proceedings of a Seminar at the International Monetary Fund (Washington, 1970): 87, 214, 221

International Monetary Reform and Latin America, report to Inter-American Committee on the Alliance for Progress (CIAP), 1966: 85, 198

J

Jacobsson, Per. "Fund Report at ECOSOC," *International Financial News Survey*, Vol. 13 (1961), pp. 121–27: 21

——. "The Two Functions of an International Monetary Standard: Stability and Liquidity," in *World Monetary Reform: Plans and Issues*, Herbert G. Grubel, ed. (Stanford, 1963), pp. 227–37: 22

Jones, Edgar. "The Fund and the GATT," *Finance and Development*, September 1972, pp. 30–33: 607

Junz, Helen B., and Rudolf R. Rhomberg, "Price Competitiveness in Export Trade Among Industrial Countries," *American Economic Review* (Papers and Proceedings of the Eighty-Fifth Annual Meeting of the American Economic Association), Vol. 63 (1973), pp. 412–18: 445

K

Khatkhate, Deena R. "Analytic Basis of the Working of Monetary Policy in Less Developed Countries," *Staff Papers*, Vol. 19 (1972), pp. 533–58: 368

M

Machlup, Fritz. *Plans for Reform of the International Monetary System*, Special Papers in International Economics, No. 3 (Princeton, 1962): 21

——. *Remaking the International Monetary System: The Rio Agreement and Beyond*, Committee for Economic Development, Supplementary Paper No. 24 (Baltimore, 1968): 155

——, and Burton G. Malkiel, eds. *International Monetary Arrangements—The Problem of Choice: Report on the Deliberations of an International Study Group of 32 Economists* (Princeton, 1964): 29, 38

Morgan Guaranty Trust Company, *World Financial Markets:* 497

Le Monde, Paris, February 6 and 13, 1965: 61

O

Onitsuke, Yusuke. *See* Bhagwat, Avinash, and Yusuke Onitsuke

PUBLICATIONS CITED

P

Park, Yung Chul. "Some Current Issues on the Transmission Process of Monetary Policy," *Staff Papers*, Vol. 19 (1972), pp. 1–45: 368

——. "The Variability of Velocity: An International Comparison," *Staff Papers*, Vol. 17 (1970), pp. 620–37: 367

Partners in Development, Report of the Commission on International Development (New York, 1969), p. 220: 613

Polak, J. J. "Monetary Analysis of Income Formation and Payments Problems," *Staff Papers*, Vol. 6 (1957–58), pp. 1–50: 366

——. "The Report of the International Monetary Fund," *American Economic Review* (Papers and Proceedings of the Seventy-Seventh Annual Meeting of the American Economic Association), Vol. 55 (1965), pp. 158–65: 61

——. *Some Reflections on the Nature of Special Drawing Rights*, IMF Pamphlet Series, No. 16 (Washington, 1971): 178

——, and Victor Argy. "Credit Policy and the Balance of Payments," *Staff Papers*, Vol. 18 (1971), pp. 1–24: 366

——, and Lorette Boissonneault. "Monetary Analysis of Income and Imports and Its Statistical Application," *Staff Papers*, Vol. 7 (1959–60), pp. 349–415: 366

Posthuma, S. "The International Monetary System," *Quarterly Review*, Banca Nazionale del Lavoro (Rome), September 1963, pp. 239–61: 53

Q

Questions and Answers on the International Monetary Fund (June 10, 1944), *History, 1945–64*, Vol. III, pp. 136–82: 188

Quinn, Brian. *See* Bhatia, Rattan J., Gyorgy Szapary, and Brian Quinn

R

[Radcliffe] Committee on the Working of the Monetary System, *Report* (London, Cmnd. 827, 1959), pp. 241 and 247–48: 20

Rhomberg, Rudolf R. *See* Artus, Jacques R., and Rudolf R. Rhomberg; Junz, Helen B., and Rudolf R. Rhomberg

Robichek, E. Walter, and Carlos E. Sansón. "The Balance of Payments Performance of Latin America and the Caribbean, 1966–70," *Staff Papers*, Vol. 19 (1972), pp. 286–343: 367

Roosa, Robert V. *Monetary Reform for the World Economy*, The Elihu Root Lectures, 1964–65 (New York, 1965): 54

S

Sakakibara, Eisuke. "The Euro-Currency Market in Perspective," *Finance and Development*, September 1975, pp. 11–13: 498

Sansón, Carlos E. *See* Robichek, E. Walter, and Carlos E. Sansón

Schweitzer, Pierre-Paul. Speech, Ecosoc, February 24, 1966, *International Financial News Survey*, Vol. 18 (1966), Supplement, pp. 65–68: 90

——. Speech, Federation of German Industries, April 25, 1966, *International Financial News Survey*, Vol. 18 (1966), Supplement, pp. 141–44: 90, 91

——. Speech, Institut d'Etudes Bancaires et Financières, June 2, 1965, *International Financial News Survey*, Vol. 17 (1965), Supplement, pp. 209–16: 64

——. Speech, National Foreign Trade Convention, November 16, 1964, *International Financial News Survey*, Vol. 16 (1964), pp. 441–45: 45, 46

——. Speech, University School of Economics, Bombay University, September 29, 1964, *International Financial News Survey*, Vol. 16 (1964), Supplement, pp. 361–64: 45

Shonfield, Andrew, ed. *International Economic Relations of the Western World, 1959–1971*, Vol. 2—*International Monetary Relations*, by Susan Strange (London, 1976), Chap. 6: 498

Southard, Frank A., Jr. Speech, Jno. E. Owens Memorial Foundation, March 27, 1964, *International Financial News Survey*, Vol. 16 (1964), Supplement, pp. 113–16: 44

Staff Papers, International Monetary Fund (Washington): *see* various articles listed by author

Stamp, Maxwell. "Changes in the World's Payments System," *Moorgate and Wall Street* (London), Spring 1961, pp. 3–22: 19

——. "The Fund and the Future," *Lloyds Bank Review* (London), October 1958, pp. 1–20: 19

——. "The Stamp Plan—1962 Version," *Moorgate and Wall Street* (London), Autumn 1962, pp. 5–17: 19

Summary Proceedings: *see* International Monetary Fund

Szapary, Gyorgy. *See* Bhatia, Rattan J., Gyorgy Szapary, and Brian Quinn

T

Teigeiro, José D., and R. Anthony Elson. "The Export Promotion System and the Growth of Minor Exports in Colombia," *Staff Papers*, Vol. 20 (1973), pp. 419–70: 359

Triffin, Robert. "An Agreed International Monetary Standard," *Annals of International Studies*, Alumni Association of the Graduate Institute of International Studies (Geneva, 1970), pp. 214–23: 246

——. "Altman on Triffin: A Rebuttal," *Quarterly Review*, Banca Nazionale del Lavoro (Rome), March 1961, pp. 31–50: 22

——. "A Brief for the Defense," *Staff Papers*, Vol. 8 (1960–61), pp. 192–94: 22

——. *Gold and the Dollar Crisis: The Future of Convertibility* (New Haven, 1960): 17

——. "The Return to Convertibility: 1926–1931 and 1958—? or, Convertibility and the Morning After," *Quarterly Review*, Banca Nazionale del Lavoro (Rome), March 1959, pp. 3–57: 17

——. "Statement," in *Employment, Growth and Price Levels*, U.S. Congress, Joint Economic Committee, Hearings, 86th Cong., 1st sess., October 26–30, 1959 (Washington, 1959), Part 9A, pp. 2905–54: 17

——. "Tomorrow's Convertibility: Aims and Means of International Monetary Policy," *Quarterly Review*, Banca Nazionale del Lavoro (Rome), June 1959, pp. 131–200: 17

U

United Nations. Document A/C.2/270 (1971): 618

——. Document A/C.2/L.1104/Rev.1 (1970): 245

——. Document TD/11/RES/19 (1968): 273

——. Document TD/143 (1971): 618

——. Document TD/B/32 (1965): 83, 197

——. Document TD/B/75 (1966): 85

——. Document TD/B/C.3/6 (1965): 83, 197

——. General Assembly Resolution (International Monetary Reform) 2208 (XXI), December 17, 1966: 84

————. *A Study of the Capacity of the United Nations Development System* (Geneva, 1969), 2 vols.: 605

United Nations Conference on Trade and Development (UNCTAD). *Proceedings of the United Nations Conference on Trade and Development, Volume I: Final Act and Report* (New York, 1964): 617
See also Expert Group on International Monetary Issues; Group of Seventy-Seven; *and* United Nations. Documents

U.S. Commission on International Trade and Investment Policy, *United States International Economic Policy in an Interdependent World: Report to the President* (Washington, 1971): 529, 537

U.S. Congress, Joint Economic Committee. *Action Now to Strengthen the U.S. Dollar: Report of the Subcommittee on International Exchange and Payments*, 92nd Cong., 1st sess. (Washington, 1971): 528, 537
See also Bernstein, Edward M., Day, A. C. L., and Triffin, Robert

U.S. Department of Commerce. *News*, May 17, 1971: 527

U.S. Department of State. *Department of State Bulletin*, Vol. 49 (1963) and Vol. 59 (1968): 26, 187

W

The World Bank Since Bretton Woods, by Edward S. Mason and Robert E. Asher (Washington, 1973), Chap. 16: 615

World Monetary Reform: Plans and Issues, Herbert G. Grubel, ed. (Stanford, 1963): 21, 22

Z

"Zehner-Gruppe und Reform des Weltwährungssystems," *Auszüge aus Presseartikeln*, Deutsche Bundesbank, January 26, 1966, pp. 1–6: 81